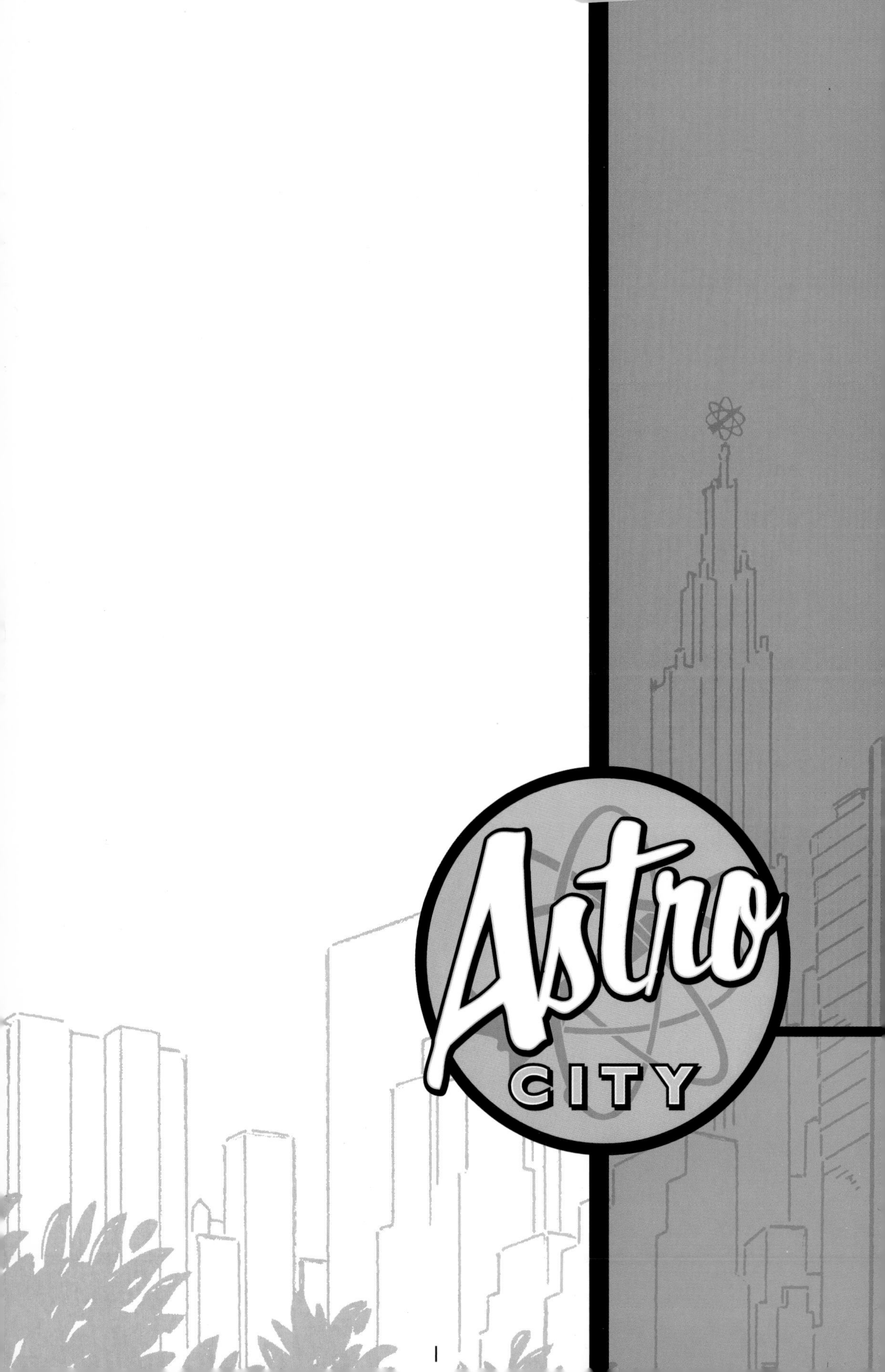
Astro
CITY

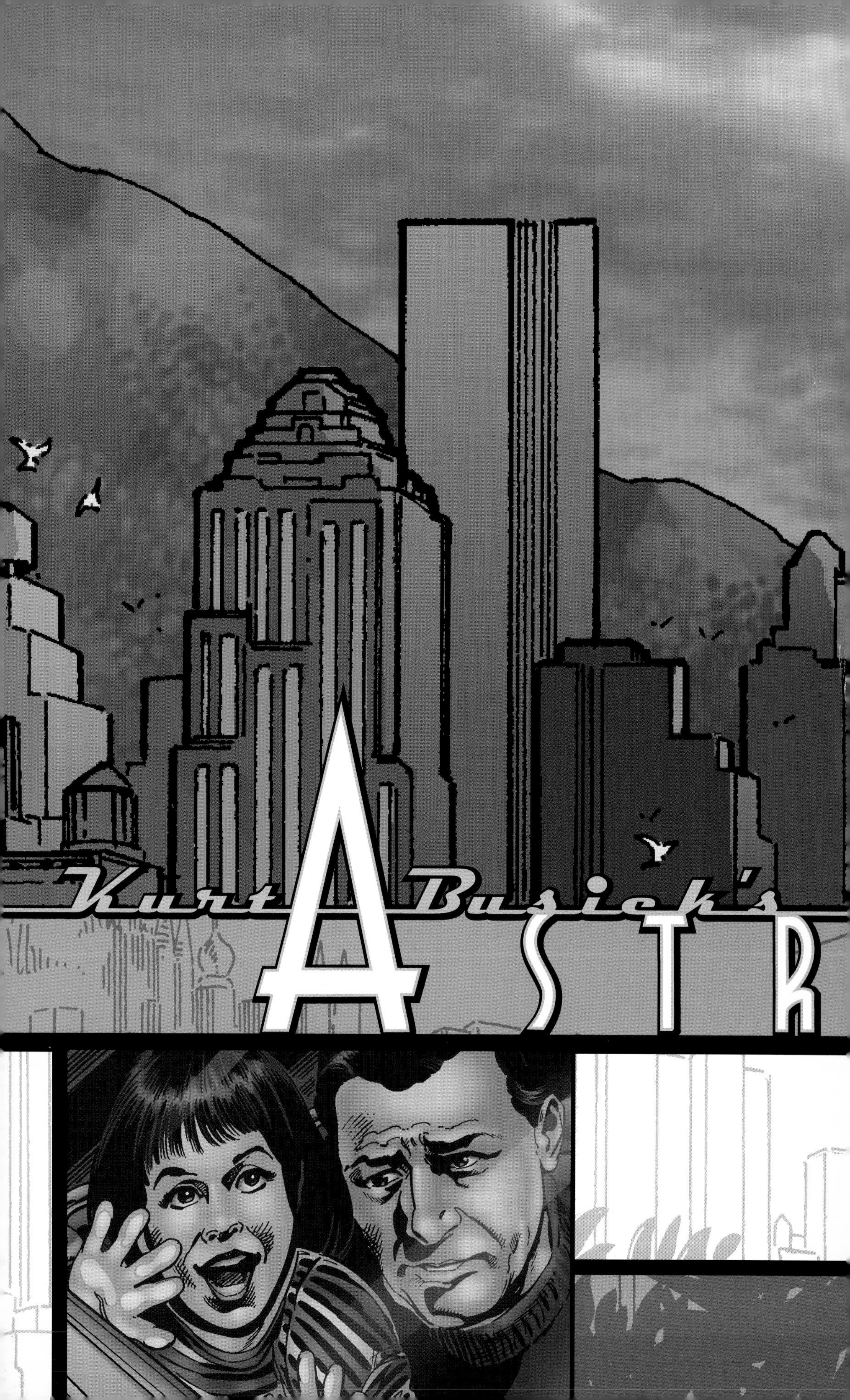
Kurt Busiek's
ASTR

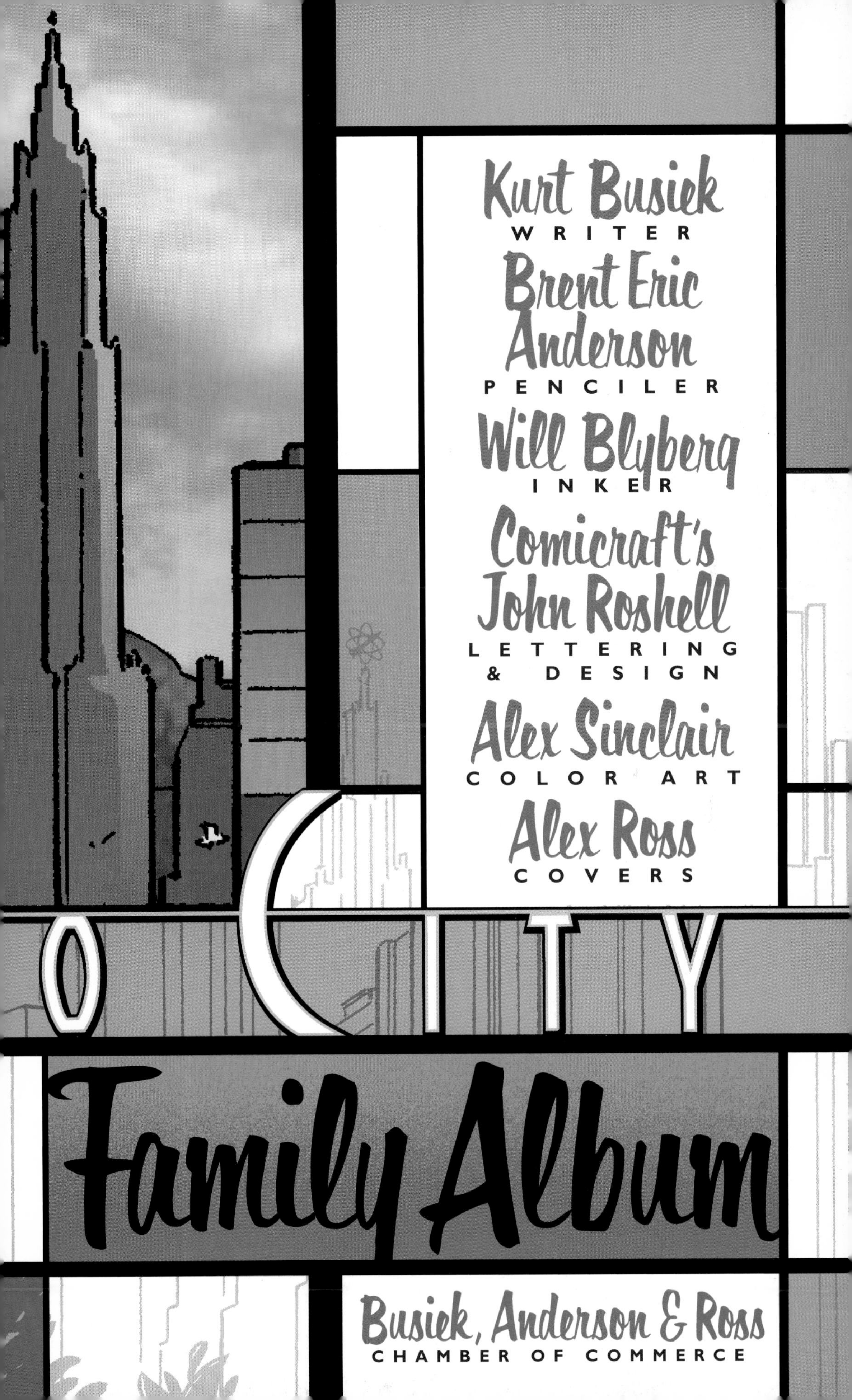
Kurt Busiek
WRITER
Brent Eric Anderson
PENCILER
Will Blyberg
INKER
Comicraft's John Roshell
LETTERING & DESIGN
Alex Sinclair
COLOR ART
Alex Ross
COVERS
O CITY
Family Album
Busiek, Anderson & Ross
CHAMBER OF COMMERCE

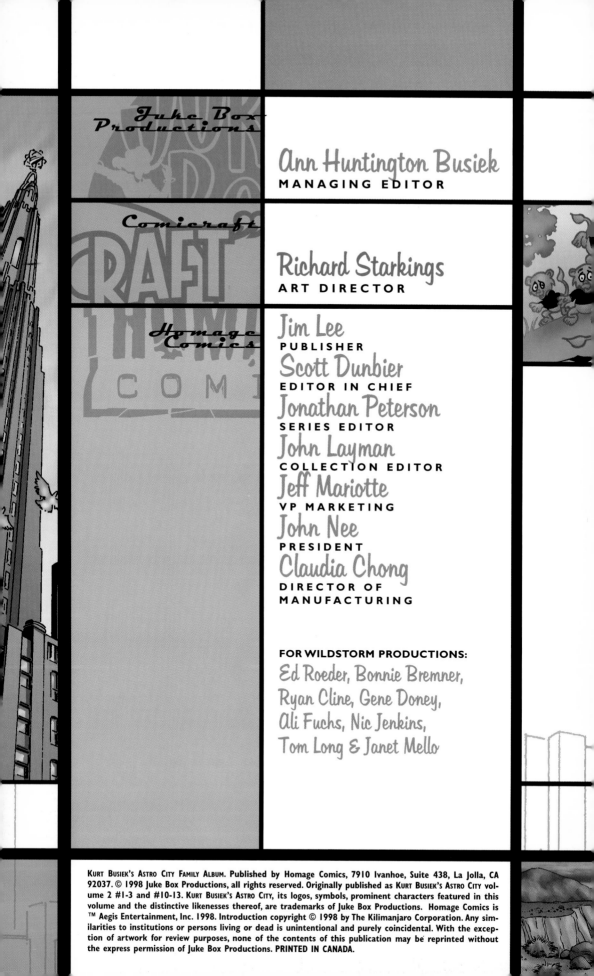

Juke Box Productions

Ann Huntington Busiek
MANAGING EDITOR

Comicraft

Richard Starkings
ART DIRECTOR

Homage Comics

Jim Lee
PUBLISHER

Scott Dunbier
EDITOR IN CHIEF

Jonathan Peterson
SERIES EDITOR

John Layman
COLLECTION EDITOR

Jeff Mariotte
VP MARKETING

John Nee
PRESIDENT

Claudia Chong
DIRECTOR OF MANUFACTURING

FOR WILDSTORM PRODUCTIONS:
Ed Roeder, Bonnie Bremner,
Ryan Cline, Gene Doney,
Ali Fuchs, Nic Jenkins,
Tom Long & Janet Mello

Dedications

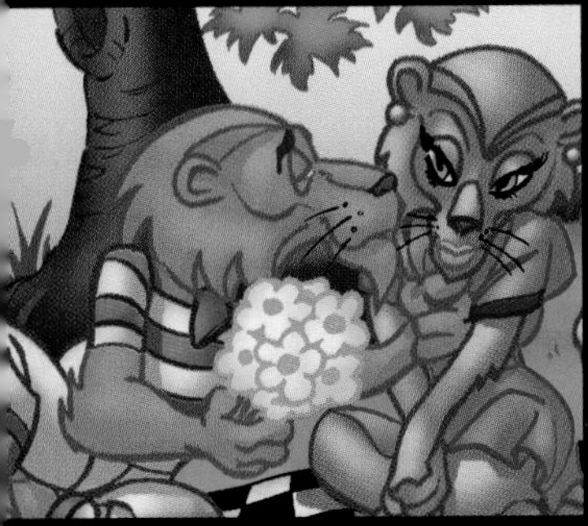

To my sisters – Amy, Robin, Faith and Jennifer – who gave me a thorough grounding in family life, and to Sydney Ann, my impending daughter, who'll teach me all about it from a new perspective.

— KURT

To Sydney, Liberty, and Stone, the newest members of the Astro City family; and to Grace and Blythe Sinclair, our most colorful additions.

— BRENT

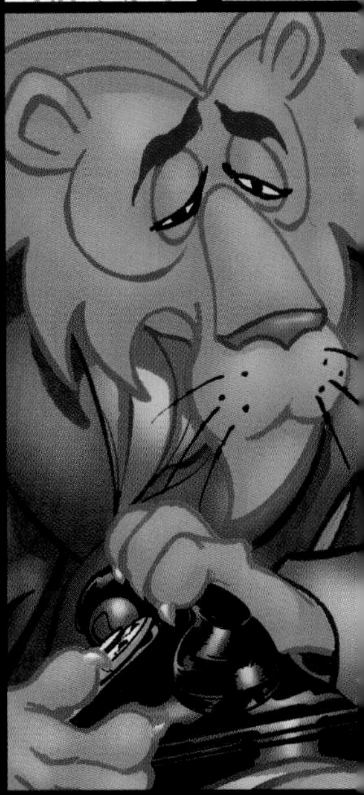

I'm so very alone.

— ALEX

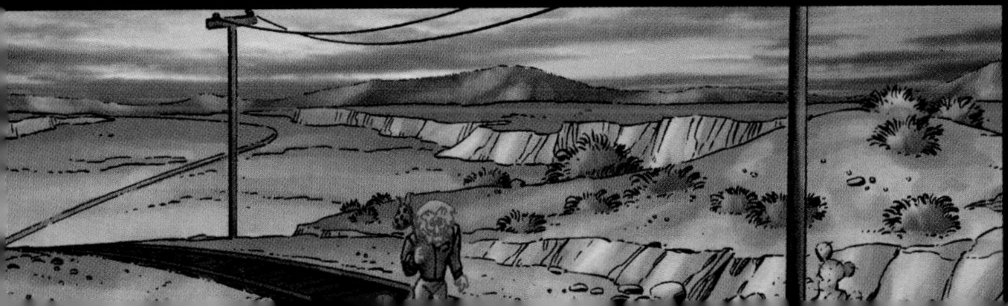

By the Same Creators:

Astro City: Life In The Big City
Astro City: Confession

by Kurt Busiek

Marvels
(with Ross)
Untold Tales of Spider-Man
(with Patrick Olliffe)
The Wizard's Tale
(with David Wenzel)

by Brent Anderson

Somerset Holmes
(with Bruce Jones)
X-Men: God Loves, Man Kills
(with Chris Claremont)

by Alex Ross

Kingdom Come
(with Mark Waid)
Superman: Peace on Earth
(with Paul Dini)
Uncle Sam
(with Steve Darnall)
Terminator: The Burning Earth
(with Ron Fortier)

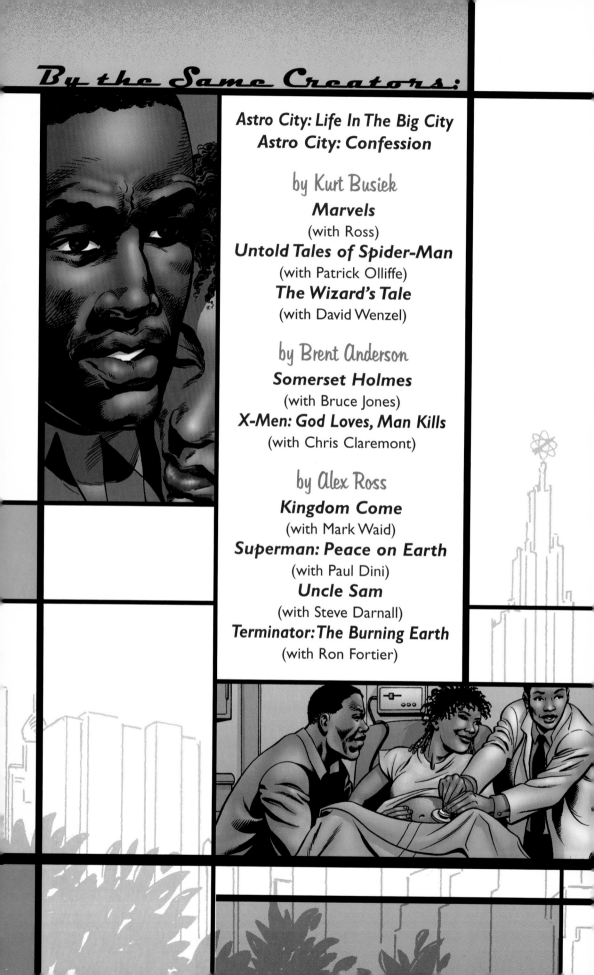

Contents

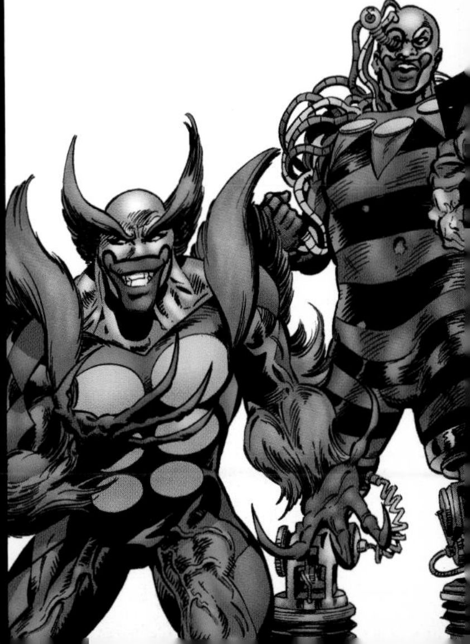

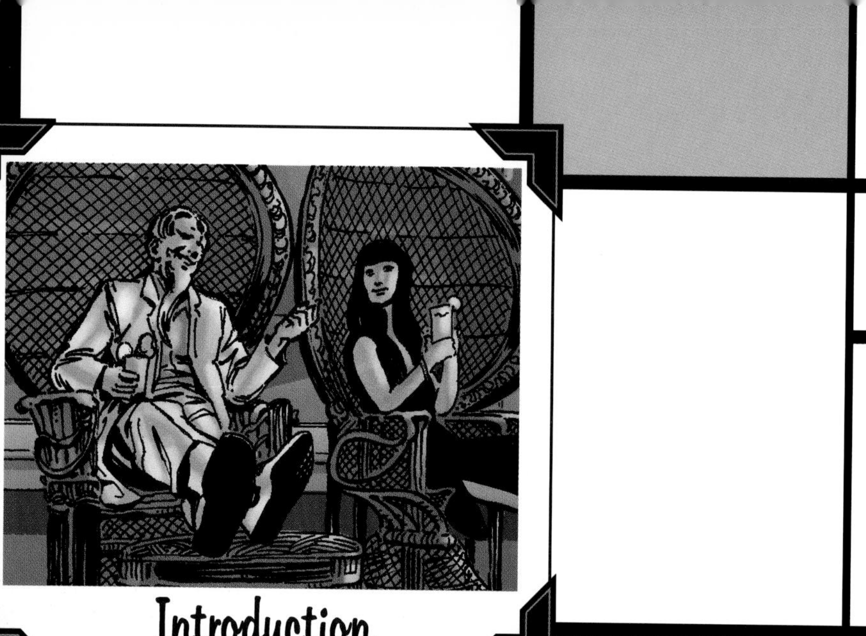

Introduction

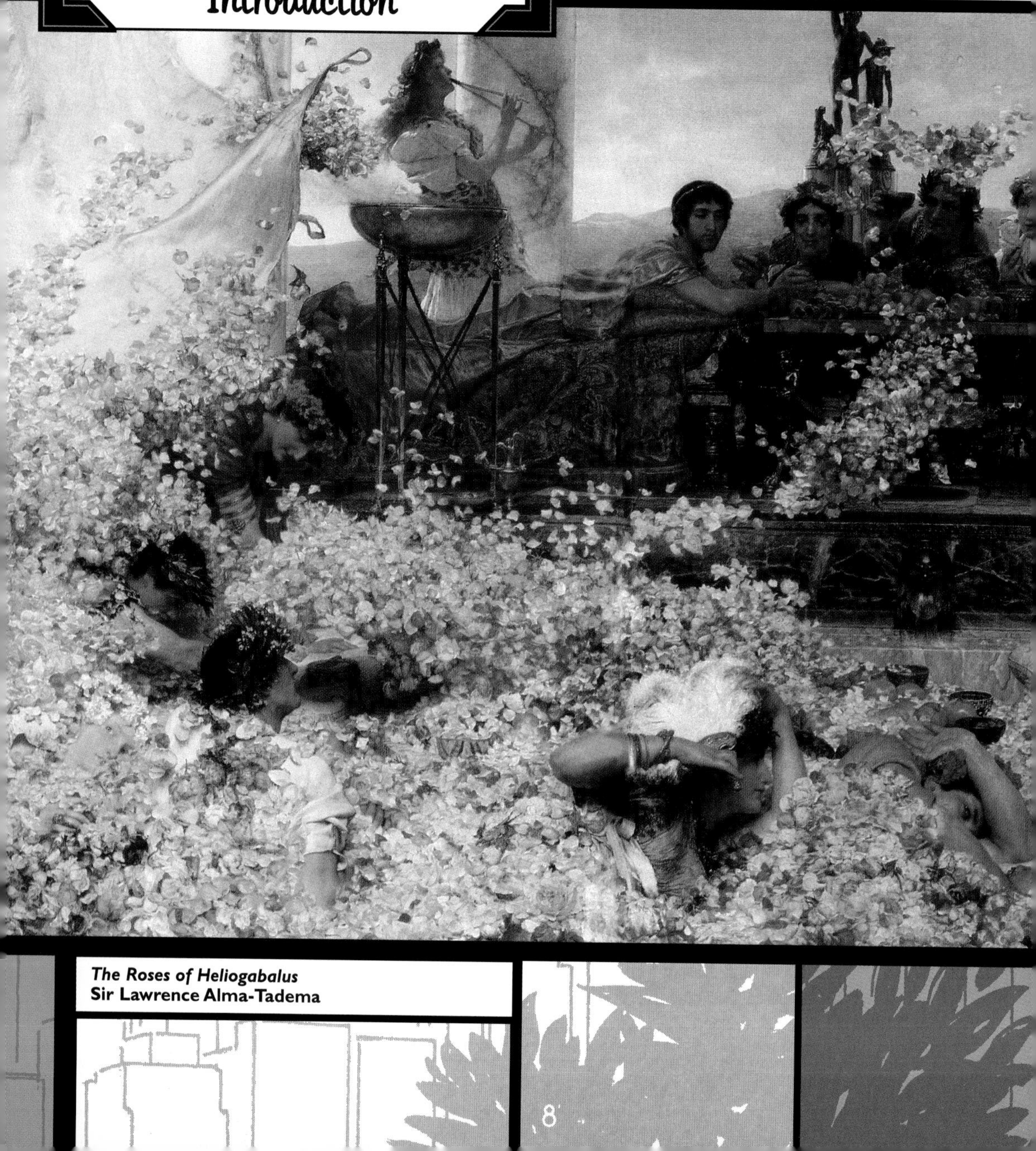

The Roses of Heliogabalus
Sir Lawrence Alma-Tadema

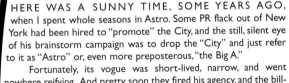

THERE WAS A SUNNY TIME, SOME YEARS AGO, when I spent whole seasons in Astro. Some PR flack out of New York had been hired to "promote" the City, and the still, silent eye of his brainstorm campaign was to drop the "City" and just refer to it as "Astro" or, even more preposterous, "the Big A."

Fortunately, its vogue was short-lived, narrow, and went nowhere reifying. And pretty soon they fired his agency, and the billboards were gone, and the cardboard stand-ups turned yellow in barbershop windows, and those with good sense dropped it; and now, the only people who call it "the Big A" are the same species of parvenus and arrivistes who call San Francisco "Frisco" or pronounce Oregon "*ore*-uh-gawn." But some of us still fall back on calling it Astro…when no one's looking.

Don't get over to Astro City much these days. Not since I had the quadruple bypass. Can't stand travel much—and it *is* something like twelve hundred miles from L.A.—and so I've had to postpone over and over again what used to be a fairly regular hegira: to Astro City, to hang out with Kurt and Alex and, especially, Brent, who only gets goofier with age.

But there were times when we sat, all four of us, looking out on the Raboy Esplanade, in that elegant lobby cafe (the name of which I cannot, for the life of me, remember) in the big glass-and-steel office building across from the Museum, staring at the sweep and swirl of the Deco facade, talking shop, talking art, talking superfolk and dreams, talking about all the things that pass out of one's mind half an hour beyond the brilliance of camaraderie.

Oftentimes I reminisce and am lured to the conclusion that it was the presence of the Finlay-Cartier Museum of Fine Arts that inspired us so. I can't remember similar sessions of chat with other friends, in other venues, being nearly as scintillant or filled with cheer. And so, I *miss* Astro.

Good times there, good people—even if Busiek was always *kvetching* about some deadline or other—as well as something constantly happening. And the thing that *always* amazed me was that never did I—or anyone else I talked to—feel inferior to the "powered people," what citizens of Astro called "the costumes." Oh, we'd see them all the time, here and there…but mostly over there, doing their super-business, and we were over here…doing our non-super business. But it was always sort of *never the twain shall meet.*

I'll get back to all that in a minute.

Indulge me. I want to explain why it is, for me, that Astro is a very special place, a *nidus* if you will. With an explanation, by way of metaphor.

Indulge me. It's my way. I do, after all, make my not inconsiderable living by telling stories, imparting lies, cobbling up scenarios.

AFTER A BIT, SIR LAWRENCE ALMA-TADEMA, AND THAT PAINTING on loan from some private collection in the U.K. or the Netherlands, as it hung before us, the four of us, in the West Gallery of the Finlay-Cartier, many years ago. In a moment. But first. By metaphor…

In the opening decade of the twentieth century, Gustav Stickley's *The Craftsman*, a magazine that promoted lively discussion of the arts and crafts tradition in the United States, ran a series of essays by Irene Sargent, a woman of powerful critical voice, championing the design jewelry of the incomparable René Lalique. This was prior to his glass of high art we honor today.

She referred to Lalique, early on, as a "model of ingenuity, imagination, and craftsmanship." Kurt Busiek. Brent Anderson. Alex Ross. (And, one presumes, though I don't know him, Will Blyberg. Whose inclusion in all that has gone before, and all that follows, goes without saying. Because the core cadre admits no one even an iota less ingenious, imaginative, and craftwise than itself.) She said, of Lalique, that he was the avatar of "art nouveau" (a term then applied to only the most innovative in art), whose concepts "actively challenge others to surpass his achievements by setting a creative standard on a very high plateau." Kurt Busiek. Brent Anderson, goofier by the year. Alex and Will. And finally, by metaphor, this: "Taken thus for all in all, M. Lalique is an artist of that type—the creative— which appears most rarely in the course of time. He has given a new direction to the art which he practices, and indicates to those that shall succeed him alluring possibilities of beauty. He has raised the objects which he creates from the rank of toy and talismans up to that of true works of art." The cadre.

What they have done with Astro City has already become the standard to be emulated. Would that the parvenus and arrivistes had even a distant whisper of their abilities.

Imitation may well be the sincerest form of flattery, but it is also the canker on the rose. First comes the voice, then—fainter, smudged and off-key—the echo.

They have elevated toys and talismans to the very high plateau of original art. And I knew them—all but Will—when.

W E STOOD IN A LINE, THE FOUR OF US, there in the West Gallery of the Finlay-Cartier Museum on the Raboy Esplanade, and we stared at a painting on loan from some private collection in the U.K. Or the Netherlands.

It was Sir Lawrence Alma-Tadema's *The Roses of Heliogabalus.*

"Geezus!" Kurt said, softly, all breath and no syllables. "It's as if you're there. It's real. That's all it is... it's palpable."

Let me tell you about that painting. This, from the 1996 comprehensive survey of Alma-Tadema's *oeuvre*, published by the Van Gogh Museum in Amsterdam:

"Marcus Aurelius Antonius became Emperor of Rome at the age of fourteen: his more familiar name, Heliogabalus or Elagabalus, was derived from the Syrian sun god whose worship, along with Eastern court practices, he attempted to introduce to Rome. He was a voluptuary in the style of Nero and ruled Rome amidst venality and debauchery until he was murdered by the Praetorian guard after a reign of only four years (218-222 C.E.)."

Gibbon said Heliogabalus, during his brief reign,

was "alike odious and contemptible by all manner of follies and abominations." And Walter Pater called him "an embodiment of pure and unmodified evil."

Brent had the catalogue *raisonné* and, as we stood there in front of the tableau, he read to us:

"Alma-Tadema's young Emperor, dressed in saffron silk, reclines on a couch placed on a raised platform and gazes impassively at the scene below…The guests, lazily reclining on silk cushions, in an arena of pain and pleasure calmly succumb to a sea of petals and their exquisitely decadent deaths."

There was then, as there is now, such a sense of *presence* in that most chilling example of what has come to be known as the Orientalist School of painting, that I cannot express with sufficient vigor how profoundly we four were affected by that viewing, on that afternoon, so long ago.

But both Kurt and Brent—echoed by Alex—said that one day, if the opportunity presented itself, they would strive, undertake, struggle toward…a project that captured *just that* sense of time and place. A project that would encapsulate a superimposed pre-continuum, a fully-formed world.

Astro City.

C HECK OUT ONE OF THE EARLIEST SCENES in this volume. I don't know on which page the panel will fall, but it's the page on which Helia and Thunderhead leave the City and the weather clears. It's the bottom of the three panels. Take a look. That's Central Park West beyond the treetops of Central Park in Manhattan. I used to have dinner with Tony Randall in one of those buildings, and Isaac and Janet Asimov looked out of yet another, next door, directly down on The Tavern on the Green. It's New York, that panel. In Astro?

There is a street in Astro City that looks

NOW SHO

THE MONST
THE DARK CO
PLUS NEWSREEL
SHORTS & AIR ACE

THE MONSTER FROM THE DARK CON

something like this view of Central Park West. Not exactly, but close. Brent has filched, what we call in the comics biz "a swipe," and he has plugged it in, because the street he *wanted* to use, the street that *used* to exist in Astro, is now gone, razed to build the elaborate International Merchandise Towers, now the hub of the City's burgeoning clothing industry. So Brent has filched, and we have a simulacrum of the way that corner of Astro City looked oh, fifteen, twenty years ago. Just around the time the four of us studied Heliogabalus's horror show. But, ironically, it is precisely *because* Brent has been compelled to use swipes that I was asked to write the introduction to this most excellent volume of work that exists on a very high plateau.

Turn, if you will, to the fourth page of the Loony Leo story (and, again, I apologize for not being able to direct you by page number). The bottom tier. You see that lovely Brent Anderson rendering of the Ace Theater on Daigh Street? Well, it's New York, again.

But this shot is inordinately special to me.

And it is the impetus for Kurt asking me to preface these fine Astro City stories.

Because I worked directly across the street from the original scene that was snapped as a photo, that Brent swiped to approximate Daigh Street back in the 1950s. (To be exact, in the photo, it's about 1939, and the film playing at the movie house Brent has recast as the Ace was *King Kong*.)

But there was virtually no change on that street between 1939 and 1954 when I worked at the Broadway Book Shop, between the Victoria and Astor Theaters, between 45th and 46th Streets, on Broadway. It's *Broadway*, folks...it's Times Square...and I hadn't yet sold my first story, I had been thrown out of Ohio State University and had come to New York to make my fortune...and I was working the most fascinating hours anyone could work in that town...seven p.m. till two in the morning. And what a time in my life that was!

I was very poor, I was living in a one-room flat 'way uptown at 611 West 114th Street, off Broadway, across from Columbia University; and every day I would take the IRT subway down to Times Square. First, I'd stop off at the Clam Bar and Flea Circus on 42nd, and say hi to Tiny Tim—yes, the singer who became ultra-famous later with *Tiptoe Through the Tulips* and got married on the Johnny Carson show—but his name wasn't Tiny Tim in those days—but I'm afraid I can't remember what stage-name he was using when he was at the Flea Circus, singing in the basement theater—and then I'd go across 42nd and walk about two doors uptown to the pizza joint where Caruso would give me a terrific slice for 15¢, and add a large papaya juice for another dime. And that was my dinner.

Well, to be precise, it was my *early*, pre-job snack.

Then I'd stroll on uptown to the Broadway Book Shop, and begin selling switchblade knives and the Modern Library editions to tourists and passersby and actors heading to their shows up and down Schubert Alley.

And about ten or ten-thirty, I'd dash between cars on Broadway and the parallel 7th Avenue, and I'd find myself right there in the middle of Brent's swipe, at the Buitoni Spaghetti House, where I could get a swell meal—a plate of *al dente* spaghettini, with one meatball, a chunk of French bread and butter, and an iced tea—for a buck.

Look at that dear panel in the Loony Leo saga. Is it possible that I can convey to you, merest words only, what it meant to me, as I was reading that issue of *Astro City*, and turned the page and found myself staring back through the lens of memory to a scene I hadn't seen in more than forty years? I tell you only this: I am hardly the world's most sentimental soul. No patsy, I. But as I turned that page for the first time, and I let my eyes drift toward the bottom tier, I began to cry. Not hard, not painfully, but my eyes welled, and I was whisked back four decades and more, to my fledgling days as a writer, when I was struggling not only to break into print, to *become* somebody, but to scratch out a living at thirty-five dollars a week, writing all night, sleeping only two or three hours in the early afternoon, hustling my manuscripts to editors in the late afternoon and early evening, and then going off to work my brains out just to pay for that fifteen-dollar-a-week room.

All in that moment. All in that swipe Brent used to recapture the glory of the Ace in the days when Daigh Street was lively and colorful...and not a surrogate Hard Rock Disney Trump Supermall of soulless hotels and tourist crap slop shops.

You see, times change and not all change is

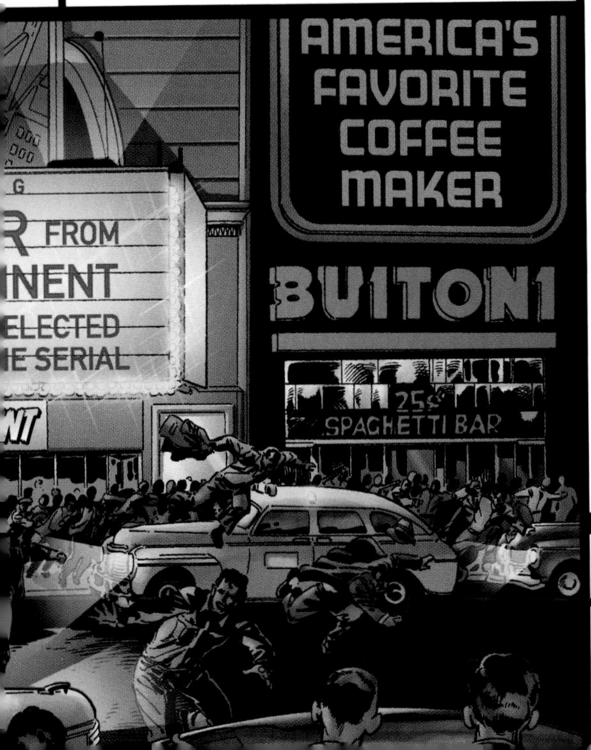
AMERICA'S
FAVORITE
COFFEE
MAKER
BUITONI
25¢
SPAGHETTI BAR
FROM
INENT
ELECTED
HE SERIAL

progress. But Brent had to reconstruct the dreamtime of Daigh Street, as this panel reconstructed for me the memory of Times Square in 1954. He *had* to filch and fudge it, to give you the panel correctly. I know he broke his ass trying to find a comparable photo of Daigh and the Ace…but it wasn't to be. So he took a photo of New York in 1939 (unchanged in 1954) and he retouched it. But *that's* why *Astro City* is the uncommon marvel that it is, no matter how many imitators think they can coat-tail themselves into that winner's circle.

It's the touchstone that brings together my tropes of Lalique and Alma-Tadema and the very high plateau upon which *Astro City* sits.

There is a reality to Astro. It is a series of comic book journeys to a *real* place. Realer (yes, improper grammar) than Metropolis or Gotham City or the New York of *Spider-Man*. Realer, perhaps, than many of the places in which you now sit, reading this.

Brent and Kurt and Alex (and now Will, too) go to Astro with regularity. They commute to that real place—as I no longer can, save in reading their work—and they come back with true snapshots of a marvelous land as exotic as Skull Island or Oz or Ultima Thule or Atlantis. They return with stories and anecdotes of ordinary folk like you and me, and the "costumes" who are anything *but* ordinary.

And the *realness* they transcribe is as much sense of place as falling into that sensuous and awful scene in which the depraved Heliogabalus suffocates his courtiers with a *tsunami* of rose petals. As exquisitely as rendered in minute detail as René Lalique created his immortal jewelry.

Astro exists.

No minuscule wonder, that.

How difficult it is, as a writer—I tell you absolutely—to create that which *seems* authentic, palpable… *real*. I've been doing it most of my life, and it never grows easier. And Kurt and Brent and Alex and Will do it every issue. They go to the City, and they return with treasures, each one as small and perfect as a Lalique.

I remember my days spent with the cadre in that city of costumes and caring, decades ago, and I dream of the past, and I revel in their presentations of the present. And when Brent has to go back to my past to bring forth a view of Astro that no longer exists, well, it puts me blood and bones and mouth and marrow right in the middle of a work of creativity that exists on a very high plateau indeed.

And that is why I am here. Because I used to spend a buck for dinner at the Buitoni Spaghetti House, when I was young, and the world was filled with costumes and wonder and the awe of standing before a painting that made us all understand that…it's real…geez, it's palpable!

When someone asks you "what is Art?" well, you can hand them this book; and I do not think they will treat you less than nobly for the consideration.

HARLAN ELLISON
Madison, Wisconsin
26 September 1998

HARLAN ELLISON, during a forty-plus-year career, has written 74 books, a dozen or so motion pictures, several dozen teleplays, and more than 1700 stories, essays, articles, columns and commentaries, for which he has won more awards than any other living fantasist. He is the creator of the DREAM CORRIDOR comics from Dark Horse, and a frequent, if controversial, "talking head" on such network tv shows as POLITICALLY INCORRECT and THE LATE LATE SHOW WITH TOM SNYDER. He began reading comic books in 1939.

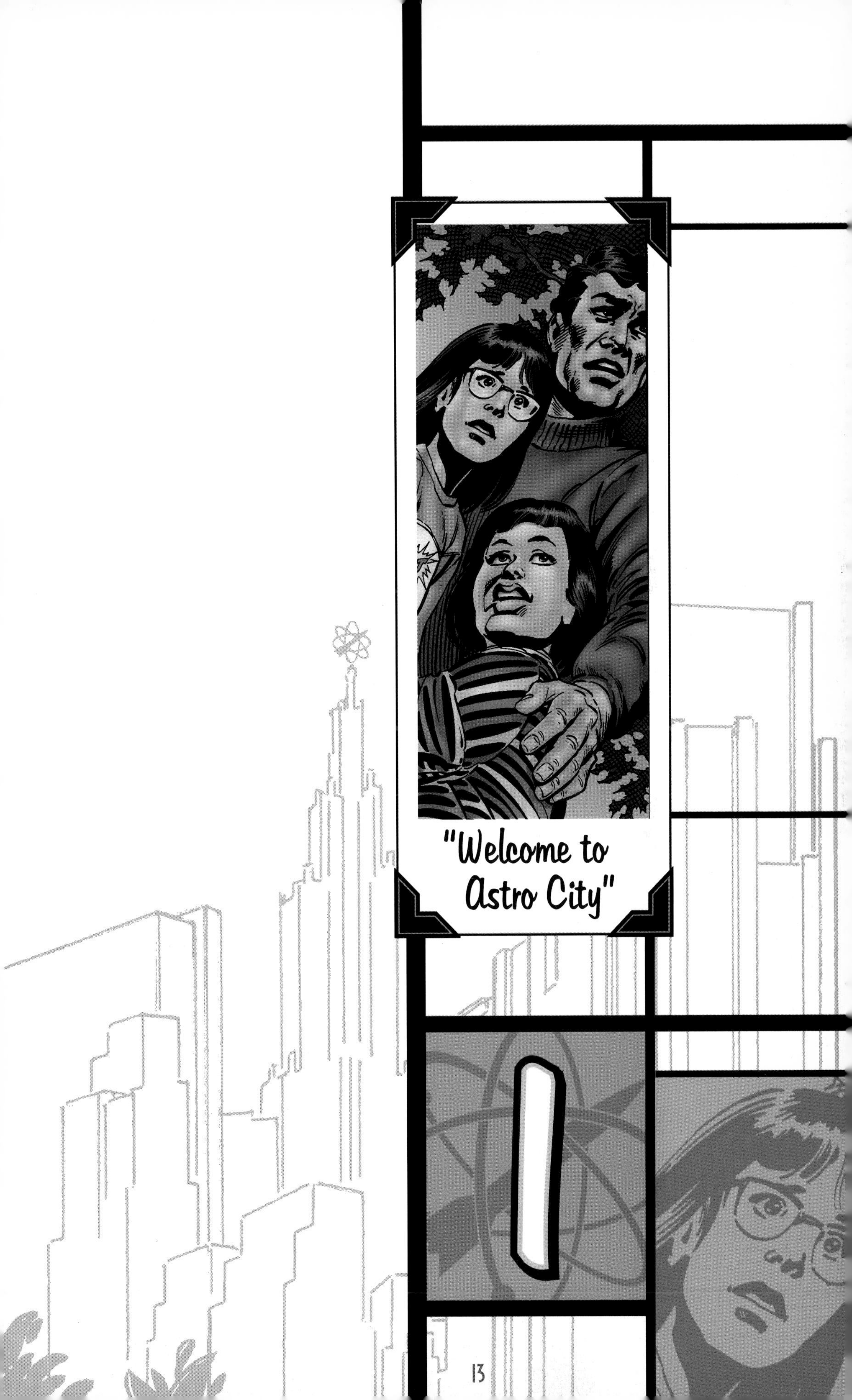
"Welcome to Astro City"

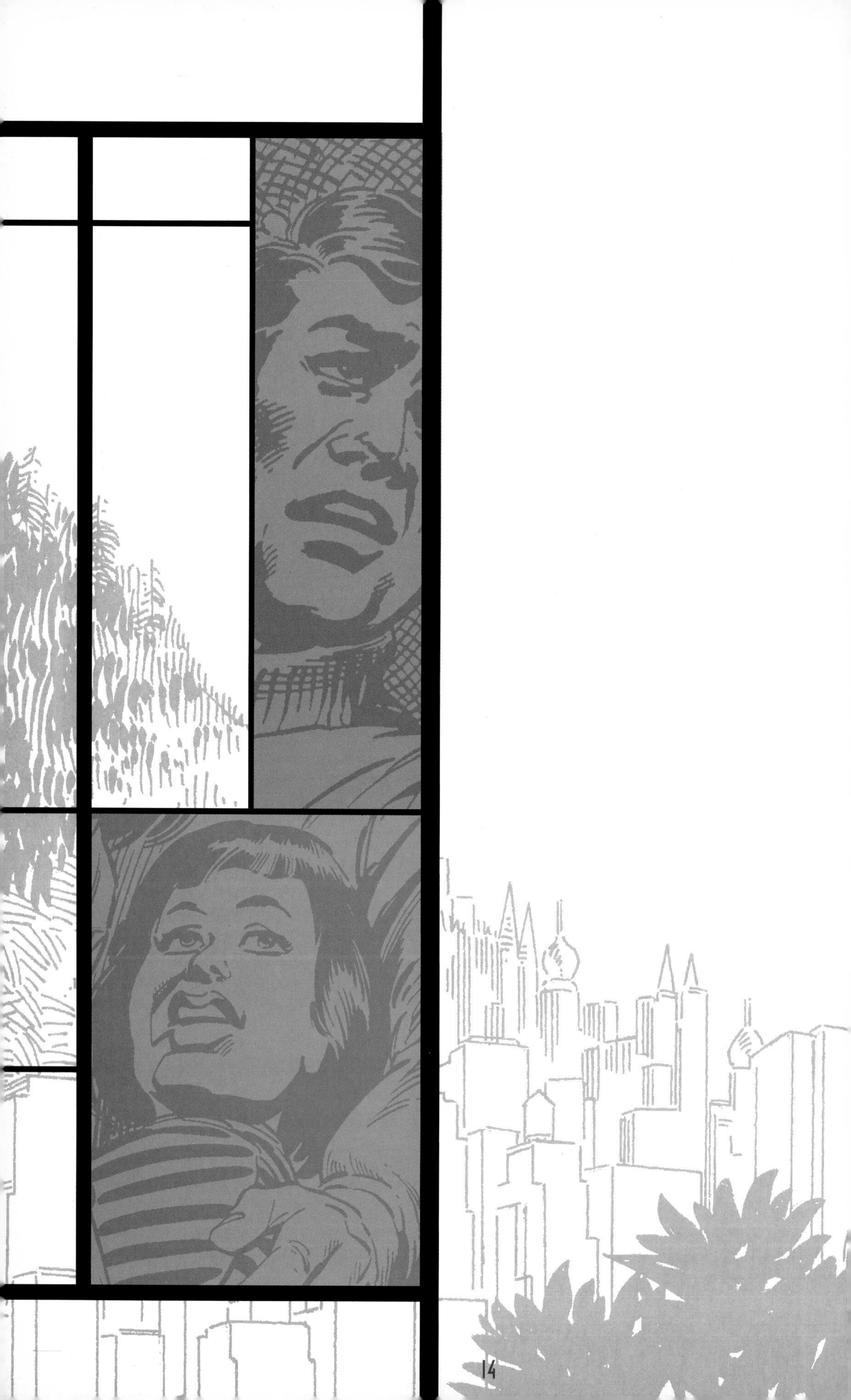

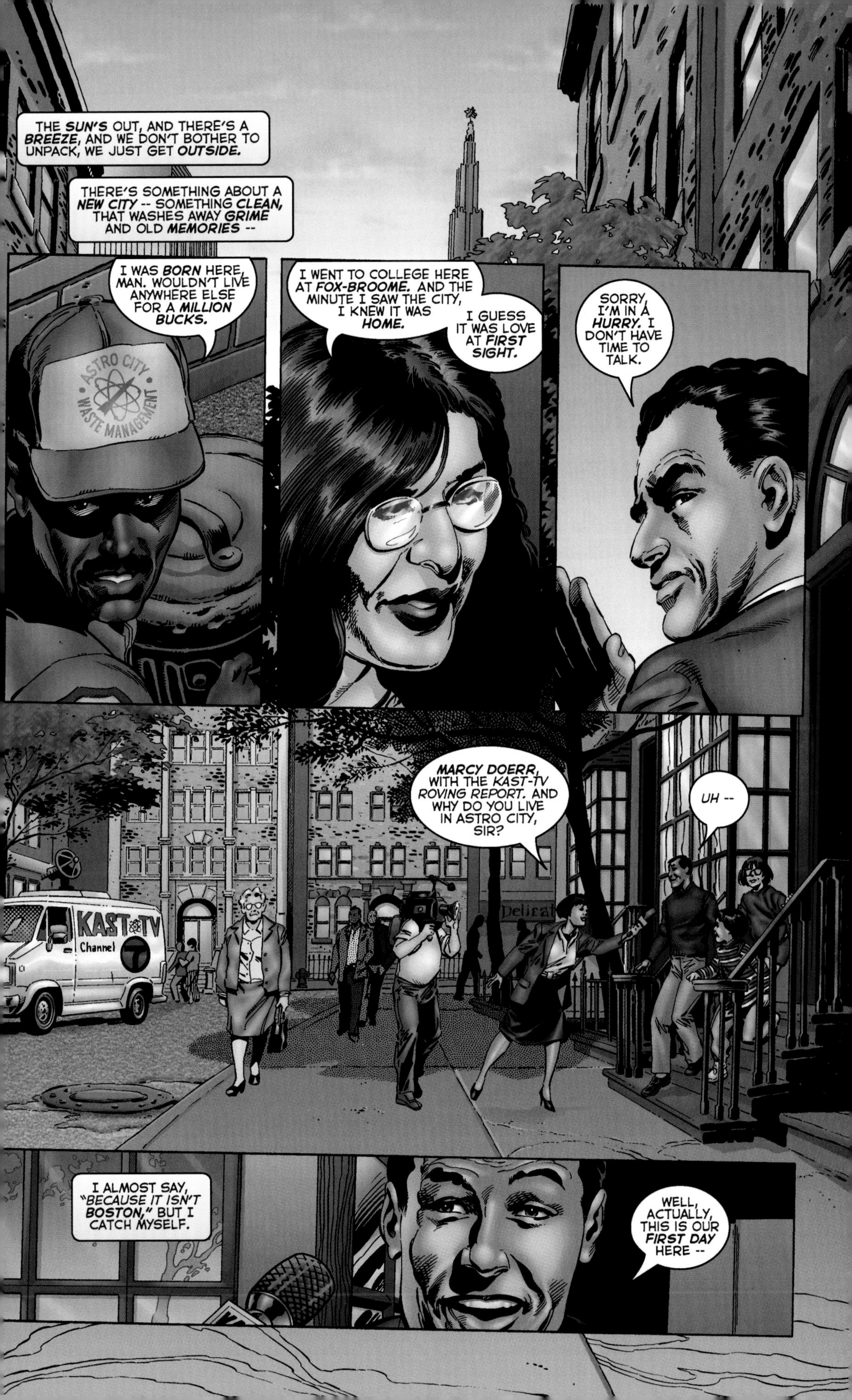
THE SUN'S OUT, AND THERE'S A BREEZE, AND WE DON'T BOTHER TO UNPACK, WE JUST GET OUTSIDE.
THERE'S SOMETHING ABOUT A NEW CITY -- SOMETHING CLEAN, THAT WASHES AWAY GRIME AND OLD MEMORIES --
I WAS BORN HERE, MAN. WOULDN'T LIVE ANYWHERE ELSE FOR A MILLION BUCKS.
ASTRO CITY WASTE MANAGEMENT
I WENT TO COLLEGE HERE AT FOX-BROOME. AND THE MINUTE I SAW THE CITY, I KNEW IT WAS HOME.
I GUESS IT WAS LOVE AT FIRST SIGHT.
SORRY, I'M IN A HURRY. I DON'T HAVE TIME TO TALK.
MARCY DOERR, WITH THE KAST-TV ROVING REPORT. AND WHY DO YOU LIVE IN ASTRO CITY, SIR?
UH --
KAST TV
Channel
I ALMOST SAY, "BECAUSE IT ISN'T BOSTON," BUT I CATCH MYSELF.
WELL, ACTUALLY, THIS IS OUR FIRST DAY HERE --

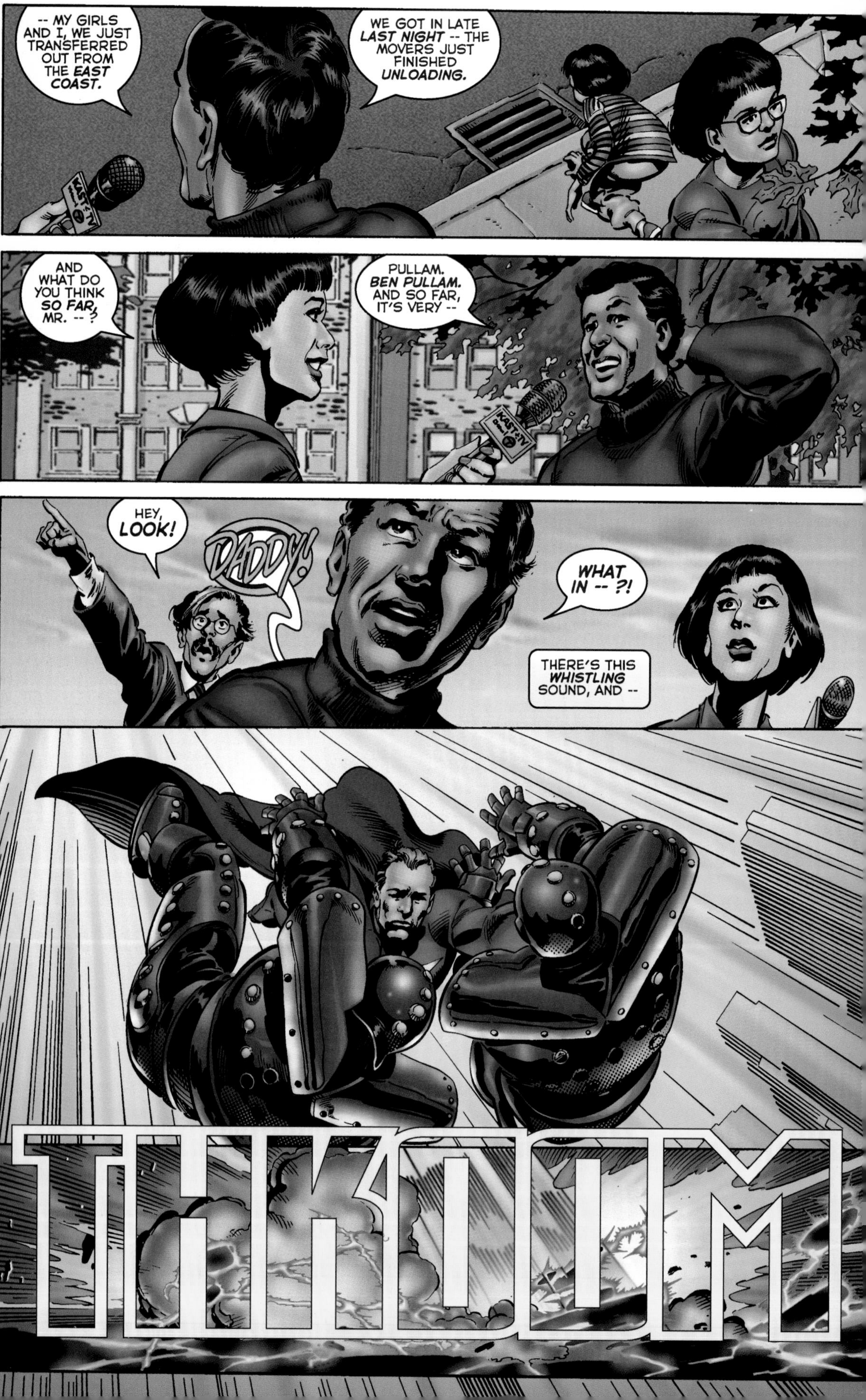
-- MY GIRLS AND I, WE JUST TRANSFERRED OUT FROM THE EAST COAST.
WE GOT IN LATE LAST NIGHT -- THE MOVERS JUST FINISHED UNLOADING.
KAST TV
AND WHAT DO YOU THINK SO FAR, MR. -- ?
PULLAM. BEN PULLAM. AND SO FAR, IT'S VERY --
KAST TV
HEY, LOOK!
DADDY!
WHAT IN -- ?!
THERE'S THIS WHISTLING SOUND, AND --
THKOOM

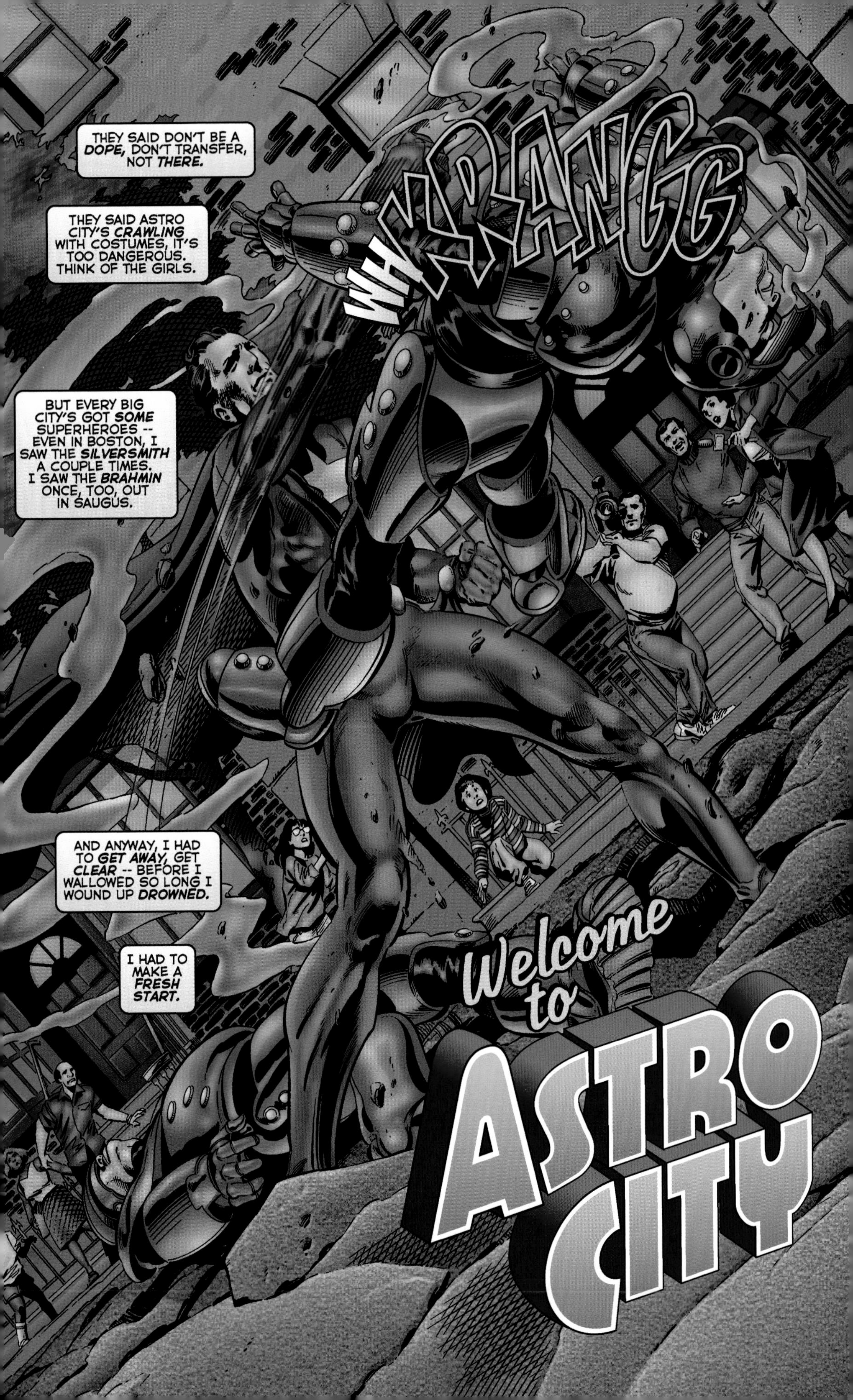

THEY SAID DON'T BE A DOPE, DON'T TRANSFER, NOT THERE.
THEY SAID ASTRO CITY'S CRAWLING WITH COSTUMES, IT'S TOO DANGEROUS. THINK OF THE GIRLS.
WHKRANGG
BUT EVERY BIG CITY'S GOT SOME SUPERHEROES -- EVEN IN BOSTON, I SAW THE SILVERSMITH A COUPLE TIMES. I SAW THE BRAHMIN ONCE, TOO, OUT IN SAUGUS.
AND ANYWAY, I HAD TO GET AWAY, GET CLEAR -- BEFORE I WALLOWED SO LONG I WOUND UP DROWNED.
I HAD TO MAKE A FRESH START.
Welcome to
ASTRO CITY

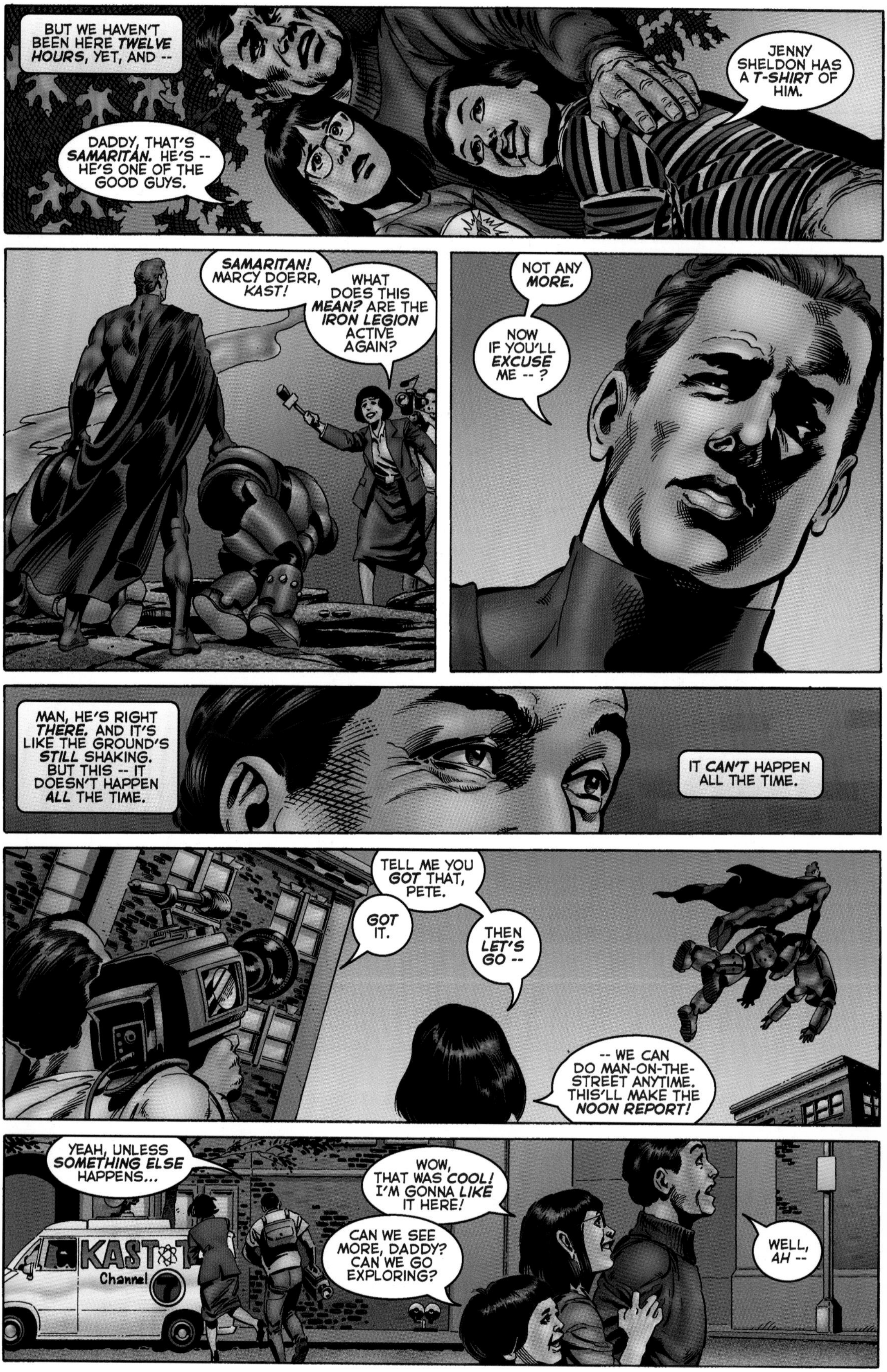
BUT WE HAVEN'T BEEN HERE TWELVE HOURS, YET, AND --
DADDY, THAT'S SAMARITAN. HE'S -- HE'S ONE OF THE GOOD GUYS.
JENNY SHELDON HAS A T-SHIRT OF HIM.
SAMARITAN! MARCY DOERR, KAST!
WHAT DOES THIS MEAN? ARE THE IRON LEGION ACTIVE AGAIN?
NOT ANY MORE.
NOW IF YOU'LL EXCUSE ME -- ?
MAN, HE'S RIGHT THERE. AND IT'S LIKE THE GROUND'S STILL SHAKING. BUT THIS -- IT DOESN'T HAPPEN ALL THE TIME.
IT CAN'T HAPPEN ALL THE TIME.
TELL ME YOU GOT THAT, PETE.
GOT IT.
THEN LET'S GO --
-- WE CAN DO MAN-ON-THE-STREET ANYTIME. THIS'LL MAKE THE NOON REPORT!
YEAH, UNLESS SOMETHING ELSE HAPPENS...
KAST-TV
Channel 7
WOW, THAT WAS COOL! I'M GONNA LIKE IT HERE!
CAN WE SEE MORE, DADDY? CAN WE GO EXPLORING?
WELL, AH --

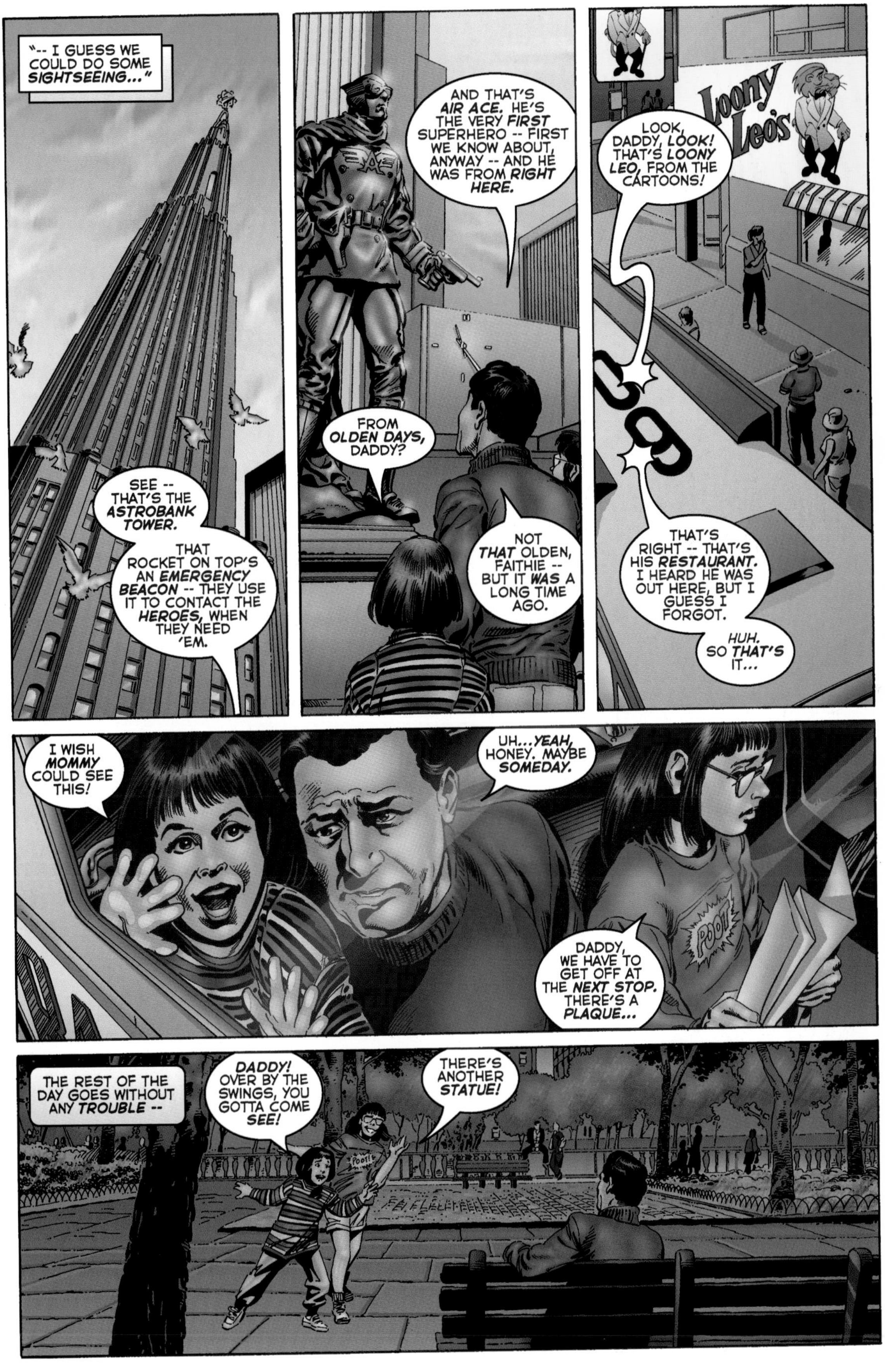
"-- I GUESS WE COULD DO SOME SIGHTSEEING..."
SEE -- THAT'S THE ASTROBANK TOWER.
THAT ROCKET ON TOP'S AN EMERGENCY BEACON -- THEY USE IT TO CONTACT THE HEROES, WHEN THEY NEED 'EM.
AND THAT'S AIR ACE. HE'S THE VERY FIRST SUPERHERO -- FIRST WE KNOW ABOUT, ANYWAY -- AND HE WAS FROM RIGHT HERE.
FROM OLDEN DAYS, DADDY?
NOT THAT OLDEN, FAITHIE -- BUT IT WAS A LONG TIME AGO.
Loony Leo's
LOOK, DADDY, LOOK! THAT'S LOONY LEO, FROM THE CARTOONS!
THAT'S RIGHT -- THAT'S HIS RESTAURANT. I HEARD HE WAS OUT HERE, BUT I GUESS I FORGOT.
HUH. SO THAT'S IT...
I WISH MOMMY COULD SEE THIS!
UH...YEAH, HONEY. MAYBE SOMEDAY.
DADDY, WE HAVE TO GET OFF AT THE NEXT STOP. THERE'S A PLAQUE...
THE REST OF THE DAY GOES WITHOUT ANY TROUBLE --
DADDY! OVER BY THE SWINGS, YOU GOTTA COME SEE!
THERE'S ANOTHER STATUE!

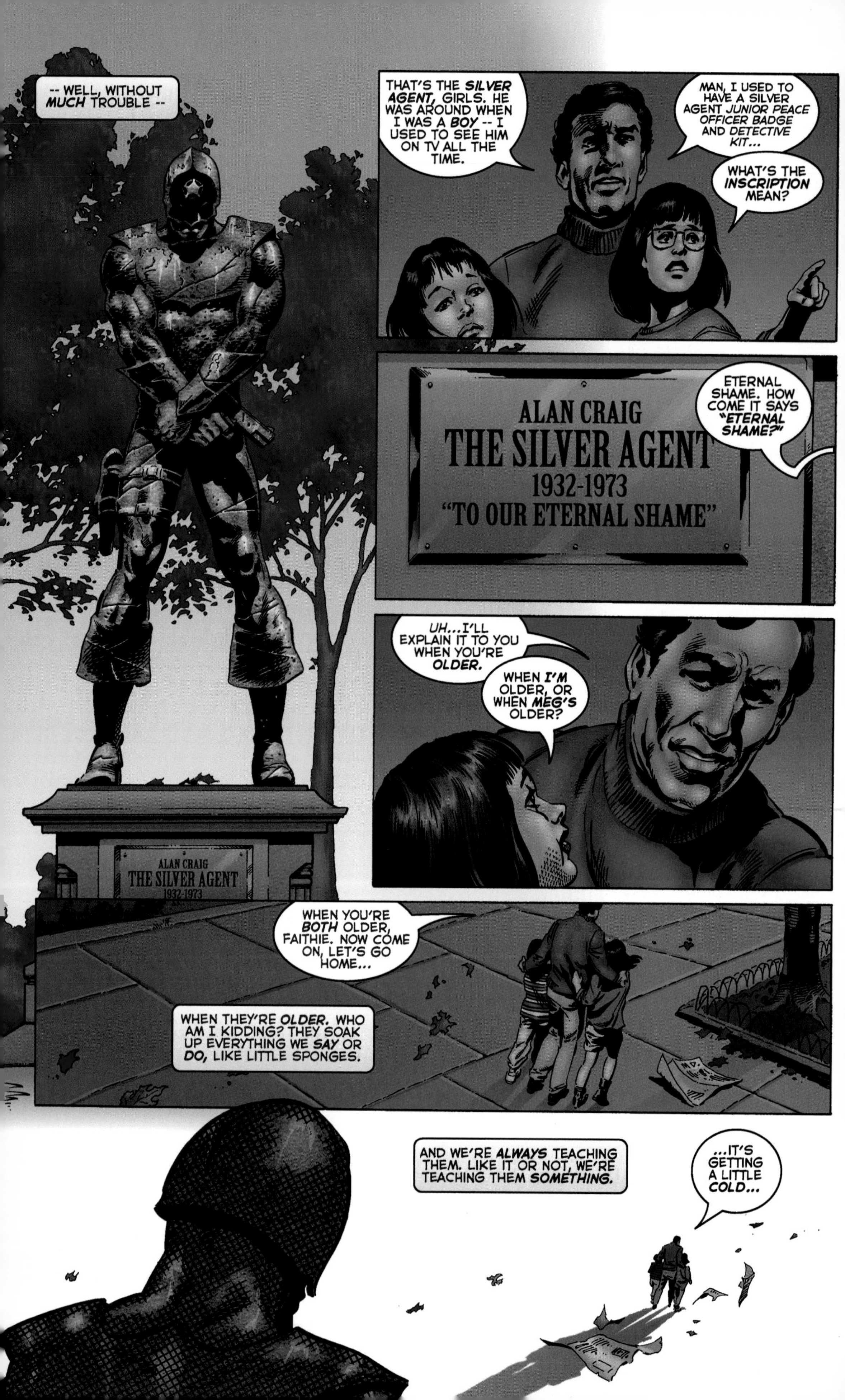

-- WELL, WITHOUT MUCH TROUBLE --
ALAN CRAIG
THE SILVER AGENT
1932-1973
THAT'S THE SILVER AGENT, GIRLS. HE WAS AROUND WHEN I WAS A BOY -- I USED TO SEE HIM ON TV ALL THE TIME.
MAN, I USED TO HAVE A SILVER AGENT JUNIOR PEACE OFFICER BADGE AND DETECTIVE KIT...
WHAT'S THE INSCRIPTION MEAN?
ALAN CRAIG
THE SILVER AGENT
1932-1973
"TO OUR ETERNAL SHAME"
ETERNAL SHAME. HOW COME IT SAYS "ETERNAL SHAME?"
UH...I'LL EXPLAIN IT TO YOU WHEN YOU'RE OLDER.
WHEN I'M OLDER, OR WHEN MEG'S OLDER?
WHEN YOU'RE BOTH OLDER, FAITHIE. NOW COME ON, LET'S GO HOME...
WHEN THEY'RE OLDER. WHO AM I KIDDING? THEY SOAK UP EVERYTHING WE SAY OR DO, LIKE LITTLE SPONGES.
AND WE'RE ALWAYS TEACHING THEM. LIKE IT OR NOT, WE'RE TEACHING THEM SOMETHING.
...IT'S GETTING A LITTLE COLD...

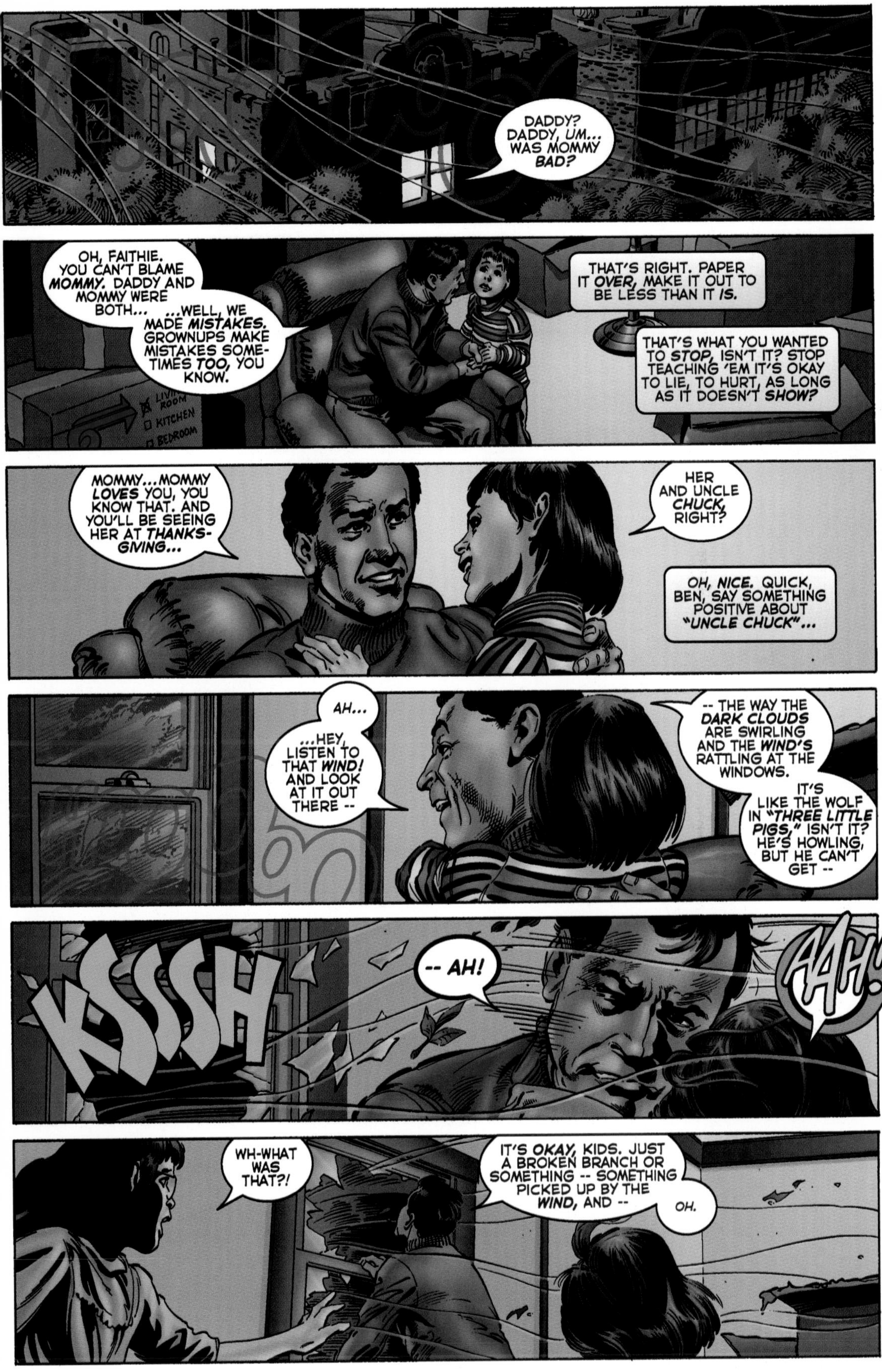
DADDY? DADDY, UM... WAS MOMMY BAD?
OH, FAITHIE. YOU CAN'T BLAME MOMMY. DADDY AND MOMMY WERE BOTH... ...WELL, WE MADE MISTAKES. GROWNUPS MAKE MISTAKES SOMETIMES TOO, YOU KNOW.
LIVING ROOM
KITCHEN
BEDROOM
THAT'S RIGHT. PAPER IT OVER, MAKE IT OUT TO BE LESS THAN IT IS.
THAT'S WHAT YOU WANTED TO STOP, ISN'T IT? STOP TEACHING 'EM IT'S OKAY TO LIE, TO HURT, AS LONG AS IT DOESN'T SHOW?
MOMMY...MOMMY LOVES YOU, YOU KNOW THAT. AND YOU'LL BE SEEING HER AT THANKSGIVING...
HER AND UNCLE CHUCK, RIGHT?
OH, NICE. QUICK, BEN, SAY SOMETHING POSITIVE ABOUT "UNCLE CHUCK"...
AH...
...HEY, LISTEN TO THAT WIND! AND LOOK AT IT OUT THERE --
-- THE WAY THE DARK CLOUDS ARE SWIRLING AND THE WIND'S RATTLING AT THE WINDOWS.
IT'S LIKE THE WOLF IN "THREE LITTLE PIGS," ISN'T IT? HE'S HOWLING, BUT HE CAN'T GET --
KSSSH
-- AH!
AAH!
WH-WHAT WAS THAT?!
IT'S OKAY, KIDS. JUST A BROKEN BRANCH OR SOMETHING -- SOMETHING PICKED UP BY THE WIND, AND --
OH.

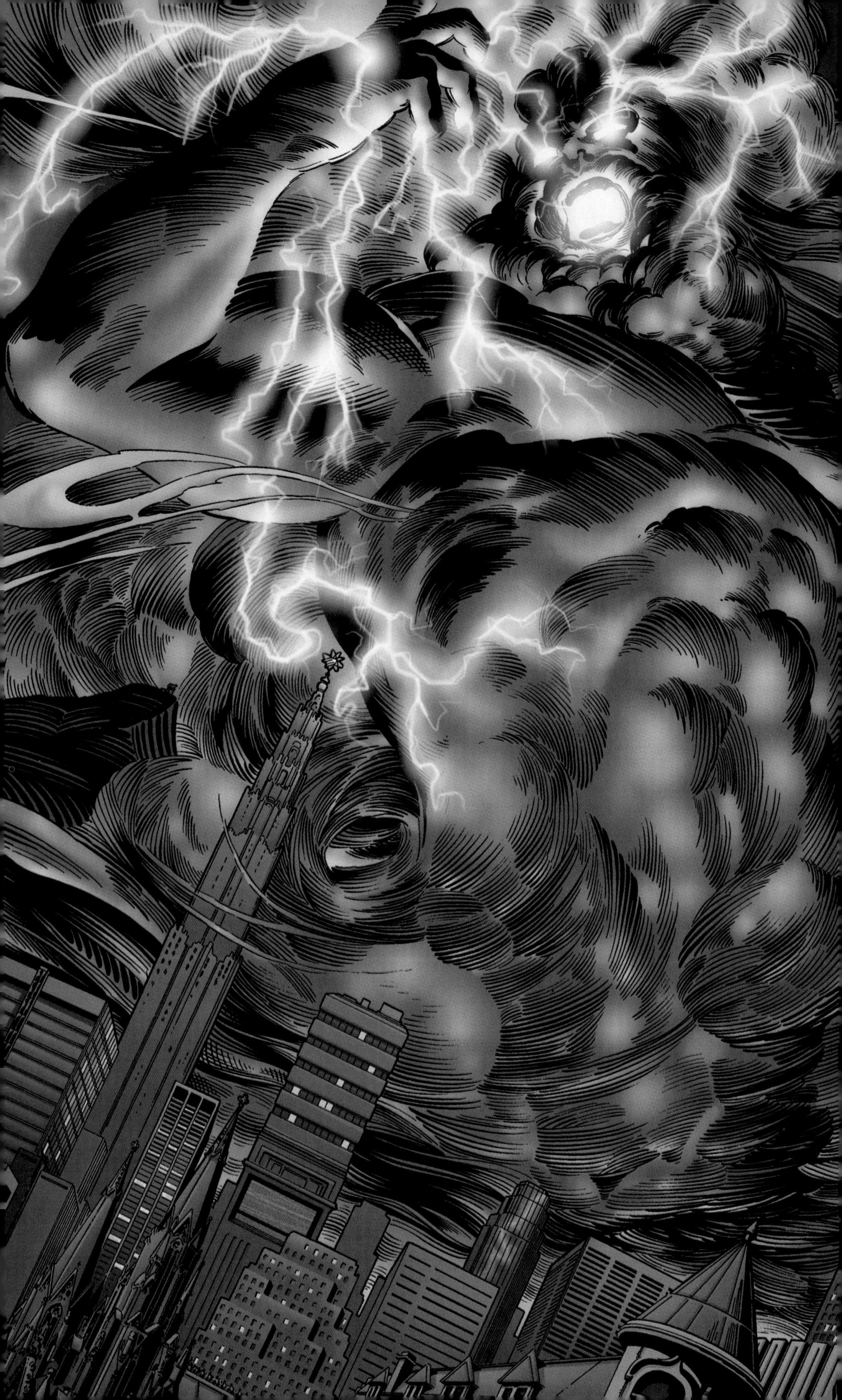

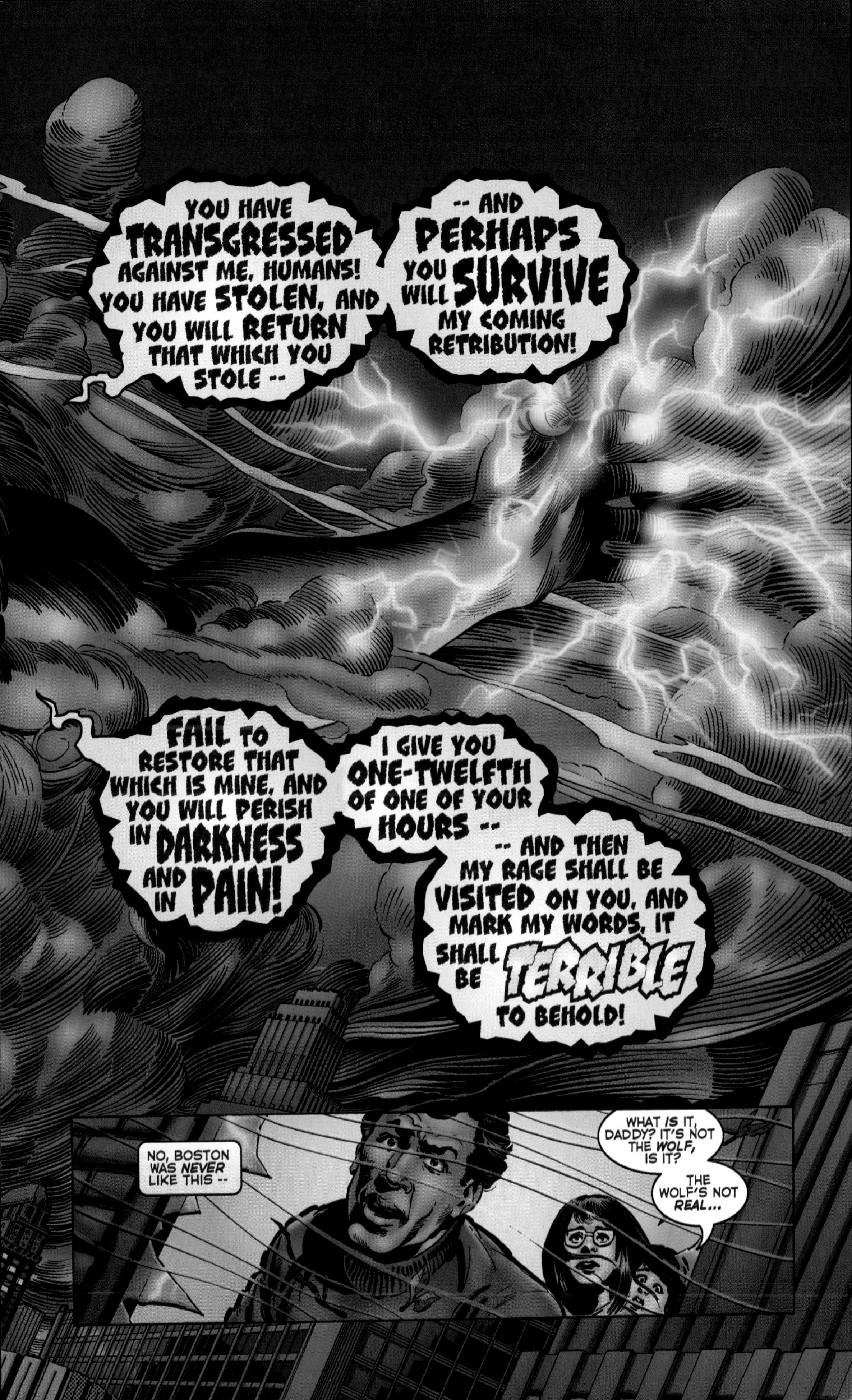
YOU HAVE TRANSGRESSED AGAINST ME, HUMANS! YOU HAVE STOLEN, AND YOU WILL RETURN THAT WHICH YOU STOLE --
-- AND PERHAPS YOU WILL SURVIVE MY COMING RETRIBUTION!
FAIL TO RESTORE THAT WHICH IS MINE, AND YOU WILL PERISH IN DARKNESS AND IN PAIN!
I GIVE YOU ONE-TWELFTH OF ONE OF YOUR HOURS --
-- AND THEN MY RAGE SHALL BE VISITED ON YOU, AND MARK MY WORDS, IT SHALL BE TERRIBLE TO BEHOLD!
NO, BOSTON WAS NEVER LIKE THIS --
WHAT IS IT, DADDY? IT'S NOT THE WOLF, IS IT?
THE WOLF'S NOT REAL...

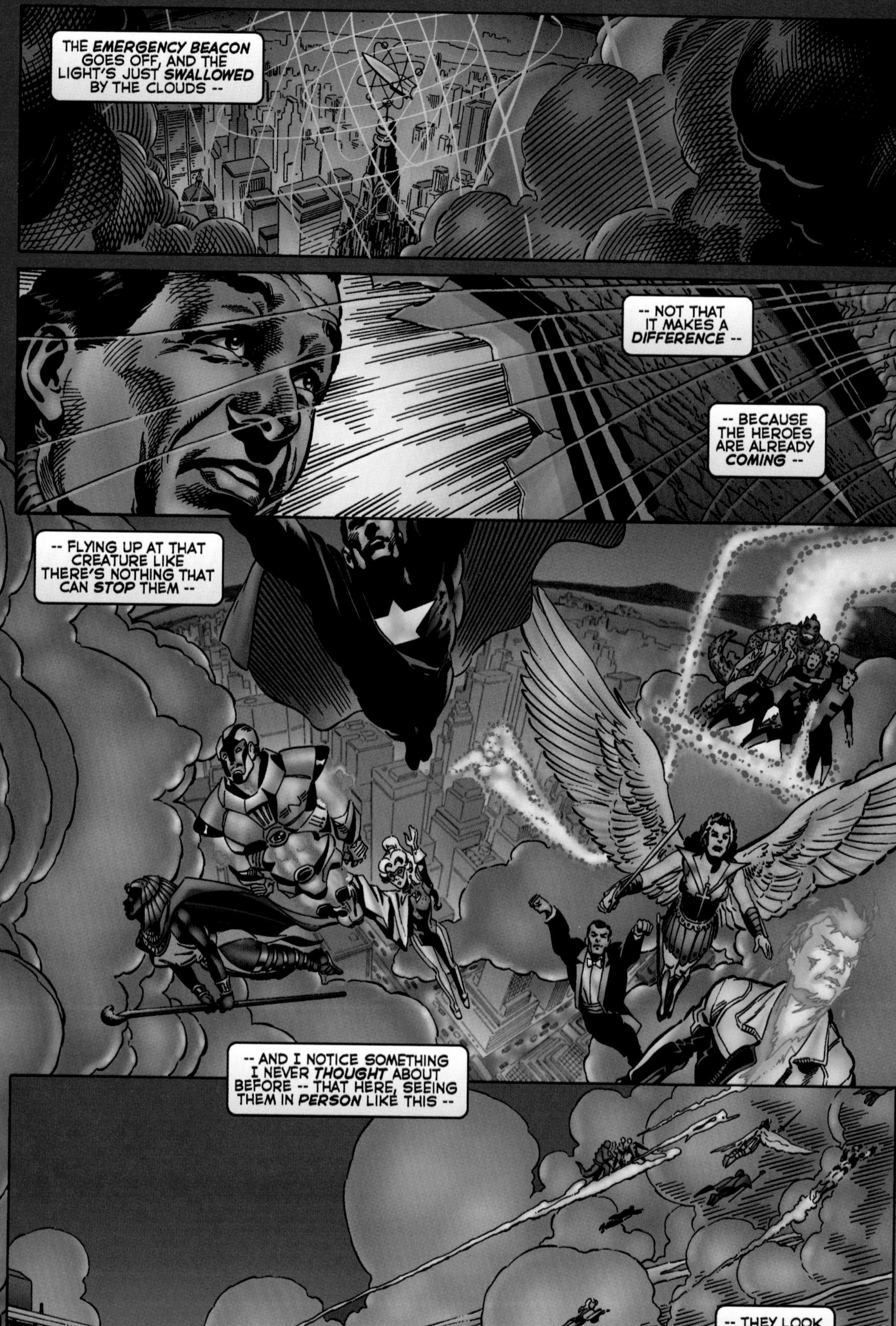
THE EMERGENCY BEACON GOES OFF, AND THE LIGHT'S JUST SWALLOWED BY THE CLOUDS --
-- NOT THAT IT MAKES A DIFFERENCE --
-- BECAUSE THE HEROES ARE ALREADY COMING --
-- FLYING UP AT THAT CREATURE LIKE THERE'S NOTHING THAT CAN STOP THEM --
-- AND I NOTICE SOMETHING I NEVER THOUGHT ABOUT BEFORE -- THAT HERE, SEEING THEM IN PERSON LIKE THIS --
-- THEY LOOK SO SMALL --

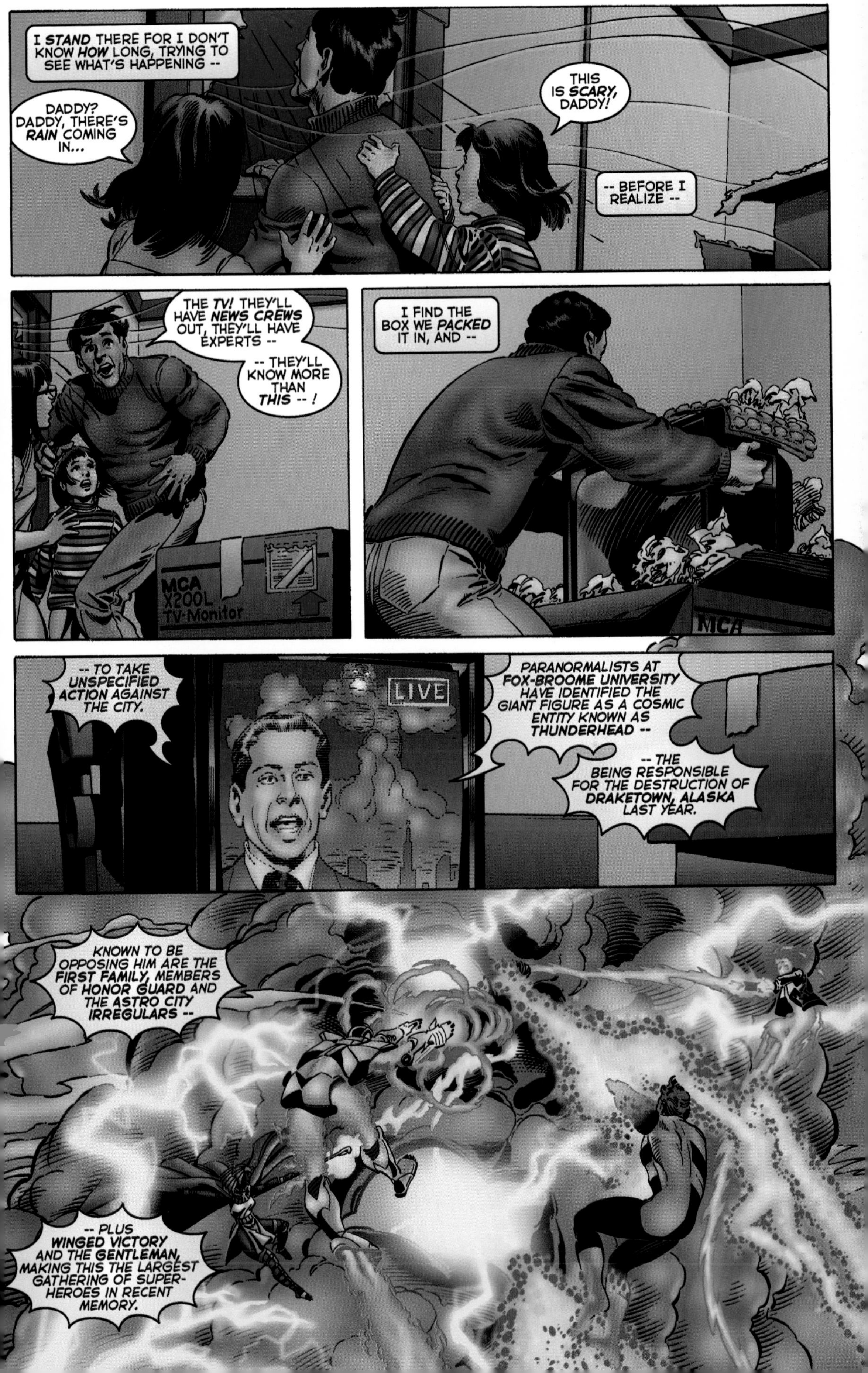
I STAND THERE FOR I DON'T KNOW HOW LONG, TRYING TO SEE WHAT'S HAPPENING --
DADDY? DADDY, THERE'S RAIN COMING IN...
THIS IS SCARY, DADDY!
-- BEFORE I REALIZE --
THE TV! THEY'LL HAVE NEWS CREWS OUT, THEY'LL HAVE EXPERTS --
-- THEY'LL KNOW MORE THAN THIS -- !
MCA X200L TV·Monitor
I FIND THE BOX WE PACKED IT IN, AND --
MCA
-- TO TAKE UNSPECIFIED ACTION AGAINST THE CITY.
LIVE
PARANORMALISTS AT FOX-BROOME UNIVERSITY HAVE IDENTIFIED THE GIANT FIGURE AS A COSMIC ENTITY KNOWN AS THUNDERHEAD --
-- THE BEING RESPONSIBLE FOR THE DESTRUCTION OF DRAKETOWN, ALASKA LAST YEAR.
KNOWN TO BE OPPOSING HIM ARE THE FIRST FAMILY, MEMBERS OF HONOR GUARD AND THE ASTRO CITY IRREGULARS --
-- PLUS WINGED VICTORY AND THE GENTLEMAN, MAKING THIS THE LARGEST GATHERING OF SUPER-HEROES IN RECENT MEMORY.

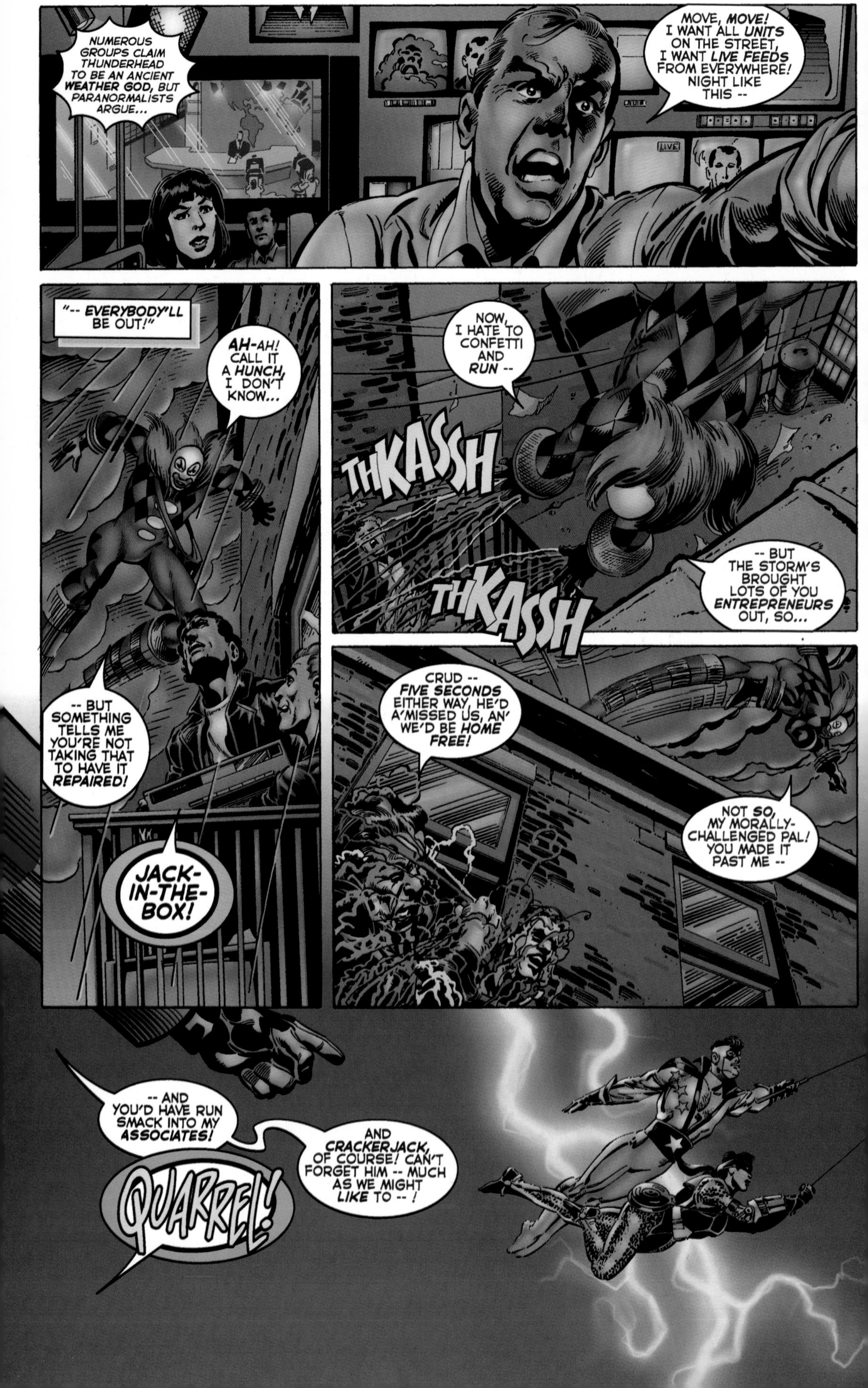
NUMEROUS GROUPS CLAIM THUNDERHEAD TO BE AN ANCIENT WEATHER GOD, BUT PARANORMALISTS ARGUE...
MOVE, MOVE! I WANT ALL UNITS ON THE STREET, I WANT LIVE FEEDS FROM EVERYWHERE! NIGHT LIKE THIS --
LIVE
"-- EVERYBODY'LL BE OUT!"
AH-AH! CALL IT A HUNCH, I DON'T KNOW...
-- BUT SOMETHING TELLS ME YOU'RE NOT TAKING THAT TO HAVE IT REPAIRED!
JACK-IN-THE-BOX!
NOW, I HATE TO CONFETTI AND RUN --
THKASSH
THKASSH
-- BUT THE STORM'S BROUGHT LOTS OF YOU ENTREPRENEURS OUT, SO...
CRUD -- FIVE SECONDS EITHER WAY, HE'D A'MISSED US, AN' WE'D BE HOME FREE!
NOT SO, MY MORALLY-CHALLENGED PAL! YOU MADE IT PAST ME --
-- AND YOU'D HAVE RUN SMACK INTO MY ASSOCIATES!
QUARREL!
AND CRACKERJACK, OF COURSE! CAN'T FORGET HIM -- MUCH AS WE MIGHT LIKE TO -- !

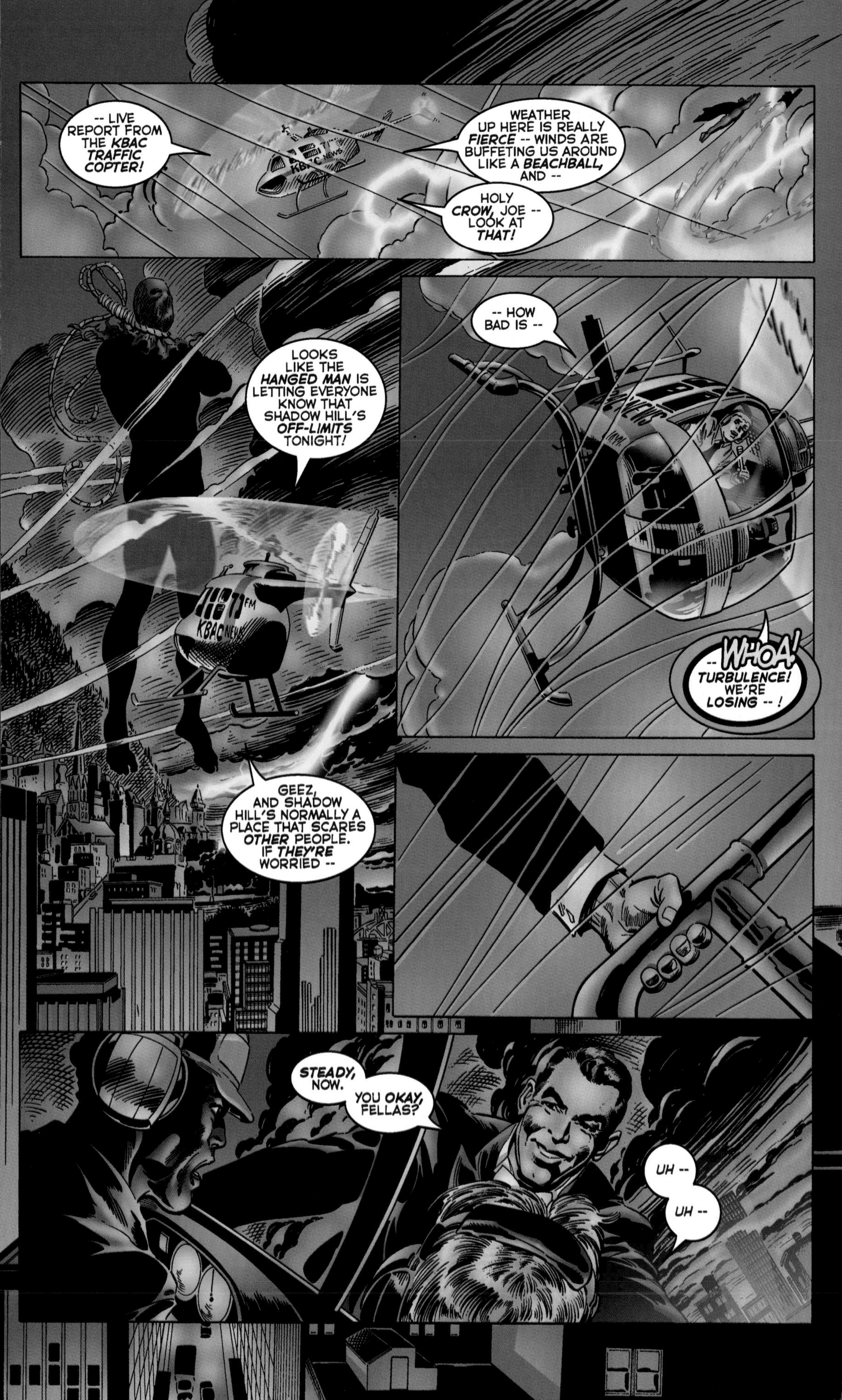
-- LIVE REPORT FROM THE KBAC TRAFFIC COPTER!
WEATHER UP HERE IS REALLY FIERCE -- WINDS ARE BUFFETING US AROUND LIKE A BEACHBALL, AND --
HOLY CROW, JOE -- LOOK AT THAT!
KBAC NEWS
LOOKS LIKE THE HANGED MAN IS LETTING EVERYONE KNOW THAT SHADOW HILL'S OFF-LIMITS TONIGHT!
GEEZ, AND SHADOW HILL'S NORMALLY A PLACE THAT SCARES OTHER PEOPLE. IF THEY'RE WORRIED --
-- HOW BAD IS --
-- WHOA! TURBULENCE! WE'RE LOSING -- !
STEADY, NOW.
YOU OKAY, FELLAS?
UH --
UH --

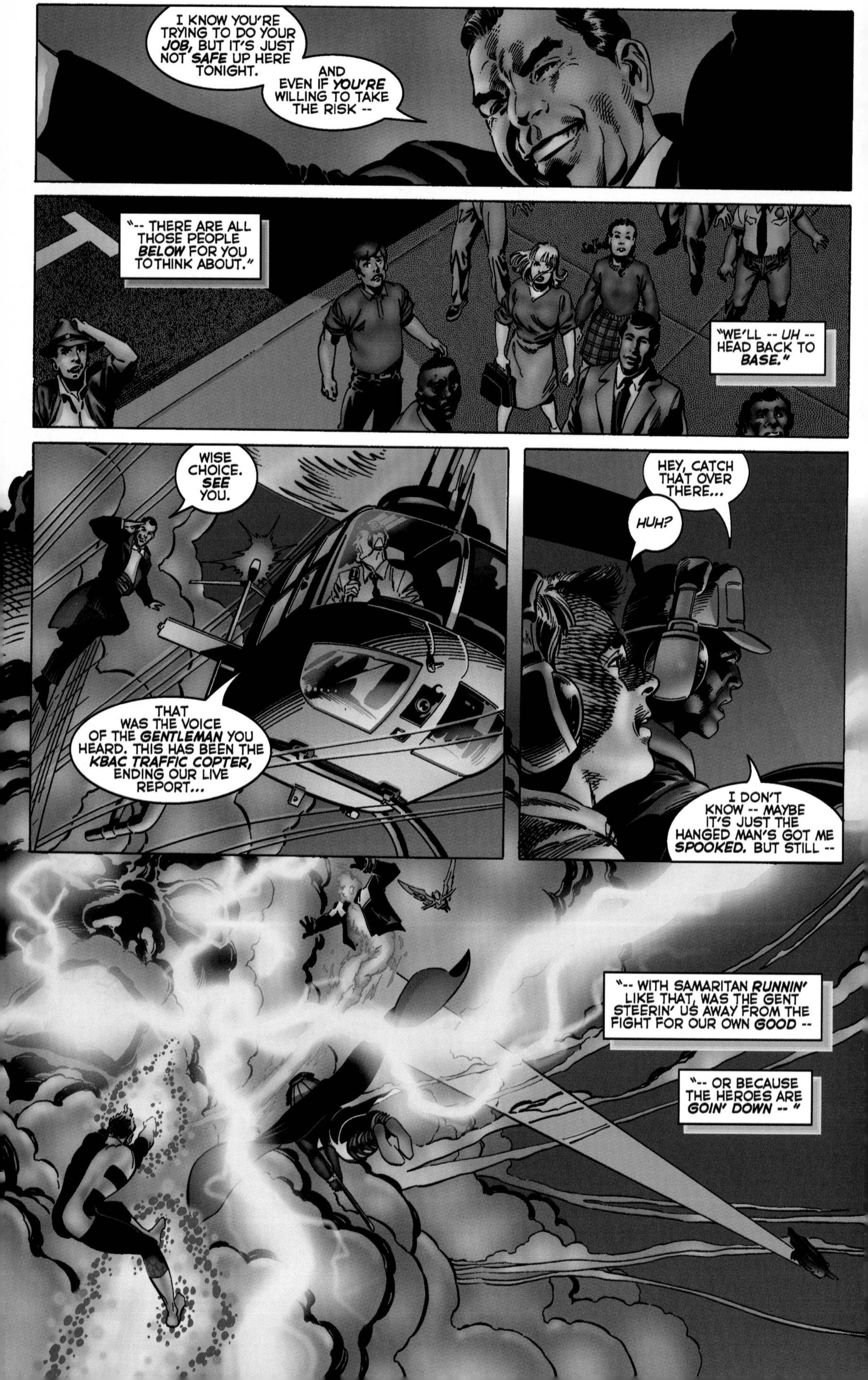
I KNOW YOU'RE TRYING TO DO YOUR JOB, BUT IT'S JUST NOT SAFE UP HERE TONIGHT.
AND EVEN IF YOU'RE WILLING TO TAKE THE RISK --
"-- THERE ARE ALL THOSE PEOPLE BELOW FOR YOU TO THINK ABOUT."
"WE'LL -- UH -- HEAD BACK TO BASE."
WISE CHOICE. SEE YOU.
THAT WAS THE VOICE OF THE GENTLEMAN YOU HEARD. THIS HAS BEEN THE KBAC TRAFFIC COPTER, ENDING OUR LIVE REPORT...
HEY, CATCH THAT OVER THERE...
HUH?
I DON'T KNOW -- MAYBE IT'S JUST THE HANGED MAN'S GOT ME SPOOKED. BUT STILL --
"-- WITH SAMARITAN RUNNIN' LIKE THAT, WAS THE GENT STEERIN' US AWAY FROM THE FIGHT FOR OUR OWN GOOD --
"-- OR BECAUSE THE HEROES ARE GOIN' DOWN -- "

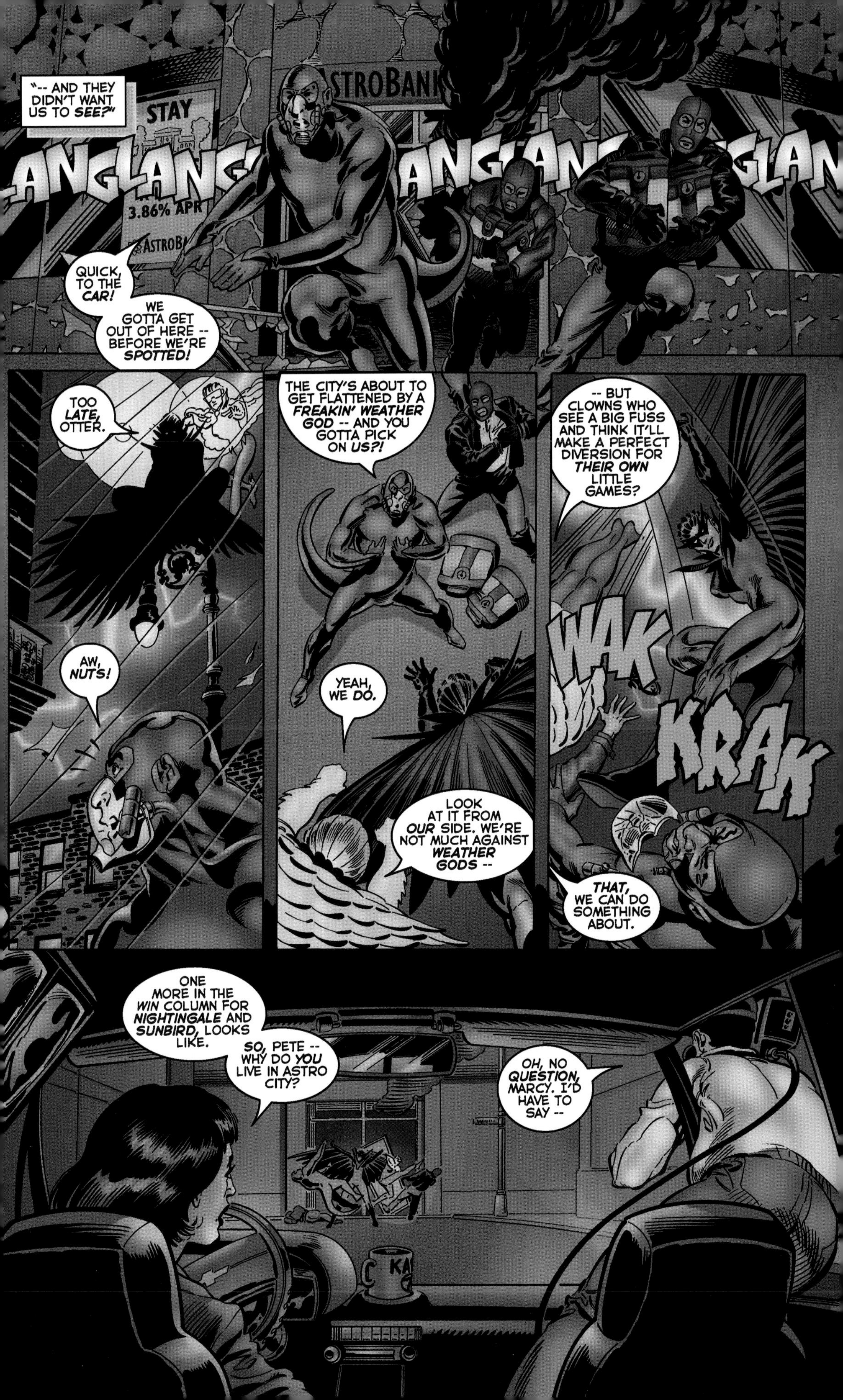
"-- AND THEY DIDN'T WANT US TO SEE?"
ASTROBANK
STAY
3.86% APR
ASTROBA
-ANGLANGLANGLANGLANGLANGLAN
QUICK, TO THE CAR!
WE GOTTA GET OUT OF HERE -- BEFORE WE'RE SPOTTED!
TOO LATE, OTTER.
AW, NUTS!
THE CITY'S ABOUT TO GET FLATTENED BY A FREAKIN' WEATHER GOD -- AND YOU GOTTA PICK ON US?!
YEAH, WE DO.
LOOK AT IT FROM OUR SIDE. WE'RE NOT MUCH AGAINST WEATHER GODS --
-- BUT CLOWNS WHO SEE A BIG FUSS AND THINK IT'LL MAKE A PERFECT DIVERSION FOR THEIR OWN LITTLE GAMES?
WAK
KRAK
THAT, WE CAN DO SOMETHING ABOUT.
ONE MORE IN THE WIN COLUMN FOR NIGHTINGALE AND SUNBIRD, LOOKS LIKE.
SO, PETE -- WHY DO YOU LIVE IN ASTRO CITY?
OH, NO QUESTION, MARCY. I'D HAVE TO SAY --

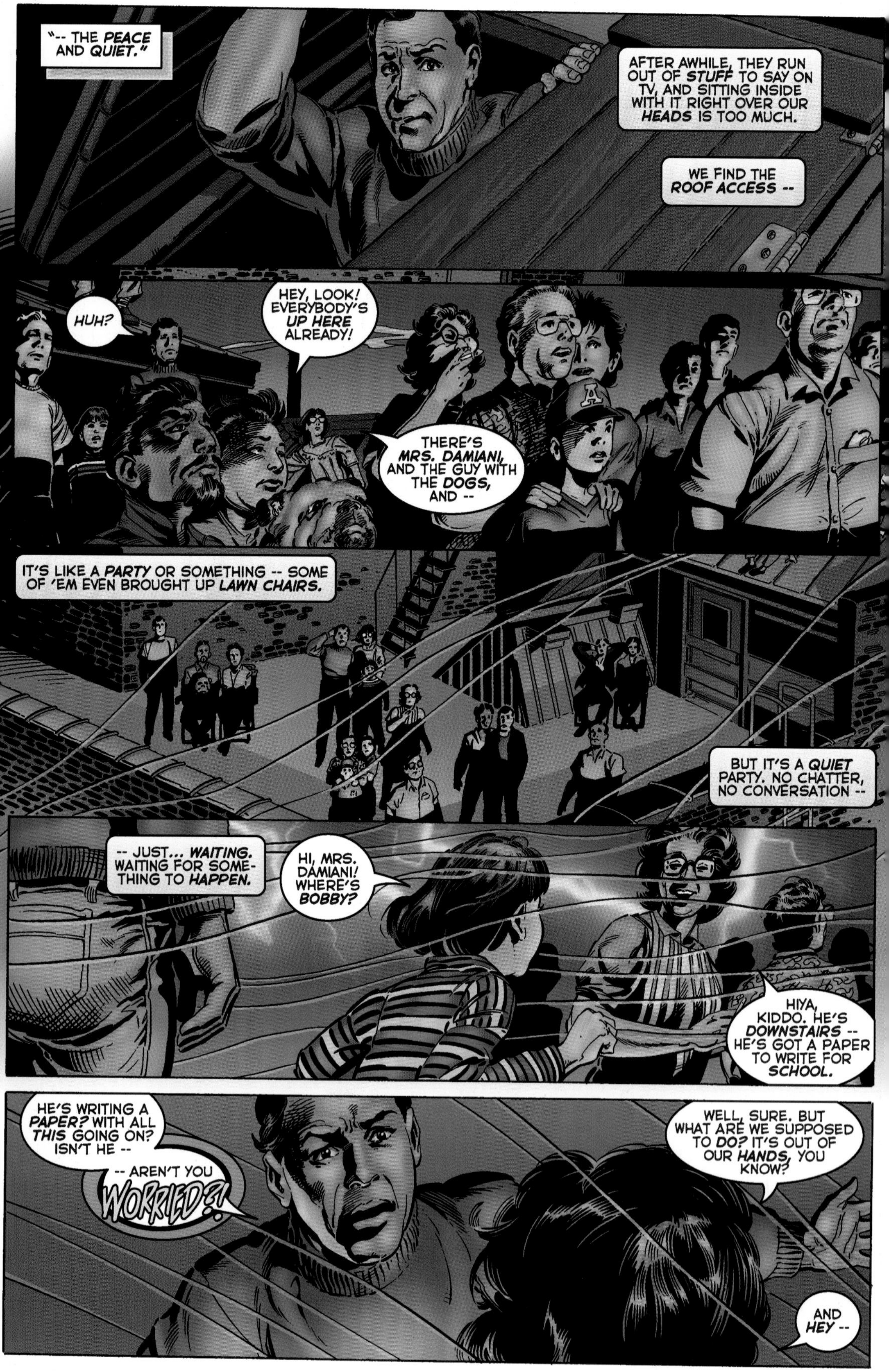
"-- THE PEACE AND QUIET."
AFTER AWHILE, THEY RUN OUT OF STUFF TO SAY ON TV, AND SITTING INSIDE WITH IT RIGHT OVER OUR HEADS IS TOO MUCH.
WE FIND THE ROOF ACCESS --
HUH?
HEY, LOOK! EVERYBODY'S UP HERE ALREADY!
THERE'S MRS. DAMIANI, AND THE GUY WITH THE DOGS, AND --
IT'S LIKE A PARTY OR SOMETHING -- SOME OF 'EM EVEN BROUGHT UP LAWN CHAIRS.
BUT IT'S A QUIET PARTY. NO CHATTER, NO CONVERSATION --
-- JUST... WAITING. WAITING FOR SOMETHING TO HAPPEN.
HI, MRS. DAMIANI! WHERE'S BOBBY?
HIYA, KIDDO. HE'S DOWNSTAIRS -- HE'S GOT A PAPER TO WRITE FOR SCHOOL.
HE'S WRITING A PAPER? WITH ALL THIS GOING ON? ISN'T HE --
-- AREN'T YOU WORRIED?!
WELL, SURE. BUT WHAT ARE WE SUPPOSED TO DO? IT'S OUT OF OUR HANDS, YOU KNOW?
AND HEY --

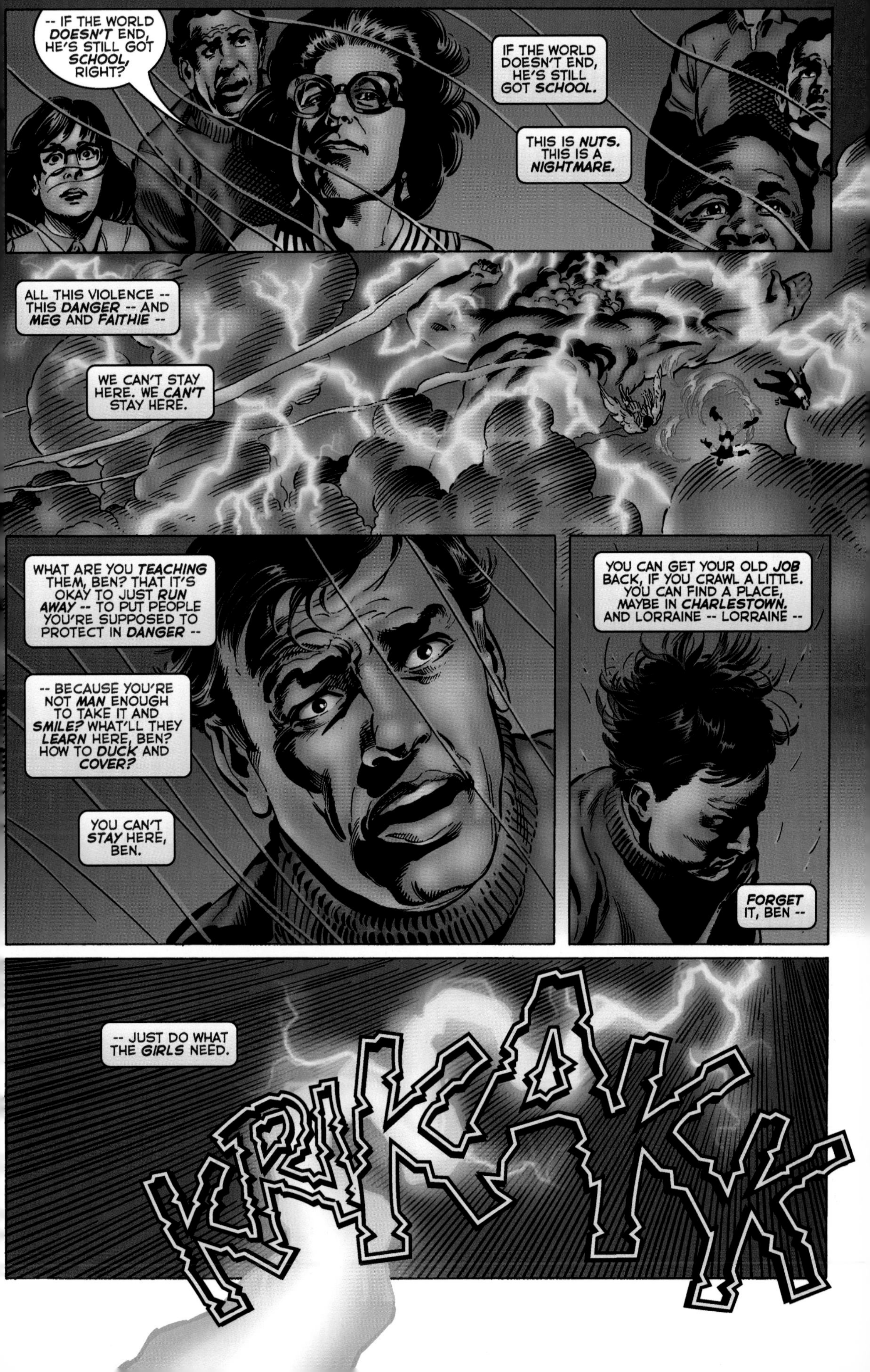
-- IF THE WORLD DOESN'T END, HE'S STILL GOT SCHOOL, RIGHT?
IF THE WORLD DOESN'T END, HE'S STILL GOT SCHOOL.
THIS IS NUTS. THIS IS A NIGHTMARE.
ALL THIS VIOLENCE -- THIS DANGER -- AND MEG AND FAITHIE --
WE CAN'T STAY HERE. WE CAN'T STAY HERE.
WHAT ARE YOU TEACHING THEM, BEN? THAT IT'S OKAY TO JUST RUN AWAY -- TO PUT PEOPLE YOU'RE SUPPOSED TO PROTECT IN DANGER --
-- BECAUSE YOU'RE NOT MAN ENOUGH TO TAKE IT AND SMILE? WHAT'LL THEY LEARN HERE, BEN? HOW TO DUCK AND COVER?
YOU CAN'T STAY HERE, BEN.
YOU CAN GET YOUR OLD JOB BACK, IF YOU CRAWL A LITTLE. YOU CAN FIND A PLACE, MAYBE IN CHARLESTOWN. AND LORRAINE -- LORRAINE --
FORGET IT, BEN --
-- JUST DO WHAT THE GIRLS NEED.
KRRKAKK

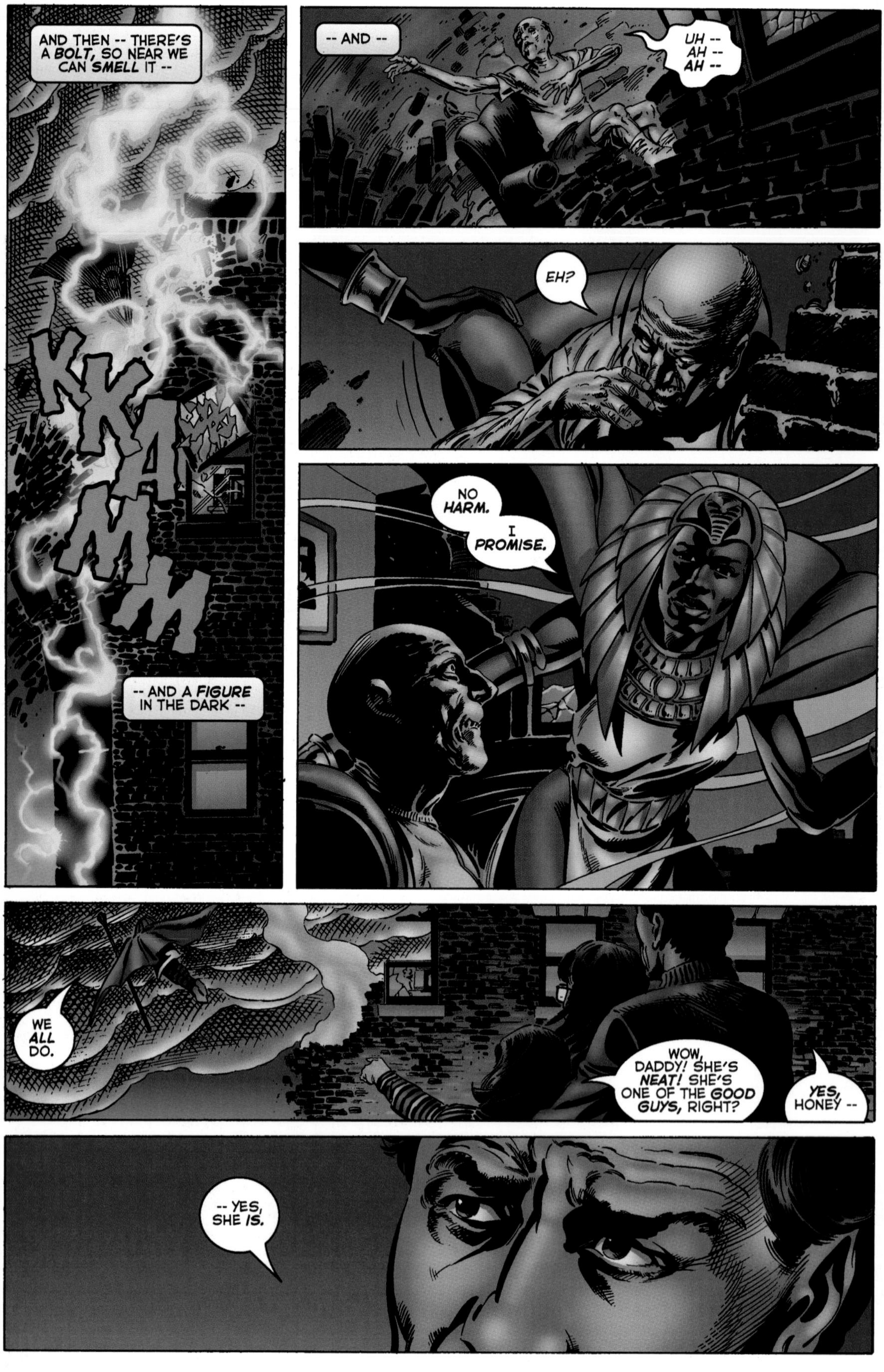

AND THEN -- THERE'S A BOLT, SO NEAR WE CAN SMELL IT --
KKAMMM
-- AND A FIGURE IN THE DARK --
-- AND --
UH -- AH -- AH --
EH?
NO HARM.
I PROMISE.
WE ALL DO.
WOW, DADDY! SHE'S NEAT! SHE'S ONE OF THE GOOD GUYS, RIGHT?
YES, HONEY --
-- YES, SHE IS.

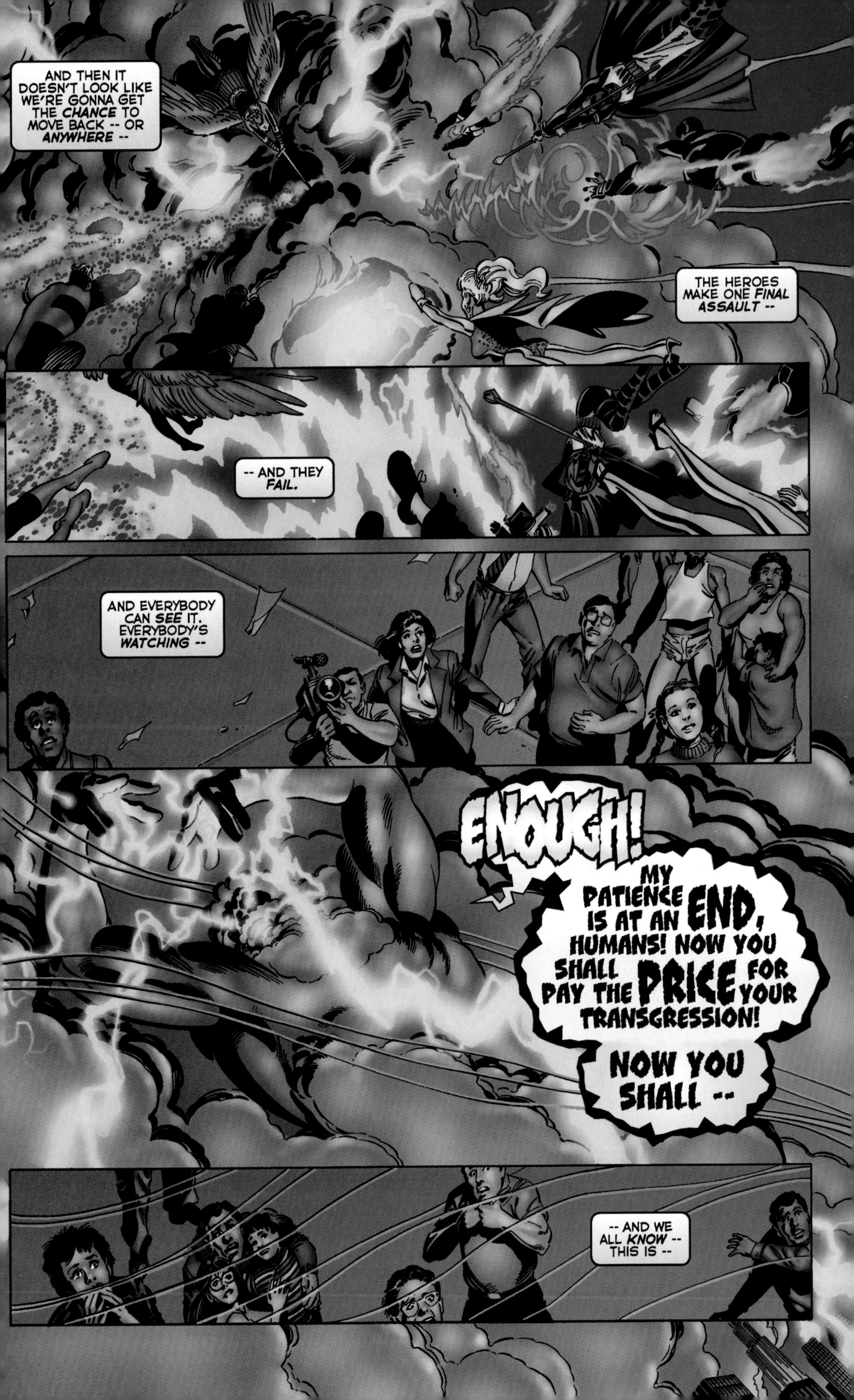
AND THEN IT DOESN'T LOOK LIKE WE'RE GONNA GET THE CHANCE TO MOVE BACK -- OR ANYWHERE --
THE HEROES MAKE ONE FINAL ASSAULT --
-- AND THEY FAIL.
AND EVERYBODY CAN SEE IT. EVERYBODY'S WATCHING --
ENOUGH!
MY PATIENCE IS AT AN END, HUMANS! NOW YOU SHALL PAY THE PRICE FOR YOUR TRANSGRESSION!
NOW YOU SHALL --
-- AND WE ALL KNOW -- THIS IS --

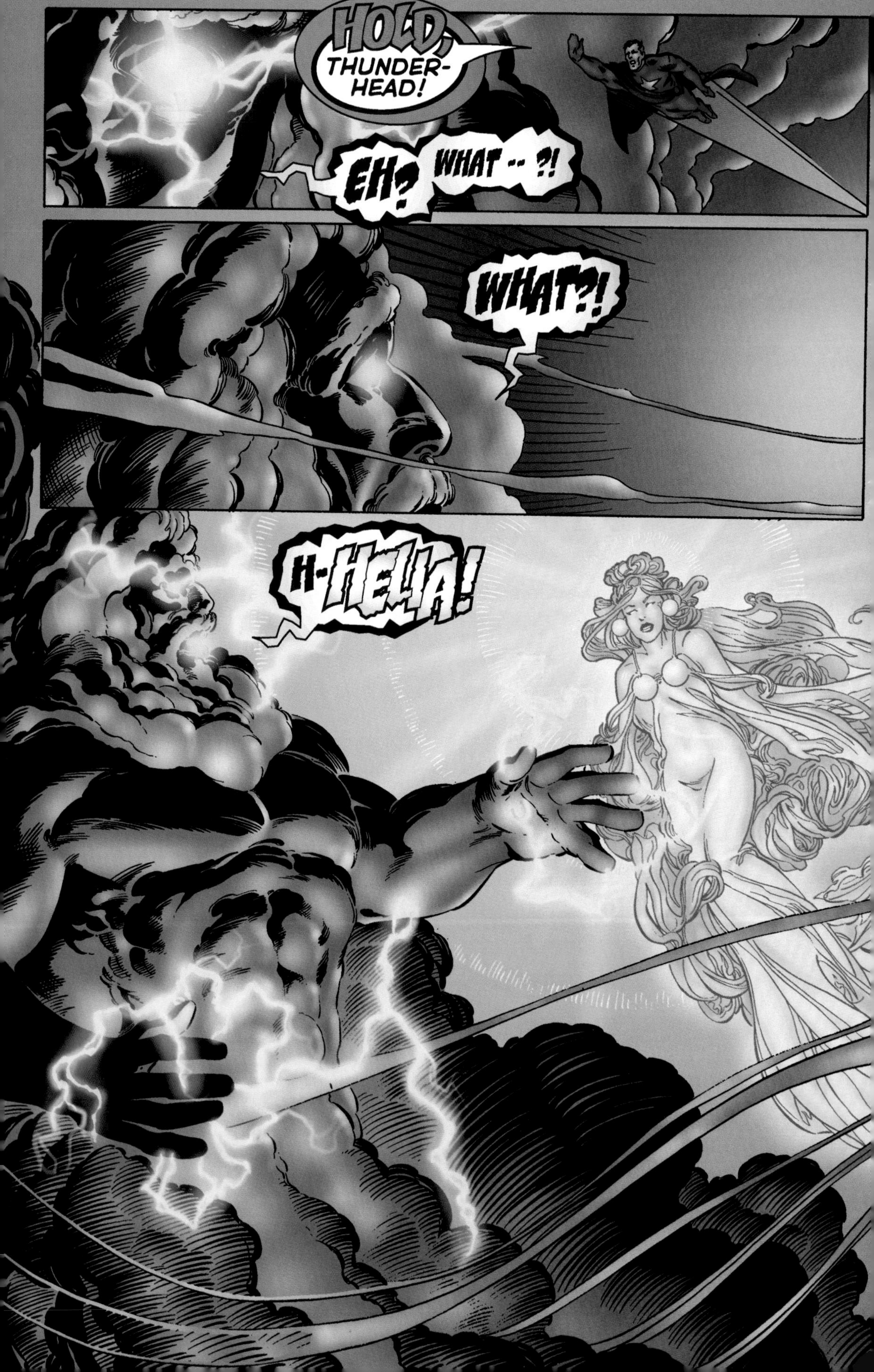
HOLD, THUNDER-HEAD!
EH?
WHAT -- ?!
WHAT?!
H-HELIA!

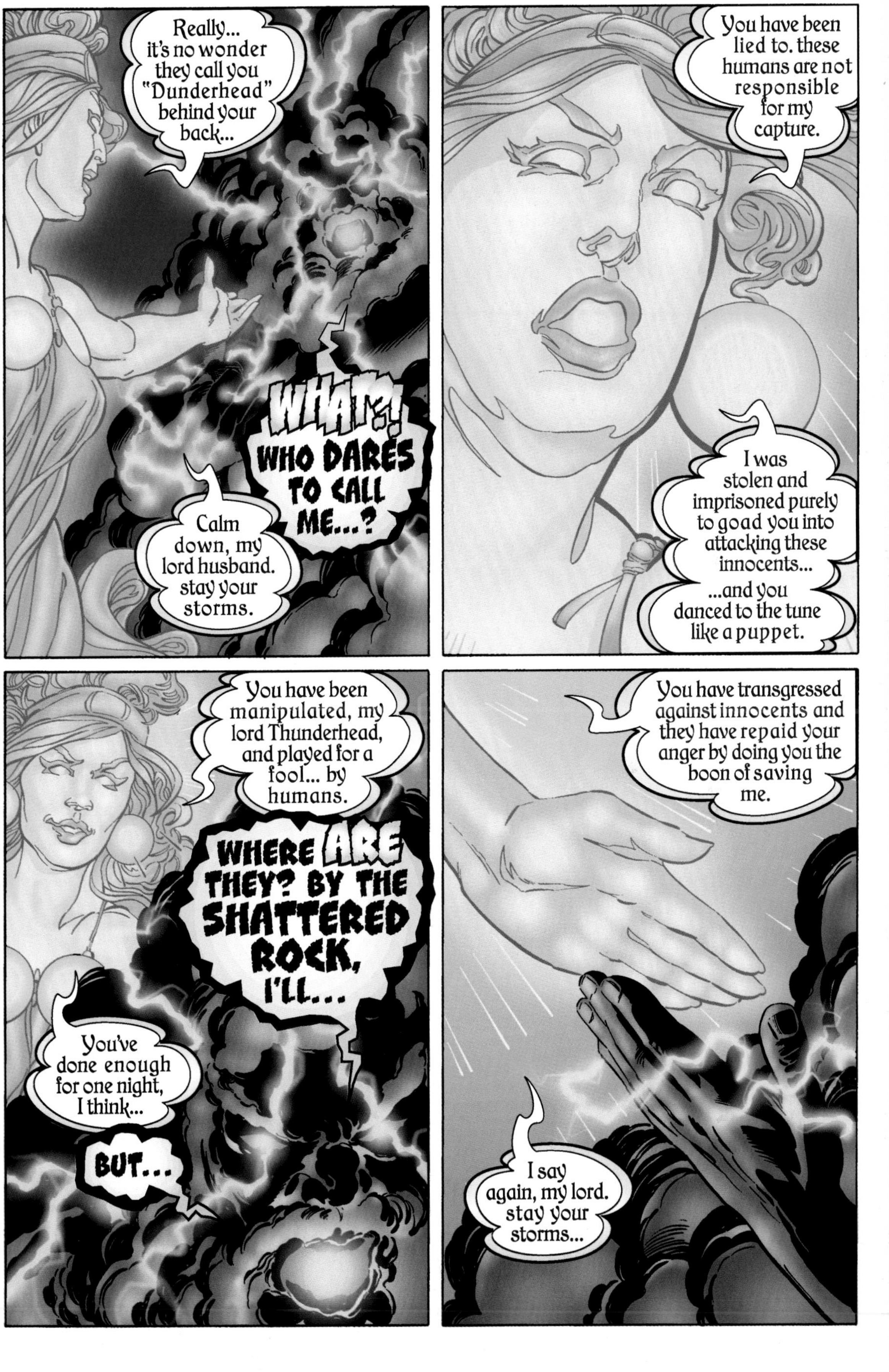
Really... it's no wonder they call you "Dunderhead" behind your back...
WHAT?! WHO DARES TO CALL ME...?
Calm down, my lord husband. stay your storms.
You have been lied to. these humans are not responsible for my capture.
I was stolen and imprisoned purely to goad you into attacking these innocents...
...and you danced to the tune like a puppet.
You have been manipulated, my lord Thunderhead, and played for a fool... by humans.
WHERE ARE THEY? BY THE SHATTERED ROCK, I'LL...
You've done enough for one night, I think...
BUT...
You have transgressed against innocents and they have repaid your anger by doing you the boon of saving me.
I say again, my lord. stay your storms...

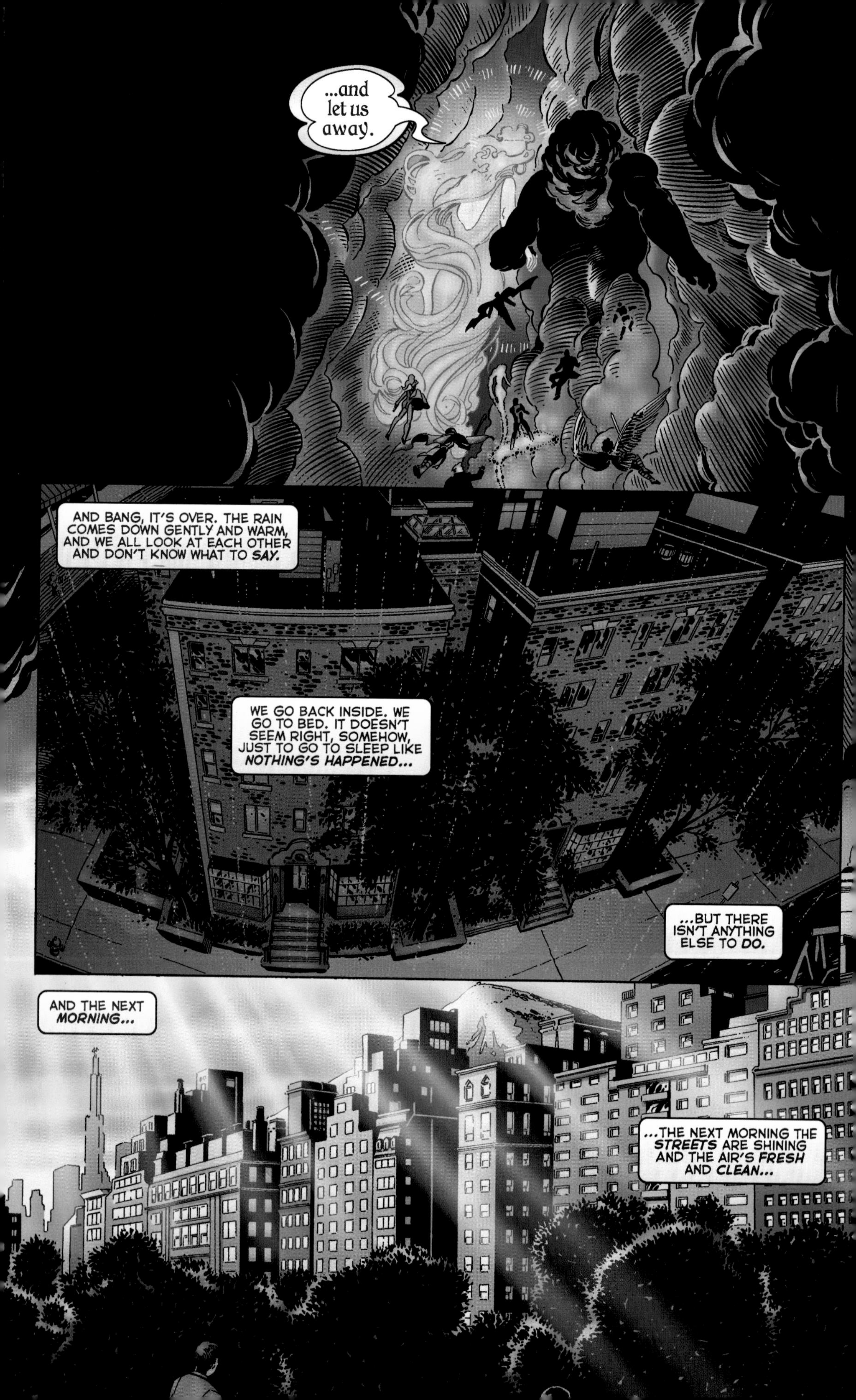
...and let us away.
AND BANG, IT'S OVER. THE RAIN COMES DOWN GENTLY AND WARM, AND WE ALL LOOK AT EACH OTHER AND DON'T KNOW WHAT TO SAY.
WE GO BACK INSIDE. WE GO TO BED. IT DOESN'T SEEM RIGHT, SOMEHOW, JUST TO GO TO SLEEP LIKE NOTHING'S HAPPENED...
...BUT THERE ISN'T ANYTHING ELSE TO DO.
AND THE NEXT MORNING...
...THE NEXT MORNING THE STREETS ARE SHINING AND THE AIR'S FRESH AND CLEAN...

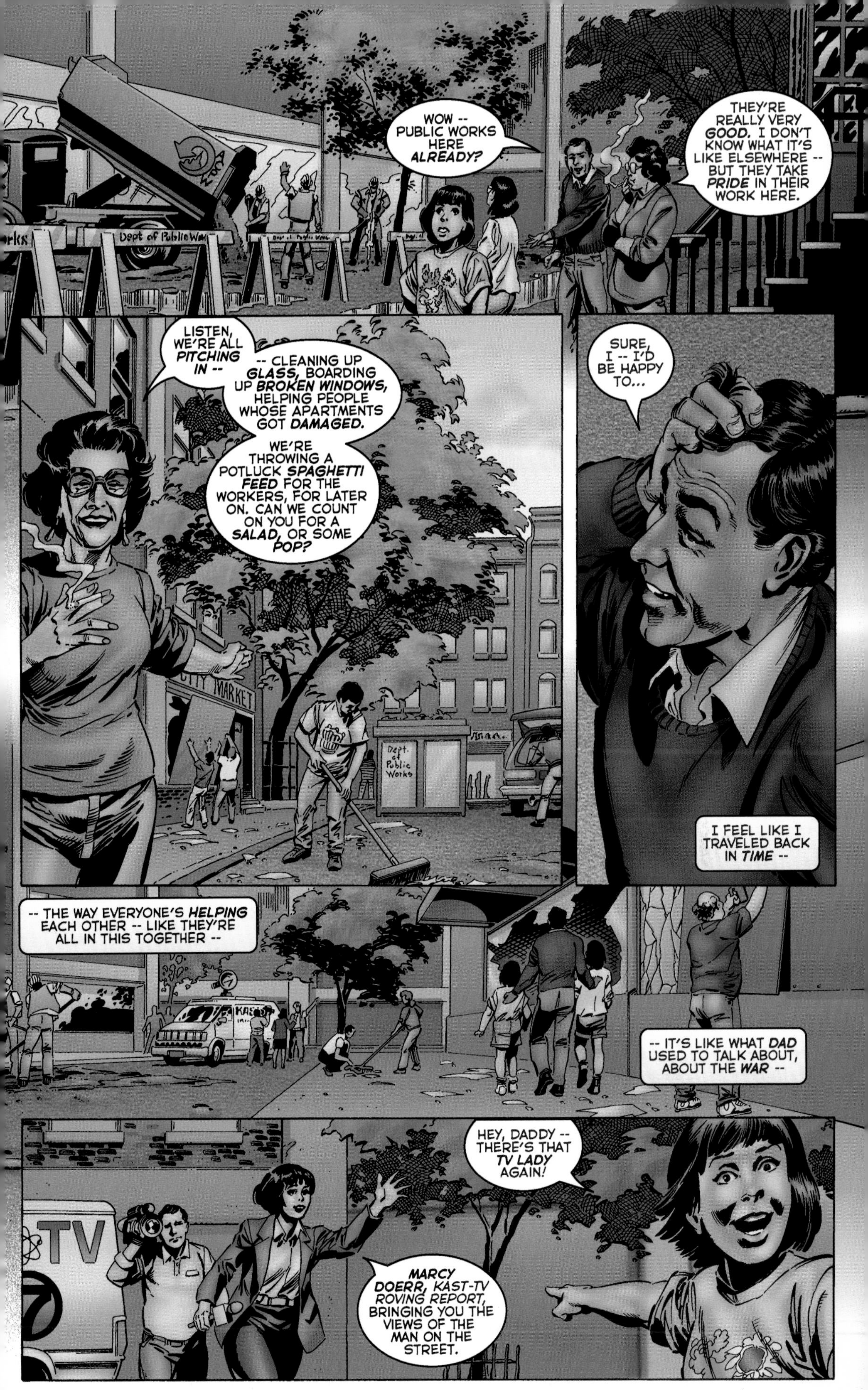

WOW -- PUBLIC WORKS HERE ALREADY?
THEY'RE REALLY VERY GOOD. I DON'T KNOW WHAT IT'S LIKE ELSEWHERE -- BUT THEY TAKE PRIDE IN THEIR WORK HERE.
Dept of Public Works
LISTEN, WE'RE ALL PITCHING IN --
-- CLEANING UP GLASS, BOARDING UP BROKEN WINDOWS, HELPING PEOPLE WHOSE APARTMENTS GOT DAMAGED.
WE'RE THROWING A POTLUCK SPAGHETTI FEED FOR THE WORKERS, FOR LATER ON. CAN WE COUNT ON YOU FOR A SALAD, OR SOME POP?
CITY MARKET
Dept. of Public Works
SURE, I -- I'D BE HAPPY TO...
I FEEL LIKE I TRAVELED BACK IN TIME --
-- THE WAY EVERYONE'S HELPING EACH OTHER -- LIKE THEY'RE ALL IN THIS TOGETHER --
-- IT'S LIKE WHAT DAD USED TO TALK ABOUT, ABOUT THE WAR --
HEY, DADDY -- THERE'S THAT TV LADY AGAIN!
TV
7
MARCY DOERR, KAST-TV ROVING REPORT, BRINGING YOU THE VIEWS OF THE MAN ON THE STREET.

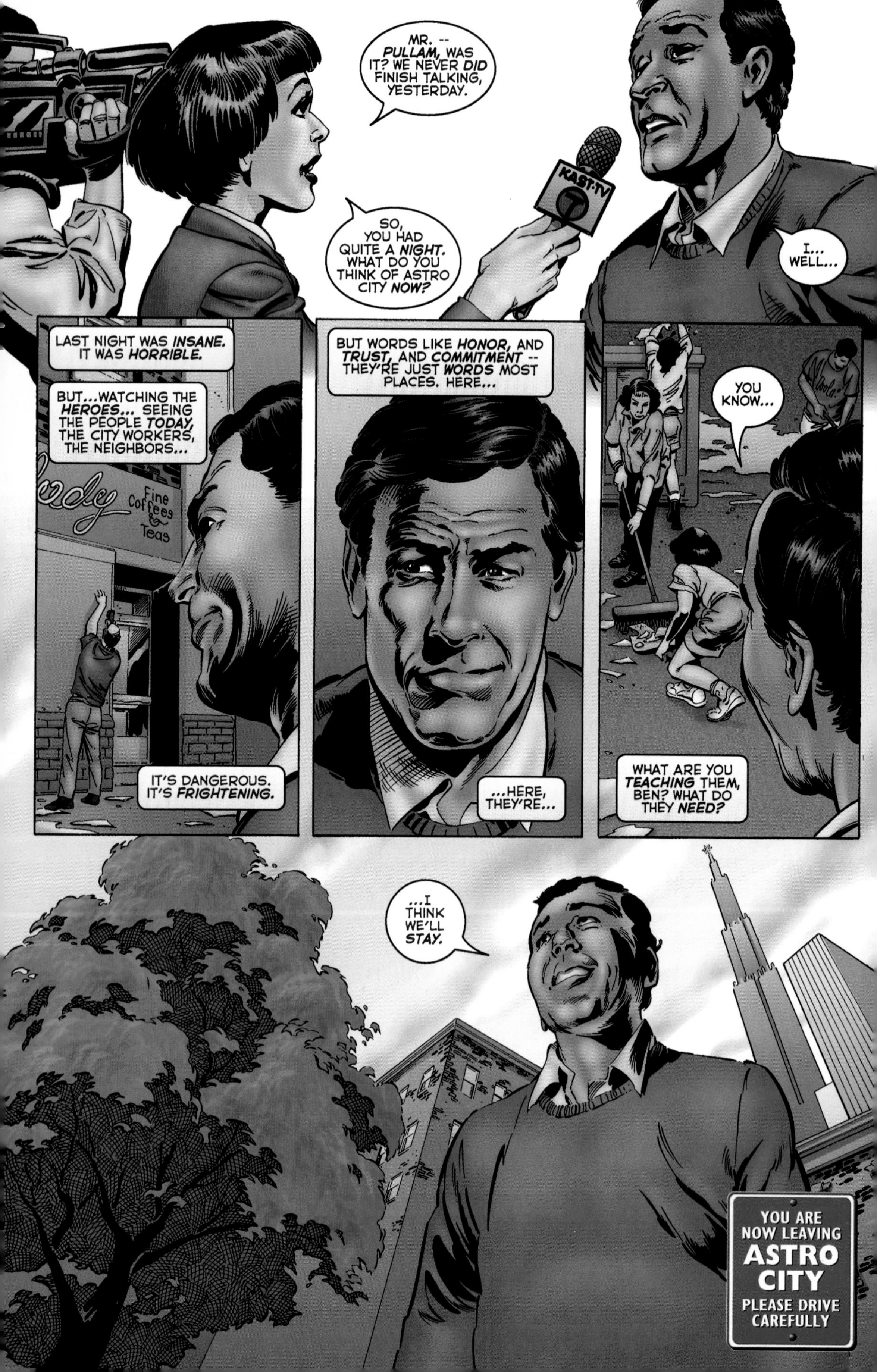
MR. -- PULLAM, WAS IT? WE NEVER DID FINISH TALKING, YESTERDAY.
SO, YOU HAD QUITE A NIGHT. WHAT DO YOU THINK OF ASTRO CITY NOW?
KAST·TV 7
I... WELL...
LAST NIGHT WAS INSANE. IT WAS HORRIBLE.
BUT...WATCHING THE HEROES... SEEING THE PEOPLE TODAY, THE CITY WORKERS, THE NEIGHBORS...
Fine Coffees & Teas
IT'S DANGEROUS. IT'S FRIGHTENING.
BUT WORDS LIKE HONOR, AND TRUST, AND COMMITMENT -- THEY'RE JUST WORDS MOST PLACES. HERE...
...HERE, THEY'RE...
YOU KNOW...
WHAT ARE YOU TEACHING THEM, BEN? WHAT DO THEY NEED?
...I THINK WE'LL STAY.
YOU ARE NOW LEAVING ASTRO CITY PLEASE DRIVE CAREFULLY

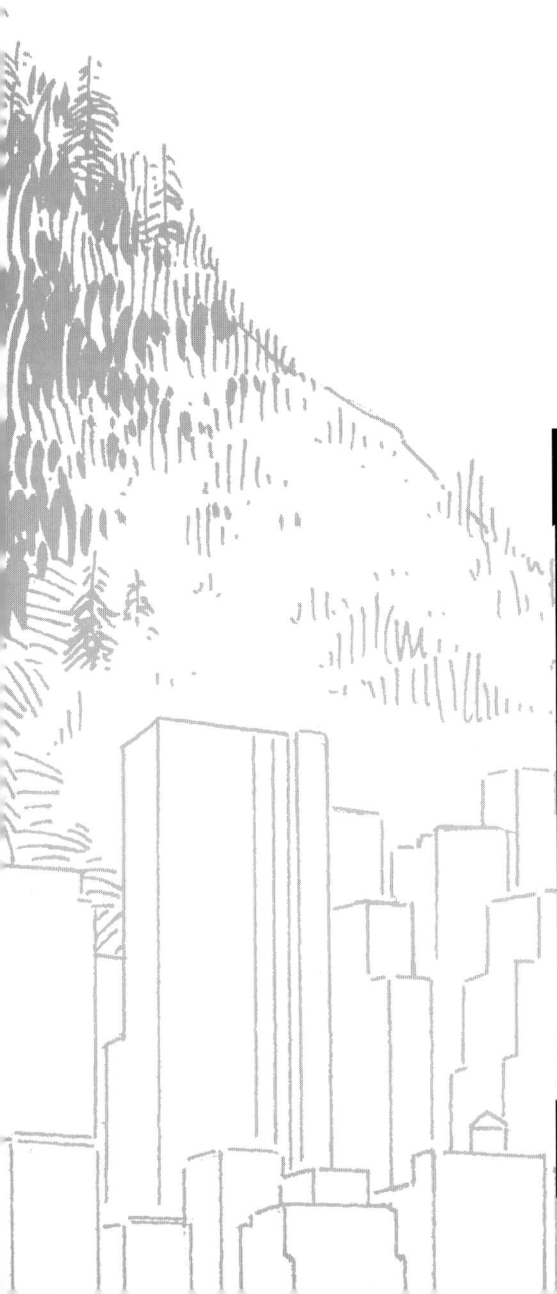

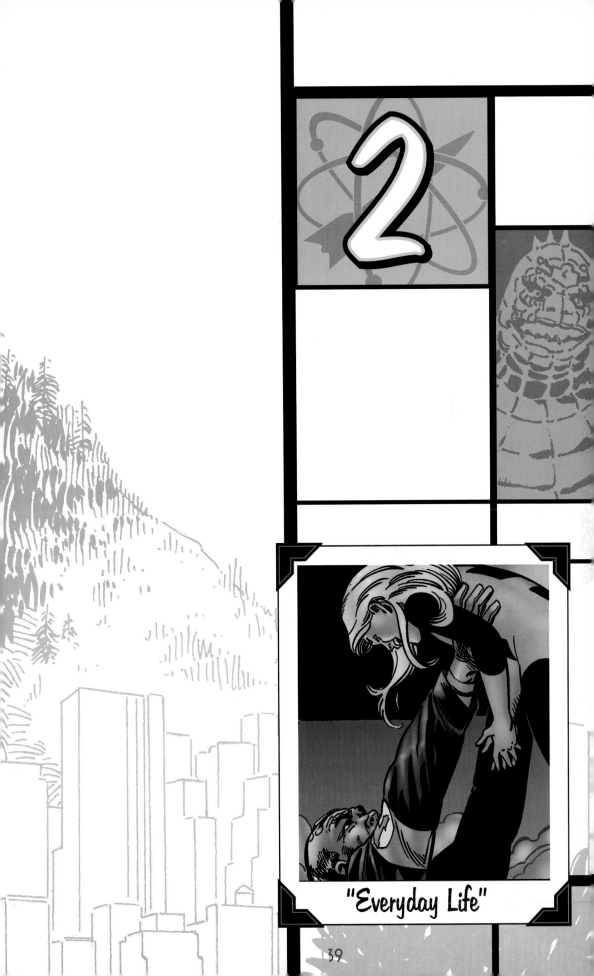

2

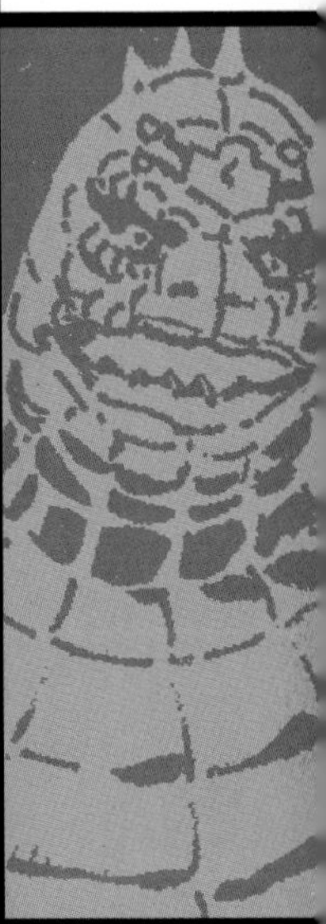

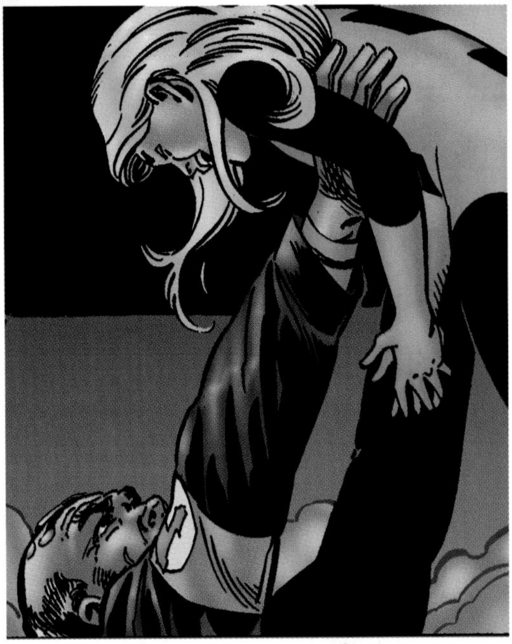

"Everyday Life"

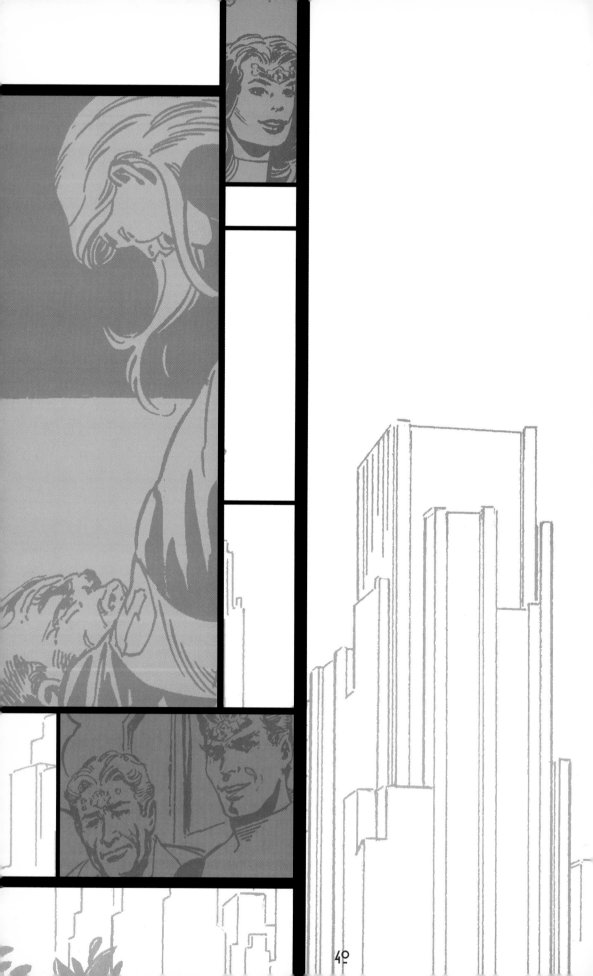

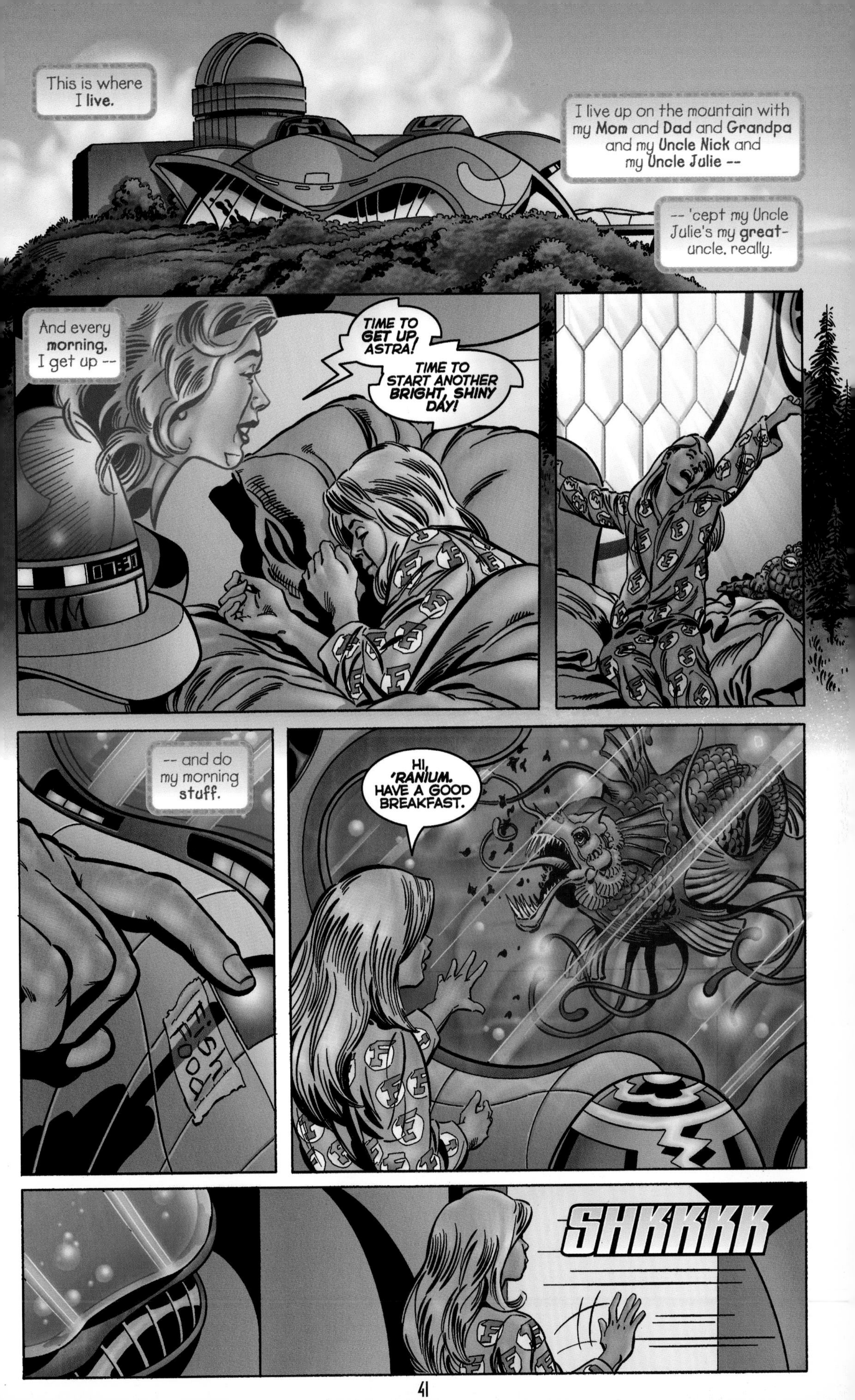
This is where I live.
I live up on the mountain with my Mom and Dad and Grandpa and my Uncle Nick and my Uncle Julie --
-- 'cept my Uncle Julie's my great-uncle, really.
And every morning, I get up --
TIME TO GET UP, ASTRA!
TIME TO START ANOTHER BRIGHT, SHINY DAY!
-- and do my morning stuff.
FISH FOOD
HI, 'RANIUM. HAVE A GOOD BREAKFAST.
SHKKKK

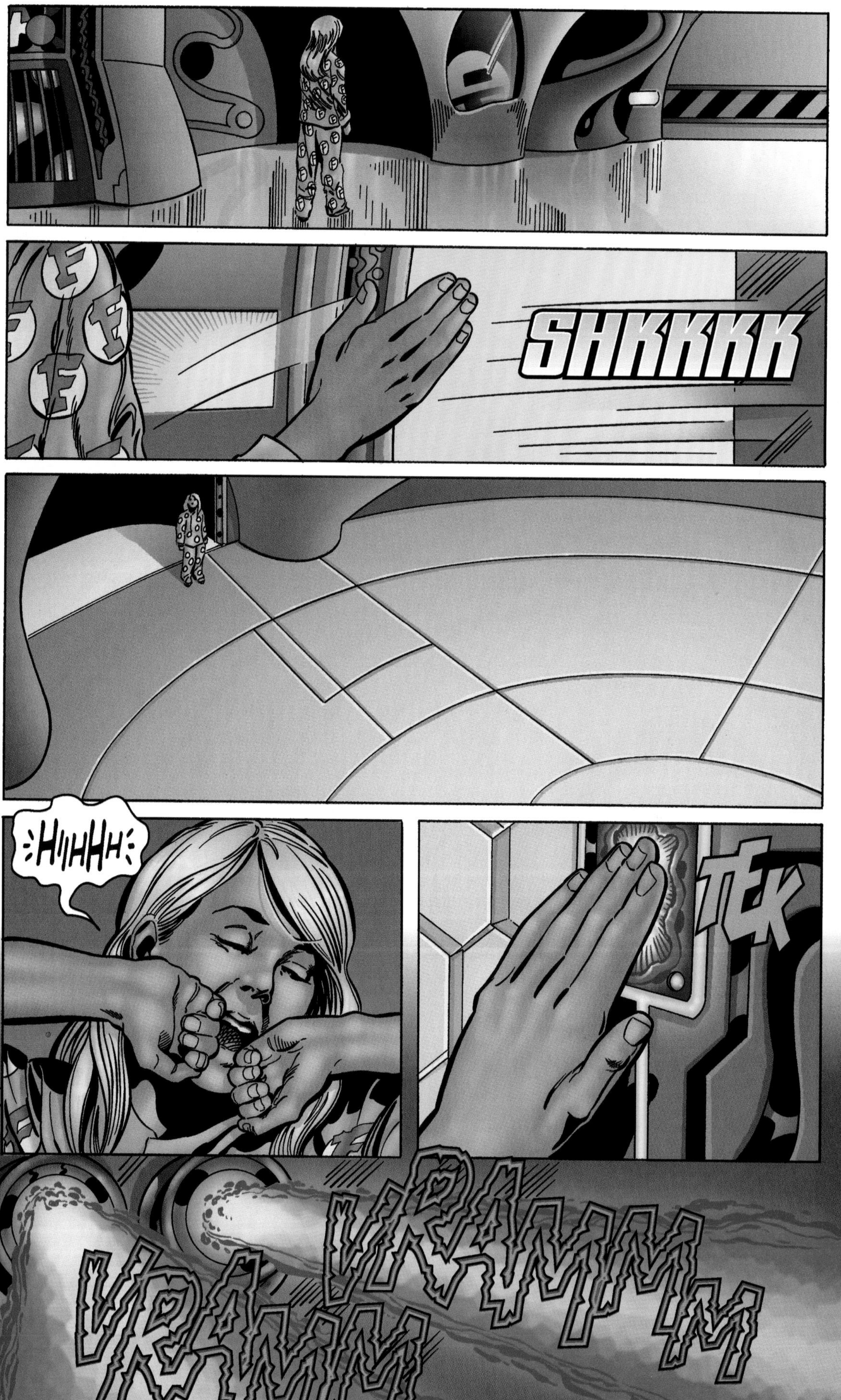
SHKKKK
HHHHH
TEK
VRAMMM
VRAMMM

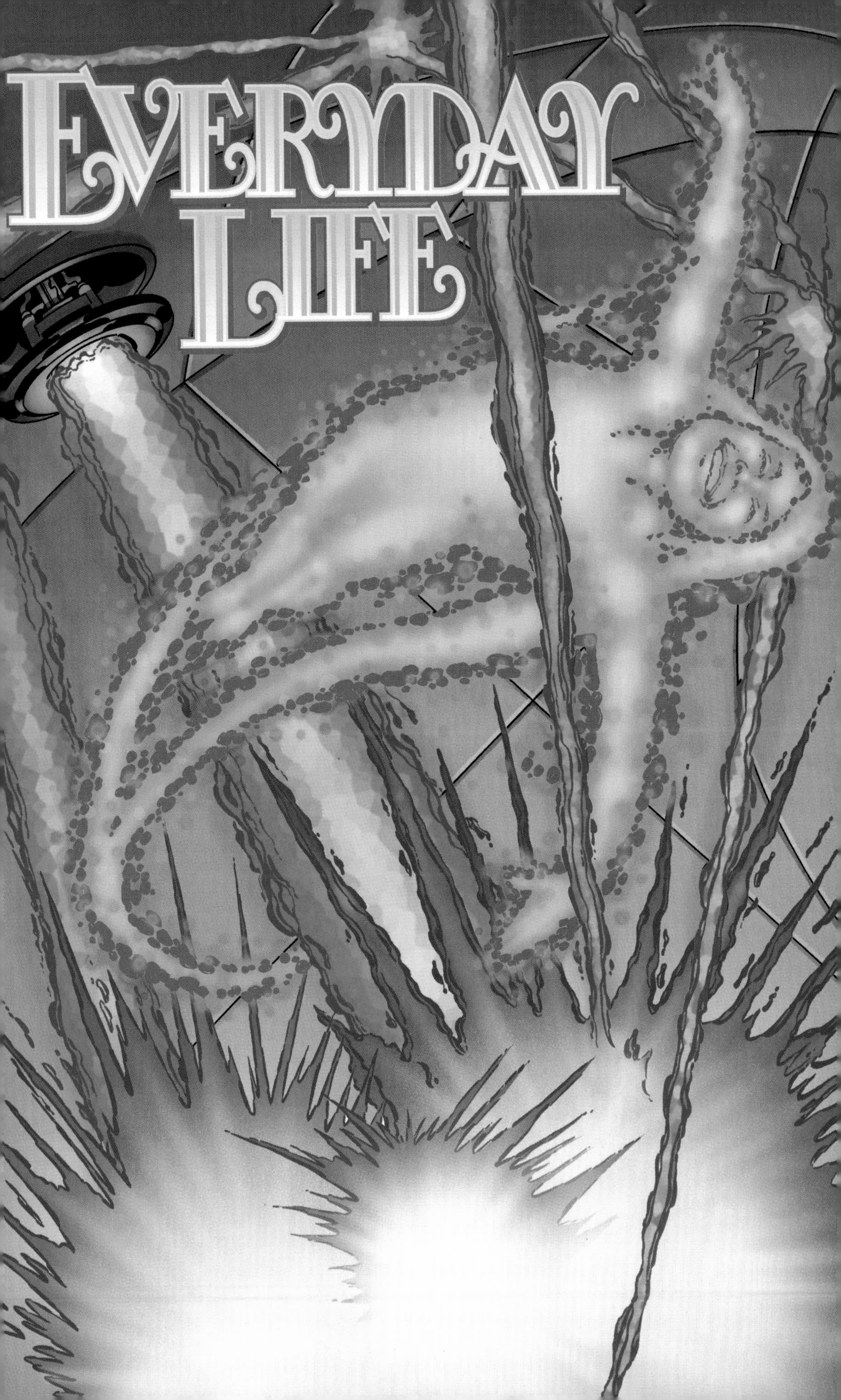
EVERYDAY
LIFE

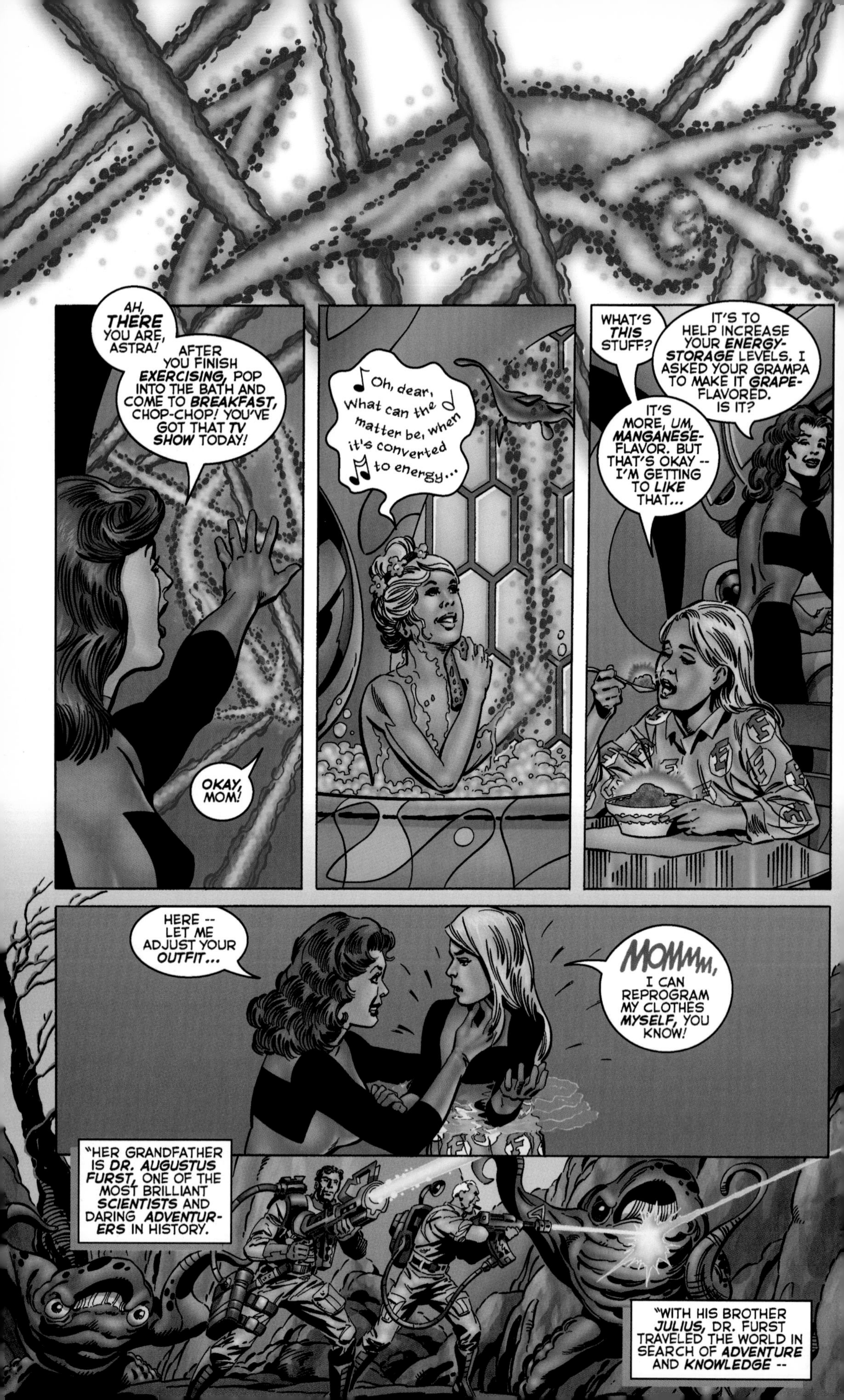

AH, THERE YOU ARE, ASTRA!
AFTER YOU FINISH EXERCISING, POP INTO THE BATH AND COME TO BREAKFAST, CHOP-CHOP! YOU'VE GOT THAT TV SHOW TODAY!
OKAY, MOM!
Oh, dear, What can the matter be, when it's converted to energy...
WHAT'S THIS STUFF?
IT'S TO HELP INCREASE YOUR ENERGY-STORAGE LEVELS. I ASKED YOUR GRAMPA TO MAKE IT GRAPE-FLAVORED. IS IT?
IT'S MORE, UM, MANGANESE-FLAVOR. BUT THAT'S OKAY -- I'M GETTING TO LIKE THAT...
HERE -- LET ME ADJUST YOUR OUTFIT...
MOMMMM, I CAN REPROGRAM MY CLOTHES MYSELF, YOU KNOW!
"HER GRANDFATHER IS DR. AUGUSTUS FURST, ONE OF THE MOST BRILLIANT SCIENTISTS AND DARING ADVENTURERS IN HISTORY.
"WITH HIS BROTHER JULIUS, DR. FURST TRAVELED THE WORLD IN SEARCH OF ADVENTURE AND KNOWLEDGE --

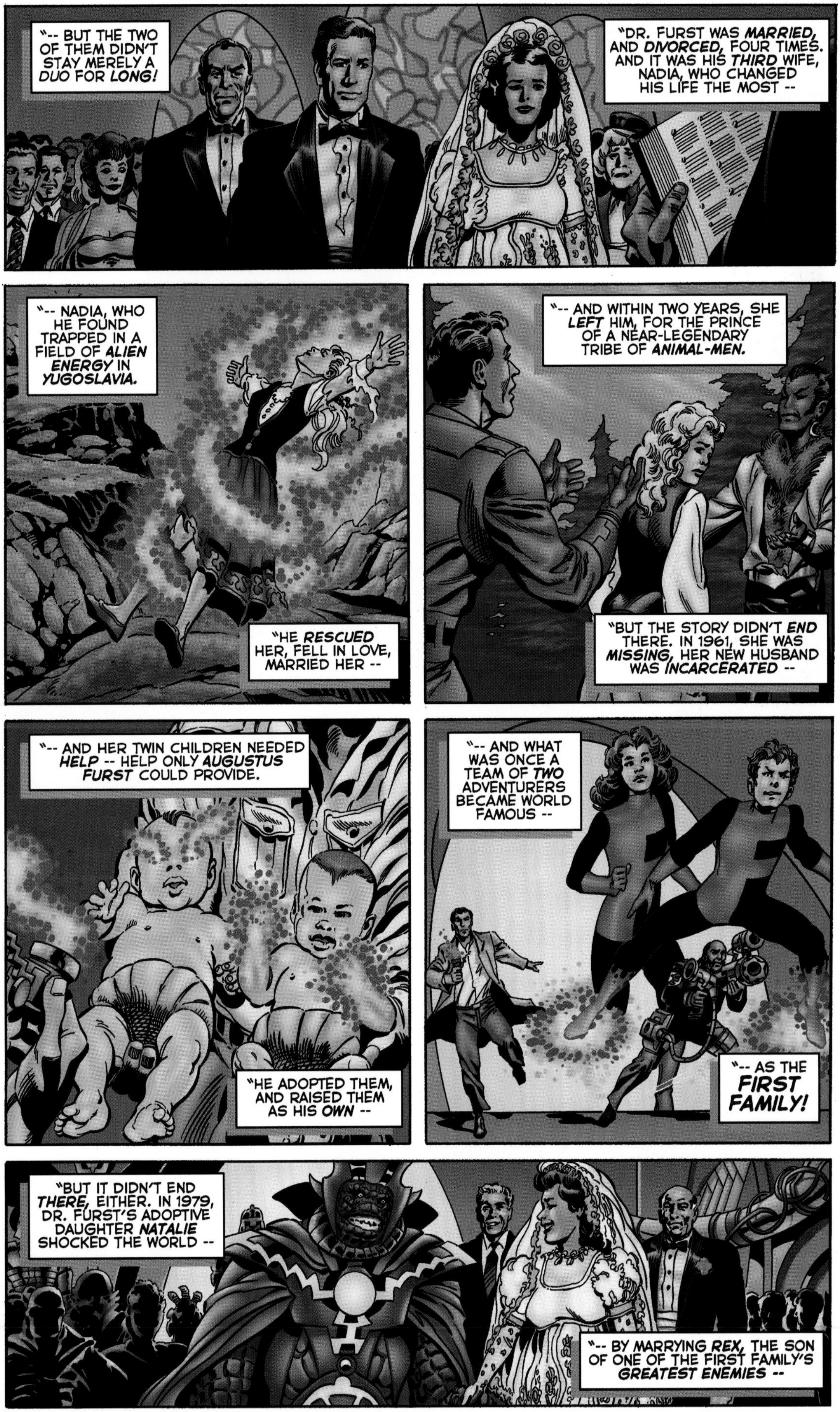
"-- BUT THE TWO OF THEM DIDN'T STAY MERELY A DUO FOR LONG!
"DR. FURST WAS MARRIED, AND DIVORCED, FOUR TIMES. AND IT WAS HIS THIRD WIFE, NADIA, WHO CHANGED HIS LIFE THE MOST --
"-- NADIA, WHO HE FOUND TRAPPED IN A FIELD OF ALIEN ENERGY IN YUGOSLAVIA.
"HE RESCUED HER, FELL IN LOVE, MARRIED HER --
"-- AND WITHIN TWO YEARS, SHE LEFT HIM, FOR THE PRINCE OF A NEAR-LEGENDARY TRIBE OF ANIMAL-MEN.
"BUT THE STORY DIDN'T END THERE. IN 1961, SHE WAS MISSING, HER NEW HUSBAND WAS INCARCERATED --
"-- AND HER TWIN CHILDREN NEEDED HELP -- HELP ONLY AUGUSTUS FURST COULD PROVIDE.
"HE ADOPTED THEM, AND RAISED THEM AS HIS OWN --
"-- AND WHAT WAS ONCE A TEAM OF TWO ADVENTURERS BECAME WORLD FAMOUS --
"-- AS THE FIRST FAMILY!
"BUT IT DIDN'T END THERE, EITHER. IN 1979, DR. FURST'S ADOPTIVE DAUGHTER NATALIE SHOCKED THE WORLD --
"-- BY MARRYING REX, THE SON OF ONE OF THE FIRST FAMILY'S GREATEST ENEMIES --

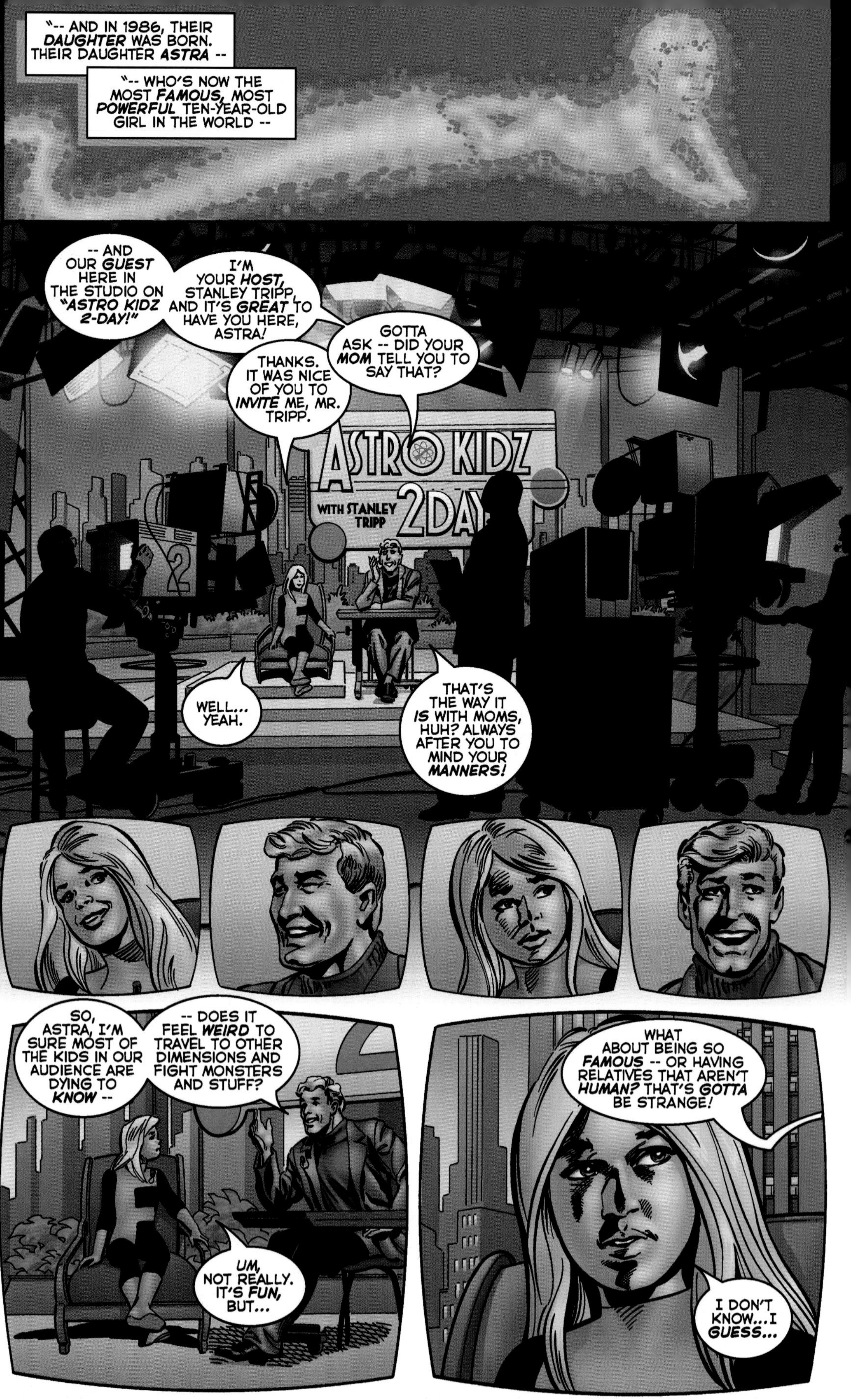
"-- AND IN 1986, THEIR DAUGHTER WAS BORN. THEIR DAUGHTER ASTRA --
"-- WHO'S NOW THE MOST FAMOUS, MOST POWERFUL TEN-YEAR-OLD GIRL IN THE WORLD --
-- AND OUR GUEST HERE IN THE STUDIO ON "ASTRO KIDZ 2-DAY!"
I'M YOUR HOST, STANLEY TRIPP, AND IT'S GREAT TO HAVE YOU HERE, ASTRA!
THANKS. IT WAS NICE OF YOU TO INVITE ME, MR. TRIPP.
GOTTA ASK -- DID YOUR MOM TELL YOU TO SAY THAT?
ASTRO KIDZ
WITH STANLEY TRIPP
2DAY
WELL... YEAH.
THAT'S THE WAY IT IS WITH MOMS, HUH? ALWAYS AFTER YOU TO MIND YOUR MANNERS!
SO, ASTRA, I'M SURE MOST OF THE KIDS IN OUR AUDIENCE ARE DYING TO KNOW --
-- DOES IT FEEL WEIRD TO TRAVEL TO OTHER DIMENSIONS AND FIGHT MONSTERS AND STUFF?
UM, NOT REALLY. IT'S FUN, BUT...
WHAT ABOUT BEING SO FAMOUS -- OR HAVING RELATIVES THAT AREN'T HUMAN? THAT'S GOTTA BE STRANGE!
I DON'T KNOW... I GUESS...

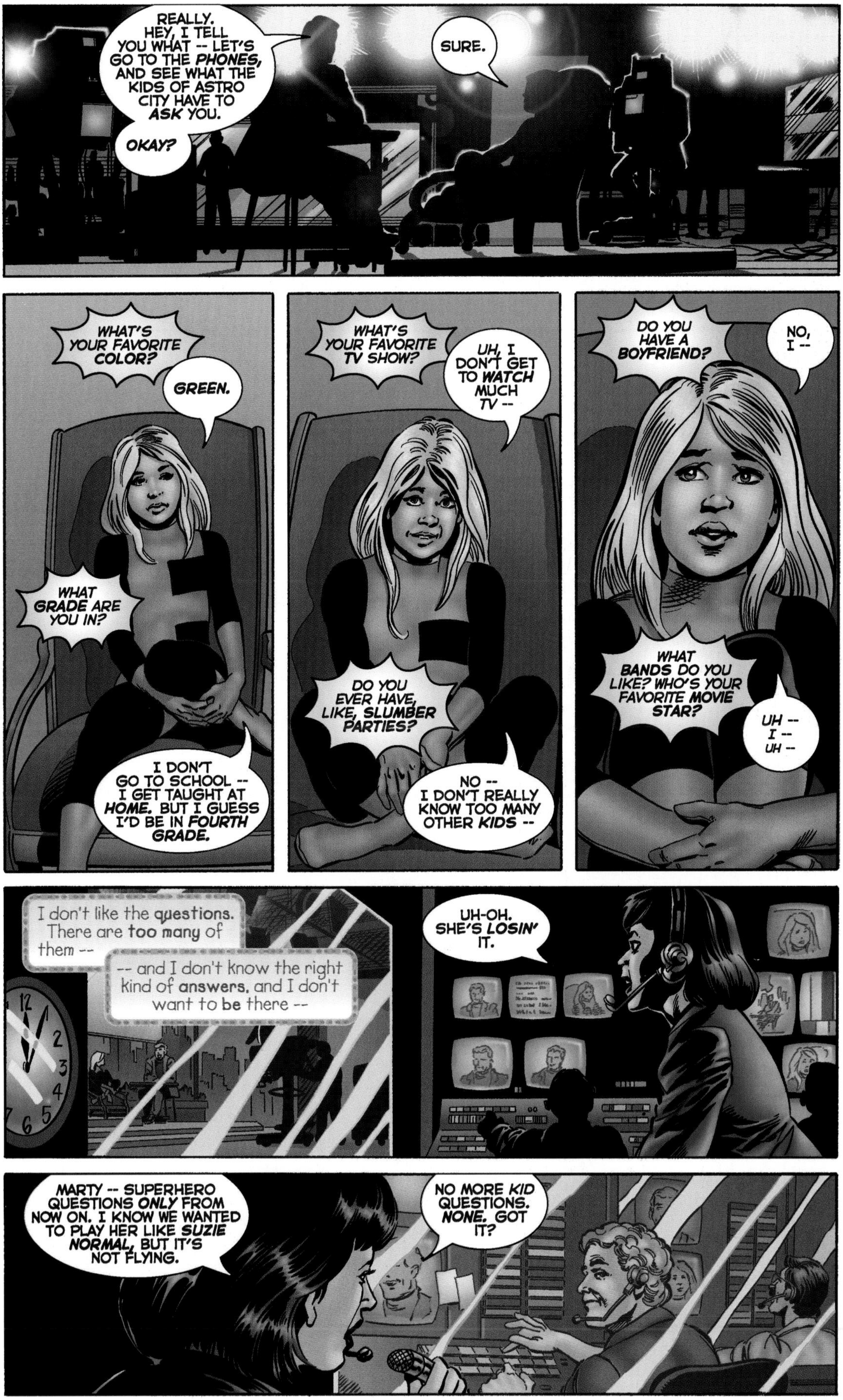
REALLY. HEY, I TELL YOU WHAT -- LET'S GO TO THE PHONES, AND SEE WHAT THE KIDS OF ASTRO CITY HAVE TO ASK YOU.
OKAY?
SURE.
WHAT'S YOUR FAVORITE COLOR?
GREEN.
WHAT GRADE ARE YOU IN?
I DON'T GO TO SCHOOL -- I GET TAUGHT AT HOME. BUT I GUESS I'D BE IN FOURTH GRADE.
WHAT'S YOUR FAVORITE TV SHOW?
UH, I DON'T GET TO WATCH MUCH TV --
DO YOU EVER HAVE, LIKE, SLUMBER PARTIES?
NO -- I DON'T REALLY KNOW TOO MANY OTHER KIDS --
DO YOU HAVE A BOYFRIEND?
NO, I --
WHAT BANDS DO YOU LIKE? WHO'S YOUR FAVORITE MOVIE STAR?
UH -- I -- UH --
I don't like the questions. There are too many of them --
-- and I don't know the right kind of answers, and I don't want to be there --
UH-OH. SHE'S LOSIN' IT.
MARTY -- SUPERHERO QUESTIONS ONLY FROM NOW ON. I KNOW WE WANTED TO PLAY HER LIKE SUZIE NORMAL, BUT IT'S NOT FLYING.
NO MORE KID QUESTIONS. NONE. GOT IT?

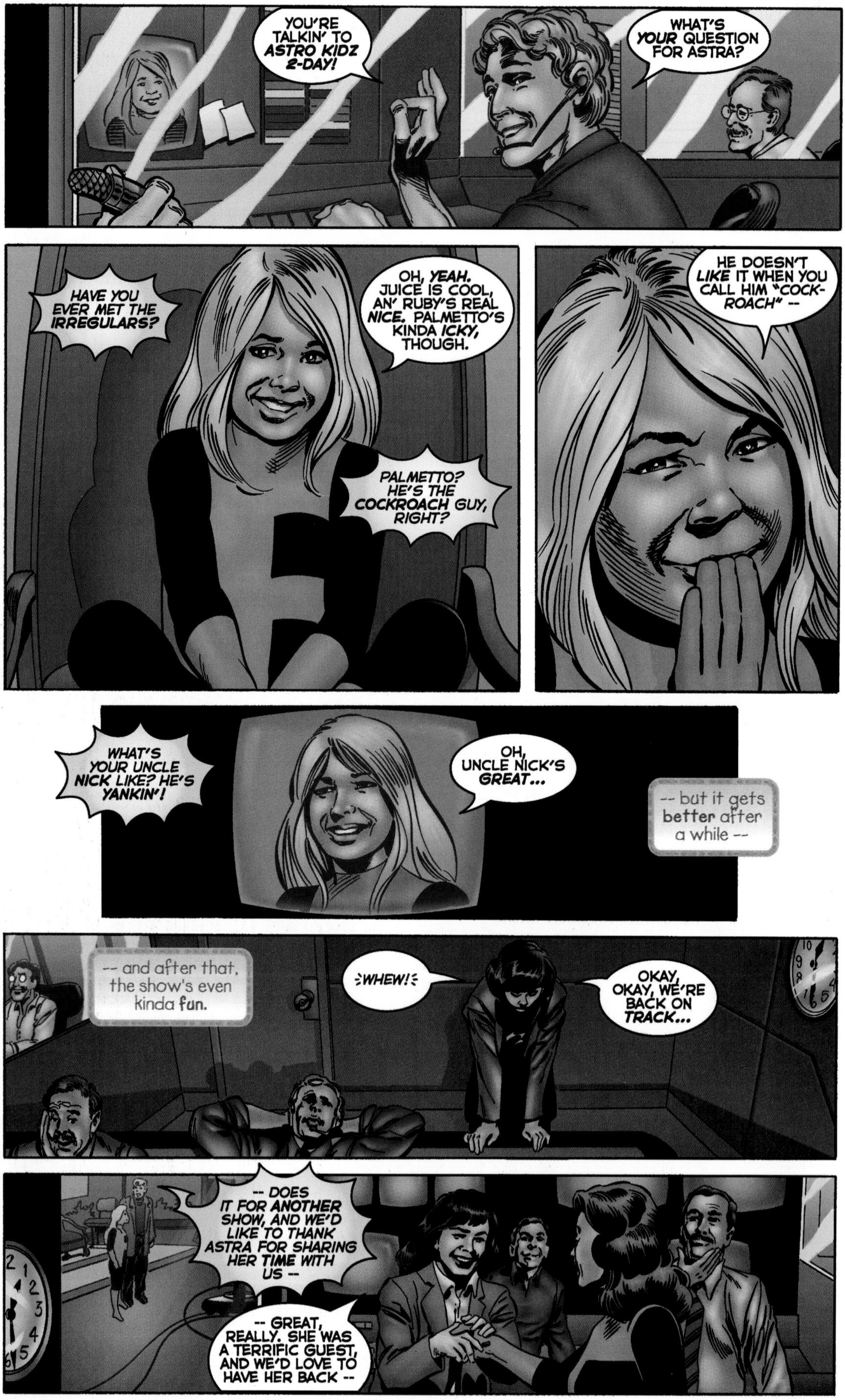

YOU'RE TALKIN' TO ASTRO KIDZ 2-DAY!
WHAT'S YOUR QUESTION FOR ASTRA?
HAVE YOU EVER MET THE IRREGULARS?
OH, YEAH. JUICE IS COOL, AN' RUBY'S REAL NICE. PALMETTO'S KINDA ICKY, THOUGH.
PALMETTO? HE'S THE COCKROACH GUY, RIGHT?
HE DOESN'T LIKE IT WHEN YOU CALL HIM "COCK-ROACH" --
WHAT'S YOUR UNCLE NICK LIKE? HE'S YANKIN'!
OH, UNCLE NICK'S GREAT...
-- but it gets better after a while --
-- and after that, the show's even kinda fun.
WHEW!
OKAY, OKAY, WE'RE BACK ON TRACK...
-- DOES IT FOR ANOTHER SHOW, AND WE'D LIKE TO THANK ASTRA FOR SHARING HER TIME WITH US --
-- GREAT, REALLY. SHE WAS A TERRIFIC GUEST, AND WE'D LOVE TO HAVE HER BACK --

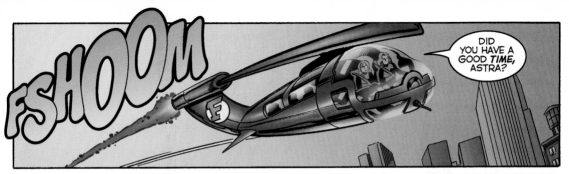

FSHOOM

DID YOU HAVE A GOOD *TIME*, ASTRA?

I *GUESS*.

HOME
7 8
6
4 5
3
2
1

Those *kids* down there -- they know all about T.V. and *boyfriends* and *slumber parties* and bands.

And me -- I know how a T.V. *works* --

-- but I don't even know what *game* they're playing.

MOM?

HOLD ON A SECOND, DEAR. I'M DOCKING *FAMILY-1...*

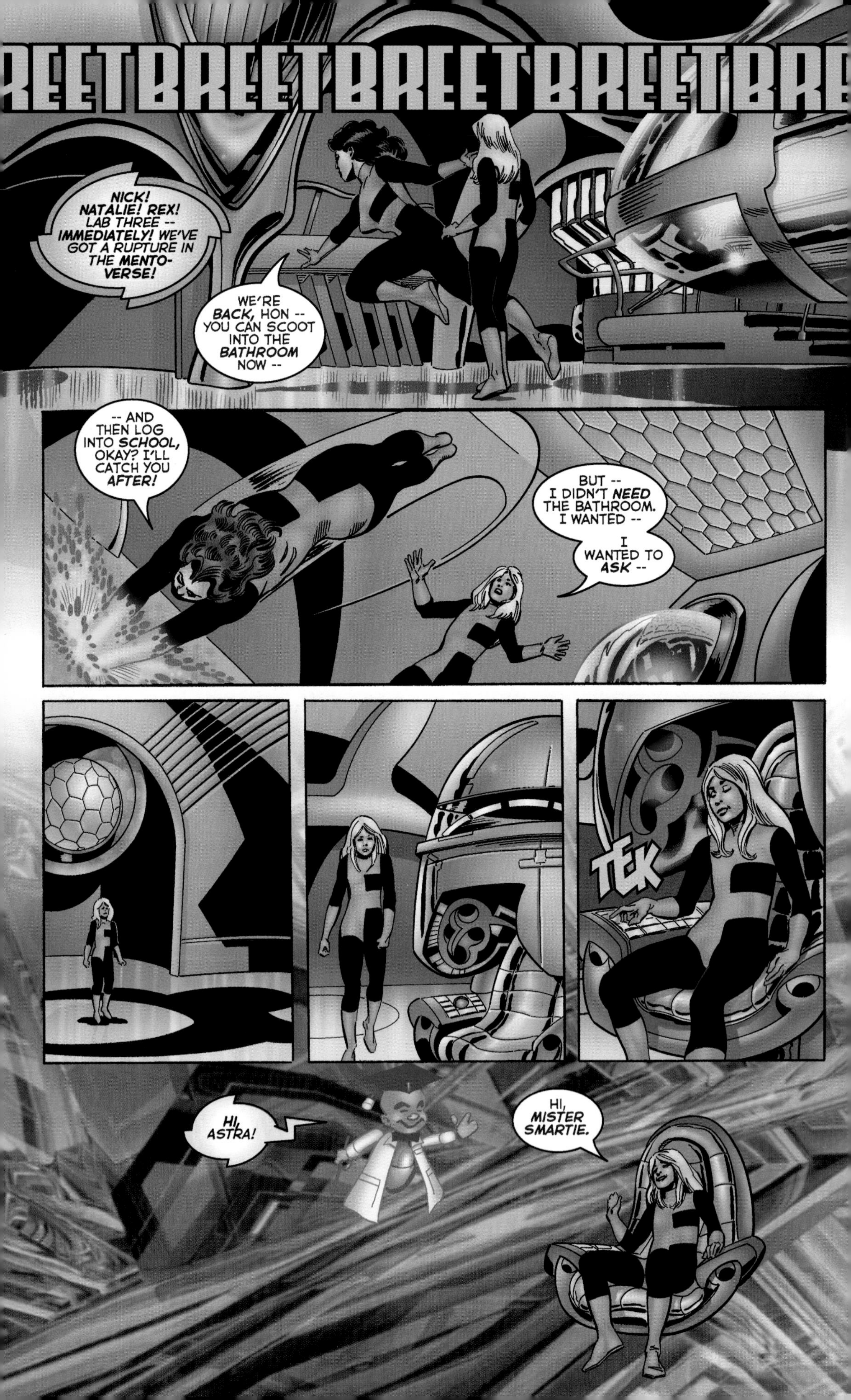
BREETBREETBREETBREETBRE
NICK! NATALIE! REX! LAB THREE -- IMMEDIATELY! WE'VE GOT A RUPTURE IN THE MENTO-VERSE!
WE'RE BACK, HON -- YOU CAN SCOOT INTO THE BATHROOM NOW --
-- AND THEN LOG INTO SCHOOL, OKAY? I'LL CATCH YOU AFTER!
BUT -- I DIDN'T NEED THE BATHROOM. I WANTED --
I WANTED TO ASK --
TEK
HI, ASTRA!
HI, MISTER SMARTIE.

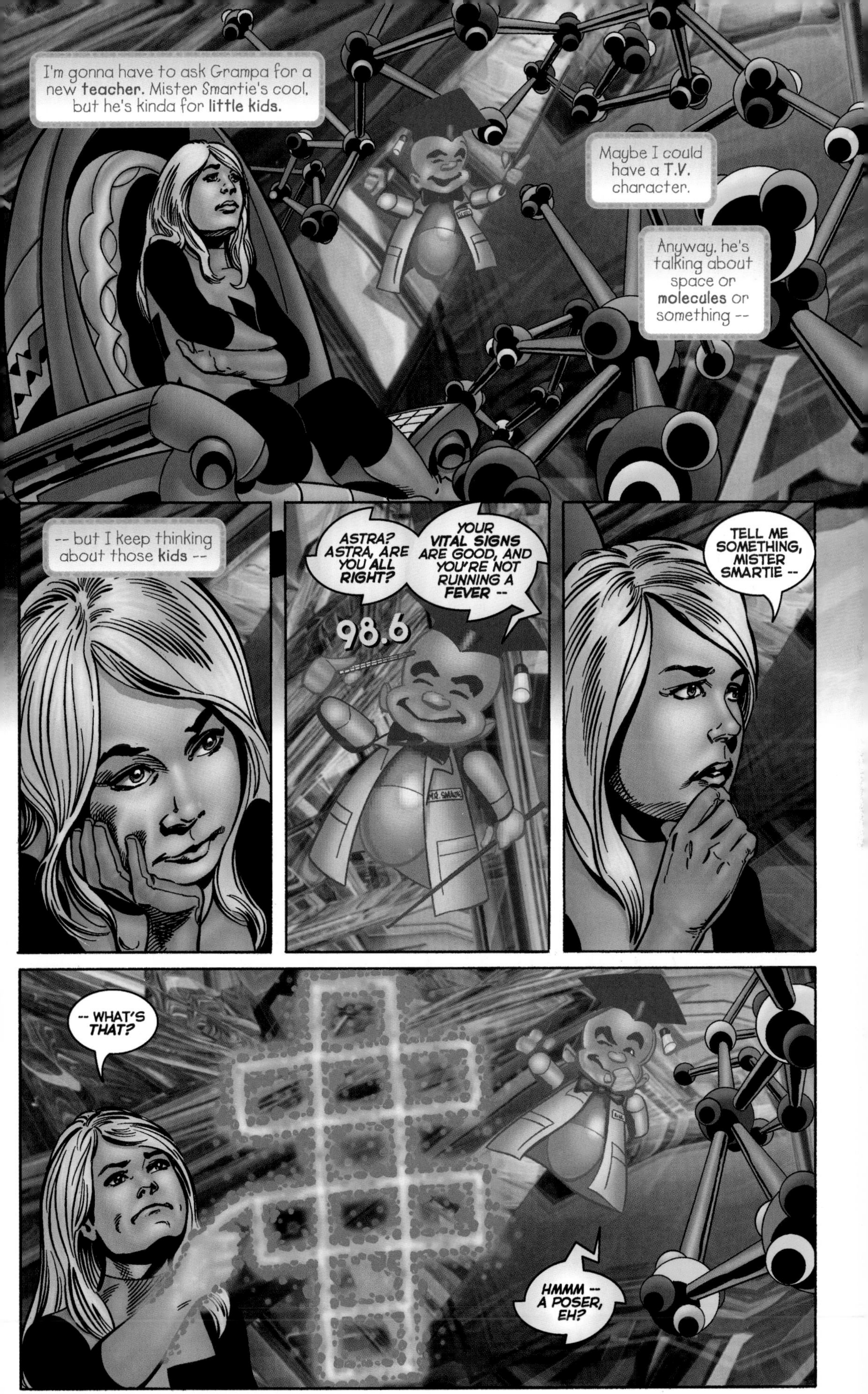
I'm gonna have to ask Grampa for a new teacher. Mister Smartie's cool, but he's kinda for little kids.
Maybe I could have a T.V. character.
Anyway, he's talking about space or molecules or something --
-- but I keep thinking about those kids --
ASTRA? ASTRA, ARE YOU ALL RIGHT?
YOUR VITAL SIGNS ARE GOOD, AND YOU'RE NOT RUNNING A FEVER --
98.6
TELL ME SOMETHING, MISTER SMARTIE --
-- WHAT'S THAT?
HMMM -- A POSER, EH?

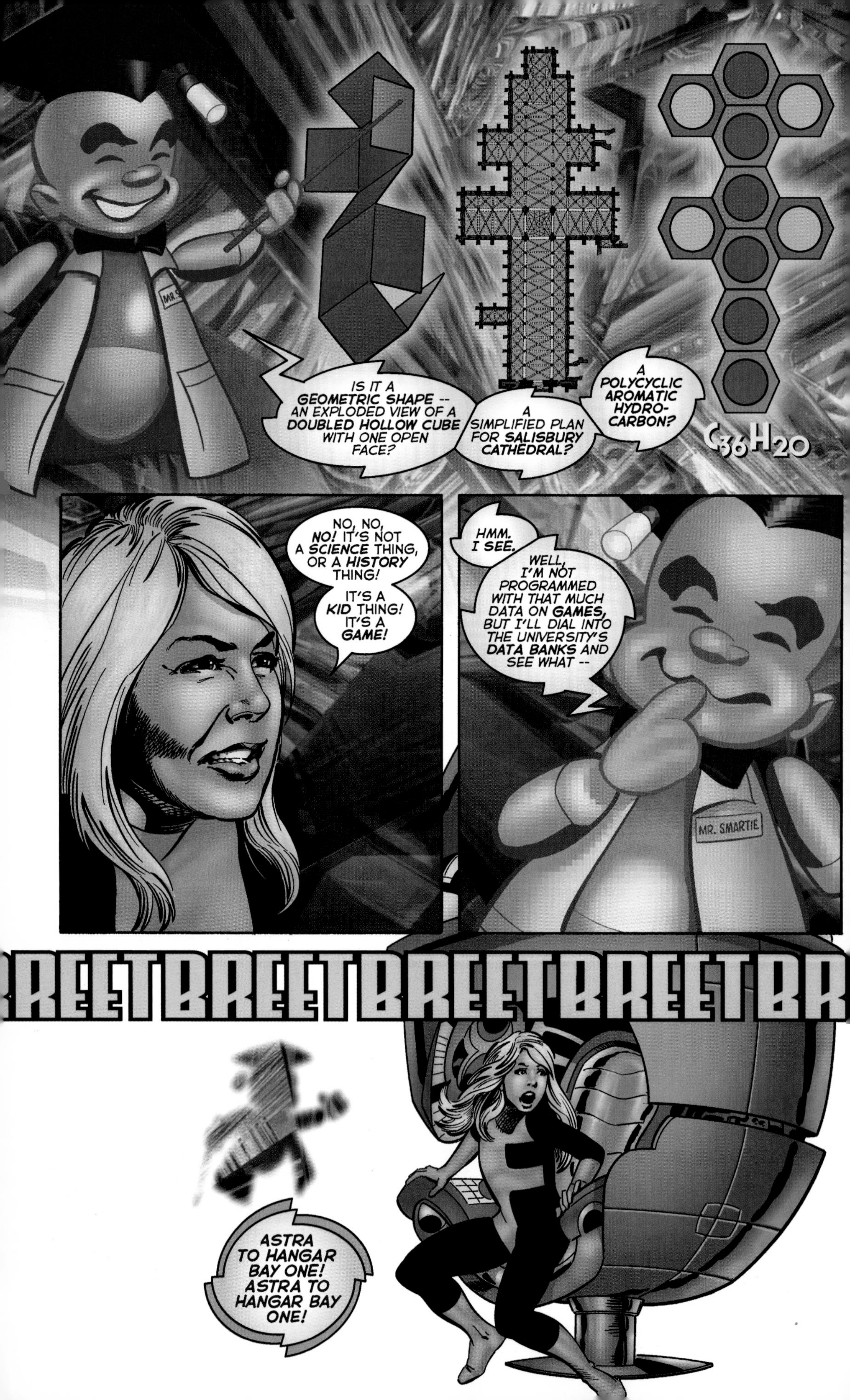
IS IT A GEOMETRIC SHAPE -- AN EXPLODED VIEW OF A DOUBLED HOLLOW CUBE WITH ONE OPEN FACE?
A SIMPLIFIED PLAN FOR SALISBURY CATHEDRAL?
A POLYCYCLIC AROMATIC HYDRO-CARBON?
C36H20
MR. S
NO, NO, NO! IT'S NOT A SCIENCE THING, OR A HISTORY THING!
IT'S A KID THING! IT'S A GAME!
HMM. I SEE.
WELL, I'M NOT PROGRAMMED WITH THAT MUCH DATA ON GAMES, BUT I'LL DIAL INTO THE UNIVERSITY'S DATA BANKS AND SEE WHAT --
MR. SMARTIE
REETBREETBREETBREETBR
ASTRA TO HANGAR BAY ONE! ASTRA TO HANGAR BAY ONE!

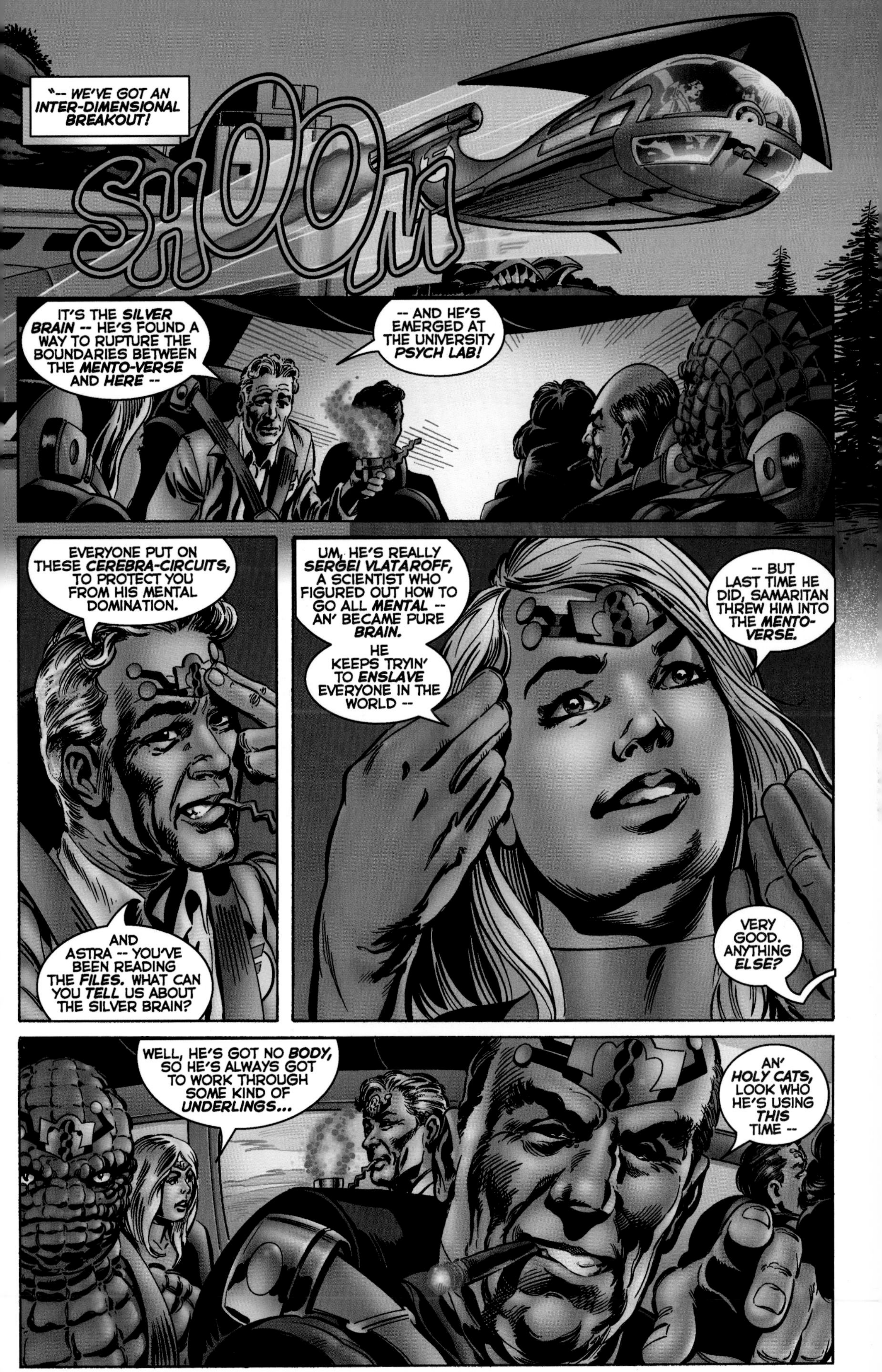
"-- WE'VE GOT AN INTER-DIMENSIONAL BREAKOUT!
SHOOM
IT'S THE SILVER BRAIN -- HE'S FOUND A WAY TO RUPTURE THE BOUNDARIES BETWEEN THE MENTO-VERSE AND HERE --
-- AND HE'S EMERGED AT THE UNIVERSITY PSYCH LAB!
EVERYONE PUT ON THESE CEREBRA-CIRCUITS, TO PROTECT YOU FROM HIS MENTAL DOMINATION.
AND ASTRA -- YOU'VE BEEN READING THE FILES. WHAT CAN YOU TELL US ABOUT THE SILVER BRAIN?
UM, HE'S REALLY SERGEI VLATAROFF, A SCIENTIST WHO FIGURED OUT HOW TO GO ALL MENTAL -- AN' BECAME PURE BRAIN.
HE KEEPS TRYIN' TO ENSLAVE EVERYONE IN THE WORLD --
-- BUT LAST TIME HE DID, SAMARITAN THREW HIM INTO THE MENTO-VERSE.
VERY GOOD. ANYTHING ELSE?
WELL, HE'S GOT NO BODY, SO HE'S ALWAYS GOT TO WORK THROUGH SOME KIND OF UNDERLINGS...
AN' HOLY CATS, LOOK WHO HE'S USING THIS TIME --

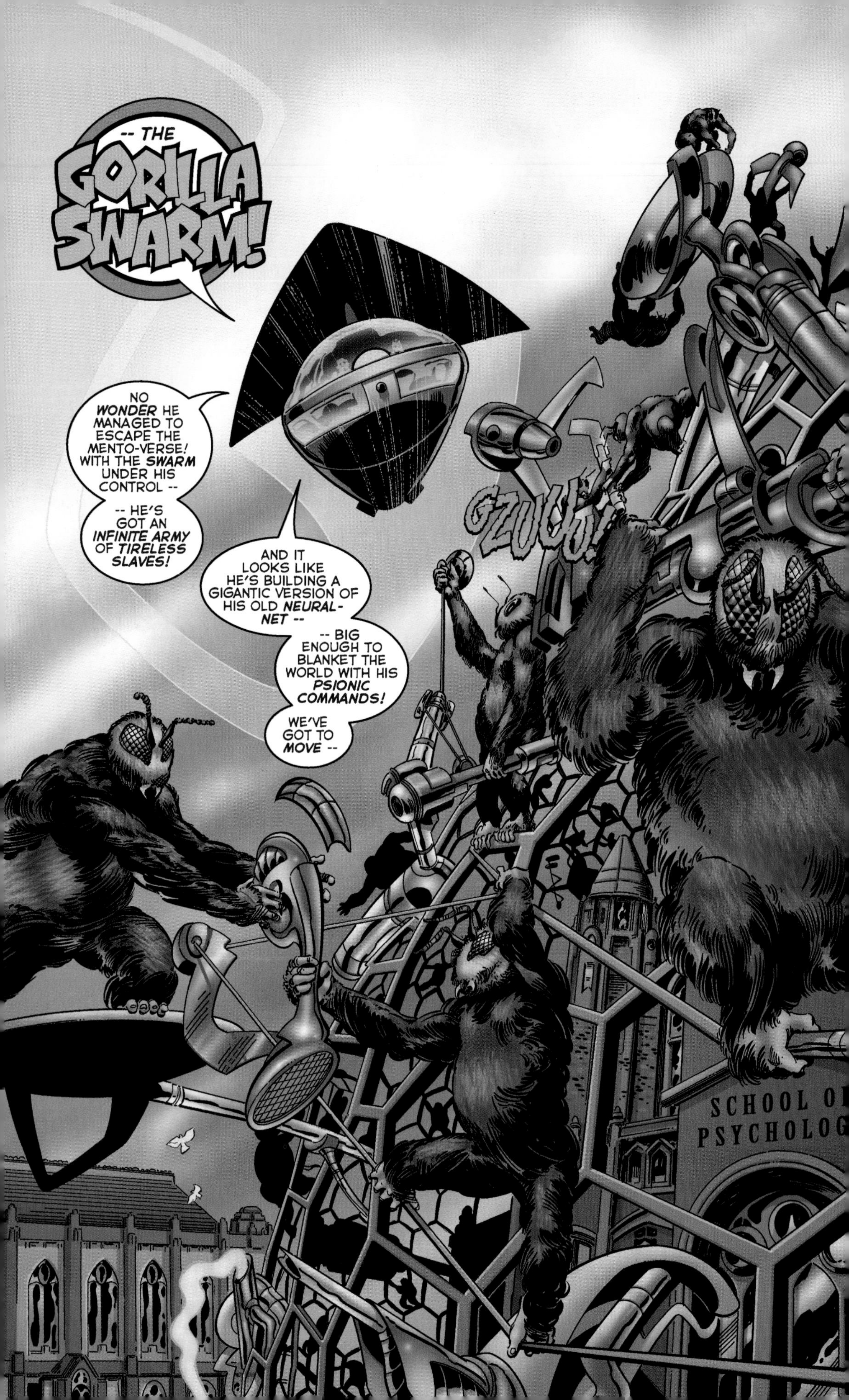

-- THE GORILLA SWARM!
NO WONDER HE MANAGED TO ESCAPE THE MENTO-VERSE! WITH THE SWARM UNDER HIS CONTROL --
-- HE'S GOT AN INFINITE ARMY OF TIRELESS SLAVES!
AND IT LOOKS LIKE HE'S BUILDING A GIGANTIC VERSION OF HIS OLD NEURAL-NET --
-- BIG ENOUGH TO BLANKET THE WORLD WITH HIS PSIONIC COMMANDS!
WE'VE GOT TO MOVE --
GZUUUU!
SCHOOL OF
PSYCHOLOG

--NOW! ASTRA -- MANEUVER **EPSILON-SEVEN!**

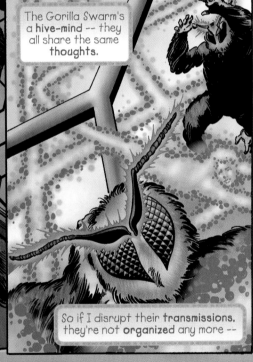

The Gorilla Swarm's a **hive-mind** -- they all share the same thoughts.

So if I disrupt their **transmissions,** they're not **organized** any more --

-- an' they go berserk!

OKAY! IN THIS STATE, NATALIE AND I CAN HANDLE THEM -- NO **PROBLEM!**

THE REST OF YOU --

GZAA!

UHRZZ!

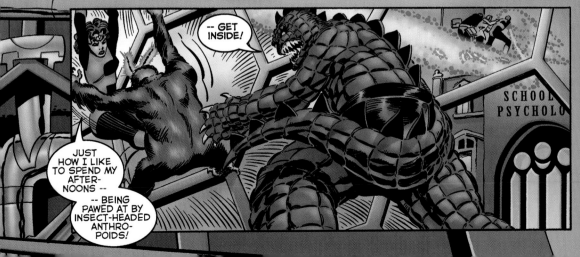

-- **GET INSIDE!**

JUST HOW I LIKE TO SPEND MY AFTER-NOONS -- -- BEING **PAWED** AT BY INSECT-HEADED ANTHRO-POIDS!

SCHOOL PSYCHOLO

KRASSCH!!
AH, DR. FURST AND HIS EXTENDED BROOD!
YOU THINK YOU'RE PROTECTED BY THOSE SILLY CIRCUITS, NO DOUBT -- BUT THAT'S ONE OF THE ADVANTAGES OF A PERFECT MEMORY!
ALL THAT TIME IN THE MENTO-VERSE, I REPLAYED OUR ENCOUNTERS --
-- UNTIL I DEDUCED YOUR CIRCUITS' FREQUENCY!
GUS?!
GRAMPA!
YOU SHOT MY GRAMPA!
ASTRA, WAIT! YOU'VE FORGOTTEN THE BRAIN'S LAST LINE OF DEFENSE --

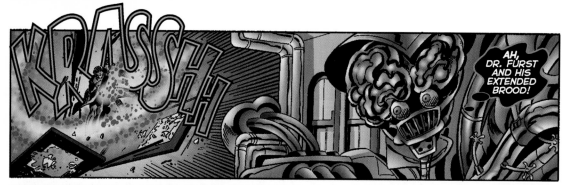

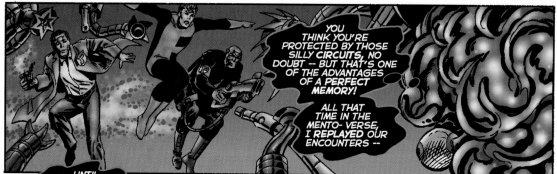

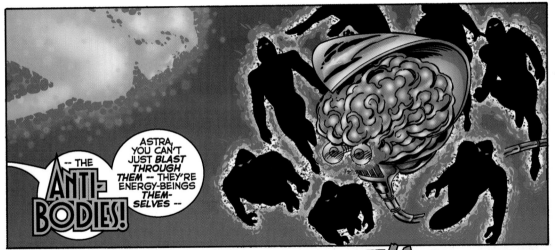

-- THE **ANTI-BODIES!**

ASTRA, YOU CAN'T JUST *BLAST THROUGH THEM* -- THEY'RE ENERGY-BEINGS THEM-SELVES --

-- AND THEY CAN GRAB *HOLD* OF YOU!

Yeah, *duh!*

ZKAK ZKAK

SHOOM

ASTRA!

WE'LL GETCHA BACK, KID!

Uncle Nick an' Uncle Julie are the ones who've forgotten what the Anti-Bodies do.

They grab onto the energy-blasts, just like they do *any* loose energy -- take us all to the power core --

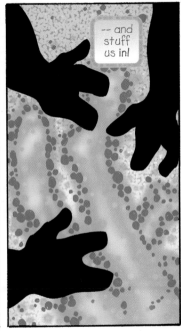

-- and stuff us *in!*

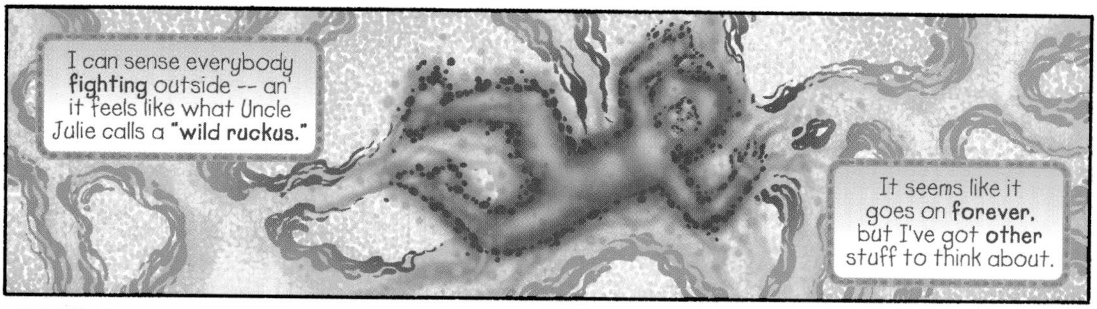
I can sense everybody fighting outside -- an' it feels like what Uncle Julie calls a "wild ruckus."
It seems like it goes on forever, but I've got other stuff to think about.

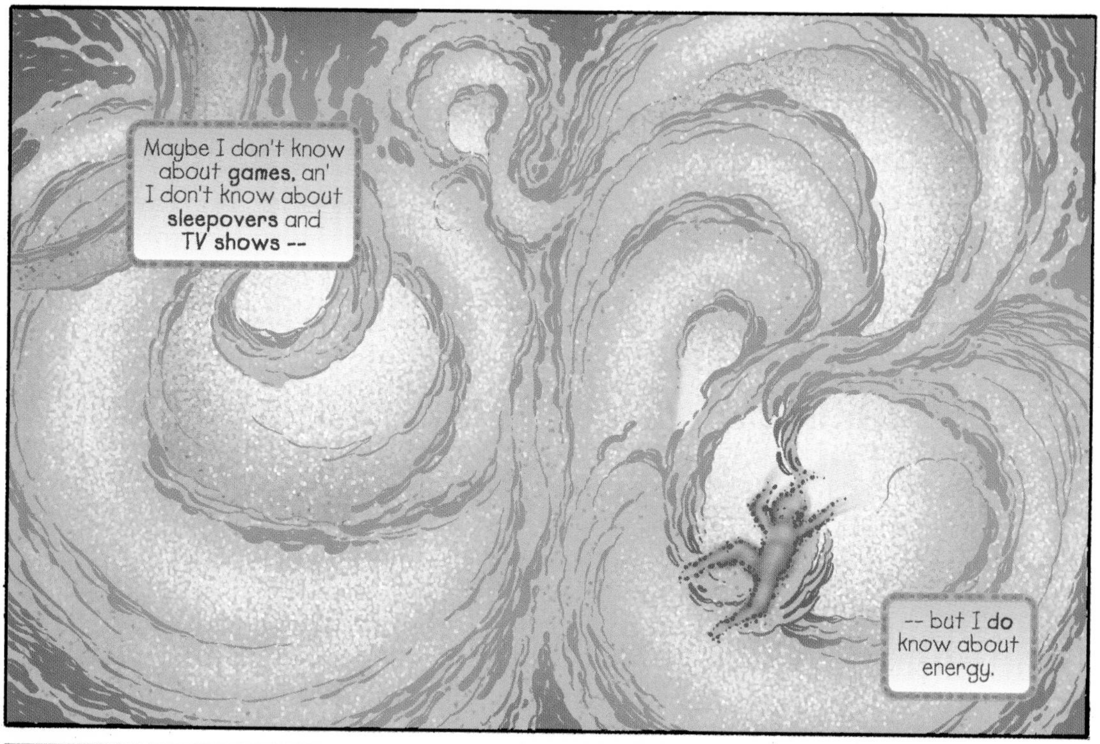
Maybe I don't know about games, an' I don't know about sleepovers and TV shows --
-- but I do know about energy.

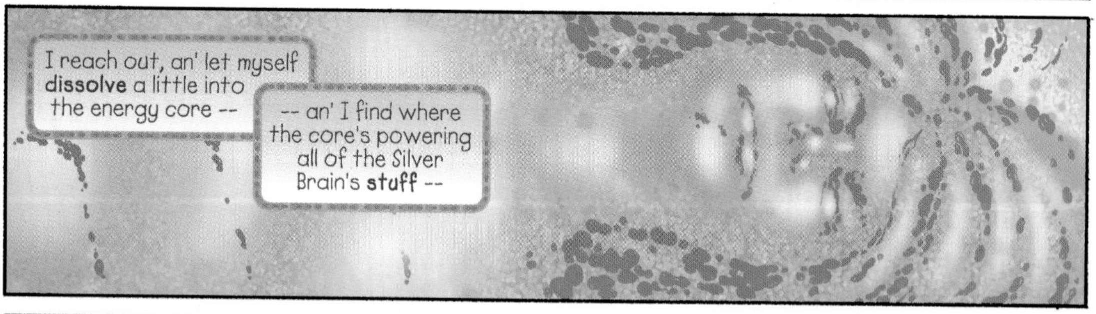
I reach out, an' let myself dissolve a little into the energy core --
-- an' I find where the core's powering all of the Silver Brain's stuff --

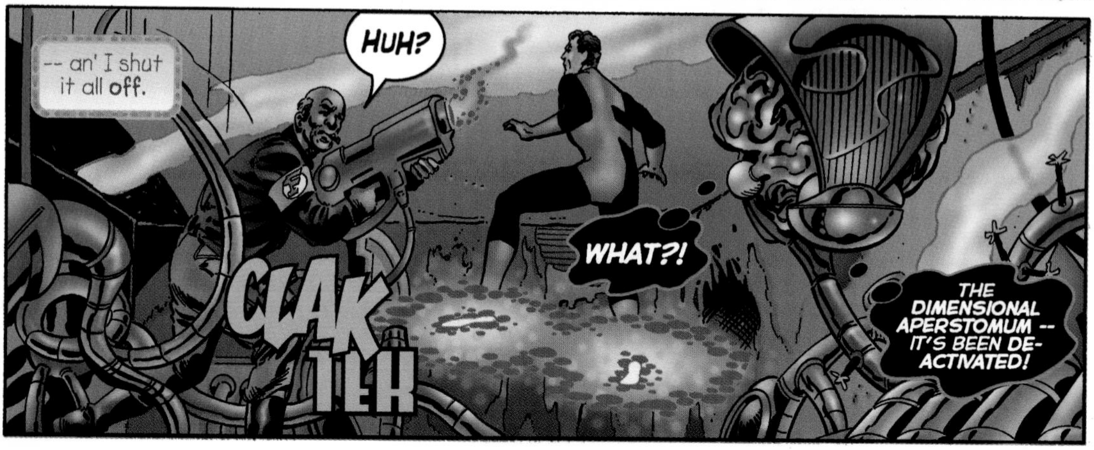
-- an' I shut it all off.
HUH?
WHAT?!
CLAK
TEK
THE DIMENSIONAL APERSTOMUM -- IT'S BEEN DE-ACTIVATED!

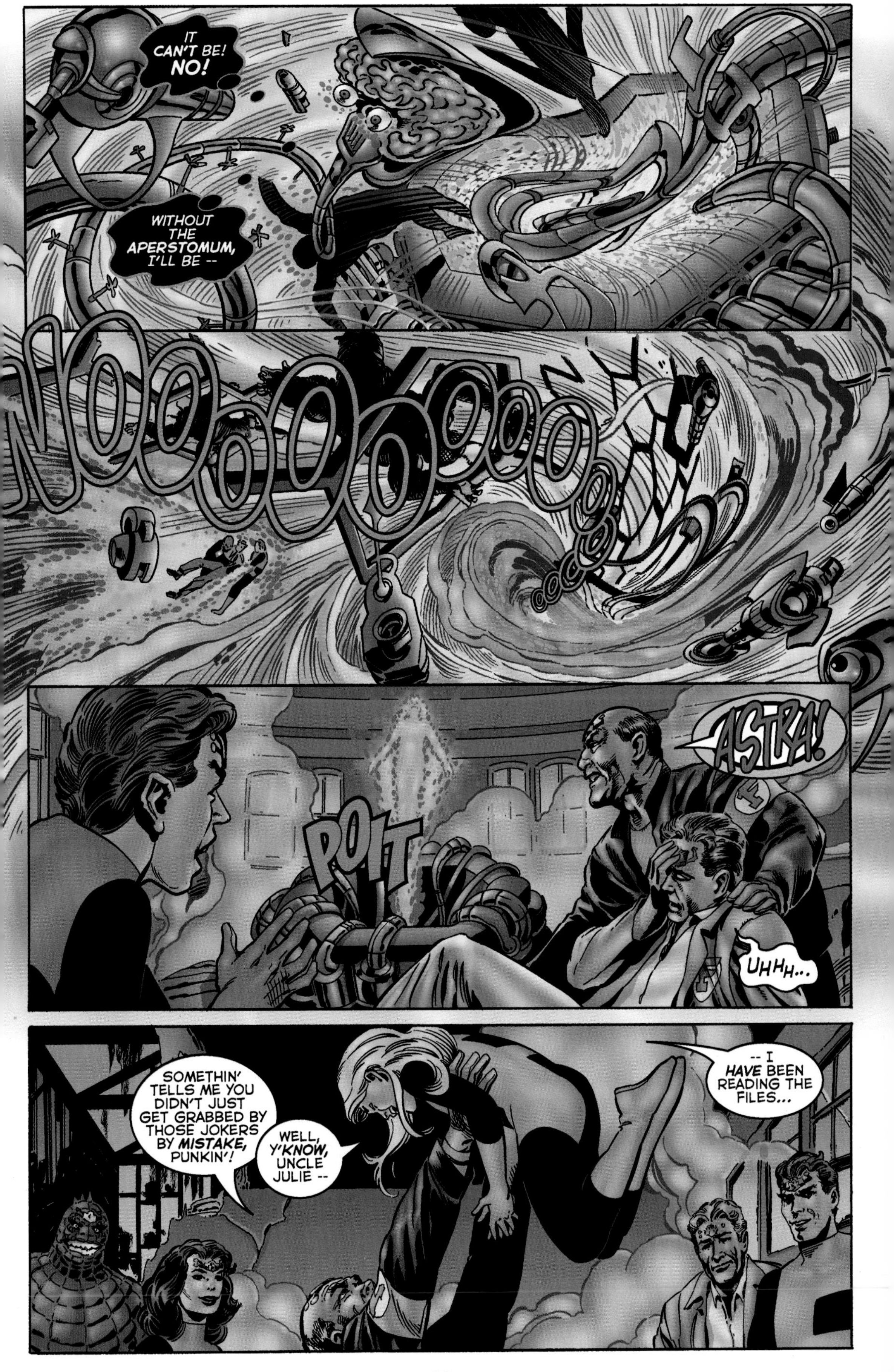
IT CAN'T BE! **NO!**
WITHOUT THE APERSTOMUM, I'LL BE --
NOOOOOOOOOOOOOOOOOOOO
POIT
ASTRA!
UHHH...
SOMETHIN' TELLS ME YOU DIDN'T JUST GET GRABBED BY THOSE JOKERS BY ***MISTAKE***, PUNKIN'!
WELL, ***Y'KNOW***, UNCLE JULIE --
-- I ***HAVE*** BEEN READING THE FILES...

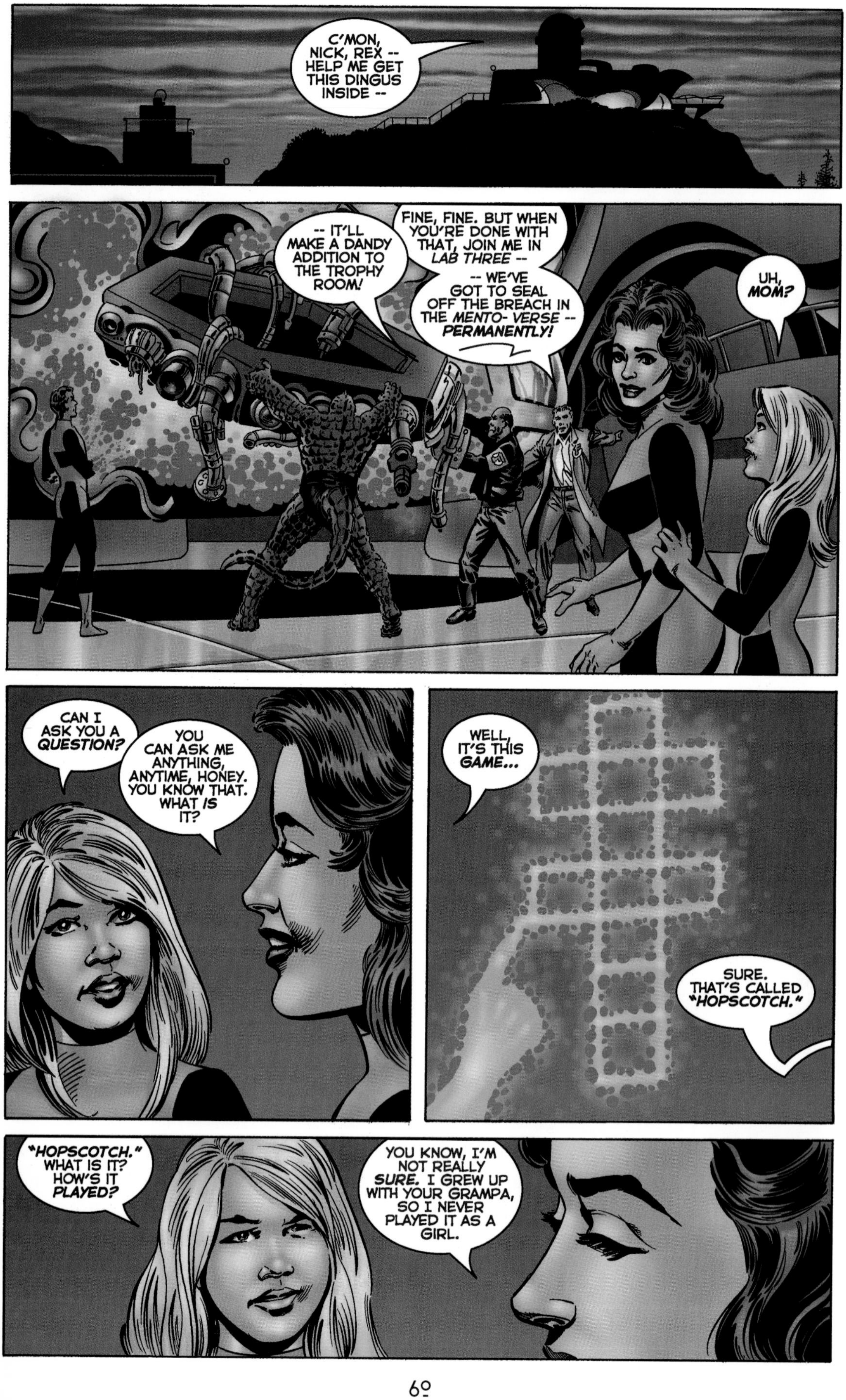
C'MON, NICK, REX -- HELP ME GET THIS DINGUS INSIDE --
-- IT'LL MAKE A DANDY ADDITION TO THE TROPHY ROOM!
FINE, FINE. BUT WHEN YOU'RE DONE WITH THAT, JOIN ME IN LAB THREE --
-- WE'VE GOT TO SEAL OFF THE BREACH IN THE MENTO- VERSE -- PERMANENTLY!
UH, MOM?
CAN I ASK YOU A QUESTION?
YOU CAN ASK ME ANYTHING, ANYTIME, HONEY. YOU KNOW THAT. WHAT IS IT?
WELL, IT'S THIS GAME...
SURE. THAT'S CALLED "HOPSCOTCH."
"HOPSCOTCH." WHAT IS IT? HOW'S IT PLAYED?
YOU KNOW, I'M NOT REALLY SURE. I GREW UP WITH YOUR GRAMPA, SO I NEVER PLAYED IT AS A GIRL.

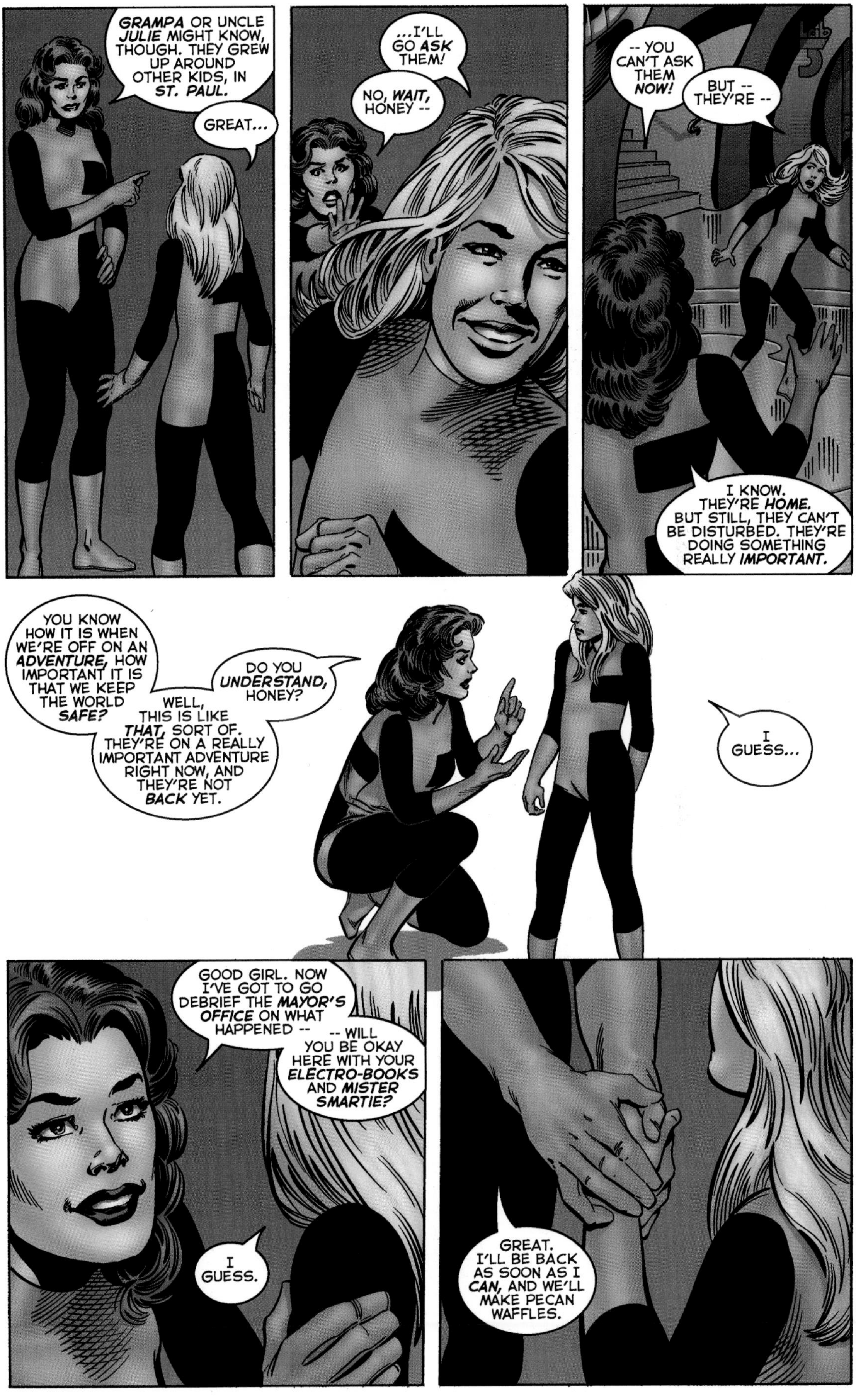
GRAMPA OR UNCLE JULIE MIGHT KNOW, THOUGH. THEY GREW UP AROUND OTHER KIDS, IN ST. PAUL.
GREAT...
...I'LL GO ASK THEM!
NO, WAIT, HONEY --
-- YOU CAN'T ASK THEM NOW!
BUT -- THEY'RE --
I KNOW. THEY'RE HOME. BUT STILL, THEY CAN'T BE DISTURBED. THEY'RE DOING SOMETHING REALLY IMPORTANT.
YOU KNOW HOW IT IS WHEN WE'RE OFF ON AN ADVENTURE, HOW IMPORTANT IT IS THAT WE KEEP THE WORLD SAFE?
WELL, THIS IS LIKE THAT, SORT OF. THEY'RE ON A REALLY IMPORTANT ADVENTURE RIGHT NOW, AND THEY'RE NOT BACK YET.
DO YOU UNDERSTAND, HONEY?
I GUESS...
GOOD GIRL. NOW I'VE GOT TO GO DEBRIEF THE MAYOR'S OFFICE ON WHAT HAPPENED --
-- WILL YOU BE OKAY HERE WITH YOUR ELECTRO-BOOKS AND MISTER SMARTIE?
I GUESS.
GREAT. I'LL BE BACK AS SOON AS I CAN, AND WE'LL MAKE PECAN WAFFLES.

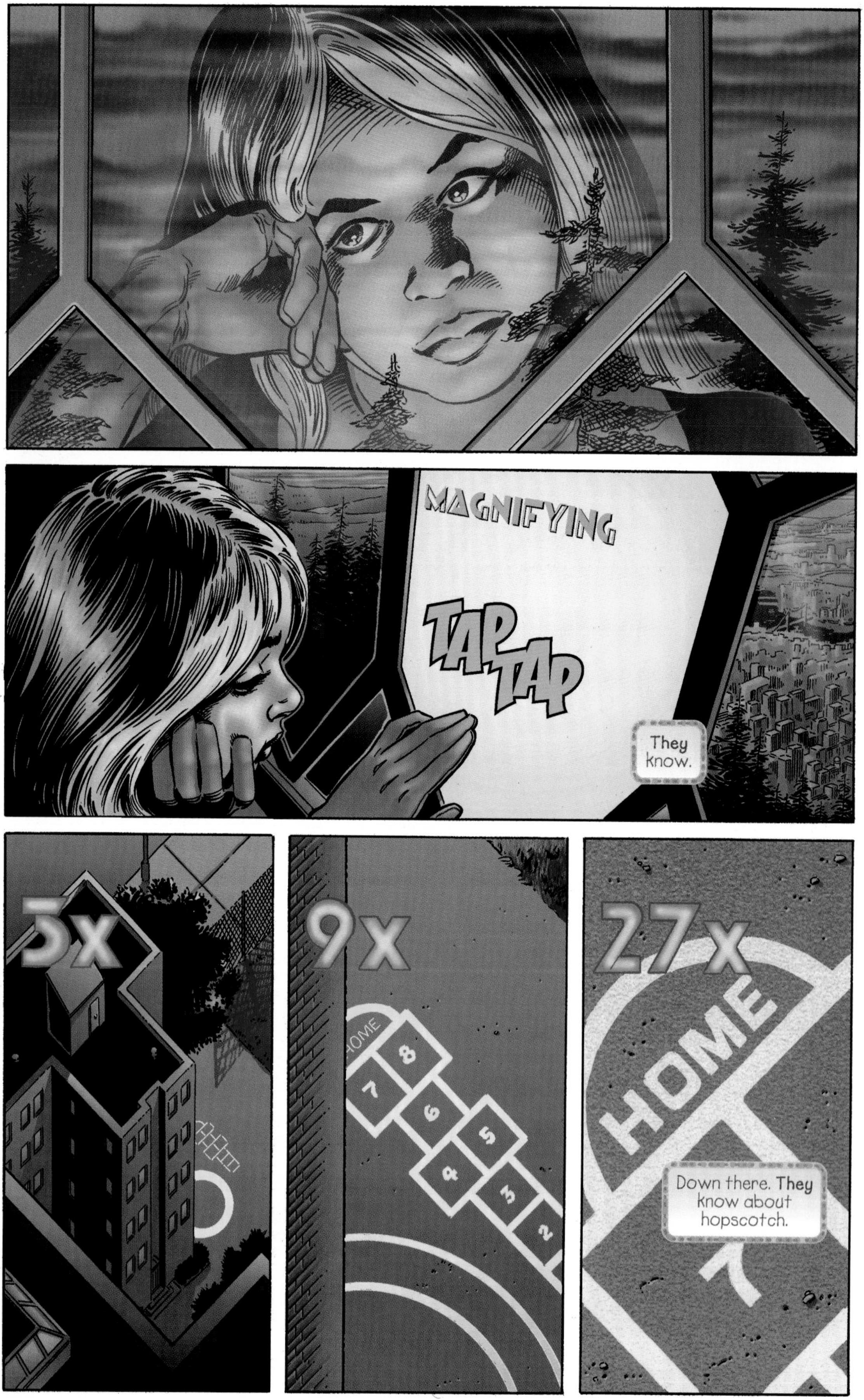
MAGNIFYING
TAP TAP
They know.
3x
9x
HOME
27x
HOME
Down there. They know about hopscotch.

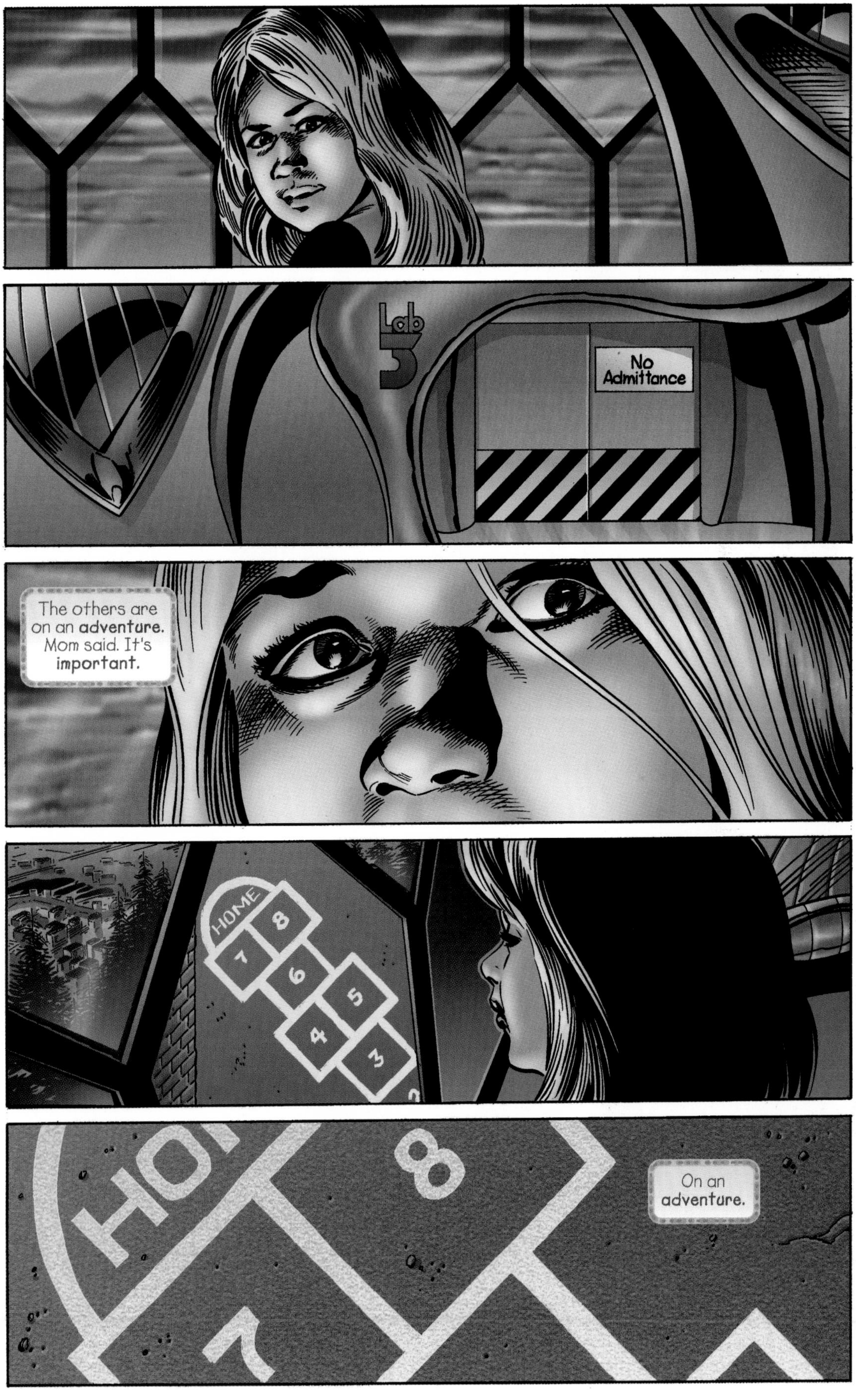
Lab 3
No Admittance
The others are on an adventure. Mom said. It's important.
HOME
8
7
6
5
4
3
On an adventure.

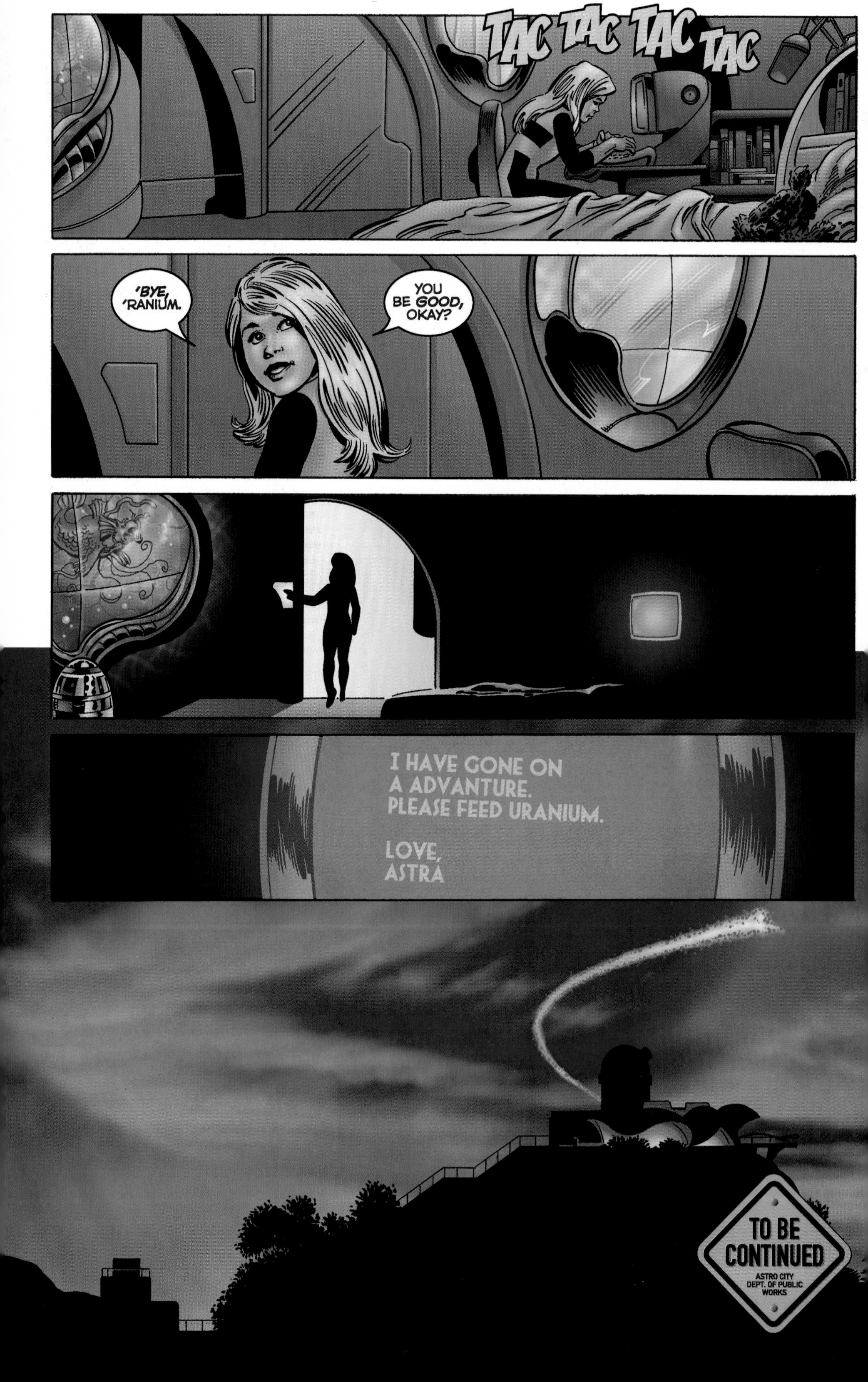
TAC TAC TAC TAC
'BYE, 'RANIUM.
YOU BE GOOD, OKAY?
I HAVE GONE ON A ADVANTURE. PLEASE FEED URANIUM.
LOVE, ASTRA
TO BE CONTINUED
ASTRO CITY DEPT. OF PUBLIC WORKS

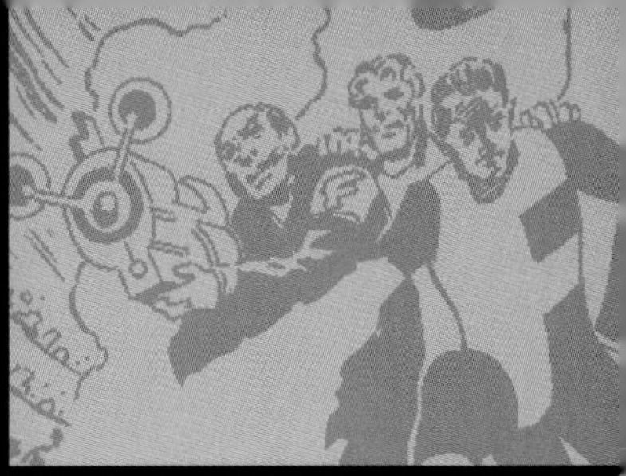

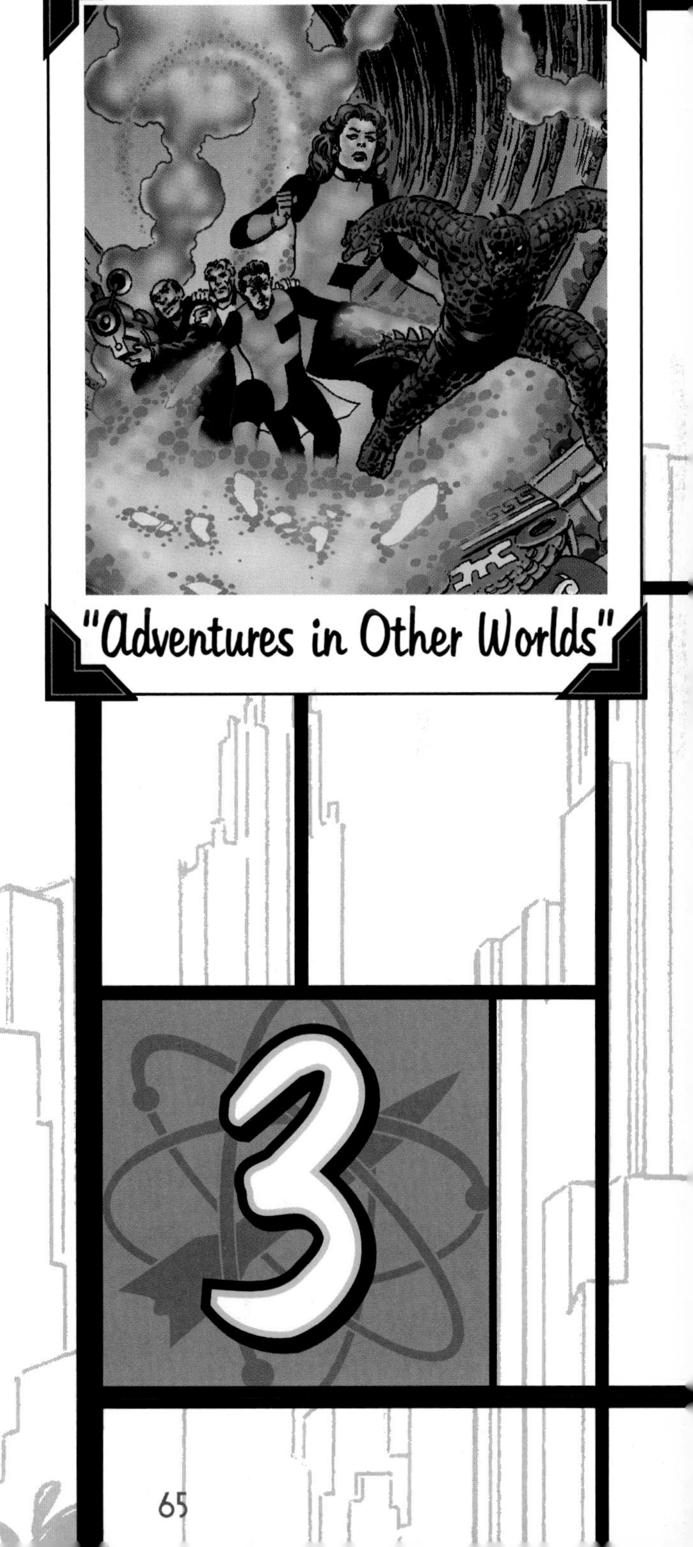

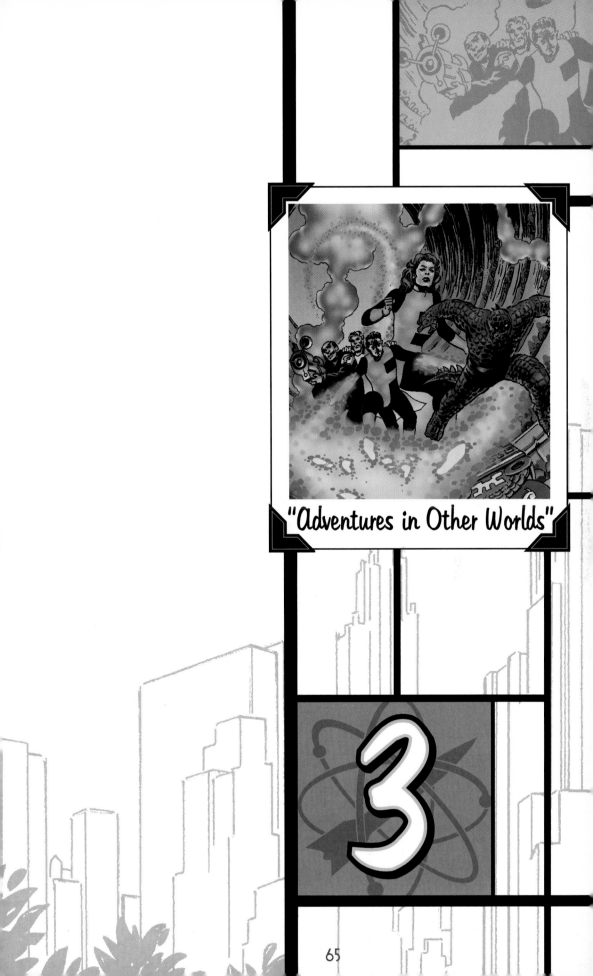

"Adventures in Other Worlds"

3

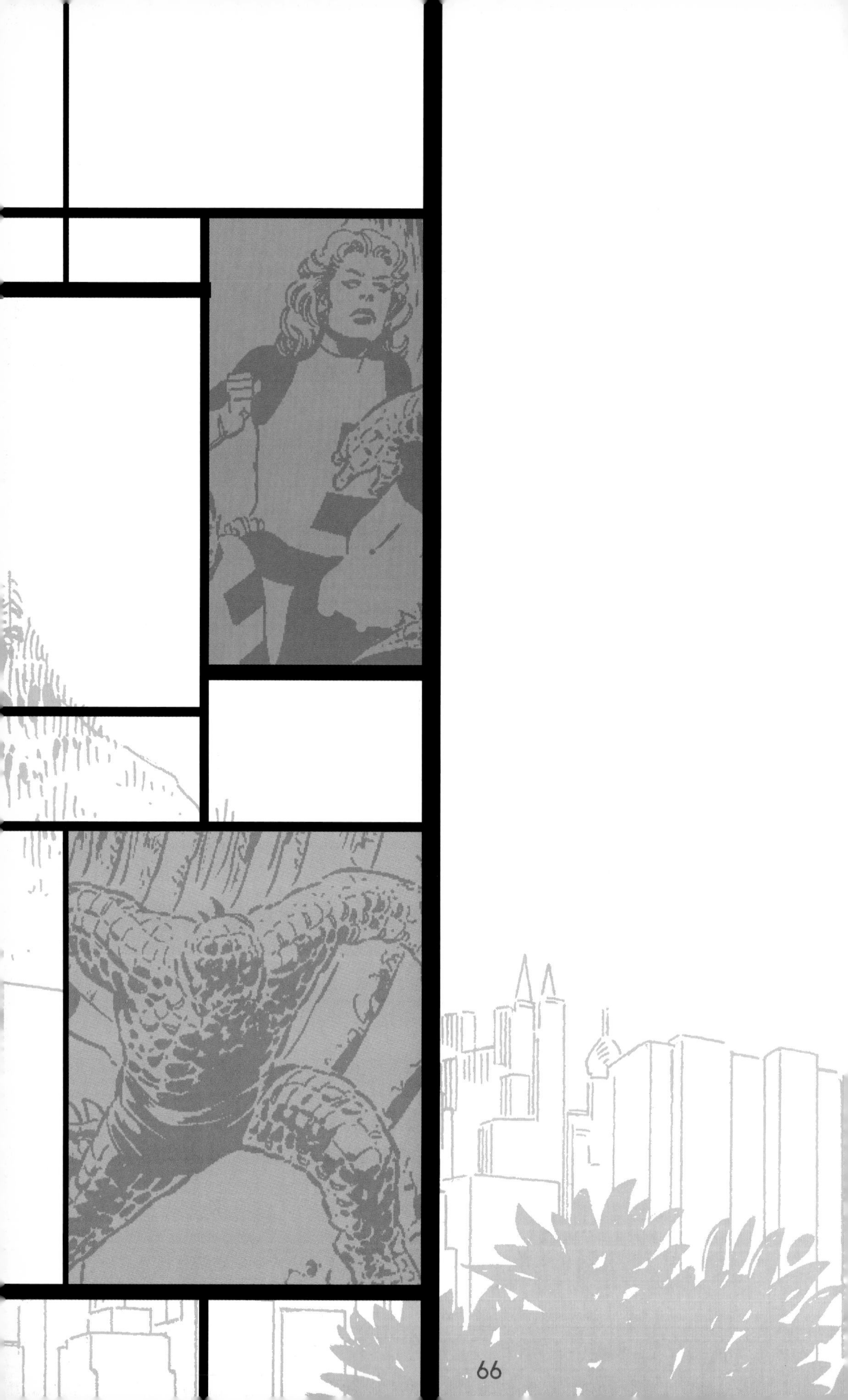

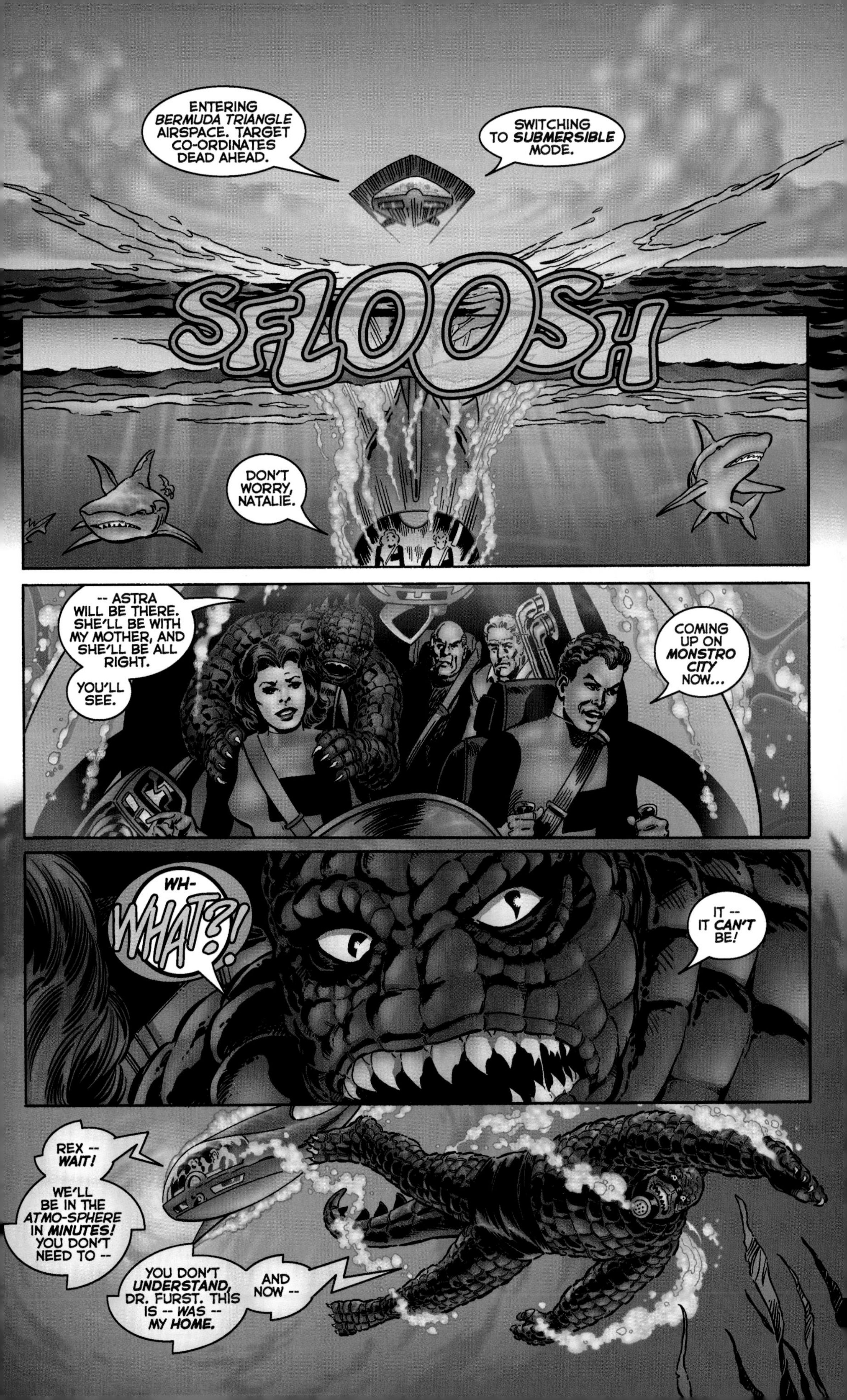
ENTERING BERMUDA TRIANGLE AIRSPACE. TARGET CO-ORDINATES DEAD AHEAD.
SWITCHING TO SUBMERSIBLE MODE.
SFLOOSH
DON'T WORRY, NATALIE.
-- ASTRA WILL BE THERE. SHE'LL BE WITH MY MOTHER, AND SHE'LL BE ALL RIGHT.
YOU'LL SEE.
COMING UP ON MONSTRO CITY NOW...
WH- WHAT?!
IT -- IT CAN'T BE!
REX -- WAIT!
WE'LL BE IN THE ATMO-SPHERE IN MINUTES! YOU DON'T NEED TO --
YOU DON'T UNDERSTAND, DR. FURST. THIS IS -- WAS -- MY HOME.
AND NOW --

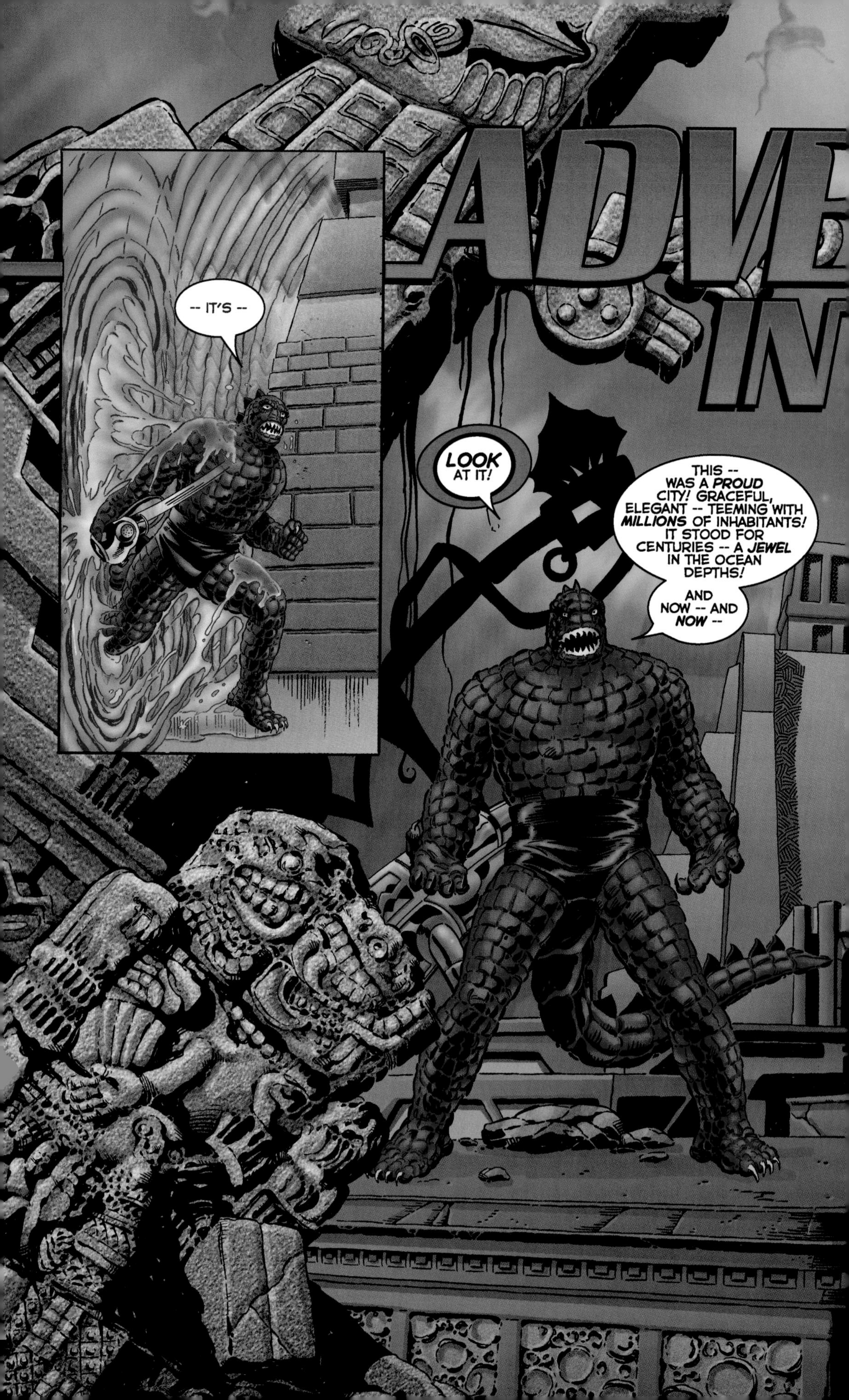

-- IT'S --
ADVE
IN
LOOK AT IT!
THIS -- WAS A PROUD CITY! GRACEFUL, ELEGANT -- TEEMING WITH MILLIONS OF INHABITANTS! IT STOOD FOR CENTURIES -- A JEWEL IN THE OCEAN DEPTHS!
AND NOW -- AND NOW --

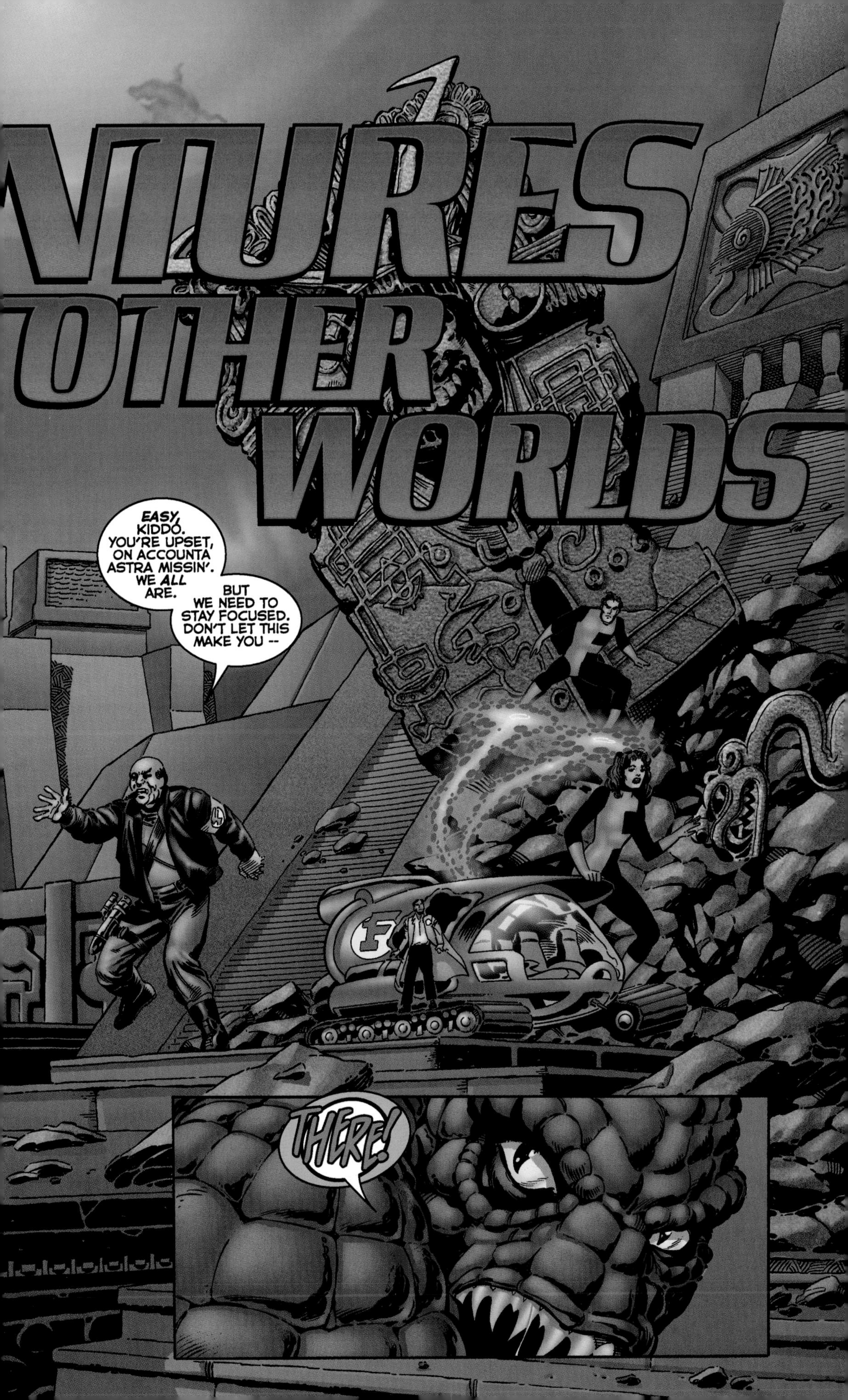
NTURES
OTHER
WORLDS
EASY, KIDDO. YOU'RE UPSET, ON ACCOUNTA ASTRA MISSIN'. WE ALL ARE.
BUT WE NEED TO STAY FOCUSED. DON'T LET THIS MAKE YOU --
THERE!

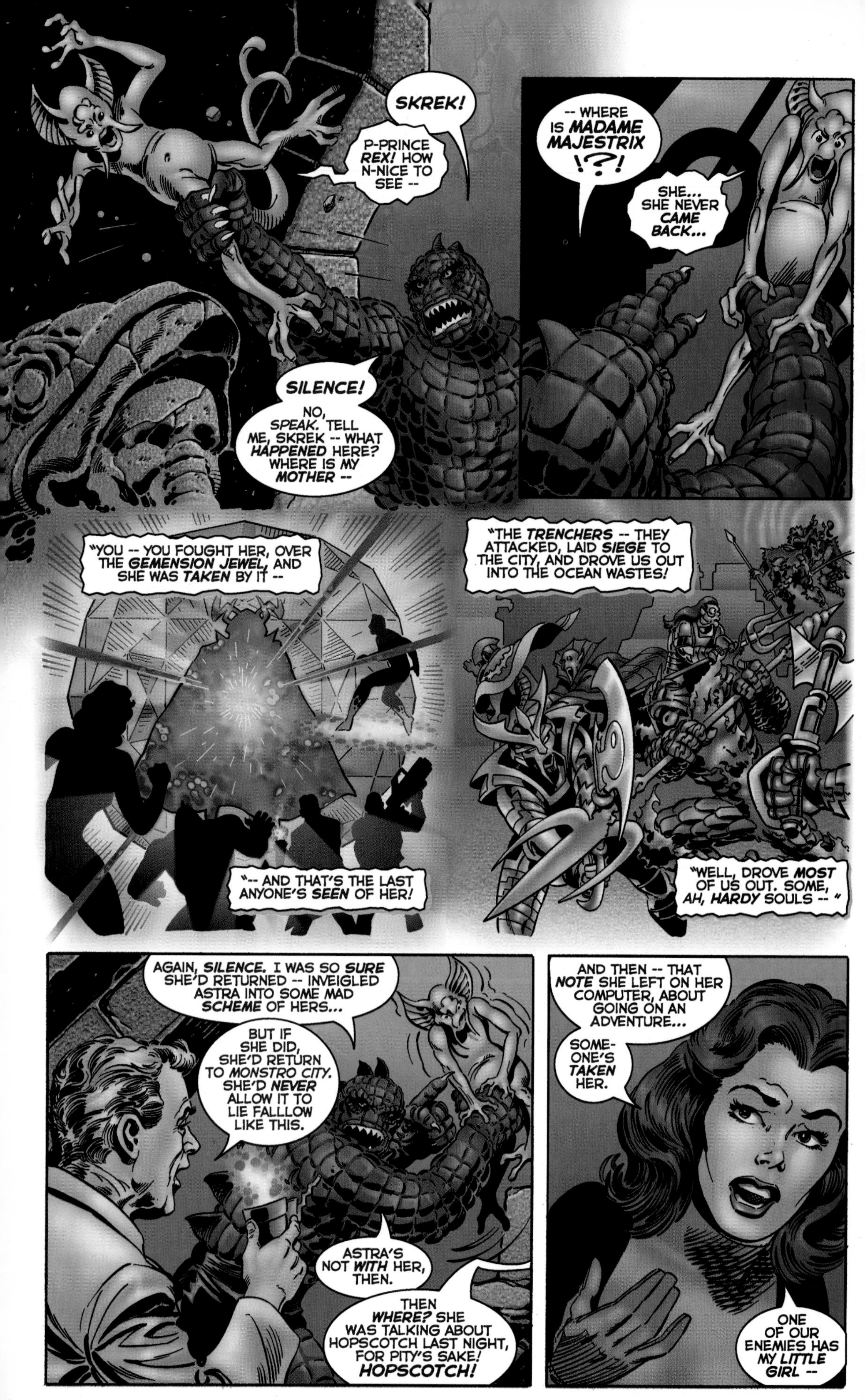
SKREK!
P-PRINCE REX! HOW N-NICE TO SEE --
SILENCE!
NO, SPEAK. TELL ME, SKREK -- WHAT HAPPENED HERE? WHERE IS MY MOTHER --
-- WHERE IS MADAME MAJESTRIX !?!
SHE... SHE NEVER CAME BACK...
"YOU -- YOU FOUGHT HER, OVER THE GEMENSION JEWEL, AND SHE WAS TAKEN BY IT --
"-- AND THAT'S THE LAST ANYONE'S SEEN OF HER!
"THE TRENCHERS -- THEY ATTACKED, LAID SIEGE TO THE CITY, AND DROVE US OUT INTO THE OCEAN WASTES!
"WELL, DROVE MOST OF US OUT. SOME, AH, HARDY SOULS -- "
AGAIN, SILENCE. I WAS SO SURE SHE'D RETURNED -- INVEIGLED ASTRA INTO SOME MAD SCHEME OF HERS...
BUT IF SHE DID, SHE'D RETURN TO MONSTRO CITY. SHE'D NEVER ALLOW IT TO LIE FALLLOW LIKE THIS.
ASTRA'S NOT WITH HER, THEN.
THEN WHERE? SHE WAS TALKING ABOUT HOPSCOTCH LAST NIGHT, FOR PITY'S SAKE! HOPSCOTCH!
AND THEN -- THAT NOTE SHE LEFT ON HER COMPUTER, ABOUT GOING ON AN ADVENTURE...
SOME-ONE'S TAKEN HER.
ONE OF OUR ENEMIES HAS MY LITTLE GIRL --

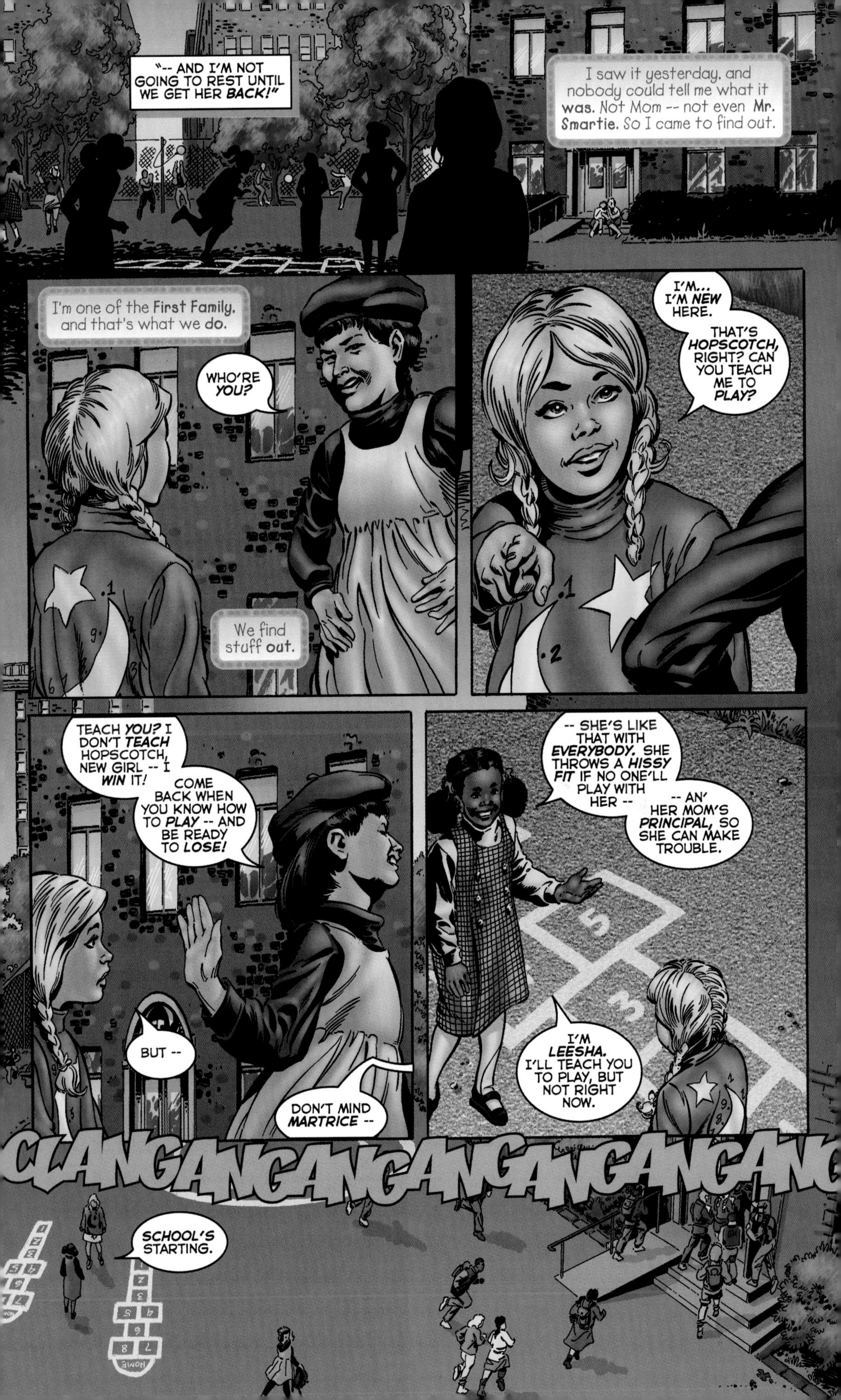
"-- AND I'M NOT GOING TO REST UNTIL WE GET HER BACK!"
I saw it yesterday, and nobody could tell me what it was. Not Mom -- not even Mr. Smartie. So I came to find out.
I'm one of the First Family, and that's what we do.
WHO'RE YOU?
We find stuff out.
I'M... I'M NEW HERE.
THAT'S HOPSCOTCH, RIGHT? CAN YOU TEACH ME TO PLAY?
TEACH YOU? I DON'T TEACH HOPSCOTCH, NEW GIRL -- I WIN IT!
COME BACK WHEN YOU KNOW HOW TO PLAY -- AND BE READY TO LOSE!
BUT --
DON'T MIND MARTRICE --
-- SHE'S LIKE THAT WITH EVERYBODY. SHE THROWS A HISSY FIT IF NO ONE'LL PLAY WITH HER --
-- AN' HER MOM'S PRINCIPAL, SO SHE CAN MAKE TROUBLE.
I'M LEESHA. I'LL TEACH YOU TO PLAY, BUT NOT RIGHT NOW.
CLANGANGANGANGANGANGANGANG
SCHOOL'S STARTING.

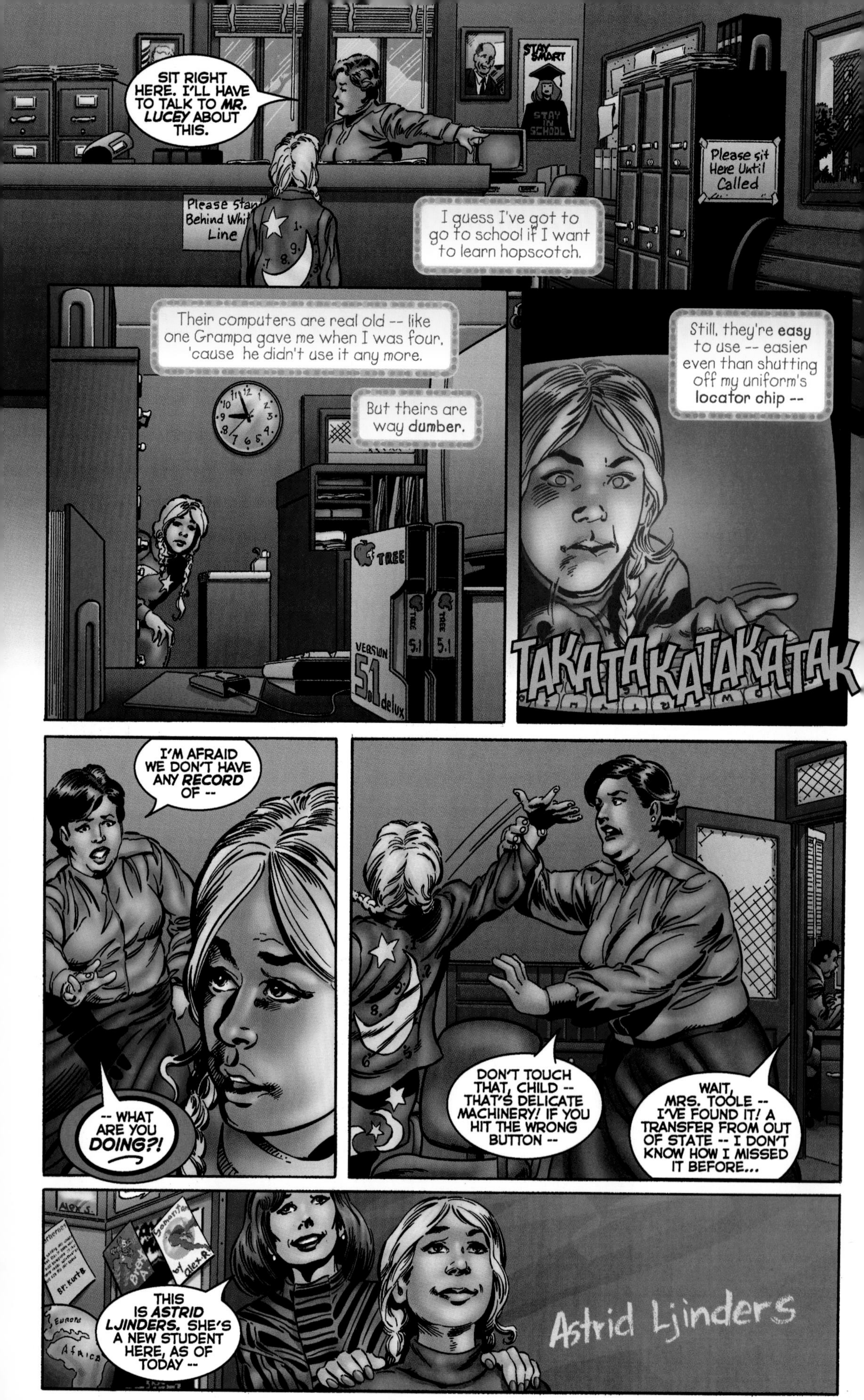

SIT RIGHT HERE. I'LL HAVE TO TALK TO MR. LUCEY ABOUT THIS.
STAY SMART
STAY IN SCHOOL
Please sit Here Until Called
Please Stand Behind White Line
I guess I've got to go to school if I want to learn hopscotch.
Their computers are real old -- like one Grampa gave me when I was four, 'cause he didn't use it any more.
But theirs are way dumber.
TREE
VERSION 5.1 delux
Still, they're easy to use -- easier even than shutting off my uniform's locator chip --
TAKATAKATAKATAK
I'M AFRAID WE DON'T HAVE ANY RECORD OF --
-- WHAT ARE YOU DOING?!
DON'T TOUCH THAT, CHILD -- THAT'S DELICATE MACHINERY! IF YOU HIT THE WRONG BUTTON --
WAIT, MRS. TOOLE -- I'VE FOUND IT! A TRANSFER FROM OUT OF STATE -- I DON'T KNOW HOW I MISSED IT BEFORE...
THIS IS ASTRID LJINDERS. SHE'S A NEW STUDENT HERE, AS OF TODAY --
Astrid Ljinders

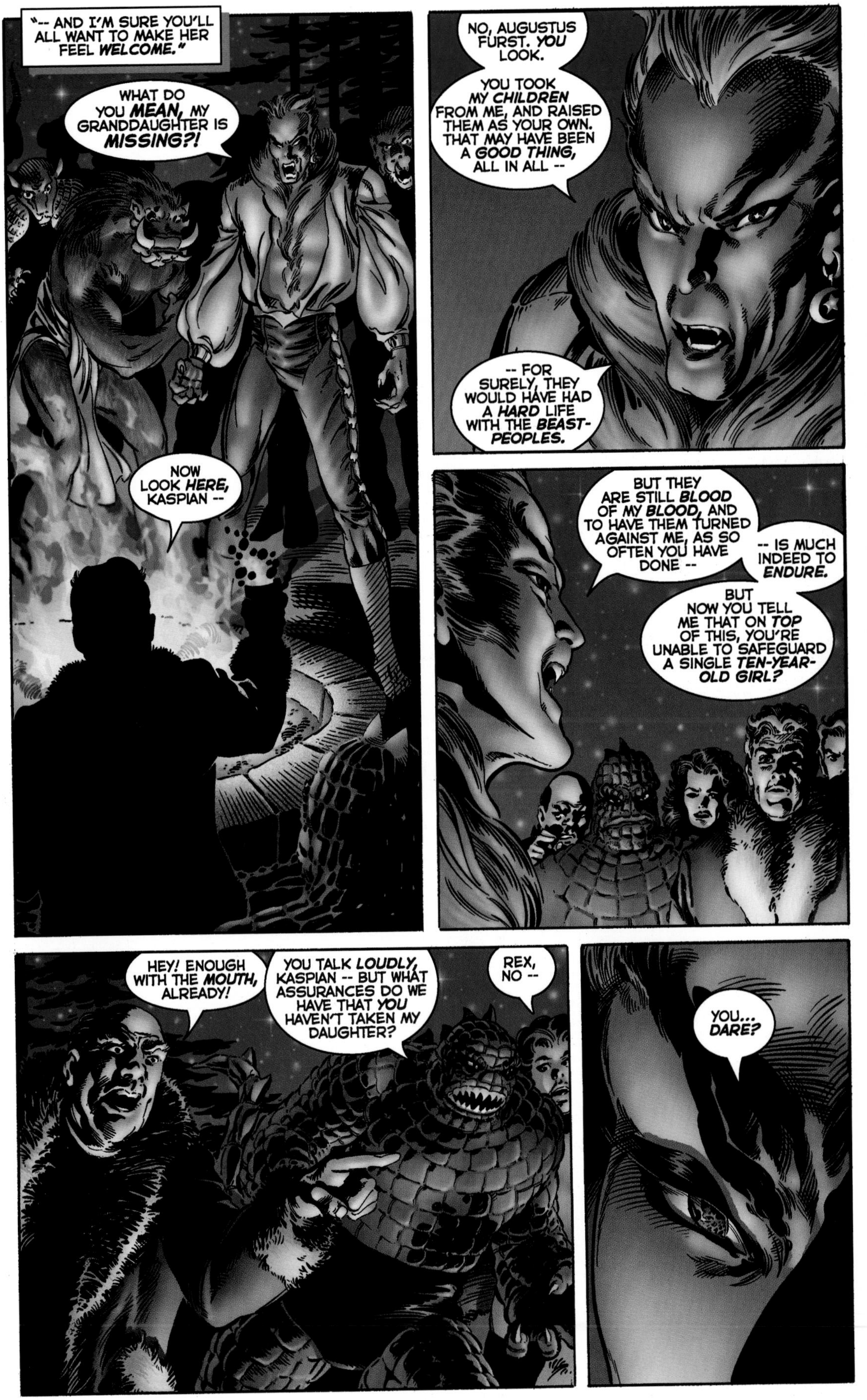
"-- AND I'M SURE YOU'LL ALL WANT TO MAKE HER FEEL WELCOME."
WHAT DO YOU MEAN, MY GRANDDAUGHTER IS MISSING?!
NOW LOOK HERE, KASPIAN --
NO, AUGUSTUS FURST. YOU LOOK.
YOU TOOK MY CHILDREN FROM ME, AND RAISED THEM AS YOUR OWN. THAT MAY HAVE BEEN A GOOD THING, ALL IN ALL --
-- FOR SURELY, THEY WOULD HAVE HAD A HARD LIFE WITH THE BEAST-PEOPLES.
BUT THEY ARE STILL BLOOD OF MY BLOOD, AND TO HAVE THEM TURNED AGAINST ME, AS SO OFTEN YOU HAVE DONE --
-- IS MUCH INDEED TO ENDURE.
BUT NOW YOU TELL ME THAT ON TOP OF THIS, YOU'RE UNABLE TO SAFEGUARD A SINGLE TEN-YEAR-OLD GIRL?
HEY! ENOUGH WITH THE MOUTH, ALREADY!
YOU TALK LOUDLY, KASPIAN -- BUT WHAT ASSURANCES DO WE HAVE THAT YOU HAVEN'T TAKEN MY DAUGHTER?
REX, NO --
YOU... DARE?

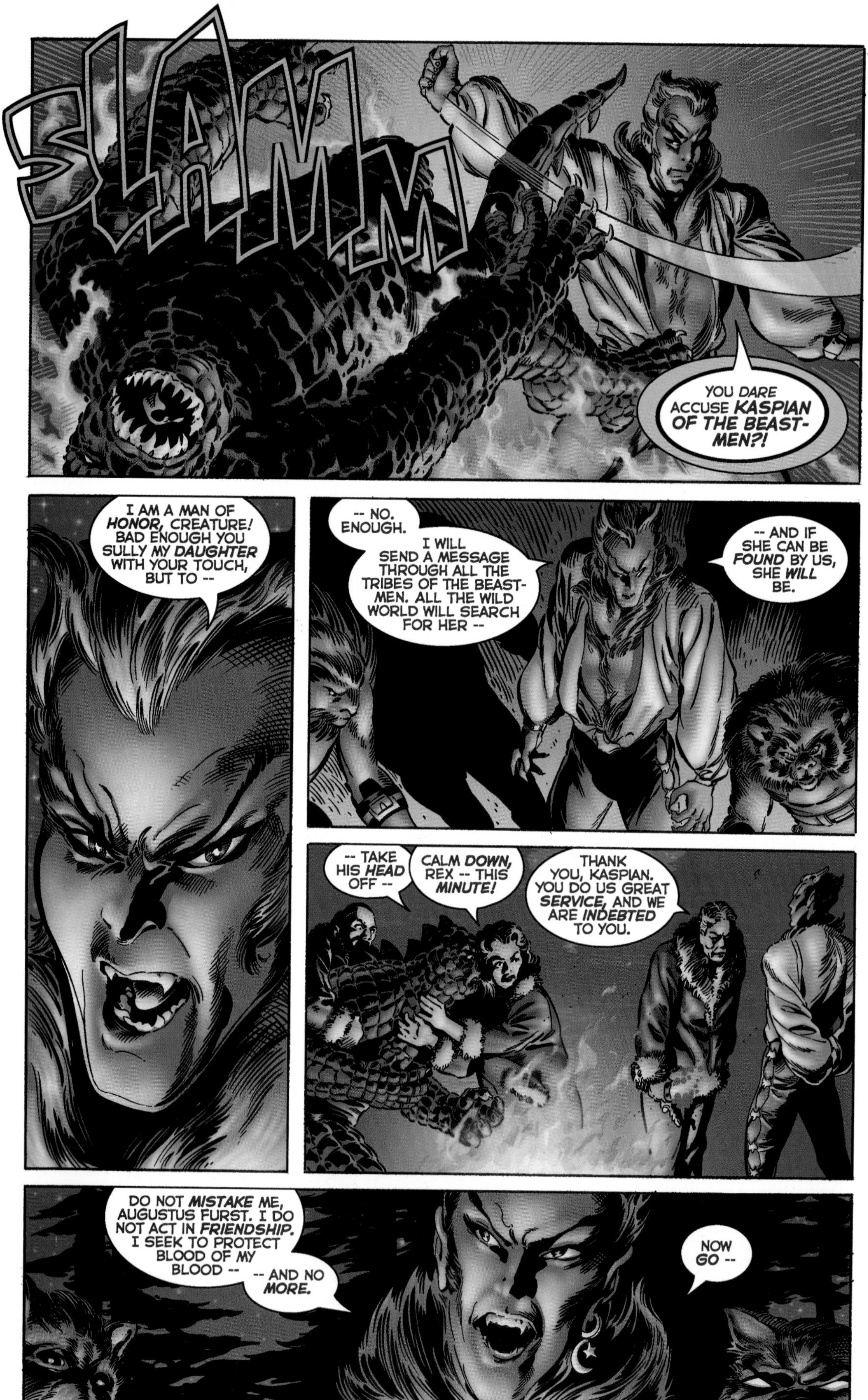
SLAMM
YOU DARE ACCUSE KASPIAN OF THE BEAST-MEN?!
I AM A MAN OF HONOR, CREATURE! BAD ENOUGH YOU SULLY MY DAUGHTER WITH YOUR TOUCH, BUT TO --
-- NO. ENOUGH.
I WILL SEND A MESSAGE THROUGH ALL THE TRIBES OF THE BEAST-MEN. ALL THE WILD WORLD WILL SEARCH FOR HER --
-- AND IF SHE CAN BE FOUND BY US, SHE WILL BE.
-- TAKE HIS HEAD OFF --
CALM DOWN, REX -- THIS MINUTE!
THANK YOU, KASPIAN. YOU DO US GREAT SERVICE, AND WE ARE INDEBTED TO YOU.
DO NOT MISTAKE ME, AUGUSTUS FURST. I DO NOT ACT IN FRIENDSHIP. I SEEK TO PROTECT BLOOD OF MY BLOOD --
-- AND NO MORE.
NOW GO --

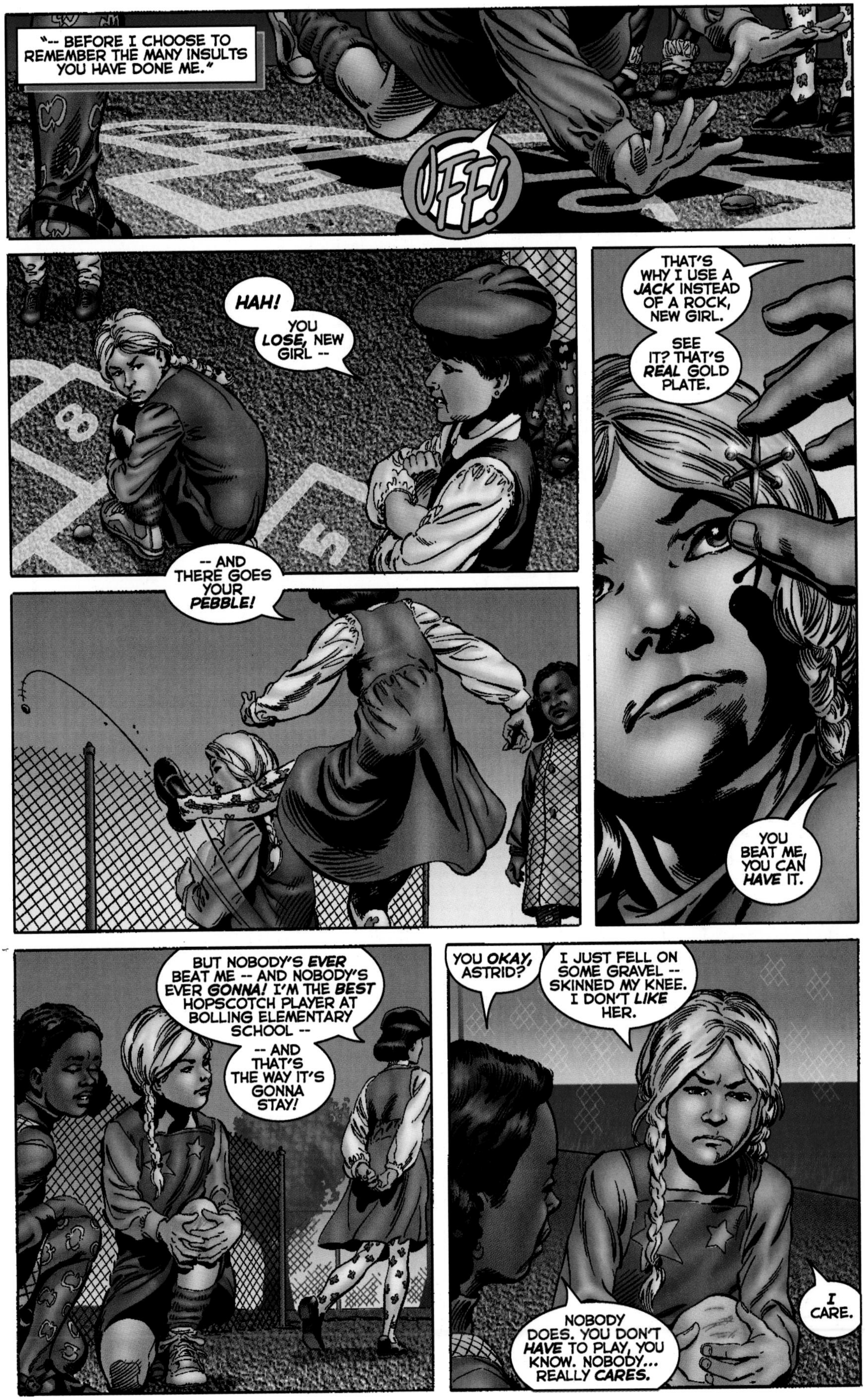
"-- BEFORE I CHOOSE TO REMEMBER THE MANY INSULTS YOU HAVE DONE ME."
UFF!
HAH!
YOU LOSE, NEW GIRL --
-- AND THERE GOES YOUR PEBBLE!
THAT'S WHY I USE A JACK INSTEAD OF A ROCK, NEW GIRL.
SEE IT? THAT'S REAL GOLD PLATE.
YOU BEAT ME, YOU CAN HAVE IT.
BUT NOBODY'S EVER BEAT ME -- AND NOBODY'S EVER GONNA! I'M THE BEST HOPSCOTCH PLAYER AT BOLLING ELEMENTARY SCHOOL --
-- AND THAT'S THE WAY IT'S GONNA STAY!
YOU OKAY, ASTRID?
I JUST FELL ON SOME GRAVEL -- SKINNED MY KNEE. I DON'T LIKE HER.
NOBODY DOES. YOU DON'T HAVE TO PLAY, YOU KNOW. NOBODY... REALLY CARES.
I CARE.

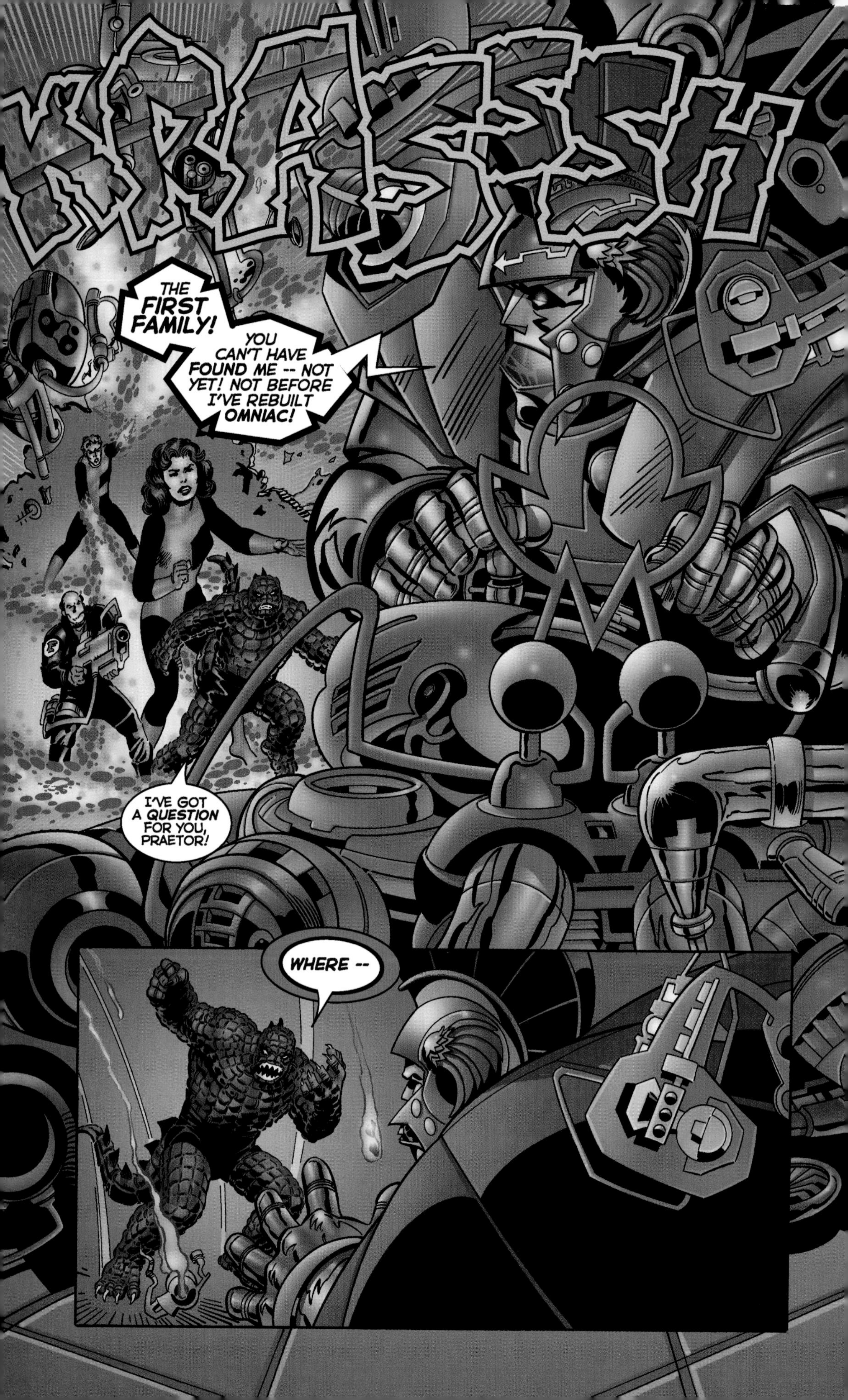

KRASSH
THE FIRST FAMILY!
YOU CAN'T HAVE FOUND ME -- NOT YET! NOT BEFORE I'VE REBUILT OMNIAC!
I'VE GOT A QUESTION FOR YOU, PRAETOR!
WHERE --

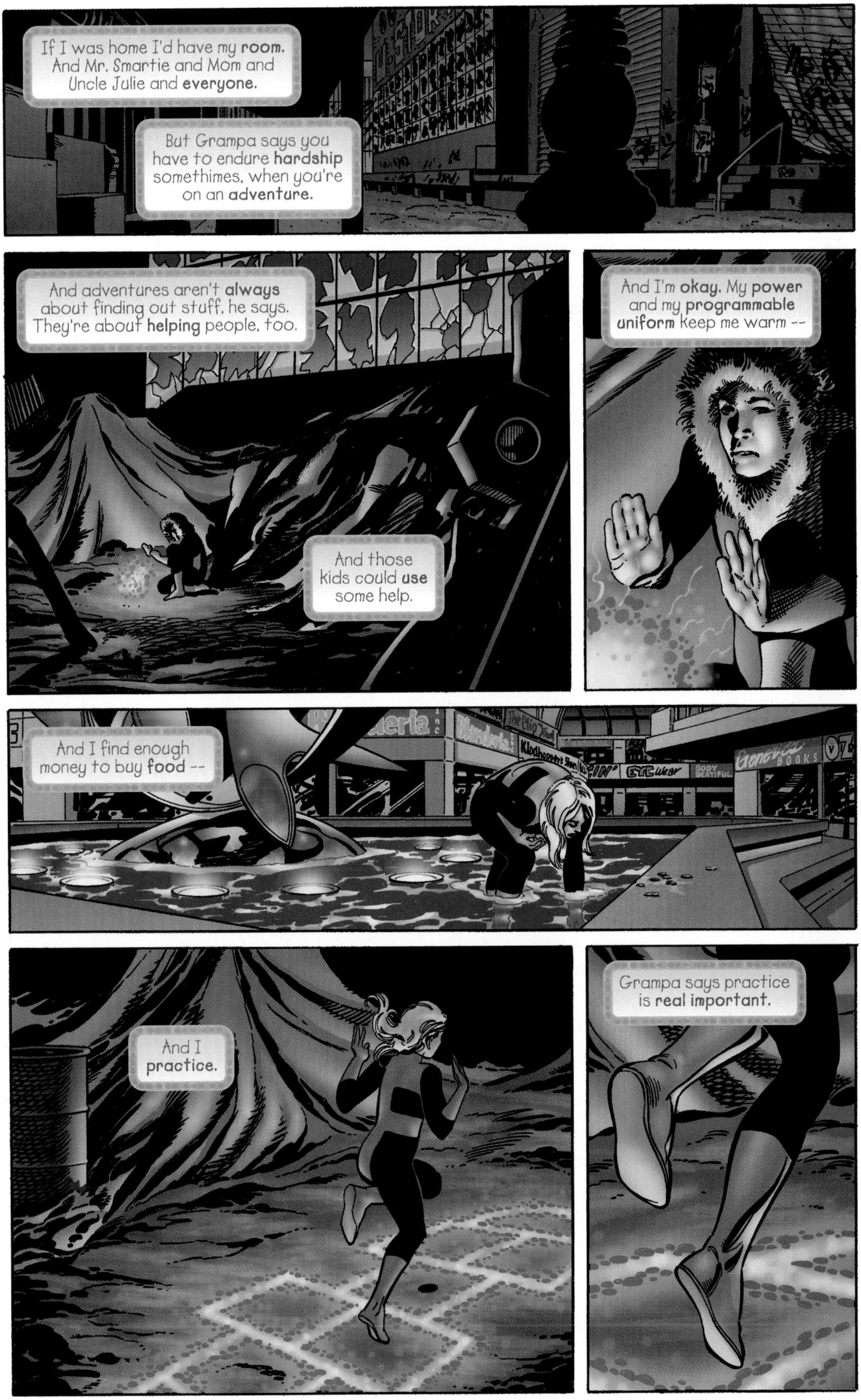
If I was home I'd have my room. And Mr. Smartie and Mom and Uncle Julie and everyone.
But Grampa says you have to endure hardship somethimes, when you're on an adventure.
And adventures aren't always about finding out stuff, he says. They're about helping people, too.
And those kids could use some help.
And I'm okay. My power and my programmable uniform keep me warm --
And I find enough money to buy food --
And I practice.
Grampa says practice is real important.

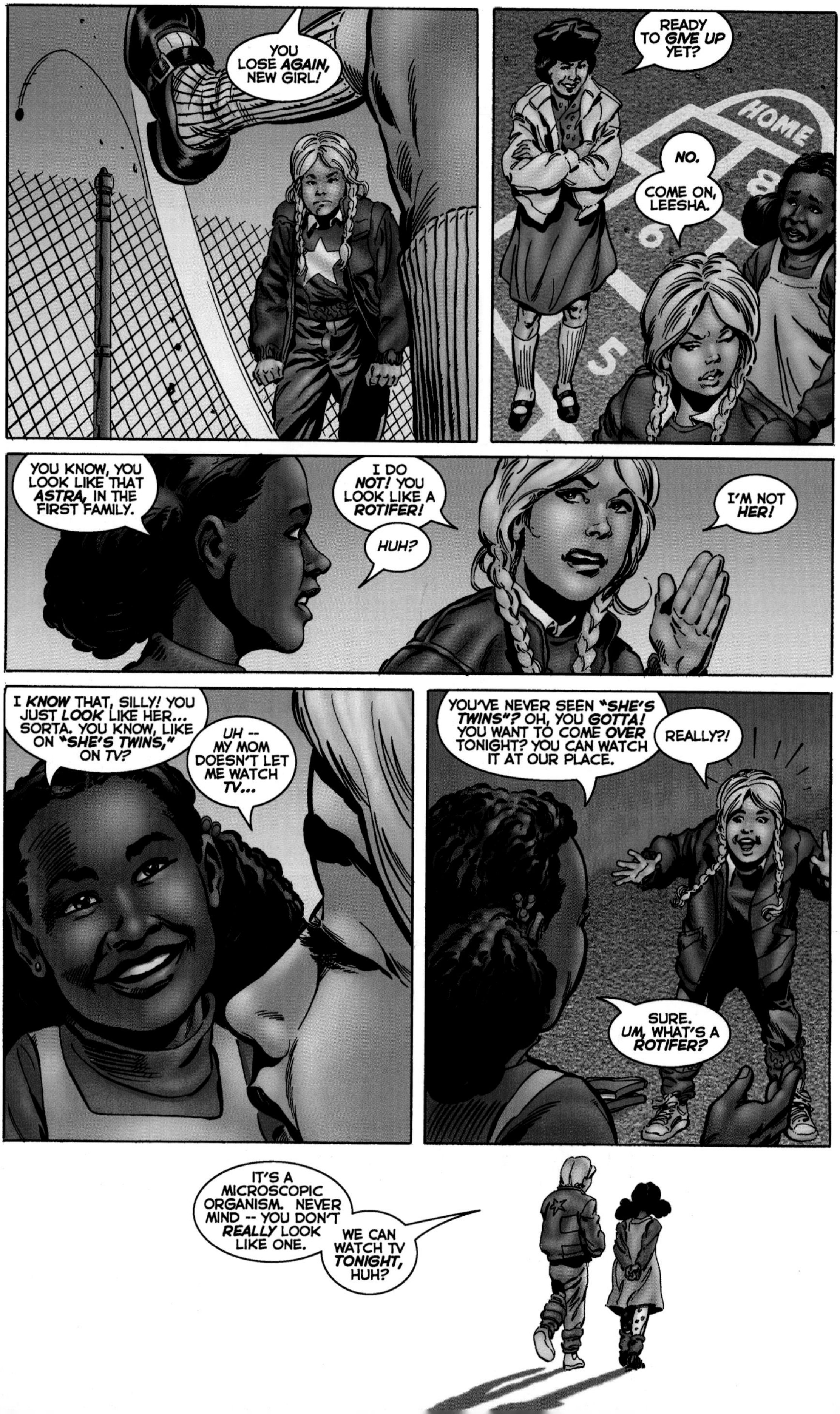
YOU LOSE AGAIN, NEW GIRL!
READY TO GIVE UP YET?
NO.
COME ON, LEESHA.
YOU KNOW, YOU LOOK LIKE THAT ASTRA, IN THE FIRST FAMILY.
I DO NOT! YOU LOOK LIKE A ROTIFER!
HUH?
I'M NOT HER!
I KNOW THAT, SILLY! YOU JUST LOOK LIKE HER... SORTA. YOU KNOW, LIKE ON "SHE'S TWINS," ON TV?
UH -- MY MOM DOESN'T LET ME WATCH TV...
YOU'VE NEVER SEEN "SHE'S TWINS"? OH, YOU GOTTA! YOU WANT TO COME OVER TONIGHT? YOU CAN WATCH IT AT OUR PLACE.
REALLY?!
SURE. UM, WHAT'S A ROTIFER?
IT'S A MICROSCOPIC ORGANISM. NEVER MIND -- YOU DON'T REALLY LOOK LIKE ONE.
WE CAN WATCH TV TONIGHT, HUH?

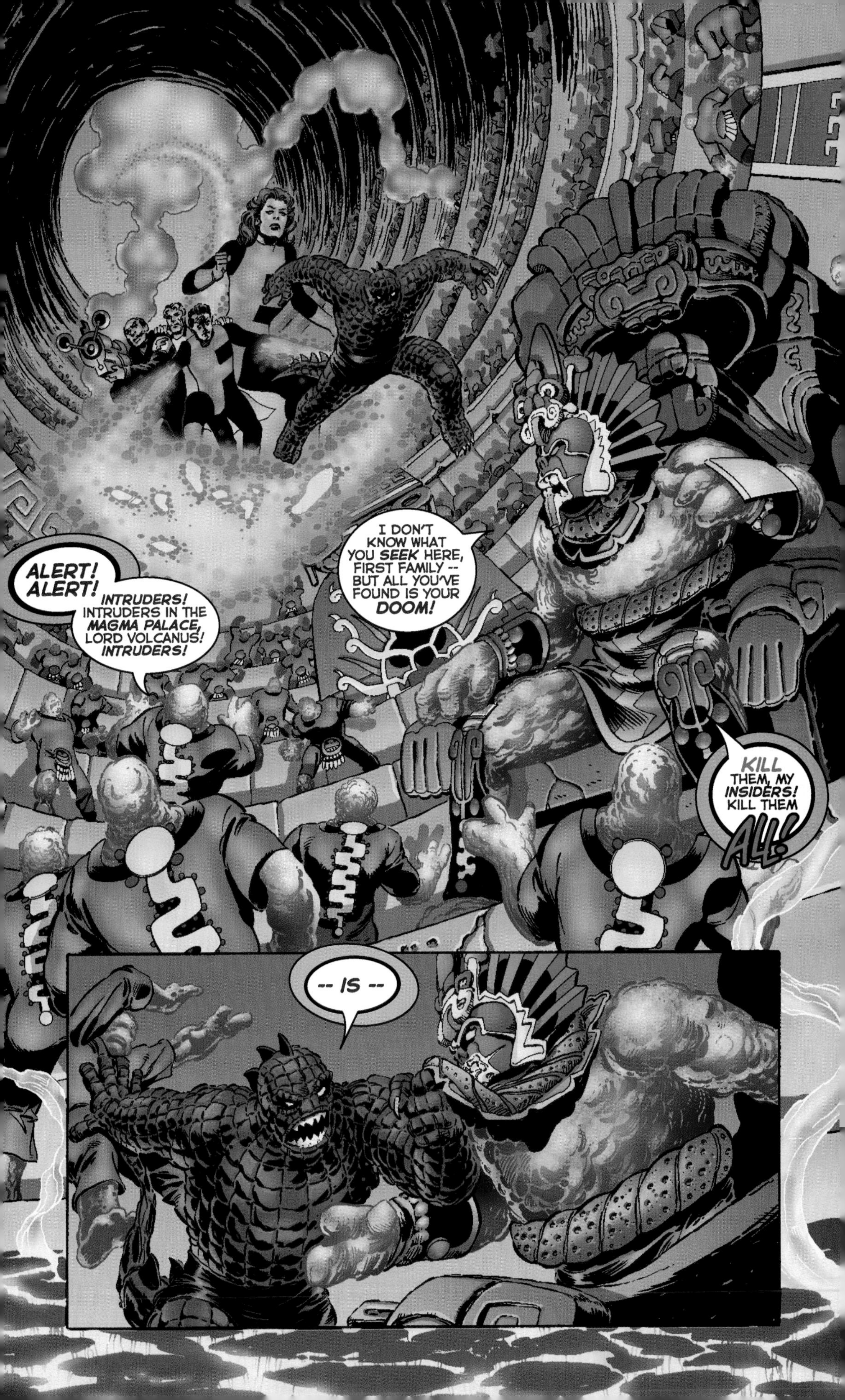
ALERT! ALERT! INTRUDERS! INTRUDERS IN THE MAGMA PALACE, LORD VOLCANUS! INTRUDERS!
I DON'T KNOW WHAT YOU SEEK HERE, FIRST FAMILY -- BUT ALL YOU'VE FOUND IS YOUR DOOM!
KILL THEM, MY INSIDERS! KILL THEM ALL!
-- IS --

I gotta be careful --

WHOALP!

HEY! YOU TRIPPED ME, MARTRICE!

I DID NOT *EITHER!*

JUST BECAUSE YOU CAN'T *PLAY* VERY WELL, THAT'S NO REASON TO BLAME *ME!*

WHINY LITTLE CRYBABY!

JUST BECAUSE YOU WERE *LOSING* -- !

I'LL SHOW *YOU*, MISS MARTRICE -- !

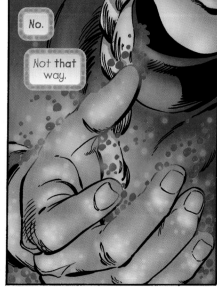

No.

Not that way.

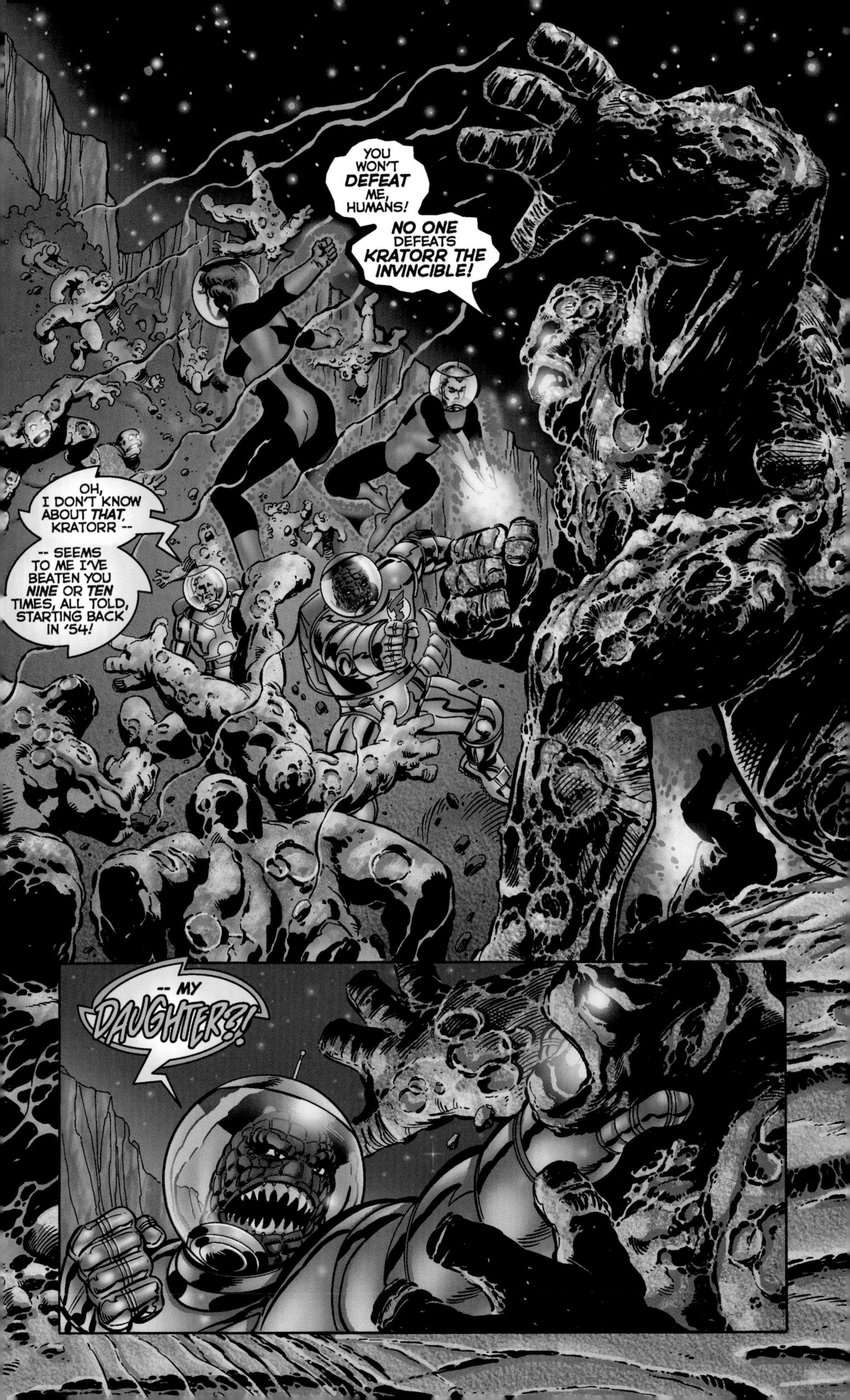
YOU WON'T DEFEAT ME, HUMANS!
NO ONE DEFEATS KRATORR THE INVINCIBLE!
OH, I DON'T KNOW ABOUT THAT, KRATORR --
-- SEEMS TO ME I'VE BEATEN YOU NINE OR TEN TIMES, ALL TOLD, STARTING BACK IN '54!
-- MY DAUGHTER?!

-- SHE DOES *NOT* LOOK LIKE ASTRA! NOT EVEN A *LITTLE*!

I THINK SHE *DOES*, MARTRICE.

Everybody's talking about me being *missing*. It was even on TV last night, during "Tooth & Claw."

HAVE YOU SEEN ME?

CALL 1-800-555-FRST

Name: Astra Nadia Furst-Zorus
D.O.B. July 8, 1988. Height 4'6"
Weight: 85 Lbs. Id Marks: None
Hair: Blonde/Straight&Long
Eye Color: Green

LOOK, IF YOU JUST CHANGED HER *HAIR*...

Mom's gonna be *mad*. She's gonna be *real* mad.

But she's always saying how Grampa and Dad and everyone can't be *interrupted* if they're on an adventure.

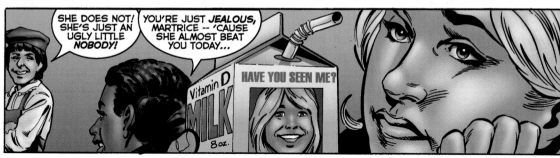

SHE DOES NOT! SHE'S JUST AN UGLY LITTLE *NOBODY*!

YOU'RE JUST *JEALOUS*, MARTRICE -- 'CAUSE SHE ALMOST BEAT YOU TODAY...

Vitamin D MILK 8 oz.

HAVE YOU SEEN ME?

SEEN ME?

1-800-555-FRST

me: Astra Nadia Furst-Zorus
B. July
ght: 85
Hair: Bl

I AM *NOT*!

And I'm on an adventure now...

... so I can't be interrupted either.

SLLLURRRPP

ILK

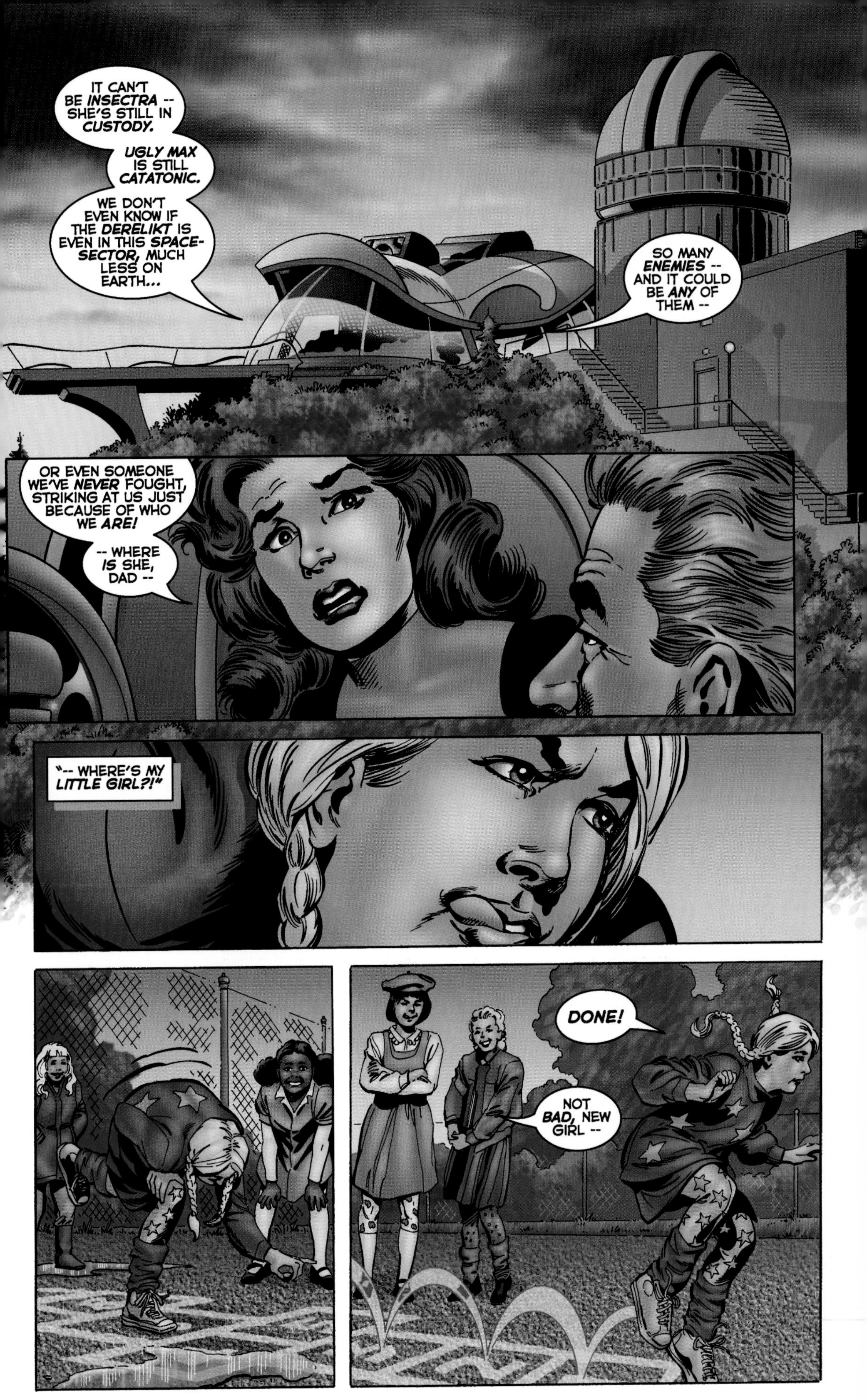
IT CAN'T BE INSECTRA -- SHE'S STILL IN CUSTODY.
UGLY MAX IS STILL CATATONIC.
WE DON'T EVEN KNOW IF THE DERELIKT IS EVEN IN THIS SPACE-SECTOR, MUCH LESS ON EARTH...
SO MANY ENEMIES -- AND IT COULD BE ANY OF THEM --
OR EVEN SOMEONE WE'VE NEVER FOUGHT, STRIKING AT US JUST BECAUSE OF WHO WE ARE!
-- WHERE IS SHE, DAD --
"-- WHERE'S MY LITTLE GIRL?!"
DONE!
NOT BAD, NEW GIRL --

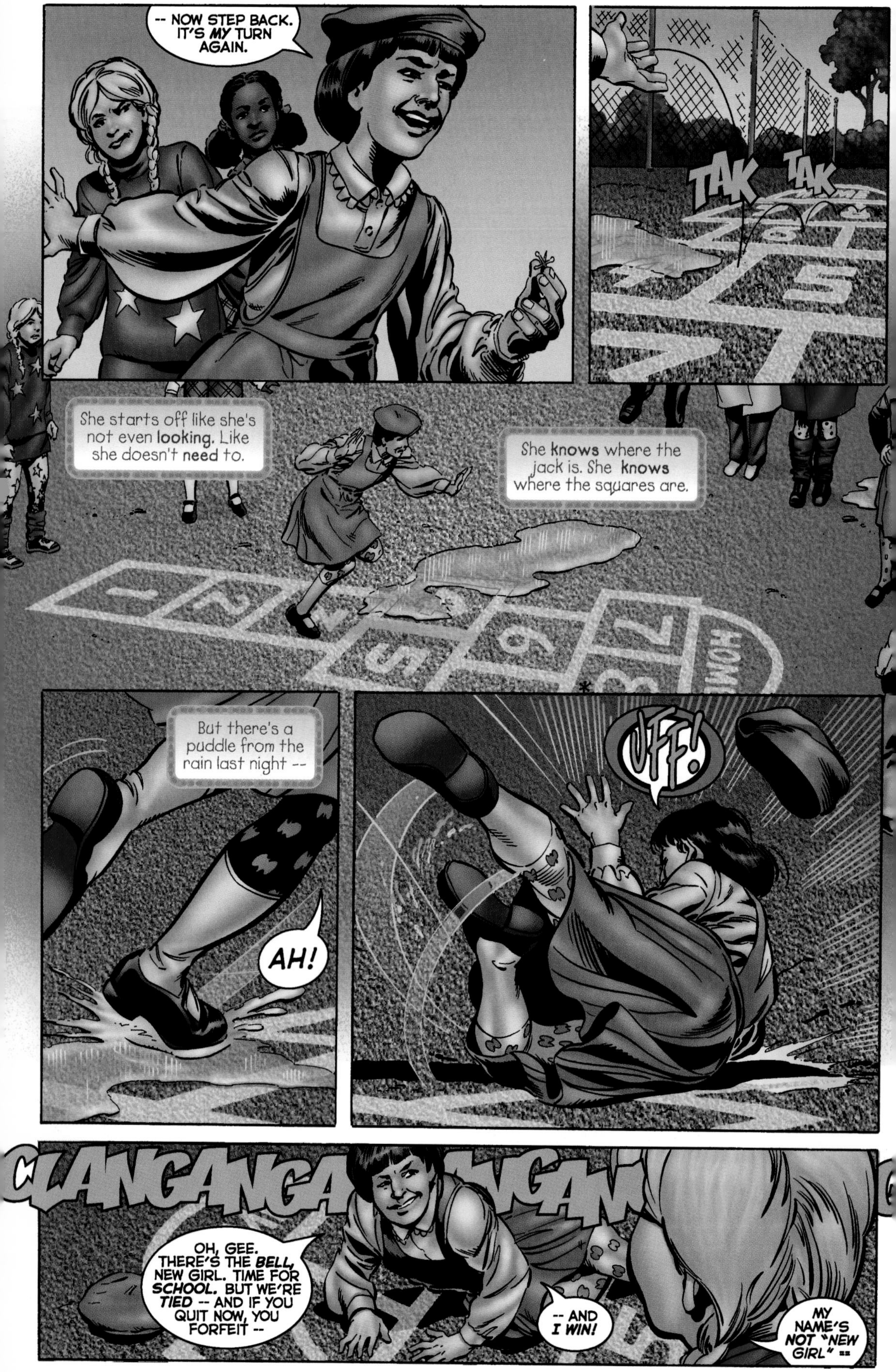
-- NOW STEP BACK. IT'S *MY* TURN AGAIN.
TAK TAK
She starts off like she's not even **looking.** Like she doesn't **need** to.
She **knows** where the jack is. She **knows** where the squares are.
But there's a puddle from the rain last night --
AH!
UFF!
CLANGANGA NGANGAN
OH, GEE. THERE'S THE *BELL*, NEW GIRL. TIME FOR *SCHOOL.* BUT WE'RE *TIED* -- AND IF YOU QUIT NOW, YOU FORFEIT --
-- AND *I WIN!*
MY NAME'S NOT "NEW GIRL" --

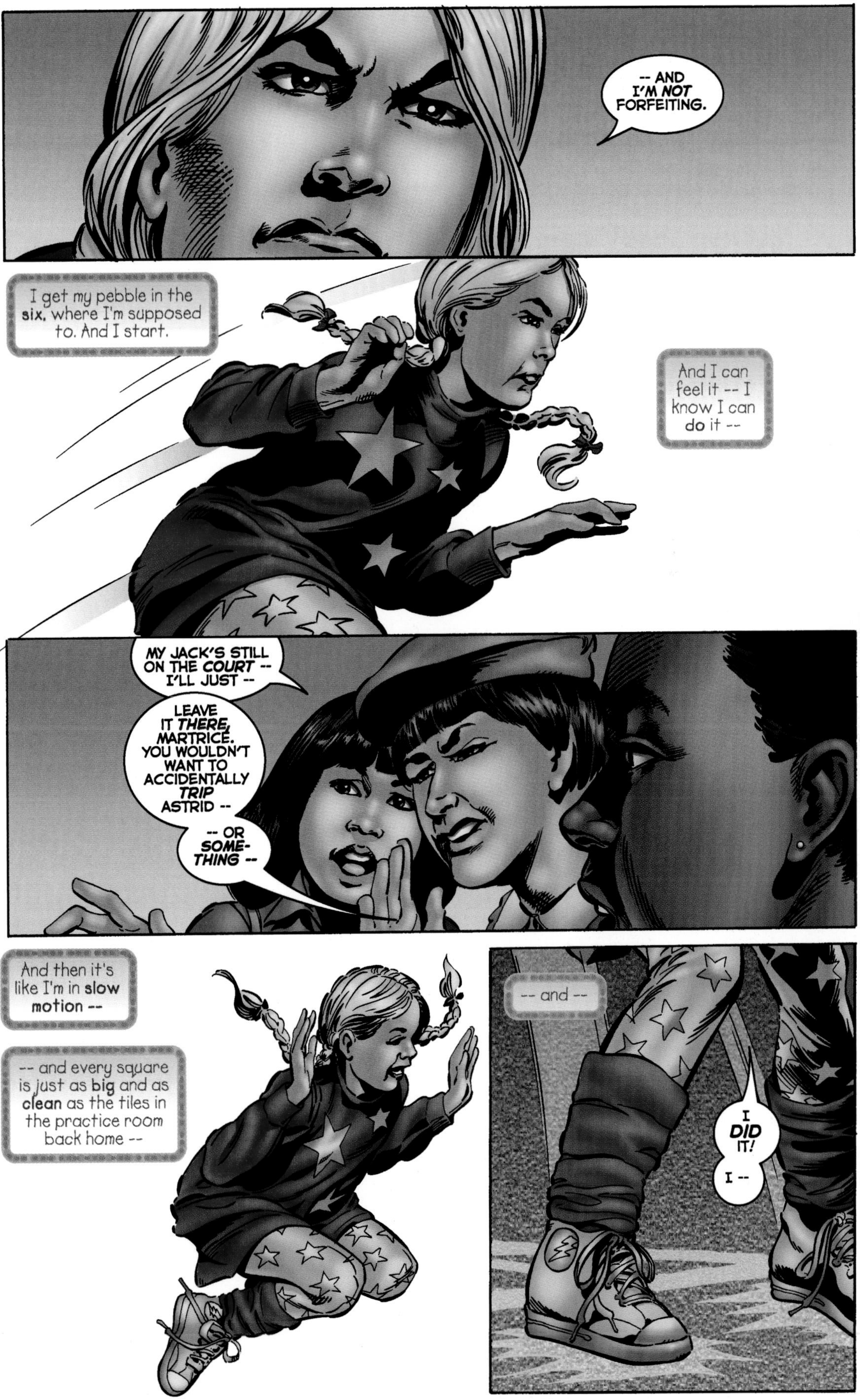

-- AND I'M *NOT* FORFEITING.
I get my pebble in the **six**, where I'm supposed to. And I start.
And I can feel it -- I know I can **do** it --
MY JACK'S STILL ON THE *COURT* -- I'LL JUST --
LEAVE IT *THERE*, MARTRICE. YOU WOULDN'T WANT TO ACCIDENTALLY *TRIP* ASTRID --
-- OR *SOMETHING* --
And then it's like I'm in **slow motion** --
-- and every square is just as **big** and as **clean** as the tiles in the practice room back home --
-- and --
I *DID* IT!
I --

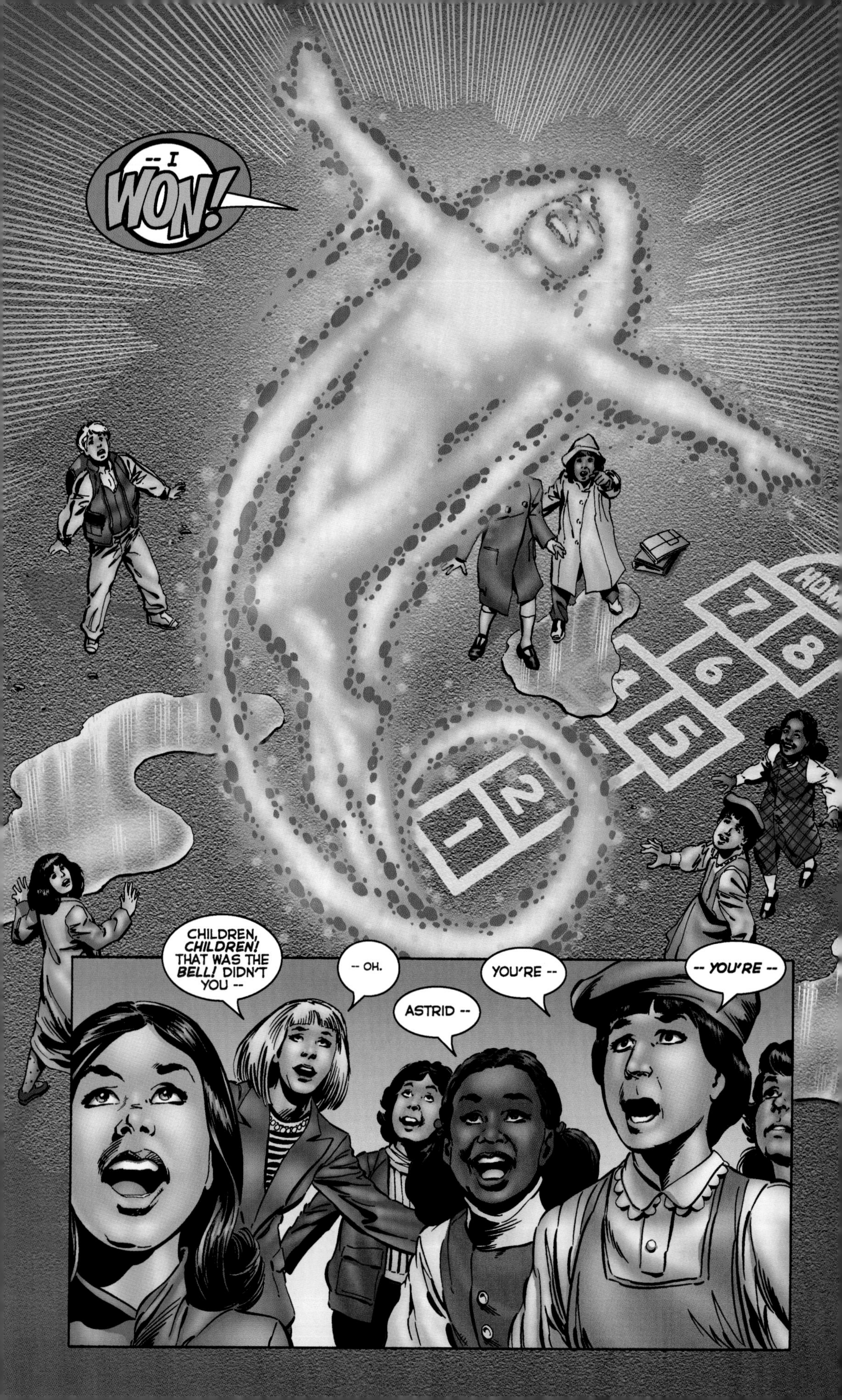

-- I WON!
CHILDREN, CHILDREN! THAT WAS THE BELL! DIDN'T YOU --
-- OH.
ASTRID --
YOU'RE --
-- YOU'RE --

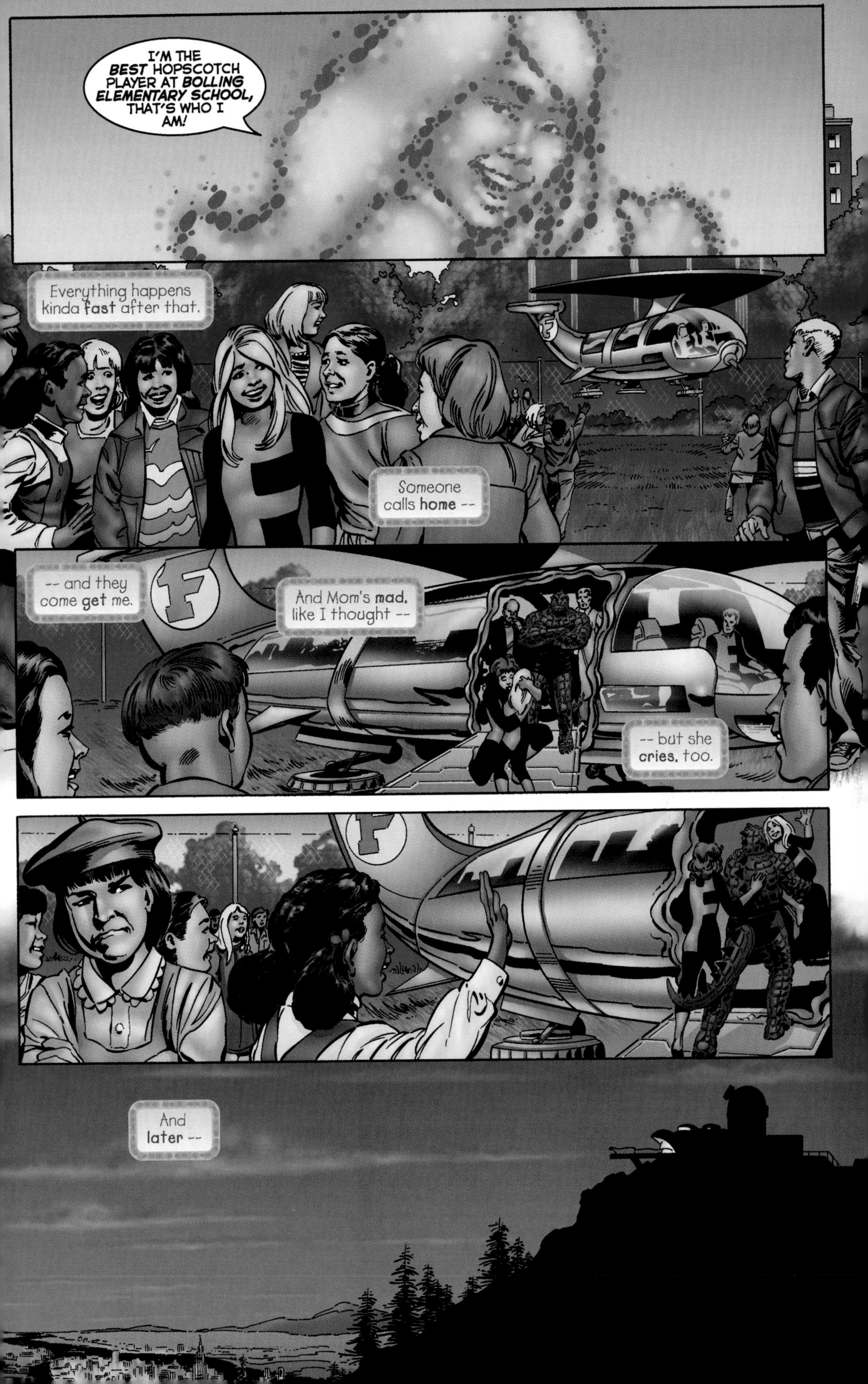
I'M THE BEST HOPSCOTCH PLAYER AT BOLLING ELEMENTARY SCHOOL, THAT'S WHO I AM!
Everything happens kinda fast after that.
Someone calls home --
-- and they come get me.
And Mom's mad, like I thought --
-- but she cries, too.
And later --

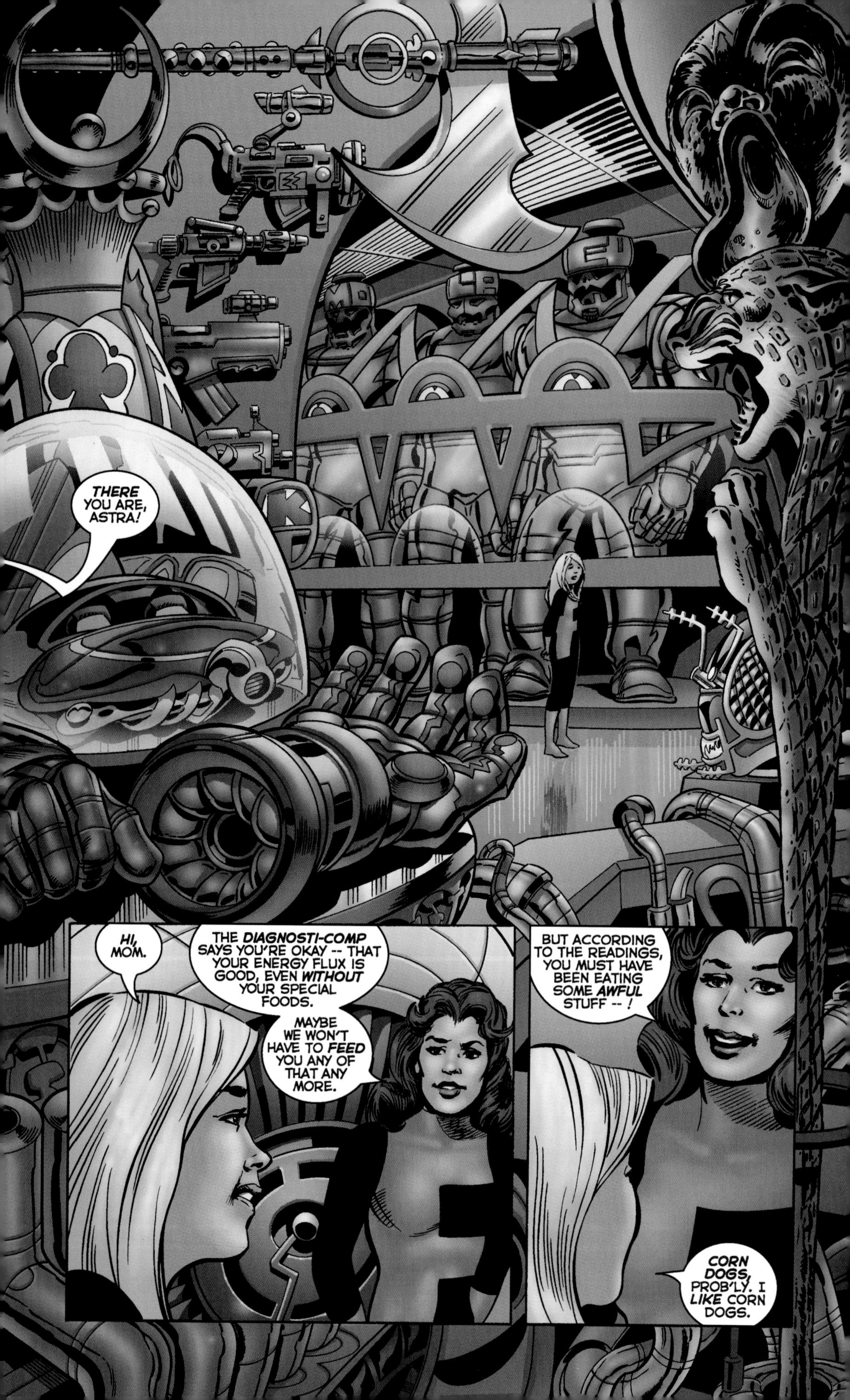
THERE YOU ARE, ASTRA!
HI, MOM.
THE DIAGNOSTI-COMP SAYS YOU'RE OKAY -- THAT YOUR ENERGY FLUX IS GOOD, EVEN WITHOUT YOUR SPECIAL FOODS.
MAYBE WE WON'T HAVE TO FEED YOU ANY OF THAT ANY MORE.
BUT ACCORDING TO THE READINGS, YOU MUST HAVE BEEN EATING SOME AWFUL STUFF -- !
CORN DOGS, PROB'LY. I LIKE CORN DOGS.

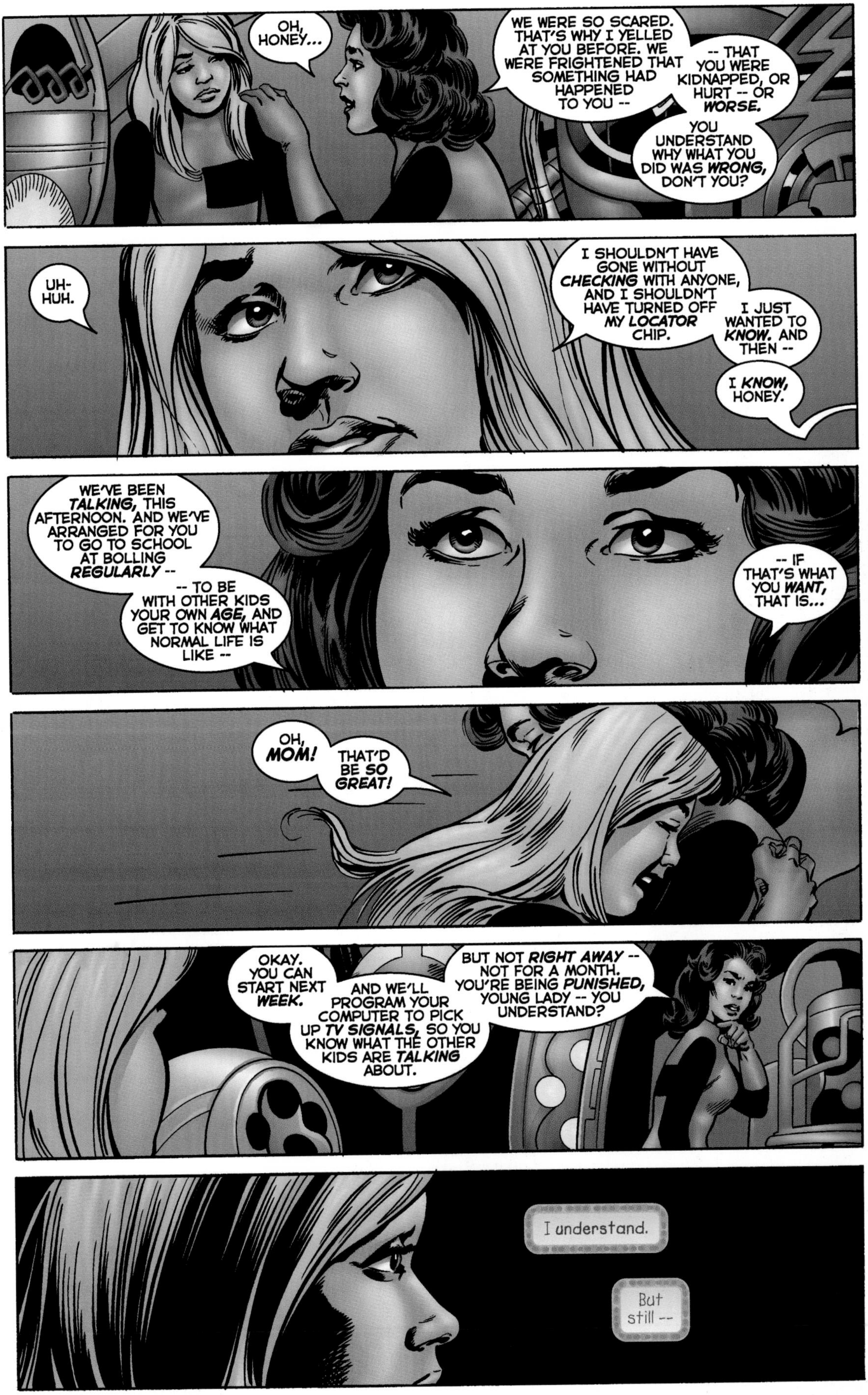
OH, HONEY...
WE WERE SO SCARED. THAT'S WHY I YELLED AT YOU BEFORE. WE WERE FRIGHTENED THAT SOMETHING HAD HAPPENED TO YOU --
-- THAT YOU WERE KIDNAPPED, OR HURT -- OR WORSE.
YOU UNDERSTAND WHY WHAT YOU DID WAS WRONG, DON'T YOU?
UH-HUH.
I SHOULDN'T HAVE GONE WITHOUT CHECKING WITH ANYONE, AND I SHOULDN'T HAVE TURNED OFF MY LOCATOR CHIP.
I JUST WANTED TO KNOW. AND THEN --
I KNOW, HONEY.
WE'VE BEEN TALKING, THIS AFTERNOON. AND WE'VE ARRANGED FOR YOU TO GO TO SCHOOL AT BOLLING REGULARLY --
-- TO BE WITH OTHER KIDS YOUR OWN AGE, AND GET TO KNOW WHAT NORMAL LIFE IS LIKE --
-- IF THAT'S WHAT YOU WANT, THAT IS...
OH, MOM!
THAT'D BE SO GREAT!
OKAY. YOU CAN START NEXT WEEK.
AND WE'LL PROGRAM YOUR COMPUTER TO PICK UP TV SIGNALS, SO YOU KNOW WHAT THE OTHER KIDS ARE TALKING ABOUT.
BUT NOT RIGHT AWAY -- NOT FOR A MONTH. YOU'RE BEING PUNISHED, YOUNG LADY -- YOU UNDERSTAND?
I understand.
But still --

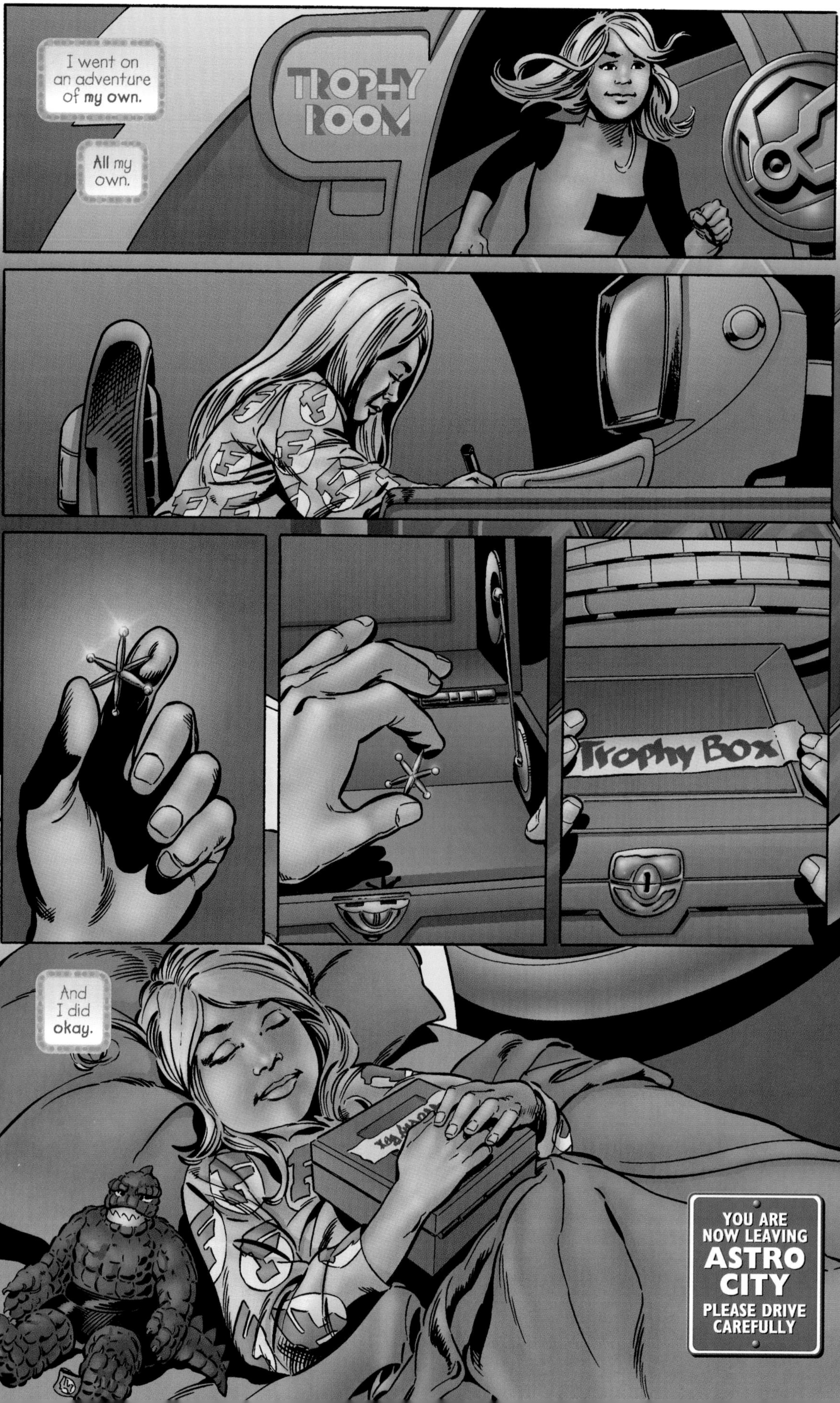

I went on an adventure of my own.
All my own.
TROPHY ROOM
Trophy Box
And I did okay.
YOU ARE NOW LEAVING ASTRO CITY PLEASE DRIVE CAREFULLY

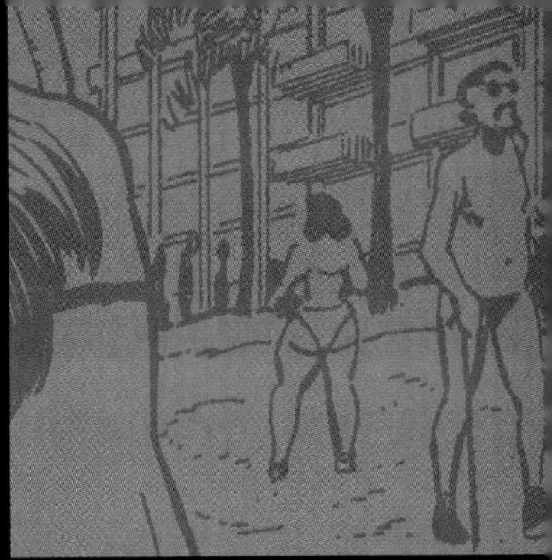

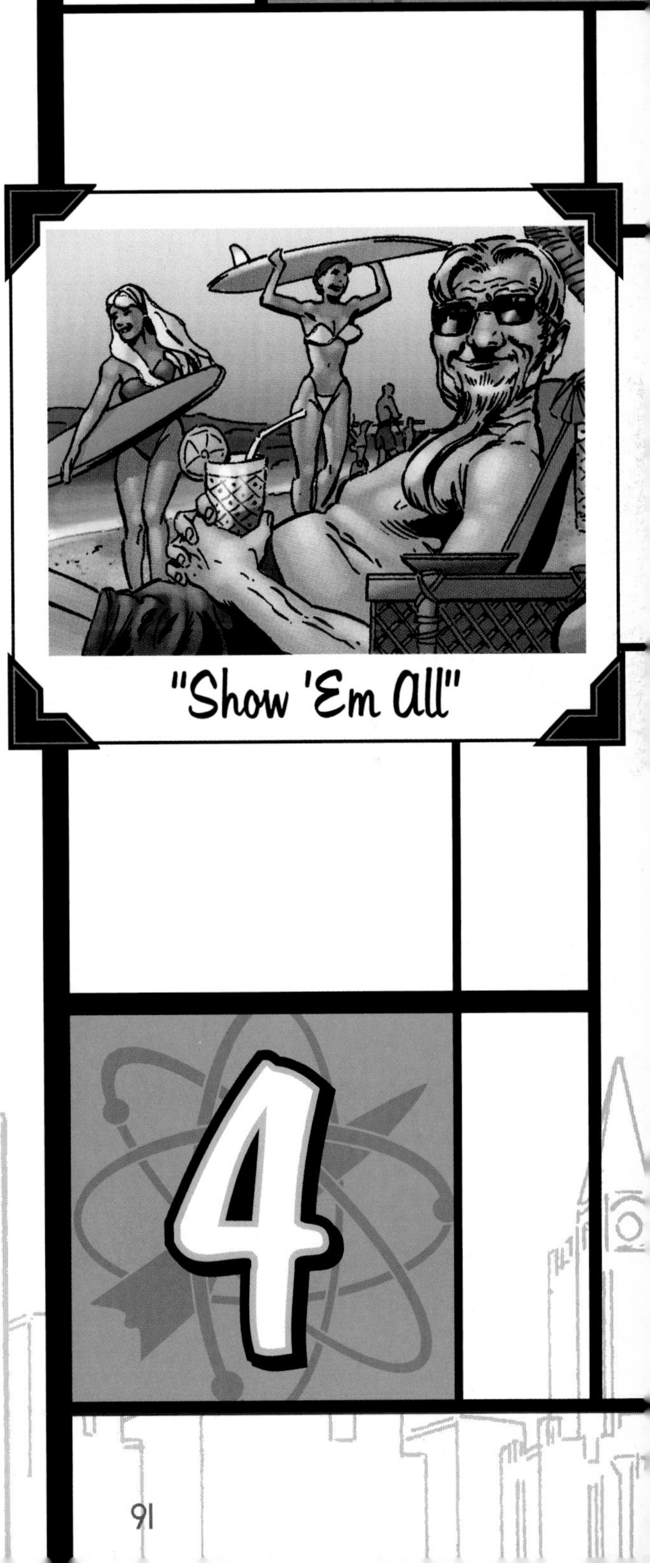

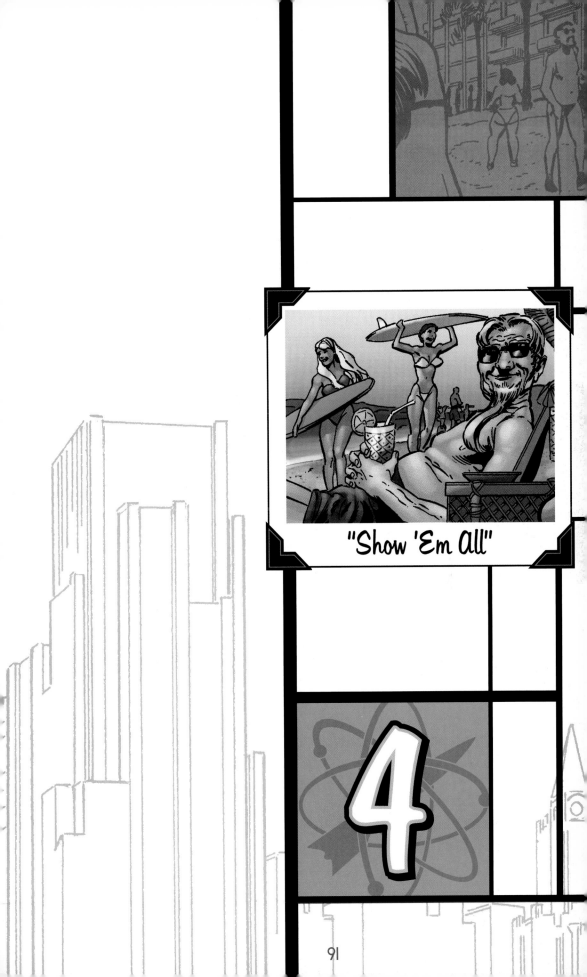

"Show 'Em All"

4

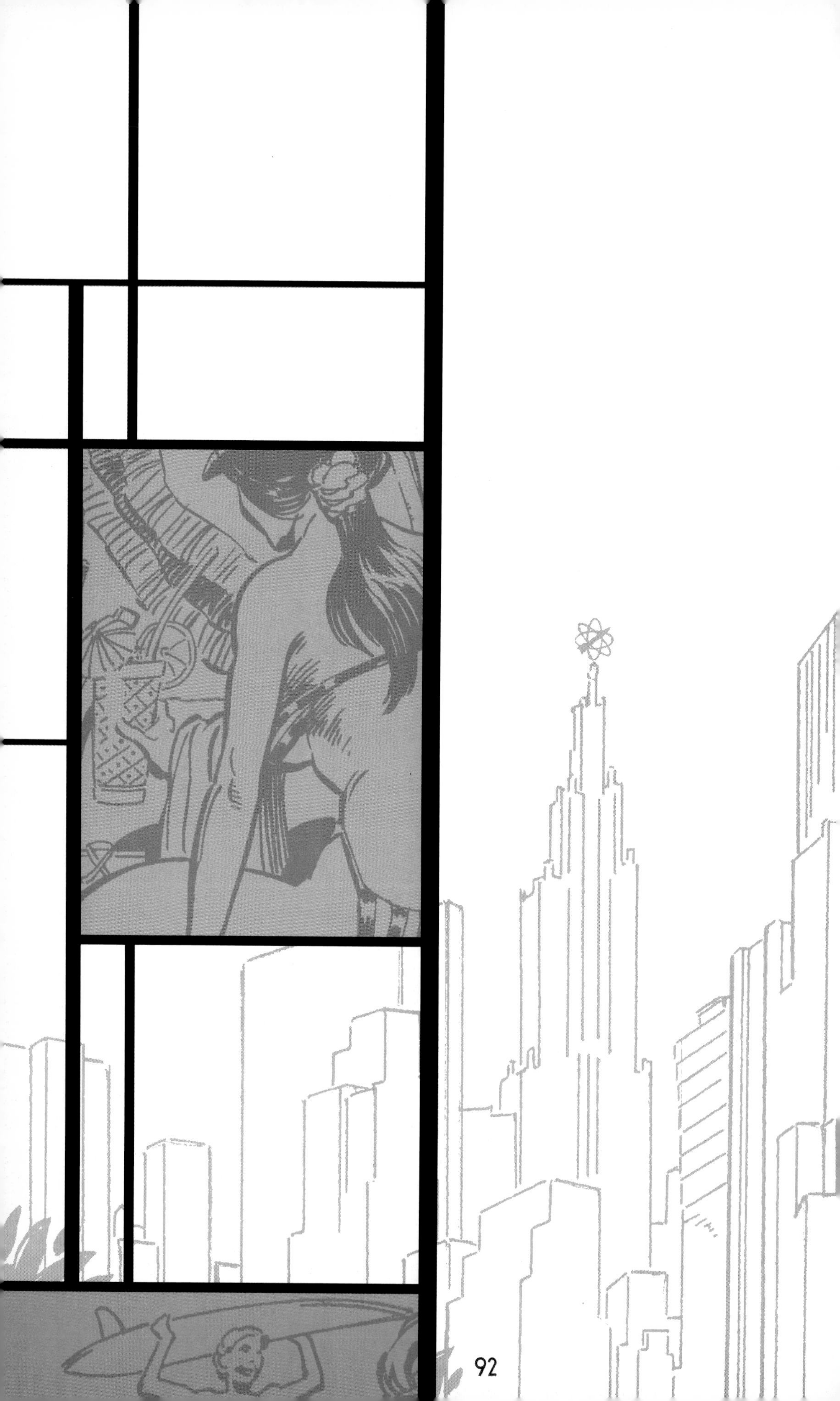

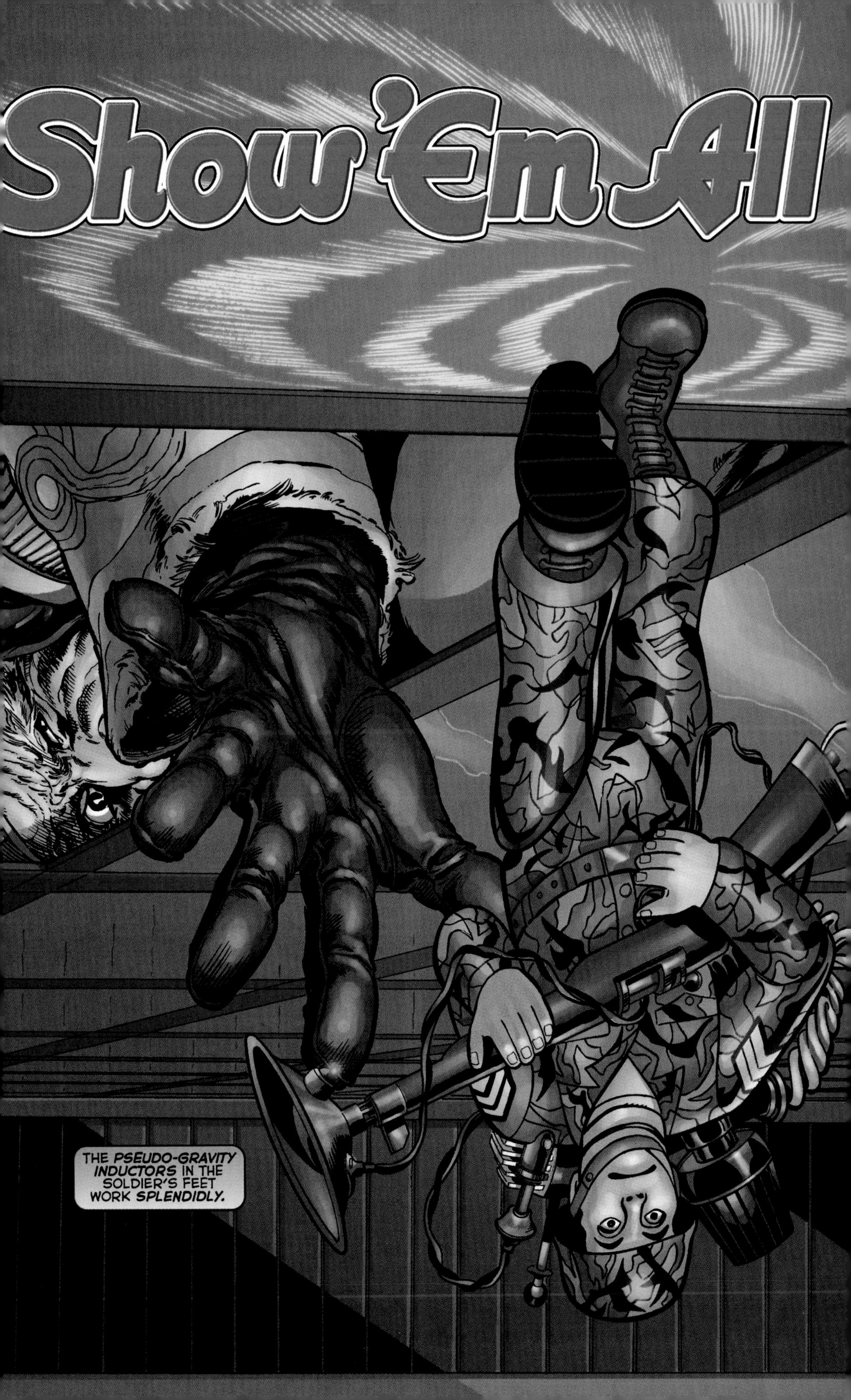
Show 'Em All
THE PSEUDO-GRAVITY INDUCTORS IN THE SOLDIER'S FEET WORK SPLENDIDLY.

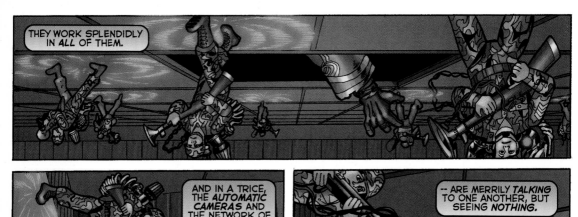

THEY WORK SPLENDIDLY IN *ALL* OF THEM.

AND IN A TRICE, THE *AUTOMATIC CAMERAS* AND THE NETWORK OF *ELECTRIC EYES* --

-- ARE MERRILY *TALKING* TO ONE ANOTHER, BUT SEEING *NOTHING.*

THEY ADDED THE ELECTRIC EYES AFTER THE *TECHSPERTS* BROKE IN, TWO YEARS AGO, AND WERE CAUGHT BY *QUARREL.*

THEY PUT *PRESSURE SENSORS* INTO THE FLOOR, TOO. BUT THEY'RE NO *GREAT DIFFICULTY.*

THE JUNKMAN COMES *PREPARED.*

HMM HMM

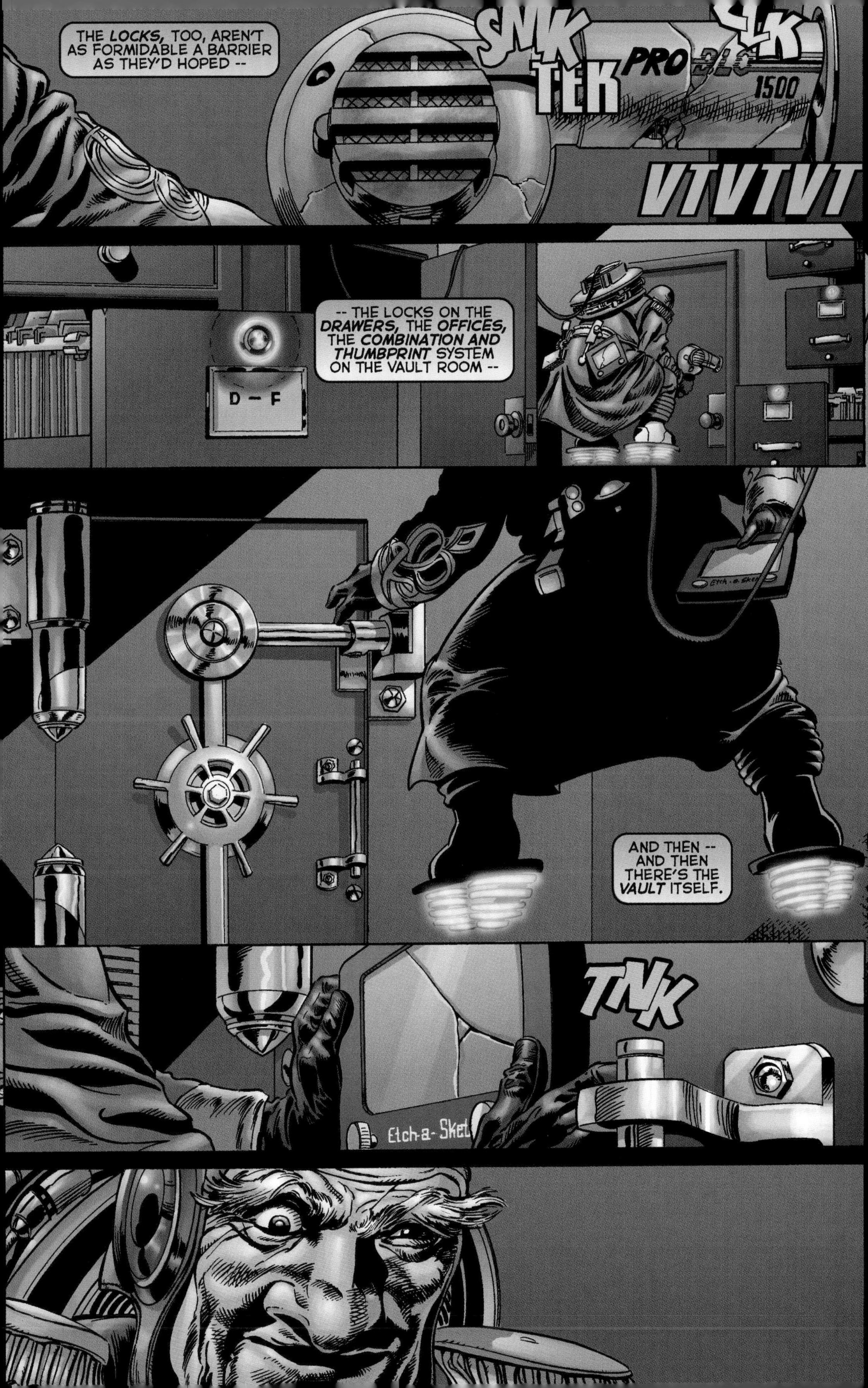
THE LOCKS, TOO, AREN'T AS FORMIDABLE A BARRIER AS THEY'D HOPED --
SNIK
TEK
PRO
1500
VTVTVT
-- THE LOCKS ON THE DRAWERS, THE OFFICES, THE COMBINATION AND THUMBPRINT SYSTEM ON THE VAULT ROOM --
D -- F
AND THEN -- AND THEN THERE'S THE VAULT ITSELF.
TNK
Etch-a-Sket

IT'S ACTUALLY *FUN.*

Etch - a - Sketch

IT TAKES *HOURS* TO HAUL IT ALL OUT. ONE ELDERLY MAN, WORKING ALONE -- OF *COURSE* IT DOES.

AND MY BACK WILL LET ME *KNOW* ABOUT IT, THE NEXT FEW DAYS.

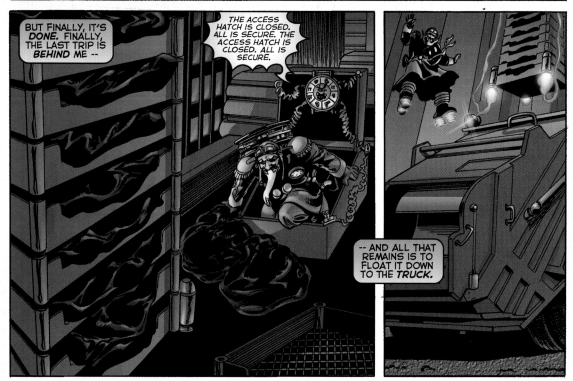

BUT FINALLY, IT'S *DONE.* FINALLY, THE LAST TRIP IS *BEHIND* ME --

THE ACCESS HATCH IS CLOSED. ALL IS SECURE. THE ACCESS HATCH IS CLOSED. ALL IS SECURE.

-- AND ALL THAT REMAINS IS TO FLOAT IT DOWN TO THE *TRUCK.*

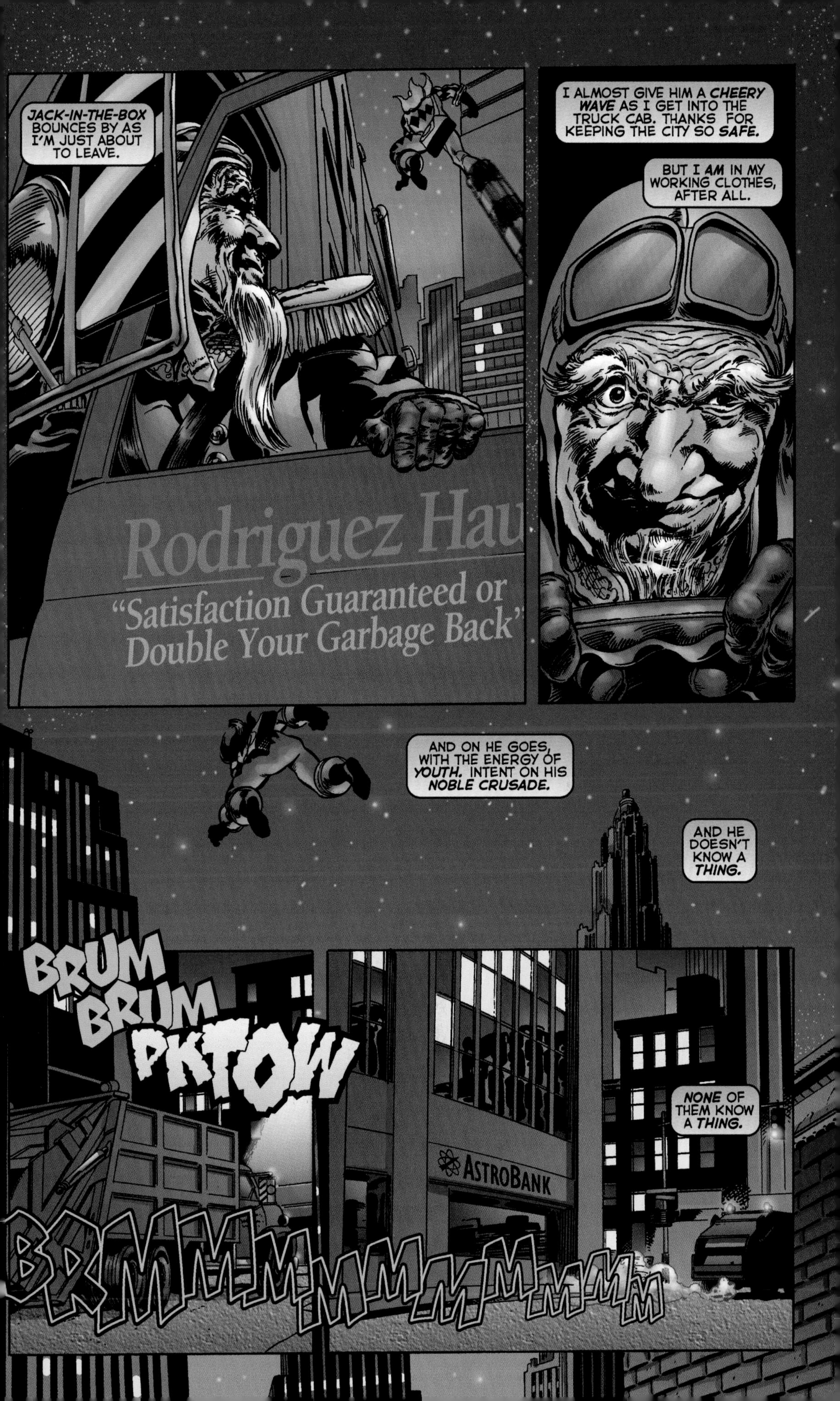

JACK-IN-THE-BOX BOUNCES BY AS I'M JUST ABOUT TO LEAVE.
Rodriguez Hau
"Satisfaction Guaranteed or Double Your Garbage Back"
I ALMOST GIVE HIM A CHEERY WAVE AS I GET INTO THE TRUCK CAB. THANKS FOR KEEPING THE CITY SO SAFE.
BUT I AM IN MY WORKING CLOTHES, AFTER ALL.
AND ON HE GOES, WITH THE ENERGY OF YOUTH. INTENT ON HIS NOBLE CRUSADE.
AND HE DOESN'T KNOW A THING.
BRUM BRUM PKTOW
ASTROBANK
NONE OF THEM KNOW A THING.
BRMMMMMMMMMMMMMMM

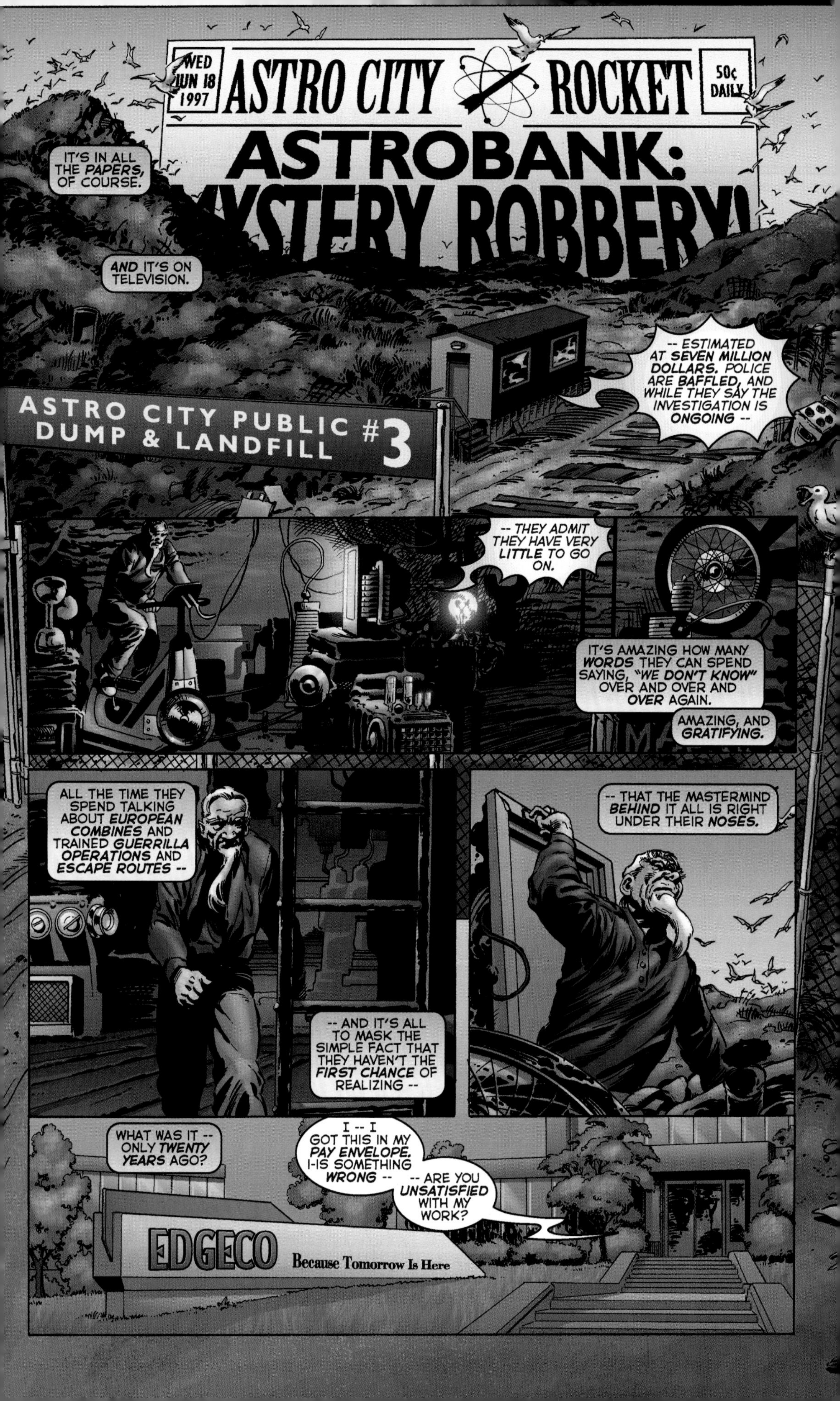
WED JUN 18 1997
ASTRO CITY ROCKET
50¢ DAILY
ASTROBANK: MYSTERY ROBBERY!
IT'S IN ALL THE *PAPERS,* OF COURSE.
AND IT'S ON TELEVISION.
-- ESTIMATED AT **SEVEN MILLION DOLLARS.** POLICE ARE **BAFFLED,** AND WHILE THEY SAY THE INVESTIGATION IS **ONGOING** --
ASTRO CITY PUBLIC DUMP & LANDFILL #3
-- THEY ADMIT THEY HAVE VERY *LITTLE* TO GO ON.
IT'S AMAZING HOW MANY **WORDS** THEY CAN SPEND SAYING, **"WE DON'T KNOW"** OVER AND OVER AND **OVER** AGAIN.
AMAZING, AND **GRATIFYING.**
ALL THE TIME THEY SPEND TALKING ABOUT **EUROPEAN COMBINES** AND TRAINED **GUERRILLA OPERATIONS** AND **ESCAPE ROUTES** --
-- AND IT'S ALL TO MASK THE SIMPLE FACT THAT THEY HAVEN'T THE **FIRST CHANCE** OF REALIZING --
-- THAT THE MASTERMIND **BEHIND** IT ALL IS RIGHT UNDER THEIR **NOSES.**
WHAT WAS IT -- ONLY **TWENTY YEARS** AGO?
I -- I GOT THIS IN MY **PAY ENVELOPE.** I-IS SOMETHING **WRONG** --
-- ARE YOU **UNSATISFIED** WITH MY WORK?
EDGECO
Because Tomorrow Is Here

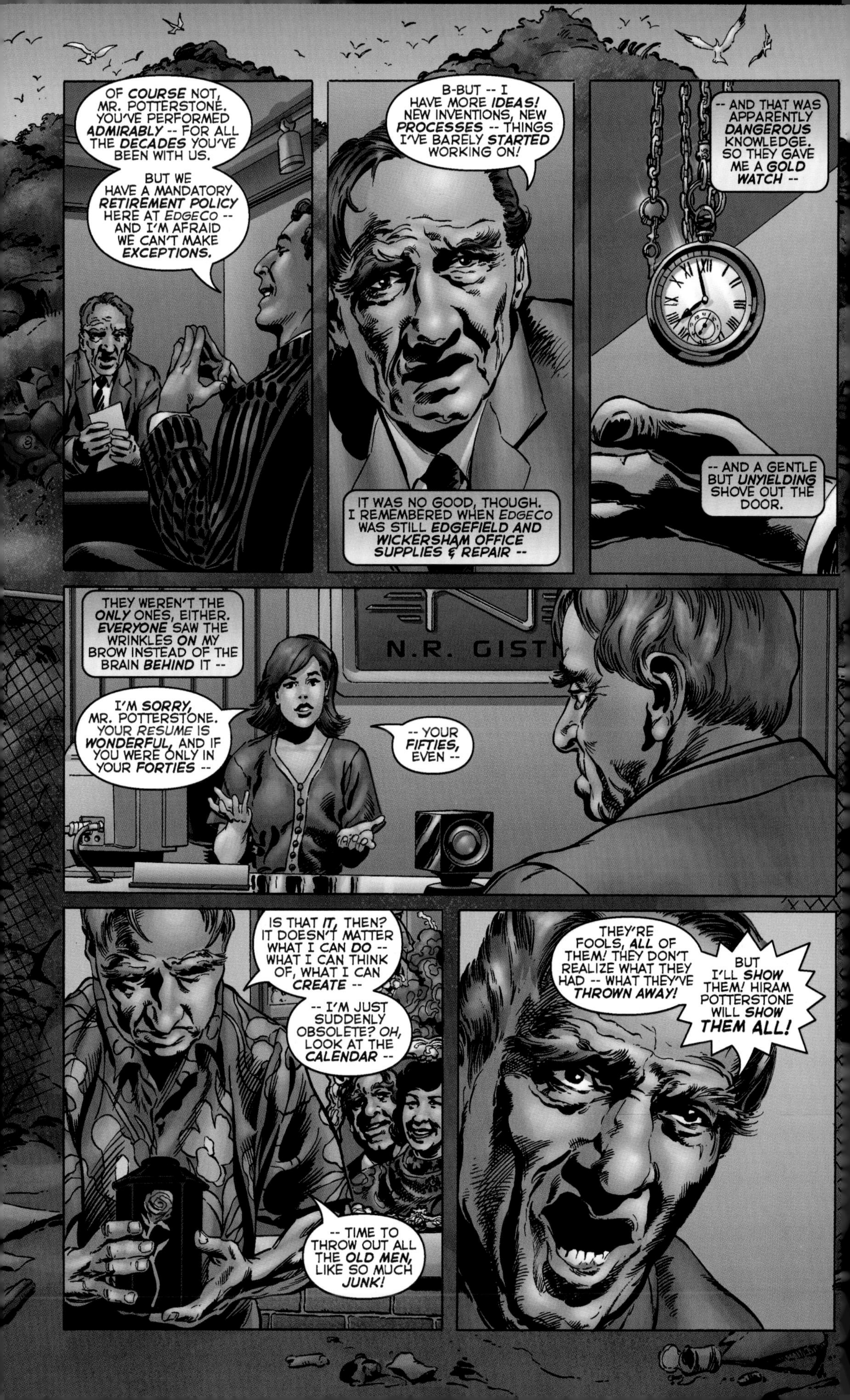

OF COURSE NOT, MR. POTTERSTONE. YOU'VE PERFORMED ADMIRABLY -- FOR ALL THE DECADES YOU'VE BEEN WITH US.
BUT WE HAVE A MANDATORY RETIREMENT POLICY HERE AT EDGECO -- AND I'M AFRAID WE CAN'T MAKE EXCEPTIONS.
B-BUT -- I HAVE MORE IDEAS! NEW INVENTIONS, NEW PROCESSES -- THINGS I'VE BARELY STARTED WORKING ON!
IT WAS NO GOOD, THOUGH. I REMEMBERED WHEN EDGECO WAS STILL EDGEFIELD AND WICKERSHAM OFFICE SUPPLIES & REPAIR --
-- AND THAT WAS APPARENTLY DANGEROUS KNOWLEDGE. SO THEY GAVE ME A GOLD WATCH --
-- AND A GENTLE BUT UNYIELDING SHOVE OUT THE DOOR.
THEY WEREN'T THE ONLY ONES, EITHER. EVERYONE SAW THE WRINKLES ON MY BROW INSTEAD OF THE BRAIN BEHIND IT --
N.R. GIST
I'M SORRY, MR. POTTERSTONE. YOUR RESUME IS WONDERFUL, AND IF YOU WERE ONLY IN YOUR FORTIES --
-- YOUR FIFTIES, EVEN --
IS THAT IT, THEN? IT DOESN'T MATTER WHAT I CAN DO -- WHAT I CAN THINK OF, WHAT I CAN CREATE --
-- I'M JUST SUDDENLY OBSOLETE? OH, LOOK AT THE CALENDAR --
-- TIME TO THROW OUT ALL THE OLD MEN, LIKE SO MUCH JUNK!
THEY'RE FOOLS, ALL OF THEM! THEY DON'T REALIZE WHAT THEY HAD -- WHAT THEY'VE THROWN AWAY!
BUT I'LL SHOW THEM! HIRAM POTTERSTONE WILL SHOW THEM ALL!

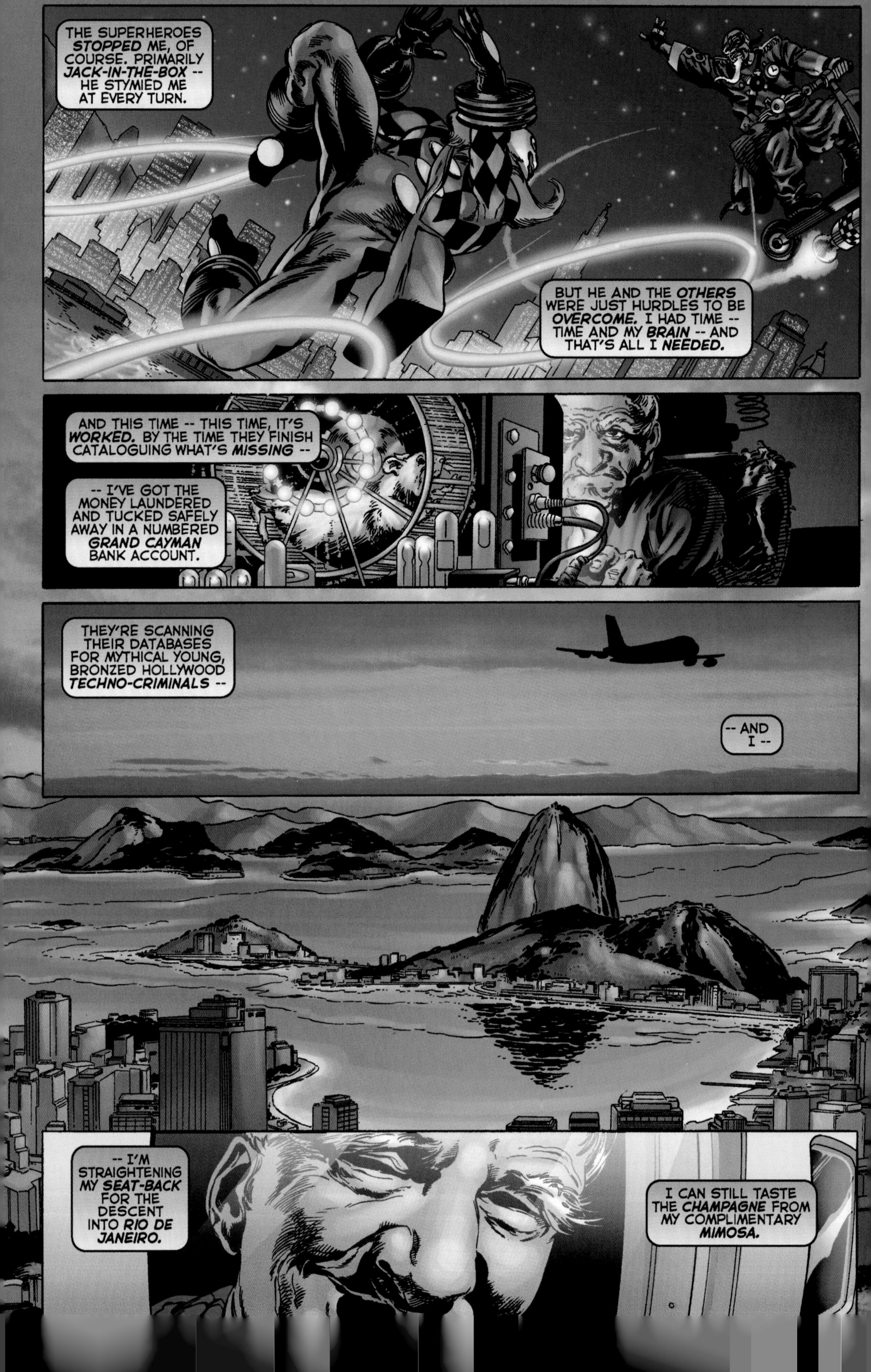
THE SUPERHEROES STOPPED ME, OF COURSE. PRIMARILY JACK-IN-THE-BOX -- HE STYMIED ME AT EVERY TURN.
BUT HE AND THE OTHERS WERE JUST HURDLES TO BE OVERCOME. I HAD TIME -- TIME AND MY BRAIN -- AND THAT'S ALL I NEEDED.
AND THIS TIME -- THIS TIME, IT'S WORKED. BY THE TIME THEY FINISH CATALOGUING WHAT'S MISSING --
-- I'VE GOT THE MONEY LAUNDERED AND TUCKED SAFELY AWAY IN A NUMBERED GRAND CAYMAN BANK ACCOUNT.
THEY'RE SCANNING THEIR DATABASES FOR MYTHICAL YOUNG, BRONZED HOLLYWOOD TECHNO-CRIMINALS --
-- AND I --
-- I'M STRAIGHTENING MY SEAT-BACK FOR THE DESCENT INTO RIO DE JANEIRO.
I CAN STILL TASTE THE CHAMPAGNE FROM MY COMPLIMENTARY MIMOSA.

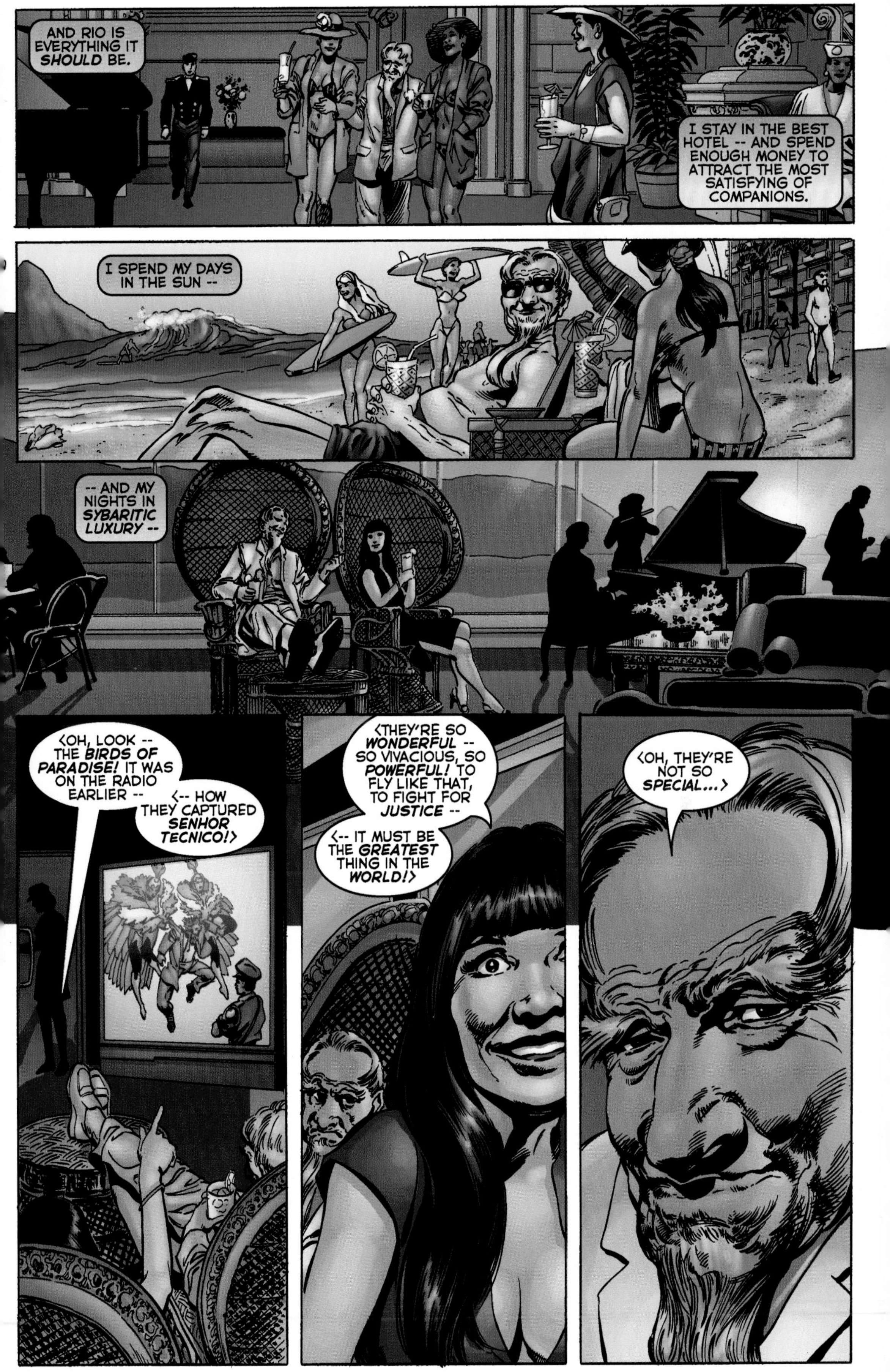
AND RIO IS EVERYTHING IT *SHOULD* BE.
I STAY IN THE BEST HOTEL -- AND SPEND ENOUGH MONEY TO ATTRACT THE MOST SATISFYING OF COMPANIONS.
I SPEND MY DAYS IN THE SUN --
-- AND MY NIGHTS IN *SYBARITIC LUXURY* --
<OH, LOOK -- THE *BIRDS OF PARADISE!* IT WAS ON THE RADIO EARLIER --
<-- HOW THEY CAPTURED *SENHOR TECNICO!*>
<THEY'RE SO *WONDERFUL* -- SO VIVACIOUS, SO *POWERFUL!* TO FLY LIKE THAT, TO FIGHT FOR *JUSTICE* --
<-- IT MUST BE THE *GREATEST* THING IN THE *WORLD!*>
<OH, THEY'RE NOT SO *SPECIAL...*>

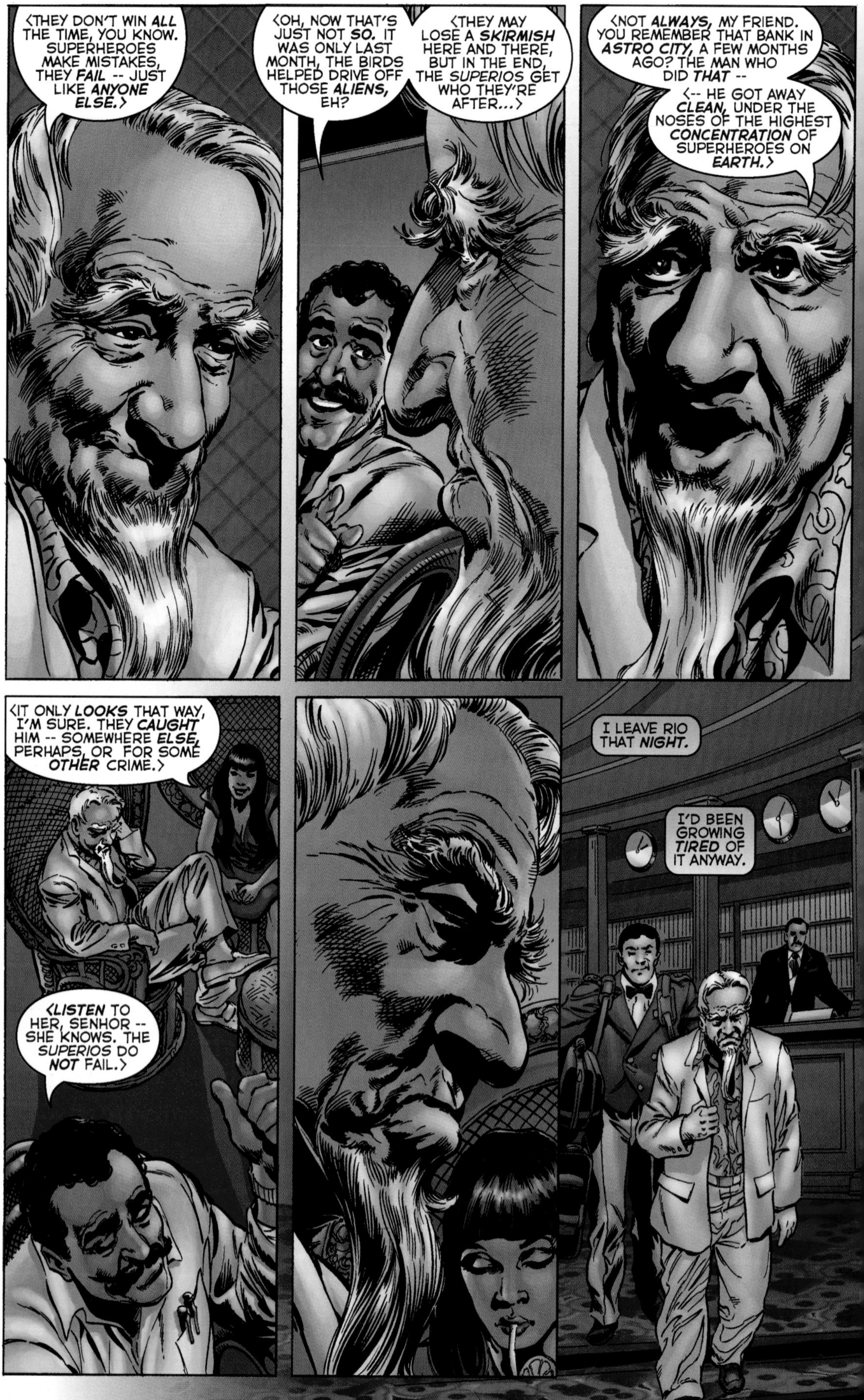
<THEY DON'T WIN ALL THE TIME, YOU KNOW. SUPERHEROES MAKE MISTAKES, THEY FAIL -- JUST LIKE ANYONE ELSE.>
<OH, NOW THAT'S JUST NOT SO. IT WAS ONLY LAST MONTH, THE BIRDS HELPED DRIVE OFF THOSE ALIENS, EH?
<THEY MAY LOSE A SKIRMISH HERE AND THERE, BUT IN THE END, THE SUPERIOS GET WHO THEY'RE AFTER...>
<NOT ALWAYS, MY FRIEND. YOU REMEMBER THAT BANK IN ASTRO CITY, A FEW MONTHS AGO? THE MAN WHO DID THAT --
<-- HE GOT AWAY CLEAN, UNDER THE NOSES OF THE HIGHEST CONCENTRATION OF SUPERHEROES ON EARTH.>
<IT ONLY LOOKS THAT WAY, I'M SURE. THEY CAUGHT HIM -- SOMEWHERE ELSE, PERHAPS, OR FOR SOME OTHER CRIME.>
<LISTEN TO HER, SENHOR -- SHE KNOWS. THE SUPERIOS DO NOT FAIL.>
I LEAVE RIO THAT NIGHT.
I'D BEEN GROWING TIRED OF IT ANYWAY.

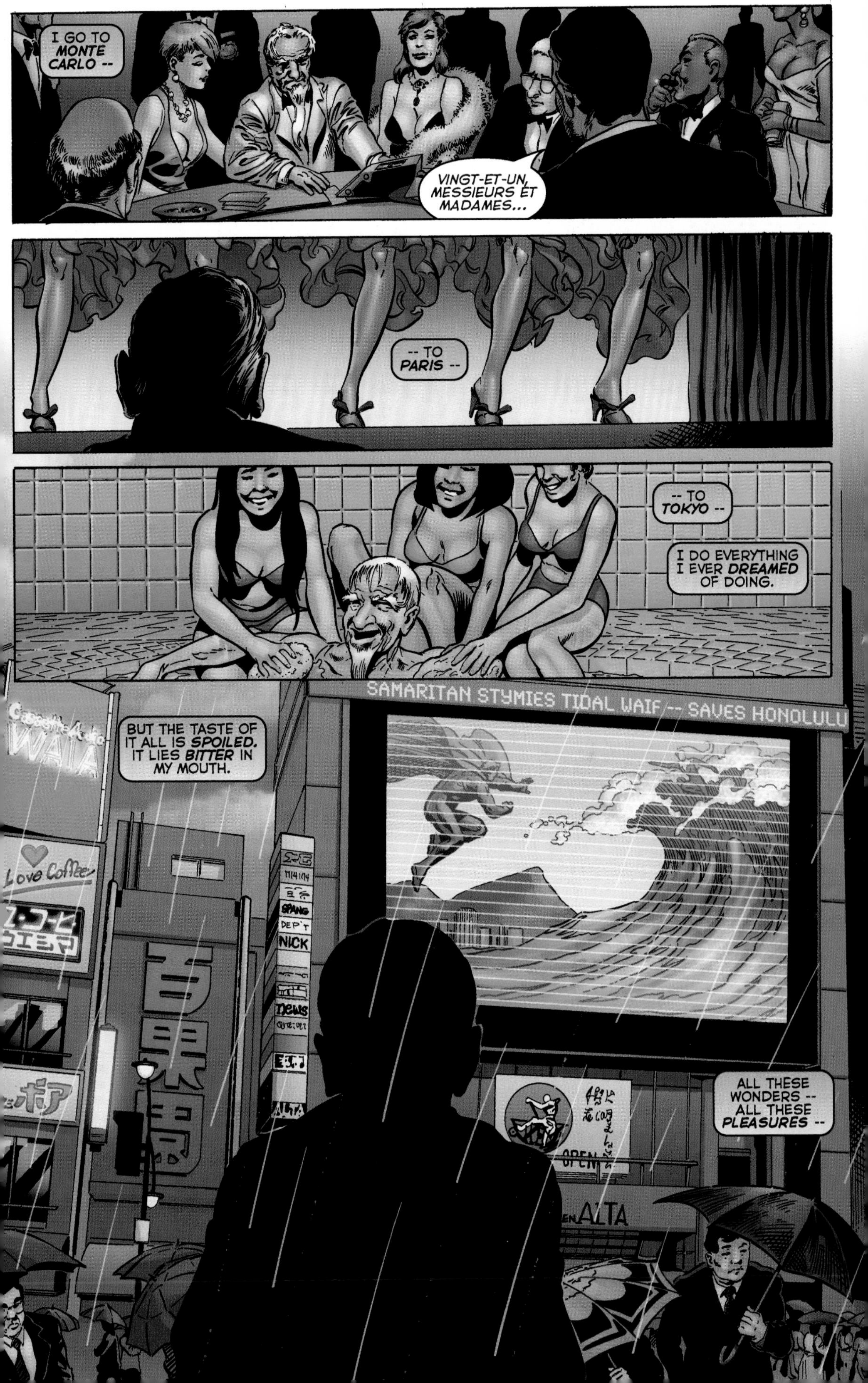

I GO TO MONTE CARLO --
VINGT-ET-UN, MESSIEURS ET MADAMES...
-- TO PARIS --
-- TO TOKYO --
I DO EVERYTHING I EVER DREAMED OF DOING.
SAMARITAN STYMIES TIDAL WAIF -- SAVES HONOLULU
BUT THE TASTE OF IT ALL IS SPOILED. IT LIES BITTER IN MY MOUTH.
Love Coffee
NICK
NEWS
ALTA
OPEN
ALL THESE WONDERS -- ALL THESE PLEASURES --

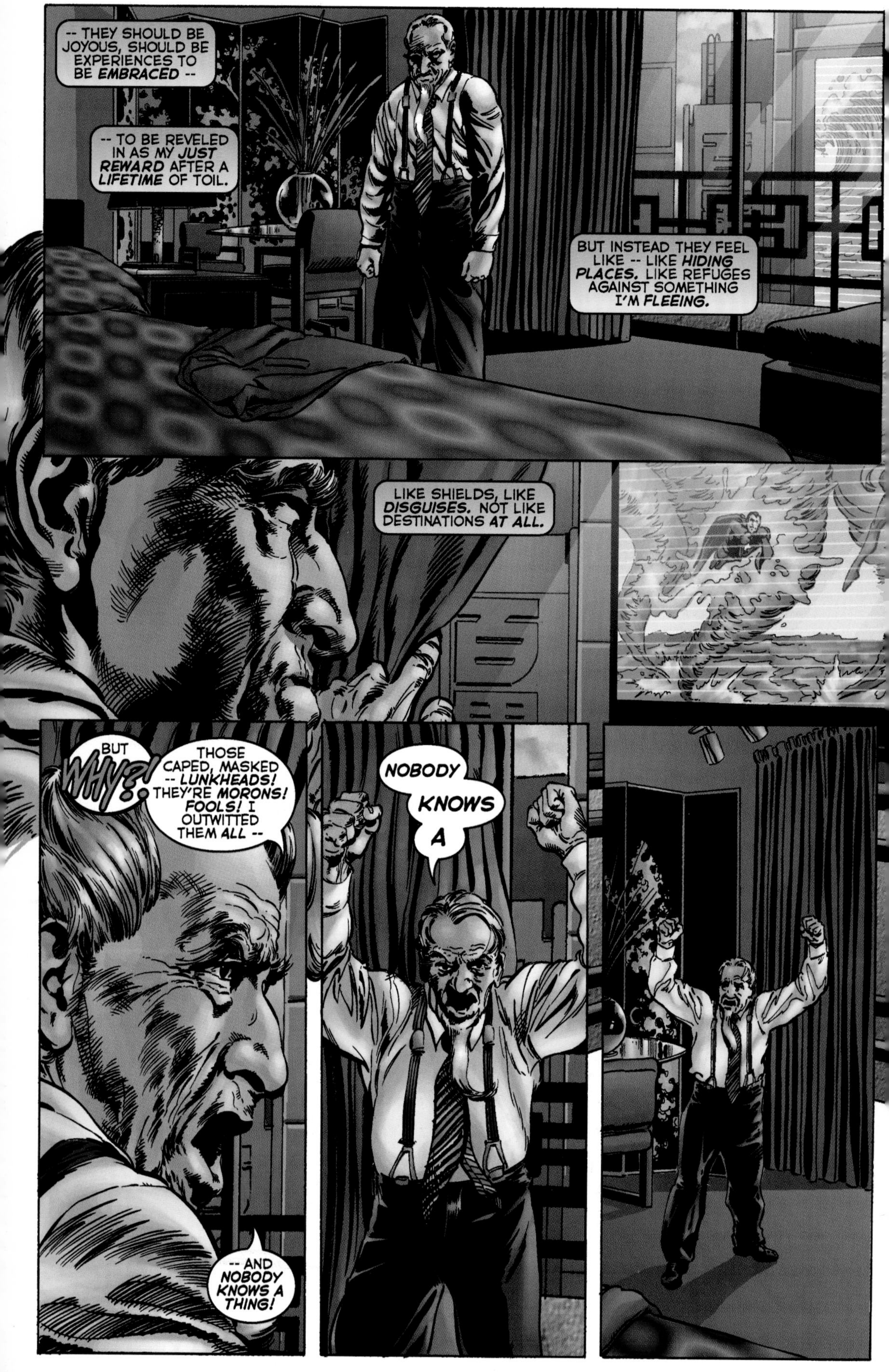
-- THEY SHOULD BE JOYOUS, SHOULD BE EXPERIENCES TO BE EMBRACED --
-- TO BE REVELED IN AS MY JUST REWARD AFTER A LIFETIME OF TOIL.
BUT INSTEAD THEY FEEL LIKE -- LIKE HIDING PLACES. LIKE REFUGES AGAINST SOMETHING I'M FLEEING.
LIKE SHIELDS, LIKE DISGUISES. NOT LIKE DESTINATIONS AT ALL.
BUT WHY?!
THOSE CAPED, MASKED -- LUNKHEADS! THEY'RE MORONS! FOOLS! I OUTWITTED THEM ALL --
-- AND NOBODY KNOWS A THING!
NOBODY KNOWS A

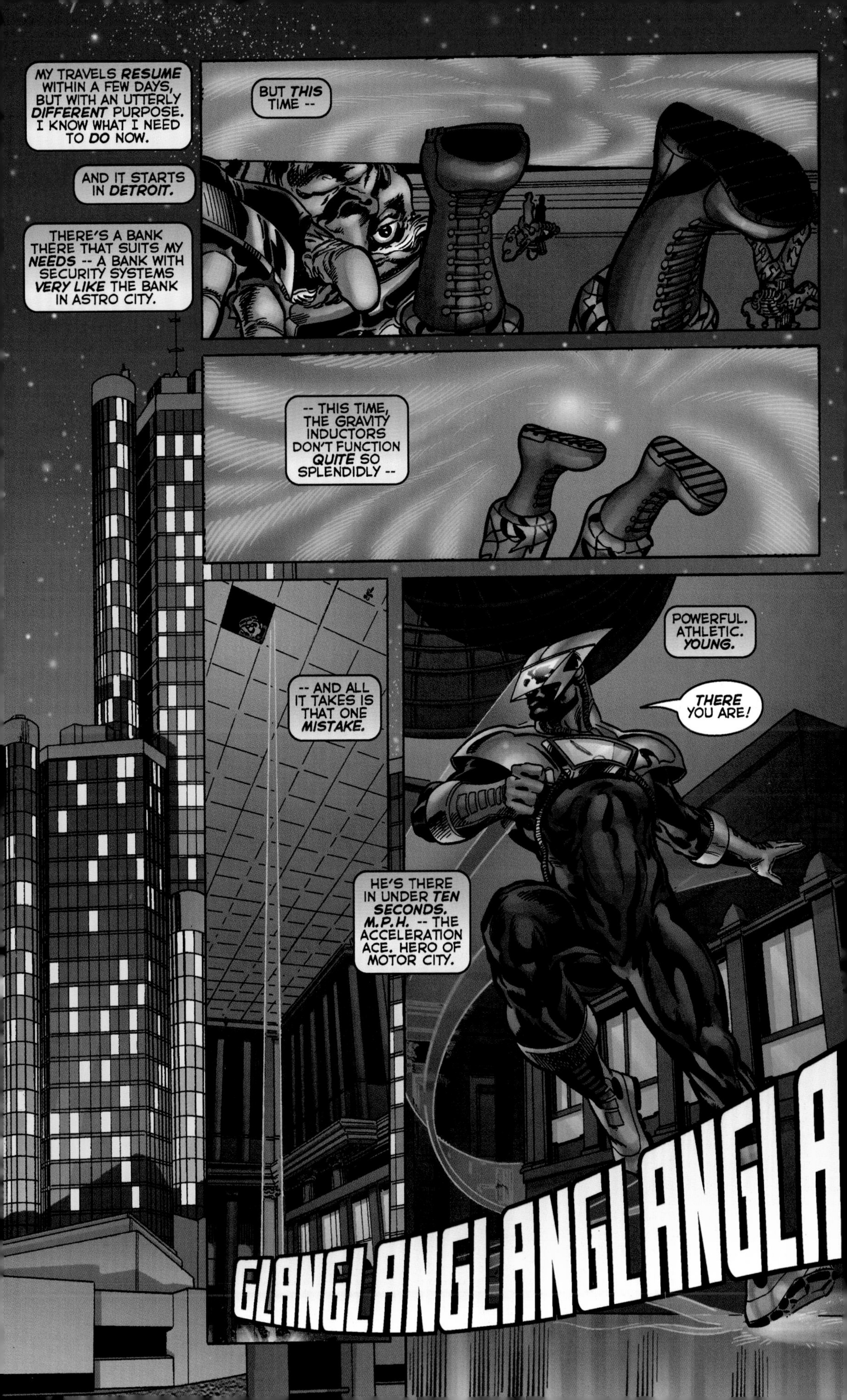
MY TRAVELS RESUME WITHIN A FEW DAYS, BUT WITH AN UTTERLY DIFFERENT PURPOSE. I KNOW WHAT I NEED TO DO NOW.
AND IT STARTS IN DETROIT.
THERE'S A BANK THERE THAT SUITS MY NEEDS -- A BANK WITH SECURITY SYSTEMS VERY LIKE THE BANK IN ASTRO CITY.
BUT THIS TIME --
-- THIS TIME, THE GRAVITY INDUCTORS DON'T FUNCTION QUITE SO SPLENDIDLY --
-- AND ALL IT TAKES IS THAT ONE MISTAKE.
GLANGLANGLANGLANGLA
HE'S THERE IN UNDER TEN SECONDS. M.P.H. -- THE ACCELERATION ACE. HERO OF MOTOR CITY.
POWERFUL. ATHLETIC. YOUNG.
THERE YOU ARE!

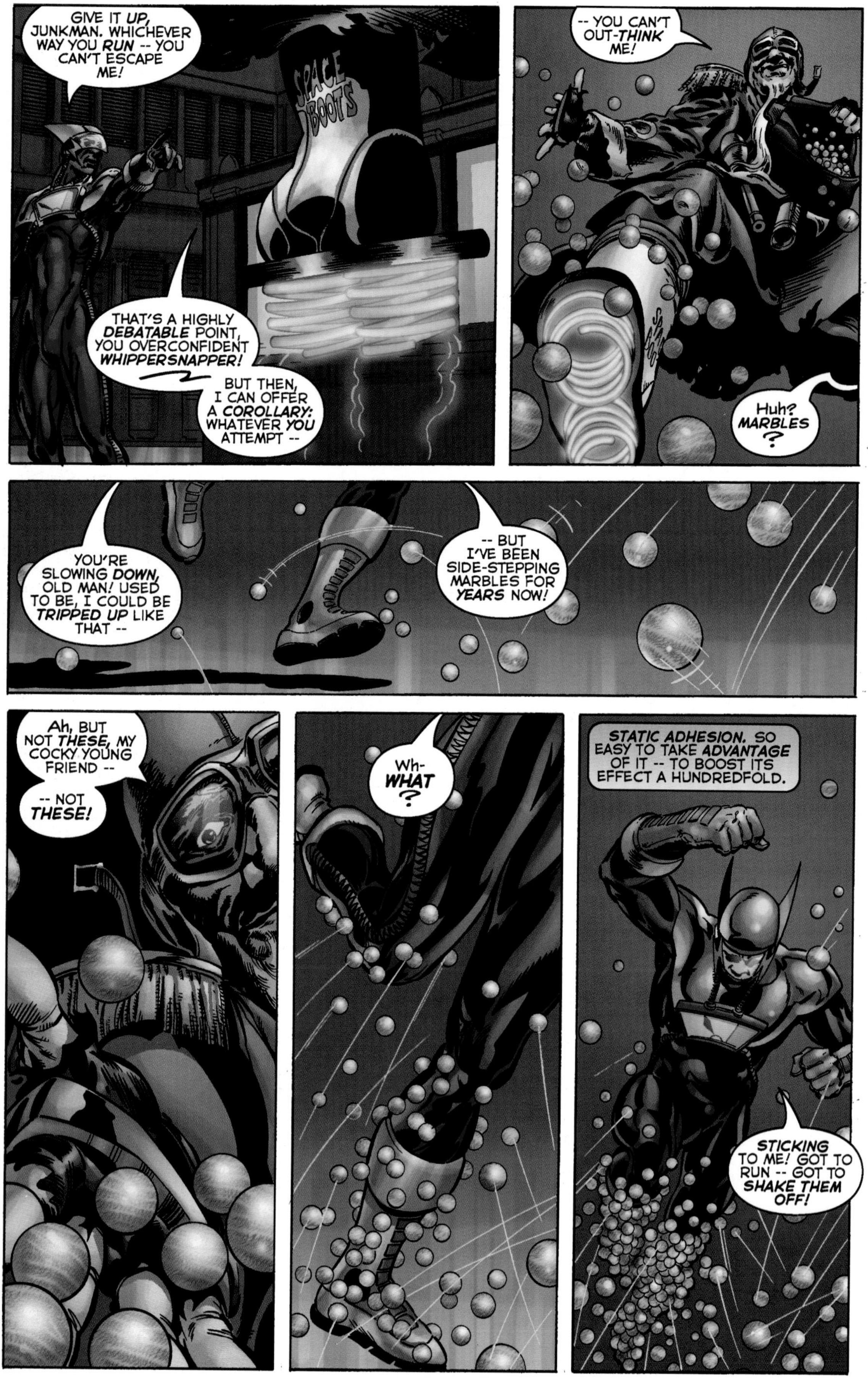
GIVE IT UP, JUNKMAN. WHICHEVER WAY YOU RUN -- YOU CAN'T ESCAPE ME!
SPACE BOOTS
THAT'S A HIGHLY DEBATABLE POINT, YOU OVERCONFIDENT WHIPPERSNAPPER!
BUT THEN, I CAN OFFER A COROLLARY: WHATEVER YOU ATTEMPT --
-- YOU CAN'T OUT-THINK ME!
Huh? MARBLES?
YOU'RE SLOWING DOWN, OLD MAN! USED TO BE, I COULD BE TRIPPED UP LIKE THAT --
-- BUT I'VE BEEN SIDE-STEPPING MARBLES FOR YEARS NOW!
Ah, BUT NOT THESE, MY COCKY YOUNG FRIEND --
-- NOT THESE!
Wh-WHAT?
STATIC ADHESION. SO EASY TO TAKE ADVANTAGE OF IT -- TO BOOST ITS EFFECT A HUNDREDFOLD.
STICKING TO ME! GOT TO RUN -- GOT TO SHAKE THEM OFF!

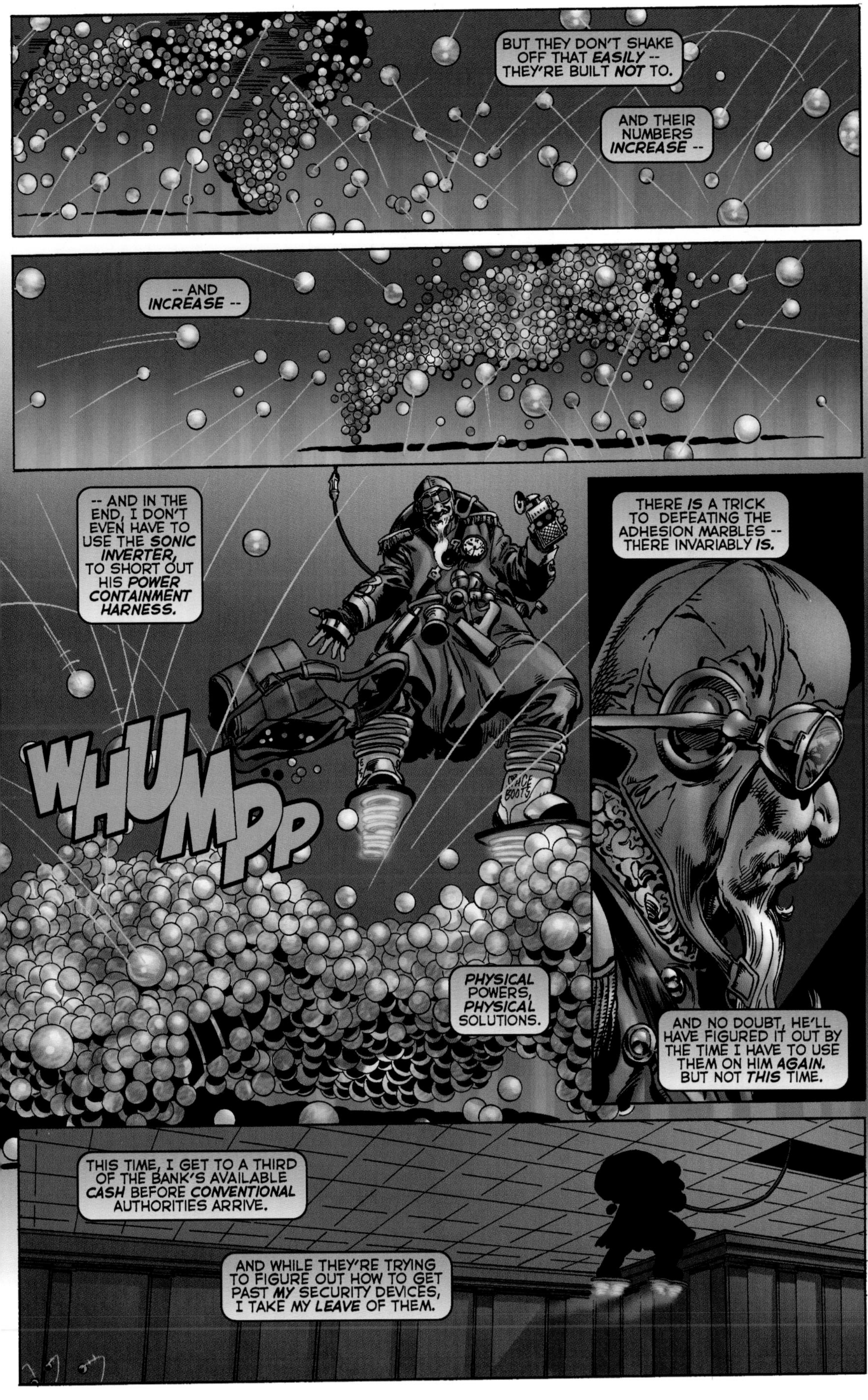

BUT THEY DON'T SHAKE OFF THAT *EASILY* -- THEY'RE BUILT *NOT* TO.
AND THEIR NUMBERS *INCREASE* --
-- AND *INCREASE* --
-- AND IN THE END, I DON'T EVEN HAVE TO USE THE *SONIC INVERTER,* TO SHORT OUT HIS *POWER CONTAINMENT HARNESS.*
WHUMPP
PHYSICAL POWERS, PHYSICAL SOLUTIONS.
THERE *IS* A TRICK TO DEFEATING THE ADHESION MARBLES -- THERE INVARIABLY *IS.*
AND NO DOUBT, HE'LL HAVE FIGURED IT OUT BY THE TIME I HAVE TO USE THEM ON HIM *AGAIN.* BUT NOT *THIS* TIME.
THIS TIME, I GET TO A THIRD OF THE BANK'S AVAILABLE *CASH* BEFORE *CONVENTIONAL* AUTHORITIES ARRIVE.
AND WHILE THEY'RE TRYING TO FIGURE OUT HOW TO GET PAST *MY* SECURITY DEVICES, I TAKE *MY LEAVE* OF THEM.

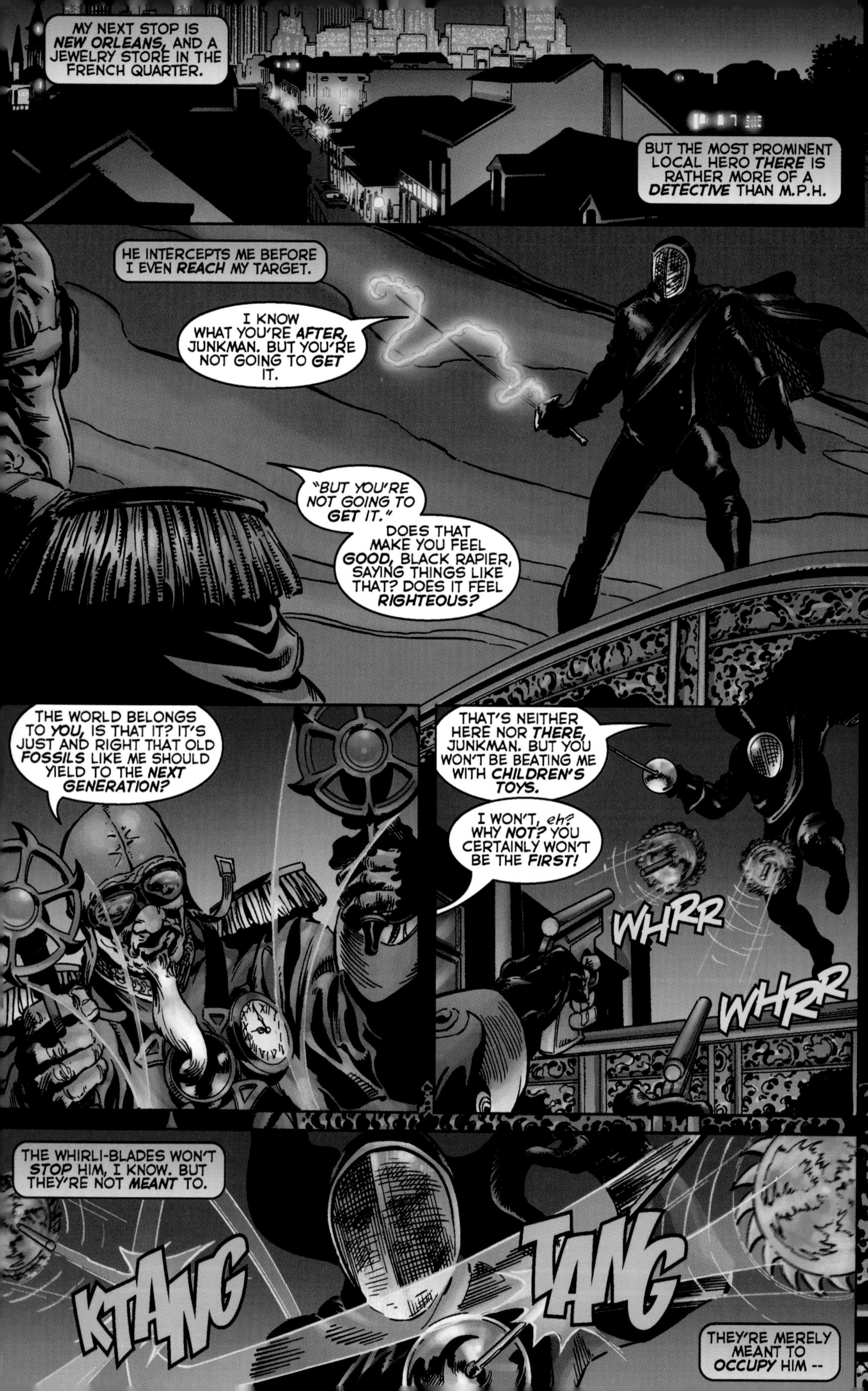
MY NEXT STOP IS NEW ORLEANS, AND A JEWELRY STORE IN THE FRENCH QUARTER.
BUT THE MOST PROMINENT LOCAL HERO THERE IS RATHER MORE OF A DETECTIVE THAN M.P.H.
HE INTERCEPTS ME BEFORE I EVEN REACH MY TARGET.
I KNOW WHAT YOU'RE AFTER, JUNKMAN. BUT YOU'RE NOT GOING TO GET IT.
"BUT YOU'RE NOT GOING TO GET IT."
DOES THAT MAKE YOU FEEL GOOD, BLACK RAPIER, SAYING THINGS LIKE THAT? DOES IT FEEL RIGHTEOUS?
THE WORLD BELONGS TO YOU, IS THAT IT? IT'S JUST AND RIGHT THAT OLD FOSSILS LIKE ME SHOULD YIELD TO THE NEXT GENERATION?
THAT'S NEITHER HERE NOR THERE, JUNKMAN. BUT YOU WON'T BE BEATING ME WITH CHILDREN'S TOYS.
I WON'T, eh? WHY NOT? YOU CERTAINLY WON'T BE THE FIRST!
WHRR
WHRR
THE WHIRLI-BLADES WON'T STOP HIM, I KNOW. BUT THEY'RE NOT MEANT TO.
KTANG
TANG
THEY'RE MERELY MEANT TO OCCUPY HIM --

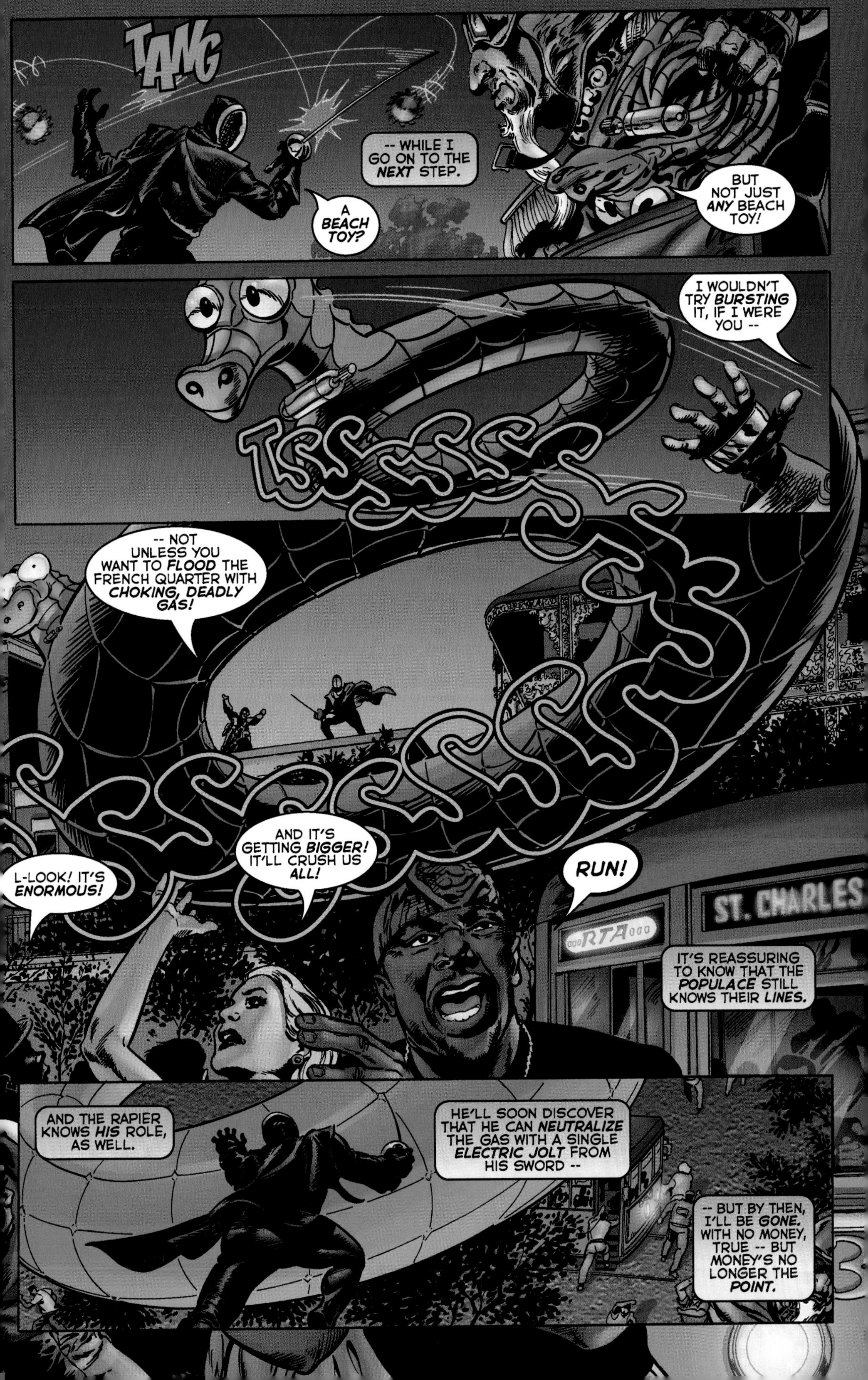
TANG
-- WHILE I GO ON TO THE NEXT STEP.
A BEACH TOY?
BUT NOT JUST ANY BEACH TOY!
I WOULDN'T TRY BURSTING IT, IF I WERE YOU --
-- NOT UNLESS YOU WANT TO FLOOD THE FRENCH QUARTER WITH CHOKING, DEADLY GAS!
L-LOOK! IT'S ENORMOUS!
AND IT'S GETTING BIGGER! IT'LL CRUSH US ALL!
RUN!
ST. CHARLES
RTA
IT'S REASSURING TO KNOW THAT THE POPULACE STILL KNOWS THEIR LINES.
AND THE RAPIER KNOWS HIS ROLE, AS WELL.
HE'LL SOON DISCOVER THAT HE CAN NEUTRALIZE THE GAS WITH A SINGLE ELECTRIC JOLT FROM HIS SWORD --
-- BUT BY THEN, I'LL BE GONE. WITH NO MONEY, TRUE -- BUT MONEY'S NO LONGER THE POINT.

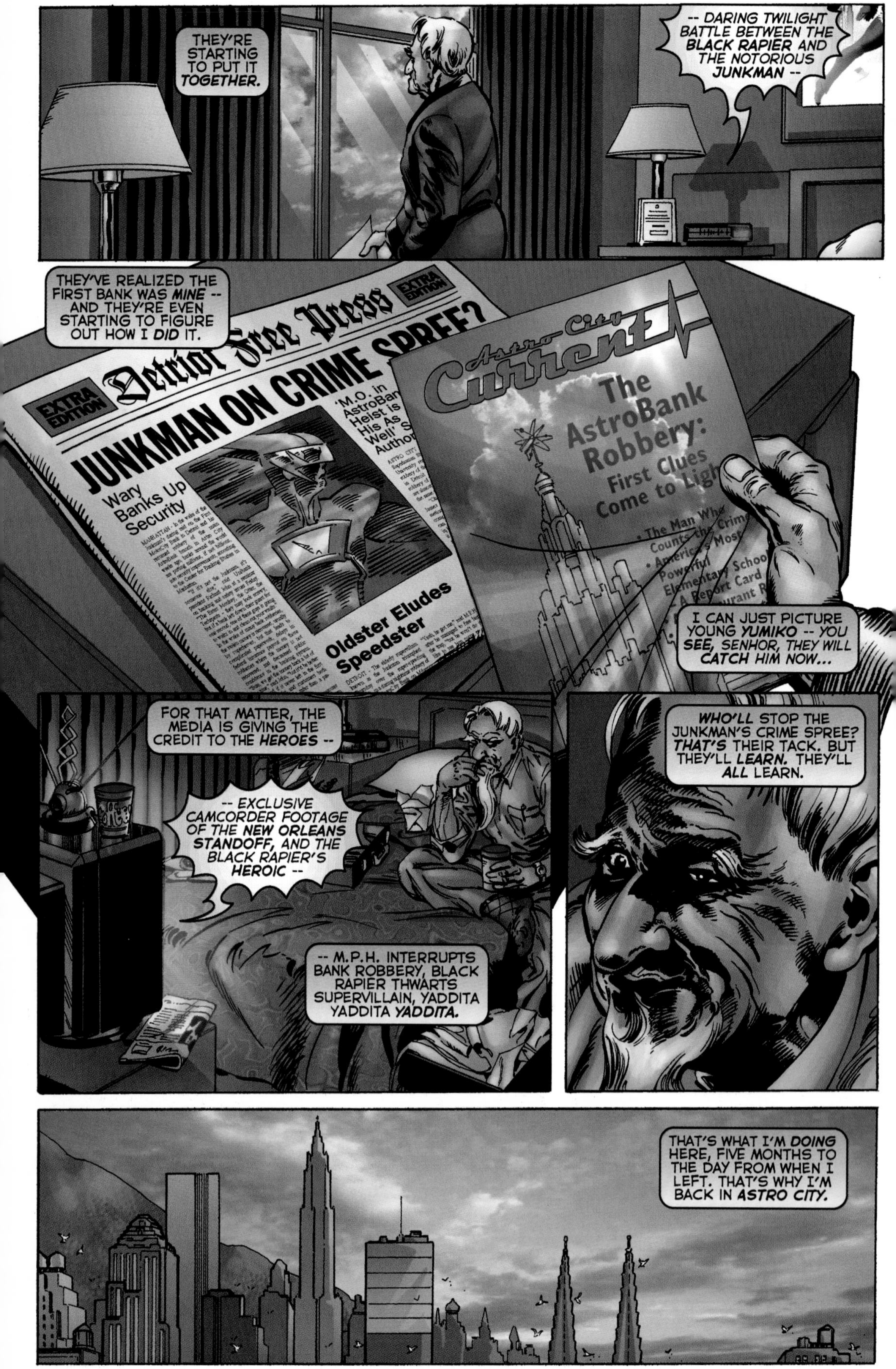
THEY'RE STARTING TO PUT IT TOGETHER.
-- DARING TWILIGHT BATTLE BETWEEN THE BLACK RAPIER AND THE NOTORIOUS JUNKMAN --
THEY'VE REALIZED THE FIRST BANK WAS MINE -- AND THEY'RE EVEN STARTING TO FIGURE OUT HOW I DID IT.
Detroit Free Press
EXTRA EDITION
JUNKMAN ON CRIME SPREE?
Wary Banks Up Security
Oldster Eludes Speedster
Astro City Current
The AstroBank Robbery:
I CAN JUST PICTURE YOUNG YUMIKO -- YOU SEE, SENHOR, THEY WILL CATCH HIM NOW...
FOR THAT MATTER, THE MEDIA IS GIVING THE CREDIT TO THE HEROES --
-- EXCLUSIVE CAMCORDER FOOTAGE OF THE NEW ORLEANS STANDOFF, AND THE BLACK RAPIER'S HEROIC --
-- M.P.H. INTERRUPTS BANK ROBBERY, BLACK RAPIER THWARTS SUPERVILLAIN, YADDITA YADDITA YADDITA.
WHO'LL STOP THE JUNKMAN'S CRIME SPREE? THAT'S THEIR TACK. BUT THEY'LL LEARN. THEY'LL ALL LEARN.
THAT'S WHAT I'M DOING HERE, FIVE MONTHS TO THE DAY FROM WHEN I LEFT. THAT'S WHY I'M BACK IN ASTRO CITY.

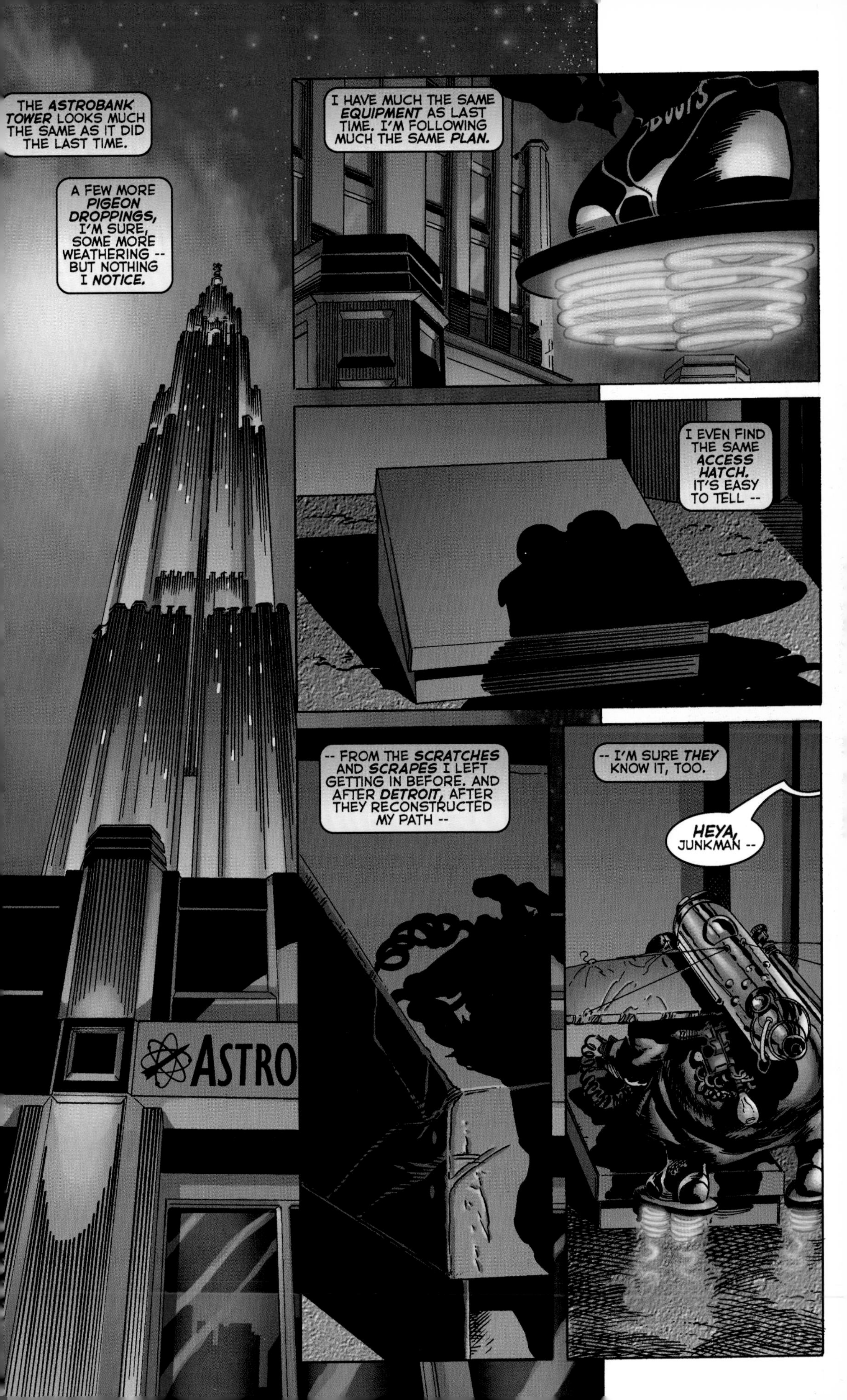
THE ASTROBANK TOWER LOOKS MUCH THE SAME AS IT DID THE LAST TIME.
A FEW MORE PIGEON DROPPINGS, I'M SURE, SOME MORE WEATHERING -- BUT NOTHING I NOTICE.
ASTRO
I HAVE MUCH THE SAME EQUIPMENT AS LAST TIME. I'M FOLLOWING MUCH THE SAME PLAN.
BOOTS
I EVEN FIND THE SAME ACCESS HATCH. IT'S EASY TO TELL --
-- FROM THE SCRATCHES AND SCRAPES I LEFT GETTING IN BEFORE. AND AFTER DETROIT, AFTER THEY RECONSTRUCTED MY PATH --
-- I'M SURE THEY KNOW IT, TOO.
HEYA, JUNKMAN --

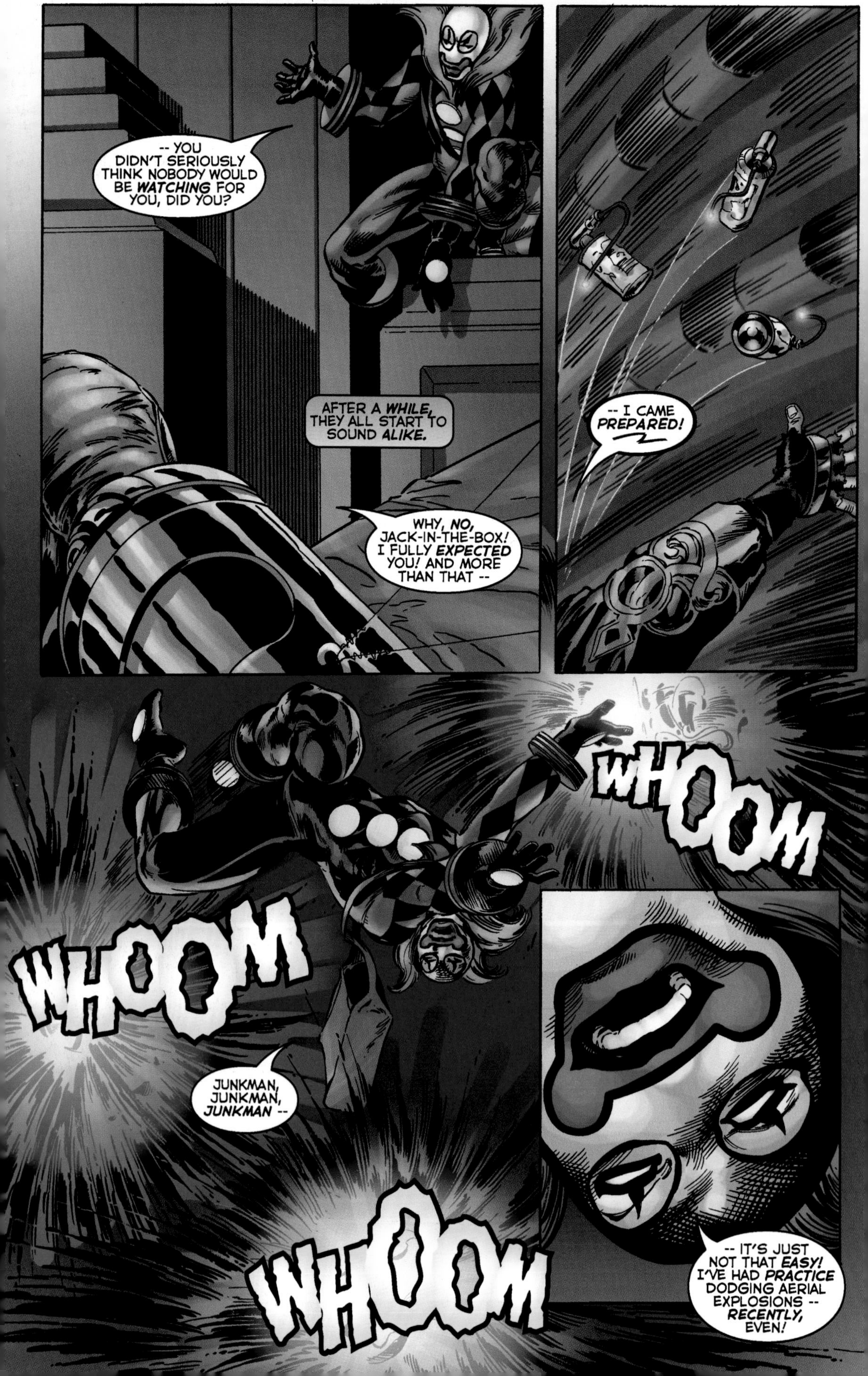
-- YOU DIDN'T SERIOUSLY THINK NOBODY WOULD BE WATCHING FOR YOU, DID YOU?
AFTER A WHILE, THEY ALL START TO SOUND ALIKE.
WHY, NO, JACK-IN-THE-BOX! I FULLY EXPECTED YOU! AND MORE THAN THAT --
-- I CAME PREPARED!
WHOOM
WHOOM
JUNKMAN, JUNKMAN, JUNKMAN --
WHOOM
-- IT'S JUST NOT THAT EASY! I'VE HAD PRACTICE DODGING AERIAL EXPLOSIONS -- RECENTLY, EVEN!

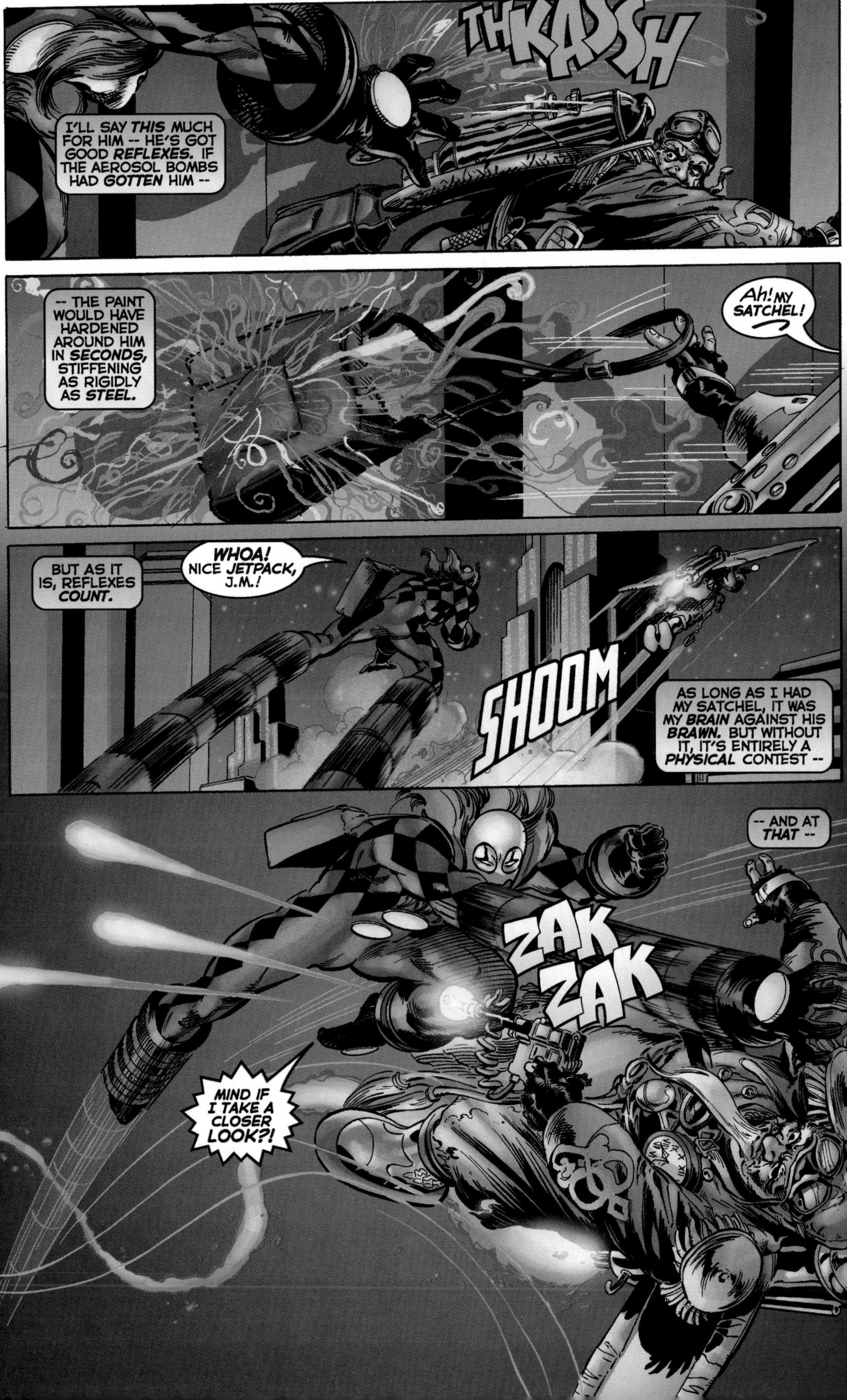
THKASSH
I'LL SAY THIS MUCH FOR HIM -- HE'S GOT GOOD REFLEXES. IF THE AEROSOL BOMBS HAD GOTTEN HIM --
-- THE PAINT WOULD HAVE HARDENED AROUND HIM IN SECONDS, STIFFENING AS RIGIDLY AS STEEL.
Ah! MY SATCHEL!
BUT AS IT IS, REFLEXES COUNT.
WHOA! NICE JETPACK, J.M.!
SHOOM
AS LONG AS I HAD MY SATCHEL, IT WAS MY BRAIN AGAINST HIS BRAWN. BUT WITHOUT IT, IT'S ENTIRELY A PHYSICAL CONTEST --
-- AND AT THAT --
ZAK
ZAK
MIND IF I TAKE A CLOSER LOOK?!

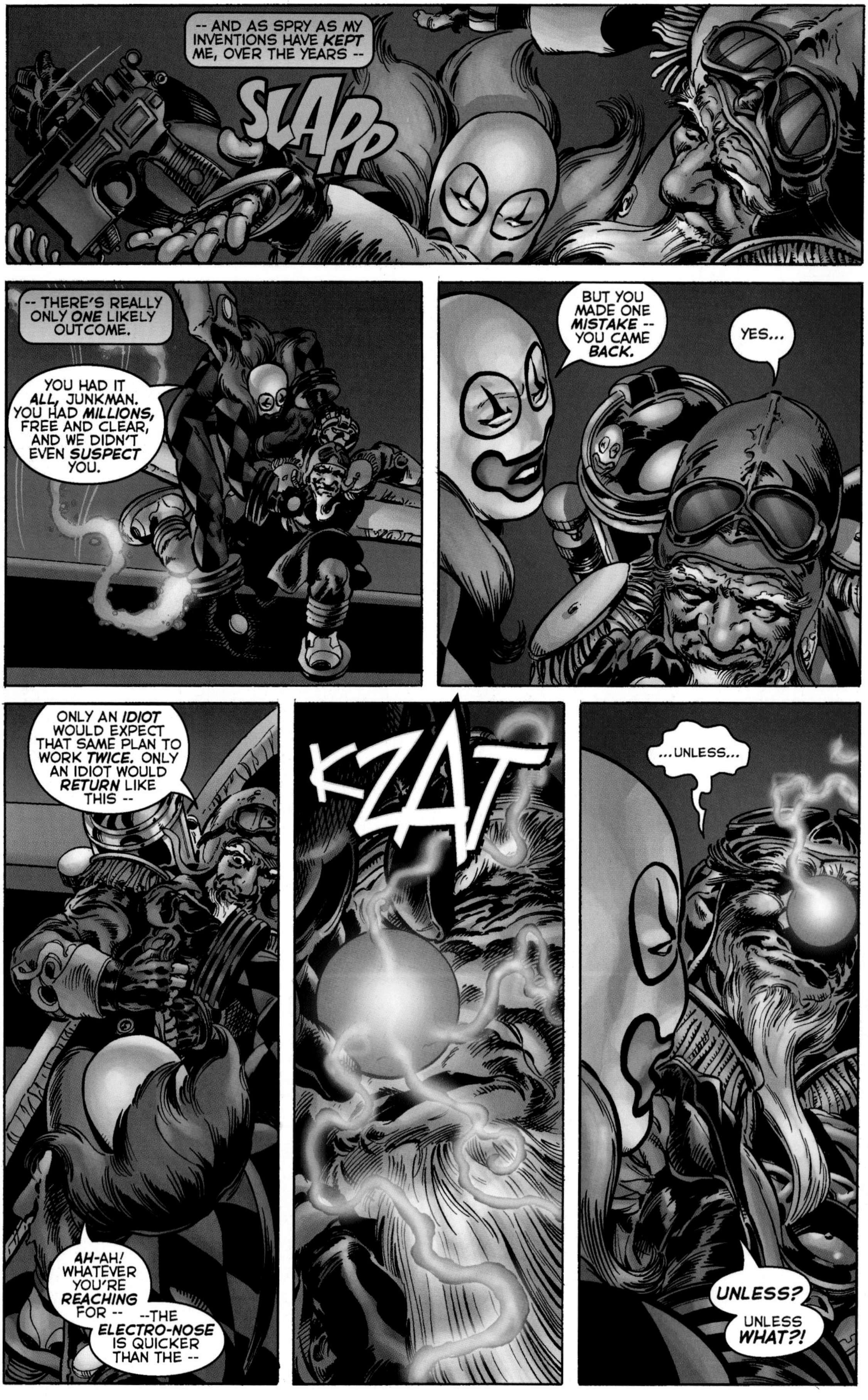
-- AND AS SPRY AS MY INVENTIONS HAVE KEPT ME, OVER THE YEARS --
SLAPP
-- THERE'S REALLY ONLY ONE LIKELY OUTCOME.
YOU HAD IT ALL, JUNKMAN. YOU HAD MILLIONS, FREE AND CLEAR, AND WE DIDN'T EVEN SUSPECT YOU.
BUT YOU MADE ONE MISTAKE -- YOU CAME BACK.
YES...
ONLY AN IDIOT WOULD EXPECT THAT SAME PLAN TO WORK TWICE. ONLY AN IDIOT WOULD RETURN LIKE THIS --
AH-AH! WHATEVER YOU'RE REACHING FOR --
--THE ELECTRO-NOSE IS QUICKER THAN THE --
KZAT
...UNLESS...
UNLESS? UNLESS WHAT?!

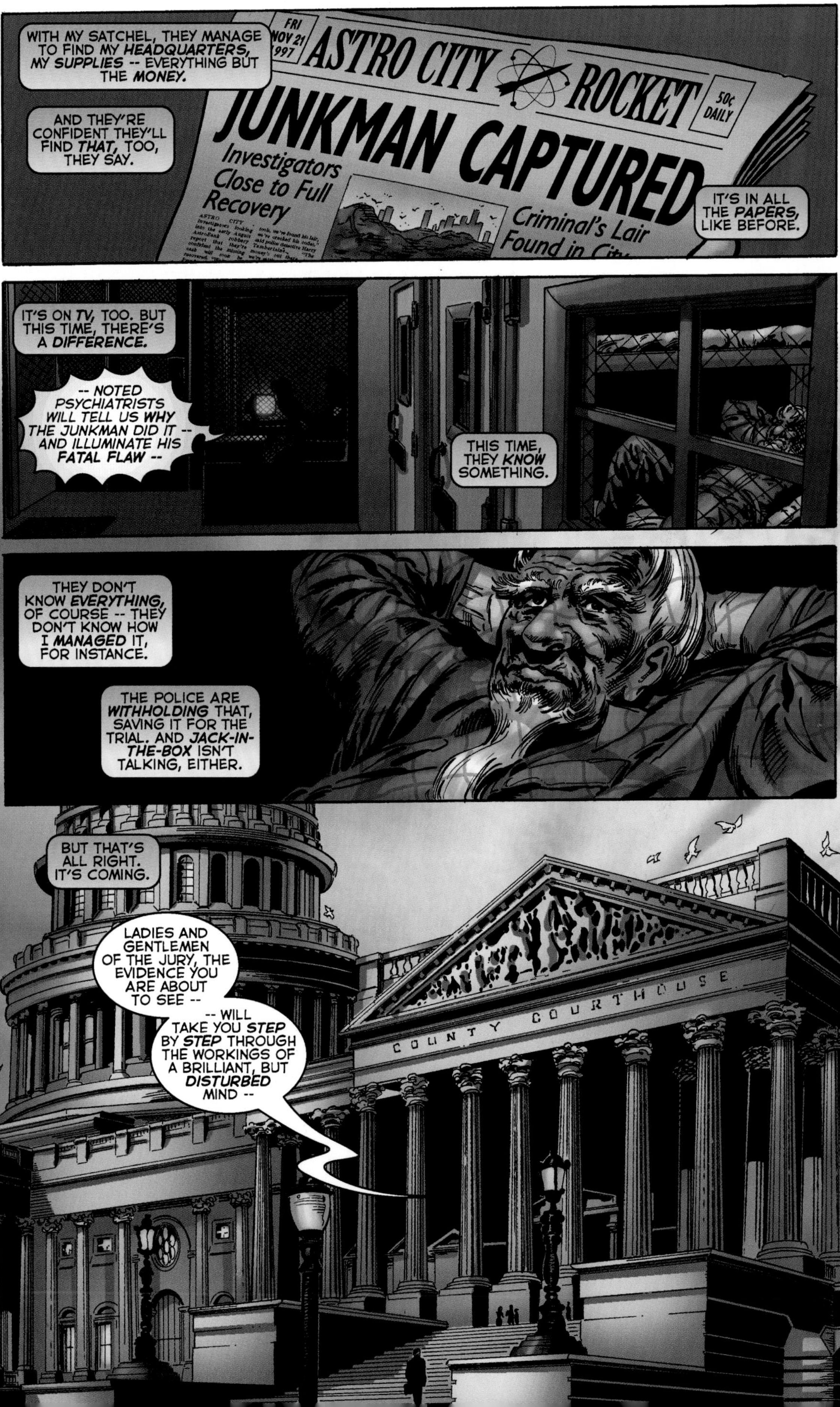
WITH MY SATCHEL, THEY MANAGE TO FIND MY HEADQUARTERS, MY SUPPLIES -- EVERYTHING BUT THE MONEY.
AND THEY'RE CONFIDENT THEY'LL FIND THAT, TOO, THEY SAY.
FRI NOV 21 1997
ASTRO CITY ROCKET
50¢ DAILY
JUNKMAN CAPTURED
Investigators Close to Full Recovery
Criminal's Lair Found in City
IT'S IN ALL THE PAPERS, LIKE BEFORE.
IT'S ON TV, TOO. BUT THIS TIME, THERE'S A DIFFERENCE.
-- NOTED PSYCHIATRISTS WILL TELL US WHY THE JUNKMAN DID IT -- AND ILLUMINATE HIS FATAL FLAW --
THIS TIME, THEY KNOW SOMETHING.
THEY DON'T KNOW EVERYTHING, OF COURSE -- THEY DON'T KNOW HOW I MANAGED IT, FOR INSTANCE.
THE POLICE ARE WITHHOLDING THAT, SAVING IT FOR THE TRIAL. AND JACK-IN-THE-BOX ISN'T TALKING, EITHER.
BUT THAT'S ALL RIGHT. IT'S COMING.
COUNTY COURTHOUSE
LADIES AND GENTLEMEN OF THE JURY, THE EVIDENCE YOU ARE ABOUT TO SEE --
-- WILL TAKE YOU STEP BY STEP THROUGH THE WORKINGS OF A BRILLIANT, BUT DISTURBED MIND --

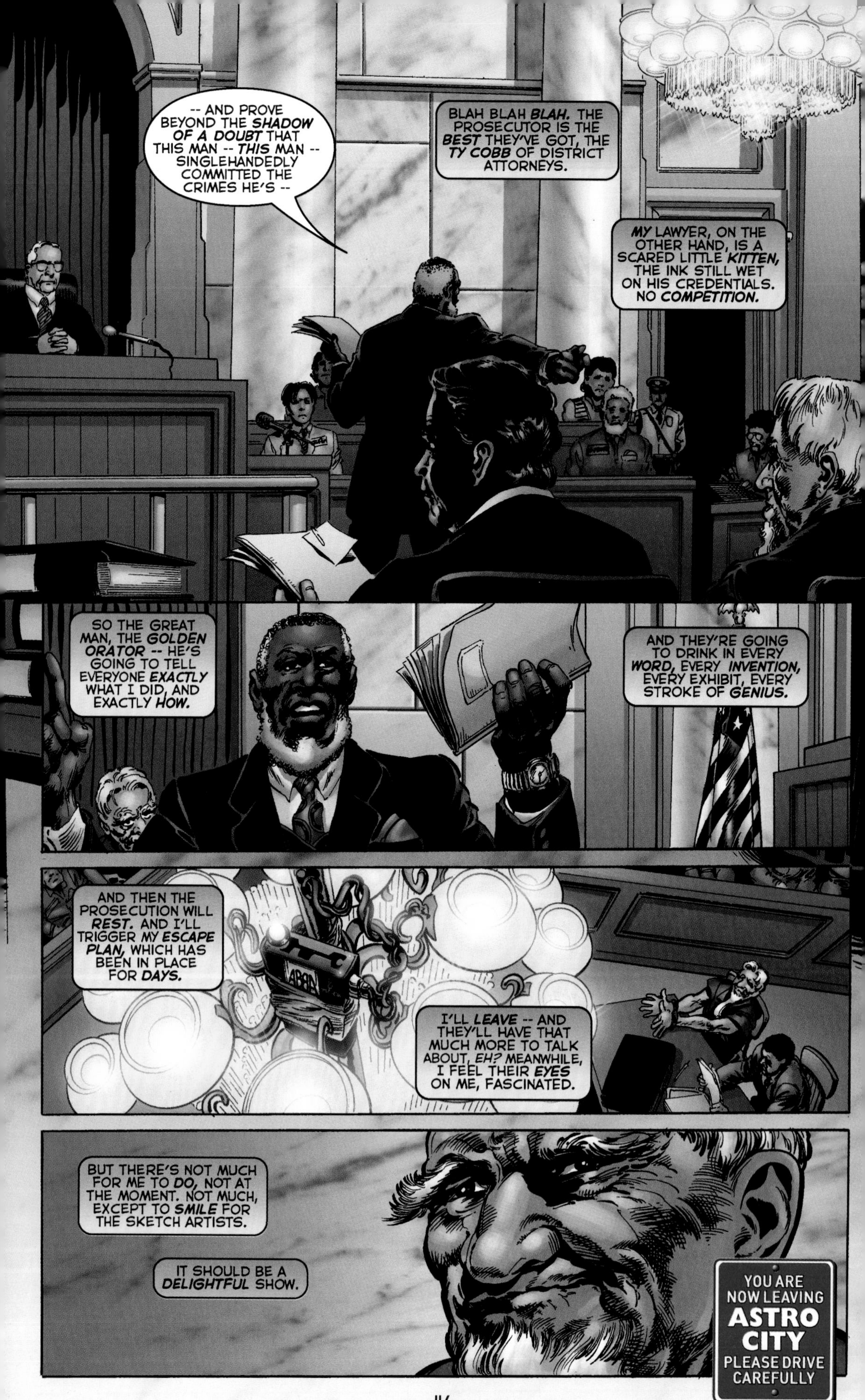
-- AND PROVE BEYOND THE SHADOW OF A DOUBT THAT THIS MAN -- THIS MAN -- SINGLEHANDEDLY COMMITTED THE CRIMES HE'S --
BLAH BLAH BLAH. THE PROSECUTOR IS THE BEST THEY'VE GOT, THE TY COBB OF DISTRICT ATTORNEYS.
MY LAWYER, ON THE OTHER HAND, IS A SCARED LITTLE KITTEN, THE INK STILL WET ON HIS CREDENTIALS. NO COMPETITION.
SO THE GREAT MAN, THE GOLDEN ORATOR -- HE'S GOING TO TELL EVERYONE EXACTLY WHAT I DID, AND EXACTLY HOW.
AND THEY'RE GOING TO DRINK IN EVERY WORD, EVERY INVENTION, EVERY EXHIBIT, EVERY STROKE OF GENIUS.
AND THEN THE PROSECUTION WILL REST. AND I'LL TRIGGER MY ESCAPE PLAN, WHICH HAS BEEN IN PLACE FOR DAYS.
I'LL LEAVE -- AND THEY'LL HAVE THAT MUCH MORE TO TALK ABOUT, EH? MEANWHILE, I FEEL THEIR EYES ON ME, FASCINATED.
BUT THERE'S NOT MUCH FOR ME TO DO, NOT AT THE MOMENT. NOT MUCH, EXCEPT TO SMILE FOR THE SKETCH ARTISTS.
IT SHOULD BE A DELIGHTFUL SHOW.
YOU ARE NOW LEAVING ASTRO CITY PLEASE DRIVE CAREFULLY

"Serpent's Teeth"

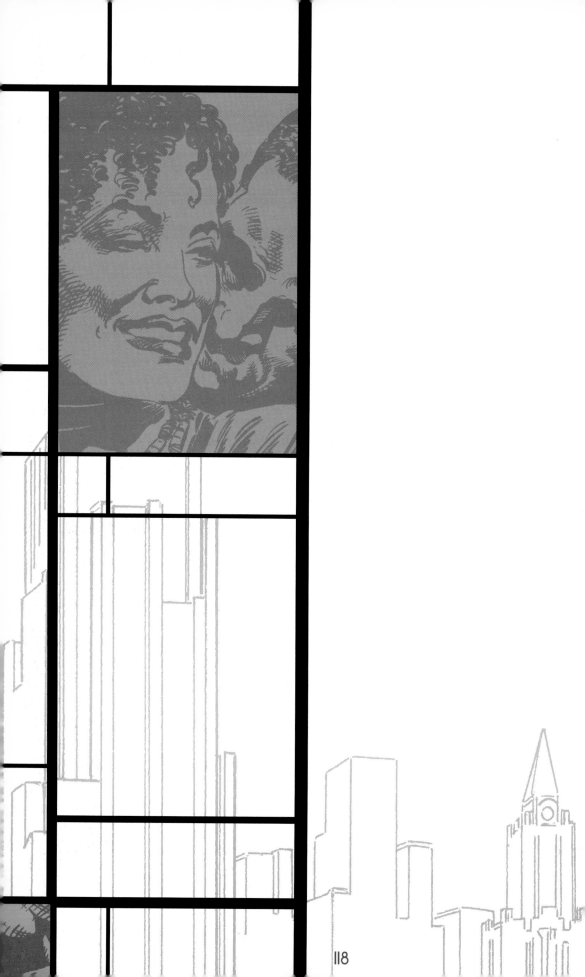

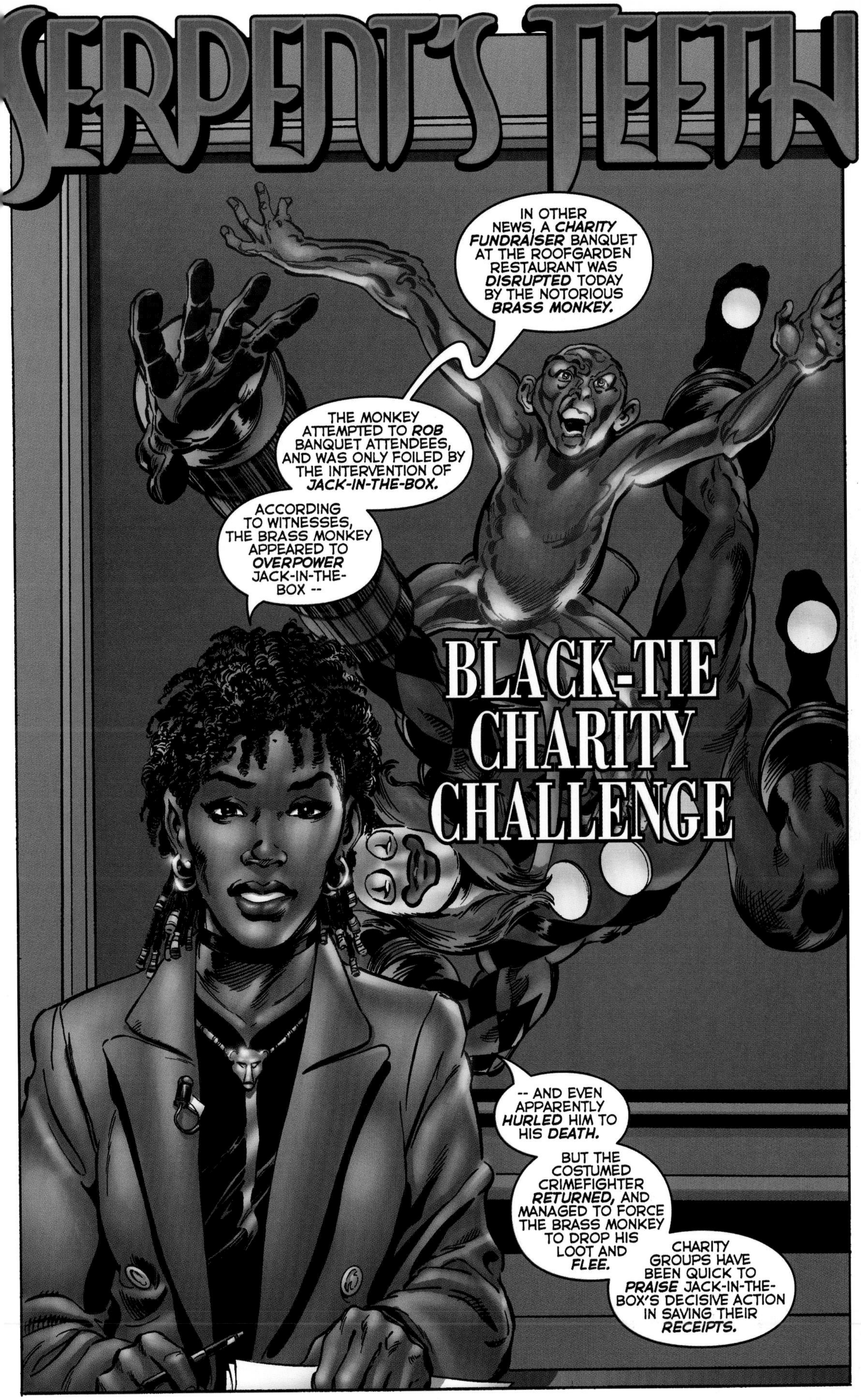
SERPENT'S TEETH
IN OTHER NEWS, A CHARITY FUNDRAISER BANQUET AT THE ROOFGARDEN RESTAURANT WAS DISRUPTED TODAY BY THE NOTORIOUS BRASS MONKEY.
THE MONKEY ATTEMPTED TO ROB BANQUET ATTENDEES, AND WAS ONLY FOILED BY THE INTERVENTION OF JACK-IN-THE-BOX.
ACCORDING TO WITNESSES, THE BRASS MONKEY APPEARED TO OVERPOWER JACK-IN-THE-BOX --
BLACK-TIE CHARITY CHALLENGE
-- AND EVEN APPARENTLY HURLED HIM TO HIS DEATH.
BUT THE COSTUMED CRIMEFIGHTER RETURNED, AND MANAGED TO FORCE THE BRASS MONKEY TO DROP HIS LOOT AND FLEE.
CHARITY GROUPS HAVE BEEN QUICK TO PRAISE JACK-IN-THE-BOX'S DECISIVE ACTION IN SAVING THEIR RECEIPTS.

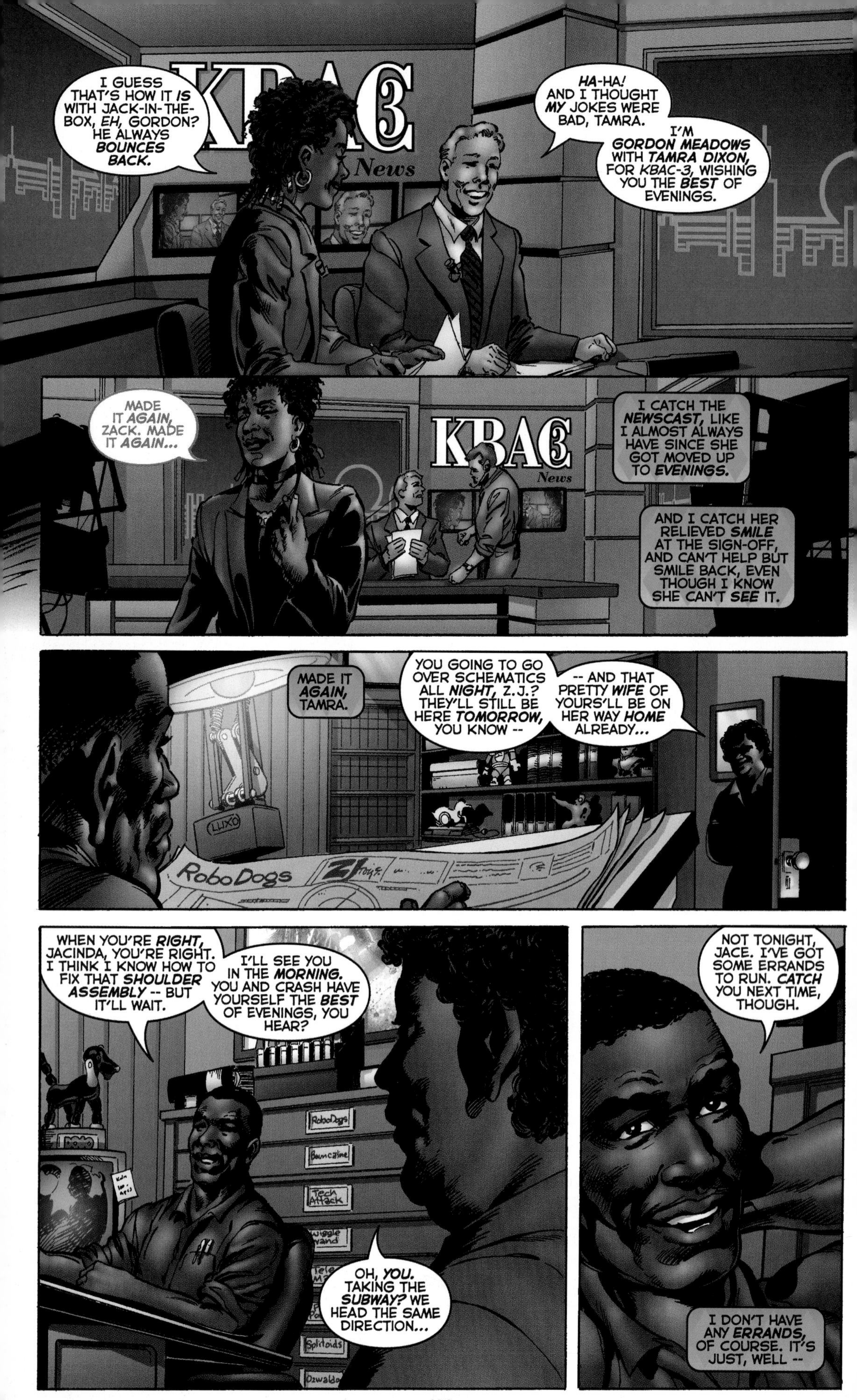

I GUESS THAT'S HOW IT IS WITH JACK-IN-THE-BOX, EH, GORDON? HE ALWAYS BOUNCES BACK.
HA-HA! AND I THOUGHT MY JOKES WERE BAD, TAMRA.
I'M GORDON MEADOWS WITH TAMRA DIXON, FOR KBAC-3, WISHING YOU THE BEST OF EVENINGS.
KBAC 3 News
MADE IT AGAIN, ZACK. MADE IT AGAIN...
I CATCH THE NEWSCAST, LIKE I ALMOST ALWAYS HAVE SINCE SHE GOT MOVED UP TO EVENINGS.
AND I CATCH HER RELIEVED SMILE AT THE SIGN-OFF, AND CAN'T HELP BUT SMILE BACK, EVEN THOUGH I KNOW SHE CAN'T SEE IT.
MADE IT AGAIN, TAMRA.
YOU GOING TO GO OVER SCHEMATICS ALL NIGHT, Z.J.? THEY'LL STILL BE HERE TOMORROW, YOU KNOW --
-- AND THAT PRETTY WIFE OF YOURS'LL BE ON HER WAY HOME ALREADY...
RoboDogs
WHEN YOU'RE RIGHT, JACINDA, YOU'RE RIGHT. I THINK I KNOW HOW TO FIX THAT SHOULDER ASSEMBLY -- BUT IT'LL WAIT.
I'LL SEE YOU IN THE MORNING. YOU AND CRASH HAVE YOURSELF THE BEST OF EVENINGS, YOU HEAR?
OH, YOU. TAKING THE SUBWAY? WE HEAD THE SAME DIRECTION...
NOT TONIGHT, JACE. I'VE GOT SOME ERRANDS TO RUN. CATCH YOU NEXT TIME, THOUGH.
I DON'T HAVE ANY ERRANDS, OF COURSE. IT'S JUST, WELL --

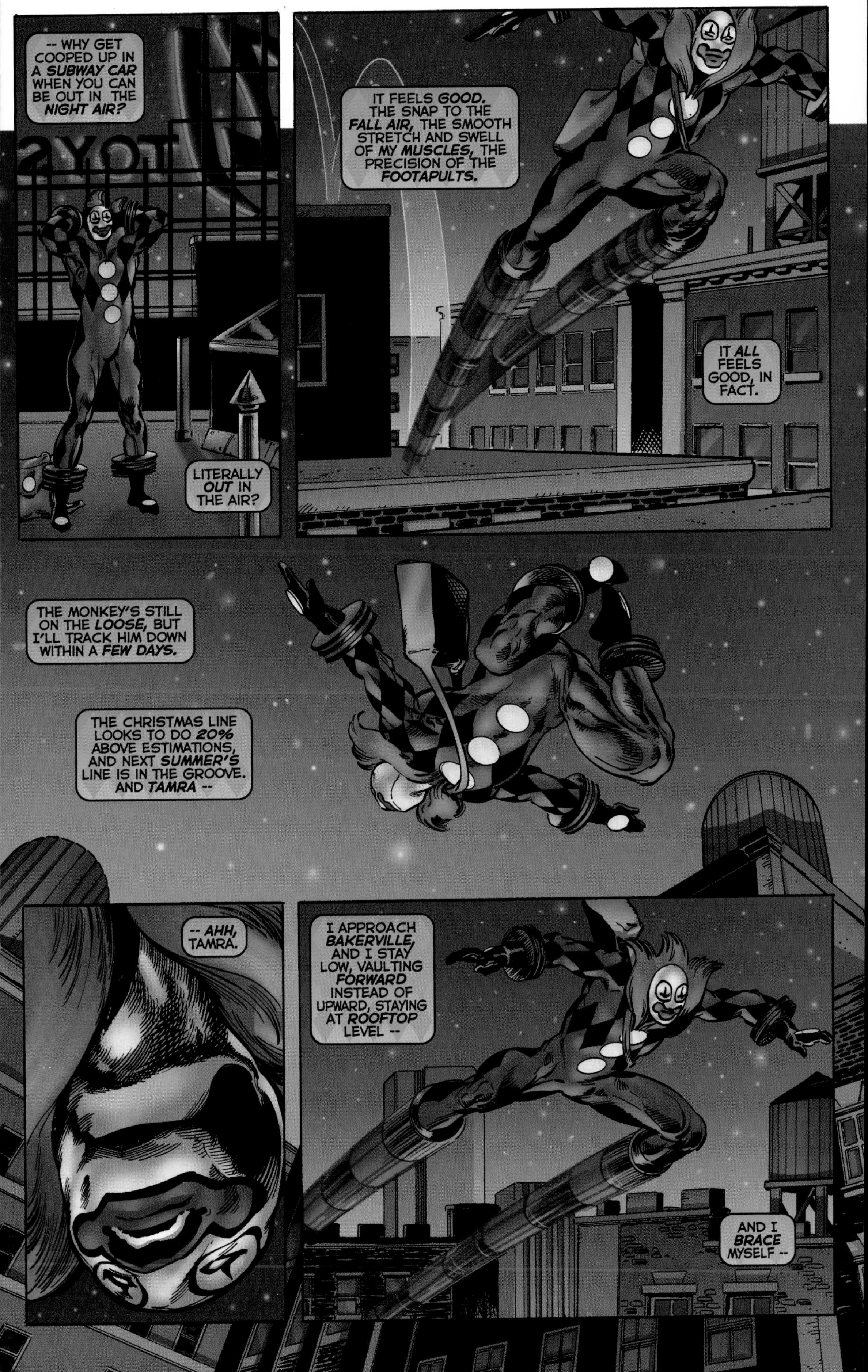

-- WHY GET COOPED UP IN A SUBWAY CAR WHEN YOU CAN BE OUT IN THE NIGHT AIR?
TOYS
LITERALLY OUT IN THE AIR?
IT FEELS GOOD. THE SNAP TO THE FALL AIR, THE SMOOTH STRETCH AND SWELL OF MY MUSCLES, THE PRECISION OF THE FOOTAPULTS.
IT ALL FEELS GOOD, IN FACT.
THE MONKEY'S STILL ON THE LOOSE, BUT I'LL TRACK HIM DOWN WITHIN A FEW DAYS.
THE CHRISTMAS LINE LOOKS TO DO 20% ABOVE ESTIMATIONS, AND NEXT SUMMER'S LINE IS IN THE GROOVE. AND TAMRA --
-- AHH, TAMRA.
I APPROACH BAKERVILLE, AND I STAY LOW, VAULTING FORWARD INSTEAD OF UPWARD, STAYING AT ROOFTOP LEVEL --
AND I BRACE MYSELF --

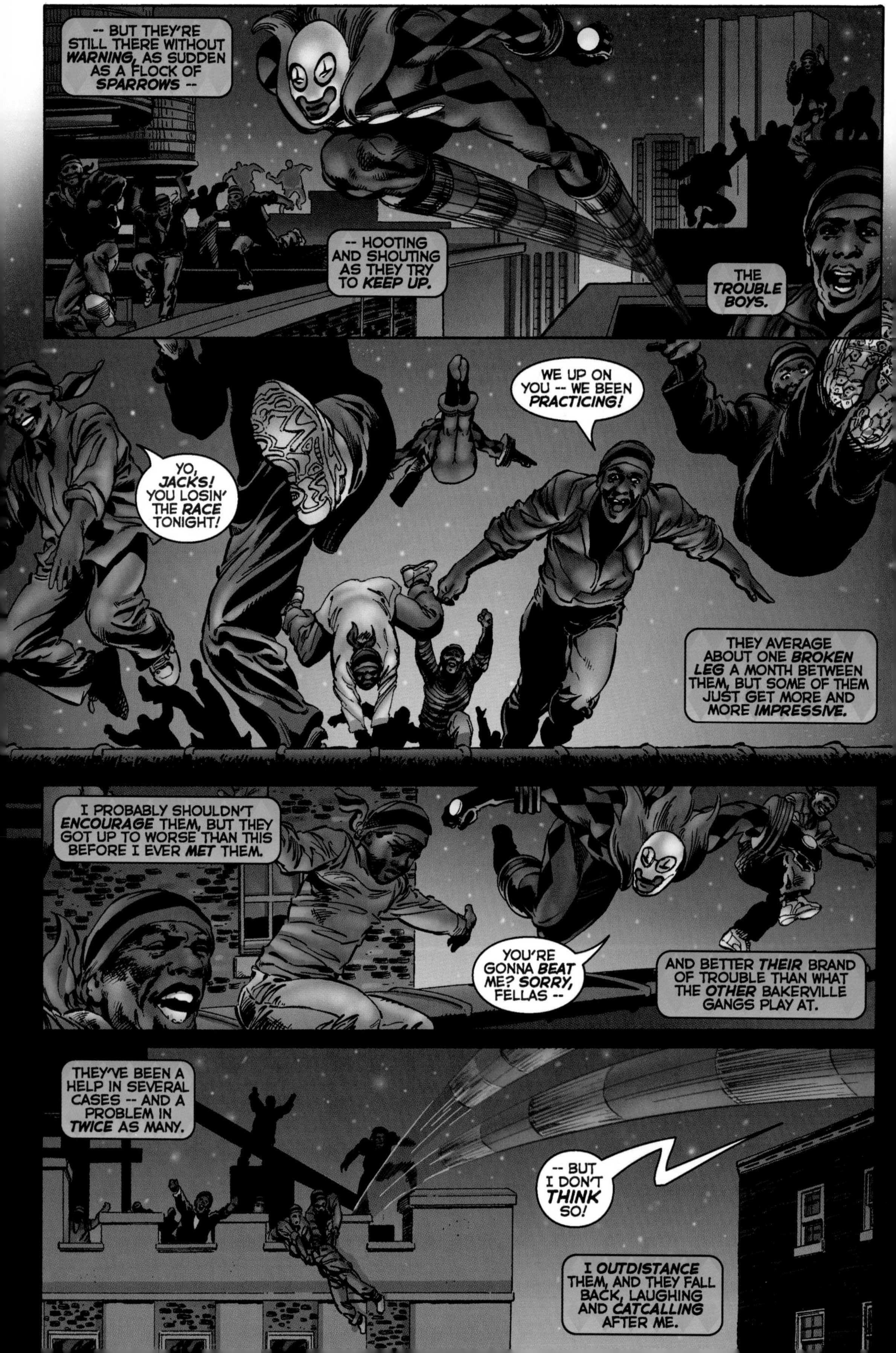
-- BUT THEY'RE STILL THERE WITHOUT WARNING, AS SUDDEN AS A FLOCK OF SPARROWS --
-- HOOTING AND SHOUTING AS THEY TRY TO KEEP UP.
THE TROUBLE BOYS.
YO, JACKS! YOU LOSIN' THE RACE TONIGHT!
WE UP ON YOU -- WE BEEN PRACTICING!
THEY AVERAGE ABOUT ONE BROKEN LEG A MONTH BETWEEN THEM, BUT SOME OF THEM JUST GET MORE AND MORE IMPRESSIVE.
I PROBABLY SHOULDN'T ENCOURAGE THEM, BUT THEY GOT UP TO WORSE THAN THIS BEFORE I EVER MET THEM.
YOU'RE GONNA BEAT ME? SORRY, FELLAS --
AND BETTER THEIR BRAND OF TROUBLE THAN WHAT THE OTHER BAKERVILLE GANGS PLAY AT.
THEY'VE BEEN A HELP IN SEVERAL CASES -- AND A PROBLEM IN TWICE AS MANY.
-- BUT I DON'T THINK SO!
I OUTDISTANCE THEM, AND THEY FALL BACK, LAUGHING AND CATCALLING AFTER ME.

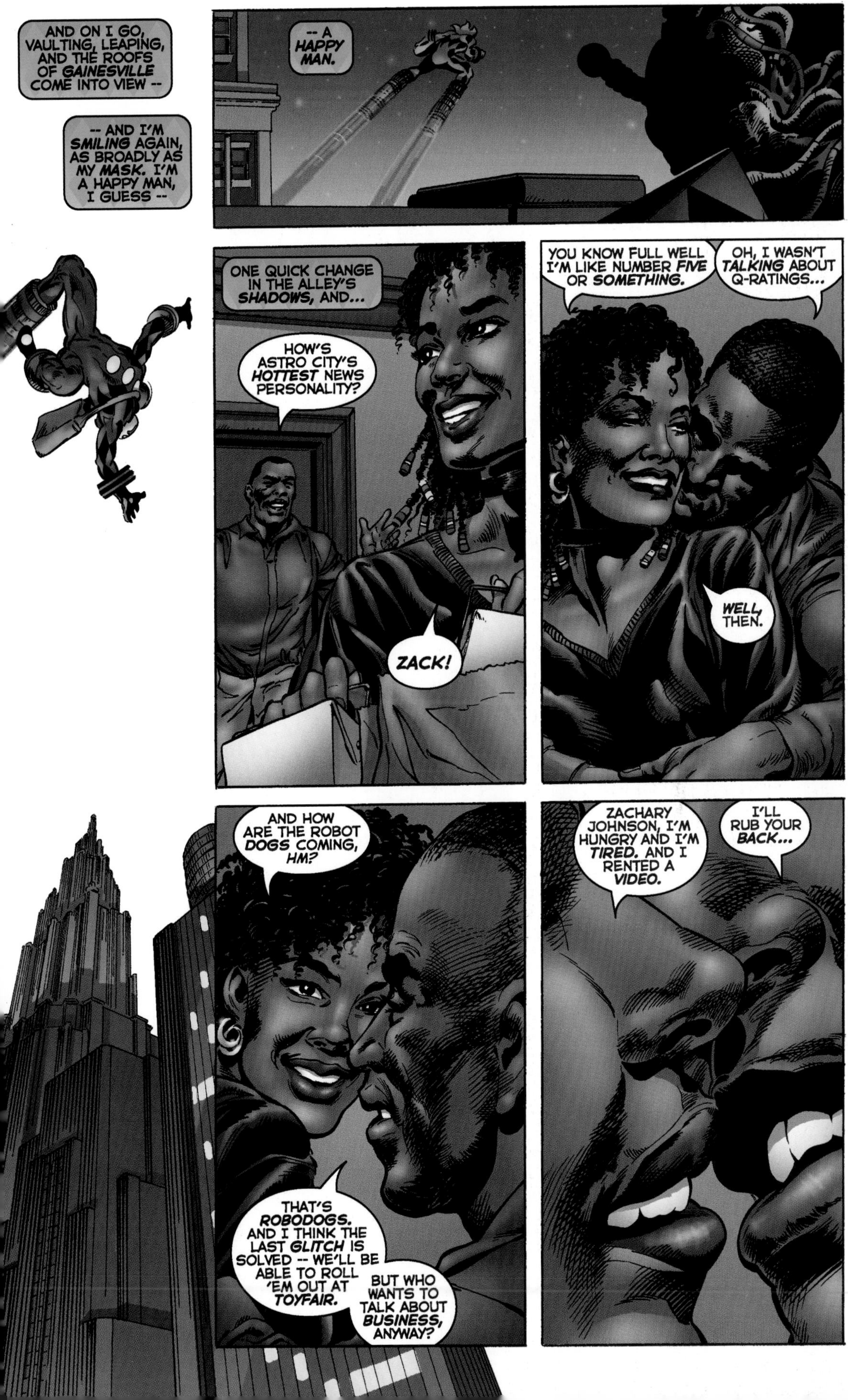
AND ON I GO, VAULTING, LEAPING, AND THE ROOFS OF GAINESVILLE COME INTO VIEW --
-- AND I'M SMILING AGAIN, AS BROADLY AS MY MASK. I'M A HAPPY MAN, I GUESS --
-- A HAPPY MAN.
ONE QUICK CHANGE IN THE ALLEY'S SHADOWS, AND...
HOW'S ASTRO CITY'S HOTTEST NEWS PERSONALITY?
ZACK!
YOU KNOW FULL WELL I'M LIKE NUMBER FIVE OR SOMETHING.
OH, I WASN'T TALKING ABOUT Q-RATINGS...
WELL, THEN.
AND HOW ARE THE ROBOT DOGS COMING, HM?
THAT'S ROBODOGS. AND I THINK THE LAST GLITCH IS SOLVED -- WE'LL BE ABLE TO ROLL 'EM OUT AT TOYFAIR.
BUT WHO WANTS TO TALK ABOUT BUSINESS, ANYWAY?
ZACHARY JOHNSON, I'M HUNGRY AND I'M TIRED. AND I RENTED A VIDEO.
I'LL RUB YOUR BACK...

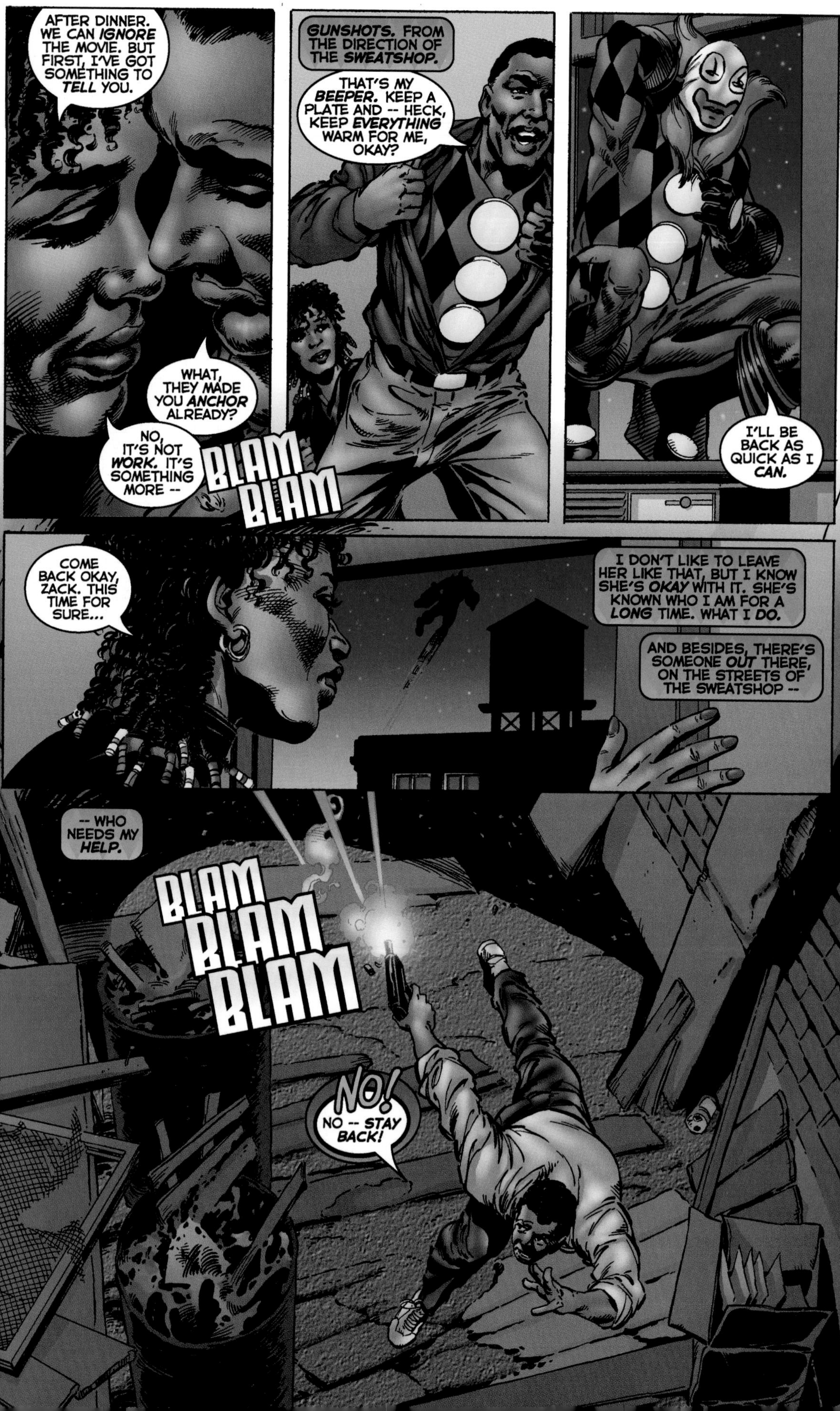
AFTER DINNER. WE CAN IGNORE THE MOVIE. BUT FIRST, I'VE GOT SOMETHING TO TELL YOU.
WHAT, THEY MADE YOU ANCHOR ALREADY?
NO, IT'S NOT WORK. IT'S SOMETHING MORE --
BLAM BLAM
GUNSHOTS. FROM THE DIRECTION OF THE SWEATSHOP.
THAT'S MY BEEPER. KEEP A PLATE AND -- HECK, KEEP EVERYTHING WARM FOR ME, OKAY?
I'LL BE BACK AS QUICK AS I CAN.
COME BACK OKAY, ZACK. THIS TIME FOR SURE...
I DON'T LIKE TO LEAVE HER LIKE THAT, BUT I KNOW SHE'S OKAY WITH IT. SHE'S KNOWN WHO I AM FOR A LONG TIME. WHAT I DO.
AND BESIDES, THERE'S SOMEONE OUT THERE, ON THE STREETS OF THE SWEATSHOP --
-- WHO NEEDS MY HELP.
BLAM BLAM BLAM
NO! NO -- STAY BACK!

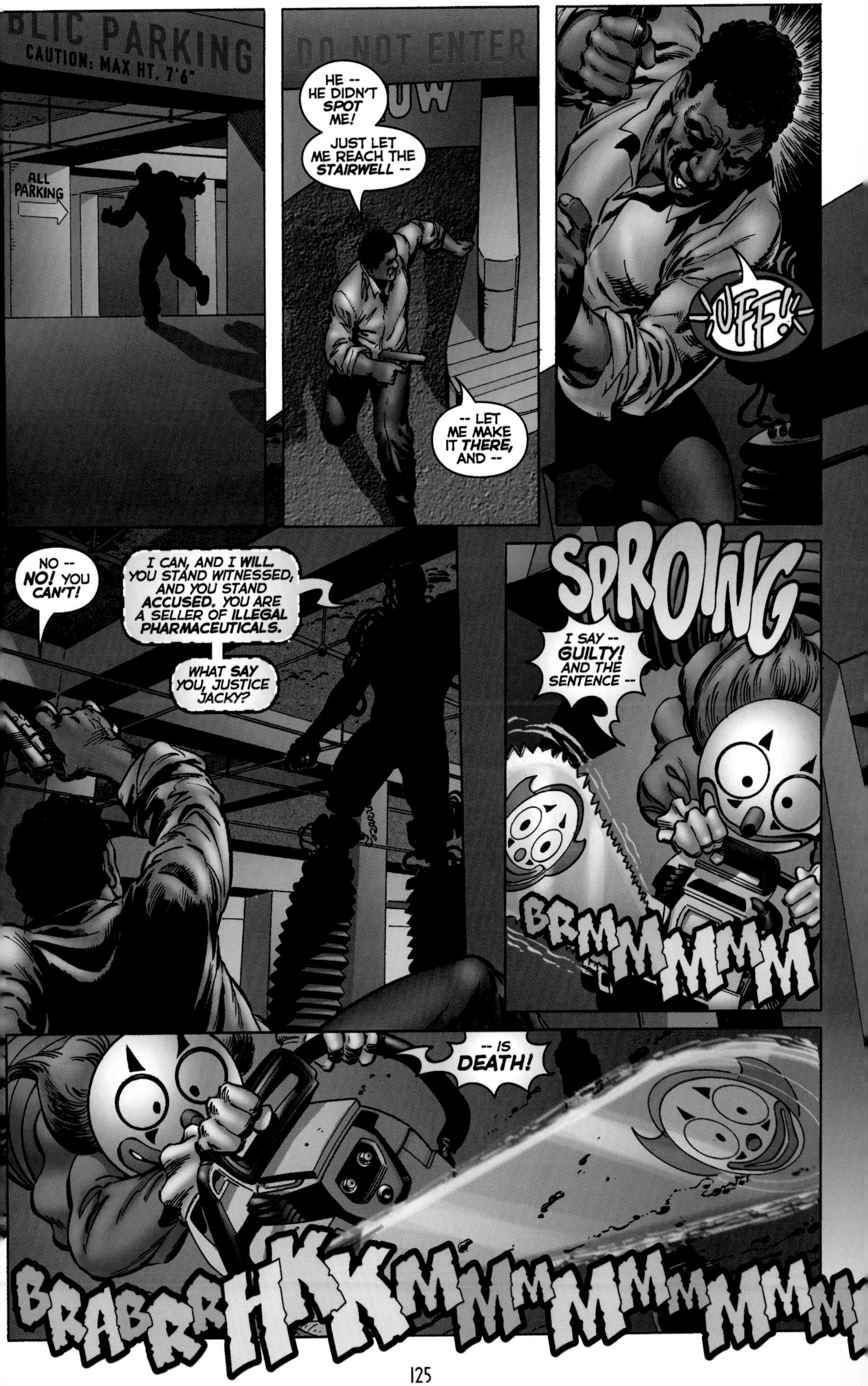
BLIC PARKING
CAUTION: MAX HT. 7'6"
ALL PARKING
DO NOT ENTER
HE -- HE DIDN'T SPOT ME!
JUST LET ME REACH THE STAIRWELL --
-- LET ME MAKE IT THERE, AND --
UFF!!
NO -- NO! YOU CAN'T!
I CAN, AND I WILL. YOU STAND WITNESSED, AND YOU STAND ACCUSED. YOU ARE A SELLER OF ILLEGAL PHARMACEUTICALS.
WHAT SAY YOU, JUSTICE JACKY?
SPROING
I SAY -- GUILTY! AND THE SENTENCE --
BRMMMMMM
-- IS DEATH!
BRABRRHKKMMMMMMMMMM

I GET THERE JUST AS THE MAN *FALLS*, WITH A WET AND FINAL GASP.

YOU -- YOU *KILLED* HIM! YOU VICIOUS --

AH. THE *TRUE* PERPETRATOR ARRIVES FOR HIS ACCUSATION -- THE CRIMINAL WE HAVE TRAVELED THE *DECADES* TO FIND.

TRUE JUSTICE --

GUILTY! *GUILTY!*

HE STEPS INTO THE LIGHT --

-- CAN FINALLY BE DONE!

-- AND MY WORLD TURNS UPSIDE DOWN.

O-OKAY, WHAT *IS* THIS? THE ARM, THE EYE -- *EVERYTHING* -- NO ONE WOULD MISTAKE YOU FOR *ME.*

SO WHO *ARE* YOU?

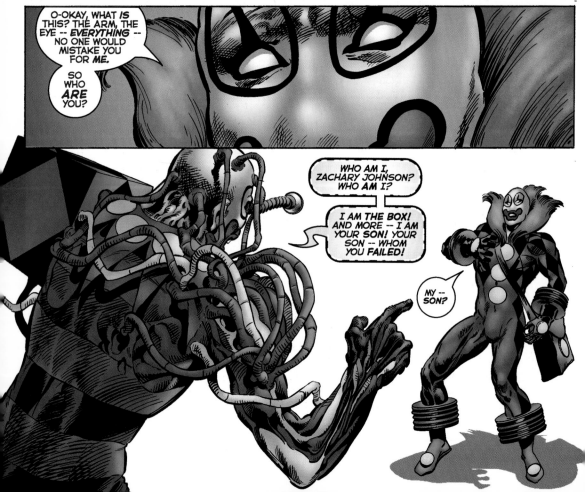

WHO AM I, ZACHARY JOHNSON? WHO AM I?

I AM THE BOX! AND MORE -- I AM YOUR SON! YOUR SON -- WHOM YOU *FAILED!*

MY -- SON?

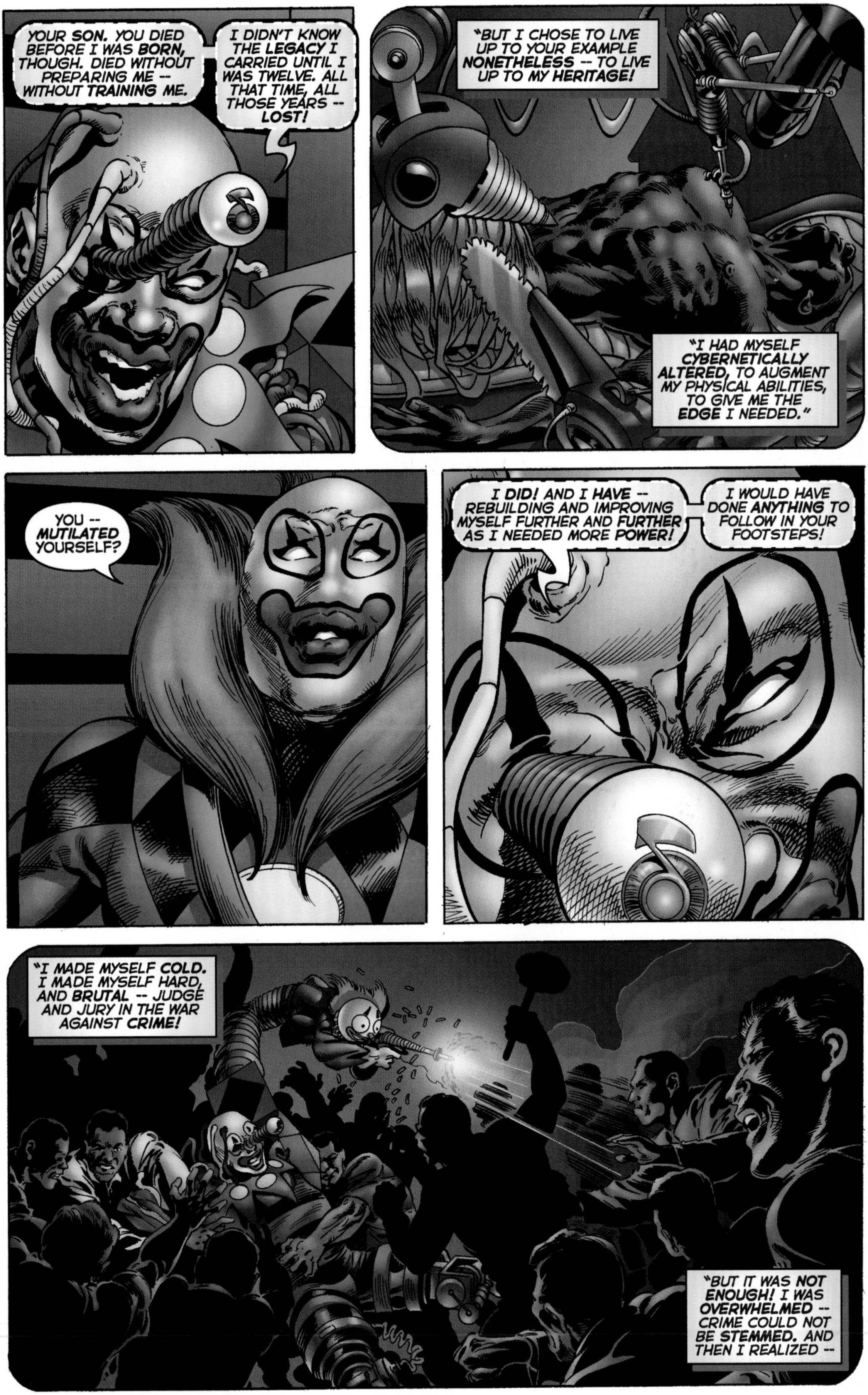
YOUR SON. YOU DIED BEFORE I WAS BORN, THOUGH. DIED WITHOUT PREPARING ME -- WITHOUT TRAINING ME.
I DIDN'T KNOW THE LEGACY I CARRIED UNTIL I WAS TWELVE. ALL THAT TIME, ALL THOSE YEARS -- LOST!
"BUT I CHOSE TO LIVE UP TO YOUR EXAMPLE NONETHELESS -- TO LIVE UP TO MY HERITAGE!
"I HAD MYSELF CYBERNETICALLY ALTERED, TO AUGMENT MY PHYSICAL ABILITIES, TO GIVE ME THE EDGE I NEEDED."
YOU -- MUTILATED YOURSELF?
I DID! AND I HAVE -- REBUILDING AND IMPROVING MYSELF FURTHER AND FURTHER AS I NEEDED MORE POWER!
I WOULD HAVE DONE ANYTHING TO FOLLOW IN YOUR FOOTSTEPS!
"I MADE MYSELF COLD. I MADE MYSELF HARD, AND BRUTAL -- JUDGE AND JURY IN THE WAR AGAINST CRIME!
"BUT IT WAS NOT ENOUGH! I WAS OVERWHELMED -- CRIME COULD NOT BE STEMMED. AND THEN I REALIZED --

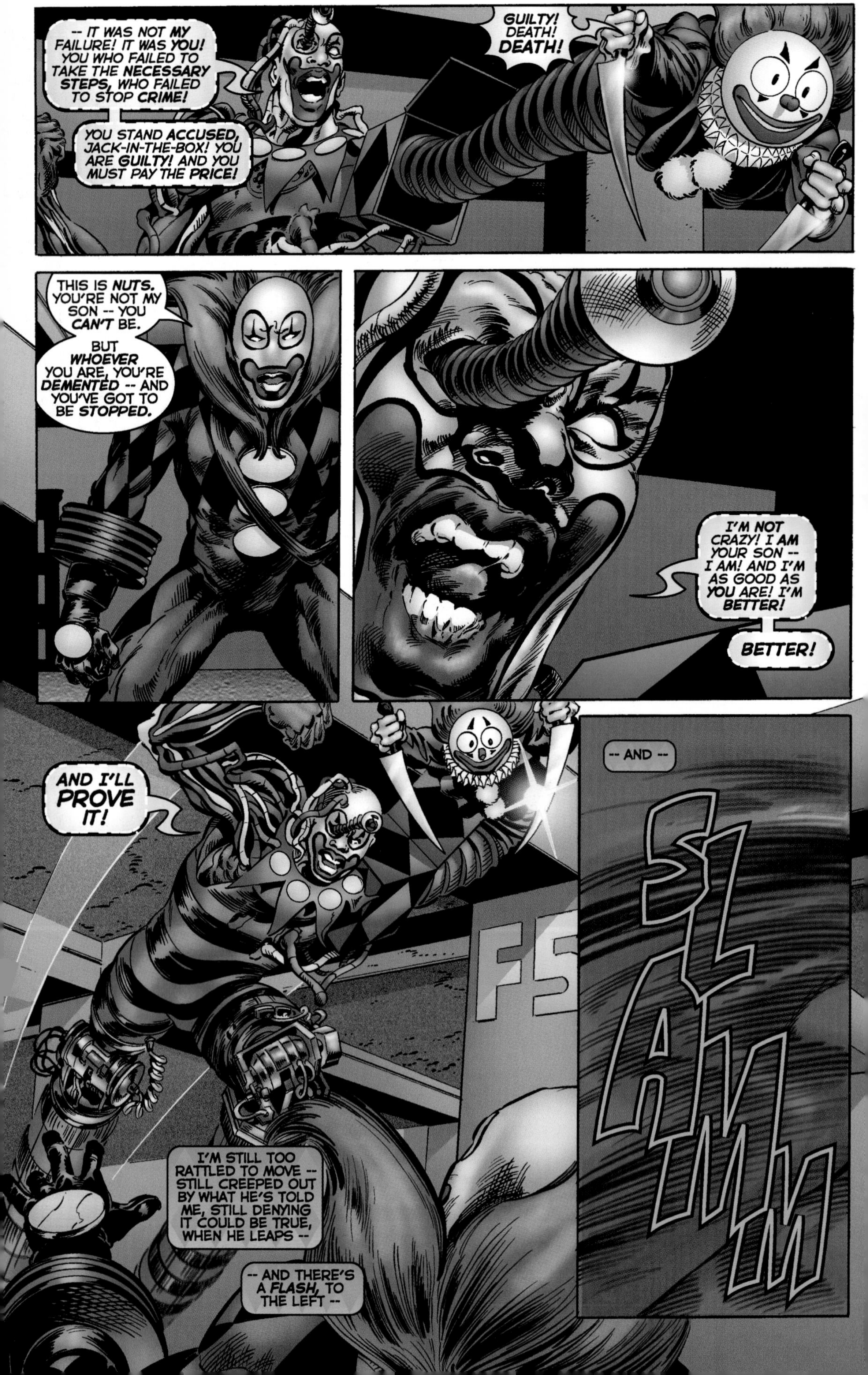
-- IT WAS NOT MY FAILURE! IT WAS YOU! YOU WHO FAILED TO TAKE THE NECESSARY STEPS, WHO FAILED TO STOP CRIME!
YOU STAND ACCUSED, JACK-IN-THE-BOX! YOU ARE GUILTY! AND YOU MUST PAY THE PRICE!
GUILTY! DEATH! DEATH!
THIS IS NUTS. YOU'RE NOT MY SON -- YOU CAN'T BE.
BUT WHOEVER YOU ARE, YOU'RE DEMENTED -- AND YOU'VE GOT TO BE STOPPED.
I'M NOT CRAZY! I AM YOUR SON -- I AM! AND I'M AS GOOD AS YOU ARE! I'M BETTER!
BETTER!
AND I'LL PROVE IT!
F5
I'M STILL TOO RATTLED TO MOVE -- STILL CREEPED OUT BY WHAT HE'S TOLD ME, STILL DENYING IT COULD BE TRUE, WHEN HE LEAPS --
-- AND THERE'S A FLASH, TO THE LEFT --
-- AND --
SLAMM

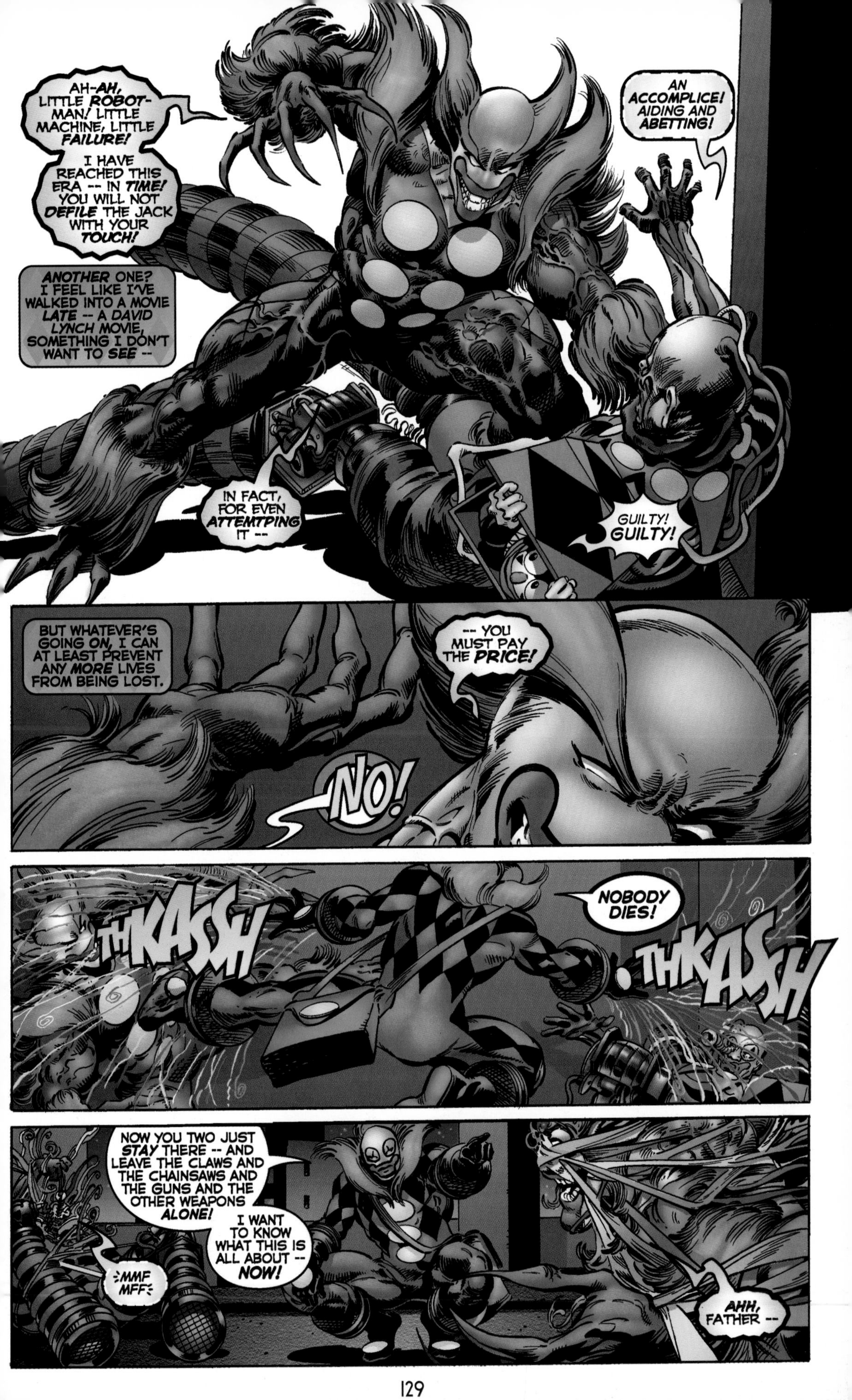
AH-AH, LITTLE ROBOT-MAN! LITTLE MACHINE, LITTLE FAILURE!
I HAVE REACHED THIS ERA -- IN TIME! YOU WILL NOT DEFILE THE JACK WITH YOUR TOUCH!
AN ACCOMPLICE! AIDING AND ABETTING!
ANOTHER ONE? I FEEL LIKE I'VE WALKED INTO A MOVIE LATE -- A DAVID LYNCH MOVIE, SOMETHING I DON'T WANT TO SEE --
IN FACT, FOR EVEN ATTEMTPING IT --
GUILTY! GUILTY!
BUT WHATEVER'S GOING ON, I CAN AT LEAST PREVENT ANY MORE LIVES FROM BEING LOST.
-- YOU MUST PAY THE PRICE!
NO!
THKASSH
NOBODY DIES!
THKASH
NOW YOU TWO JUST STAY THERE -- AND LEAVE THE CLAWS AND THE CHAINSAWS AND THE GUNS AND THE OTHER WEAPONS ALONE!
I WANT TO KNOW WHAT THIS IS ALL ABOUT -- NOW!
MMF MFF
AHH, FATHER --

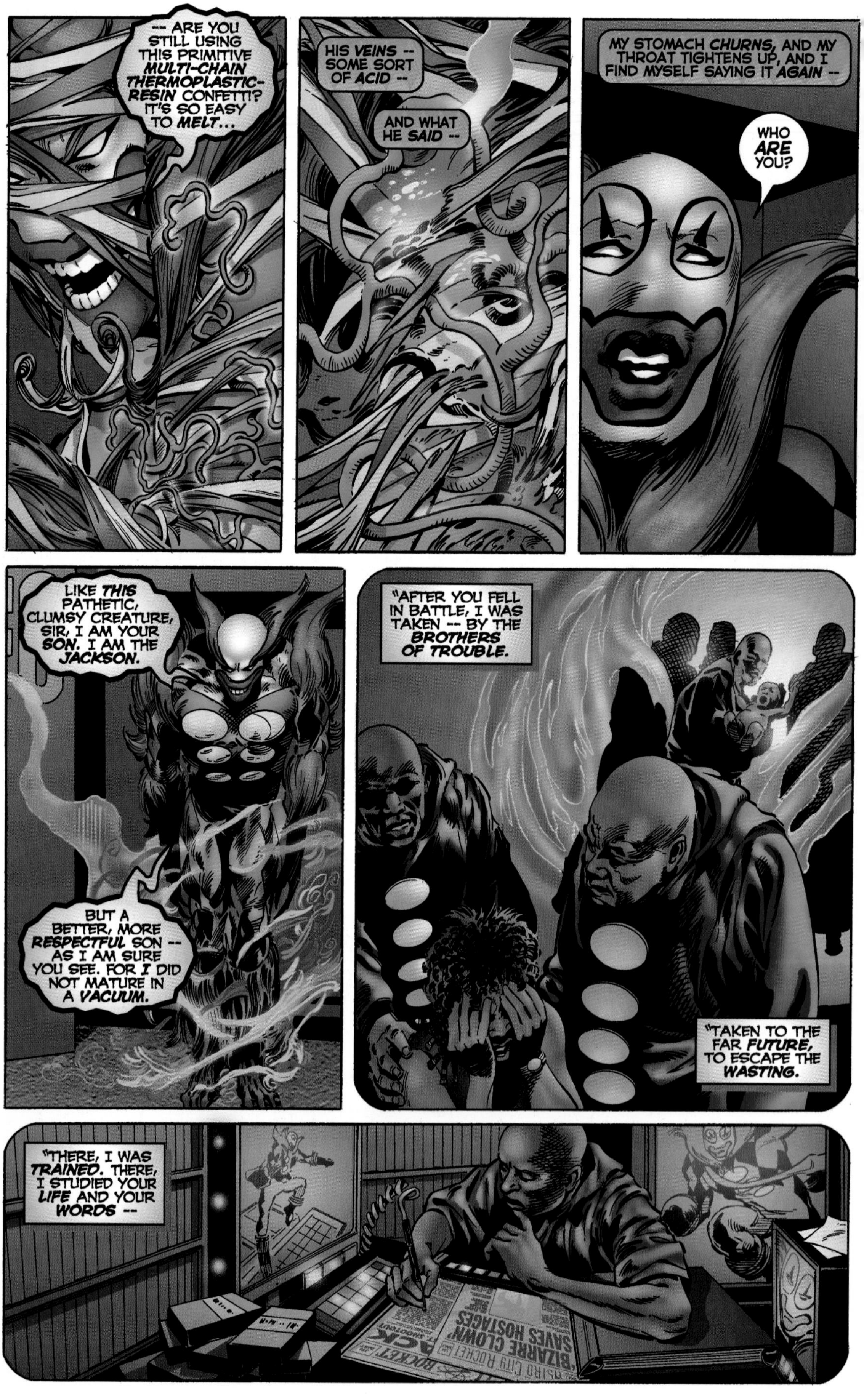

-- ARE YOU STILL USING THIS PRIMITIVE MULTI-CHAIN THERMOPLASTIC-RESIN CONFETTI!? IT'S SO EASY TO MELT...
HIS VEINS -- SOME SORT OF ACID --
AND WHAT HE SAID --
MY STOMACH CHURNS, AND MY THROAT TIGHTENS UP, AND I FIND MYSELF SAYING IT AGAIN --
WHO ARE YOU?
LIKE THIS PATHETIC, CLUMSY CREATURE, SIR, I AM YOUR SON. I AM THE JACKSON.
BUT A BETTER, MORE RESPECTFUL SON -- AS I AM SURE YOU SEE. FOR I DID NOT MATURE IN A VACUUM.
"AFTER YOU FELL IN BATTLE, I WAS TAKEN -- BY THE BROTHERS OF TROUBLE.
"TAKEN TO THE FAR FUTURE, TO ESCAPE THE WASTING.
"THERE, I WAS TRAINED. THERE, I STUDIED YOUR LIFE AND YOUR WORDS --
BIZARRE CLOWN SAVES HOSTAGES

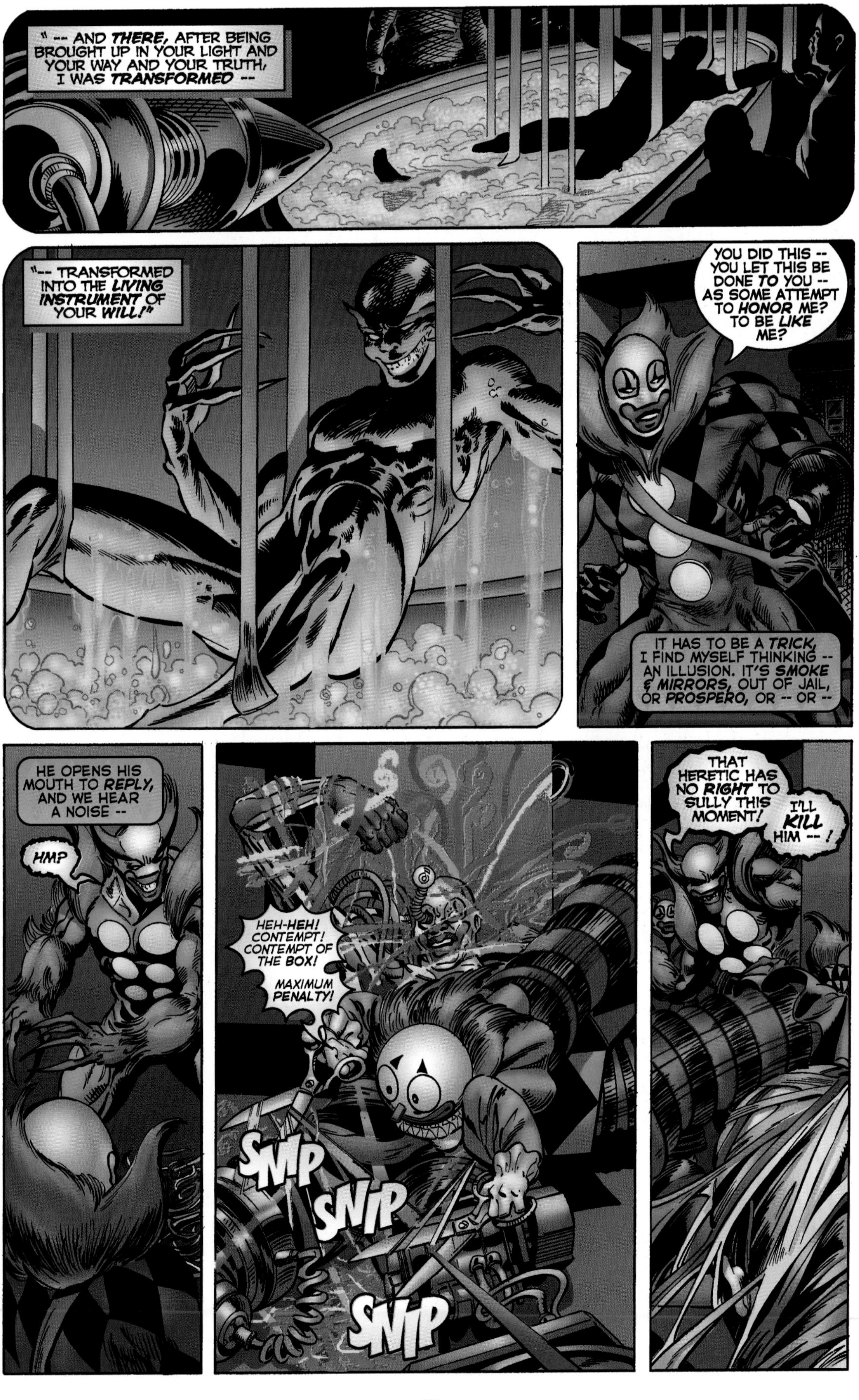

" -- AND THERE, AFTER BEING BROUGHT UP IN YOUR LIGHT AND YOUR WAY AND YOUR TRUTH, I WAS TRANSFORMED --
"-- TRANSFORMED INTO THE LIVING INSTRUMENT OF YOUR WILL!"
YOU DID THIS -- YOU LET THIS BE DONE TO YOU -- AS SOME ATTEMPT TO HONOR ME? TO BE LIKE ME?
IT HAS TO BE A TRICK, I FIND MYSELF THINKING -- AN ILLUSION. IT'S SMOKE & MIRRORS, OUT OF JAIL, OR PROSPERO, OR -- OR --
HE OPENS HIS MOUTH TO REPLY, AND WE HEAR A NOISE --
HM?
HEH-HEH! CONTEMPT! CONTEMPT OF THE BOX!
MAXIMUM PENALTY!
SNIP
SNIP
SNIP
THAT HERETIC HAS NO RIGHT TO SULLY THIS MOMENT!
I'LL KILL HIM -- !

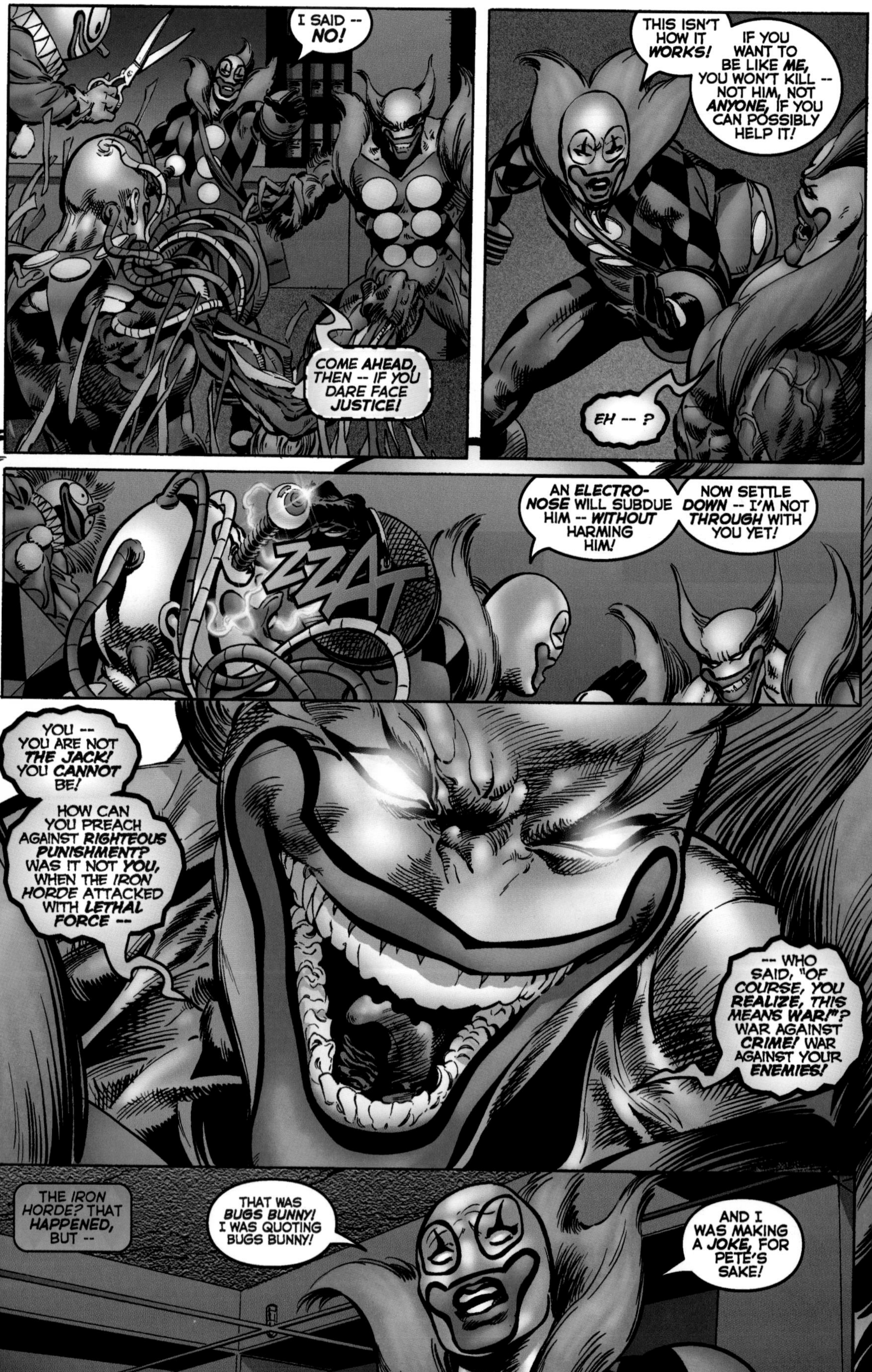
I SAID -- NO!
COME AHEAD, THEN -- IF YOU DARE FACE JUSTICE!
THIS ISN'T HOW IT WORKS!
IF YOU WANT TO BE LIKE ME, YOU WON'T KILL -- NOT HIM, NOT ANYONE, IF YOU CAN POSSIBLY HELP IT!
EH -- ?
AN ELECTRO-NOSE WILL SUBDUE HIM -- WITHOUT HARMING HIM!
NOW SETTLE DOWN -- I'M NOT THROUGH WITH YOU YET!
ZZAT
YOU -- YOU ARE NOT THE JACK! YOU CANNOT BE!
HOW CAN YOU PREACH AGAINST RIGHTEOUS PUNISHMENT? WAS IT NOT YOU, WHEN THE IRON HORDE ATTACKED WITH LETHAL FORCE --
-- WHO SAID, "OF COURSE, YOU REALIZE, THIS MEANS WAR!"? WAR AGAINST CRIME! WAR AGAINST YOUR ENEMIES!
THE IRON HORDE? THAT HAPPENED, BUT --
THAT WAS BUGS BUNNY! I WAS QUOTING BUGS BUNNY!
AND I WAS MAKING A JOKE, FOR PETE'S SAKE!

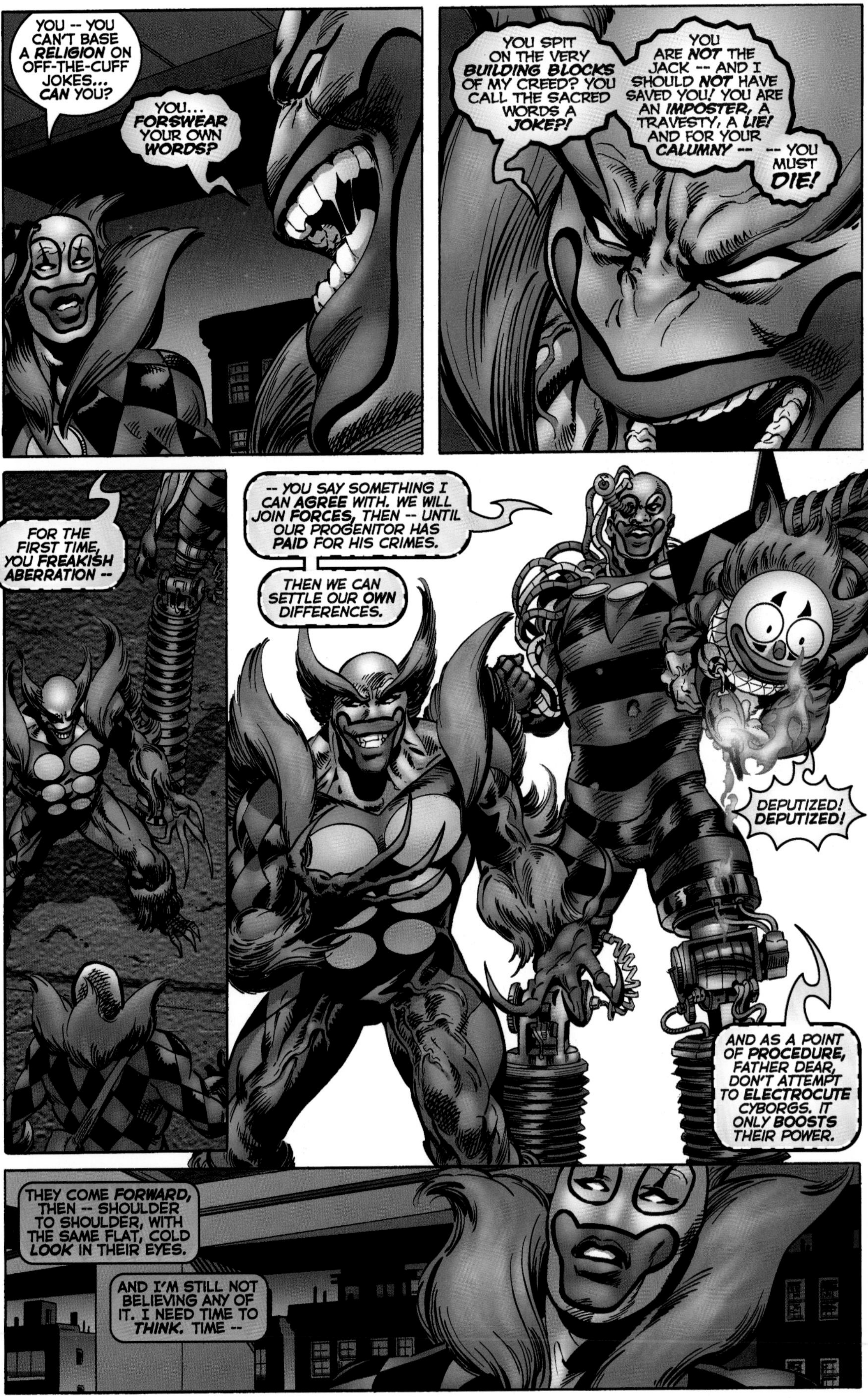
YOU -- YOU CAN'T BASE A RELIGION ON OFF-THE-CUFF JOKES... CAN YOU?
YOU... FORSWEAR YOUR OWN WORDS?
YOU SPIT ON THE VERY BUILDING BLOCKS OF MY CREED? YOU CALL THE SACRED WORDS A JOKE?!
YOU ARE NOT THE JACK -- AND I SHOULD NOT HAVE SAVED YOU! YOU ARE AN IMPOSTER, A TRAVESTY, A LIE! AND FOR YOUR CALUMNY --
-- YOU MUST DIE!
FOR THE FIRST TIME, YOU FREAKISH ABERRATION --
-- YOU SAY SOMETHING I CAN AGREE WITH. WE WILL JOIN FORCES, THEN -- UNTIL OUR PROGENITOR HAS PAID FOR HIS CRIMES.
THEN WE CAN SETTLE OUR OWN DIFFERENCES.
DEPUTIZED! DEPUTIZED!
AND AS A POINT OF PROCEDURE, FATHER DEAR, DON'T ATTEMPT TO ELECTROCUTE CYBORGS. IT ONLY BOOSTS THEIR POWER.
THEY COME FORWARD, THEN -- SHOULDER TO SHOULDER, WITH THE SAME FLAT, COLD LOOK IN THEIR EYES.
AND I'M STILL NOT BELIEVING ANY OF IT. I NEED TIME TO THINK. TIME --

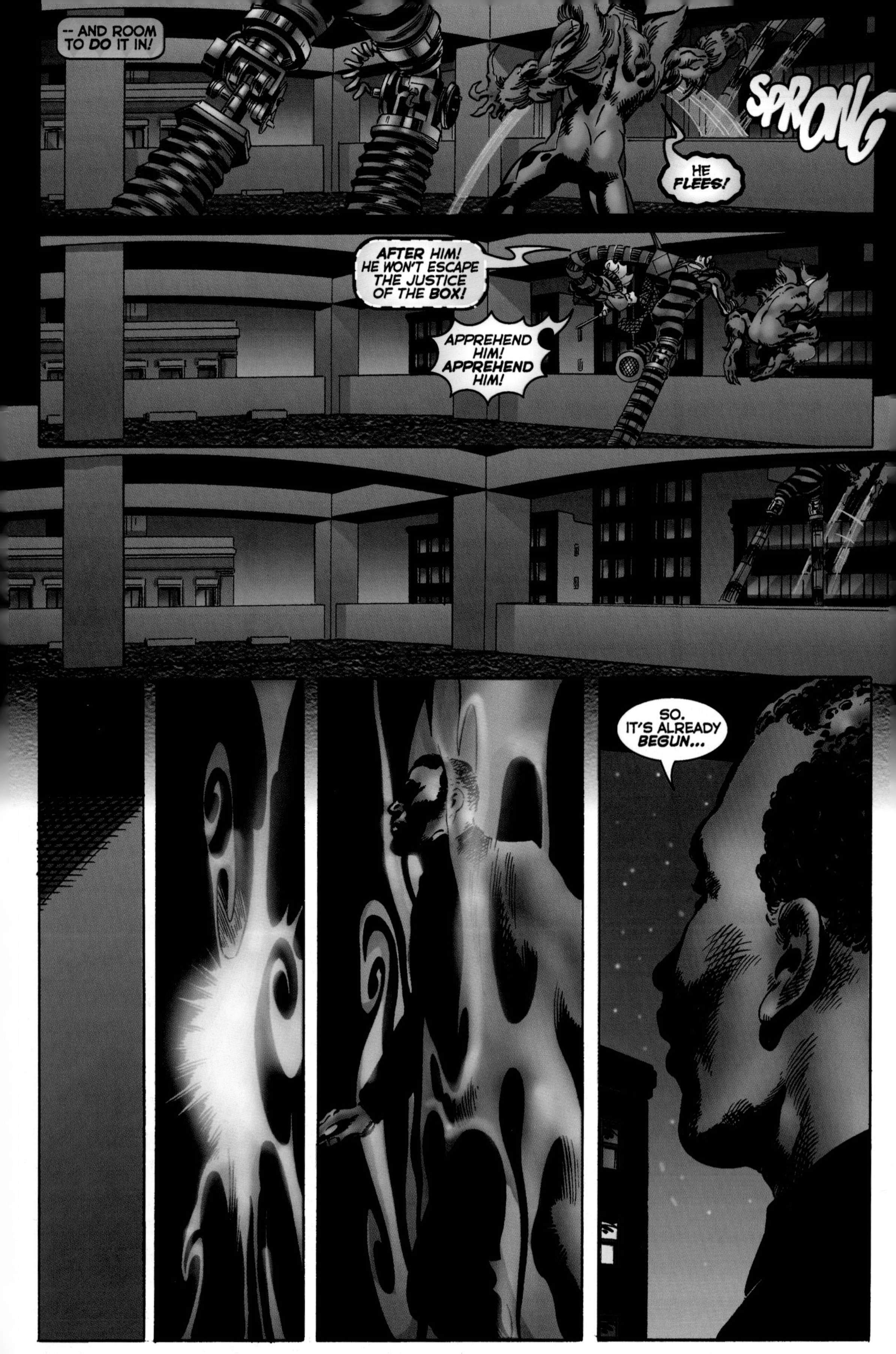
-- AND ROOM TO DO IT IN!
SPRONG
HE FLEES!
AFTER HIM! HE WON'T ESCAPE THE JUSTICE OF THE BOX!
APPREHEND HIM! APPREHEND HIM!
SO. IT'S ALREADY BEGUN...

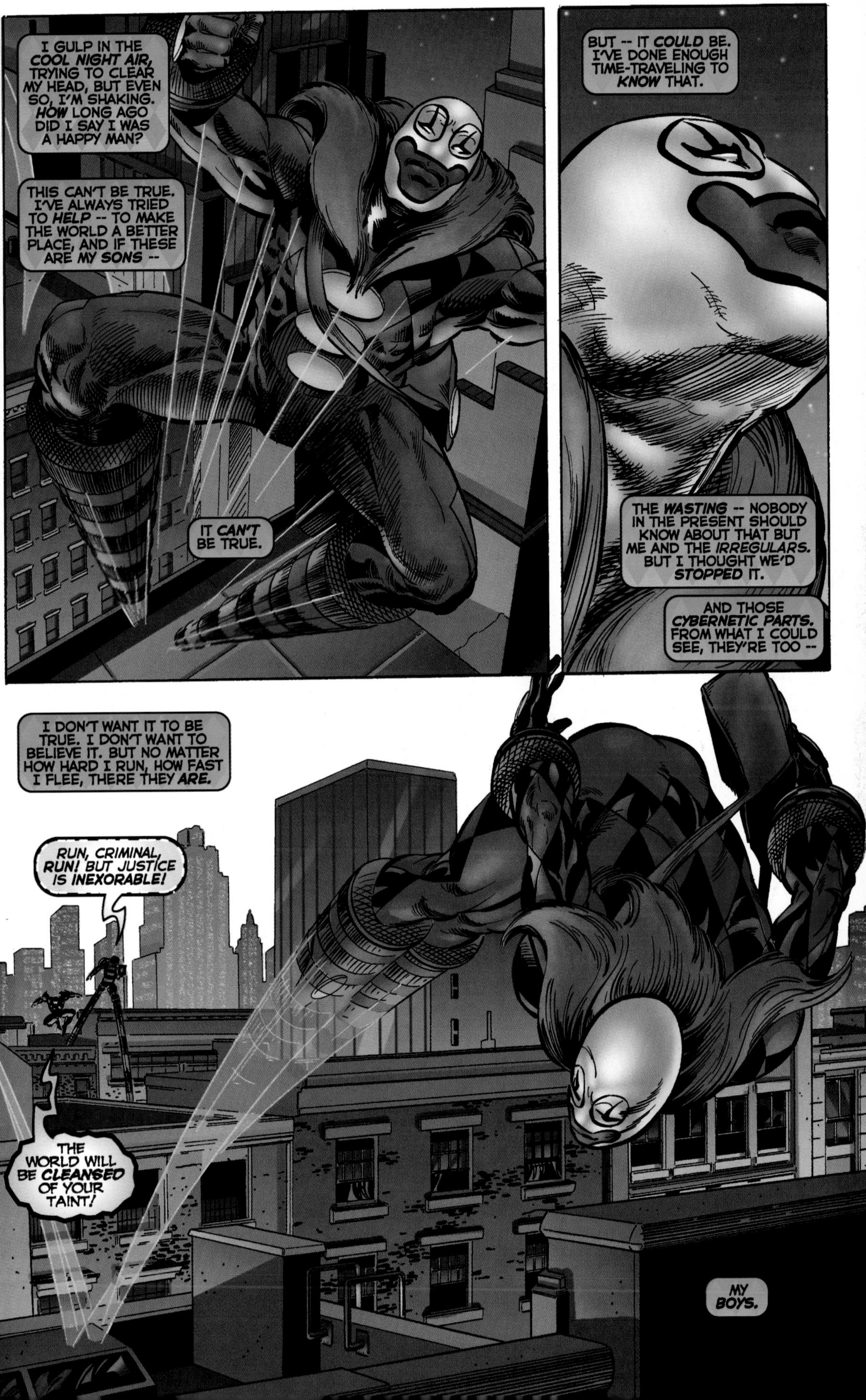
I GULP IN THE COOL NIGHT AIR, TRYING TO CLEAR MY HEAD, BUT EVEN SO, I'M SHAKING. HOW LONG AGO DID I SAY I WAS A HAPPY MAN?
THIS CAN'T BE TRUE. I'VE ALWAYS TRIED TO HELP -- TO MAKE THE WORLD A BETTER PLACE, AND IF THESE ARE MY SONS --
IT CAN'T BE TRUE.
BUT -- IT COULD BE. I'VE DONE ENOUGH TIME-TRAVELING TO KNOW THAT.
THE WASTING -- NOBODY IN THE PRESENT SHOULD KNOW ABOUT THAT BUT ME AND THE IRREGULARS. BUT I THOUGHT WE'D STOPPED IT.
AND THOSE CYBERNETIC PARTS. FROM WHAT I COULD SEE, THEY'RE TOO --
I DON'T WANT IT TO BE TRUE. I DON'T WANT TO BELIEVE IT. BUT NO MATTER HOW HARD I RUN, HOW FAST I FLEE, THERE THEY ARE.
RUN, CRIMINAL, RUN! BUT JUSTICE IS INEXORABLE!
THE WORLD WILL BE CLEANSED OF YOUR TAINT!
MY BOYS.

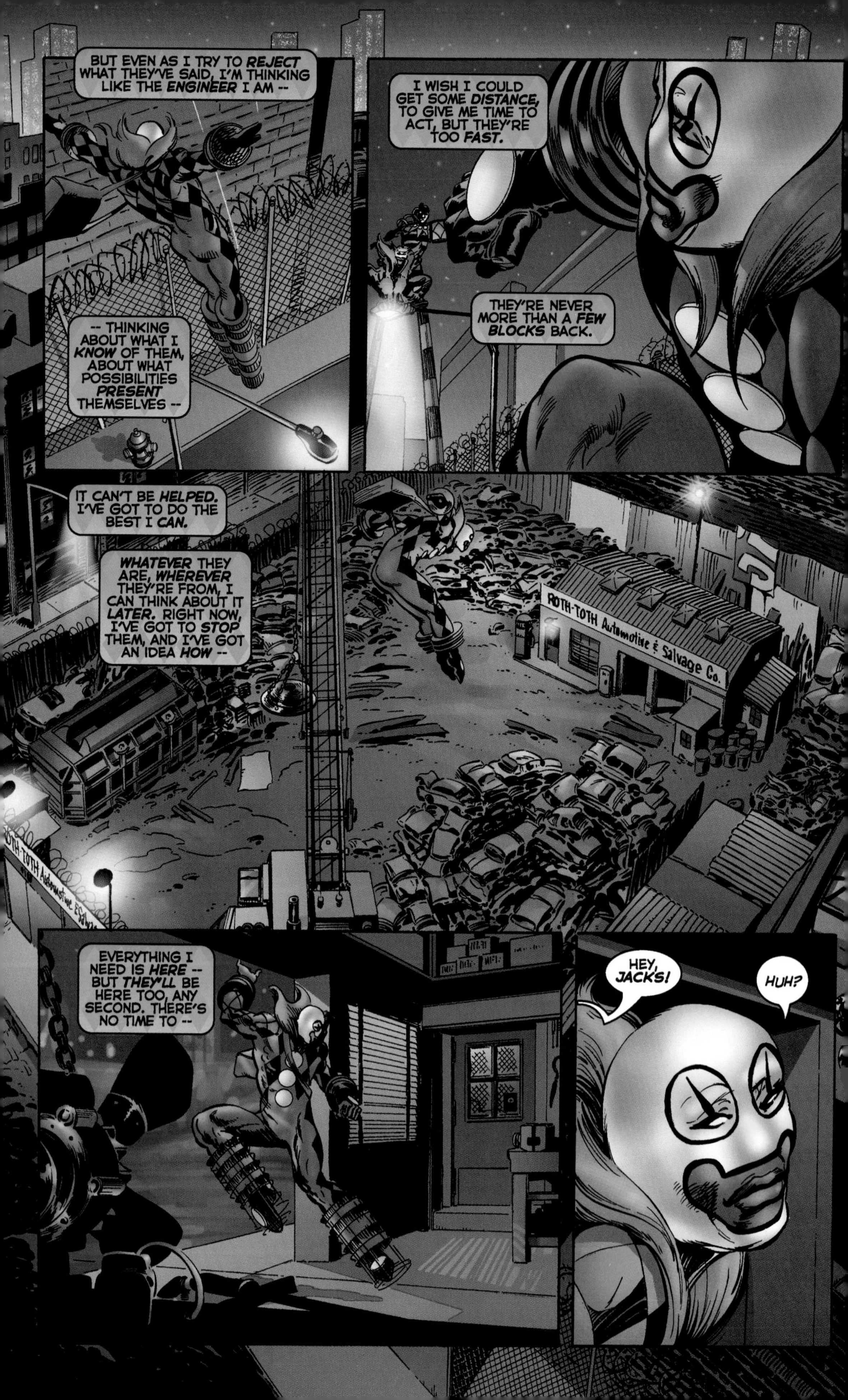
BUT EVEN AS I TRY TO REJECT WHAT THEY'VE SAID, I'M THINKING LIKE THE ENGINEER I AM --
-- THINKING ABOUT WHAT I KNOW OF THEM, ABOUT WHAT POSSIBILITIES PRESENT THEMSELVES --
I WISH I COULD GET SOME DISTANCE, TO GIVE ME TIME TO ACT, BUT THEY'RE TOO FAST.
THEY'RE NEVER MORE THAN A FEW BLOCKS BACK.
IT CAN'T BE HELPED. I'VE GOT TO DO THE BEST I CAN.
WHATEVER THEY ARE, WHEREVER THEY'RE FROM, I CAN THINK ABOUT IT LATER. RIGHT NOW, I'VE GOT TO STOP THEM, AND I'VE GOT AN IDEA HOW --
ROTH-TOTH Automotive & Salvage Co.
EVERYTHING I NEED IS HERE -- BUT THEY'LL BE HERE TOO, ANY SECOND. THERE'S NO TIME TO --
HEY, JACKS!
HUH?

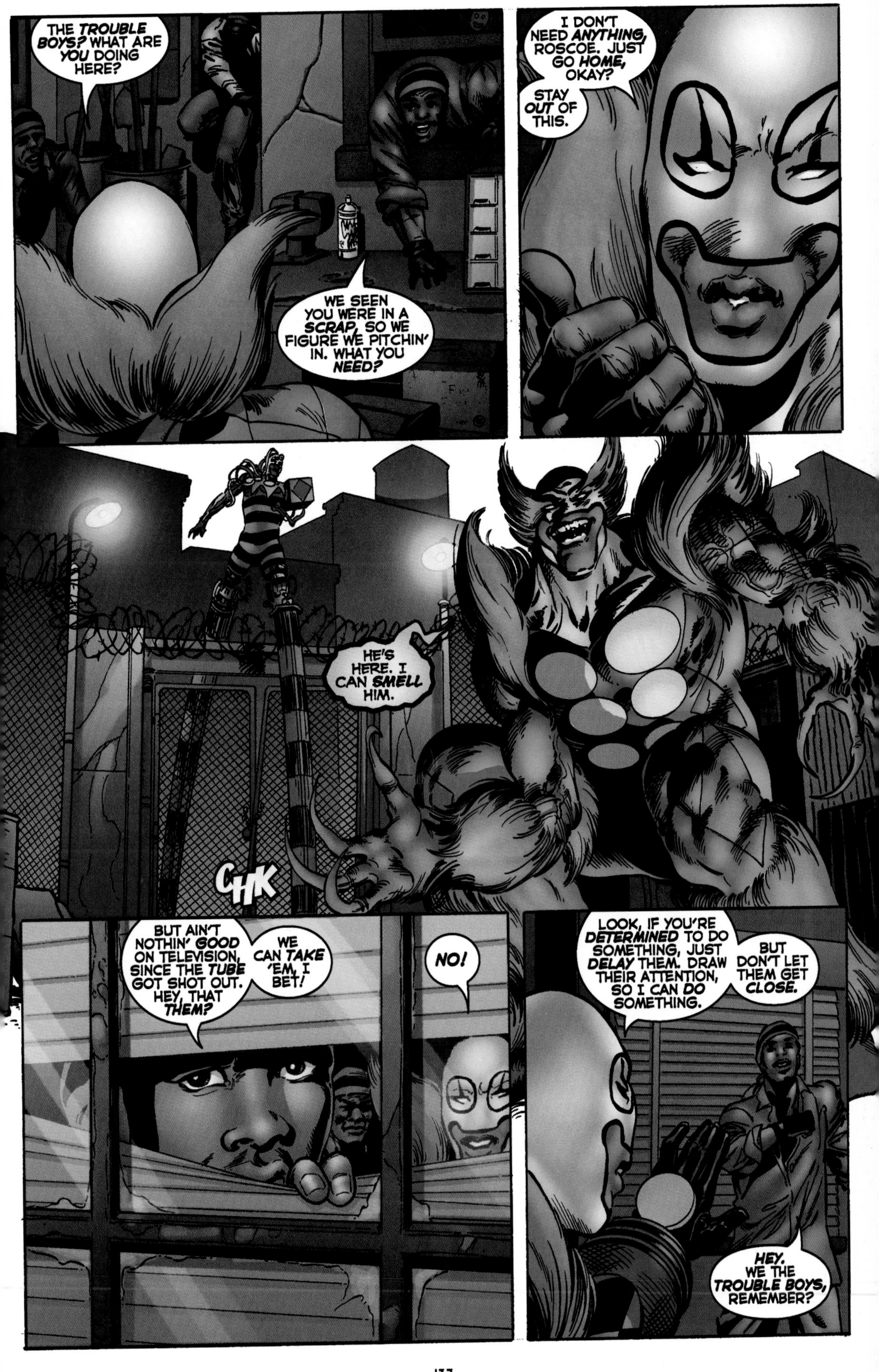

THE TROUBLE BOYS? WHAT ARE YOU DOING HERE?
WE SEEN YOU WERE IN A SCRAP, SO WE FIGURE WE PITCHIN' IN. WHAT YOU NEED?
I DON'T NEED ANYTHING, ROSCOE. JUST GO HOME, OKAY?
STAY OUT OF THIS.
HE'S HERE. I CAN SMELL HIM.
CHK
BUT AIN'T NOTHIN' GOOD ON TELEVISION, SINCE THE TUBE GOT SHOT OUT. HEY, THAT THEM?
WE CAN TAKE 'EM, I BET!
NO!
LOOK, IF YOU'RE DETERMINED TO DO SOMETHING, JUST DELAY THEM. DRAW THEIR ATTENTION, SO I CAN DO SOMETHING.
BUT DON'T LET THEM GET CLOSE.
HEY. WE THE TROUBLE BOYS, REMEMBER?

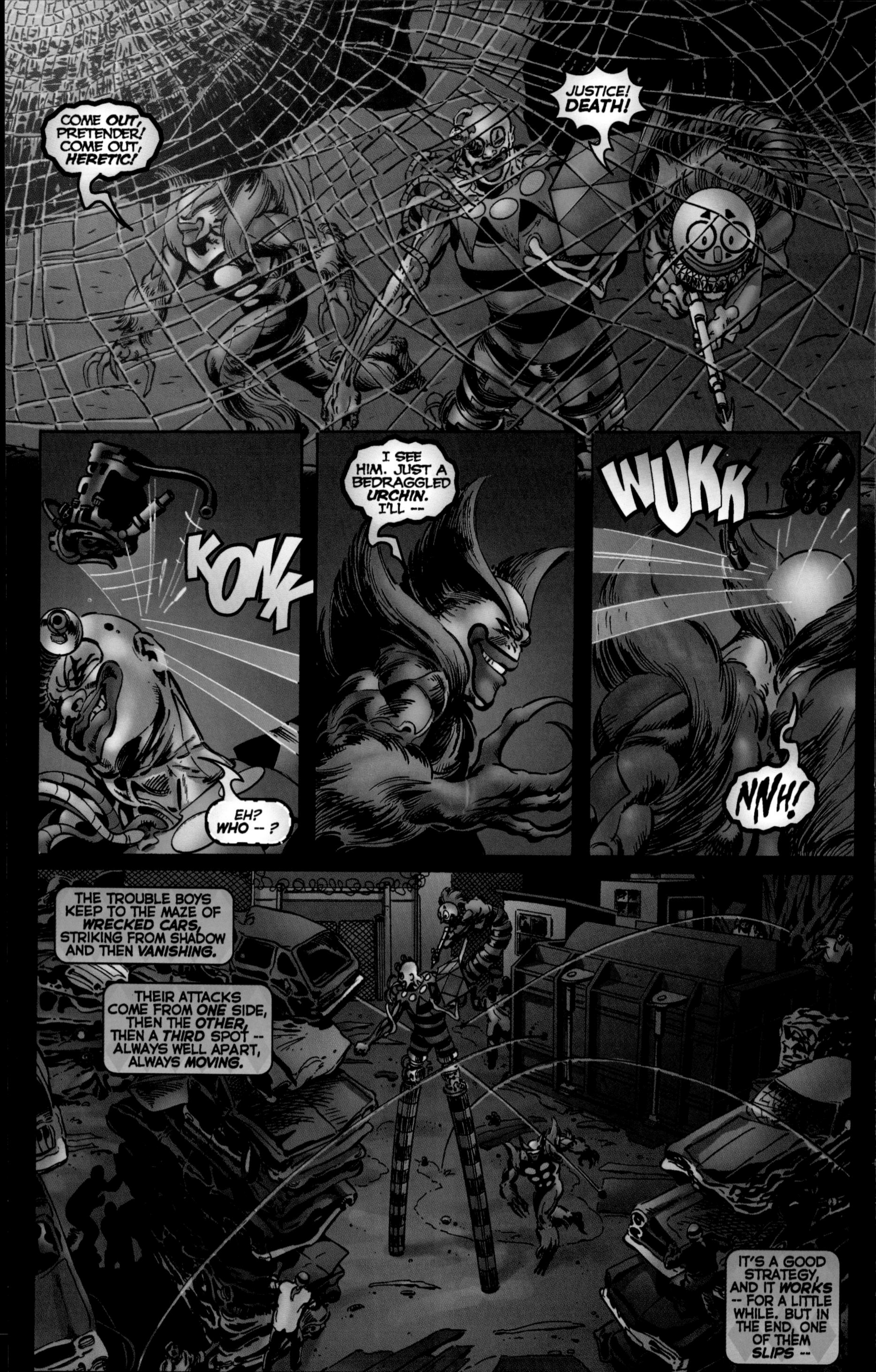
COME OUT, PRETENDER! COME OUT, HERETIC!
JUSTICE! DEATH!
KONK
EH? WHO -- ?
I SEE HIM. JUST A BEDRAGGLED URCHIN. I'LL --
WUKK
NNH!
THE TROUBLE BOYS KEEP TO THE MAZE OF WRECKED CARS, STRIKING FROM SHADOW AND THEN VANISHING.
THEIR ATTACKS COME FROM ONE SIDE, THEN THE OTHER, THEN A THIRD SPOT -- ALWAYS WELL APART, ALWAYS MOVING.
IT'S A GOOD STRATEGY, AND IT WORKS -- FOR A LITTLE WHILE. BUT IN THE END, ONE OF THEM SLIPS --

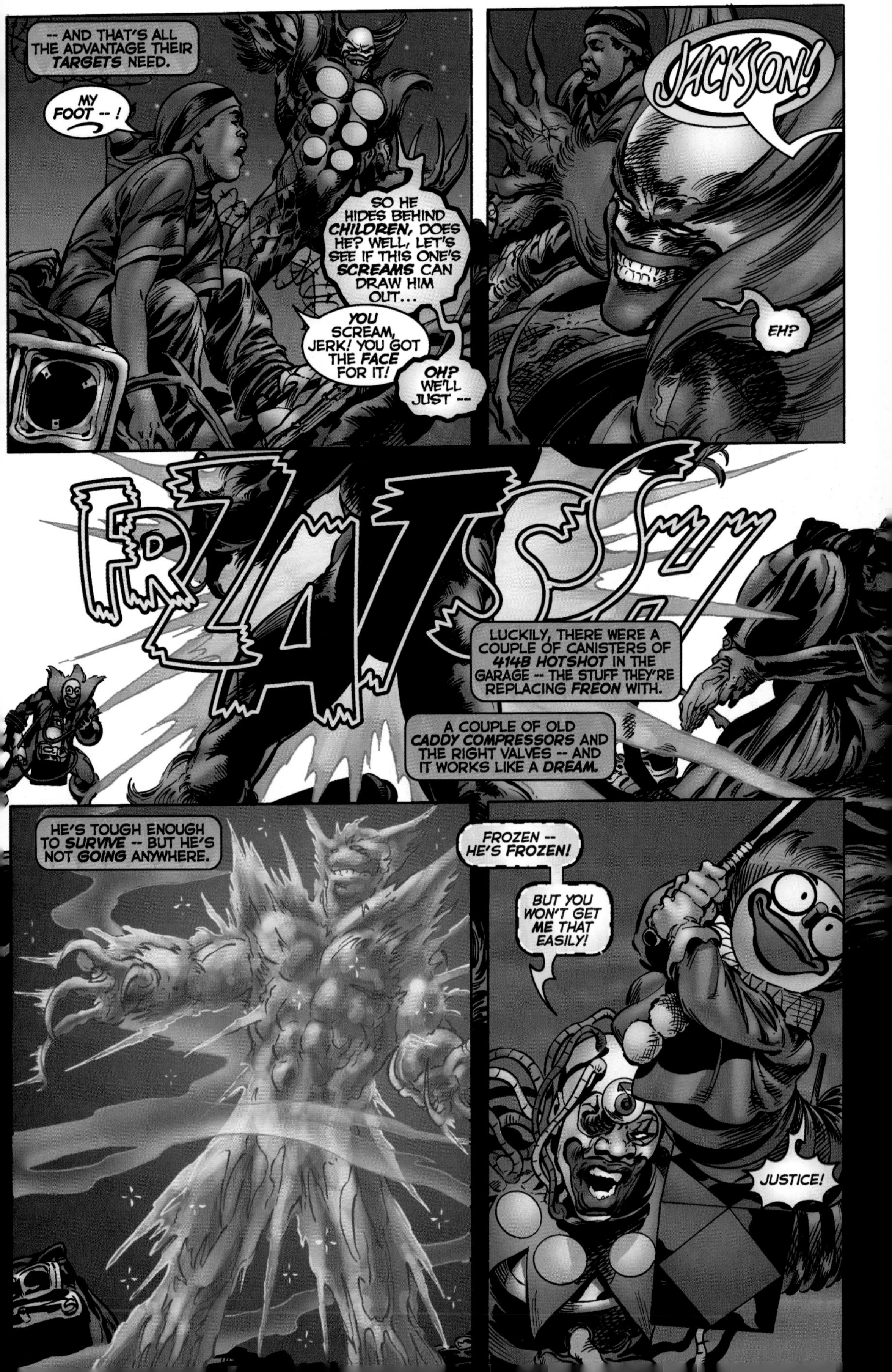
-- AND THAT'S ALL THE ADVANTAGE THEIR TARGETS NEED.
MY FOOT -- !
SO HE HIDES BEHIND CHILDREN, DOES HE? WELL, LET'S SEE IF THIS ONE'S SCREAMS CAN DRAW HIM OUT...
YOU SCREAM, JERK! YOU GOT THE FACE FOR IT!
OH? WE'LL JUST --
JACKSON!
EH?
FRZATSSH
LUCKILY, THERE WERE A COUPLE OF CANISTERS OF 414B HOTSHOT IN THE GARAGE -- THE STUFF THEY'RE REPLACING FREON WITH.
A COUPLE OF OLD CADDY COMPRESSORS AND THE RIGHT VALVES -- AND IT WORKS LIKE A DREAM.
HE'S TOUGH ENOUGH TO SURVIVE -- BUT HE'S NOT GOING ANYWHERE.
FROZEN -- HE'S FROZEN!
BUT YOU WON'T GET ME THAT EASILY!
JUSTICE!

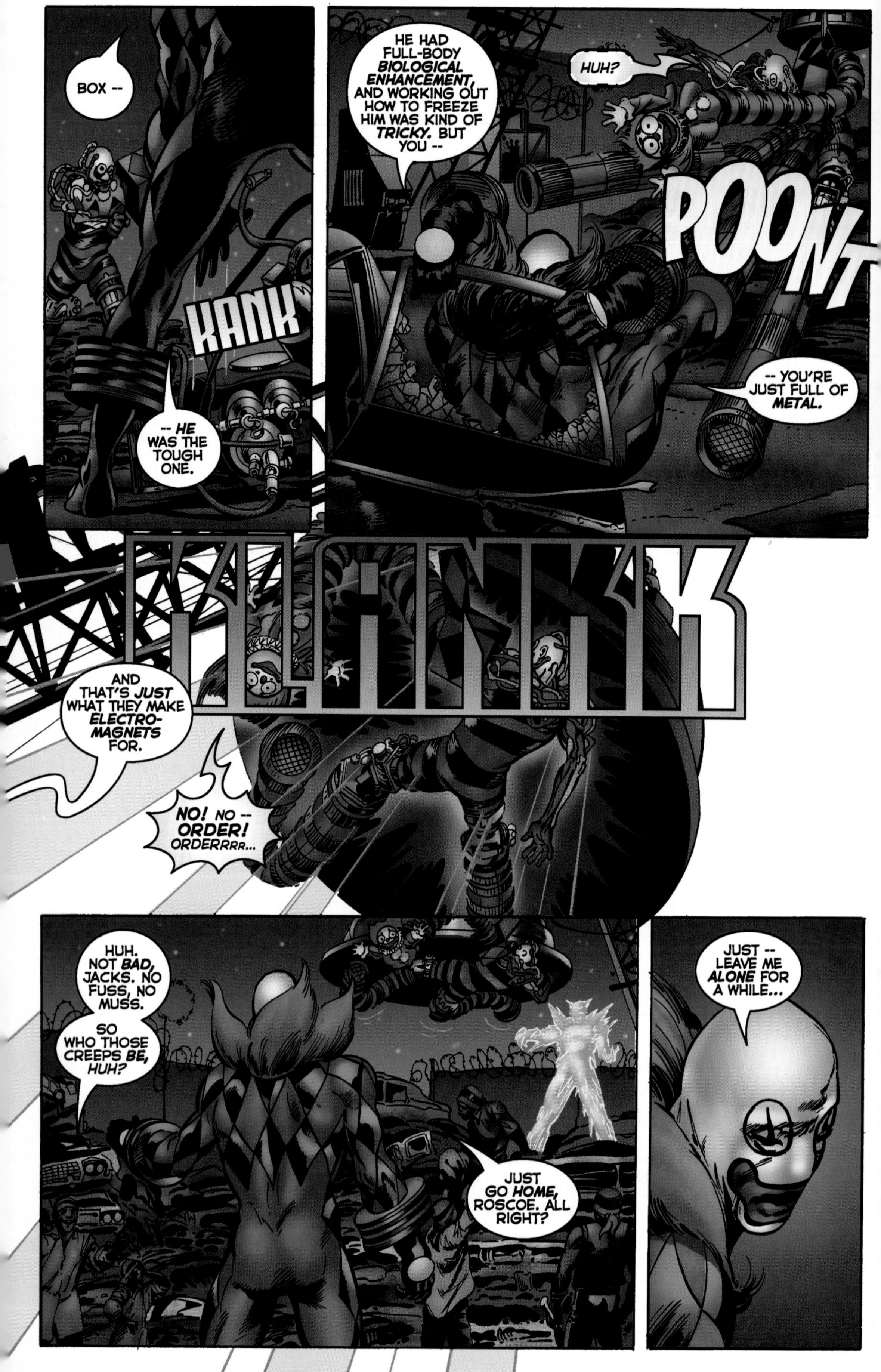
BOX --
KANK
-- HE WAS THE TOUGH ONE.
HE HAD FULL-BODY BIOLOGICAL ENHANCEMENT, AND WORKING OUT HOW TO FREEZE HIM WAS KIND OF TRICKY. BUT YOU --
HUH?
POONT
-- YOU'RE JUST FULL OF METAL.
KLANKK
AND THAT'S JUST WHAT THEY MAKE ELECTRO-MAGNETS FOR.
NO! NO -- ORDER! ORDERRRR...
HUH. NOT BAD, JACKS. NO FUSS, NO MUSS.
SO WHO THOSE CREEPS BE, HUH?
JUST GO HOME, ROSCOE. ALL RIGHT?
JUST -- LEAVE ME ALONE FOR A WHILE...

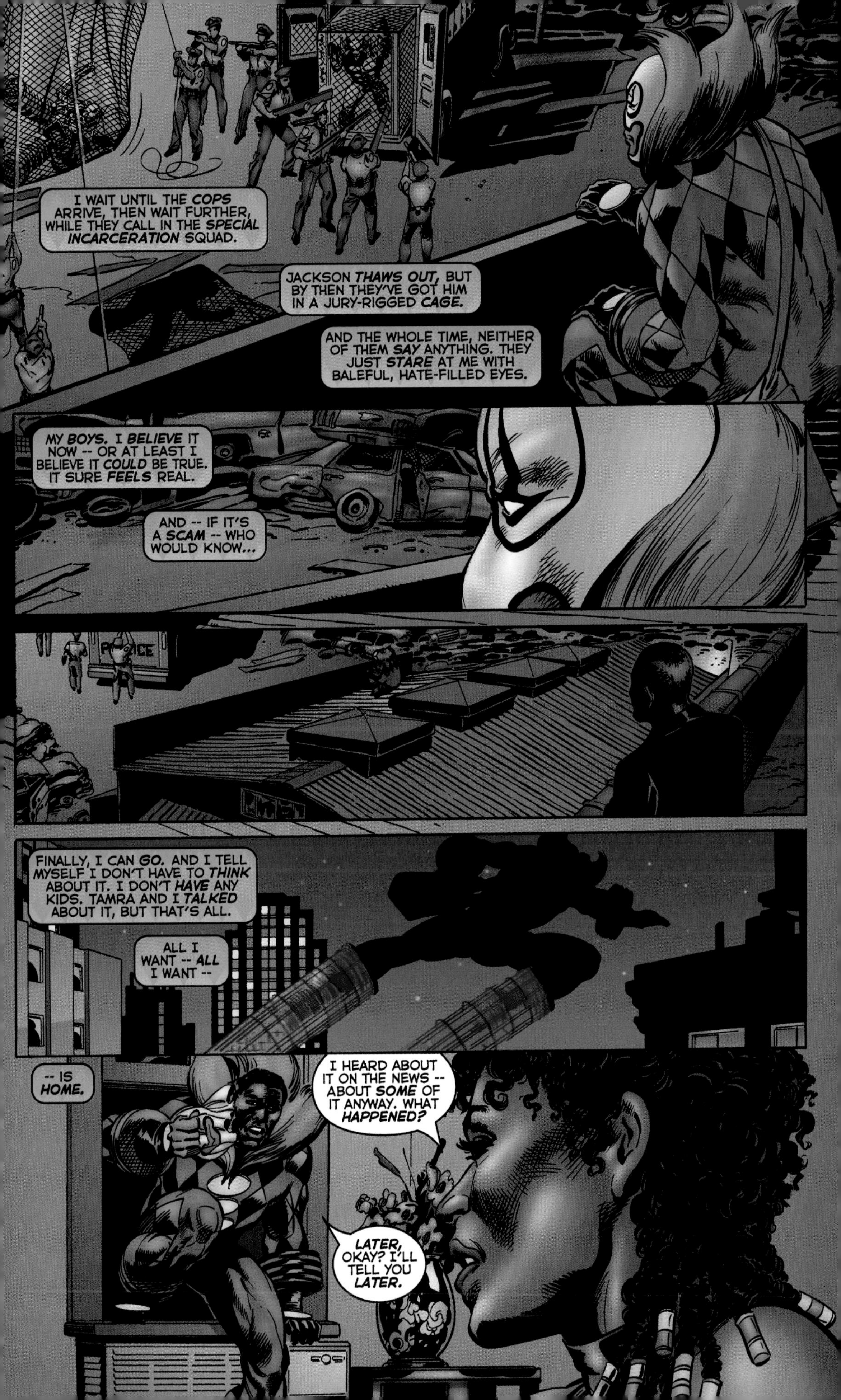
I WAIT UNTIL THE COPS ARRIVE, THEN WAIT FURTHER, WHILE THEY CALL IN THE SPECIAL INCARCERATION SQUAD.
JACKSON THAWS OUT, BUT BY THEN THEY'VE GOT HIM IN A JURY-RIGGED CAGE.
AND THE WHOLE TIME, NEITHER OF THEM SAY ANYTHING. THEY JUST STARE AT ME WITH BALEFUL, HATE-FILLED EYES.
MY BOYS. I BELIEVE IT NOW -- OR AT LEAST I BELIEVE IT COULD BE TRUE. IT SURE FEELS REAL.
AND -- IF IT'S A SCAM -- WHO WOULD KNOW...
FINALLY, I CAN GO. AND I TELL MYSELF I DON'T HAVE TO THINK ABOUT IT. I DON'T HAVE ANY KIDS. TAMRA AND I TALKED ABOUT IT, BUT THAT'S ALL.
ALL I WANT -- ALL I WANT --
-- IS HOME.
I HEARD ABOUT IT ON THE NEWS -- ABOUT SOME OF IT ANYWAY. WHAT HAPPENED?
LATER, OKAY? I'LL TELL YOU LATER.

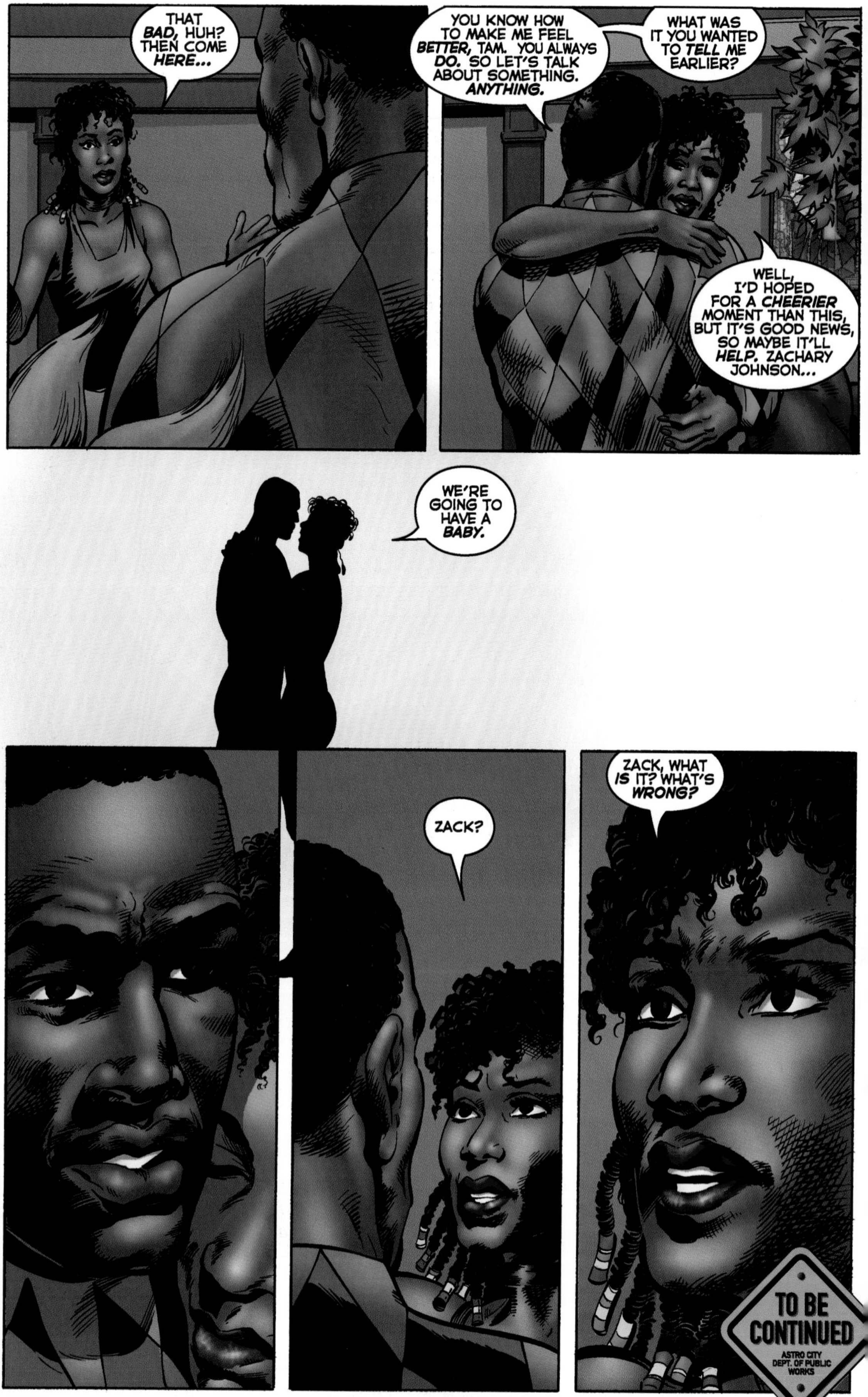
THAT BAD, HUH? THEN COME HERE...
YOU KNOW HOW TO MAKE ME FEEL BETTER, TAM. YOU ALWAYS DO. SO LET'S TALK ABOUT SOMETHING. ANYTHING.
WHAT WAS IT YOU WANTED TO TELL ME EARLIER?
WELL, I'D HOPED FOR A CHEERIER MOMENT THAN THIS, BUT IT'S GOOD NEWS, SO MAYBE IT'LL HELP. ZACHARY JOHNSON...
WE'RE GOING TO HAVE A BABY.
ZACK?
ZACK, WHAT IS IT? WHAT'S WRONG?
TO BE CONTINUED
ASTRO CITY DEPT. OF PUBLIC WORKS

"Father's Day"

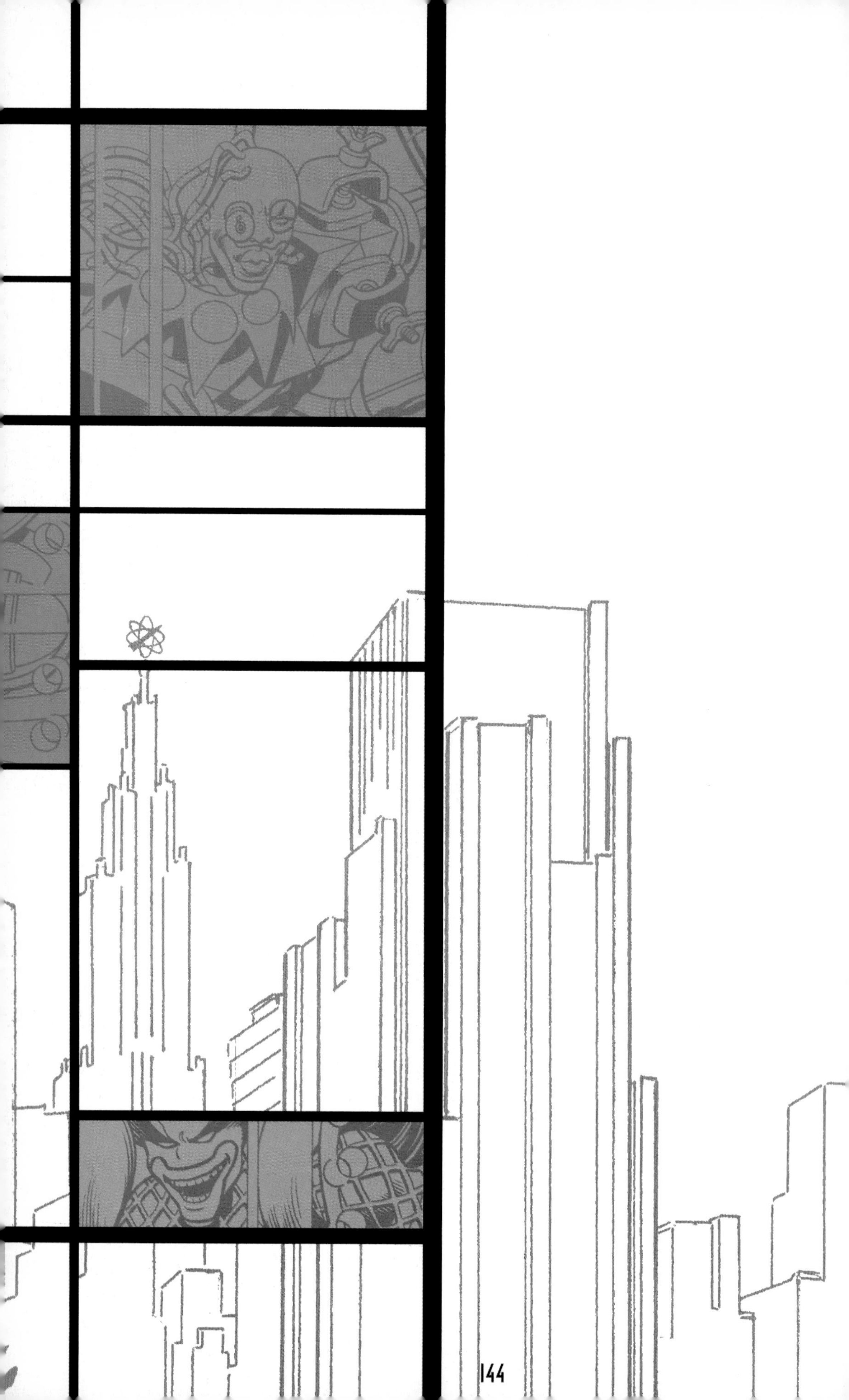

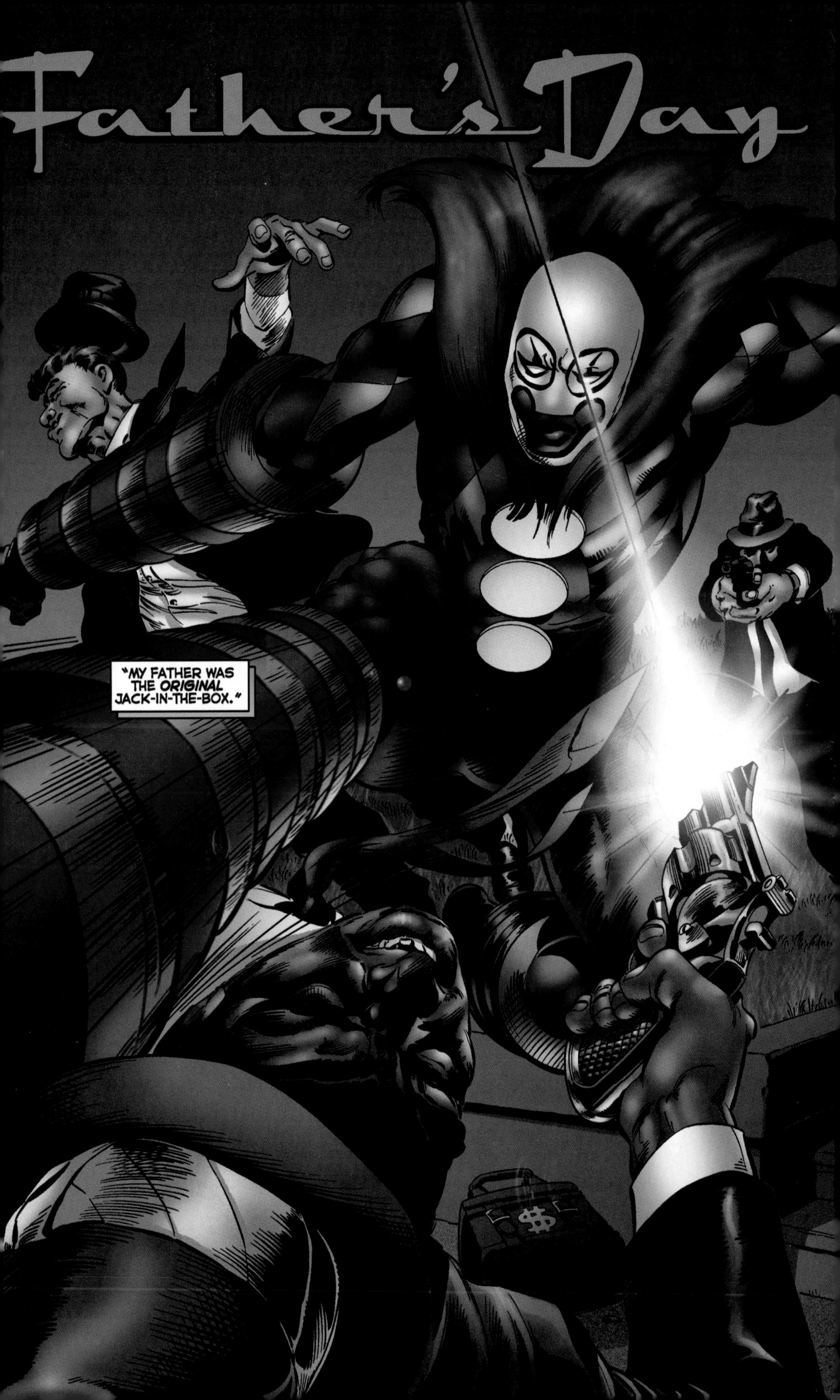

Father's Day
"MY FATHER WAS THE ORIGINAL JACK-IN-THE-BOX."

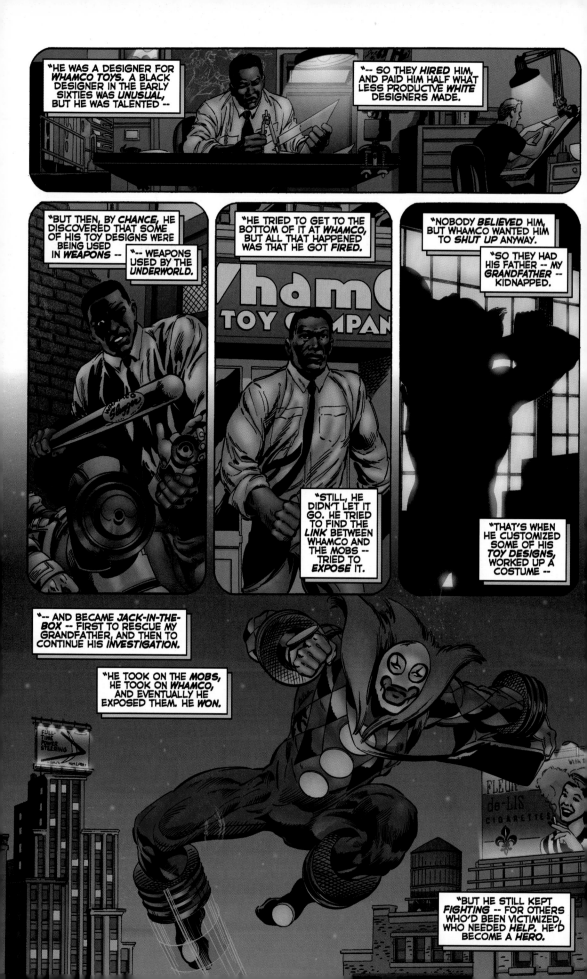

"HE WAS A DESIGNER FOR *WHAMCO TOYS.* A BLACK DESIGNER IN THE EARLY SIXTIES WAS *UNUSUAL,* BUT HE WAS TALENTED --

"-- SO THEY *HIRED* HIM, AND PAID HIM HALF WHAT LESS PRODUCTIVE *WHITE* DESIGNERS MADE.

"BUT THEN, BY *CHANCE,* HE DISCOVERED THAT SOME OF HIS TOY DESIGNS WERE BEING USED IN *WEAPONS* --

"-- *WEAPONS* USED BY THE *UNDERWORLD.*

"HE TRIED TO GET TO THE BOTTOM OF IT AT *WHAMCO,* BUT ALL THAT HAPPENED WAS THAT HE GOT *FIRED.*

"STILL, HE *DIDN'T* LET IT GO. HE TRIED TO FIND THE *LINK* BETWEEN WHAMCO AND THE MOBS -- TRIED TO *EXPOSE* IT.

"NOBODY *BELIEVED* HIM, BUT WHAMCO WANTED HIM TO *SHUT UP* ANYWAY.

"SO THEY HAD HIS FATHER -- MY *GRANDFATHER* -- KIDNAPPED.

"THAT'S WHEN HE CUSTOMIZED SOME OF HIS *TOY DESIGNS,* WORKED UP A COSTUME --

"-- AND BECAME *JACK-IN-THE-BOX* -- FIRST TO RESCUE MY GRANDFATHER -- AND THEN TO CONTINUE HIS *INVESTIGATION.*

"HE TOOK ON THE *MOBS,* HE TOOK ON *WHAMCO,* AND EVENTUALLY HE EXPOSED THEM. HE *WON.*

FULL-TIME POWER STEERING

FLEUR de-LIS CIGARETTES

"BUT HE STILL KEPT *FIGHTING* -- FOR OTHERS WHO'D BEEN VICTIMIZED, WHO NEEDED *HELP.* HE'D BECOME A *HERO.*

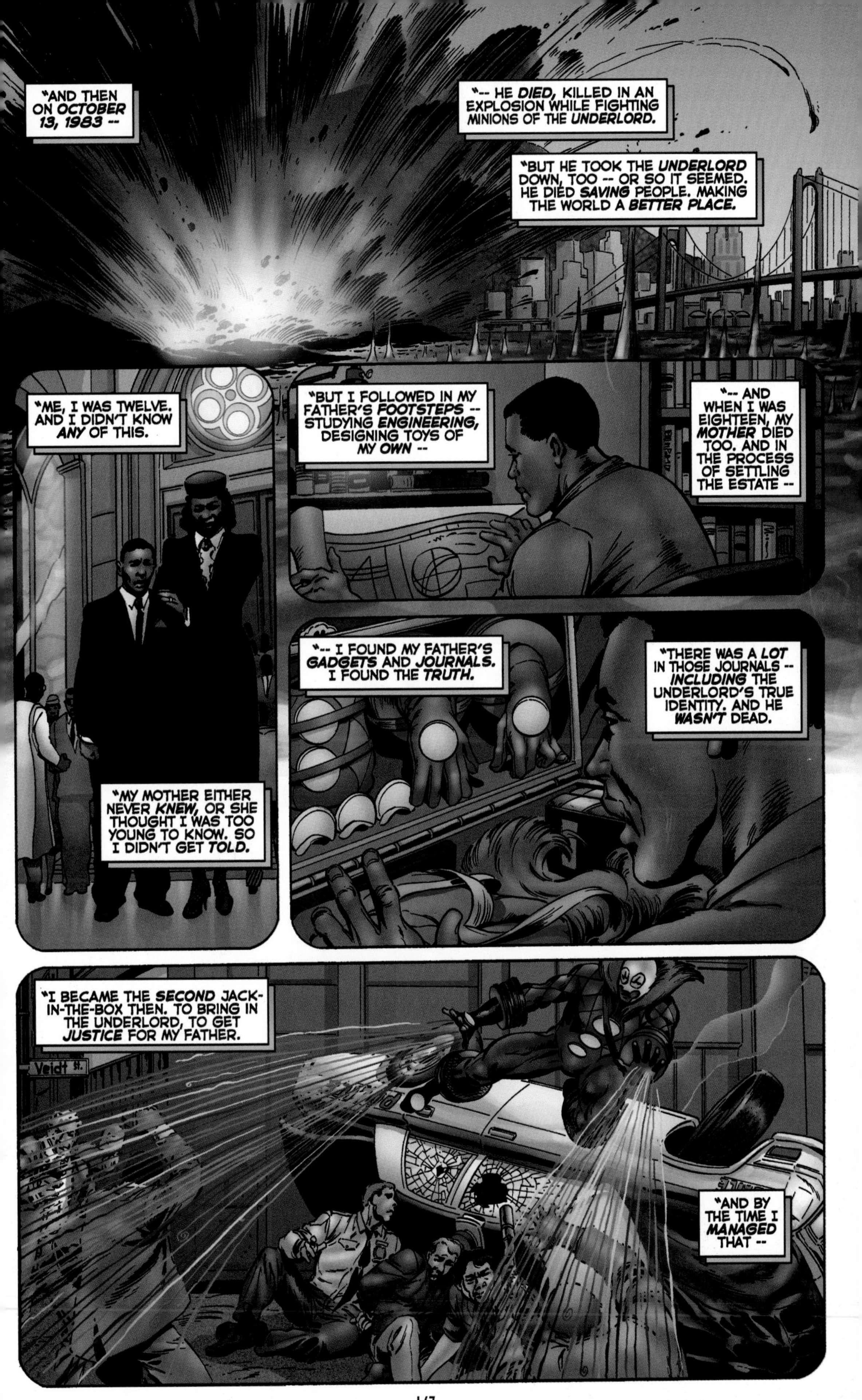
"AND THEN ON OCTOBER 13, 1983 --
"-- HE DIED, KILLED IN AN EXPLOSION WHILE FIGHTING MINIONS OF THE UNDERLORD.
"BUT HE TOOK THE UNDERLORD DOWN, TOO -- OR SO IT SEEMED. HE DIED SAVING PEOPLE. MAKING THE WORLD A BETTER PLACE.
"ME, I WAS TWELVE. AND I DIDN'T KNOW ANY OF THIS.
"MY MOTHER EITHER NEVER KNEW, OR SHE THOUGHT I WAS TOO YOUNG TO KNOW. SO I DIDN'T GET TOLD.
"BUT I FOLLOWED IN MY FATHER'S FOOTSTEPS -- STUDYING ENGINEERING, DESIGNING TOYS OF MY OWN --
"-- AND WHEN I WAS EIGHTEEN, MY MOTHER DIED TOO. AND IN THE PROCESS OF SETTLING THE ESTATE --
"-- I FOUND MY FATHER'S GADGETS AND JOURNALS. I FOUND THE TRUTH.
"THERE WAS A LOT IN THOSE JOURNALS -- INCLUDING THE UNDERLORD'S TRUE IDENTITY. AND HE WASN'T DEAD.
"I BECAME THE SECOND JACK-IN-THE-BOX THEN. TO BRING IN THE UNDERLORD, TO GET JUSTICE FOR MY FATHER.
Veidt St.
"AND BY THE TIME I MANAGED THAT --

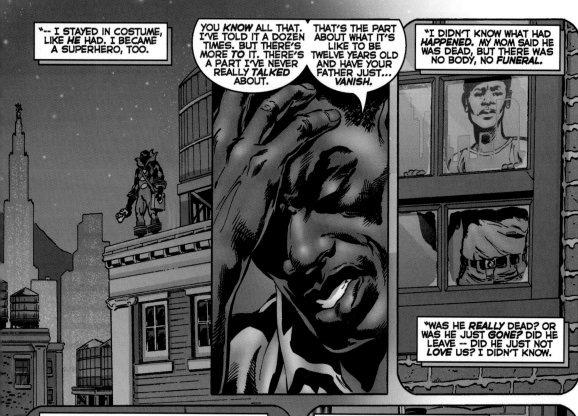

"-- I STAYED IN COSTUME, LIKE *HE* HAD. I BECAME A SUPERHERO, TOO.

"YOU *KNOW* ALL THAT. I'VE TOLD IT A DOZEN TIMES. BUT THERE'S MORE *TO* IT. THERE'S A PART I'VE NEVER REALLY *TALKED* ABOUT.

"THAT'S THE PART ABOUT WHAT IT'S LIKE TO BE TWELVE YEARS OLD AND HAVE YOUR FATHER JUST... *VANISH.*

"I DIDN'T KNOW WHAT HAD *HAPPENED.* MY MOM SAID HE WAS DEAD, BUT THERE WAS NO BODY, NO *FUNERAL.*

"WAS HE *REALLY* DEAD? OR WAS HE JUST *GONE?* DID HE LEAVE -- DID HE JUST NOT *LOVE* US? I DIDN'T KNOW.

"I CAME UP WITH ALL KINDS OF FANTASIES -- HE WAS A *SPY,* OR AN *UNDERCOVER COP.* OR IN THE *WITNESS PROTECTION PROGRAM.*

"SOMETIMES, I EVEN IMAGINED HE WAS A DARING *CRIMINAL MASTERMIND,* ON THE RUN FROM THE LAW. *STUPID,* HUH?

"BUT THE BOTTOM LINE WAS, HE WAS *GONE.* AND I SPENT SIX YEARS TRYING TO *FILL* THAT HOLE --

"-- TRYING TO WIN THE APPROVAL OF A *GHOST,* TO BE WHAT MY FATHER WOULD HAVE WANTED WITHOUT KNOWING WHAT THAT *WAS.*

"AND IN THE END, WHEN I LEARNED THAT THE TRUTH EXCEEDED *ALL MY FANTASIES,* I WAS *PROUD,* AND I WAS HONORED --

"-- BUT STILL, THERE WAS A PART OF ME THAT FELT *HOLLOW* --

"-- THAT FELT LIKE MY FATHER HAD CARED MORE ABOUT *FIGHTING CRIME* THAN ABOUT HIS *FAMILY.*"

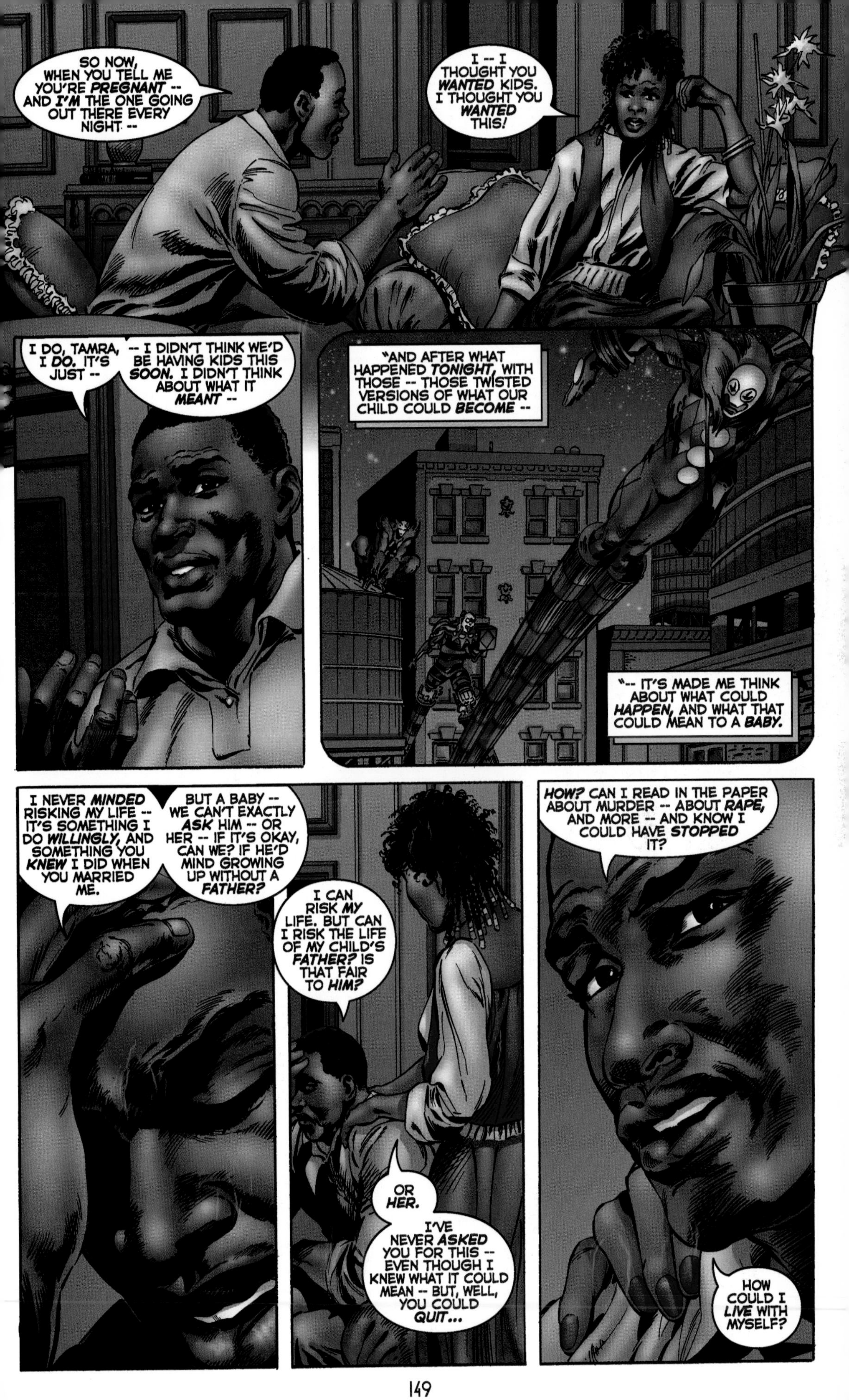
SO NOW, WHEN YOU TELL ME YOU'RE PREGNANT -- AND I'M THE ONE GOING OUT THERE EVERY NIGHT --
I -- I THOUGHT YOU WANTED KIDS. I THOUGHT YOU WANTED THIS!
I DO, TAMRA, I DO. IT'S JUST --
-- I DIDN'T THINK WE'D BE HAVING KIDS THIS SOON. I DIDN'T THINK ABOUT WHAT IT MEANT --
"AND AFTER WHAT HAPPENED TONIGHT, WITH THOSE -- THOSE TWISTED VERSIONS OF WHAT OUR CHILD COULD BECOME --
"-- IT'S MADE ME THINK ABOUT WHAT COULD HAPPEN, AND WHAT THAT COULD MEAN TO A BABY.
I NEVER MINDED RISKING MY LIFE -- IT'S SOMETHING I DO WILLINGLY, AND SOMETHING YOU KNEW I DID WHEN YOU MARRIED ME.
BUT A BABY -- WE CAN'T EXACTLY ASK HIM -- OR HER -- IF IT'S OKAY, CAN WE? IF HE'D MIND GROWING UP WITHOUT A FATHER?
I CAN RISK MY LIFE. BUT CAN I RISK THE LIFE OF MY CHILD'S FATHER? IS THAT FAIR TO HIM?
OR HER.
I'VE NEVER ASKED YOU FOR THIS -- EVEN THOUGH I KNEW WHAT IT COULD MEAN -- BUT, WELL, YOU COULD QUIT...
HOW? CAN I READ IN THE PAPER ABOUT MURDER -- ABOUT RAPE, AND MORE -- AND KNOW I COULD HAVE STOPPED IT?
HOW COULD I LIVE WITH MYSELF?

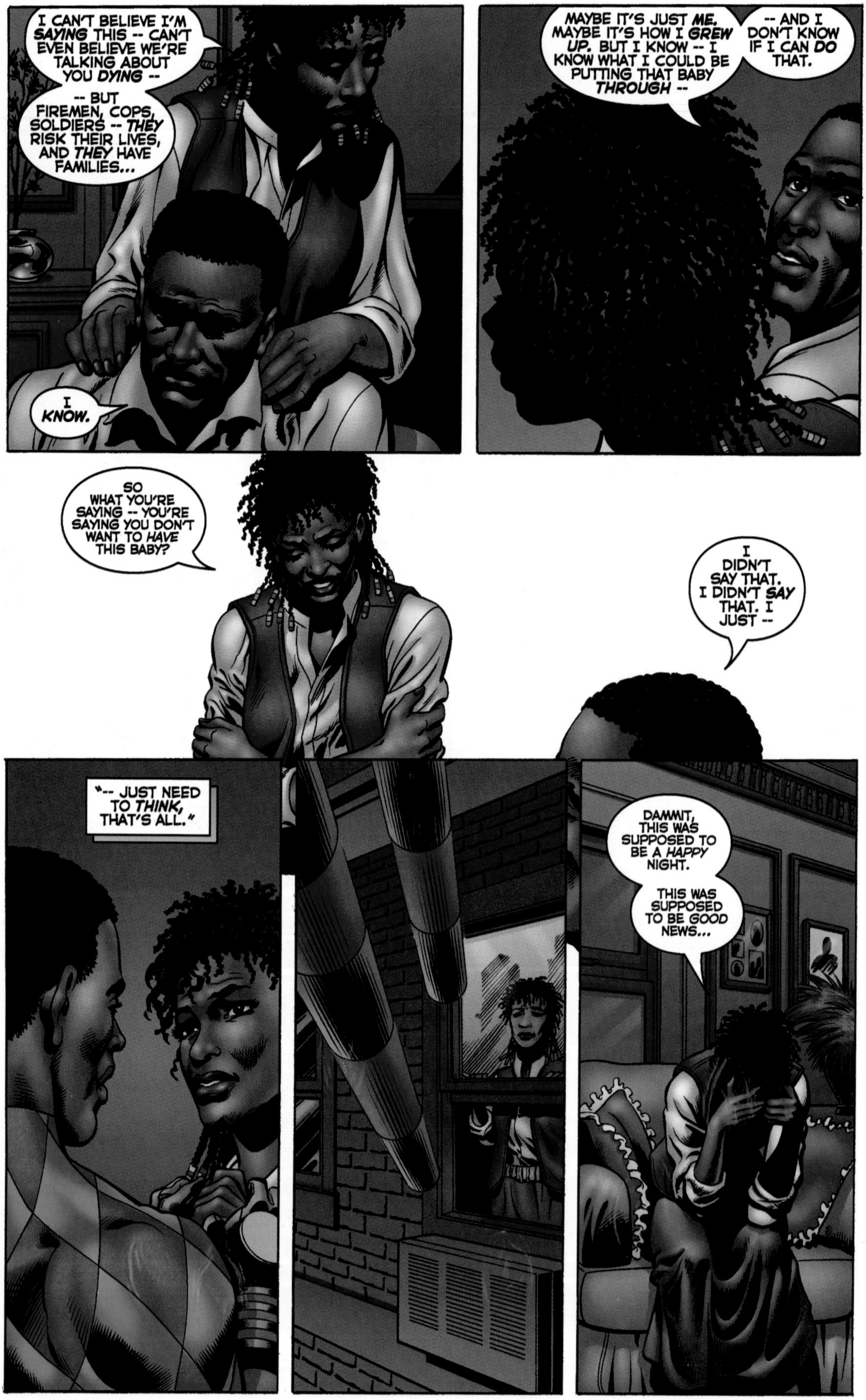
I CAN'T BELIEVE I'M SAYING THIS -- CAN'T EVEN BELIEVE WE'RE TALKING ABOUT YOU DYING --
-- BUT FIREMEN, COPS, SOLDIERS -- THEY RISK THEIR LIVES, AND THEY HAVE FAMILIES...
I KNOW.
MAYBE IT'S JUST ME. MAYBE IT'S HOW I GREW UP. BUT I KNOW -- I KNOW WHAT I COULD BE PUTTING THAT BABY THROUGH --
-- AND I DON'T KNOW IF I CAN DO THAT.
SO WHAT YOU'RE SAYING -- YOU'RE SAYING YOU DON'T WANT TO HAVE THIS BABY?
I DIDN'T SAY THAT. I DIDN'T SAY THAT. I JUST --
"-- JUST NEED TO THINK, THAT'S ALL."
DAMMIT, THIS WAS SUPPOSED TO BE A HAPPY NIGHT.
THIS WAS SUPPOSED TO BE GOOD NEWS...

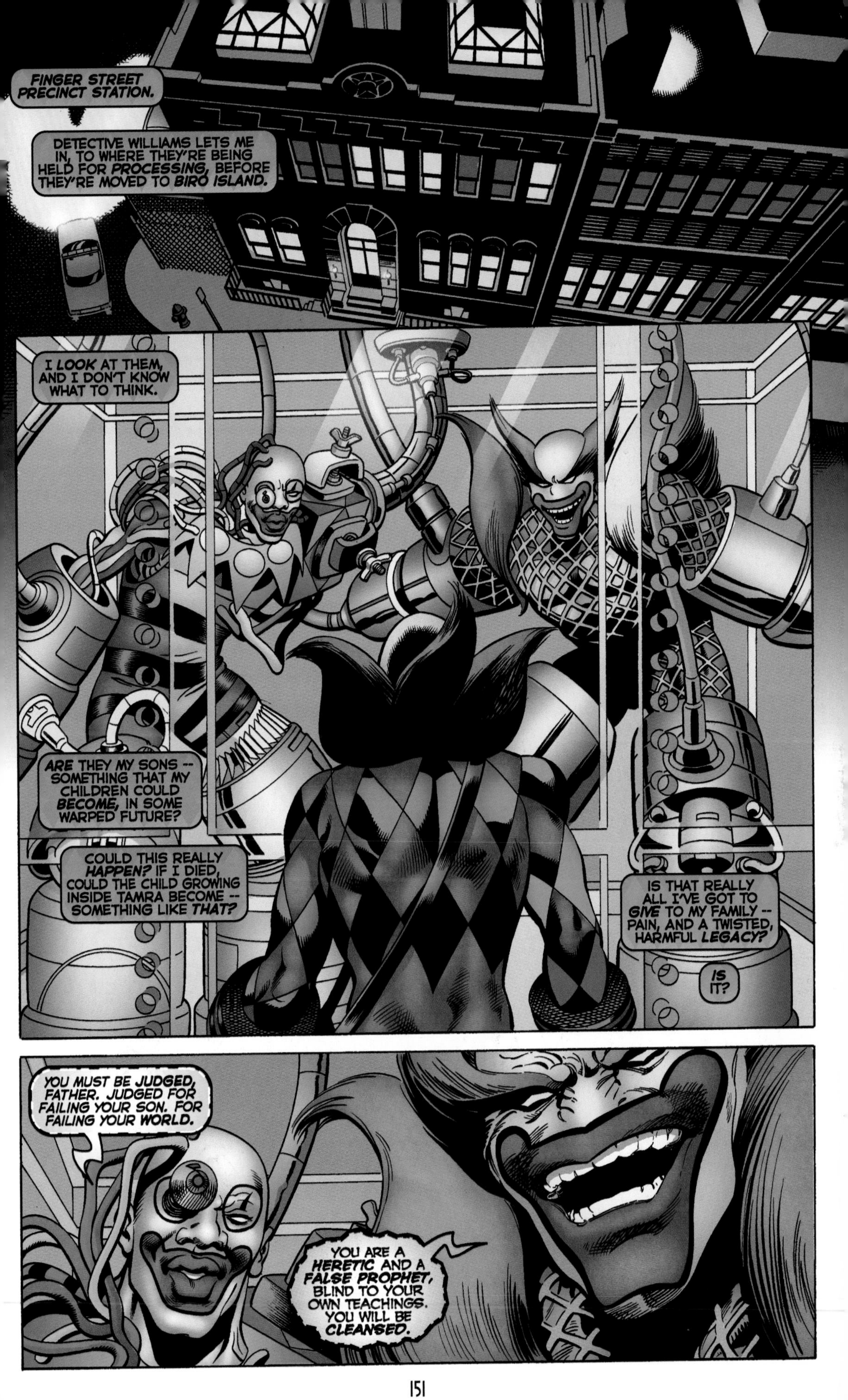
FINGER STREET PRECINCT STATION.
DETECTIVE WILLIAMS LETS ME IN, TO WHERE THEY'RE BEING HELD FOR PROCESSING, BEFORE THEY'RE MOVED TO BIRO ISLAND.
I LOOK AT THEM, AND I DON'T KNOW WHAT TO THINK.
ARE THEY MY SONS -- SOMETHING THAT MY CHILDREN COULD BECOME, IN SOME WARPED FUTURE?
COULD THIS REALLY HAPPEN? IF I DIED, COULD THE CHILD GROWING INSIDE TAMRA BECOME -- SOMETHING LIKE THAT?
IS THAT REALLY ALL I'VE GOT TO GIVE TO MY FAMILY -- PAIN, AND A TWISTED, HARMFUL LEGACY?
IS IT?
YOU MUST BE JUDGED, FATHER. JUDGED FOR FAILING YOUR SON. FOR FAILING YOUR WORLD.
YOU ARE A HERETIC AND A FALSE PROPHET, BLIND TO YOUR OWN TEACHINGS. YOU WILL BE CLEANSED.

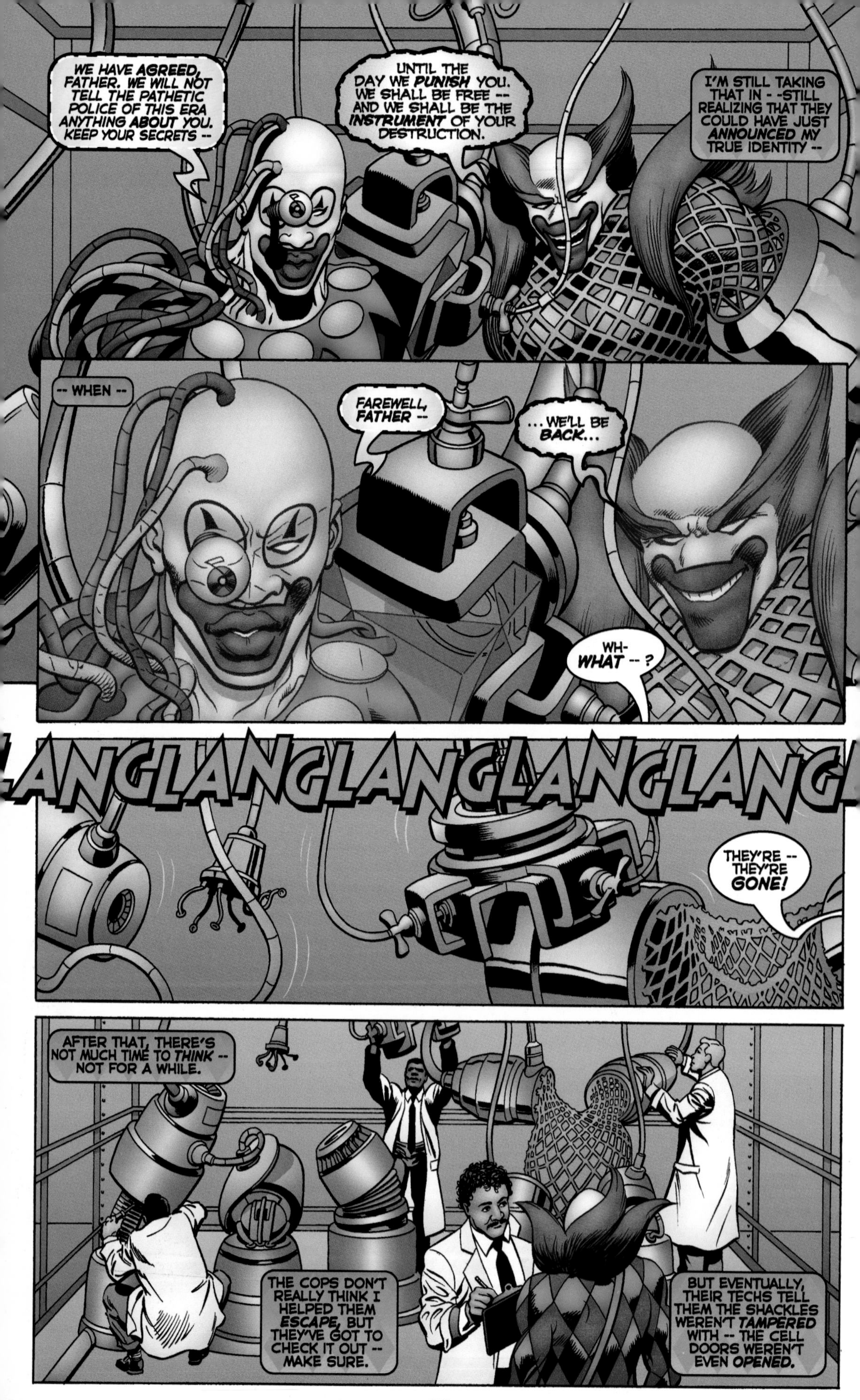
WE HAVE AGREED, FATHER. WE WILL NOT TELL THE PATHETIC POLICE OF THIS ERA ANYTHING ABOUT YOU. KEEP YOUR SECRETS --
UNTIL THE DAY WE PUNISH YOU. WE SHALL BE FREE -- AND WE SHALL BE THE INSTRUMENT OF YOUR DESTRUCTION.
I'M STILL TAKING THAT IN - -STILL REALIZING THAT THEY COULD HAVE JUST ANNOUNCED MY TRUE IDENTITY --
-- WHEN --
FAREWELL, FATHER --
...WE'LL BE BACK...
WH- WHAT -- ?
LANGLANGLANGLANGLANG
THEY'RE -- THEY'RE GONE!
AFTER THAT, THERE'S NOT MUCH TIME TO THINK -- NOT FOR A WHILE.
THE COPS DON'T REALLY THINK I HELPED THEM ESCAPE, BUT THEY'VE GOT TO CHECK IT OUT -- MAKE SURE.
BUT EVENTUALLY, THEIR TECHS TELL THEM THE SHACKLES WEREN'T TAMPERED WITH -- THE CELL DOORS WEREN'T EVEN OPENED.

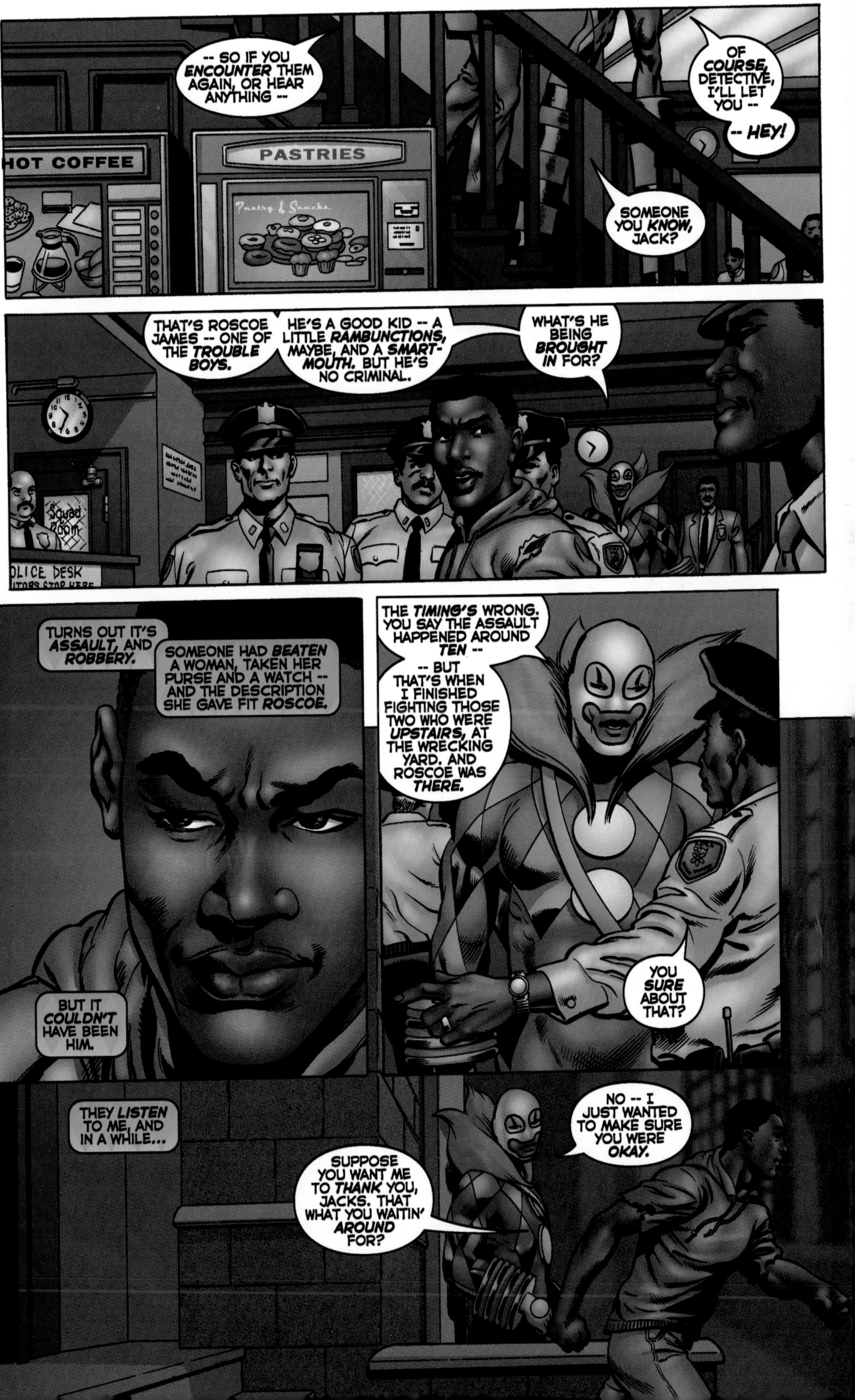

HOT COFFEE
PASTRIES
Pastry & Snacks
-- SO IF YOU ENCOUNTER THEM AGAIN, OR HEAR ANYTHING --
OF COURSE, DETECTIVE, I'LL LET YOU --
-- HEY!
SOMEONE YOU KNOW, JACK?
THAT'S ROSCOE JAMES -- ONE OF THE TROUBLE BOYS.
HE'S A GOOD KID -- A LITTLE RAMBUNCTIONS, MAYBE, AND A SMART-MOUTH. BUT HE'S NO CRIMINAL.
WHAT'S HE BEING BROUGHT IN FOR?
Squad Room
OLICE DESK
TURNS OUT IT'S ASSAULT, AND ROBBERY.
SOMEONE HAD BEATEN A WOMAN, TAKEN HER PURSE AND A WATCH -- AND THE DESCRIPTION SHE GAVE FIT ROSCOE.
BUT IT COULDN'T HAVE BEEN HIM.
THE TIMING'S WRONG. YOU SAY THE ASSAULT HAPPENED AROUND TEN --
-- BUT THAT'S WHEN I FINISHED FIGHTING THOSE TWO WHO WERE UPSTAIRS, AT THE WRECKING YARD. AND ROSCOE WAS THERE.
YOU SURE ABOUT THAT?
THEY LISTEN TO ME, AND IN A WHILE...
SUPPOSE YOU WANT ME TO THANK YOU, JACKS. THAT WHAT YOU WAITIN' AROUND FOR?
NO -- I JUST WANTED TO MAKE SURE YOU WERE OKAY.

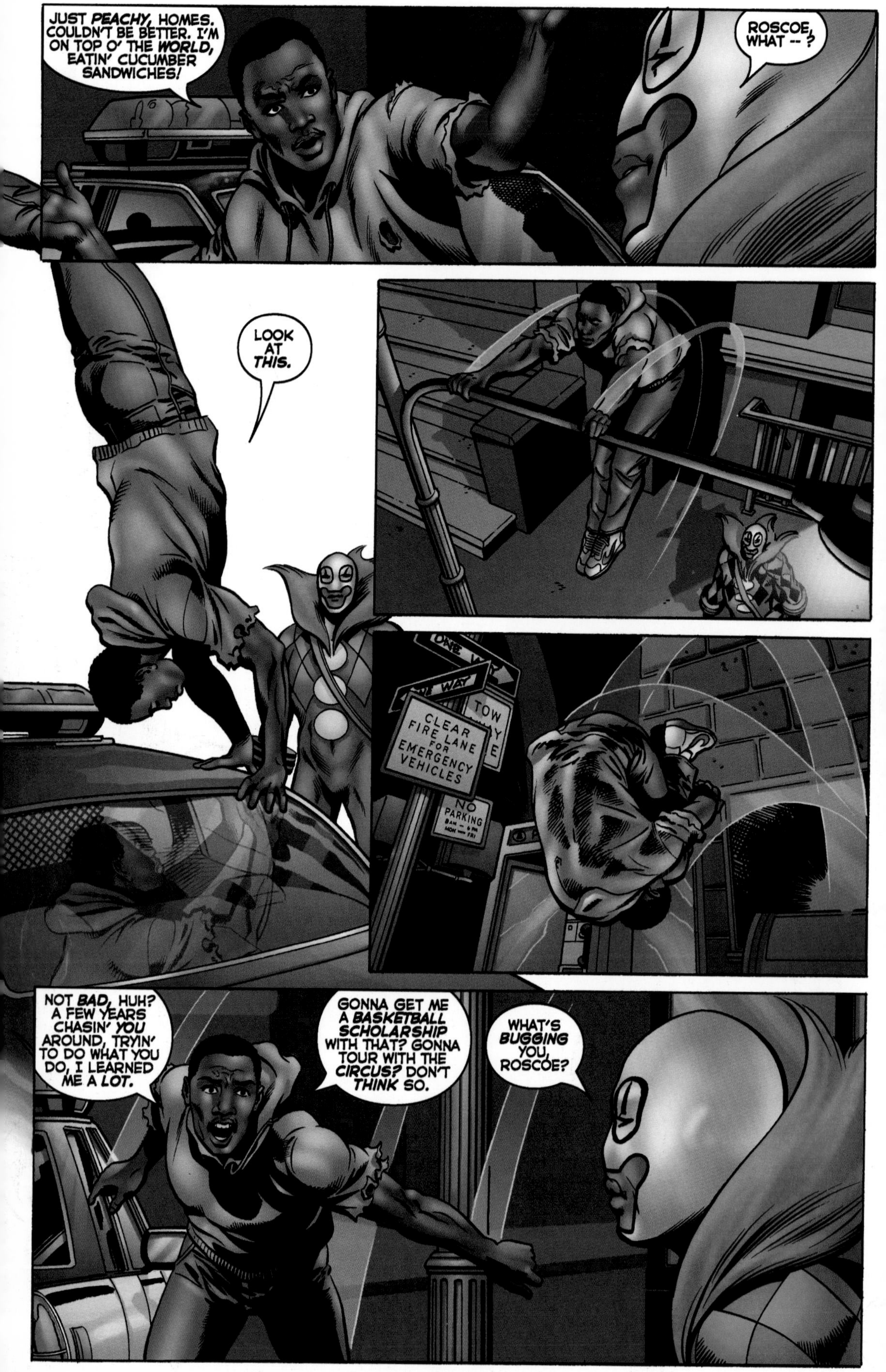
JUST PEACHY, HOMES. COULDN'T BE BETTER. I'M ON TOP O' THE WORLD, EATIN' CUCUMBER SANDWICHES!
ROSCOE, WHAT -- ?
LOOK AT THIS.
ONE WAY
ONE WAY
CLEAR FIRE LANE FOR EMERGENCY VEHICLES
NO PARKING
NOT BAD, HUH? A FEW YEARS CHASIN' YOU AROUND, TRYIN' TO DO WHAT YOU DO, I LEARNED ME A LOT.
GONNA GET ME A BASKETBALL SCHOLARSHIP WITH THAT? GONNA TOUR WITH THE CIRCUS? DON'T THINK SO.
WHAT'S BUGGING YOU, ROSCOE?

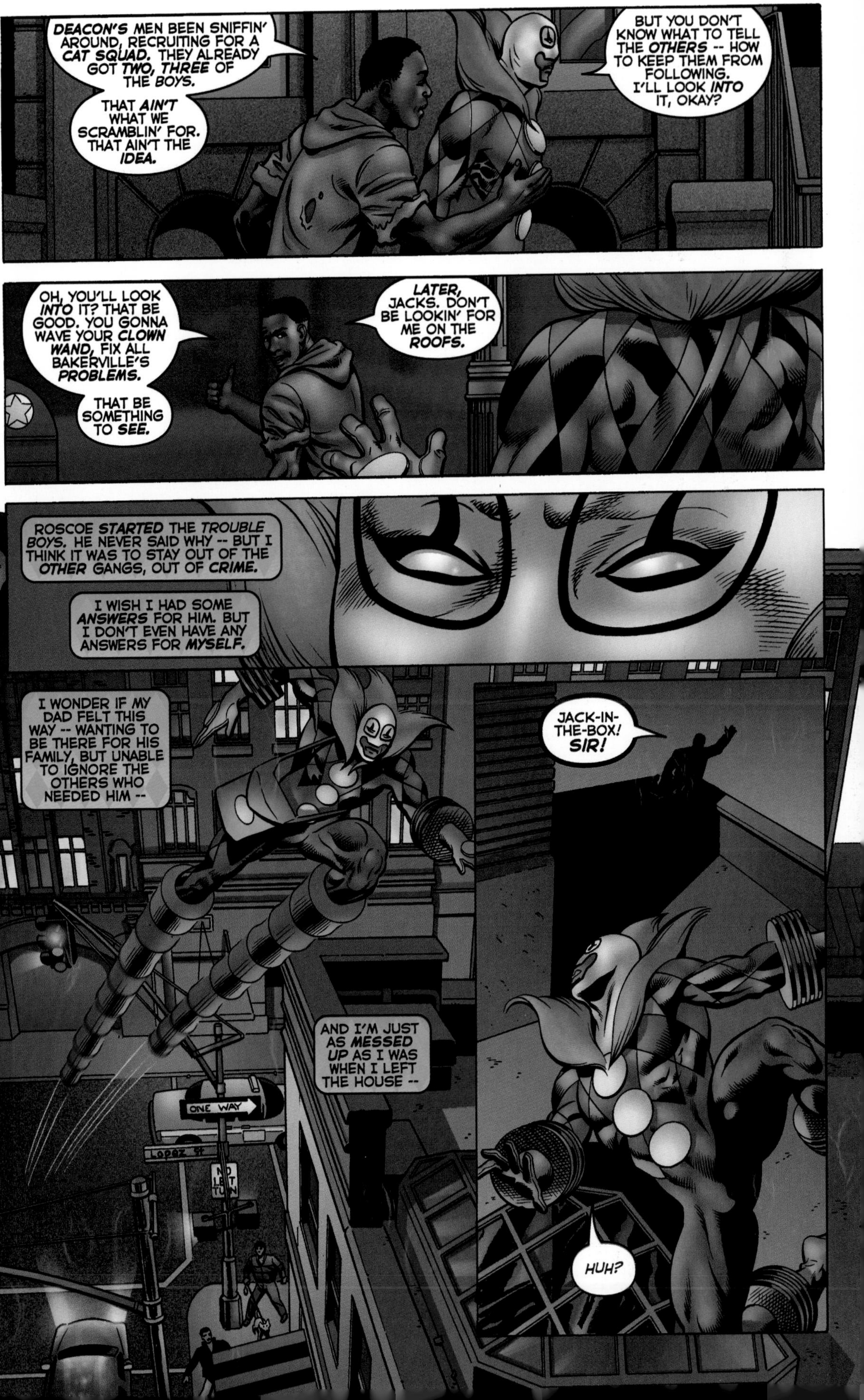
DEACON'S MEN BEEN SNIFFIN' AROUND, RECRUITING FOR A CAT SQUAD. THEY ALREADY GOT TWO, THREE OF THE BOYS.
THAT AIN'T WHAT WE SCRAMBLIN' FOR. THAT AIN'T THE IDEA.
BUT YOU DON'T KNOW WHAT TO TELL THE OTHERS -- HOW TO KEEP THEM FROM FOLLOWING. I'LL LOOK INTO IT, OKAY?
OH, YOU'LL LOOK INTO IT? THAT BE GOOD. YOU GONNA WAVE YOUR CLOWN WAND, FIX ALL BAKERVILLE'S PROBLEMS.
THAT BE SOMETHING TO SEE.
LATER, JACKS. DON'T BE LOOKIN' FOR ME ON THE ROOFS.
ROSCOE STARTED THE TROUBLE BOYS. HE NEVER SAID WHY -- BUT I THINK IT WAS TO STAY OUT OF THE OTHER GANGS, OUT OF CRIME.
I WISH I HAD SOME ANSWERS FOR HIM. BUT I DON'T EVEN HAVE ANY ANSWERS FOR MYSELF.
I WONDER IF MY DAD FELT THIS WAY -- WANTING TO BE THERE FOR HIS FAMILY, BUT UNABLE TO IGNORE THE OTHERS WHO NEEDED HIM --
AND I'M JUST AS MESSED UP AS I WAS WHEN I LEFT THE HOUSE --
ONE WAY
NO LEFT TURN
JACK-IN-THE-BOX! SIR!
HUH?

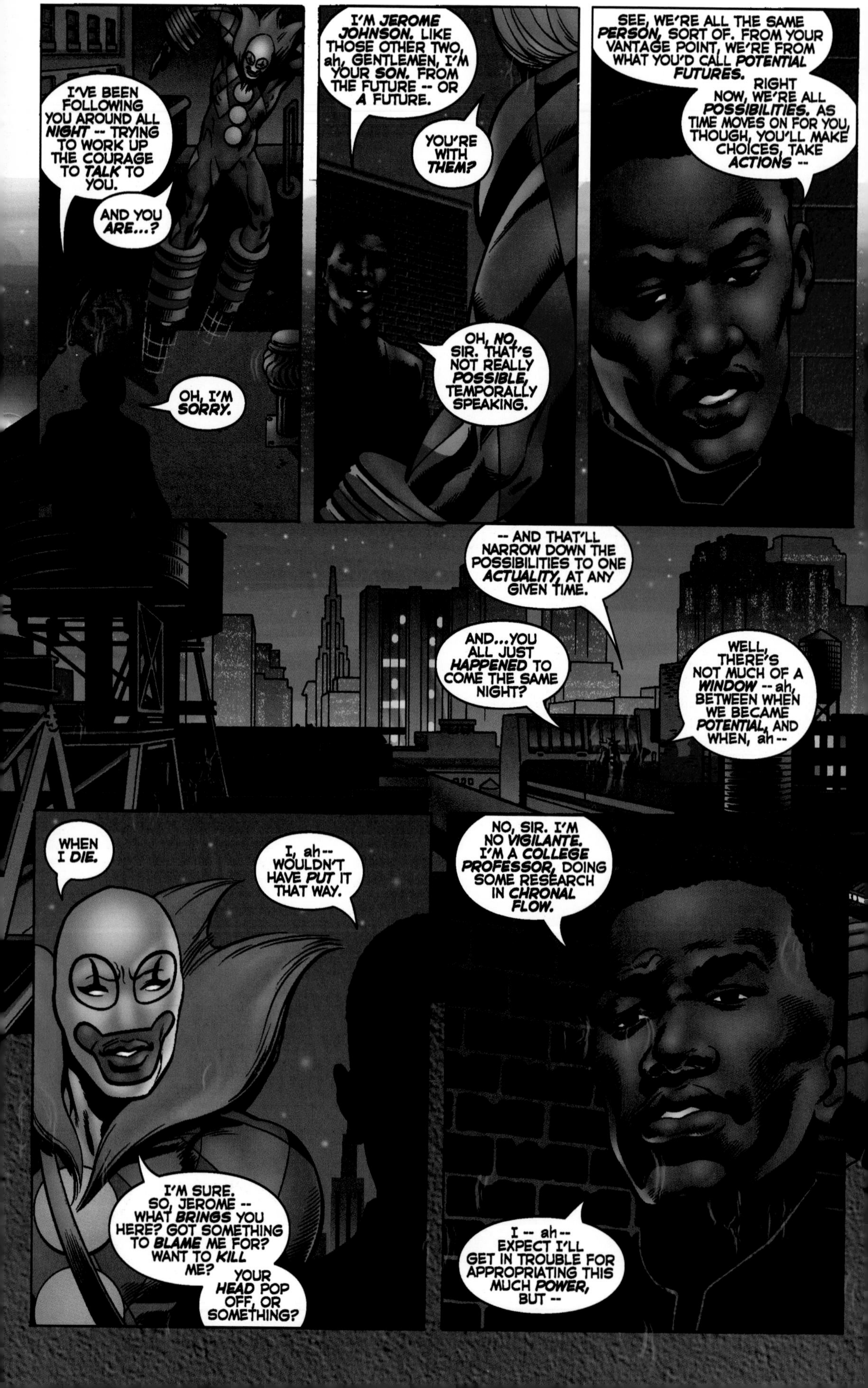
I'VE BEEN FOLLOWING YOU AROUND ALL NIGHT -- TRYING TO WORK UP THE COURAGE TO TALK TO YOU.
AND YOU ARE...?
OH, I'M SORRY.
I'M JEROME JOHNSON. LIKE THOSE OTHER TWO, ah, GENTLEMEN, I'M YOUR SON. FROM THE FUTURE -- OR A FUTURE.
YOU'RE WITH THEM?
OH, NO, SIR. THAT'S NOT REALLY POSSIBLE, TEMPORALLY SPEAKING.
SEE, WE'RE ALL THE SAME PERSON, SORT OF. FROM YOUR VANTAGE POINT, WE'RE FROM WHAT YOU'D CALL POTENTIAL FUTURES.
RIGHT NOW, WE'RE ALL POSSIBILITIES. AS TIME MOVES ON FOR YOU, THOUGH, YOU'LL MAKE CHOICES, TAKE ACTIONS --
-- AND THAT'LL NARROW DOWN THE POSSIBILITIES TO ONE ACTUALITY, AT ANY GIVEN TIME.
AND...YOU ALL JUST HAPPENED TO COME THE SAME NIGHT?
WELL, THERE'S NOT MUCH OF A WINDOW -- ah, BETWEEN WHEN WE BECAME POTENTIAL, AND WHEN, ah --
WHEN I DIE.
I, ah -- WOULDN'T HAVE PUT IT THAT WAY.
I'M SURE. SO, JEROME -- WHAT BRINGS YOU HERE? GOT SOMETHING TO BLAME ME FOR? WANT TO KILL ME?
YOUR HEAD POP OFF, OR SOMETHING?
NO, SIR. I'M NO VIGILANTE. I'M A COLLEGE PROFESSOR, DOING SOME RESEARCH IN CHRONAL FLOW.
I -- ah -- EXPECT I'LL GET IN TROUBLE FOR APPROPRIATING THIS MUCH POWER, BUT --

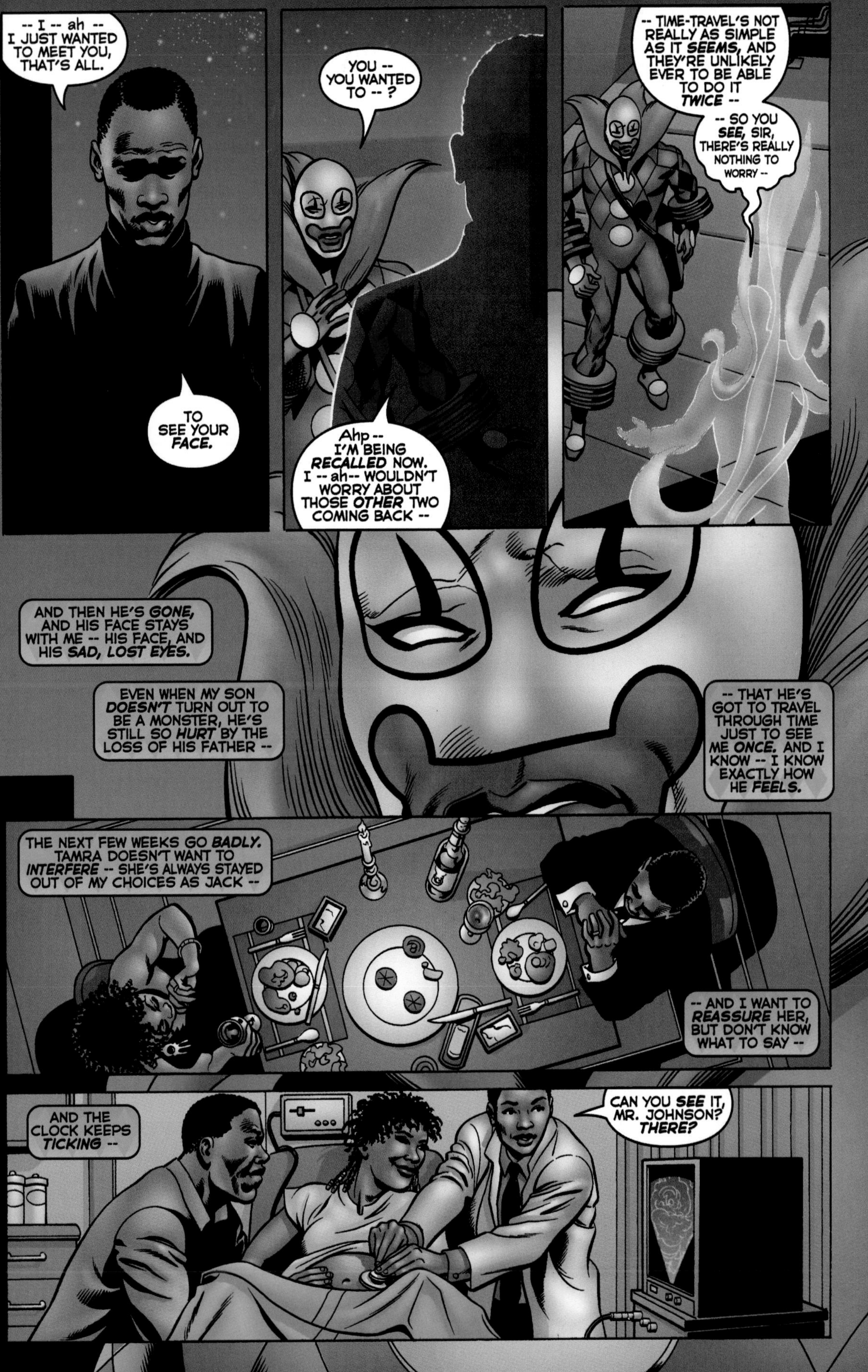
-- I -- ah -- I JUST WANTED TO MEET YOU, THAT'S ALL.
TO SEE YOUR FACE.
YOU -- YOU WANTED TO -- ?
Ahp -- I'M BEING RECALLED NOW. I -- ah-- WOULDN'T WORRY ABOUT THOSE OTHER TWO COMING BACK --
-- TIME-TRAVEL'S NOT REALLY AS SIMPLE AS IT SEEMS, AND THEY'RE UNLIKELY EVER TO BE ABLE TO DO IT TWICE --
-- SO YOU SEE, SIR, THERE'S REALLY NOTHING TO WORRY --
AND THEN HE'S GONE, AND HIS FACE STAYS WITH ME -- HIS FACE, AND HIS SAD, LOST EYES.
EVEN WHEN MY SON DOESN'T TURN OUT TO BE A MONSTER, HE'S STILL SO HURT BY THE LOSS OF HIS FATHER --
-- THAT HE'S GOT TO TRAVEL THROUGH TIME JUST TO SEE ME ONCE. AND I KNOW -- I KNOW EXACTLY HOW HE FEELS.
THE NEXT FEW WEEKS GO BADLY. TAMRA DOESN'T WANT TO INTERFERE -- SHE'S ALWAYS STAYED OUT OF MY CHOICES AS JACK --
-- AND I WANT TO REASSURE HER, BUT DON'T KNOW WHAT TO SAY --
AND THE CLOCK KEEPS TICKING --
CAN YOU SEE IT, MR. JOHNSON? THERE?

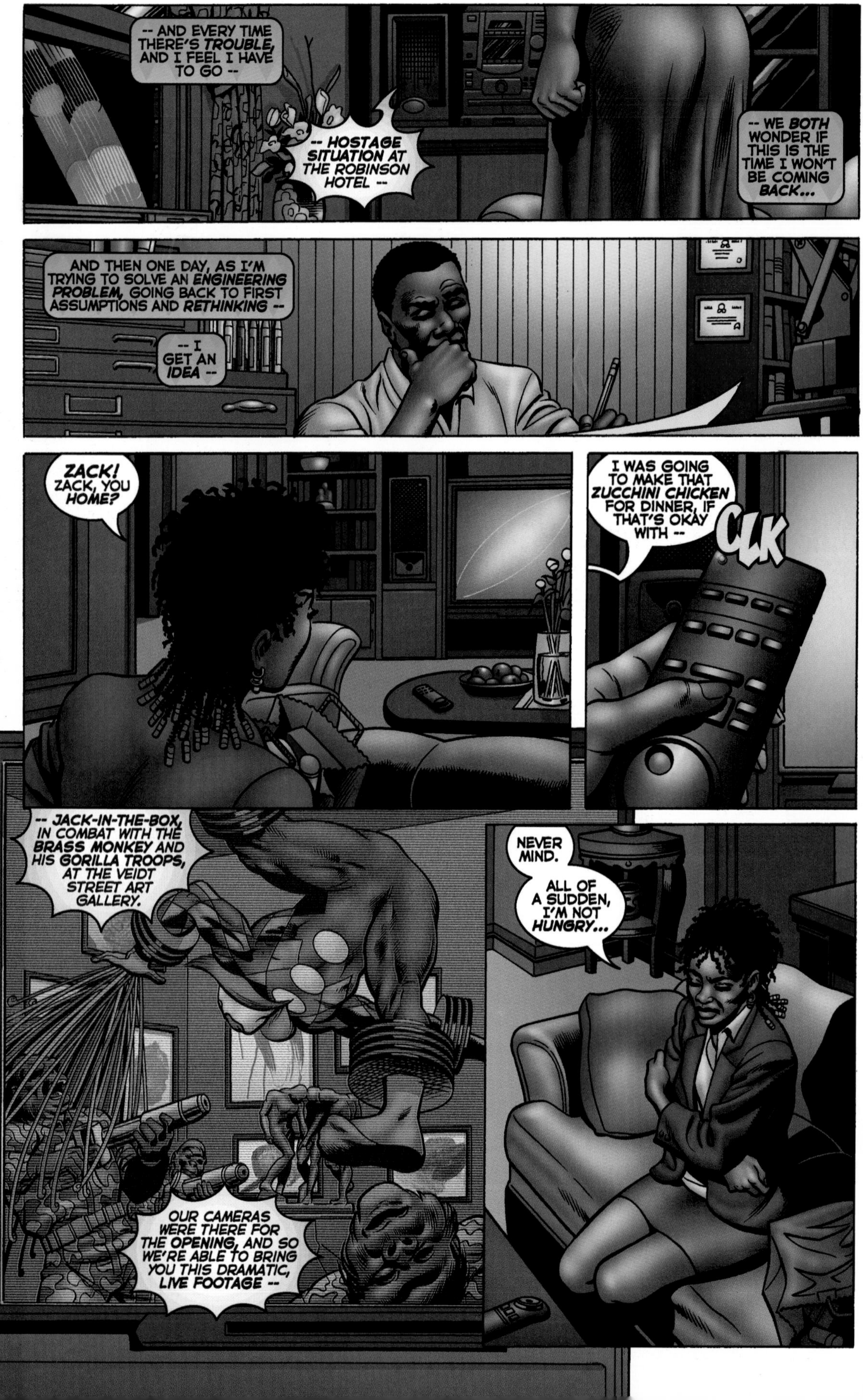
-- AND EVERY TIME THERE'S TROUBLE, AND I FEEL I HAVE TO GO --
-- HOSTAGE SITUATION AT THE ROBINSON HOTEL --
-- WE BOTH WONDER IF THIS IS THE TIME I WON'T BE COMING BACK...
AND THEN ONE DAY, AS I'M TRYING TO SOLVE AN ENGINEERING PROBLEM, GOING BACK TO FIRST ASSUMPTIONS AND RETHINKING --
-- I GET AN IDEA --
ZACK! ZACK, YOU HOME?
I WAS GOING TO MAKE THAT ZUCCHINI CHICKEN FOR DINNER, IF THAT'S OKAY WITH --
CLK
-- JACK-IN-THE-BOX, IN COMBAT WITH THE BRASS MONKEY AND HIS GORILLA TROOPS, AT THE VEIDT STREET ART GALLERY.
OUR CAMERAS WERE THERE FOR THE OPENING, AND SO WE'RE ABLE TO BRING YOU THIS DRAMATIC, LIVE FOOTAGE --
NEVER MIND.
ALL OF A SUDDEN, I'M NOT HUNGRY...

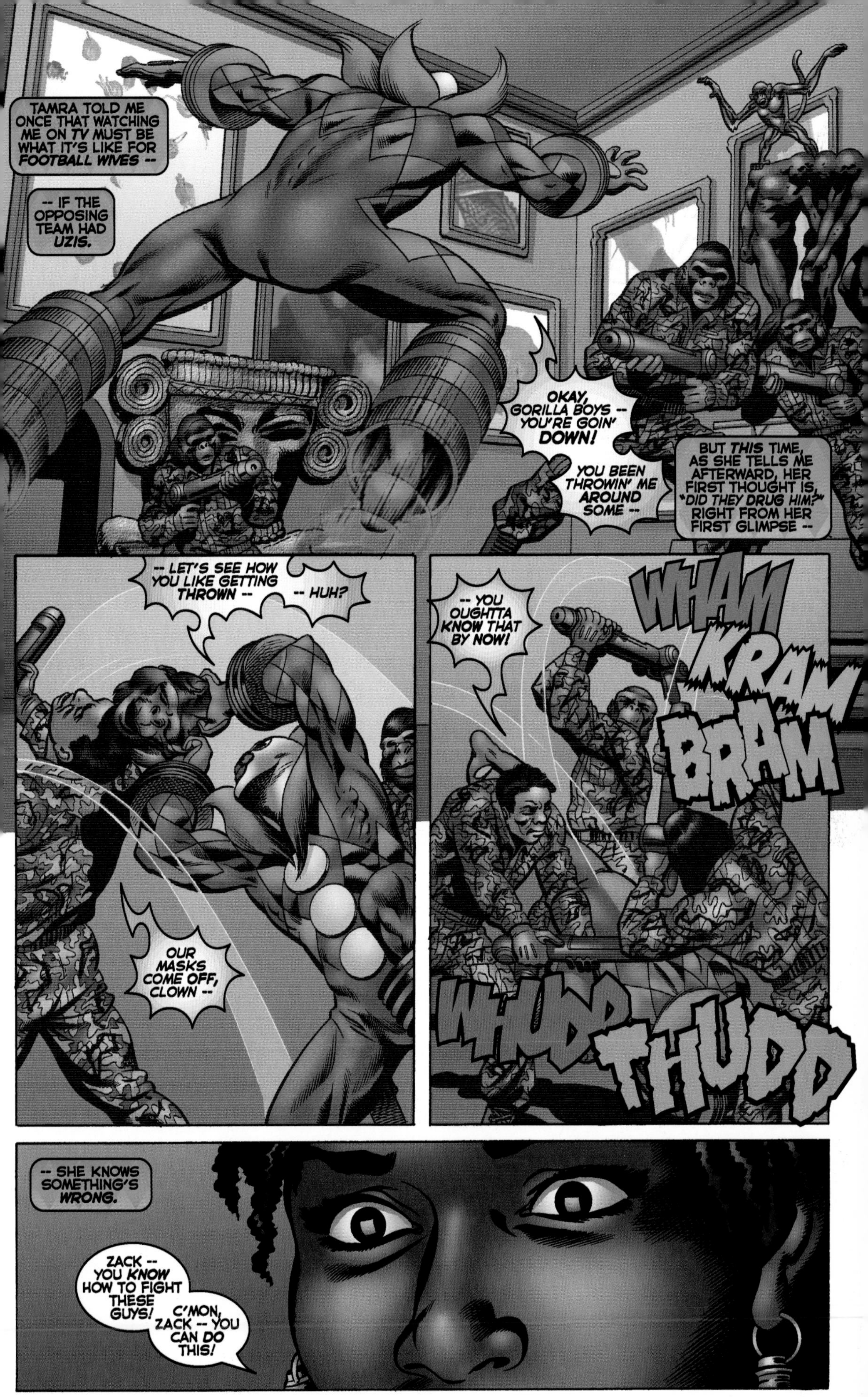
TAMRA TOLD ME ONCE THAT WATCHING ME ON TV MUST BE WHAT IT'S LIKE FOR FOOTBALL WIVES --
-- IF THE OPPOSING TEAM HAD UZIS.
OKAY, GORILLA BOYS -- YOU'RE GOIN' DOWN!
YOU BEEN THROWIN' ME AROUND SOME --
BUT THIS TIME, AS SHE TELLS ME AFTERWARD, HER FIRST THOUGHT IS, "DID THEY DRUG HIM?" RIGHT FROM HER FIRST GLIMPSE --
-- LET'S SEE HOW YOU LIKE GETTING THROWN --
-- HUH?
OUR MASKS COME OFF, CLOWN --
-- YOU OUGHTTA KNOW THAT BY NOW!
WHAM
KRAM
BRAM
WHUDD
THUDD
-- SHE KNOWS SOMETHING'S WRONG.
ZACK -- YOU KNOW HOW TO FIGHT THESE GUYS!
C'MON, ZACK -- YOU CAN DO THIS!

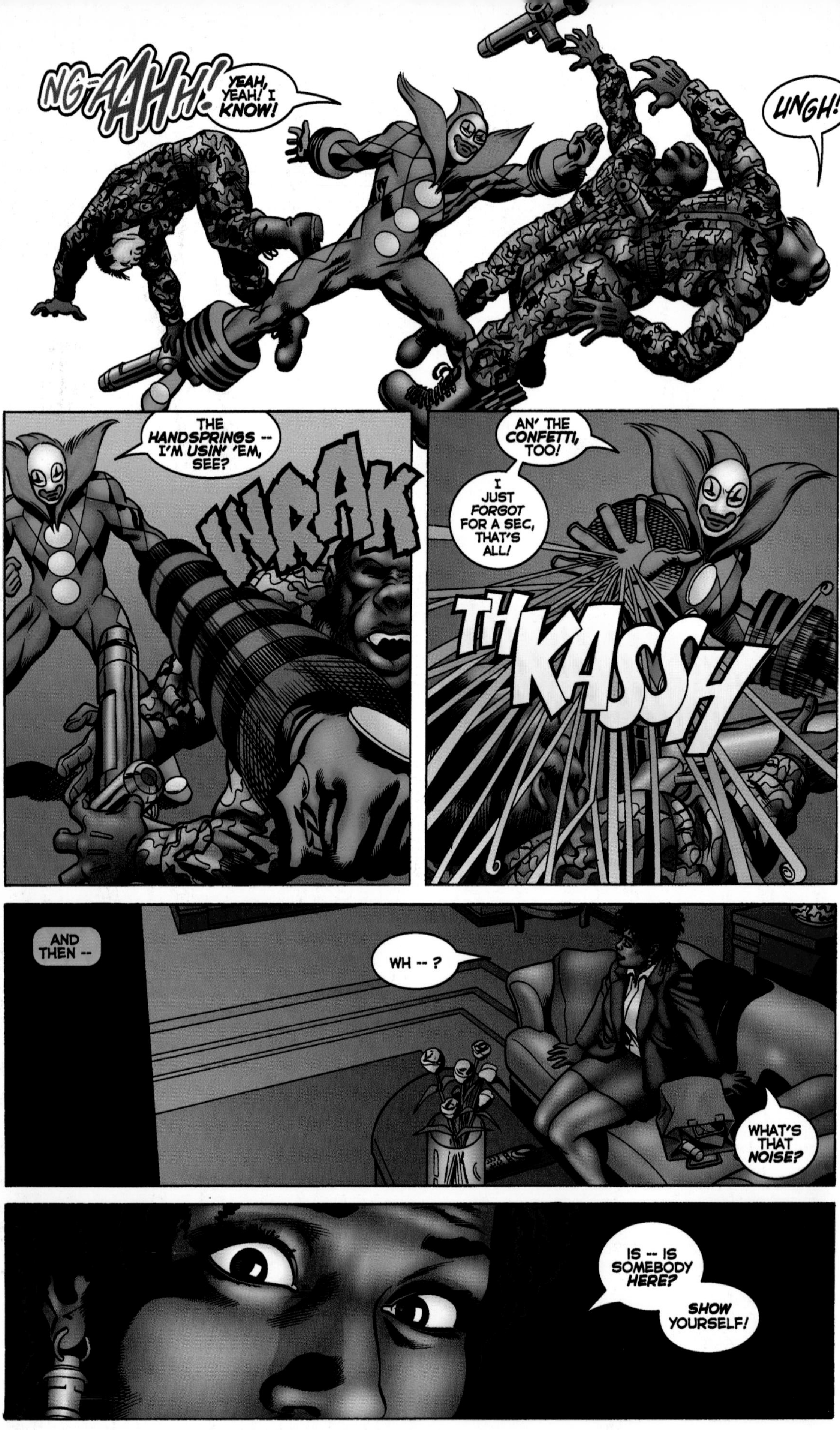
NG-AAHH!
YEAH, YEAH! I KNOW!
UNGH!
THE HANDSPRINGS -- I'M USIN' 'EM, SEE?
WRAK
AN' THE CONFETTI, TOO!
I JUST FORGOT FOR A SEC, THAT'S ALL!
THKASSH
AND THEN --
WH -- ?
WHAT'S THAT NOISE?
IS -- IS SOMEBODY HERE?
SHOW YOURSELF!

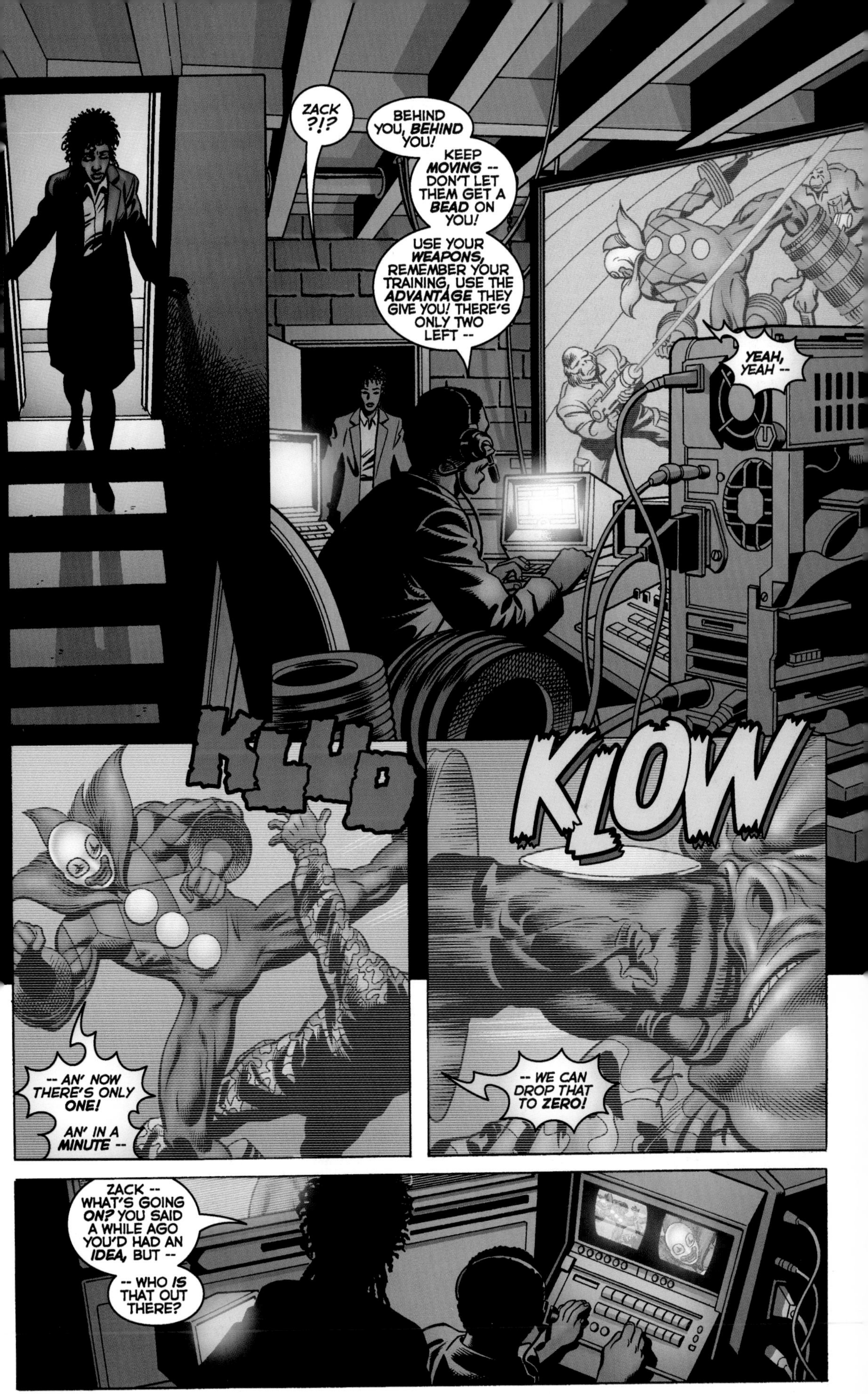
ZACK ?!?
BEHIND YOU, BEHIND YOU!
KEEP MOVING -- DON'T LET THEM GET A BEAD ON YOU!
USE YOUR WEAPONS, REMEMBER YOUR TRAINING, USE THE ADVANTAGE THEY GIVE YOU! THERE'S ONLY TWO LEFT --
YEAH, YEAH --
KLUD
-- AN' NOW THERE'S ONLY ONE!
AN' IN A MINUTE --
KLOW
-- WE CAN DROP THAT TO ZERO!
ZACK -- WHAT'S GOING ON? YOU SAID A WHILE AGO YOU'D HAD AN IDEA, BUT --
-- WHO IS THAT OUT THERE?

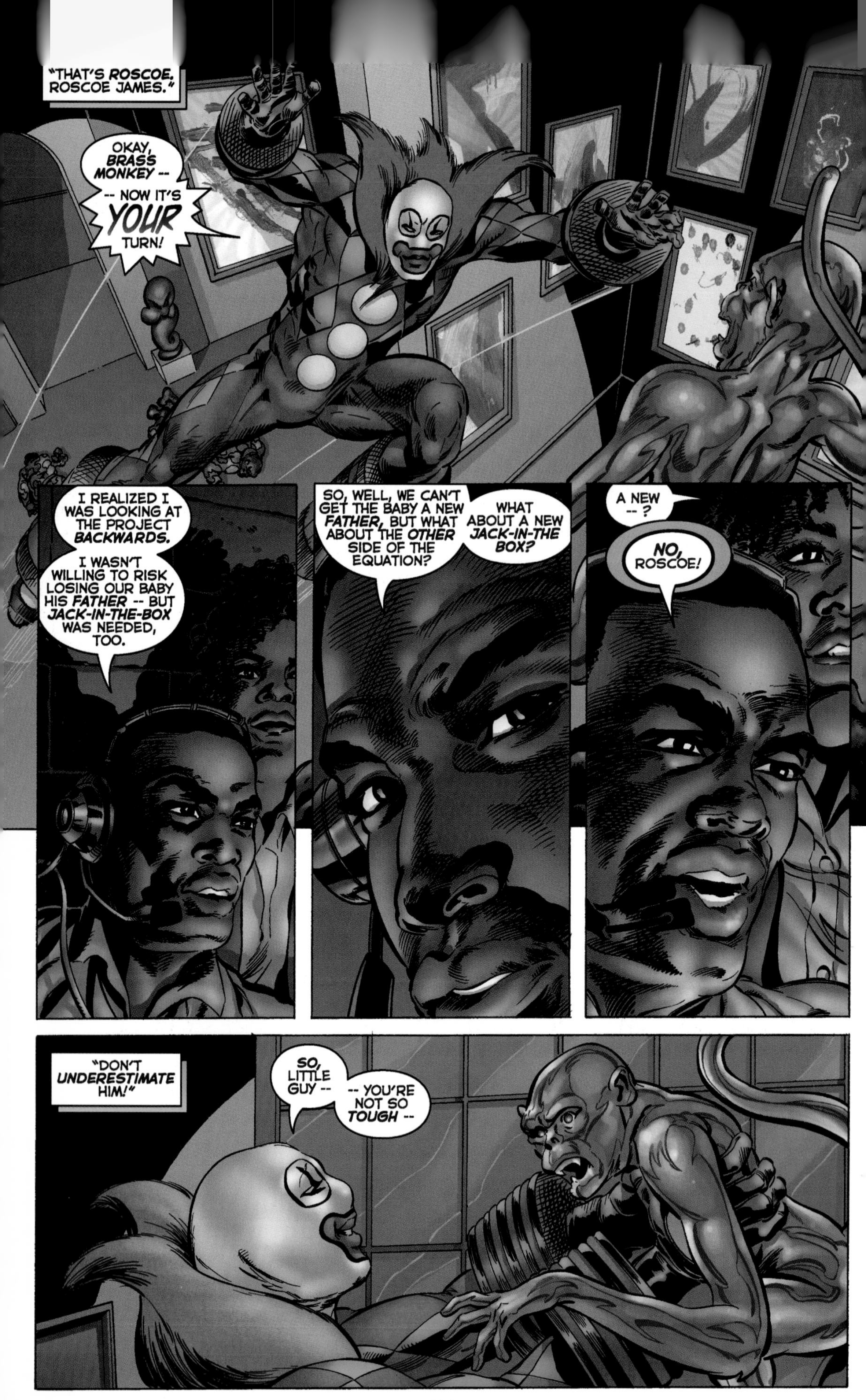
"THAT'S ROSCOE. ROSCOE JAMES."
OKAY, BRASS MONKEY --
-- NOW IT'S YOUR TURN!
I REALIZED I WAS LOOKING AT THE PROJECT BACKWARDS.
I WASN'T WILLING TO RISK LOSING OUR BABY HIS FATHER -- BUT JACK-IN-THE-BOX WAS NEEDED, TOO.
SO, WELL, WE CAN'T GET THE BABY A NEW FATHER, BUT WHAT ABOUT THE OTHER SIDE OF THE EQUATION?
WHAT ABOUT A NEW JACK-IN-THE-BOX?
A NEW -- ?
NO, ROSCOE!
"DON'T UNDERESTIMATE HIM!"
SO, LITTLE GUY --
-- YOU'RE NOT SO TOUGH --

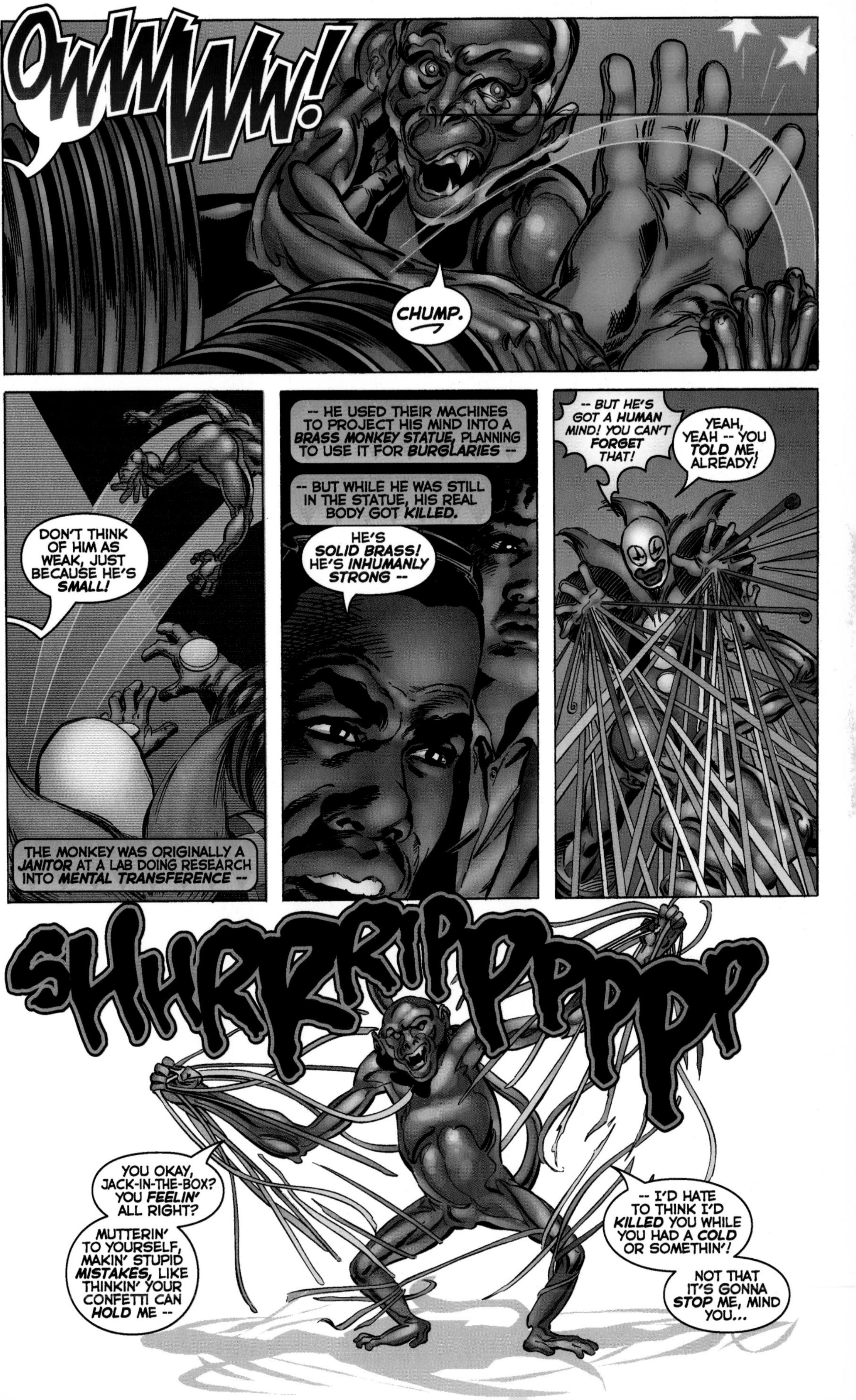
OWWWW!
CHUMP.
THE MONKEY WAS ORIGINALLY A JANITOR AT A LAB DOING RESEARCH INTO MENTAL TRANSFERENCE --
DON'T THINK OF HIM AS WEAK, JUST BECAUSE HE'S SMALL!
-- HE USED THEIR MACHINES TO PROJECT HIS MIND INTO A BRASS MONKEY STATUE, PLANNING TO USE IT FOR BURGLARIES --
-- BUT WHILE HE WAS STILL IN THE STATUE, HIS REAL BODY GOT KILLED.
HE'S SOLID BRASS! HE'S INHUMANLY STRONG --
-- BUT HE'S GOT A HUMAN MIND! YOU CAN'T FORGET THAT!
YEAH, YEAH -- YOU TOLD ME, ALREADY!
SHHRRRIPPPPPP
YOU OKAY, JACK-IN-THE-BOX? YOU FEELIN' ALL RIGHT?
MUTTERIN' TO YOURSELF, MAKIN' STUPID MISTAKES, LIKE THINKIN' YOUR CONFETTI CAN HOLD ME --
-- I'D HATE TO THINK I'D KILLED YOU WHILE YOU HAD A COLD OR SOMETHIN'!
NOT THAT IT'S GONNA STOP ME, MIND YOU...

USE THE FOOTAPULTS, ROSCOE -- STAY AWAY FROM HIM!

DON'T LET HIM GRAPPLE WITH YOU -- HE'S TOO STRONG!

ARE YOU SURE IT'S OKAY TO *RECRUIT* HIM? THE RISK --

IT'S A *RISK*, YEAH. BUT AT LEAST *HE* CAN ACCEPT IT *CONSCIOUSLY* --

-- AND IT'S NOT LIKE THE STREETS OF BAKERVILLE ARE A WALK IN THE *PARK.* BELIEVE ME, HE *KNEW* WHAT HE WAS AGREEING TO.

HE NEEDS A WAY *OUT* -- AND THIS WAY, I CAN GIVE HIM SOME MONEY FOR SCHOOL, FOR *COLLEGE* --

-- AND HE'LL *TAKE* IT. HE WOULDN'T HAVE TAKEN *CHARITY.*

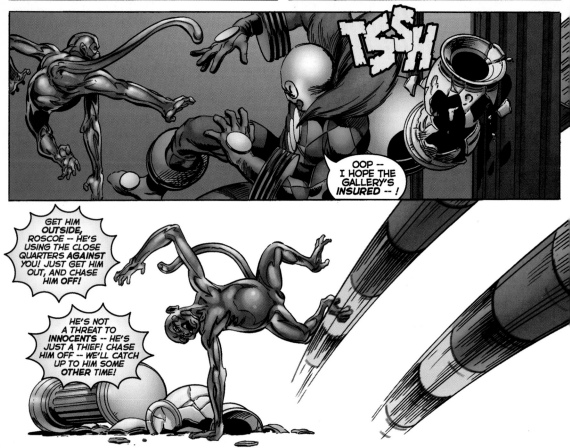

TSSH

OOP -- I HOPE THE GALLERY'S *INSURED* -- !

GET HIM *OUTSIDE,* ROSCOE -- HE'S USING THE CLOSE QUARTERS *AGAINST* YOU! JUST GET HIM OUT, AND CHASE HIM OFF!

HE'S NOT A THREAT TO *INNOCENTS* -- HE'S JUST A THIEF! CHASE HIM OFF -- WE'LL CATCH UP TO HIM SOME OTHER TIME!

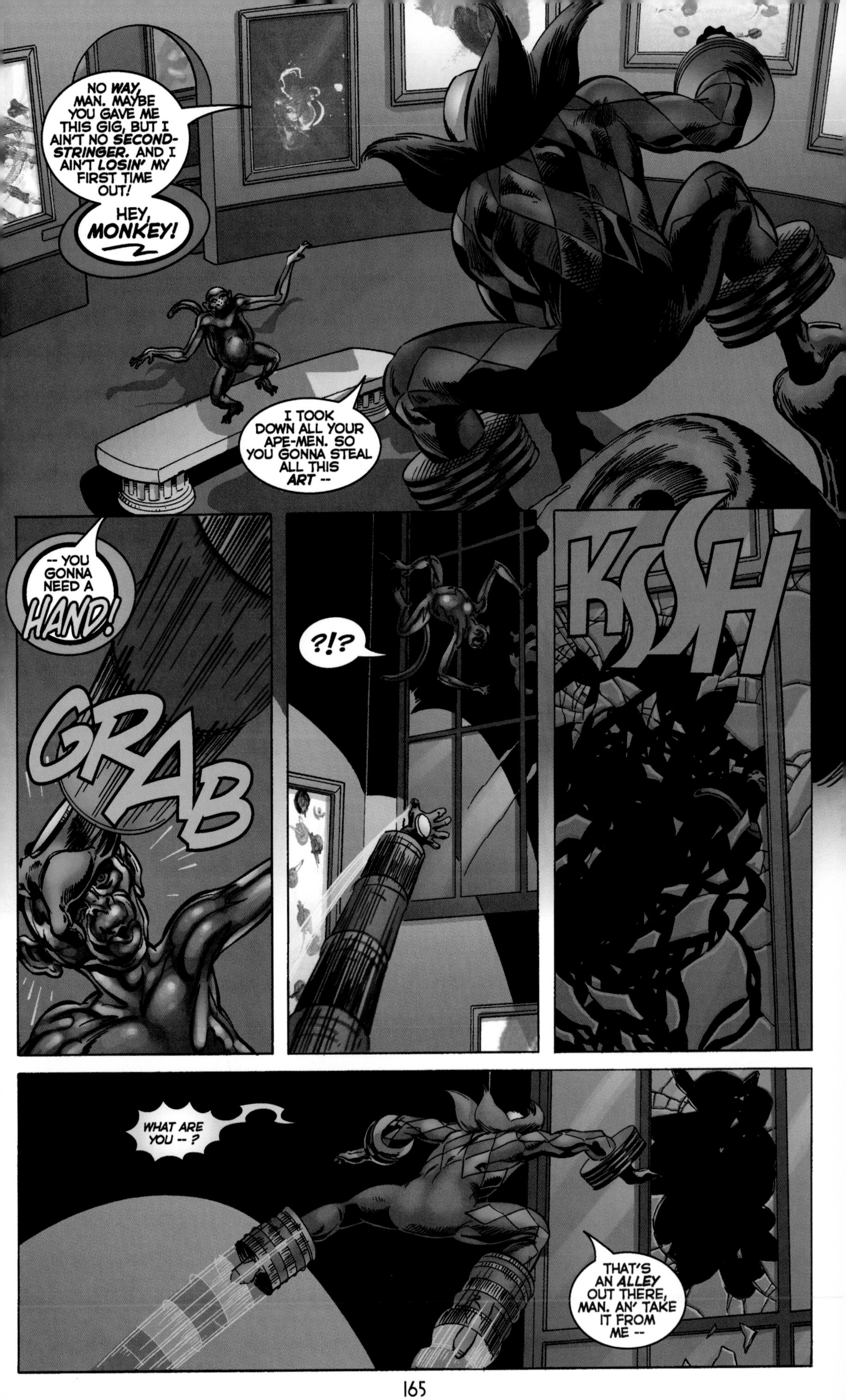
NO WAY, MAN. MAYBE YOU GAVE ME THIS GIG, BUT I AIN'T NO SECOND-STRINGER. AND I AIN'T LOSIN' MY FIRST TIME OUT!
HEY, MONKEY!
I TOOK DOWN ALL YOUR APE-MEN. SO YOU GONNA STEAL ALL THIS ART --
-- YOU GONNA NEED A HAND!
GRAB
?!?
KSSH
WHAT ARE YOU -- ?
THAT'S AN ALLEY OUT THERE, MAN. AN' TAKE IT FROM ME --

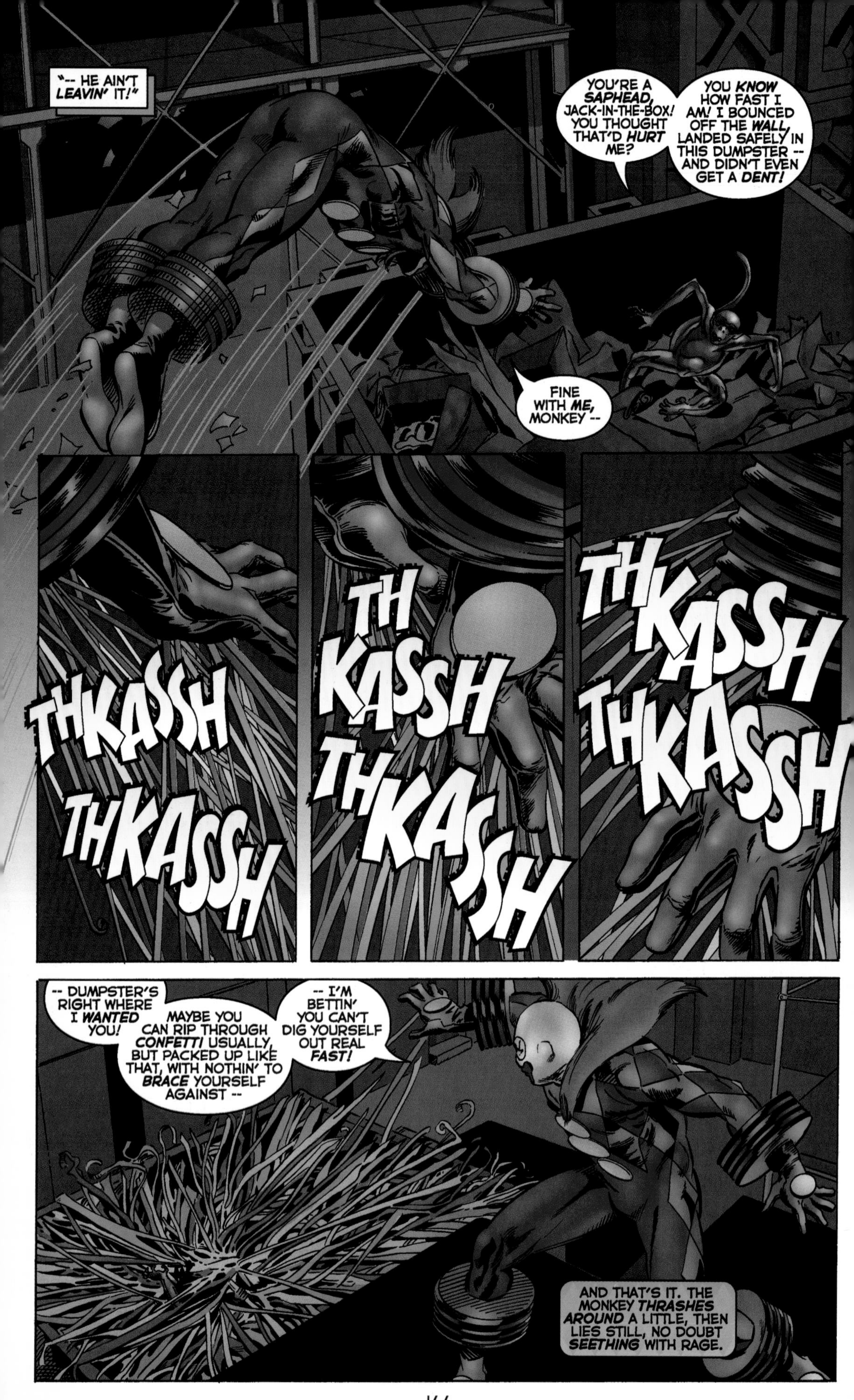
"-- HE AIN'T LEAVIN' IT!"
YOU'RE A SAPHEAD, JACK-IN-THE-BOX! YOU THOUGHT THAT'D HURT ME?
YOU KNOW HOW FAST I AM! I BOUNCED OFF THE WALL, LANDED SAFELY IN THIS DUMPSTER -- AND DIDN'T EVEN GET A DENT!
FINE WITH ME, MONKEY --
THKASSH THKASSH
THKASSH THKASSH
THKASSH THKASSH
-- DUMPSTER'S RIGHT WHERE I WANTED YOU!
MAYBE YOU CAN RIP THROUGH CONFETTI USUALLY, BUT PACKED UP LIKE THAT, WITH NOTHIN' TO BRACE YOURSELF AGAINST --
-- I'M BETTIN' YOU CAN'T DIG YOURSELF OUT REAL FAST!
AND THAT'S IT. THE MONKEY THRASHES AROUND A LITTLE, THEN LIES STILL, NO DOUBT SEETHING WITH RAGE.

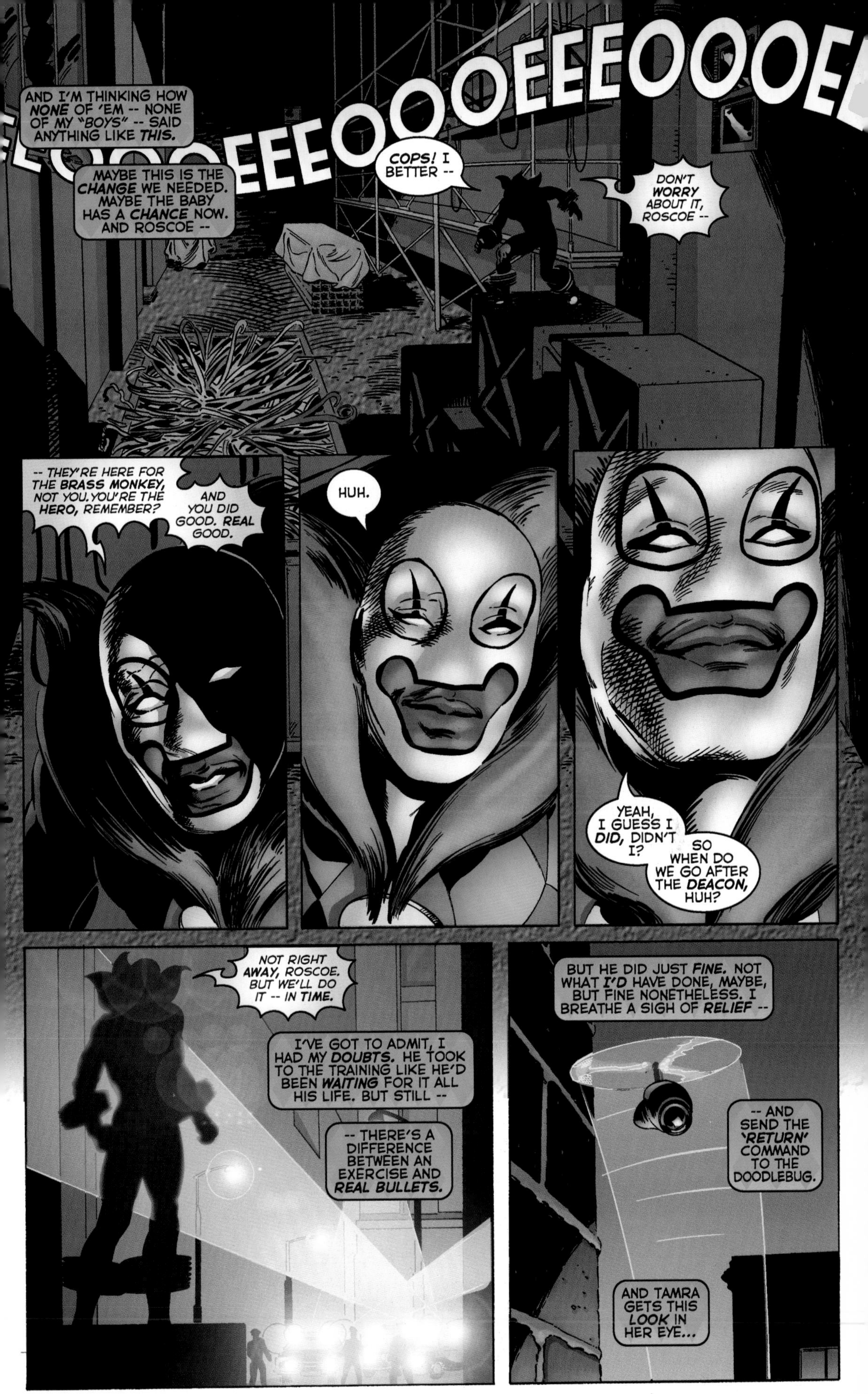
EEEOOOEEEOOOEEEOOOEEEOOOE
AND I'M THINKING HOW NONE OF 'EM -- NONE OF MY "BOYS" -- SAID ANYTHING LIKE THIS.
MAYBE THIS IS THE CHANGE WE NEEDED. MAYBE THE BABY HAS A CHANCE NOW. AND ROSCOE --
COPS! I BETTER --
DON'T WORRY ABOUT IT, ROSCOE --
-- THEY'RE HERE FOR THE BRASS MONKEY, NOT YOU. YOU'RE THE HERO, REMEMBER?
AND YOU DID GOOD. REAL GOOD.
HUH.
YEAH, I GUESS I DID, DIDN'T I?
SO WHEN DO WE GO AFTER THE DEACON, HUH?
NOT RIGHT AWAY, ROSCOE. BUT WE'LL DO IT -- IN TIME.
I'VE GOT TO ADMIT, I HAD MY DOUBTS. HE TOOK TO THE TRAINING LIKE HE'D BEEN WAITING FOR IT ALL HIS LIFE. BUT STILL --
-- THERE'S A DIFFERENCE BETWEEN AN EXERCISE AND REAL BULLETS.
BUT HE DID JUST FINE. NOT WHAT I'D HAVE DONE, MAYBE, BUT FINE NONETHELESS. I BREATHE A SIGH OF RELIEF --
-- AND SEND THE 'RETURN' COMMAND TO THE DOODLEBUG.
AND TAMRA GETS THIS LOOK IN HER EYE...

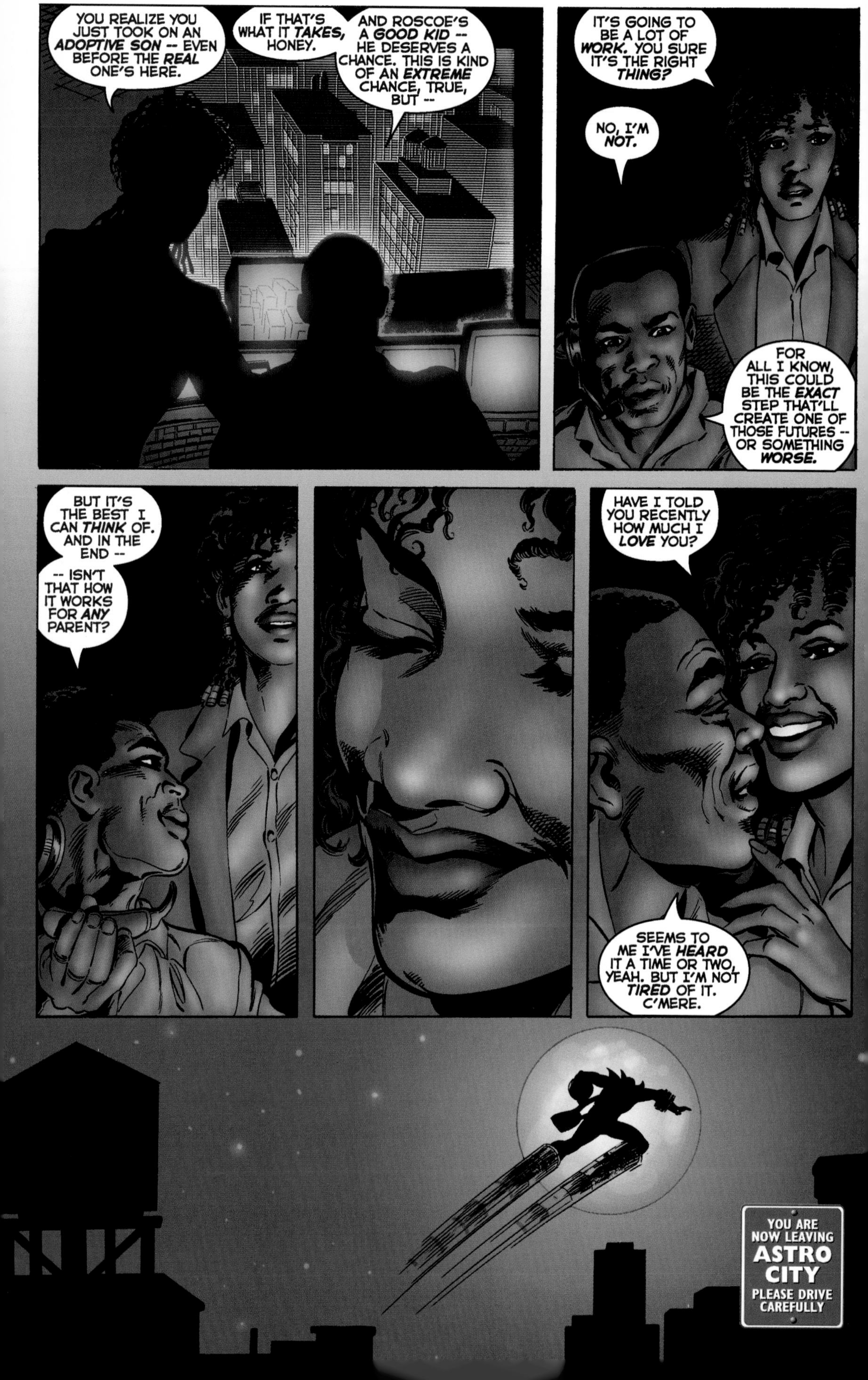
YOU REALIZE YOU JUST TOOK ON AN ADOPTIVE SON -- EVEN BEFORE THE REAL ONE'S HERE.
IF THAT'S WHAT IT TAKES, HONEY.
AND ROSCOE'S A GOOD KID -- HE DESERVES A CHANCE. THIS IS KIND OF AN EXTREME CHANCE, TRUE, BUT --
IT'S GOING TO BE A LOT OF WORK. YOU SURE IT'S THE RIGHT THING?
NO, I'M NOT.
FOR ALL I KNOW, THIS COULD BE THE EXACT STEP THAT'LL CREATE ONE OF THOSE FUTURES -- OR SOMETHING WORSE.
BUT IT'S THE BEST I CAN THINK OF. AND IN THE END --
-- ISN'T THAT HOW IT WORKS FOR ANY PARENT?
HAVE I TOLD YOU RECENTLY HOW MUCH I LOVE YOU?
SEEMS TO ME I'VE HEARD IT A TIME OR TWO, YEAH. BUT I'M NOT TIRED OF IT. C'MERE.
YOU ARE NOW LEAVING ASTRO CITY PLEASE DRIVE CAREFULLY

"In the Spotlight"

7

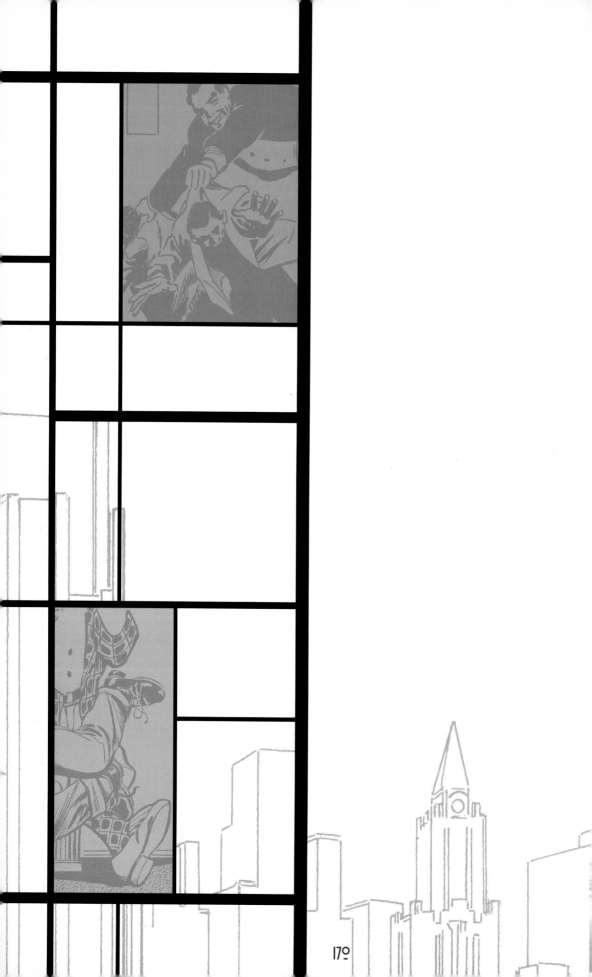

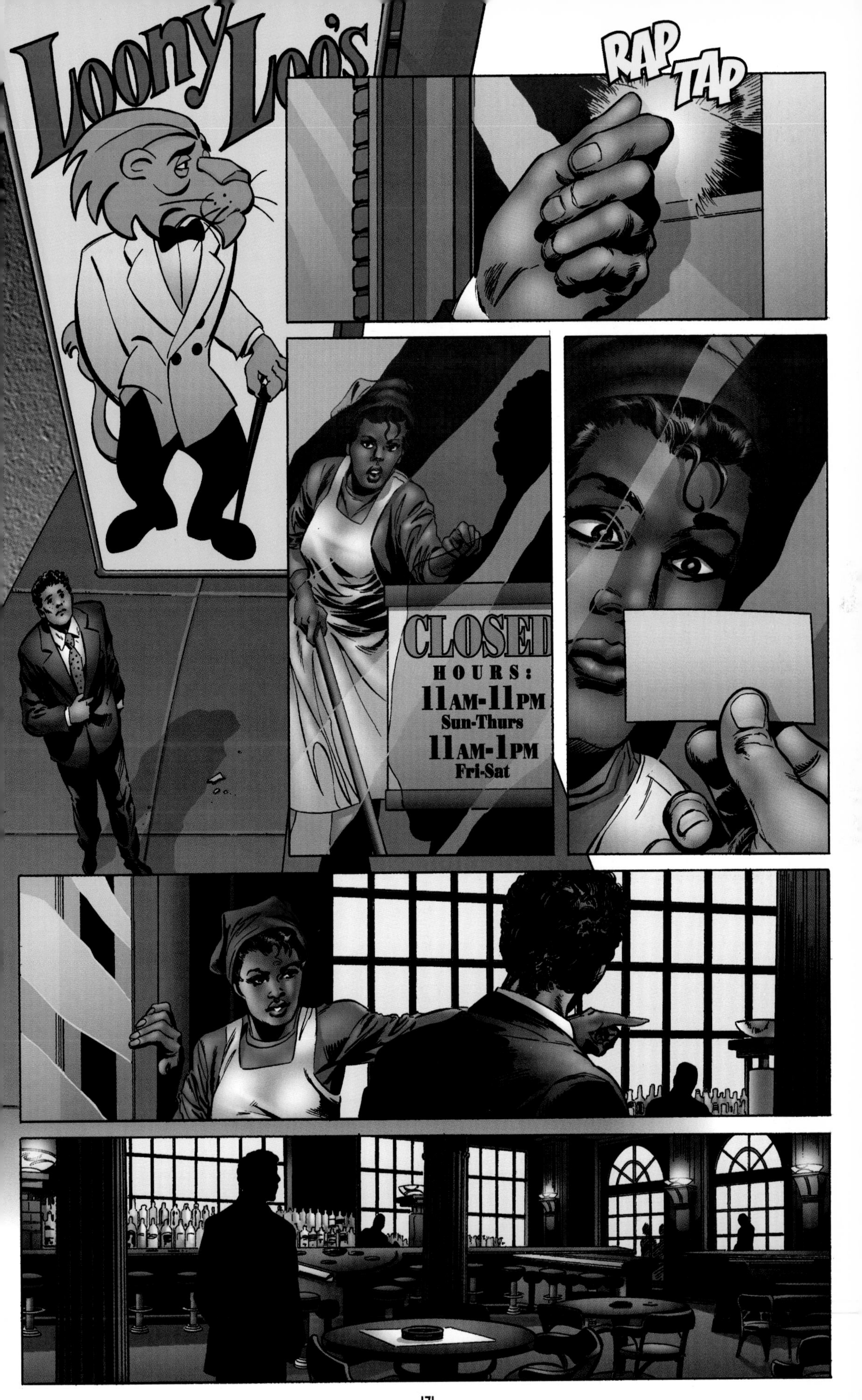
Loony Leo's
RAP TAP
CLOSED
HOURS:
11AM-11PM
Sun-Thurs
11AM-1PM
Fri-Sat

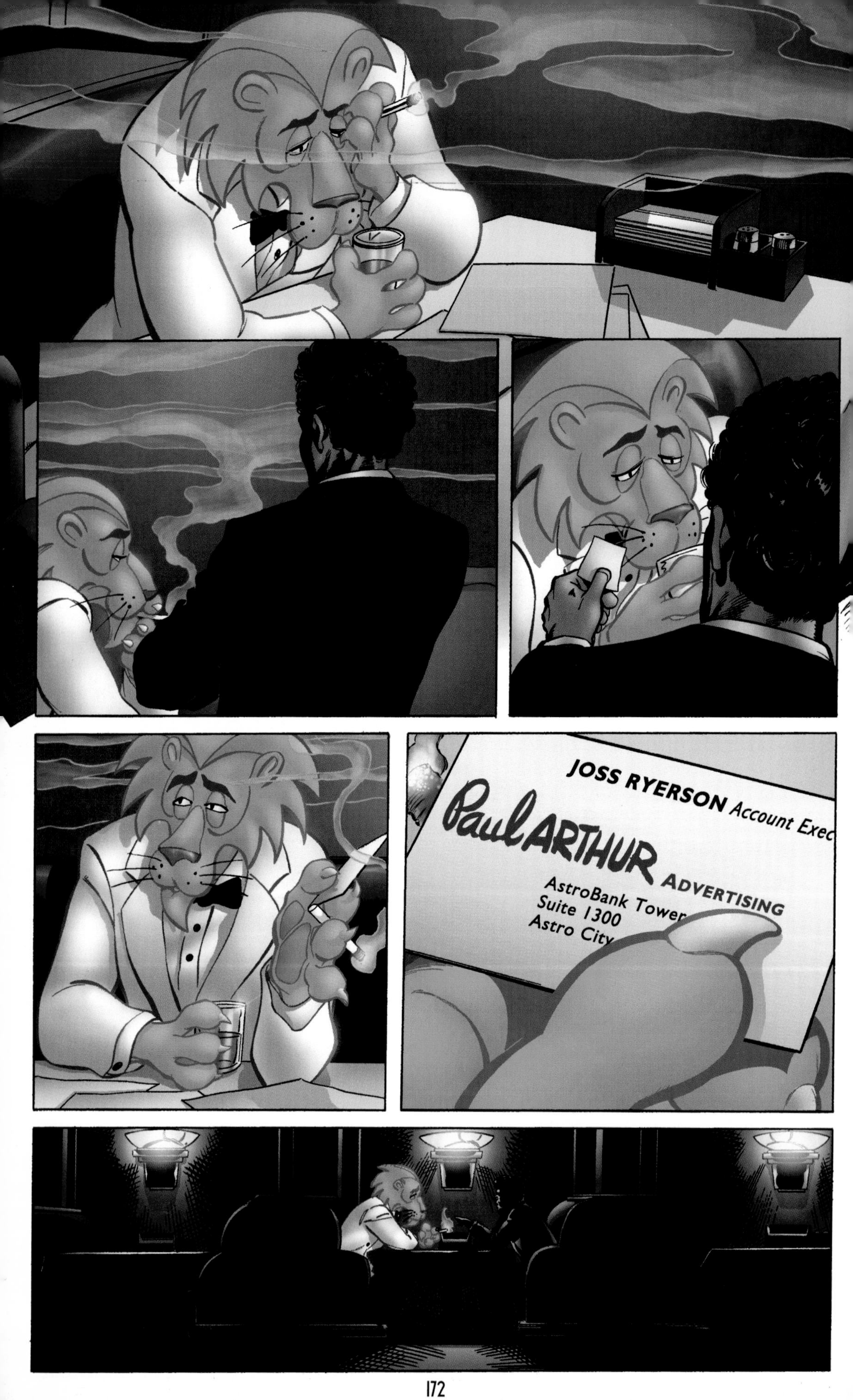
JOSS RYERSON Account Exec
Paul ARTHUR ADVERTISING
AstroBank Tower
Suite 1300
Astro City

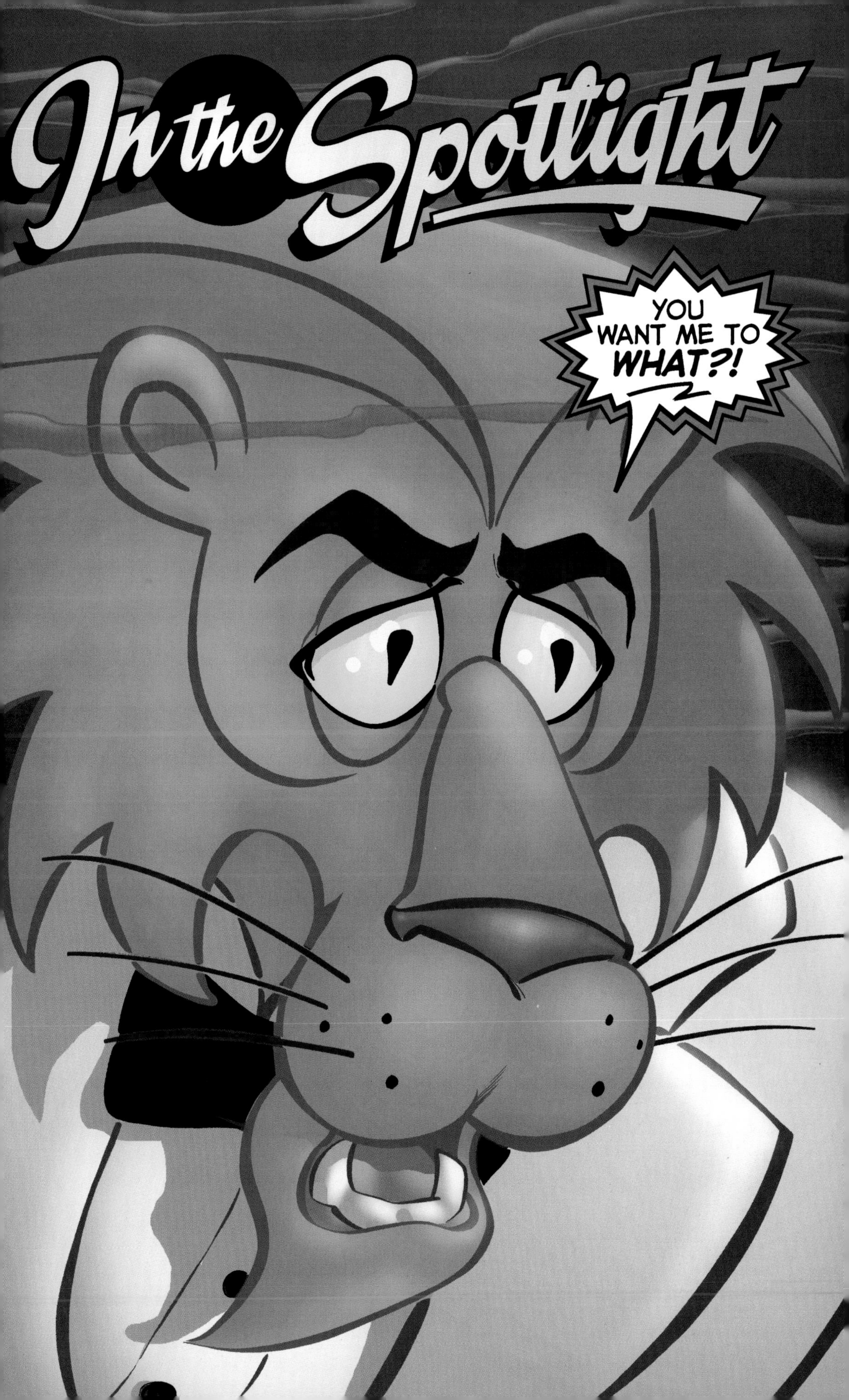
In the Spotlight
YOU WANT ME TO WHAT?!

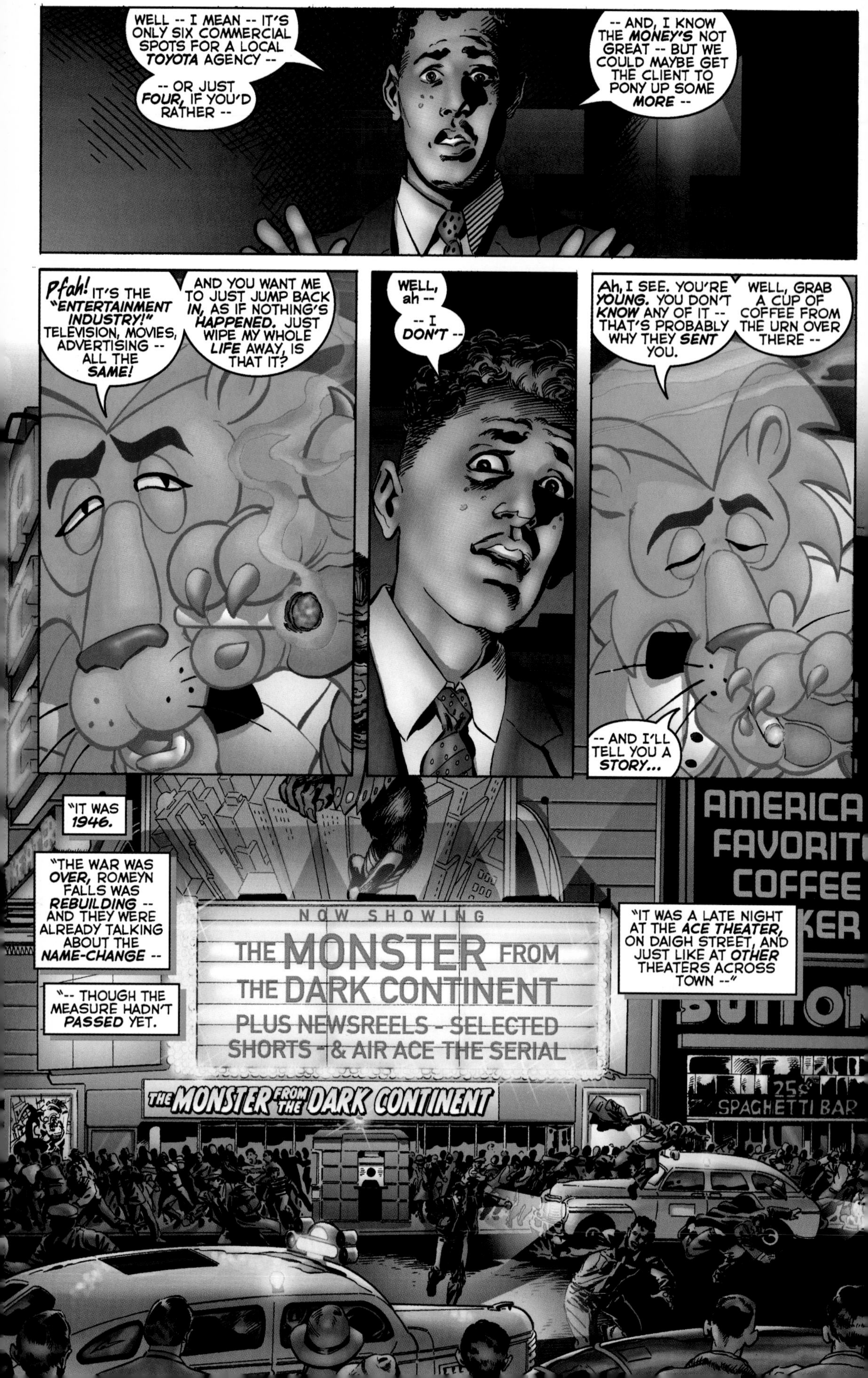

WELL -- I MEAN -- IT'S ONLY SIX COMMERCIAL SPOTS FOR A LOCAL TOYOTA AGENCY --
-- OR JUST FOUR, IF YOU'D RATHER --
-- AND, I KNOW THE MONEY'S NOT GREAT -- BUT WE COULD MAYBE GET THE CLIENT TO PONY UP SOME MORE --
Pfah! IT'S THE "ENTERTAINMENT INDUSTRY!" TELEVISION, MOVIES, ADVERTISING -- ALL THE SAME!
AND YOU WANT ME TO JUST JUMP BACK IN, AS IF NOTHING'S HAPPENED. JUST WIPE MY WHOLE LIFE AWAY, IS THAT IT?
WELL, ah --
-- I DON'T --
Ah, I SEE. YOU'RE YOUNG. YOU DON'T KNOW ANY OF IT -- THAT'S PROBABLY WHY THEY SENT YOU.
WELL, GRAB A CUP OF COFFEE FROM THE URN OVER THERE --
-- AND I'LL TELL YOU A STORY...
"IT WAS 1946.
"THE WAR WAS OVER, ROMEYN FALLS WAS REBUILDING -- AND THEY WERE ALREADY TALKING ABOUT THE NAME-CHANGE --
"-- THOUGH THE MEASURE HADN'T PASSED YET.
AMERICA FAVORIT COFFEE
NOW SHOWING
THE MONSTER FROM THE DARK CONTINENT
PLUS NEWSREELS - SELECTED SHORTS - & AIR ACE THE SERIAL
THE MONSTER FROM THE DARK CONTINENT
25¢ SPAGHETTI BAR
"IT WAS A LATE NIGHT AT THE ACE THEATER, ON DAIGH STREET, AND JUST LIKE AT OTHER THEATERS ACROSS TOWN --"

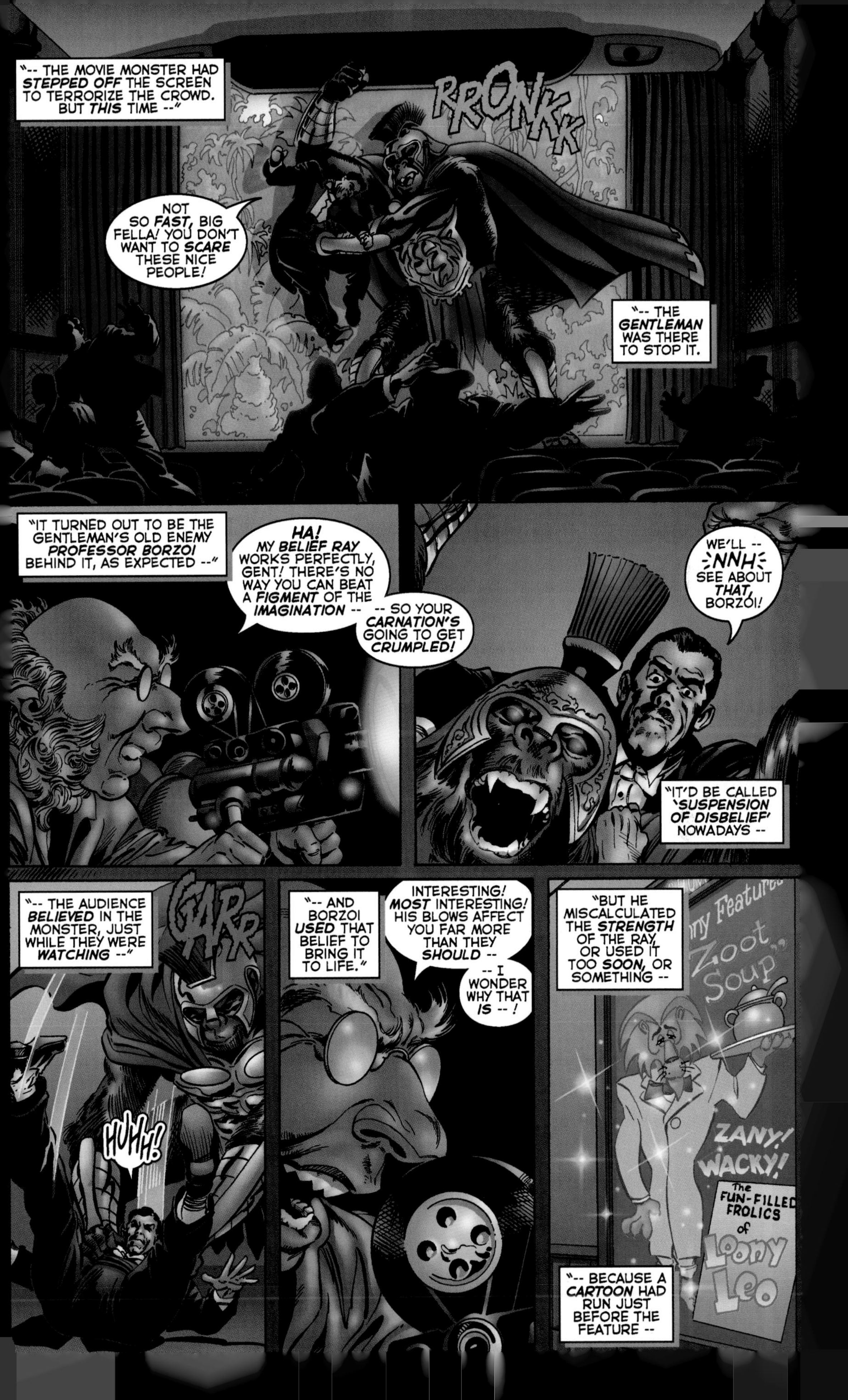
"-- THE MOVIE MONSTER HAD STEPPED OFF THE SCREEN TO TERRORIZE THE CROWD. BUT THIS TIME --"
RRONKK
NOT SO FAST, BIG FELLA! YOU DON'T WANT TO SCARE THESE NICE PEOPLE!
"-- THE GENTLEMAN WAS THERE TO STOP IT.
"IT TURNED OUT TO BE THE GENTLEMAN'S OLD ENEMY PROFESSOR BORZOI BEHIND IT, AS EXPECTED --"
HA! MY BELIEF RAY WORKS PERFECTLY, GENT! THERE'S NO WAY YOU CAN BEAT A FIGMENT OF THE IMAGINATION --
-- SO YOUR CARNATION'S GOING TO GET CRUMPLED!
WE'LL -- NNH -- SEE ABOUT THAT, BORZOI!
"IT'D BE CALLED 'SUSPENSION OF DISBELIEF' NOWADAYS --
"-- THE AUDIENCE BELIEVED IN THE MONSTER, JUST WHILE THEY WERE WATCHING --"
GARR
HUHH!
"-- AND BORZOI USED THAT BELIEF TO BRING IT TO LIFE."
INTERESTING! MOST INTERESTING! HIS BLOWS AFFECT YOU FAR MORE THAN THEY SHOULD --
-- I WONDER WHY THAT IS -- !
"BUT HE MISCALCULATED THE STRENGTH OF THE RAY, OR USED IT TOO SOON, OR SOMETHING --
Zoot Soup
ZANY! WACKY!
The FUN-FILLED FROLICS of LOONY LEO
"-- BECAUSE A CARTOON HAD RUN JUST BEFORE THE FEATURE --

"-- AND OUT IN THE *LOBBY* --"

Hm?

ZANY! WACKY!

The FUN-FILLED FROLICS of *Loony Leo*

Rita HAYWORTH as *Gilda* Glenn FORD

"I'D NEVER *EXISTED* BEFORE, NOT REALLY. AND IT WAS *BEWILDERING*."

HOW... ODD!

"I DIDN'T KNOW WHY *ANYTHING* WAS HAPPENING --"

"-- OR WHY THEY WERE *SCREAMING* AT ME."

EEEEE!

COMING SOON

ANOTHER ONE!

THEY'LL *KILL* US! THEY'LL *KILL* US ALL!

RUN! *RUN!*

PLEASE -- I DON'T --

"ALL IN ALL, IT WAS A PRETTY *CONFUSING* SCENE TO COME IN ON."

ROYAL CROWN COLA

Eat POPCORN

OH, NO YOU *DON'T!*

Happy Jack

BEVERAGES

"BUT IT WAS *FASCINATING,* TOO.

"I *WATCHED,* TRYING TO FIGURE OUT WHAT WAS *GOING ON* --

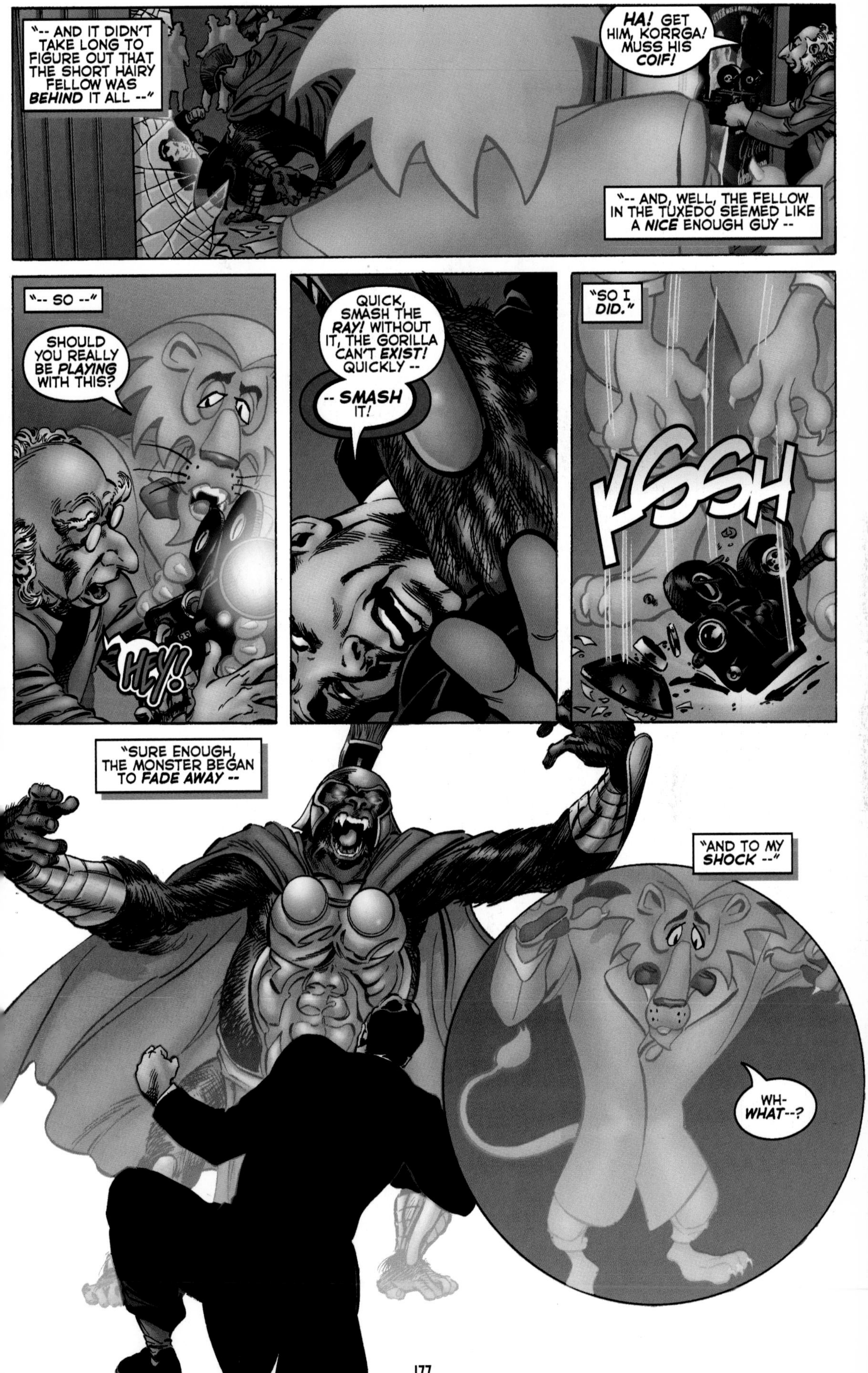

"-- AND IT DIDN'T TAKE LONG TO FIGURE OUT THAT THE SHORT HAIRY FELLOW WAS BEHIND IT ALL --"
HA! GET HIM, KORRGA! MUSS HIS COIF!
"-- AND, WELL, THE FELLOW IN THE TUXEDO SEEMED LIKE A NICE ENOUGH GUY --
"-- SO --"
SHOULD YOU REALLY BE PLAYING WITH THIS?
HEY!
QUICK, SMASH THE RAY! WITHOUT IT, THE GORILLA CAN'T EXIST! QUICKLY --
-- SMASH IT!
"SO I DID."
KSSH
"SURE ENOUGH, THE MONSTER BEGAN TO FADE AWAY --
"AND TO MY SHOCK --"
WH- WHAT--?

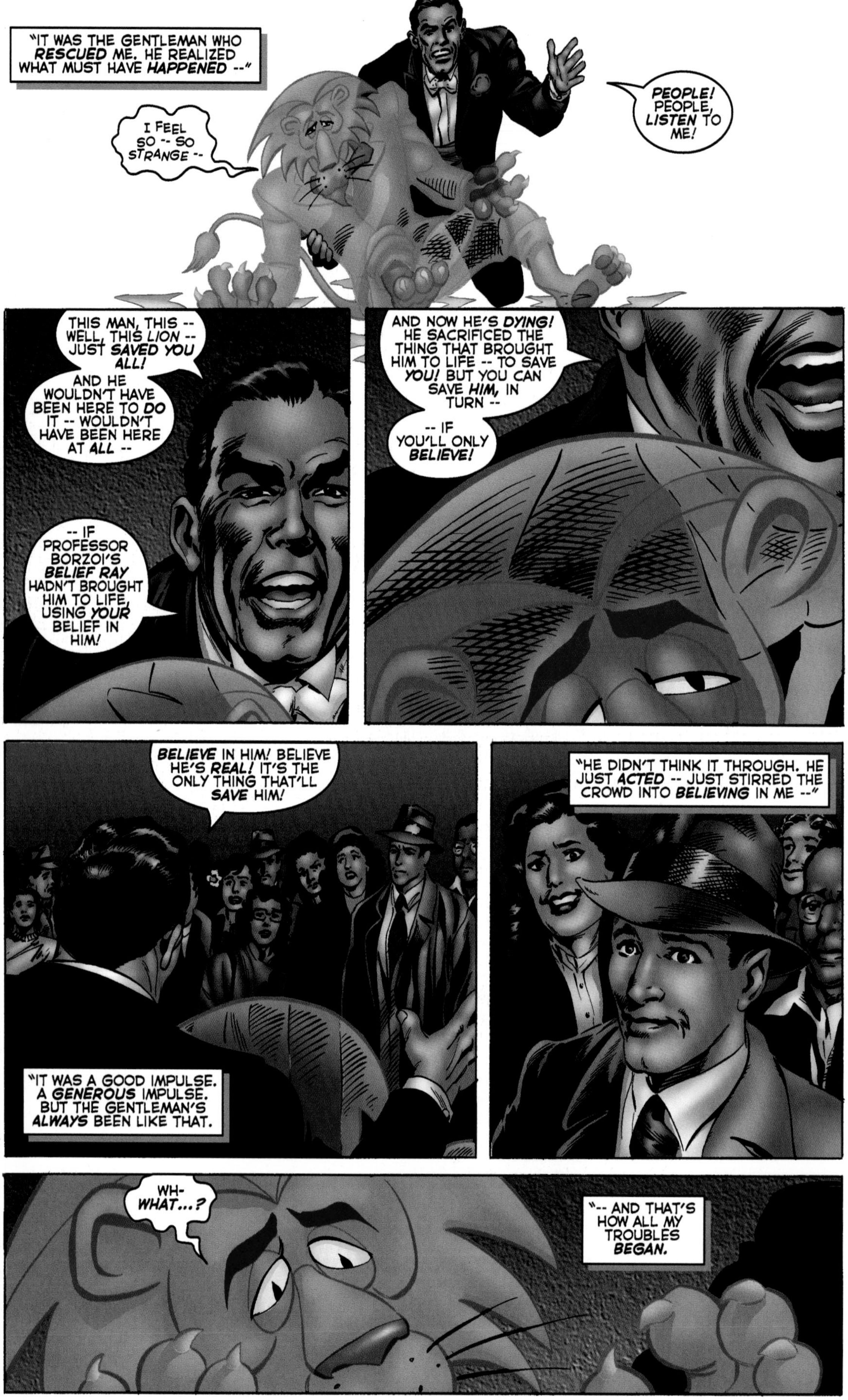
"IT WAS THE GENTLEMAN WHO RESCUED ME. HE REALIZED WHAT MUST HAVE HAPPENED --"
I FEEL SO -- SO STRANGE --
PEOPLE! PEOPLE, LISTEN TO ME!
THIS MAN, THIS -- WELL, THIS LION -- JUST SAVED YOU ALL!
AND HE WOULDN'T HAVE BEEN HERE TO DO IT -- WOULDN'T HAVE BEEN HERE AT ALL --
-- IF PROFESSOR BORZOI'S BELIEF RAY HADN'T BROUGHT HIM TO LIFE, USING YOUR BELIEF IN HIM!
AND NOW HE'S DYING! HE SACRIFICED THE THING THAT BROUGHT HIM TO LIFE -- TO SAVE YOU! BUT YOU CAN SAVE HIM, IN TURN --
-- IF YOU'LL ONLY BELIEVE!
BELIEVE IN HIM! BELIEVE HE'S REAL! IT'S THE ONLY THING THAT'LL SAVE HIM!
"IT WAS A GOOD IMPULSE. A GENEROUS IMPULSE. BUT THE GENTLEMAN'S ALWAYS BEEN LIKE THAT.
"HE DIDN'T THINK IT THROUGH. HE JUST ACTED -- JUST STIRRED THE CROWD INTO BELIEVING IN ME --"
WH- WHAT...?
"-- AND THAT'S HOW ALL MY TROUBLES BEGAN.

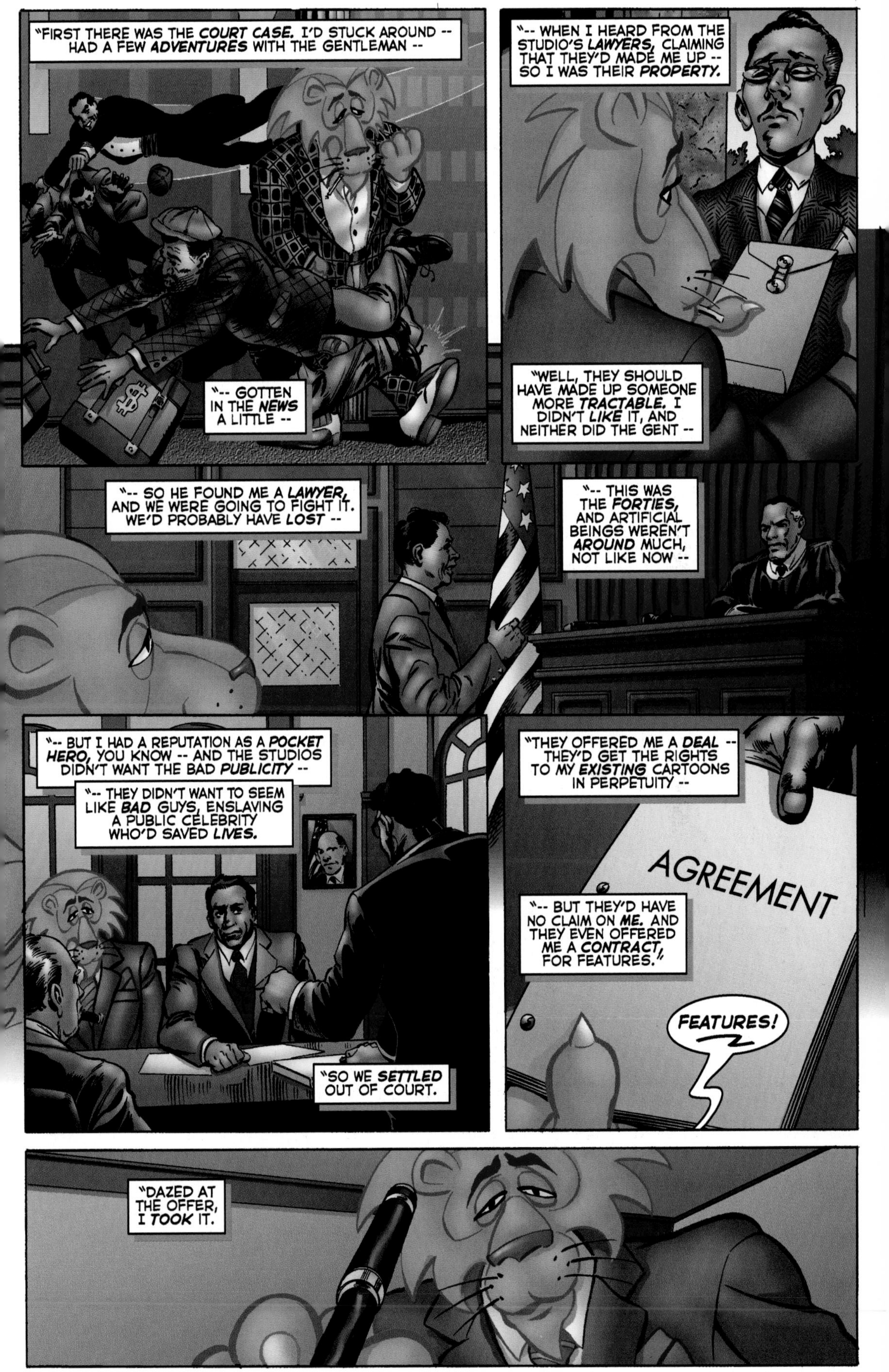
"FIRST THERE WAS THE COURT CASE. I'D STUCK AROUND -- HAD A FEW ADVENTURES WITH THE GENTLEMAN --
"-- GOTTEN IN THE NEWS A LITTLE --
"-- WHEN I HEARD FROM THE STUDIO'S LAWYERS, CLAIMING THAT THEY'D MADE ME UP -- SO I WAS THEIR PROPERTY.
"WELL, THEY SHOULD HAVE MADE UP SOMEONE MORE TRACTABLE. I DIDN'T LIKE IT, AND NEITHER DID THE GENT --
"-- SO HE FOUND ME A LAWYER, AND WE WERE GOING TO FIGHT IT. WE'D PROBABLY HAVE LOST --
"-- THIS WAS THE FORTIES, AND ARTIFICIAL BEINGS WEREN'T AROUND MUCH, NOT LIKE NOW --
"-- BUT I HAD A REPUTATION AS A POCKET HERO, YOU KNOW -- AND THE STUDIOS DIDN'T WANT THE BAD PUBLICITY --
"-- THEY DIDN'T WANT TO SEEM LIKE BAD GUYS, ENSLAVING A PUBLIC CELEBRITY WHO'D SAVED LIVES.
"SO WE SETTLED OUT OF COURT.
"THEY OFFERED ME A DEAL -- THEY'D GET THE RIGHTS TO MY EXISTING CARTOONS IN PERPETUITY --
AGREEMENT
"-- BUT THEY'D HAVE NO CLAIM ON ME. AND THEY EVEN OFFERED ME A CONTRACT, FOR FEATURES."
FEATURES!
"DAZED AT THE OFFER, I TOOK IT.

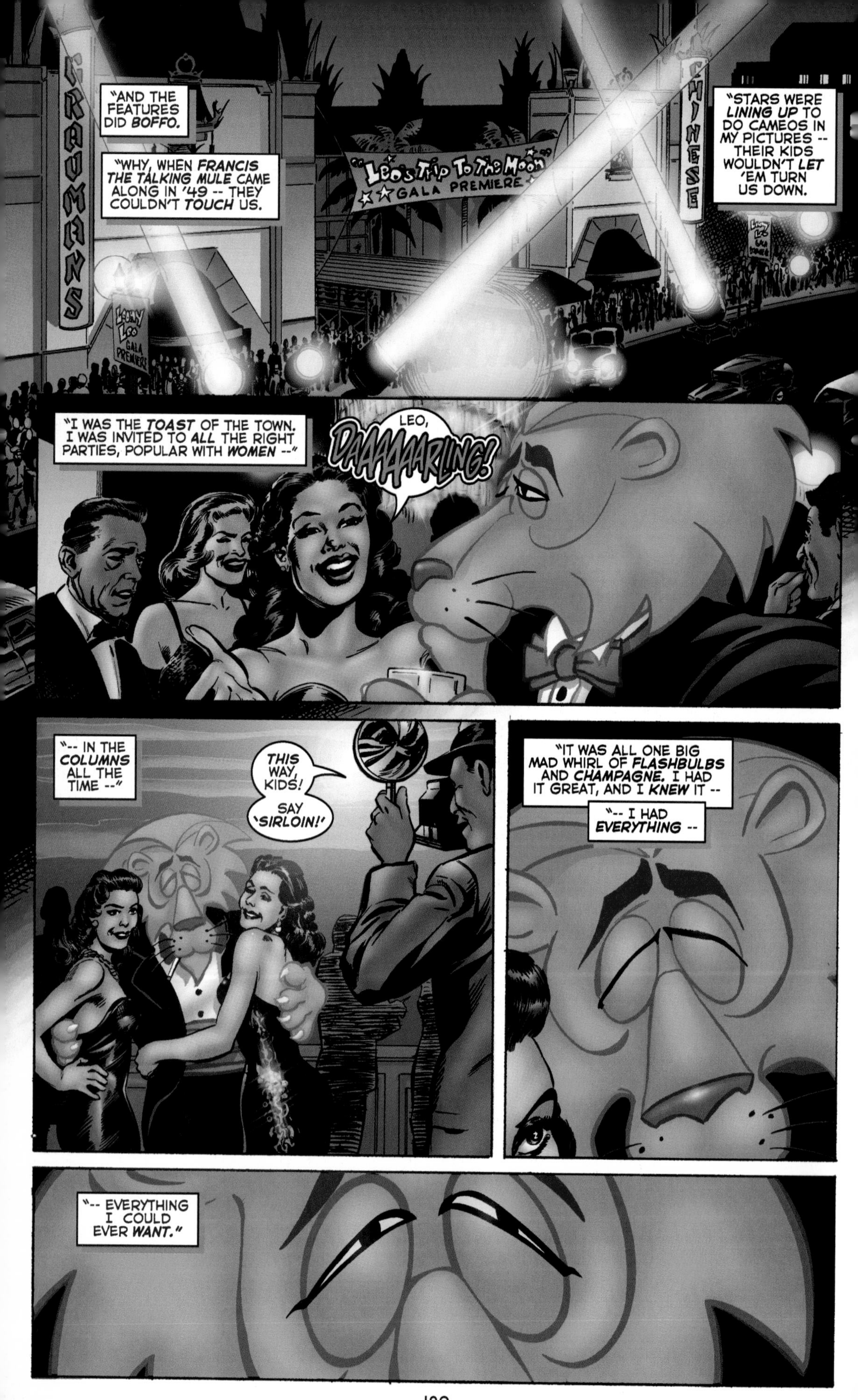
GRAUMANS
CHINESE
"AND THE FEATURES DID BOFFO.
"WHY, WHEN FRANCIS THE TALKING MULE CAME ALONG IN '49 -- THEY COULDN'T TOUCH US.
"LEO'S TRIP TO THE MOON" GALA PREMIERE
"STARS WERE LINING UP TO DO CAMEOS IN MY PICTURES -- THEIR KIDS WOULDN'T LET 'EM TURN US DOWN.
"I WAS THE TOAST OF THE TOWN. I WAS INVITED TO ALL THE RIGHT PARTIES, POPULAR WITH WOMEN --"
LEO, DAAAAAARLING!
"-- IN THE COLUMNS ALL THE TIME --"
THIS WAY, KIDS!
SAY 'SIRLOIN!'
"IT WAS ALL ONE BIG MAD WHIRL OF FLASHBULBS AND CHAMPAGNE. I HAD IT GREAT, AND I KNEW IT --
"-- I HAD EVERYTHING --
"-- EVERYTHING I COULD EVER WANT."

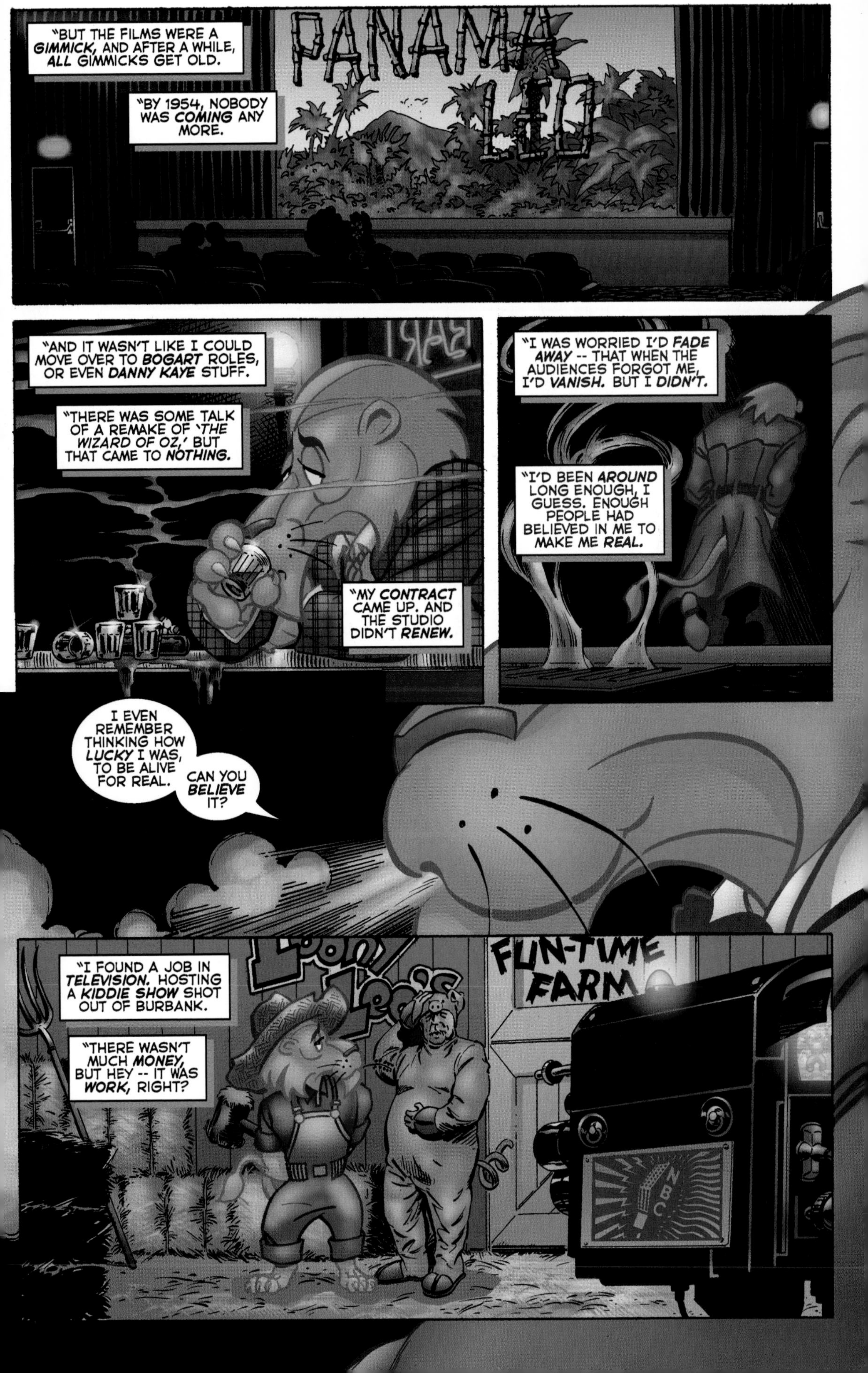
PANAMA LEO
"BUT THE FILMS WERE A GIMMICK, AND AFTER A WHILE, ALL GIMMICKS GET OLD.
"BY 1954, NOBODY WAS COMING ANY MORE.
"AND IT WASN'T LIKE I COULD MOVE OVER TO BOGART ROLES, OR EVEN DANNY KAYE STUFF.
"THERE WAS SOME TALK OF A REMAKE OF 'THE WIZARD OF OZ,' BUT THAT CAME TO NOTHING.
"MY CONTRACT CAME UP. AND THE STUDIO DIDN'T RENEW.
"I WAS WORRIED I'D FADE AWAY -- THAT WHEN THE AUDIENCES FORGOT ME, I'D VANISH. BUT I DIDN'T.
"I'D BEEN AROUND LONG ENOUGH, I GUESS. ENOUGH PEOPLE HAD BELIEVED IN ME TO MAKE ME REAL.
I EVEN REMEMBER THINKING HOW LUCKY I WAS, TO BE ALIVE FOR REAL.
CAN YOU BELIEVE IT?
"I FOUND A JOB IN TELEVISION. HOSTING A KIDDIE SHOW SHOT OUT OF BURBANK.
"THERE WASN'T MUCH MONEY, BUT HEY -- IT WAS WORK, RIGHT?
FUN-TIME FARM
NBC

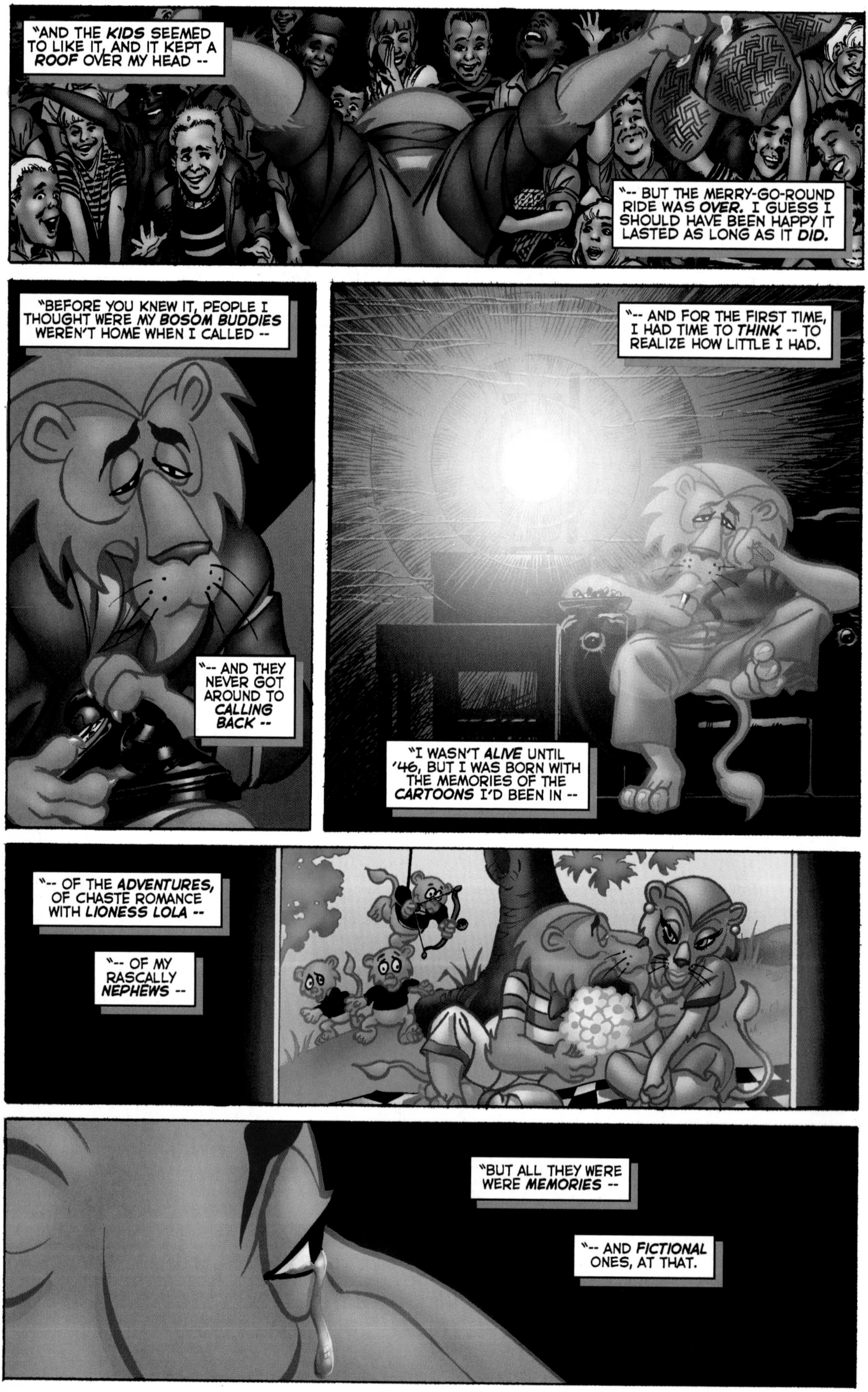
"AND THE KIDS SEEMED TO LIKE IT, AND IT KEPT A ROOF OVER MY HEAD --
"-- BUT THE MERRY-GO-ROUND RIDE WAS OVER. I GUESS I SHOULD HAVE BEEN HAPPY IT LASTED AS LONG AS IT DID.
"BEFORE YOU KNEW IT, PEOPLE I THOUGHT WERE MY BOSOM BUDDIES WEREN'T HOME WHEN I CALLED --
"-- AND THEY NEVER GOT AROUND TO CALLING BACK --
"-- AND FOR THE FIRST TIME, I HAD TIME TO THINK -- TO REALIZE HOW LITTLE I HAD.
"I WASN'T ALIVE UNTIL '46, BUT I WAS BORN WITH THE MEMORIES OF THE CARTOONS I'D BEEN IN --
"-- OF THE ADVENTURES, OF CHASTE ROMANCE WITH LIONESS LOLA --
"-- OF MY RASCALLY NEPHEWS --
"BUT ALL THEY WERE WERE MEMORIES --
"-- AND FICTIONAL ONES, AT THAT.

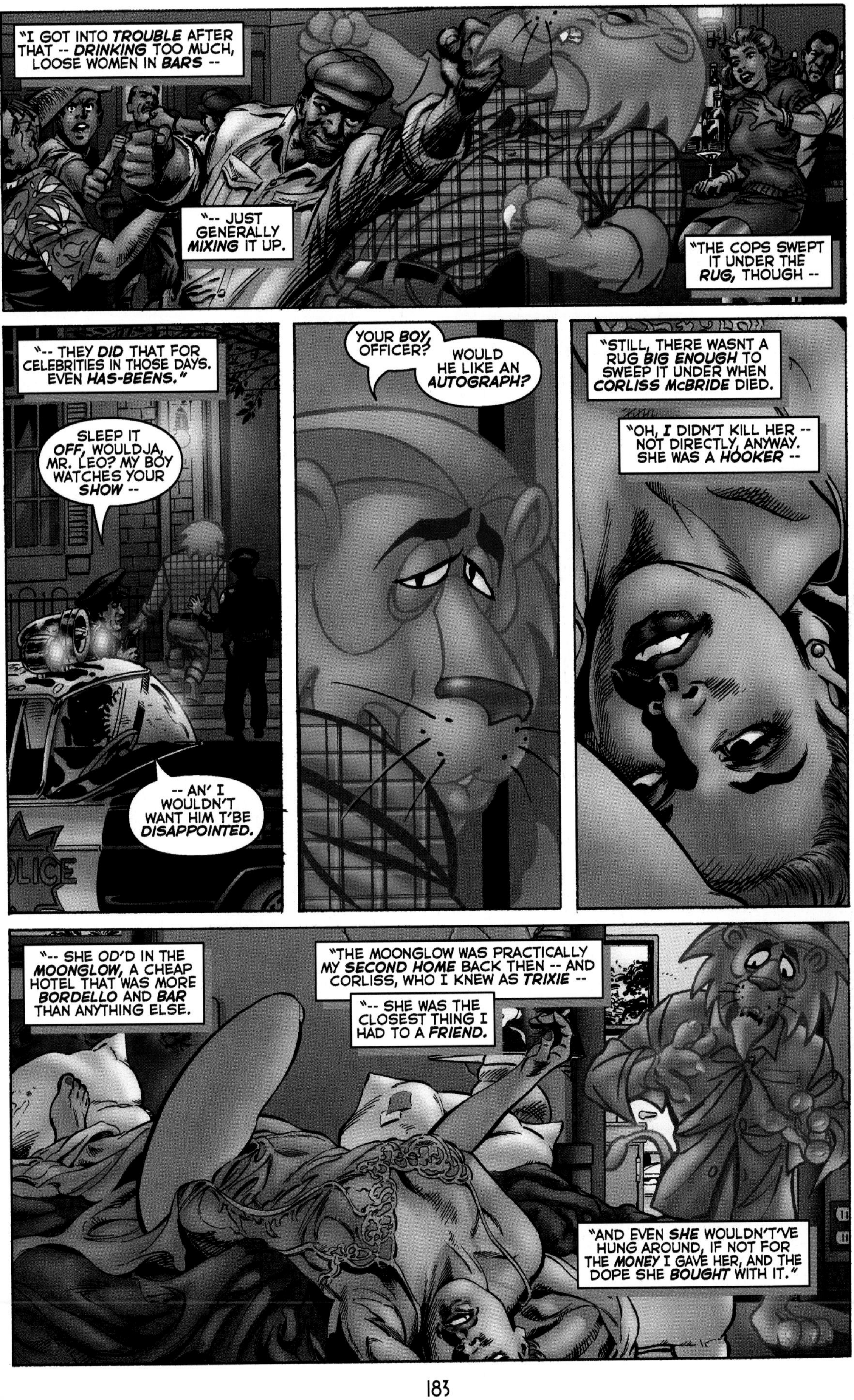
"I GOT INTO TROUBLE AFTER THAT -- DRINKING TOO MUCH, LOOSE WOMEN IN BARS --
"-- JUST GENERALLY MIXING IT UP.
"THE COPS SWEPT IT UNDER THE RUG, THOUGH --
"-- THEY DID THAT FOR CELEBRITIES IN THOSE DAYS. EVEN HAS-BEENS."
SLEEP IT OFF, WOULDJA, MR. LEO? MY BOY WATCHES YOUR SHOW --
-- AN' I WOULDN'T WANT HIM T'BE DISAPPOINTED.
POLICE
YOUR BOY, OFFICER?
WOULD HE LIKE AN AUTOGRAPH?
"STILL, THERE WASNT A RUG BIG ENOUGH TO SWEEP IT UNDER WHEN CORLISS McBRIDE DIED.
"OH, I DIDN'T KILL HER -- NOT DIRECTLY, ANYWAY. SHE WAS A HOOKER --
"-- SHE OD'D IN THE MOONGLOW, A CHEAP HOTEL THAT WAS MORE BORDELLO AND BAR THAN ANYTHING ELSE.
"THE MOONGLOW WAS PRACTICALLY MY SECOND HOME BACK THEN -- AND CORLISS, WHO I KNEW AS TRIXIE --
"-- SHE WAS THE CLOSEST THING I HAD TO A FRIEND.
"AND EVEN SHE WOULDN'T'VE HUNG AROUND, IF NOT FOR THE MONEY I GAVE HER, AND THE DOPE SHE BOUGHT WITH IT."

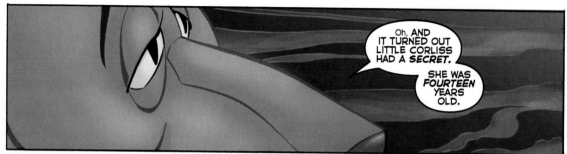

Oh, AND IT TURNED OUT LITTLE CORLISS HAD A *SECRET.*

SHE WAS *FOURTEEN* YEARS OLD.

"I WAS THE ONE WHO *FOUND* HER, AND THE POLICE LOOKED AT ME JUST LIKE *ANYONE ELSE.*

"BUT I *WASN'T* ANYONE ELSE, WAS I?"

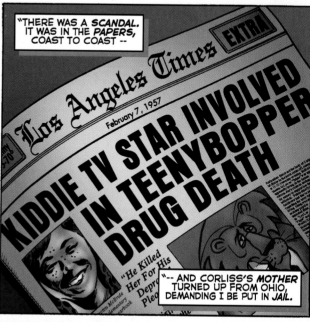

"THERE WAS A *SCANDAL.* IT WAS IN THE *PAPERS,* COAST TO COAST --

Los Angeles Times EXTRA

February 7, 1957

KIDDIE TV STAR INVOLVED IN TEENYBOPPER DRUG DEATH

"He Killed Her For His Depr Plea

"-- AND CORLISS'S *MOTHER* TURNED UP FROM OHIO, DEMANDING I BE PUT IN *JAIL.*

"THERE WAS A BOOK LATER -- IT SEEMS CORLISS'S DEAR MA *BEAT* HER, WHICH IS WHY SHE RAN OFF IN THE *FIRST PLACE* --

"-- BUT THAT DIDN'T *MATTER* BACK THEN. IT MADE GOOD *HEADLINES,* IS WHAT MATTERED."

SHE WAS A *GOOD KID,* TRIXIE. I LIKE TO THINK IF I'D KNOWN, I COULD HAVE *DONE* SOMETHING, *HELPED* MAYBE.

BUT THAT'S A *CROCK.* MAYBE I DIDN'T KILL HER, BUT I SURE *HELPED* PUT THAT NEEDLE IN HER ARM --

-- AND WOULD IT *REALLY* HAVE MADE IT BETTER IF SHE WAS AN *EIGHTEEN-YEAR-OLD* JUNKIE CORPSE?

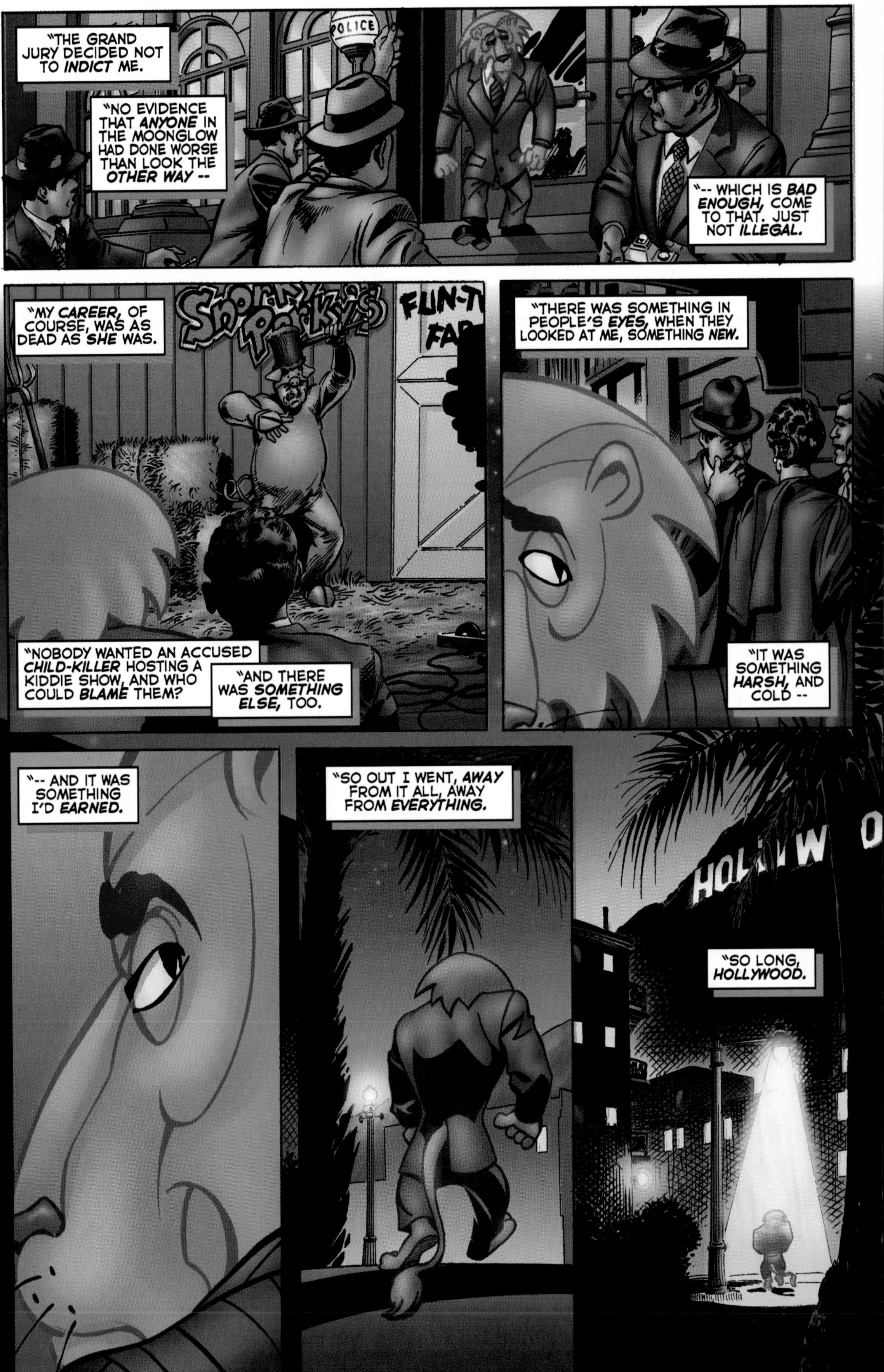
"THE GRAND JURY DECIDED NOT TO INDICT ME.
"NO EVIDENCE THAT ANYONE IN THE MOONGLOW HAD DONE WORSE THAN LOOK THE OTHER WAY --
POLICE
"-- WHICH IS BAD ENOUGH, COME TO THAT. JUST NOT ILLEGAL.
"MY CAREER, OF COURSE, WAS AS DEAD AS SHE WAS.
"NOBODY WANTED AN ACCUSED CHILD-KILLER HOSTING A KIDDIE SHOW, AND WHO COULD BLAME THEM?
"AND THERE WAS SOMETHING ELSE, TOO.
"THERE WAS SOMETHING IN PEOPLE'S EYES, WHEN THEY LOOKED AT ME, SOMETHING NEW.
"IT WAS SOMETHING HARSH, AND COLD --
"-- AND IT WAS SOMETHING I'D EARNED.
"SO OUT I WENT, AWAY FROM IT ALL, AWAY FROM EVERYTHING.
"SO LONG, HOLLYWOOD.

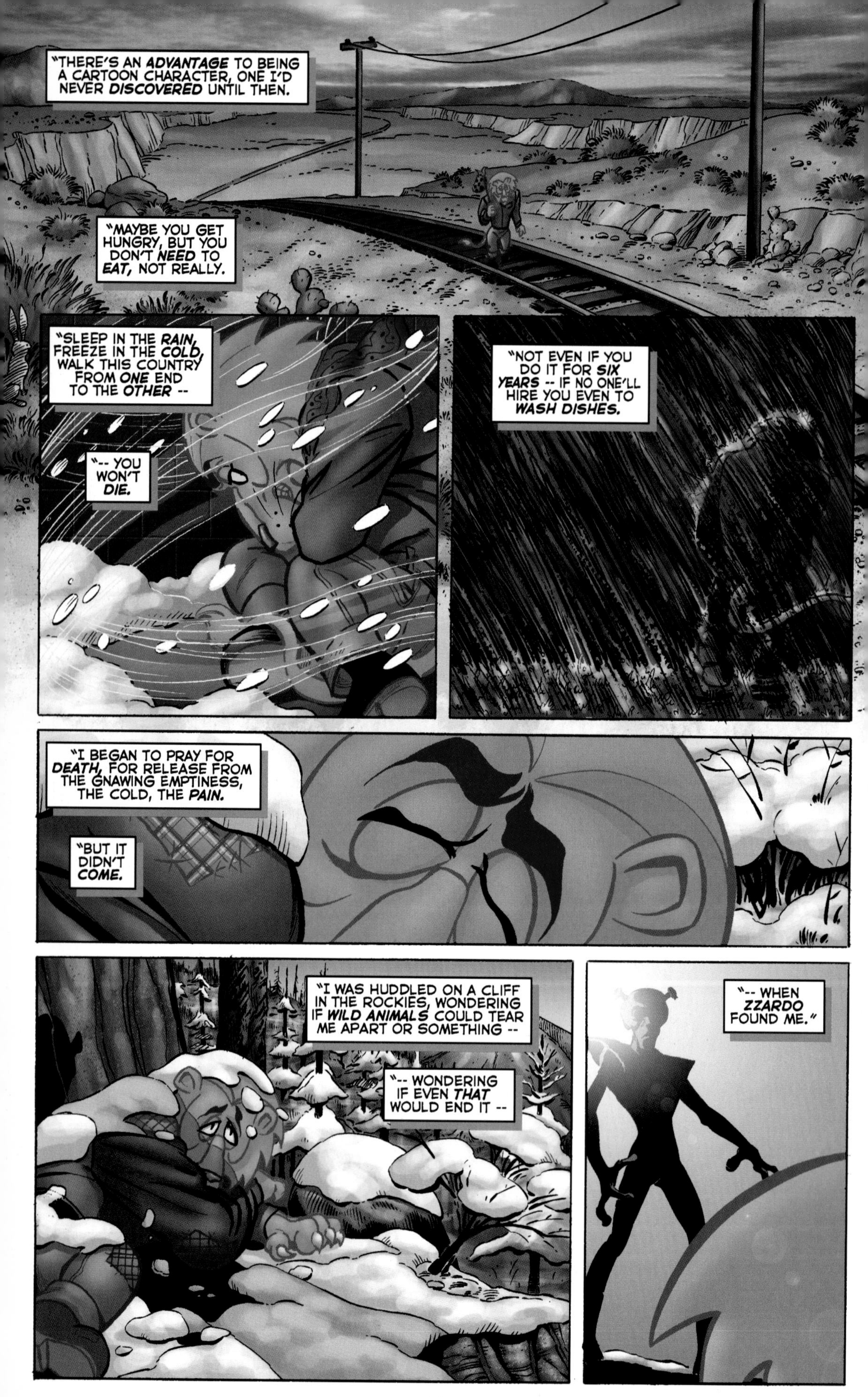
"THERE'S AN ADVANTAGE TO BEING A CARTOON CHARACTER, ONE I'D NEVER DISCOVERED UNTIL THEN.
"MAYBE YOU GET HUNGRY, BUT YOU DON'T NEED TO EAT, NOT REALLY.
"SLEEP IN THE RAIN, FREEZE IN THE COLD, WALK THIS COUNTRY FROM ONE END TO THE OTHER --
"-- YOU WON'T DIE.
"NOT EVEN IF YOU DO IT FOR SIX YEARS -- IF NO ONE'LL HIRE YOU EVEN TO WASH DISHES.
"I BEGAN TO PRAY FOR DEATH, FOR RELEASE FROM THE GNAWING EMPTINESS, THE COLD, THE PAIN.
"BUT IT DIDN'T COME.
"I WAS HUDDLED ON A CLIFF IN THE ROCKIES, WONDERING IF WILD ANIMALS COULD TEAR ME APART OR SOMETHING --
"-- WONDERING IF EVEN THAT WOULD END IT --
"-- WHEN ZZARDO FOUND ME."

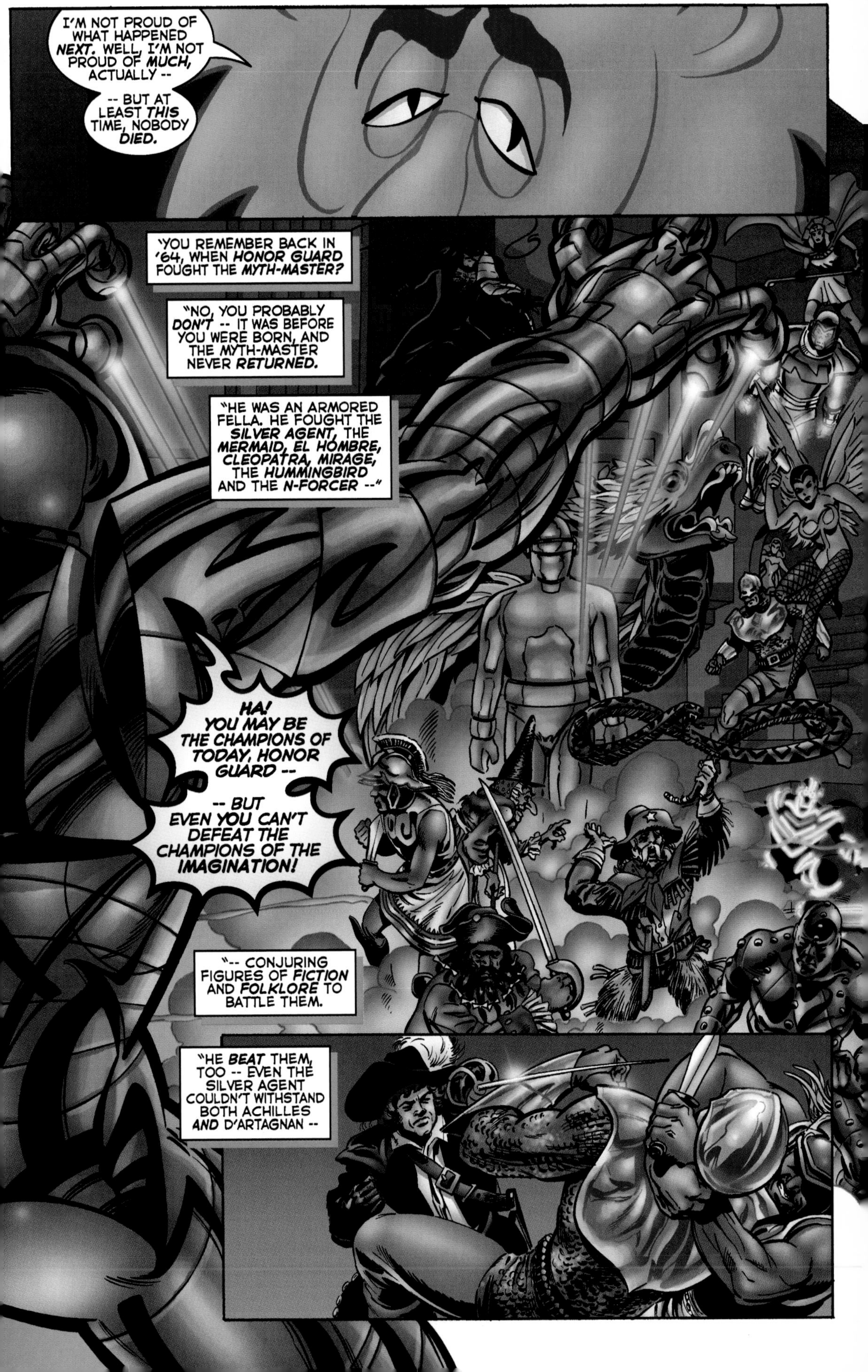

I'M NOT PROUD OF WHAT HAPPENED NEXT. WELL, I'M NOT PROUD OF MUCH, ACTUALLY --
-- BUT AT LEAST THIS TIME, NOBODY DIED.
"YOU REMEMBER BACK IN '64, WHEN HONOR GUARD FOUGHT THE MYTH-MASTER?
"NO, YOU PROBABLY DON'T -- IT WAS BEFORE YOU WERE BORN, AND THE MYTH-MASTER NEVER RETURNED.
"HE WAS AN ARMORED FELLA. HE FOUGHT THE SILVER AGENT, THE MERMAID, EL HOMBRE, CLEOPATRA, MIRAGE, THE HUMMINGBIRD AND THE N-FORCER --"
HA! YOU MAY BE THE CHAMPIONS OF TODAY, HONOR GUARD --
-- BUT EVEN YOU CAN'T DEFEAT THE CHAMPIONS OF THE IMAGINATION!
"-- CONJURING FIGURES OF FICTION AND FOLKLORE TO BATTLE THEM.
"HE BEAT THEM, TOO -- EVEN THE SILVER AGENT COULDN'T WITHSTAND BOTH ACHILLES AND D'ARTAGNAN --

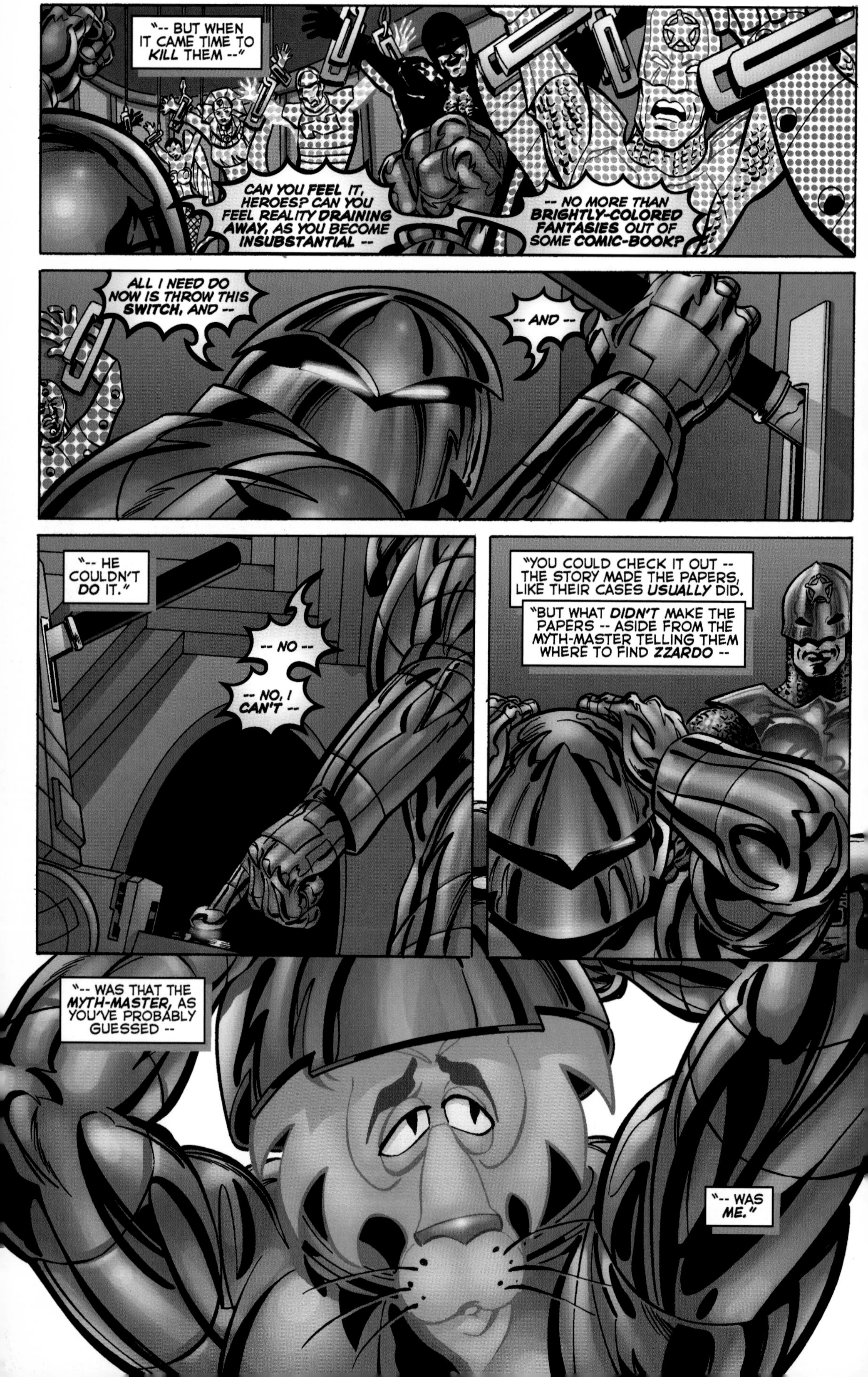
"-- BUT WHEN IT CAME TIME TO KILL THEM --"
CAN YOU FEEL IT, HEROES? CAN YOU FEEL REALITY DRAINING AWAY, AS YOU BECOME INSUBSTANTIAL --
-- NO MORE THAN BRIGHTLY-COLORED FANTASIES OUT OF SOME COMIC-BOOK?
ALL I NEED DO NOW IS THROW THIS SWITCH, AND --
-- AND --
"-- HE COULDN'T DO IT."
-- NO --
-- NO, I CAN'T --
"YOU COULD CHECK IT OUT -- THE STORY MADE THE PAPERS, LIKE THEIR CASES USUALLY DID.
"BUT WHAT DIDN'T MAKE THE PAPERS -- ASIDE FROM THE MYTH-MASTER TELLING THEM WHERE TO FIND ZZARDO --
"-- WAS THAT THE MYTH-MASTER, AS YOU'VE PROBABLY GUESSED --
"-- WAS ME."

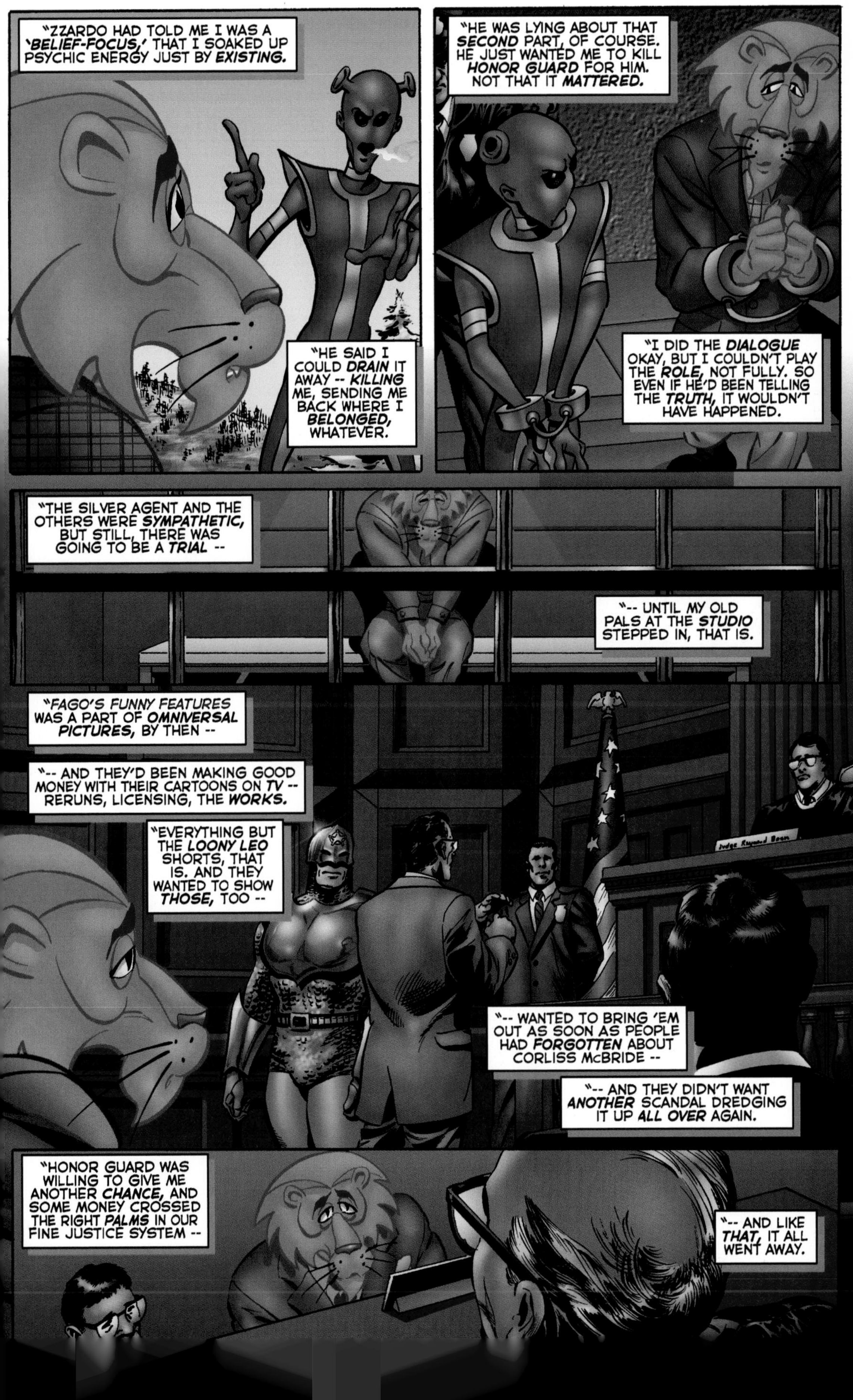
"ZZARDO HAD TOLD ME I WAS A 'BELIEF-FOCUS,' THAT I SOAKED UP PSYCHIC ENERGY JUST BY EXISTING.
"HE SAID I COULD DRAIN IT AWAY -- KILLING ME, SENDING ME BACK WHERE I BELONGED, WHATEVER.
"HE WAS LYING ABOUT THAT SECOND PART, OF COURSE. HE JUST WANTED ME TO KILL HONOR GUARD FOR HIM. NOT THAT IT MATTERED.
"I DID THE DIALOGUE OKAY, BUT I COULDN'T PLAY THE ROLE, NOT FULLY. SO EVEN IF HE'D BEEN TELLING THE TRUTH, IT WOULDN'T HAVE HAPPENED.
"THE SILVER AGENT AND THE OTHERS WERE SYMPATHETIC, BUT STILL, THERE WAS GOING TO BE A TRIAL --
"-- UNTIL MY OLD PALS AT THE STUDIO STEPPED IN, THAT IS.
"FAGO'S FUNNY FEATURES WAS A PART OF OMNIVERSAL PICTURES, BY THEN --
"-- AND THEY'D BEEN MAKING GOOD MONEY WITH THEIR CARTOONS ON TV -- RERUNS, LICENSING, THE WORKS.
"EVERYTHING BUT THE LOONY LEO SHORTS, THAT IS. AND THEY WANTED TO SHOW THOSE, TOO --
"-- WANTED TO BRING 'EM OUT AS SOON AS PEOPLE HAD FORGOTTEN ABOUT CORLISS McBRIDE --
"-- AND THEY DIDN'T WANT ANOTHER SCANDAL DREDGING IT UP ALL OVER AGAIN.
"HONOR GUARD WAS WILLING TO GIVE ME ANOTHER CHANCE, AND SOME MONEY CROSSED THE RIGHT PALMS IN OUR FINE JUSTICE SYSTEM --
"-- AND LIKE THAT, IT ALL WENT AWAY.

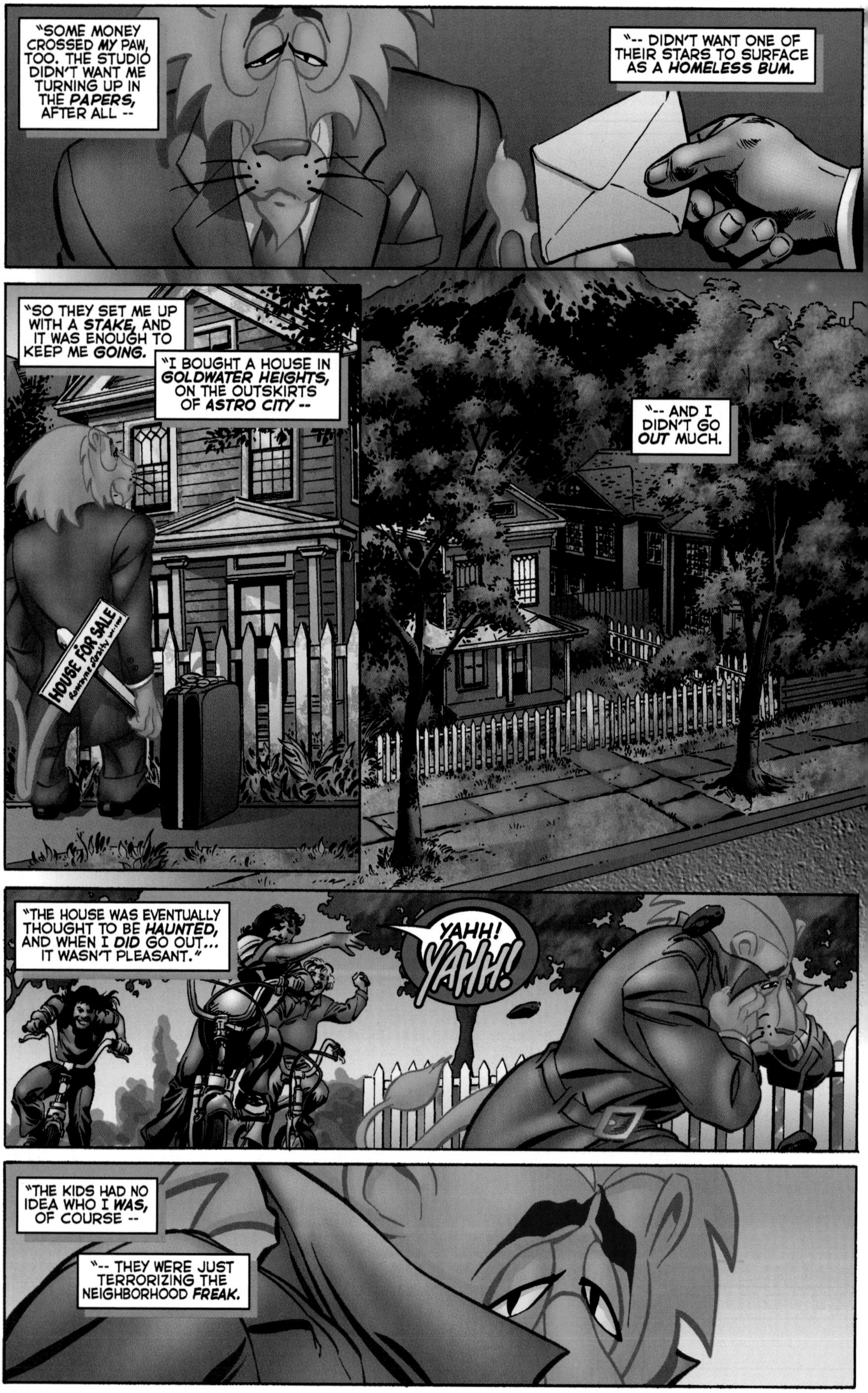
"SOME MONEY CROSSED MY PAW, TOO. THE STUDIO DIDN'T WANT ME TURNING UP IN THE PAPERS, AFTER ALL --
"-- DIDN'T WANT ONE OF THEIR STARS TO SURFACE AS A HOMELESS BUM.
"SO THEY SET ME UP WITH A STAKE, AND IT WAS ENOUGH TO KEEP ME GOING.
"I BOUGHT A HOUSE IN GOLDWATER HEIGHTS, ON THE OUTSKIRTS OF ASTRO CITY --
HOUSE FOR SALE
"-- AND I DIDN'T GO OUT MUCH.
"THE HOUSE WAS EVENTUALLY THOUGHT TO BE HAUNTED, AND WHEN I DID GO OUT... IT WASN'T PLEASANT."
YAHH! YAHH!
"THE KIDS HAD NO IDEA WHO I WAS, OF COURSE --
"-- THEY WERE JUST TERRORIZING THE NEIGHBORHOOD FREAK.

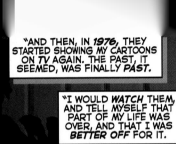

"AND THEN, IN *1976*, THEY STARTED SHOWING MY CARTOONS ON *TV* AGAIN. THE PAST, IT SEEMED, WAS FINALLY *PAST*.

"I WOULD *WATCH* THEM, AND TELL MYSELF THAT PART OF MY LIFE WAS OVER, AND THAT I WAS *BETTER OFF* FOR IT.

"BUT A FEW YEARS *LATER*, I WAS APPROACHED BY SOME BUSINESSMEN. *ENTREPRENEURS.*

"THEY'D TRACKED ME DOWN, FOUND OUT WHERE I *LIVED.*

"THEY WANTED TO OPEN A *RESTAURANT*, A FORTIES NOSTALGIA PLACE. AND THEY WANTED TO BUILD IT AROUND *ME* --

"-- TO MAKE ME A LIVING *PROMOTIONAL GIMMICK.*

"THEY LAID IT ALL *OUT* FOR ME, HOW IT WOULD *WORK.*

"THERE WAS ONLY ONE *HITCH...*"

WE NEED YOU TO BUY IN AS *PARTNER.* TO BE PART *OWNER* OF THE PLACE. IT'S PART OF THE *CONCEPT*, YOU KNOW?

LOONY LEO'S RESTAURANT -- IT'S A BETTER HOOK THAN LOONY LEO WORKING *IN* A RESTAURANT, RIGHT?

"LOOKING BACK ON IT, I WONDER IF THEY JUST DIDN'T HAVE ENOUGH MONEY *THEMSELVES.*

"BUT AT THE TIME, I WAS JUST *SCARED.* GOING OUT, FACING THE *PUBLIC* AGAIN --

"-- AND IF IT FAILED, I'D HAVE LOST MY STAKE -- I'D BE OUT ON THE *STREET* AGAIN --

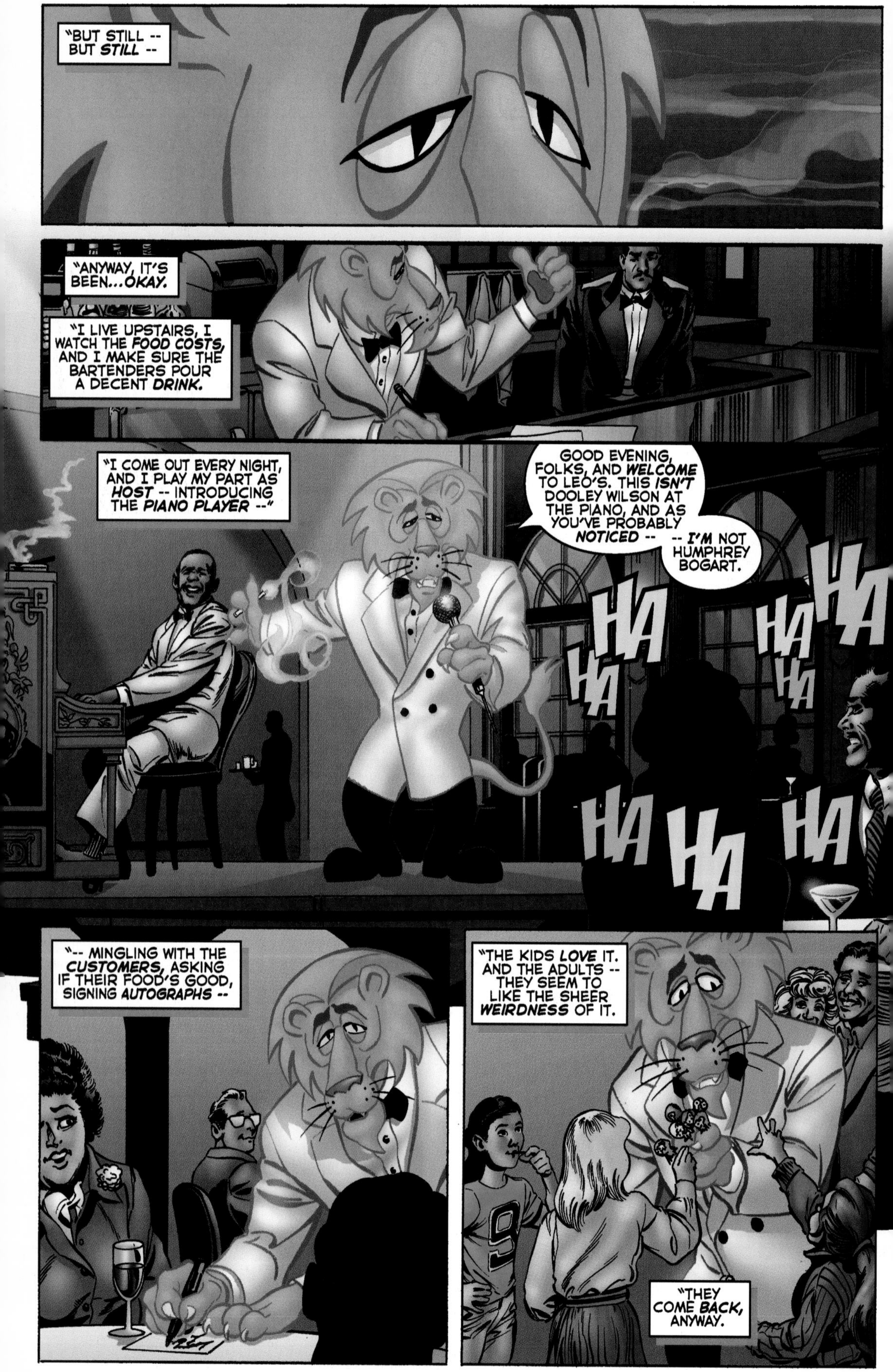
"BUT STILL -- BUT STILL --
"ANYWAY, IT'S BEEN... OKAY.
"I LIVE UPSTAIRS, I WATCH THE FOOD COSTS, AND I MAKE SURE THE BARTENDERS POUR A DECENT DRINK.
"I COME OUT EVERY NIGHT, AND I PLAY MY PART AS HOST -- INTRODUCING THE PIANO PLAYER --"
GOOD EVENING, FOLKS, AND WELCOME TO LEO'S. THIS ISN'T DOOLEY WILSON AT THE PIANO, AND AS YOU'VE PROBABLY NOTICED --
-- I'M NOT HUMPHREY BOGART.
HA HA
HA HA HA
HA HA HA
"-- MINGLING WITH THE CUSTOMERS, ASKING IF THEIR FOOD'S GOOD, SIGNING AUTOGRAPHS --
"THE KIDS LOVE IT. AND THE ADULTS -- THEY SEEM TO LIKE THE SHEER WEIRDNESS OF IT.
"THEY COME BACK, ANYWAY.

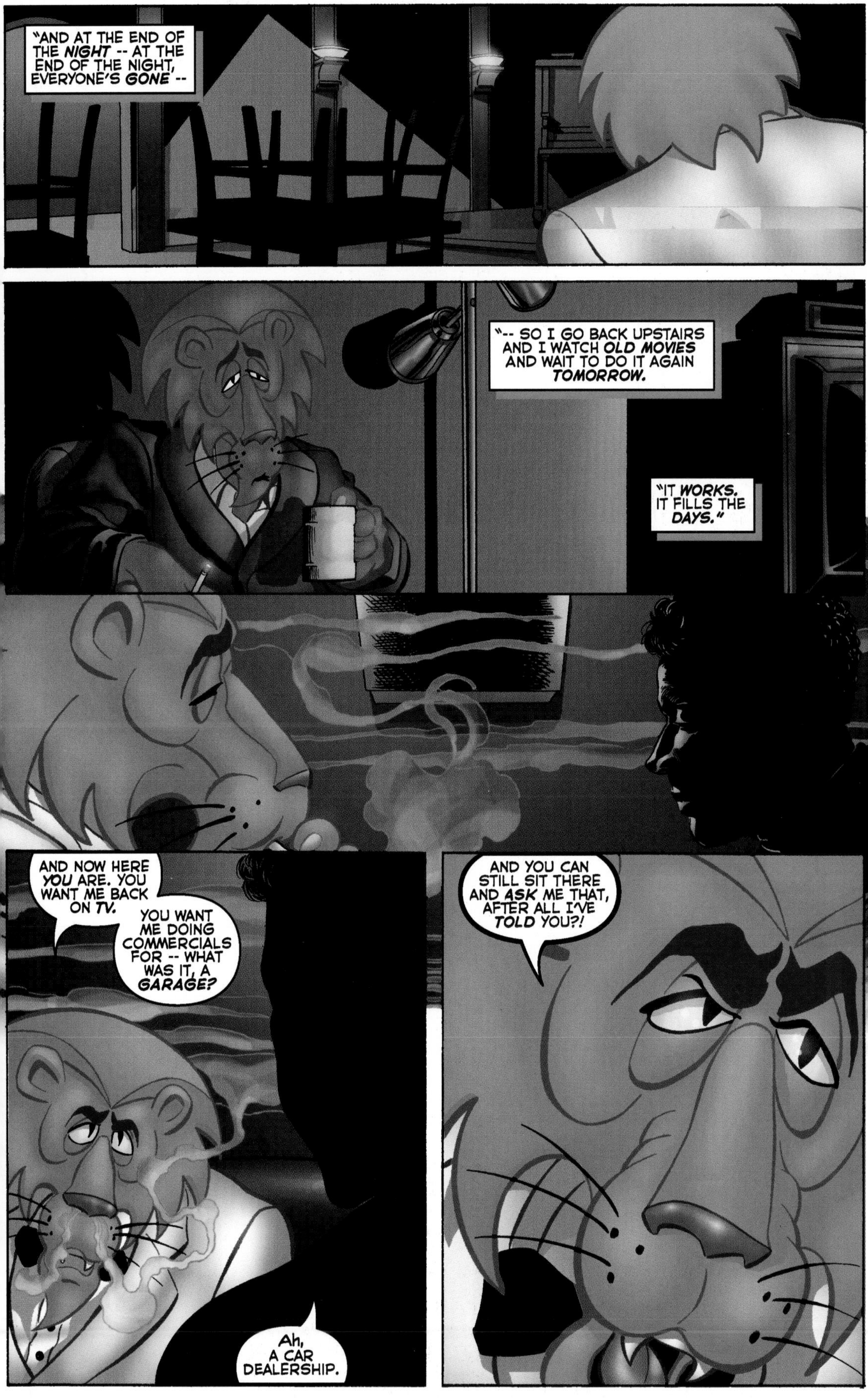
"AND AT THE END OF THE NIGHT -- AT THE END OF THE NIGHT, EVERYONE'S GONE --
"-- SO I GO BACK UPSTAIRS AND I WATCH OLD MOVIES AND WAIT TO DO IT AGAIN TOMORROW.
"IT WORKS. IT FILLS THE DAYS."
AND NOW HERE YOU ARE. YOU WANT ME BACK ON TV.
YOU WANT ME DOING COMMERCIALS FOR -- WHAT WAS IT, A GARAGE?
Ah, A CAR DEALERSHIP.
AND YOU CAN STILL SIT THERE AND ASK ME THAT, AFTER ALL I'VE TOLD YOU?!

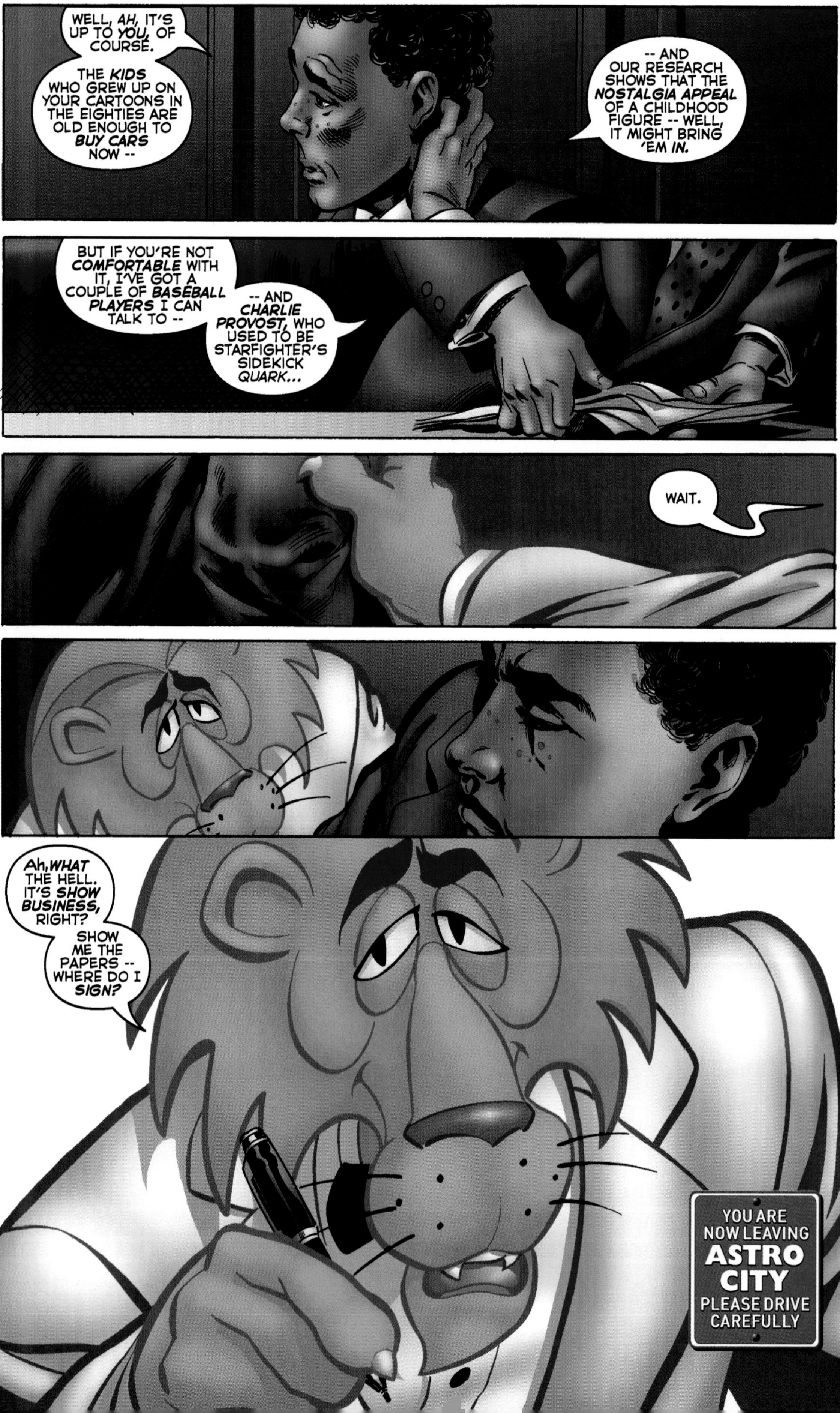
WELL, AH, IT'S UP TO YOU, OF COURSE.
THE KIDS WHO GREW UP ON YOUR CARTOONS IN THE EIGHTIES ARE OLD ENOUGH TO BUY CARS NOW --
-- AND OUR RESEARCH SHOWS THAT THE NOSTALGIA APPEAL OF A CHILDHOOD FIGURE -- WELL, IT MIGHT BRING 'EM IN.
BUT IF YOU'RE NOT COMFORTABLE WITH IT, I'VE GOT A COUPLE OF BASEBALL PLAYERS I CAN TALK TO --
-- AND CHARLIE PROVOST, WHO USED TO BE STARFIGHTER'S SIDEKICK QUARK...
WAIT.
Ah, WHAT THE HELL. IT'S SHOW BUSINESS, RIGHT?
SHOW ME THE PAPERS -- WHERE DO I SIGN?
YOU ARE NOW LEAVING
ASTRO CITY
PLEASE DRIVE CAREFULLY

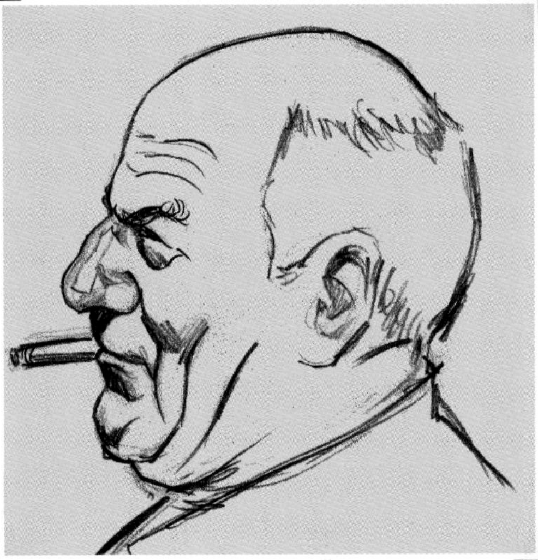

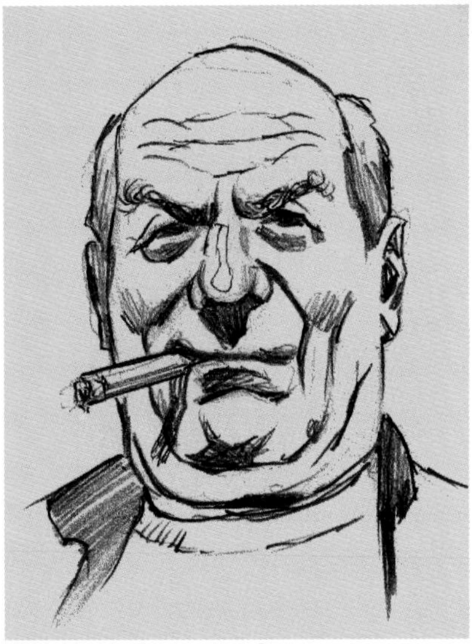

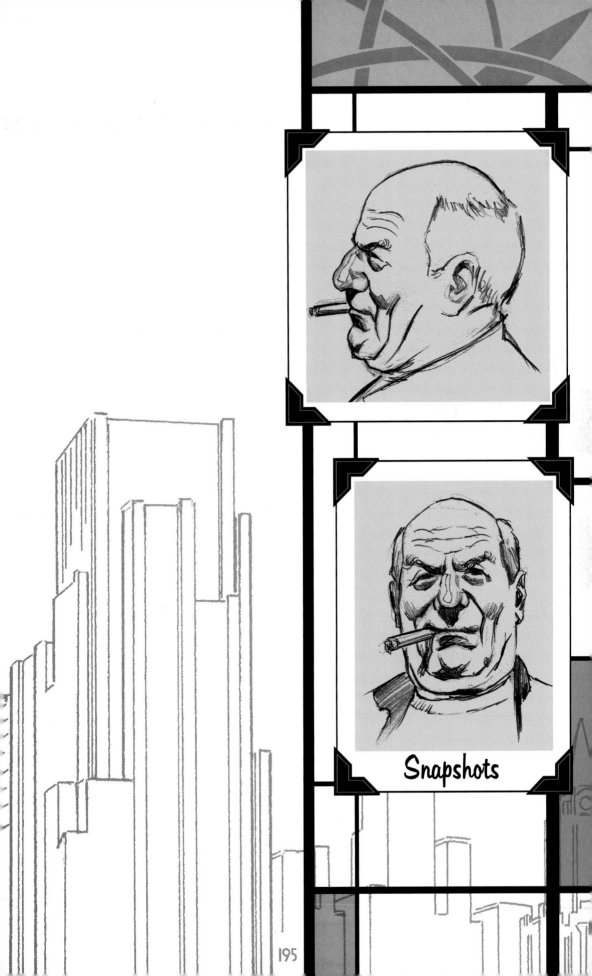

Snapshots

One of the most enjoyable parts of creating a city is filling it with people. Whether they're heroes or villains, fantasy creatures or ordinary people, they've got to be engaging, distinctive, expressive and memorable. And luckily, working with artists of the caliber of Brent and Alex makes it easy to achieve those goals, no matter what I might throw at them. Herewith, some examples...

— Kurt Busiek

Previous Page: Alex's design for Julius "Uncle Julie" Furst, the William Frawley of the First Family.

Air Ace

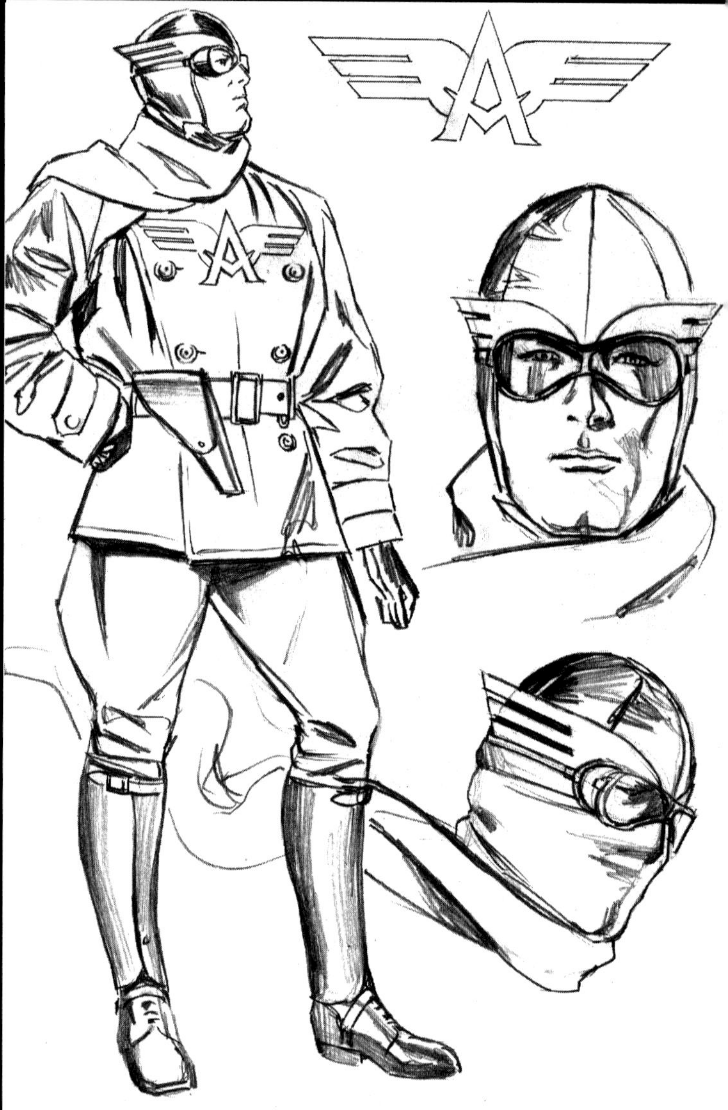

Air Ace has only appeared as a statue so far, but even a statue's got to be designed fully — and when you know the guy's going to show up in his own story someday, he's got to be designed carefully as well. For Air Ace, we wanted to combine a classic WWI pilot's look with just enough superhero elements to make him a believable bridge between a pulp hero and a superhero. The emblem on his chest and the wings on his goggles supplied just the right touch.

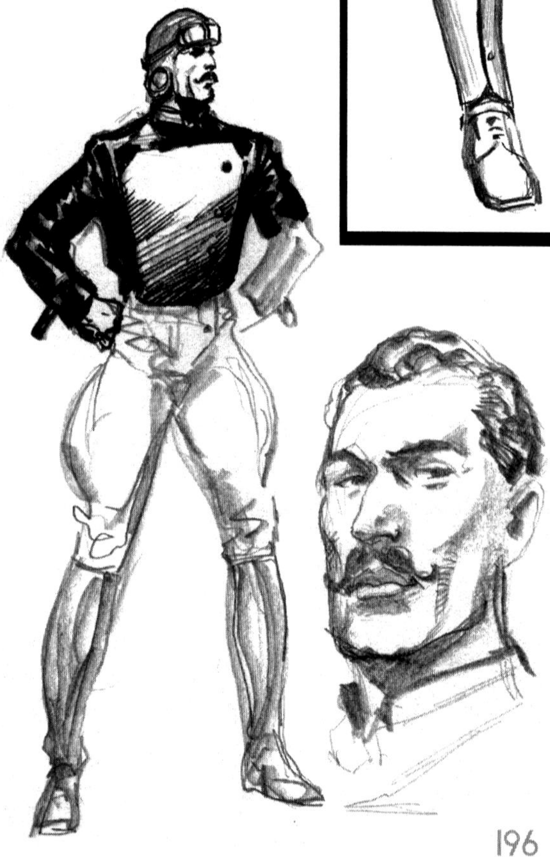

Thunderhead

It's one thing to say "a gigantic, threatening stormgod made entirely of dark clouds," and another to pull it off. To find the right look for Thunderhead, Alex was inspired by the "Night on Bald Mountain" section of Fantasia, and classical images of the Greek god Zeus. From Alex's original sketch, shown here, Brent developed the final rendition seen in "Welcome to Astro City."

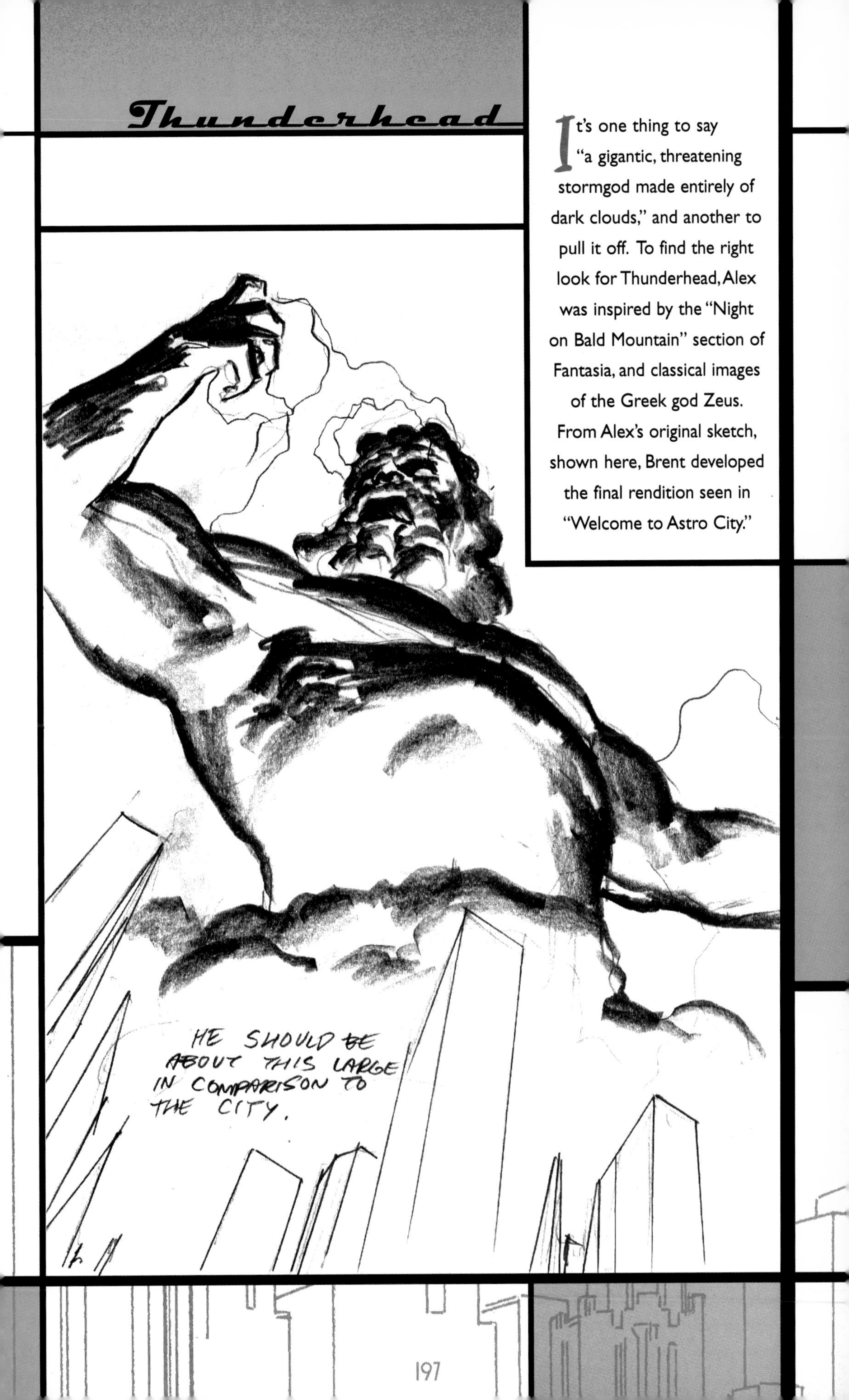
HE SHOULD BE ABOUT THIS LARGE IN COMPARISON TO THE CITY.

Astra & Mr. Smartie

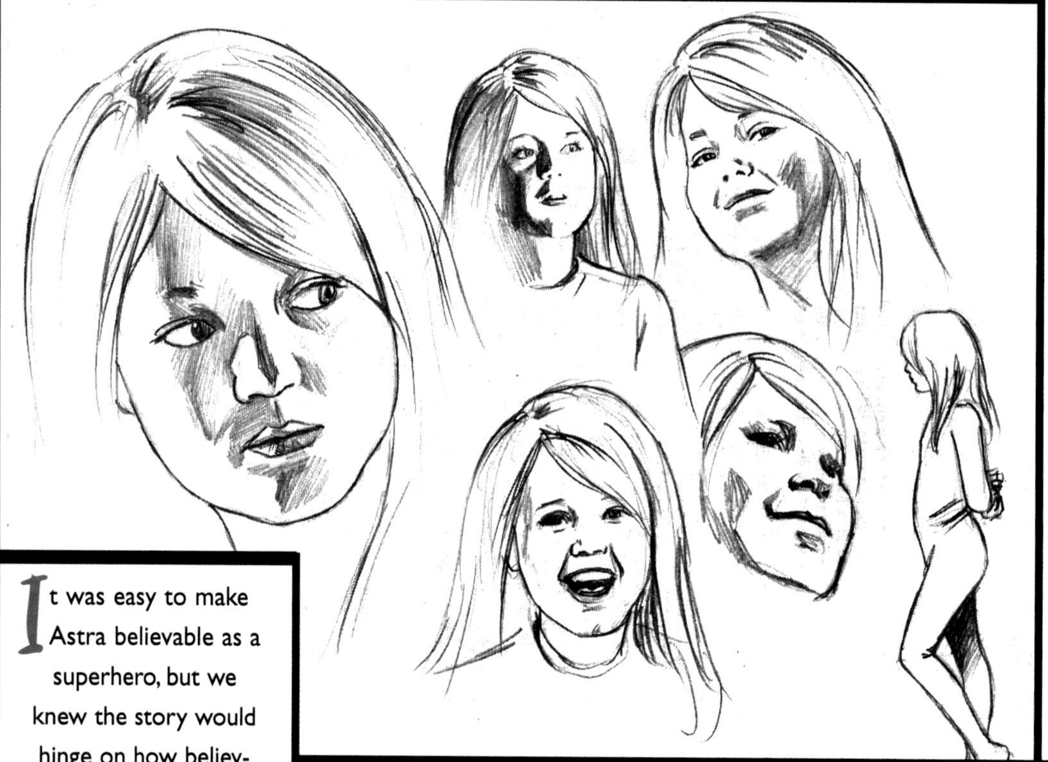

It was easy to make Astra believable as a superhero, but we knew the story would hinge on how believable she was as a little girl. Alex did these sketches to capture her youth and innocence in a variety of moods.

The trick with Mister Smartie, Astra's computer-generated schoolteacher, was to make him expressive enough to be a character, while simple enough to look like a hologram. As you can see, Brent's early sketches included hair and detailed eyebrows, but the brows were simplified and the hair eliminated in the finished version, to make him more of an abstraction.

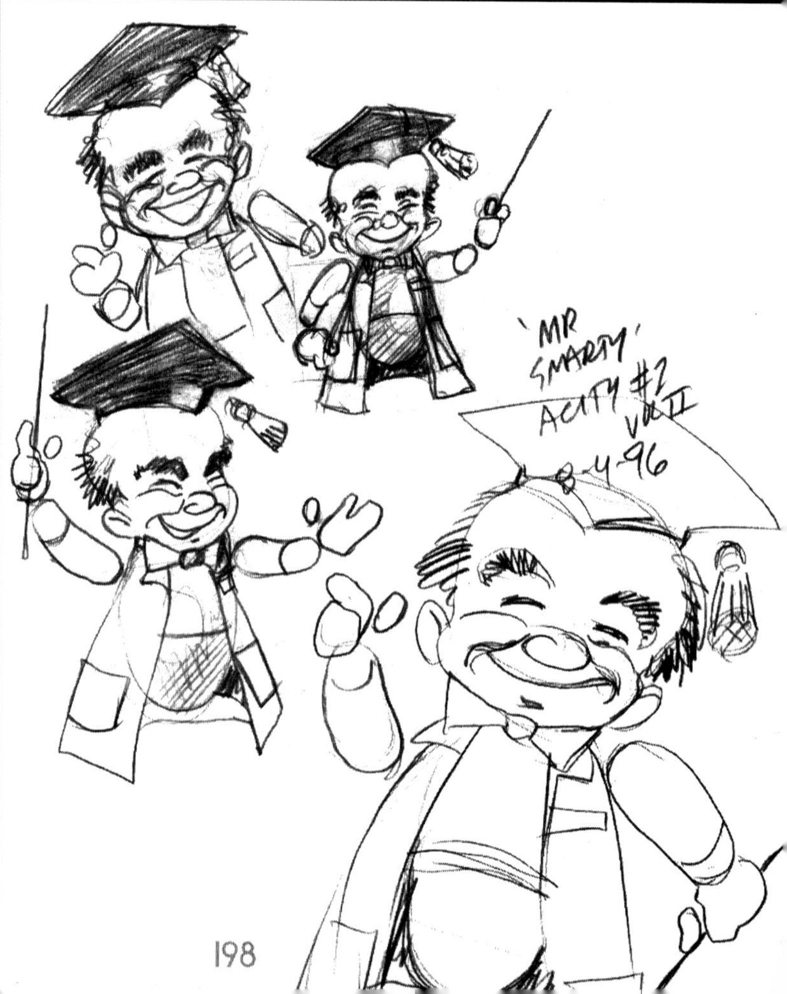
'MR SMARTY'
ACITY #2 VOL II
8-4-96

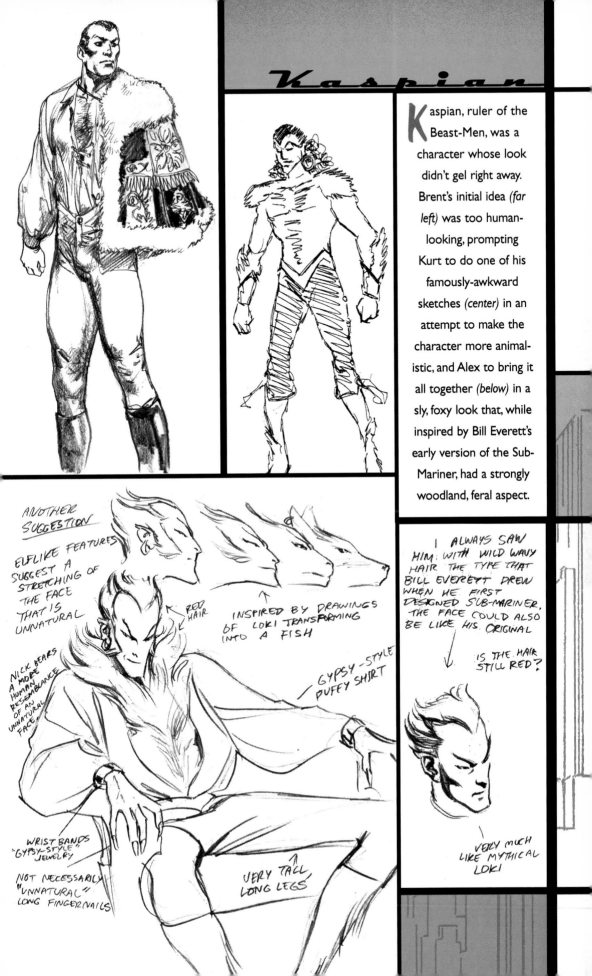

Kaspian

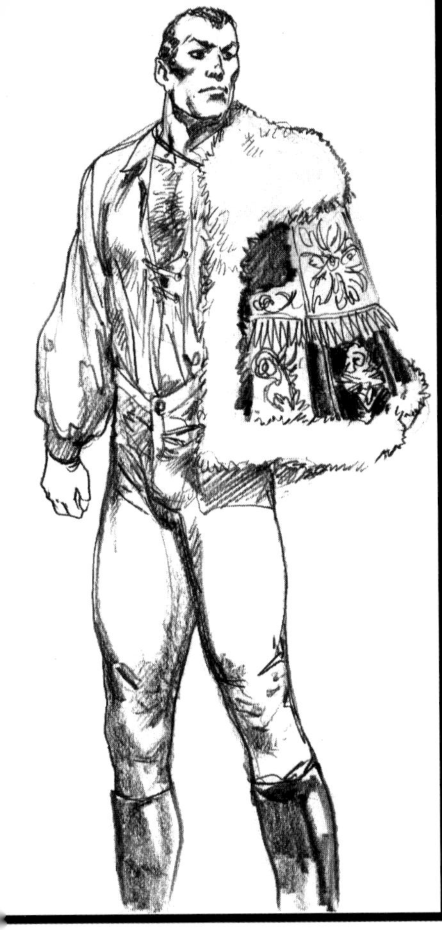

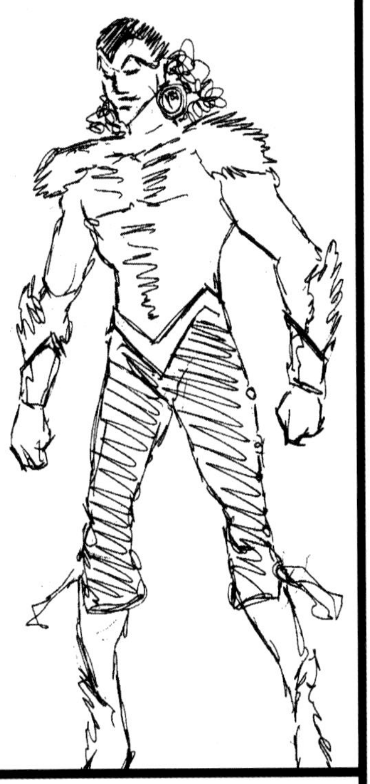

Kaspian, ruler of the Beast-Men, was a character whose look didn't gel right away. Brent's initial idea *(far left)* was too human-looking, prompting Kurt to do one of his famously-awkward sketches *(center)* in an attempt to make the character more animal-istic, and Alex to bring it all together *(below)* in a sly, foxy look that, while inspired by Bill Everett's early version of the Sub-Mariner, had a strongly woodland, feral aspect.

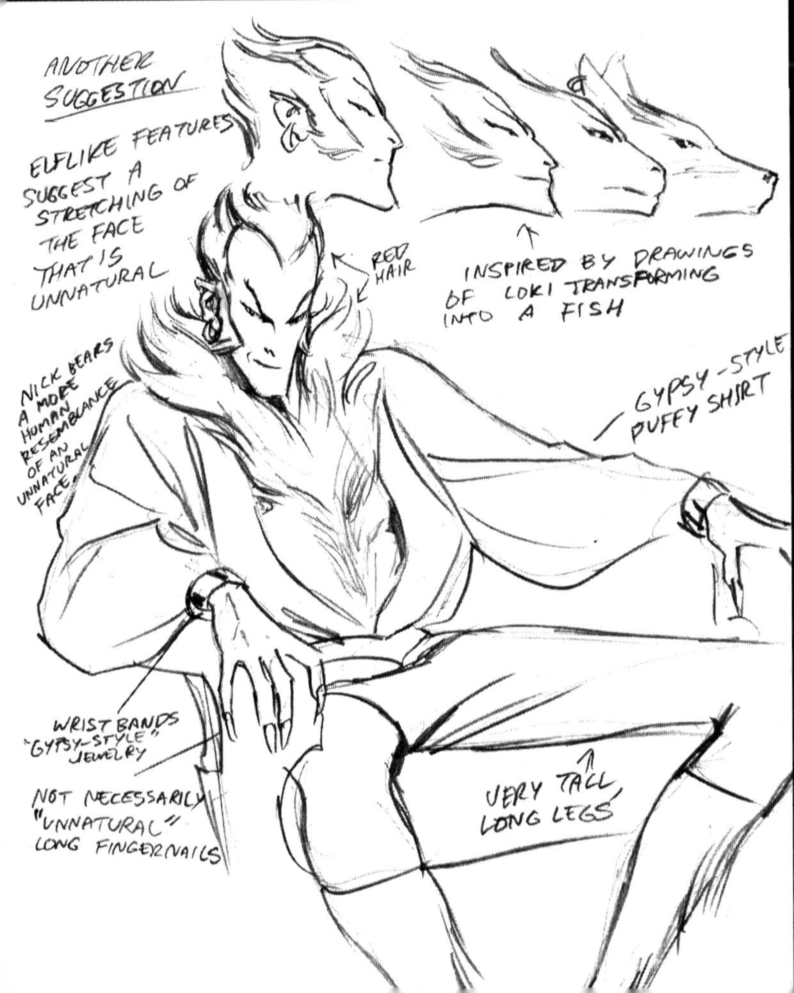
ANOTHER SUGGESTION
ELFLIKE FEATURES SUGGEST A STRETCHING OF THE FACE THAT IS UNNATURAL
RED HAIR
INSPIRED BY DRAWINGS OF LOKI TRANSFORMING INTO A FISH
NICK BEARS A MORE HUMAN RESEMBLANCE OF AN UNNATURAL FACE
GYPSY-STYLE PUFFY SHIRT
WRIST BANDS "GYPSY-STYLE" JEWELRY
NOT NECESSARILY "UNNATURAL" LONG FINGERNAILS
VERY TALL, LONG LEGS

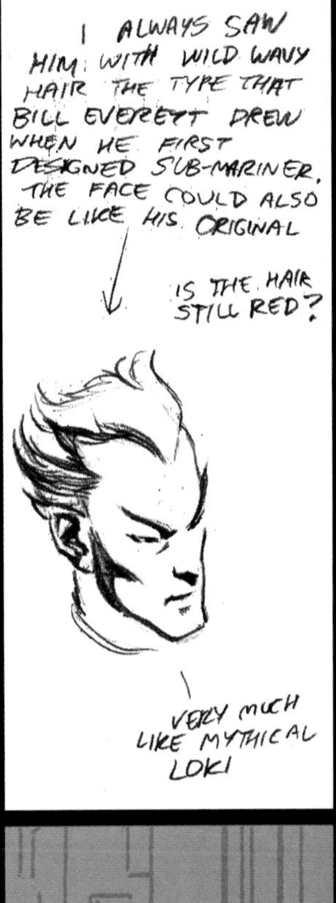
I ALWAYS SAW HIM WITH WILD WAVY HAIR THE TYPE THAT BILL EVERETT DREW WHEN HE FIRST DESIGNED SUB-MARINER. THE FACE COULD ALSO BE LIKE HIS ORIGINAL
IS THE HAIR STILL RED?
VERY MUCH LIKE MYTHICAL LOKI

The Junkman

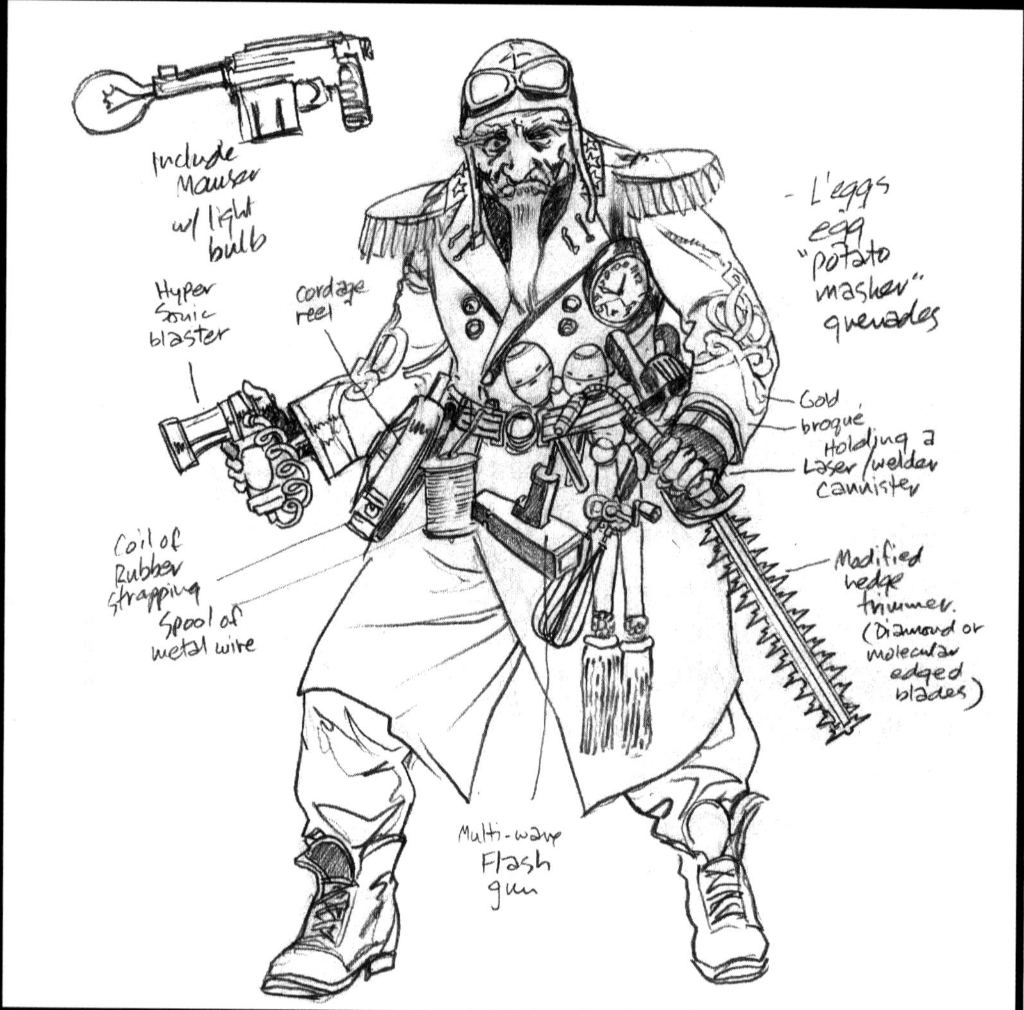
Include Mauser w/ light bulb
Hyper Sonic blaster
cordage reel
- L'eggs egg "potato masher" grenades
Gold broque
Holding a Laser/welder cannister
Modified hedge trimmer. (Diamond or molecular edged blades)
Coil of Rubber strapping
Spool of metal wire
Multi-wave Flash gun

For the Junkman, we wanted someone who looked more cranky than dangerous, but who would nevertheless be striking and memorable, and whose gadgetry would be complex and fascinating. The Uncle-Sam beard was Alex's idea (wonder where he got that, hmm?), and the vacuum-cleaner jetpack was Brent's addition. The Mauser with the light bulb was Kurt's contribution, inspired half by a dummy raygun he saw at a convention, and half by Gyro Gearloose's bulb-headed "Helper."

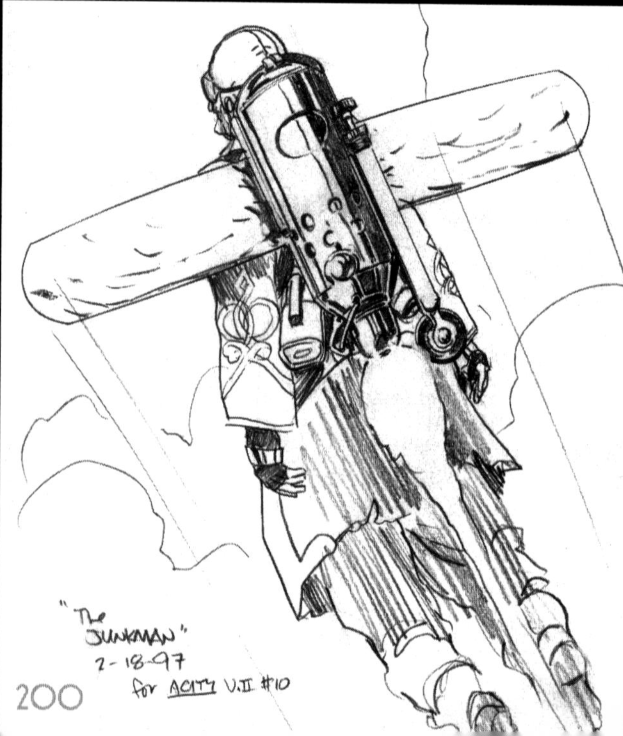
"The JUNKMAN"
2-18-97
for ACITY V.II #10

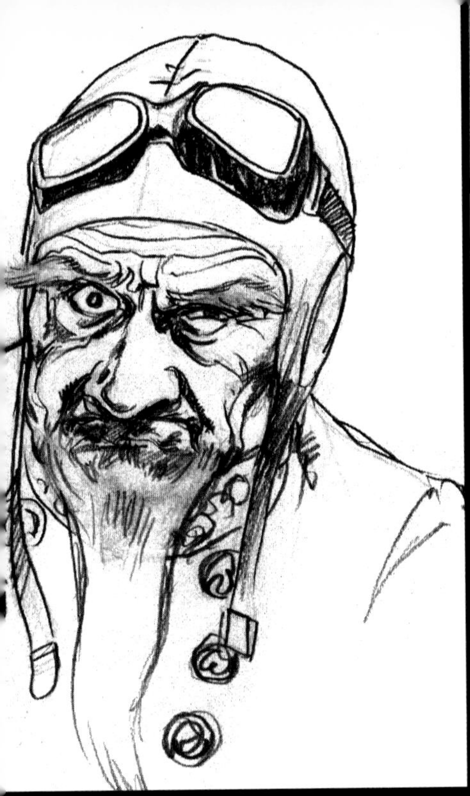

Black Rapier

As with Air Ace, we wanted the Black Rapier to look simple and elegant, and a fencer's costume seemed to be the obvious design choice. But the result was too plain, too ordinary-looking, until Alex gave him the combination sash/cape. A minor element, but it was just enough to make him a superhero, rather than simply a fencer with a different-colored outfit.

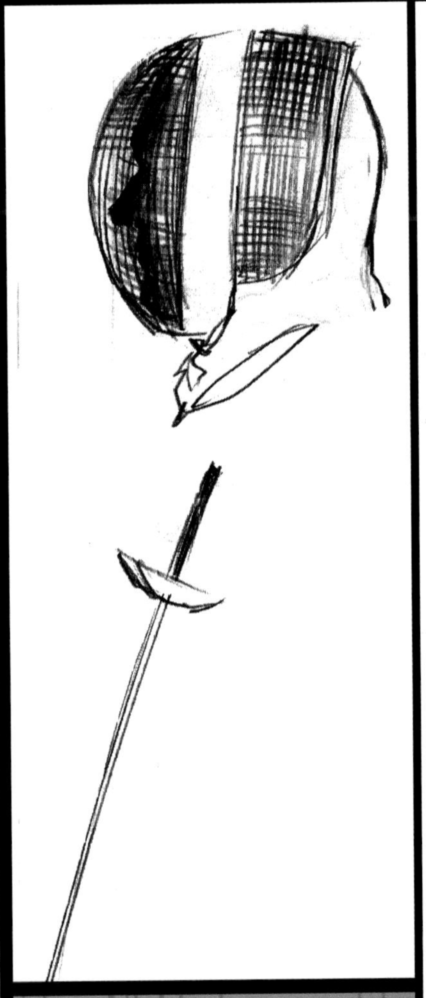

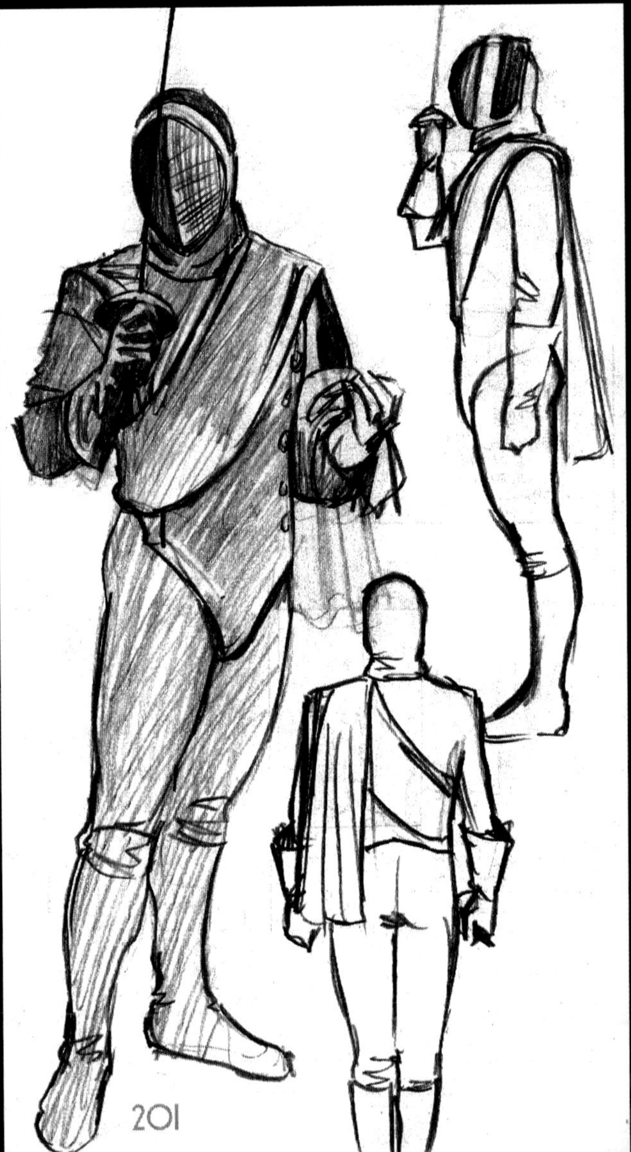

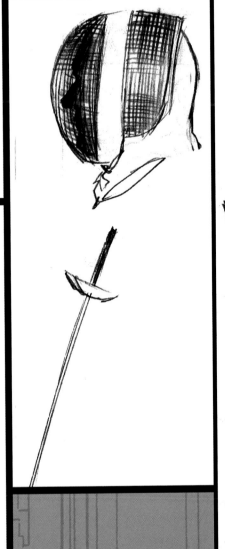

Jackson & The Box

Jack-In-The-Box's alternate-future sons, The Box and Jackson, represented different design challenges, since unlike most of Astro City's denizens, we didn't want them to look classic or elegant. Instead, we wanted to evoke modern grotesqueries like Cable, Venom and Lobo — but still with a strong family resemblance to their progenitor. Kurt decided that one of them would be an organic monster, and the other a technological one — and Alex took that to heart, delivering a Jackson that featured Jack-In-The-Box's costume elements merged with his own flesh and distorting the human shape beneath, and a Box who'd been mutilated, his body augmented with clunky, functional-but-ugly additions. Justice Jacky was an inspired addition by Alex.

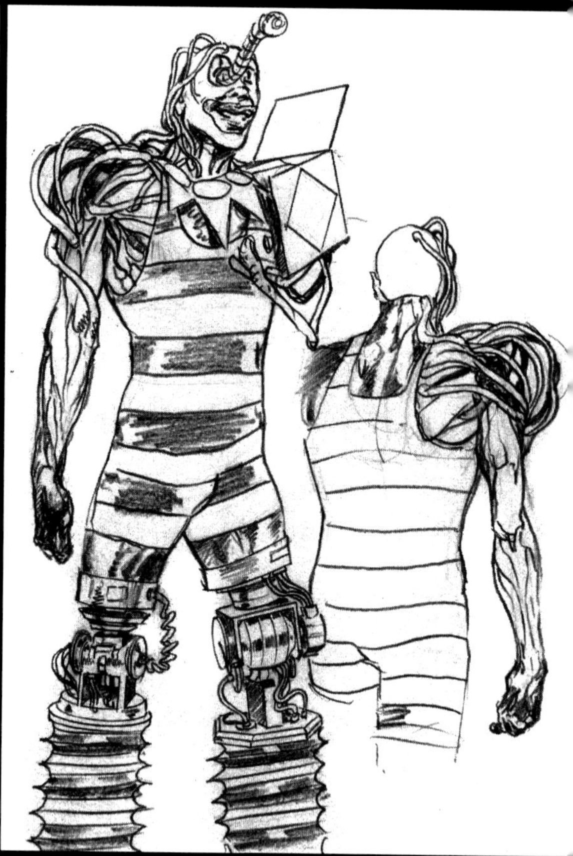

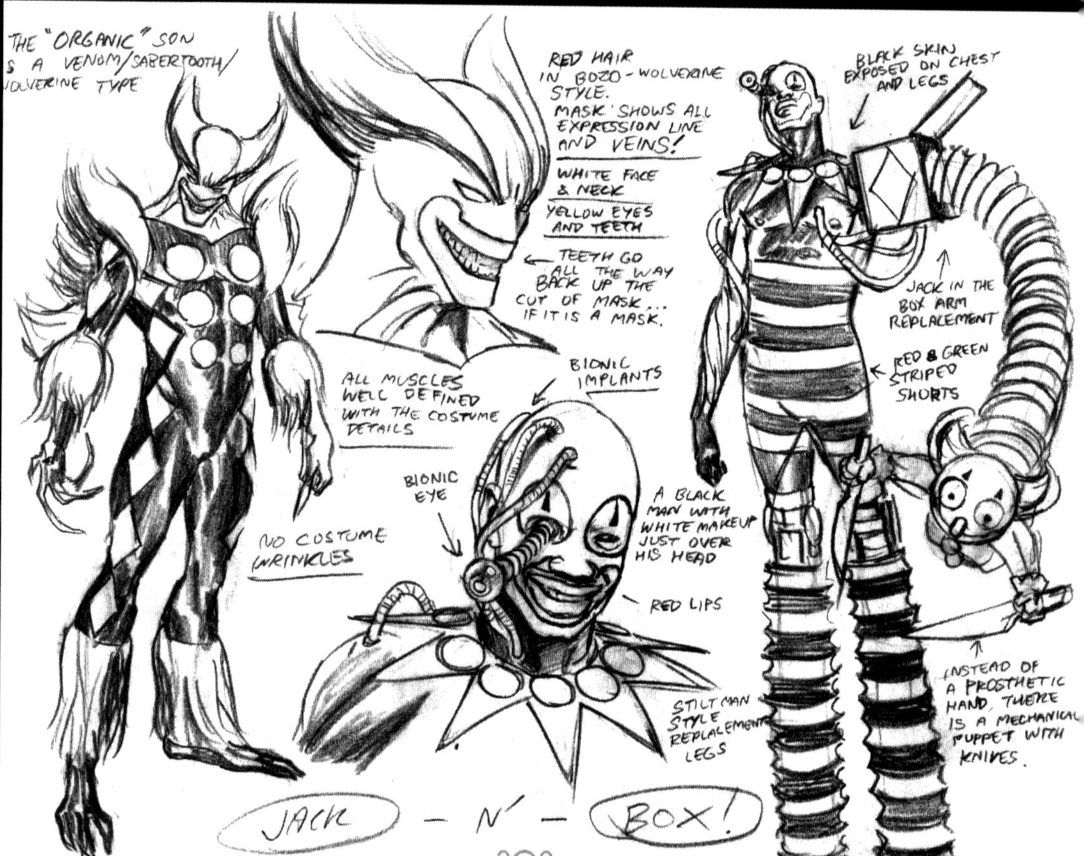

THE "ORGANIC" SON
S A VENOM/SABERTOOTH/
OLVERINE TYPE
RED HAIR IN BOZO-WOLVERINE STYLE.
MASK SHOWS ALL EXPRESSION LINE AND VEINS!
WHITE FACE & NECK
YELLOW EYES AND TEETH
TEETH GO ALL THE WAY BACK UP THE CUT OF MASK... IF IT IS A MASK.
ALL MUSCLES WELL DEFINED WITH THE COSTUME DETAILS
BIONIC IMPLANTS
BIONIC EYE
NO COSTUME WRINKLES
A BLACK MAN WITH WHITE MAKEUP JUST OVER HIS HEAD
RED LIPS
BLACK SKIN EXPOSED ON CHEST AND LEGS
JACK IN THE BOX ARM REPLACEMENT
RED & GREEN STRIPED SHORTS
STILT MAN STYLE REPLACEMENT LEGS
INSTEAD OF A PROSTHETIC HAND, THERE IS A MECHANICAL PUPPET WITH KNIVES.
JACK - N' - BOX!

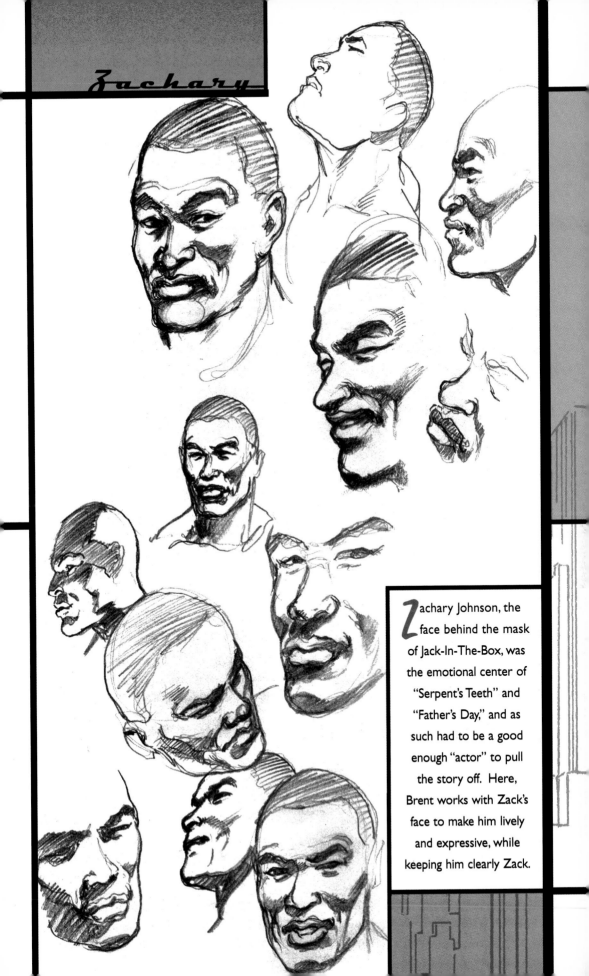

Zachary

Zachary Johnson, the face behind the mask of Jack-In-The-Box, was the emotional center of "Serpent's Teeth" and "Father's Day," and as such had to be a good enough "actor" to pull the story off. Here, Brent works with Zack's face to make him lively and expressive, while keeping him clearly Zack.

Loony Leo

The first conception of Leo was as a cartoon lion in a tux, but something about it didn't seem right. We knew his story was one of disappointment and disgrace, and this dapper fellow didn't seem like he had the range for it.

Below: Expression studies, looking for a way to give Leo the right "hangdog" look. *Below right:* Figure proportion sketches.

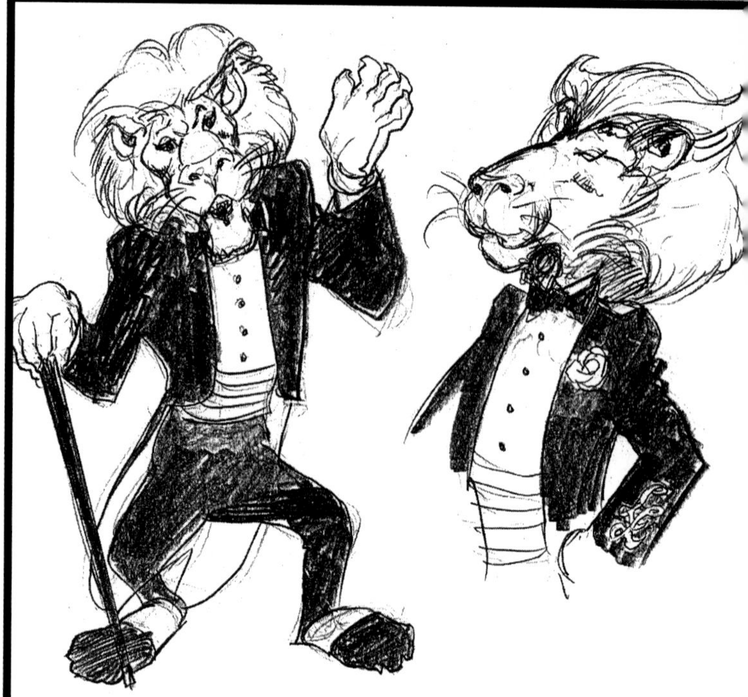

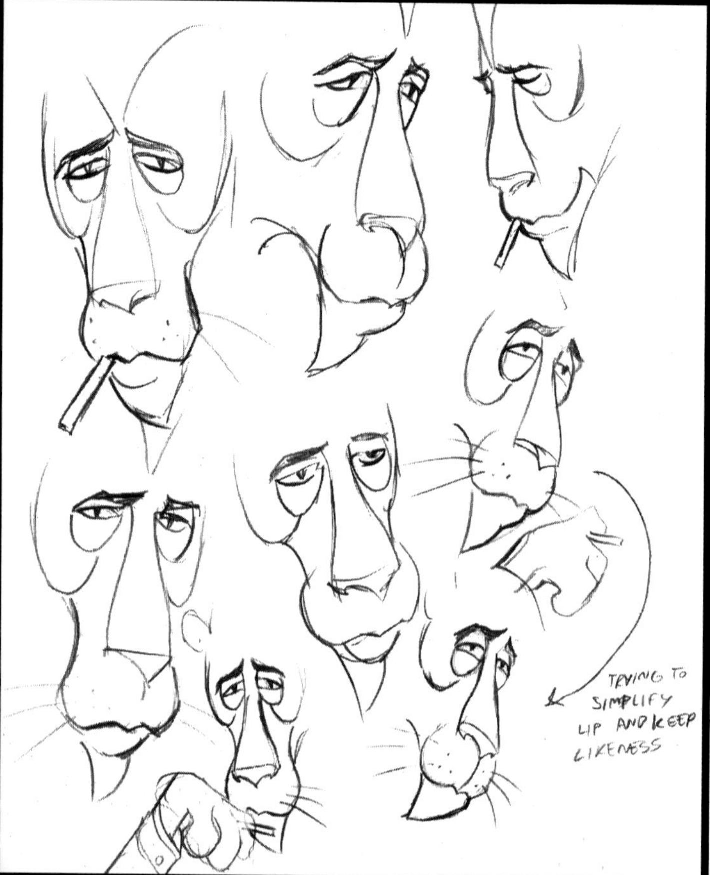
TRYING TO SIMPLIFY LIP AND KEEP LIKENESS

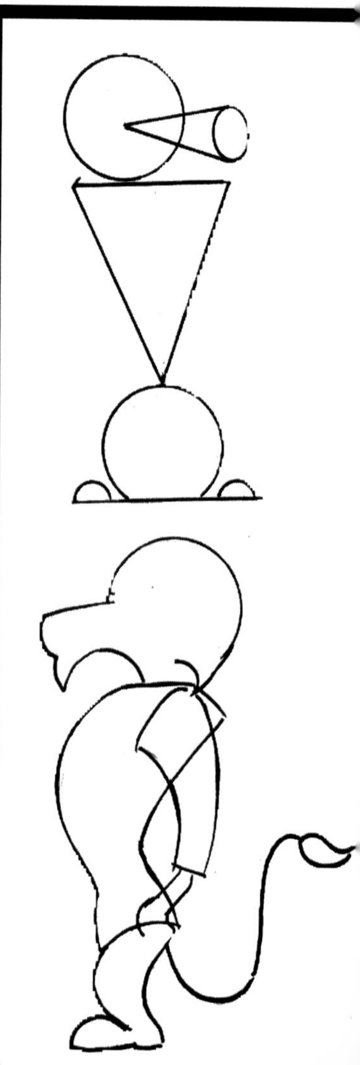

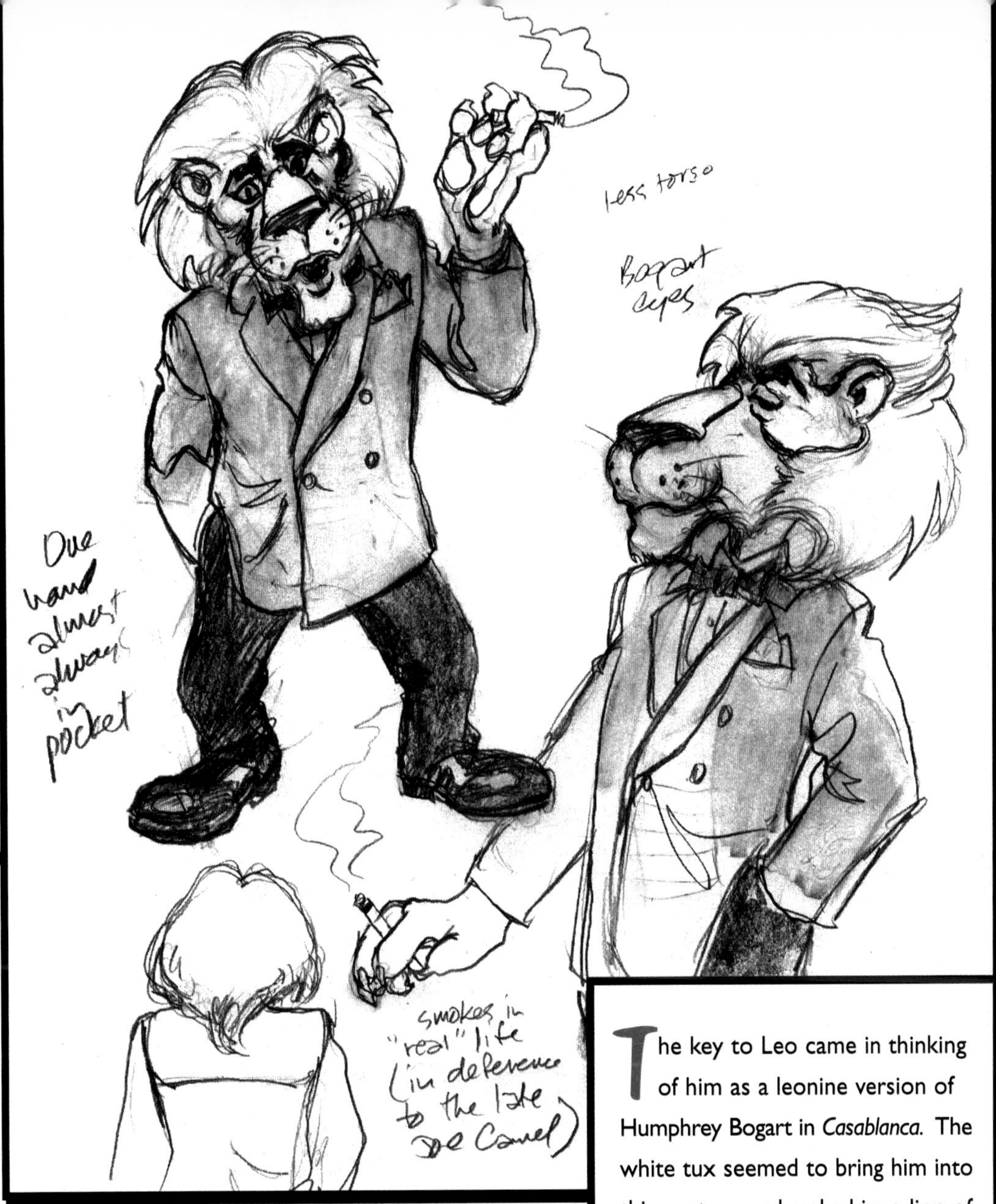
less torso
Bogart eyes
One hand almost always in pocket
smokes in "real" life (in deference to the late Joe Camel)

The key to Leo came in thinking of him as a leonine version of Humphrey Bogart in *Casablanca.* The white tux seemed to bring him into this century, and make him a lion of the people, not an elitist snob. Still, something wasn't clicking...

...until he got an abstraction of Bogart's lidded, weary eyes, and his "reality" level was cranked back far enough to make him look like a cartoon among humans, and not just an anthropomorphized jungle beast.

Left: That's a guy who can be a world-weary cartoon!

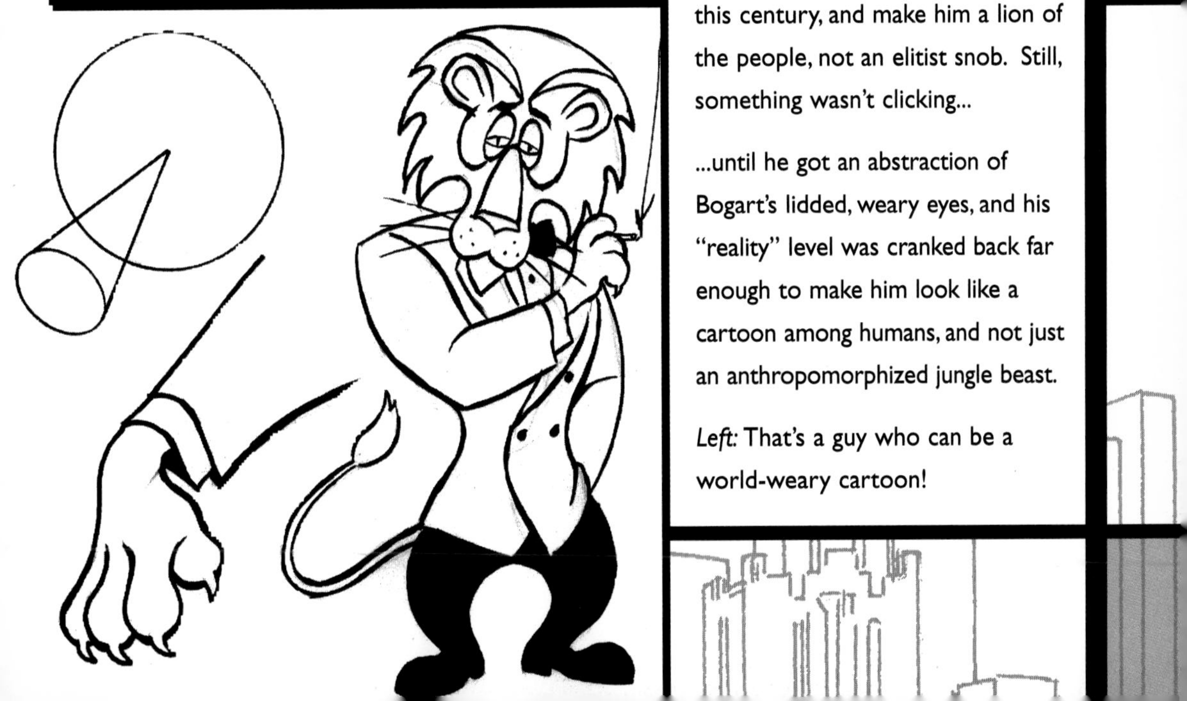

Gentleman

Alex's design for the Gentleman, the sartorially-impeccable fellow who's been performing well-mannered feats of derring-do in Astro City for coming up on six decades now. He hasn't had much of a chance at the spotlight yet, but he's got quite a history, and quite a story to tell.

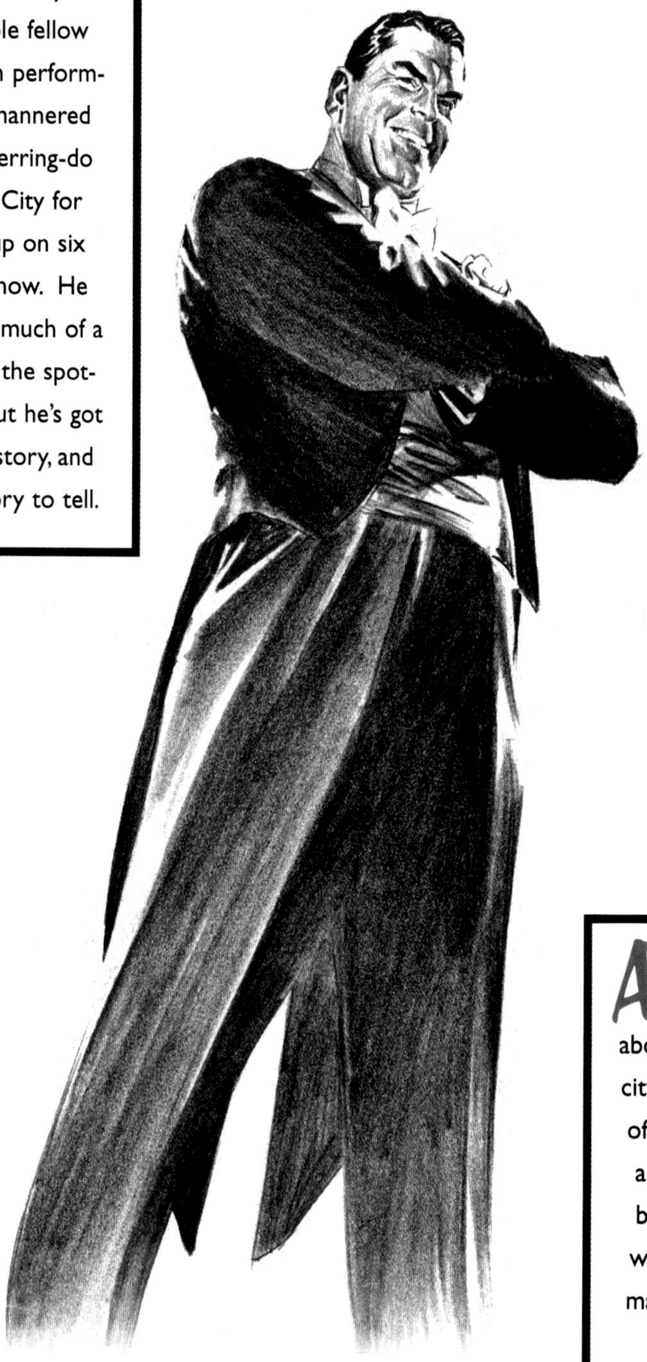

And that's the frustrating thing about filling an entire city with such a host of characters. They all have stories — but they've got to wait their turn. So many characters, so few pages...

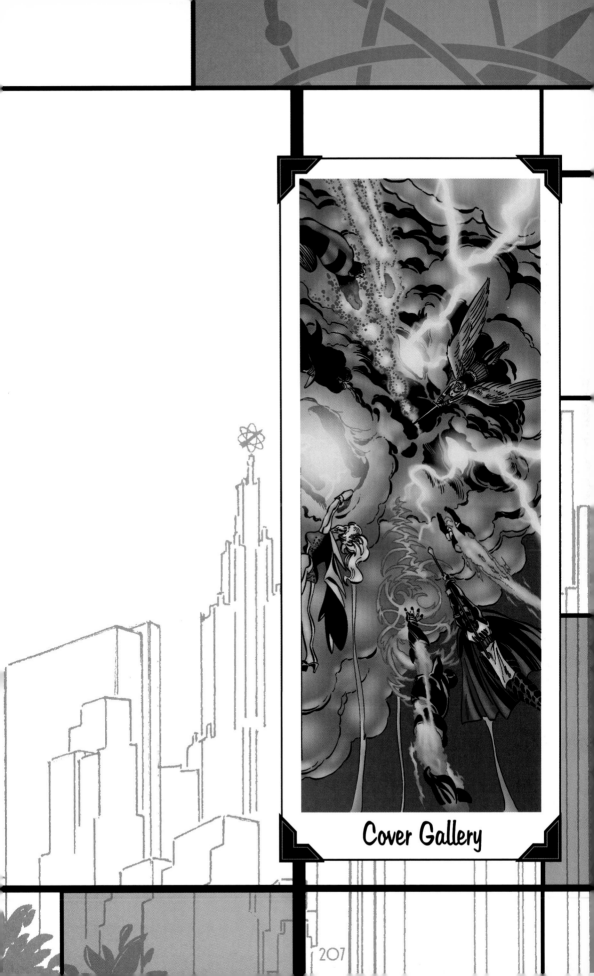

Cover Gallery

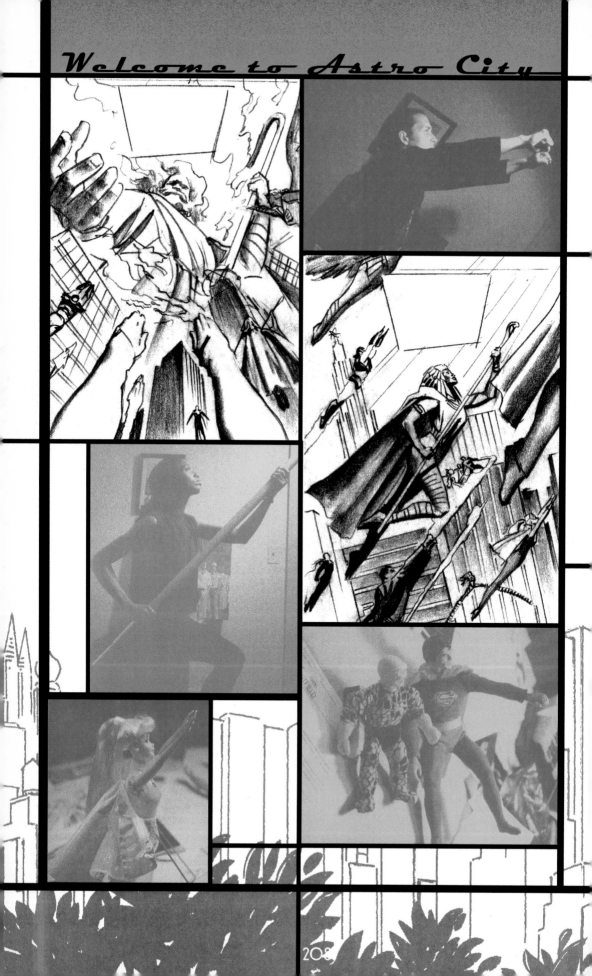

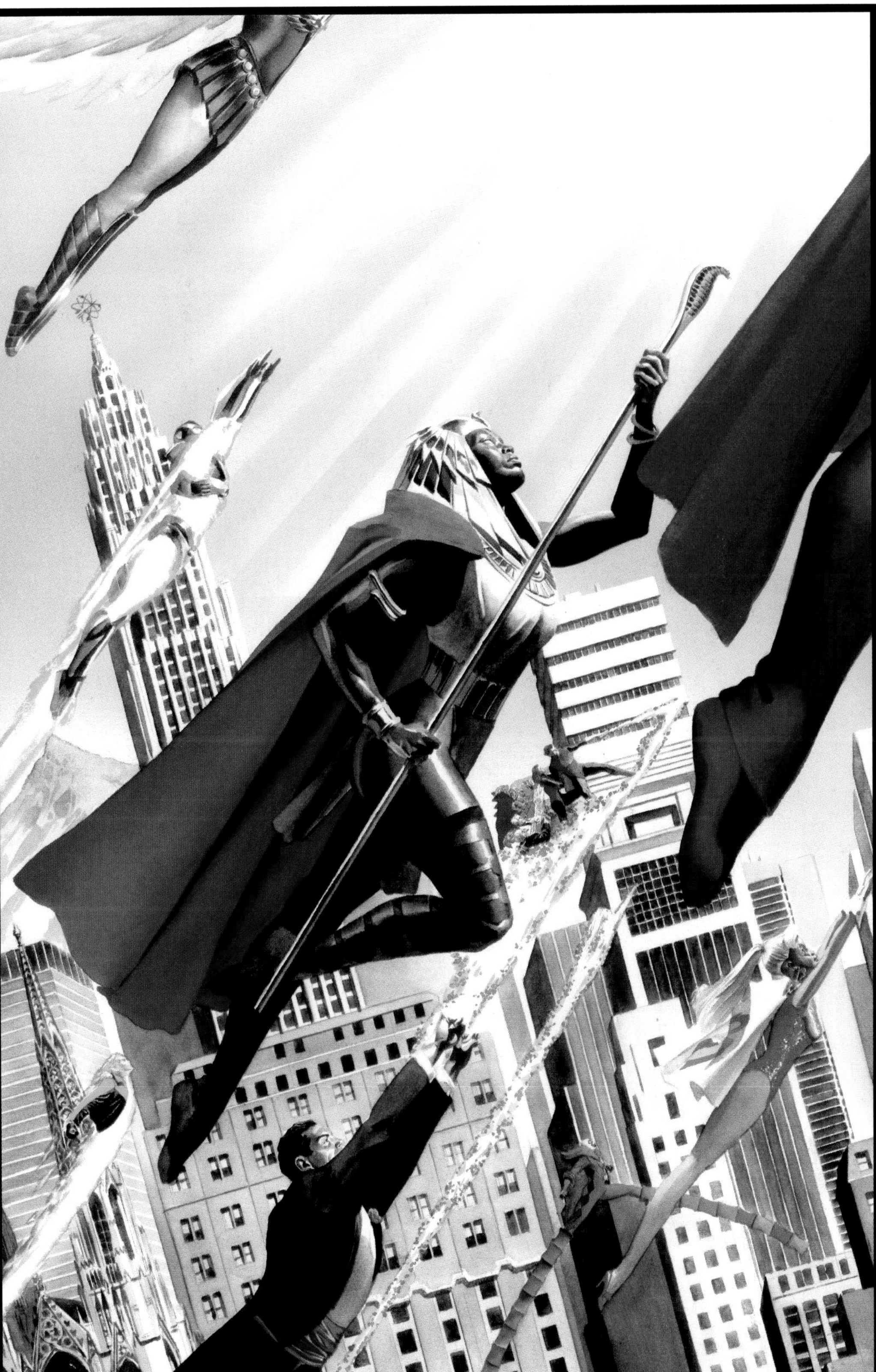

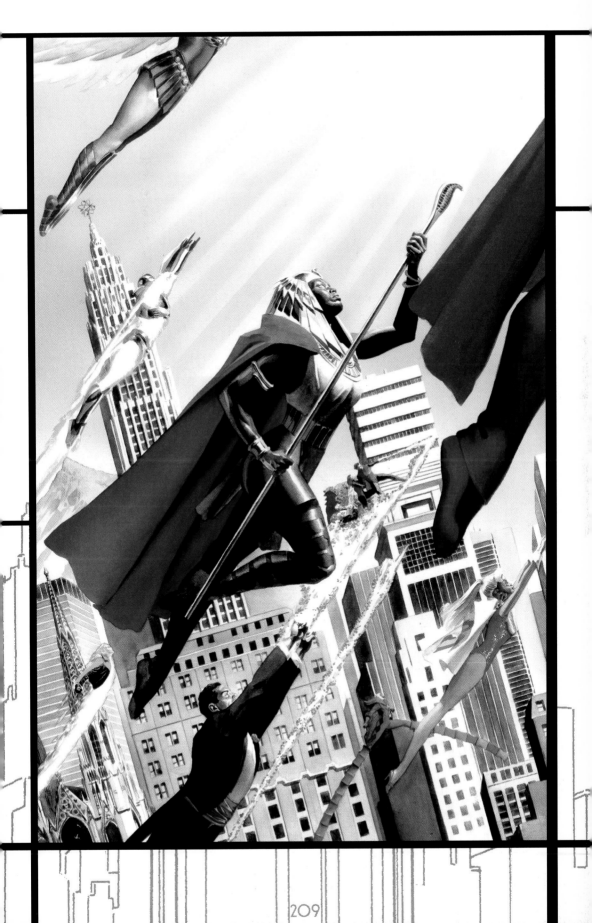

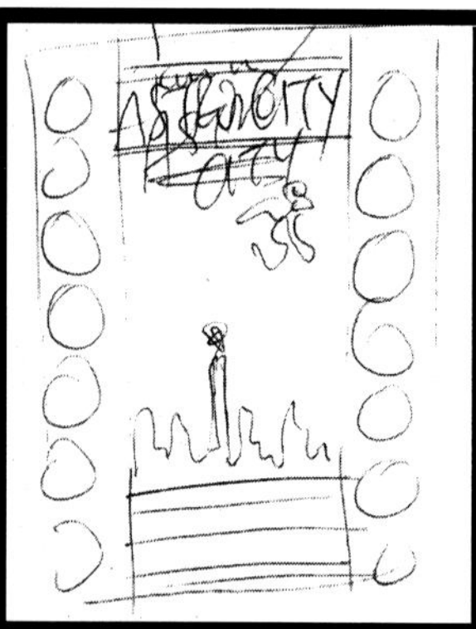

ASTRO CITY

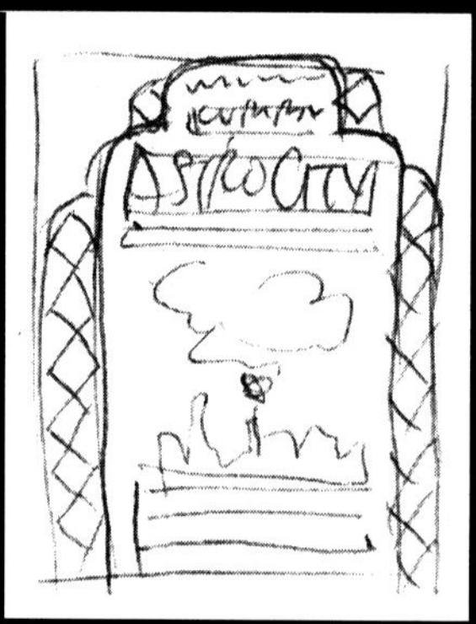

ASTRO CITY

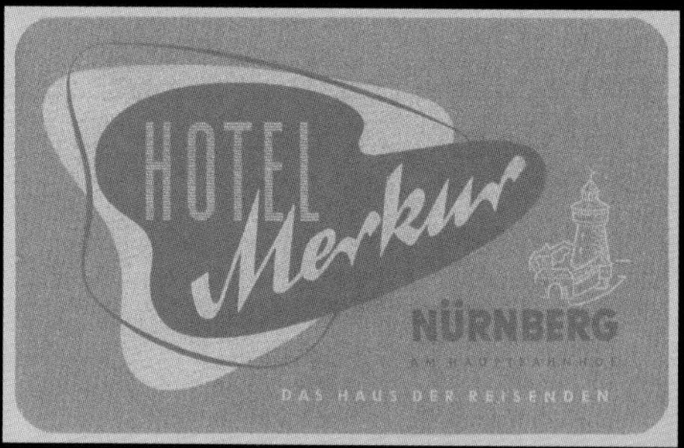

HOTEL
Merkur
NÜRNBERG
DAS HAUS DER REISENDEN

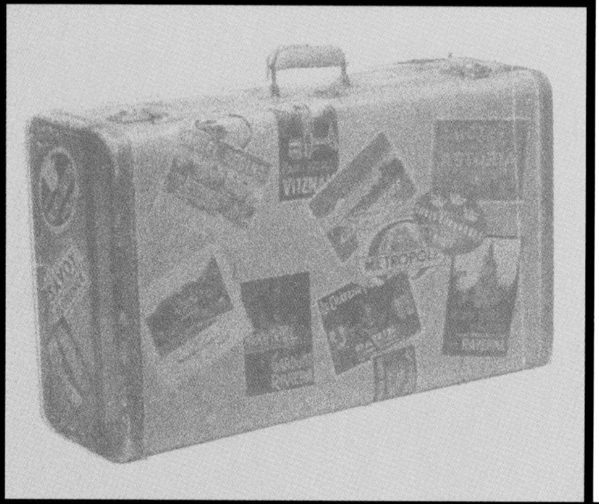

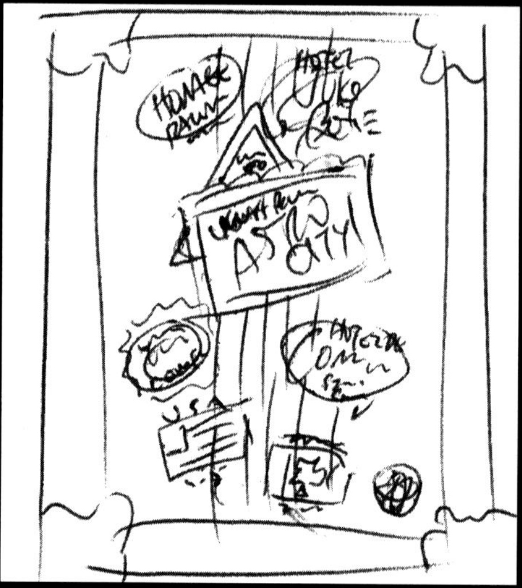

ASTRO CITY

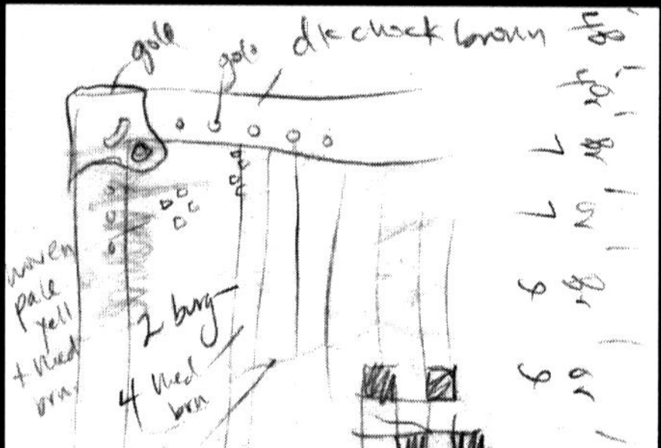

gold
gold
dk chock brown
2 burg
4 med brn
other colors replace w/med brn

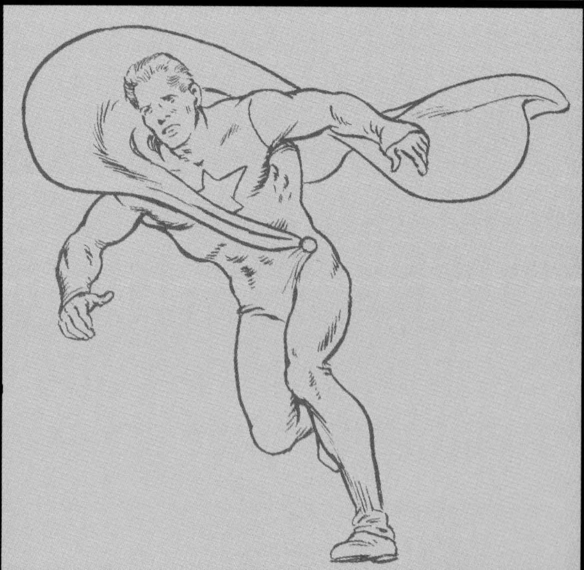

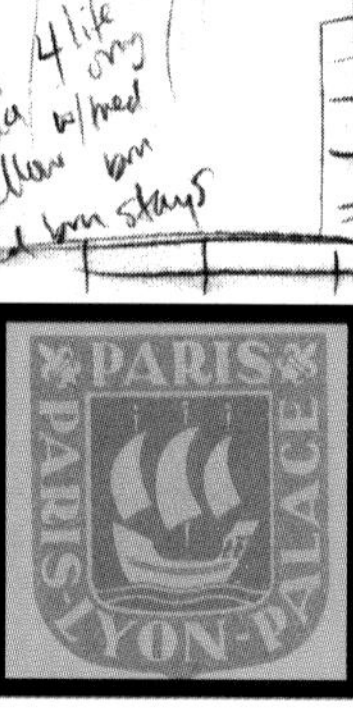

PARIS
PARIS-LYON-PALACE

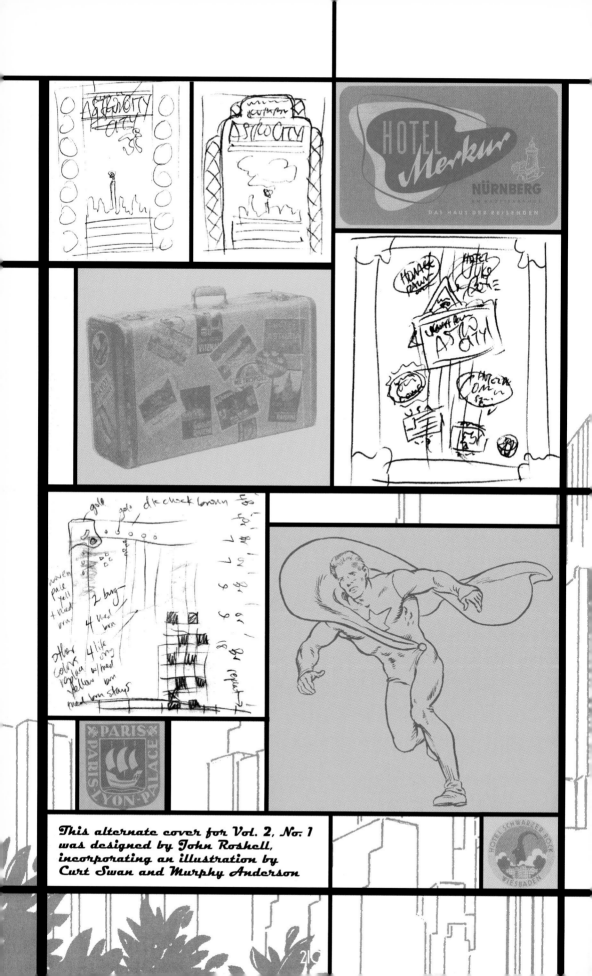

This alternate cover for Vol. 2, No. 1 was designed by John Roshell, incorporating an illustration by Curt Swan and Murphy Anderson

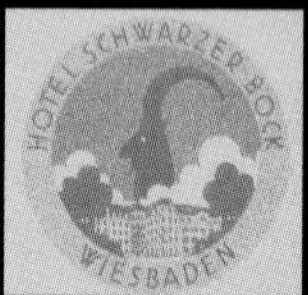

HOTEL SCHWARZER BOCK
WIESBADEN

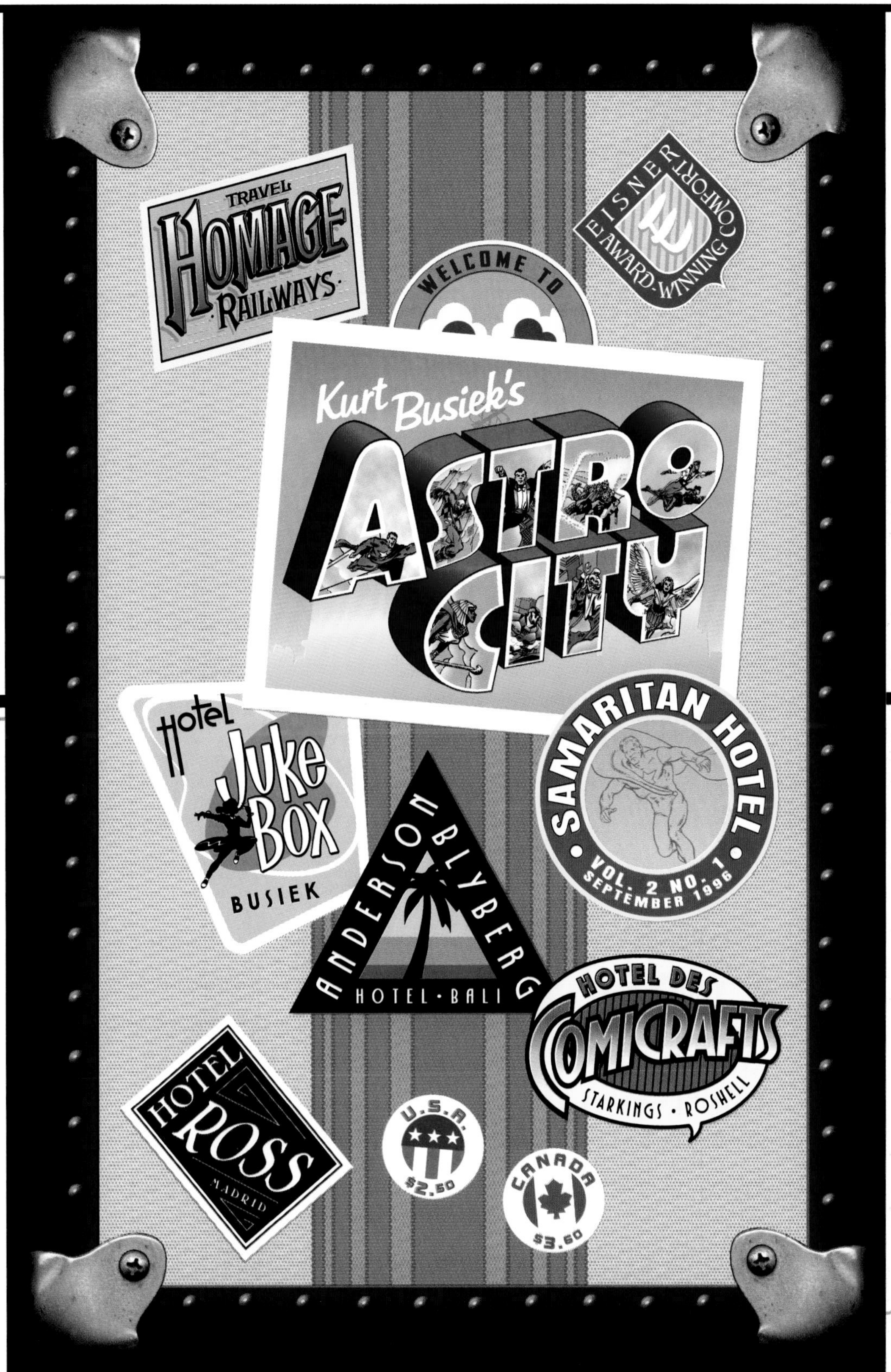

TRAVEL
HOMAGE
RAILWAYS
EISNER AWARD-WINNING COMFORT
WELCOME TO
Kurt Busiek's
ASTRO CITY
hotel
Juke Box
BUSIEK
SAMARITAN HOTEL
VOL. 2 NO. 1
SEPTEMBER 1996
ANDERSON BLYBERG
HOTEL · BALI
HOTEL DES
COMICRAFTS
STARKINGS · ROSHELL
HOTEL
ROSS
MADRID
U.S.A.
$2.50
CANADA
$3.60

Everyday Life

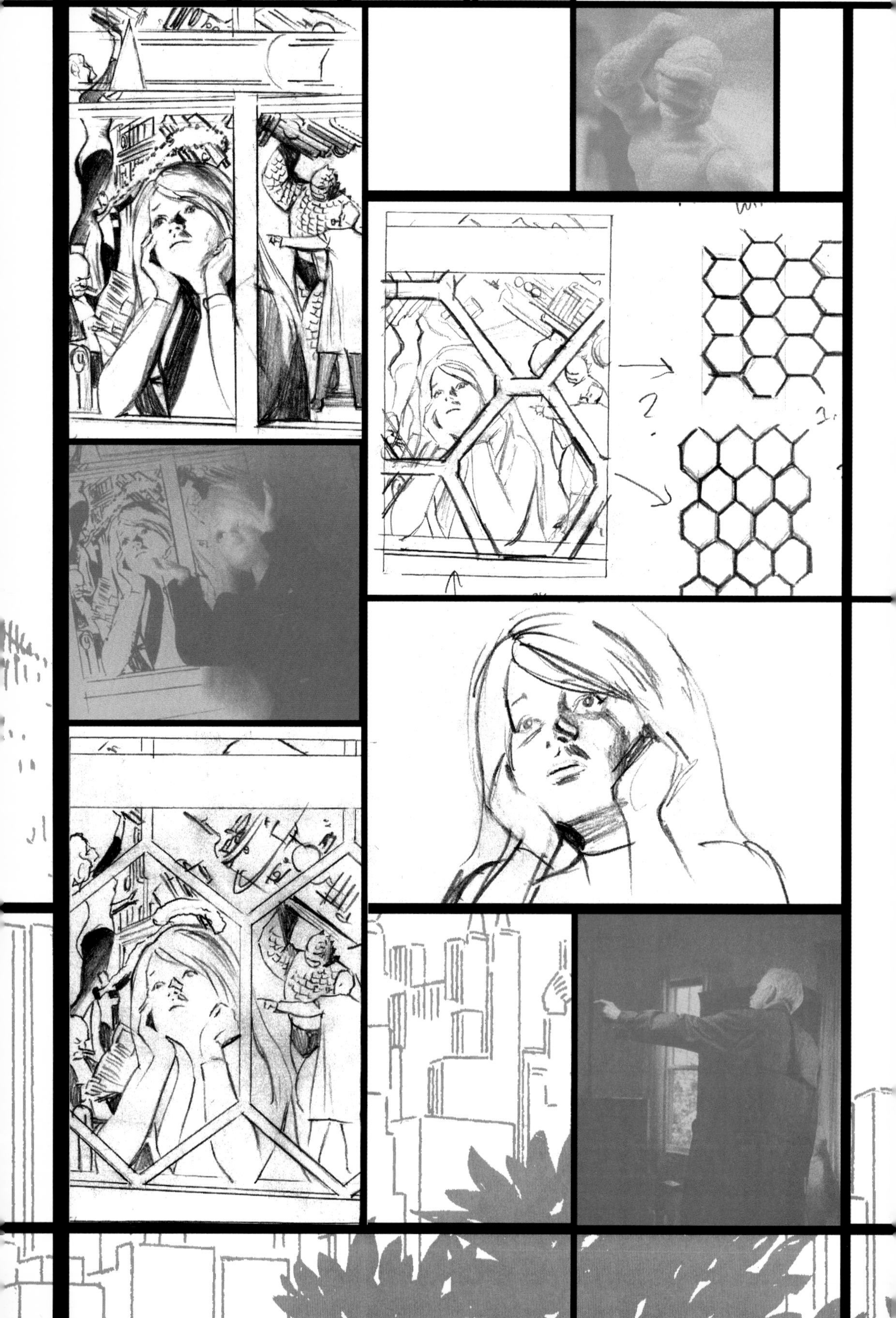

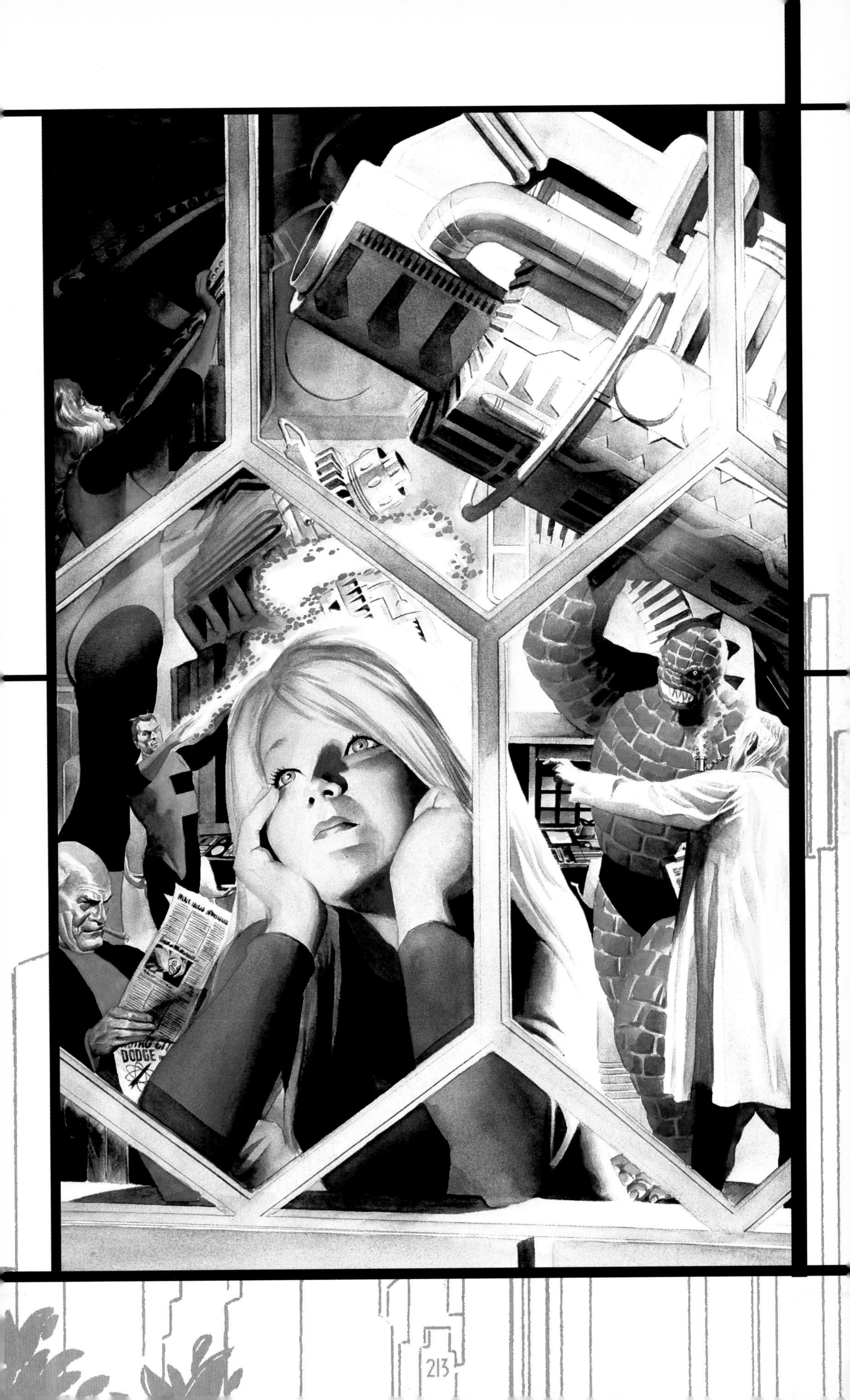
DODGE

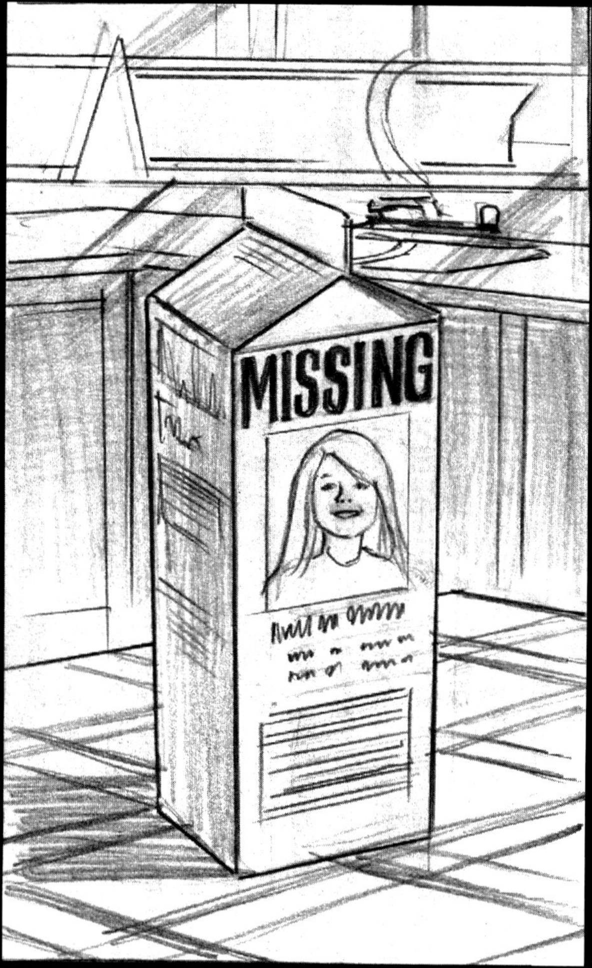
MISSING

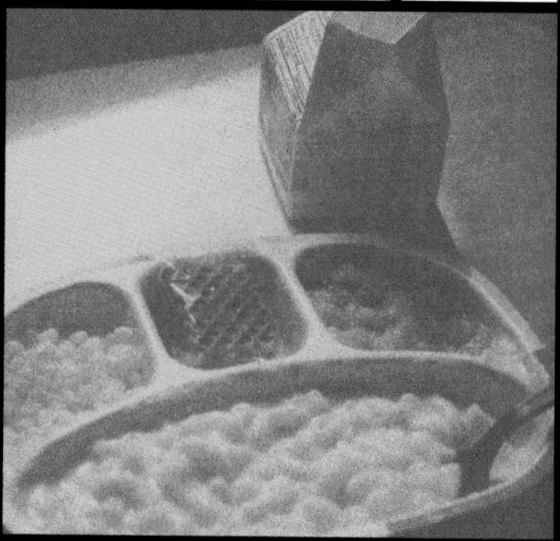

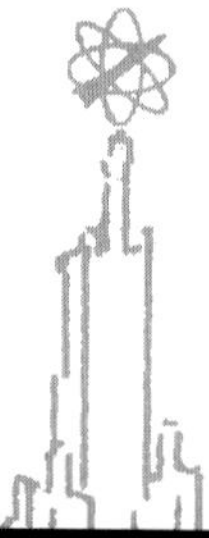

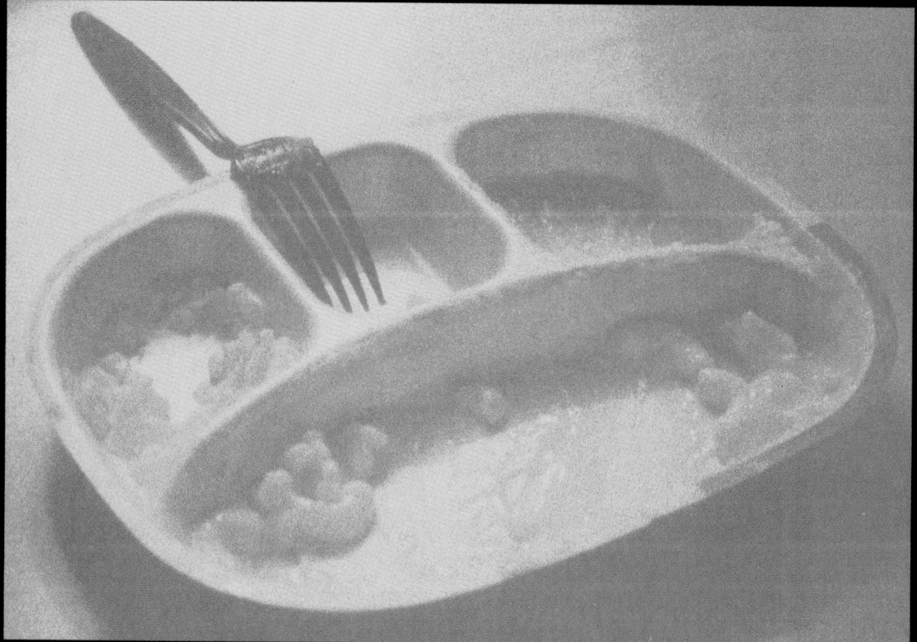

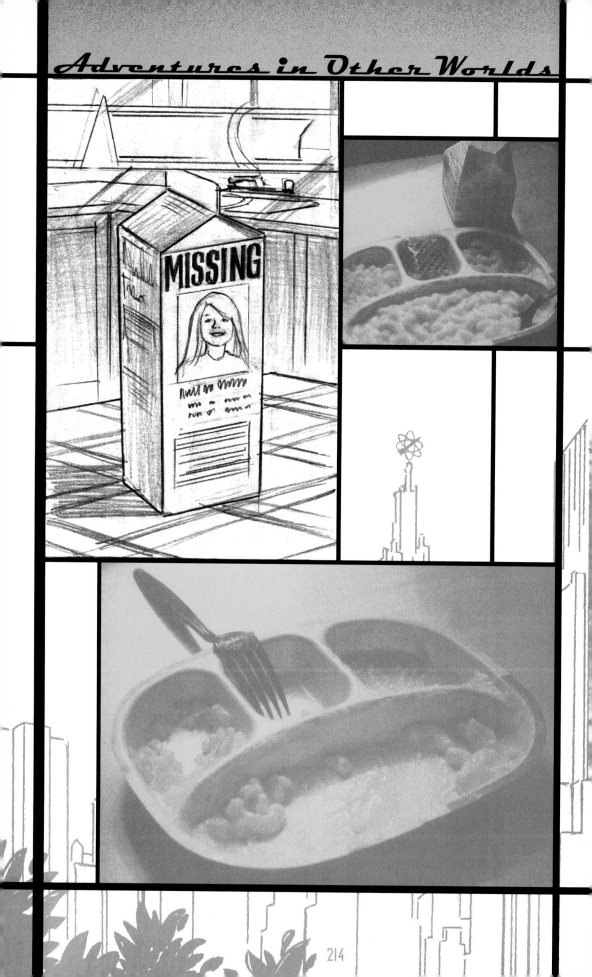

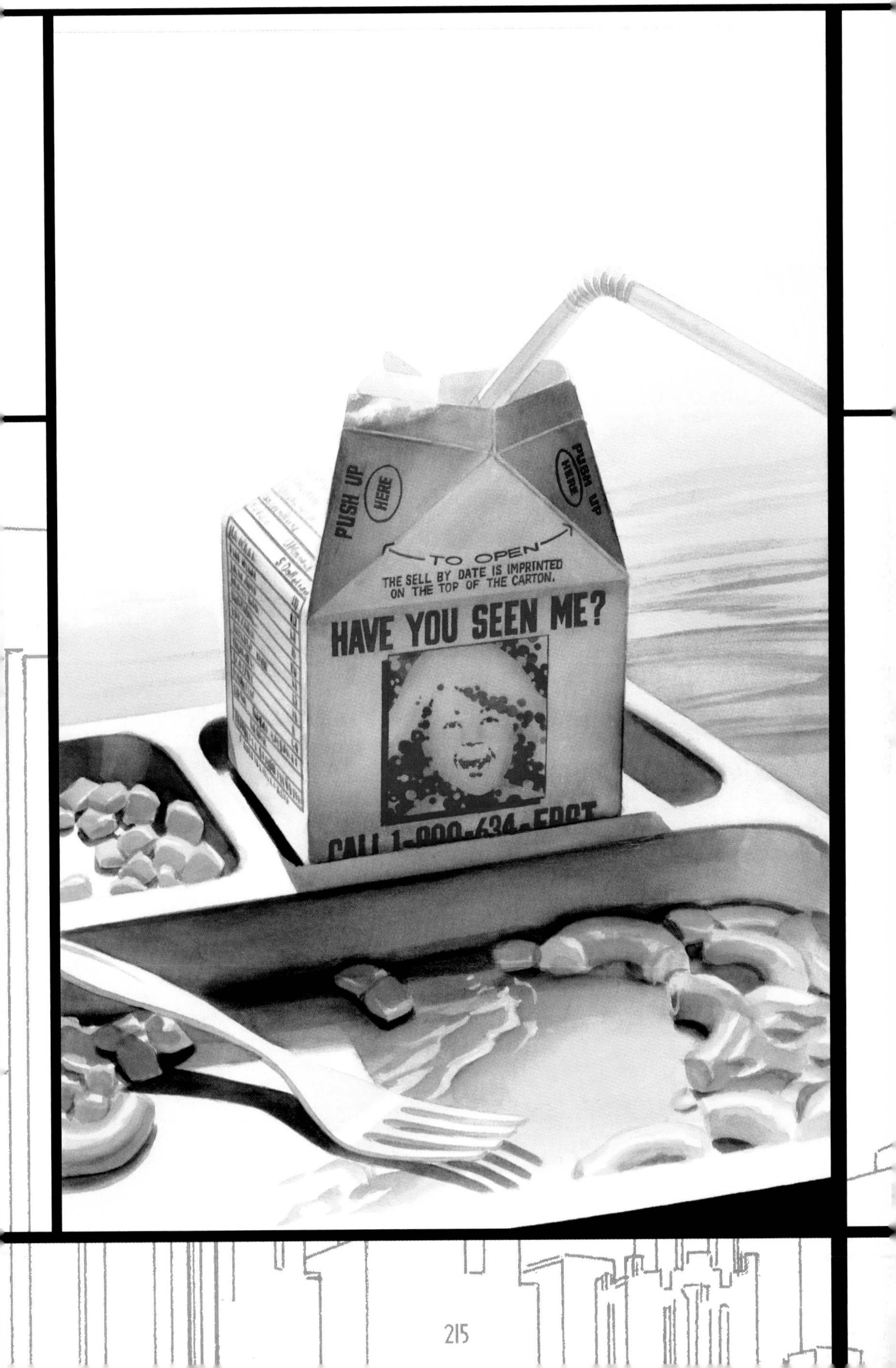
PUSH UP HERE
PUSH UP HERE
TO OPEN
THE SELL BY DATE IS IMPRINTED ON THE TOP OF THE CARTON.
HAVE YOU SEEN ME?

Show 'Em All

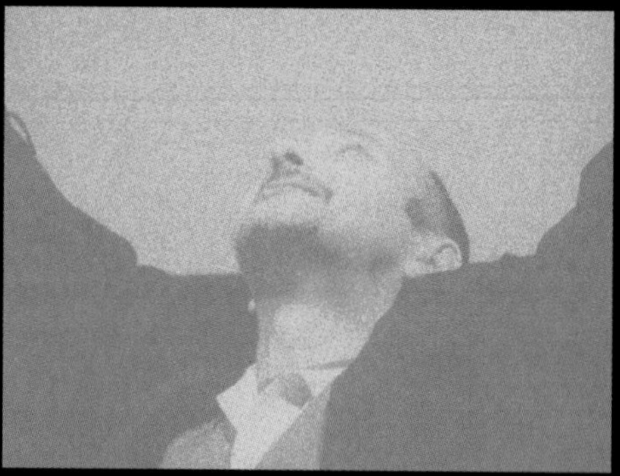

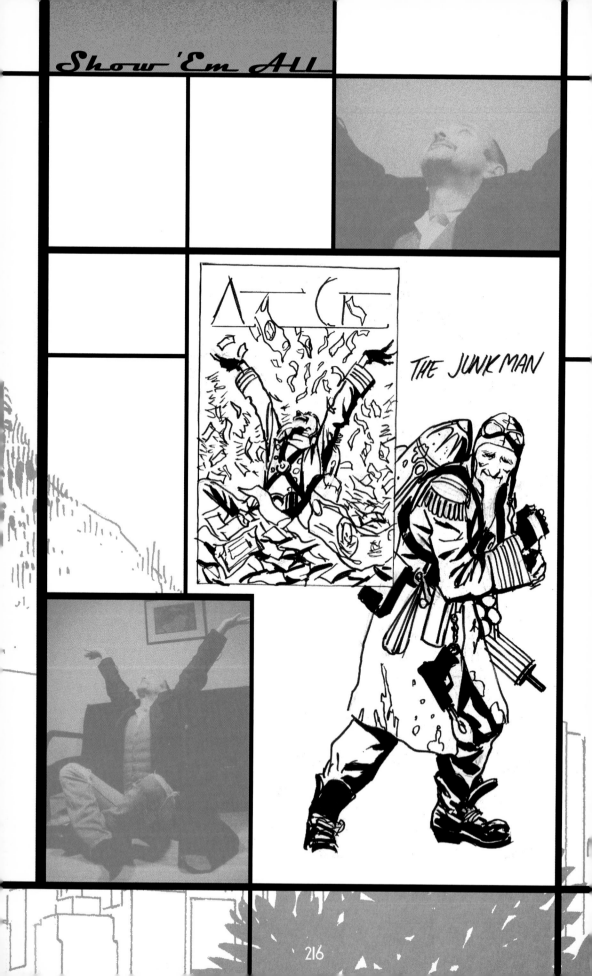

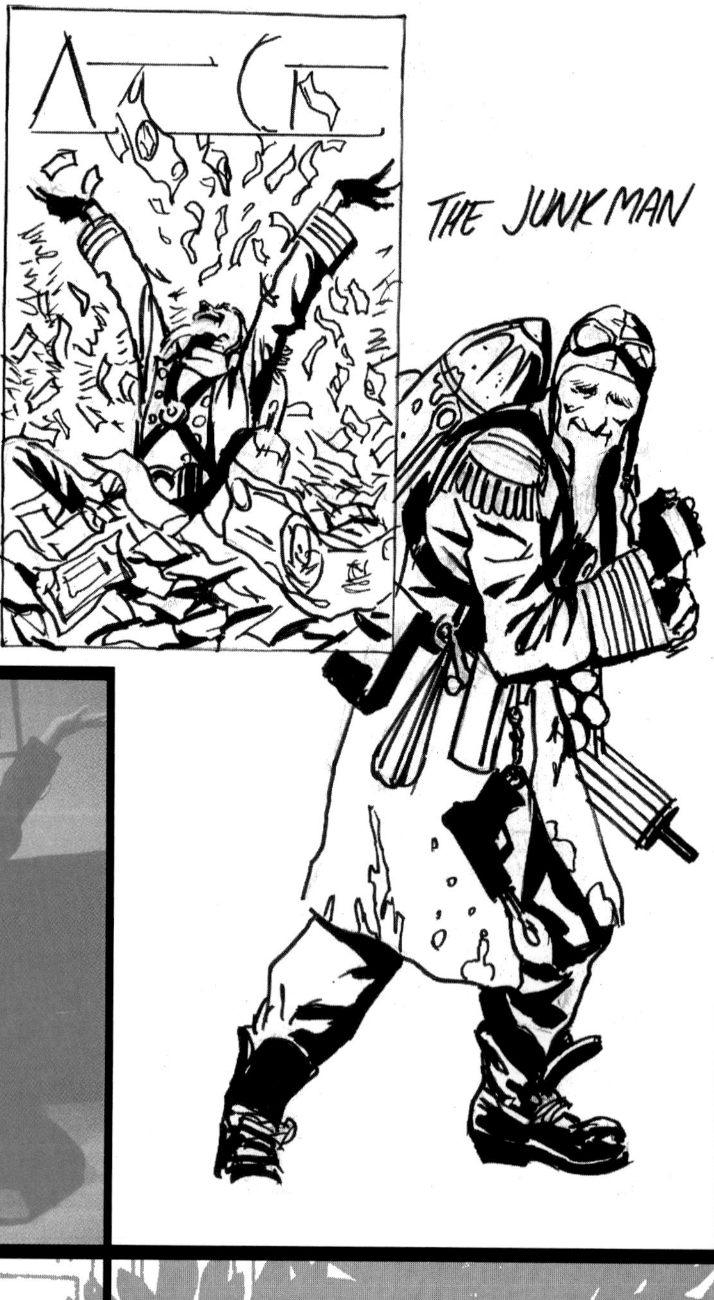
THE JUNK MAN

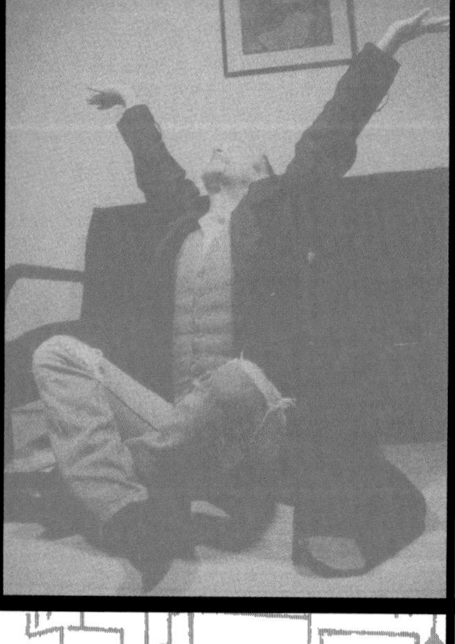

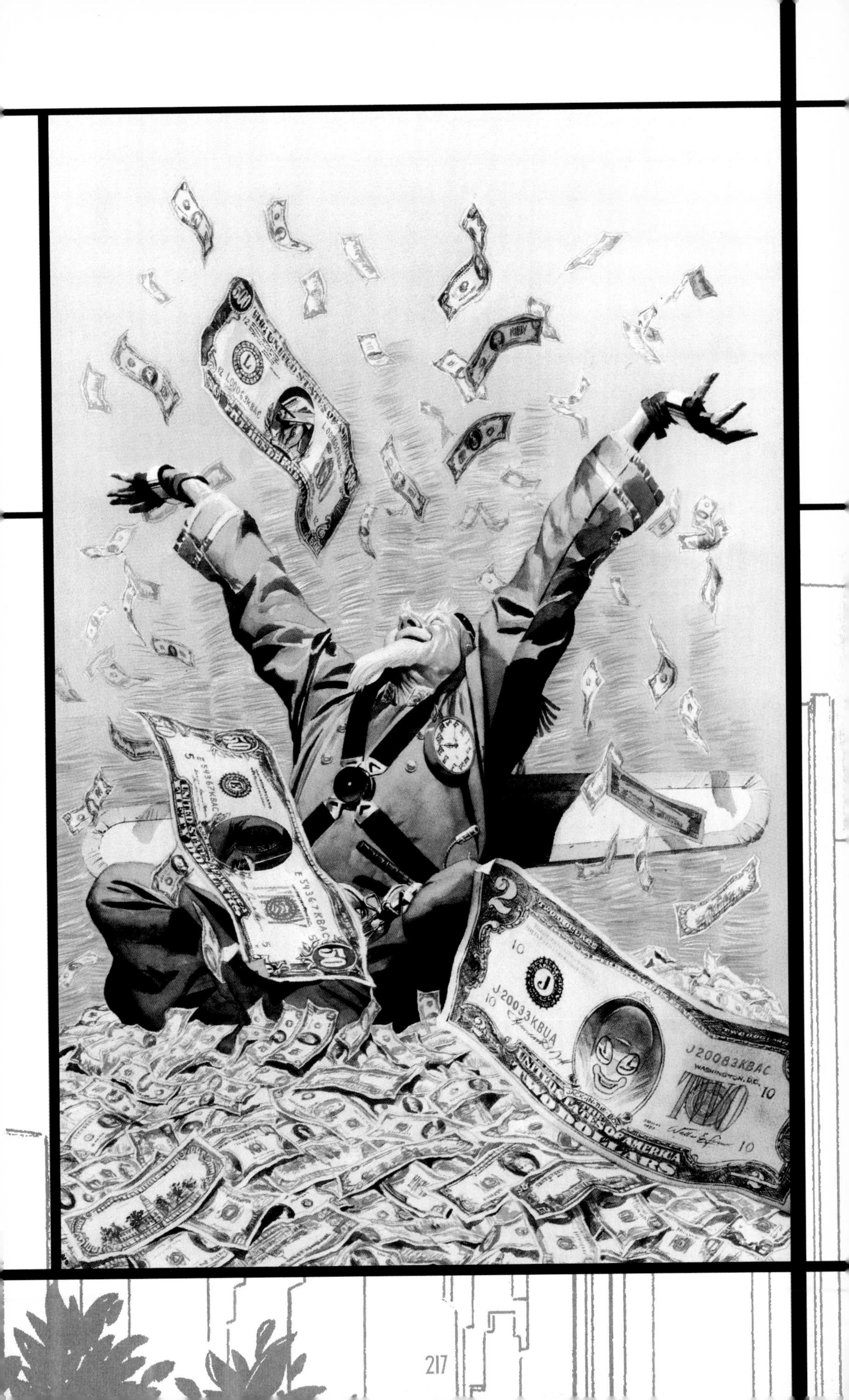

Serpent's Teeth

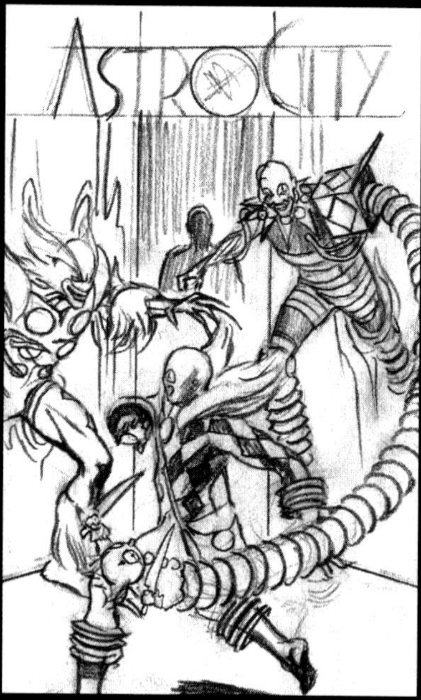
ASTRO CITY

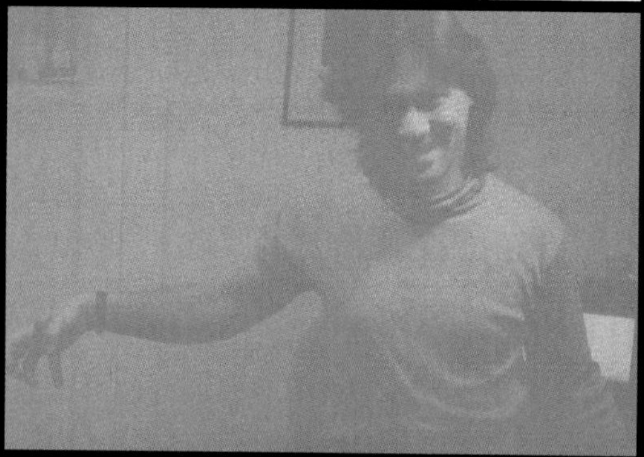

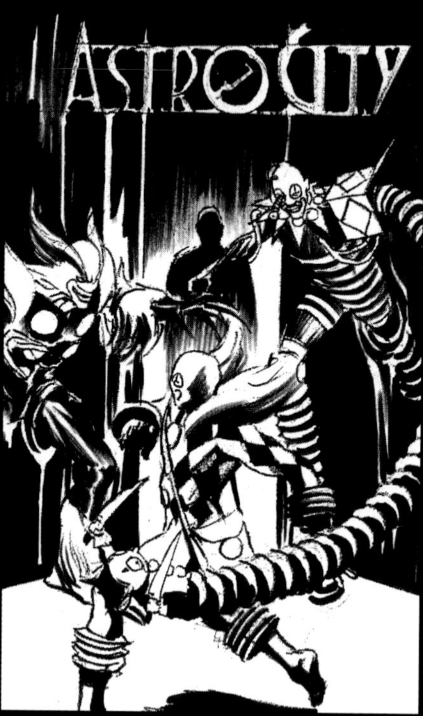
ASTRO CITY

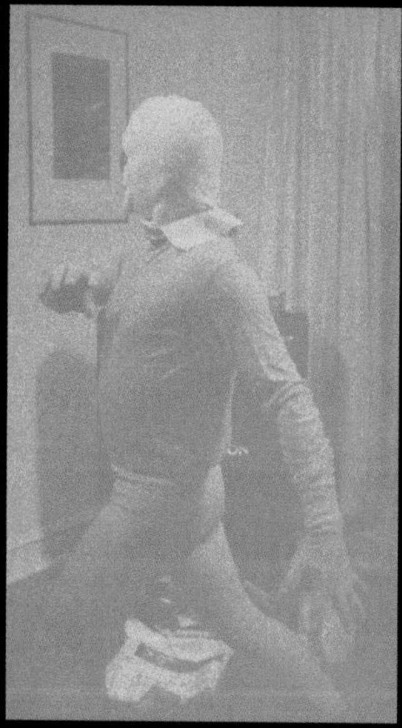

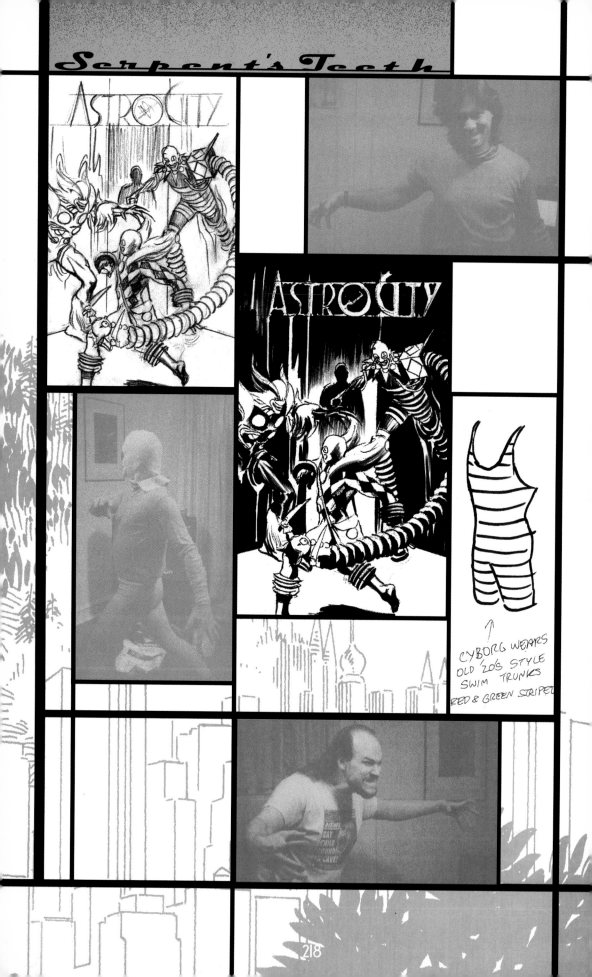

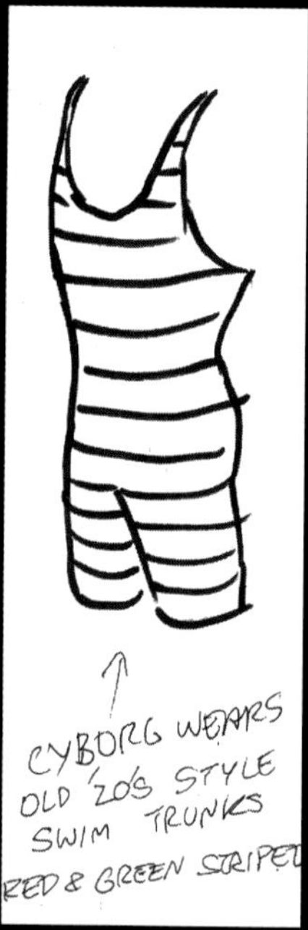
CYBORG WEARS
OLD '20'S STYLE
SWIM TRUNKS
RED & GREEN STRIPED

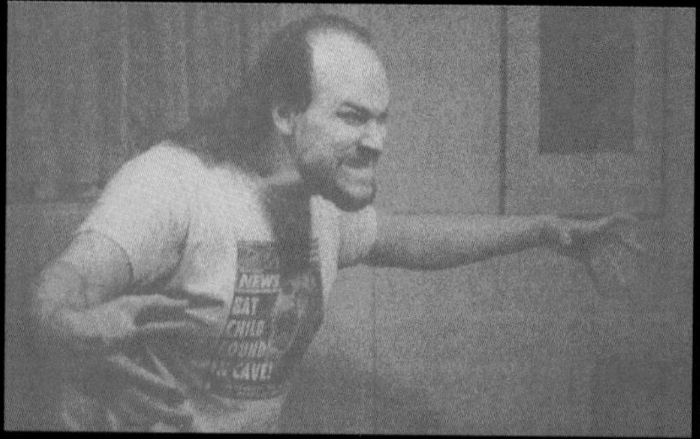

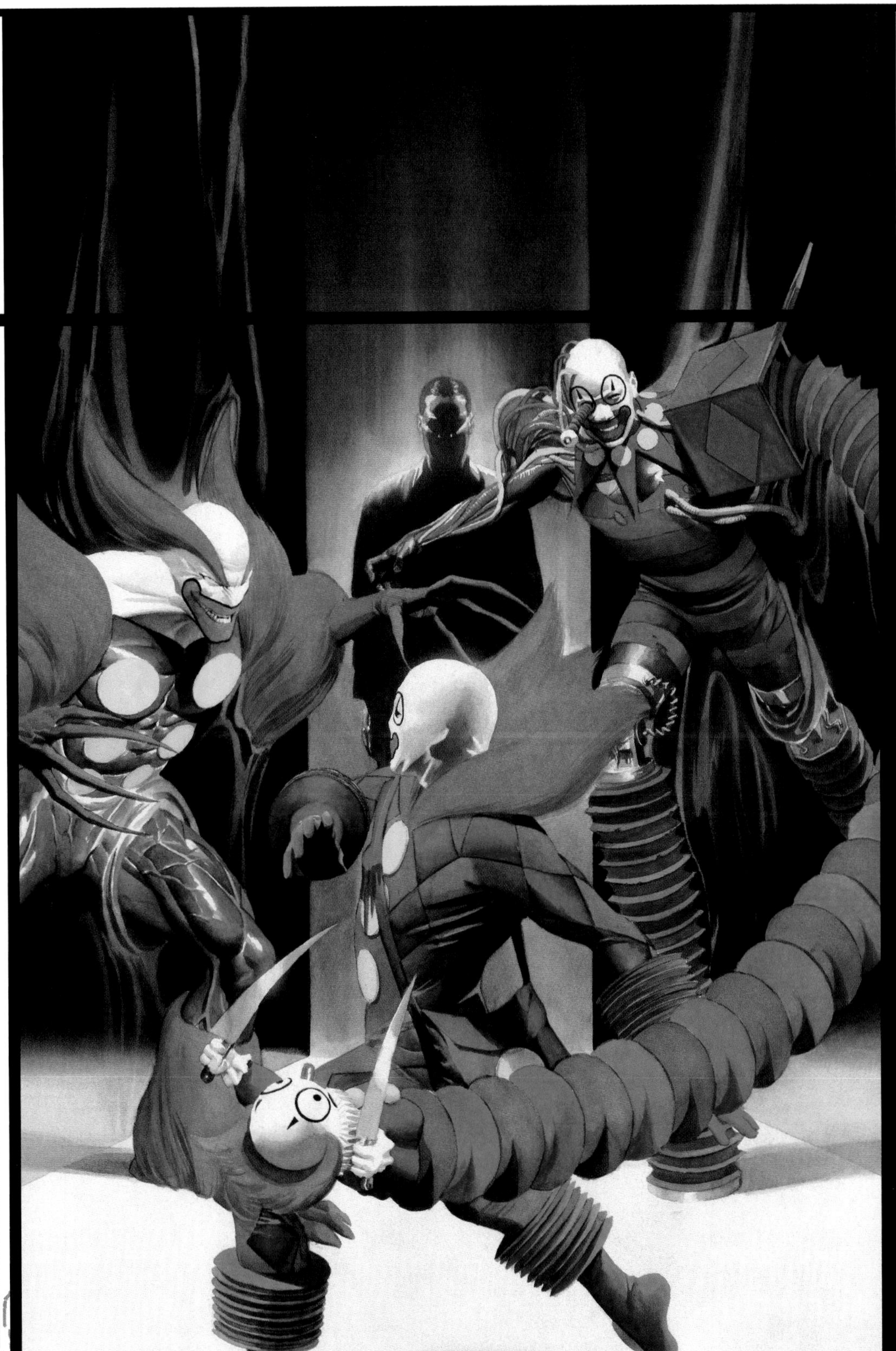

Father's Day

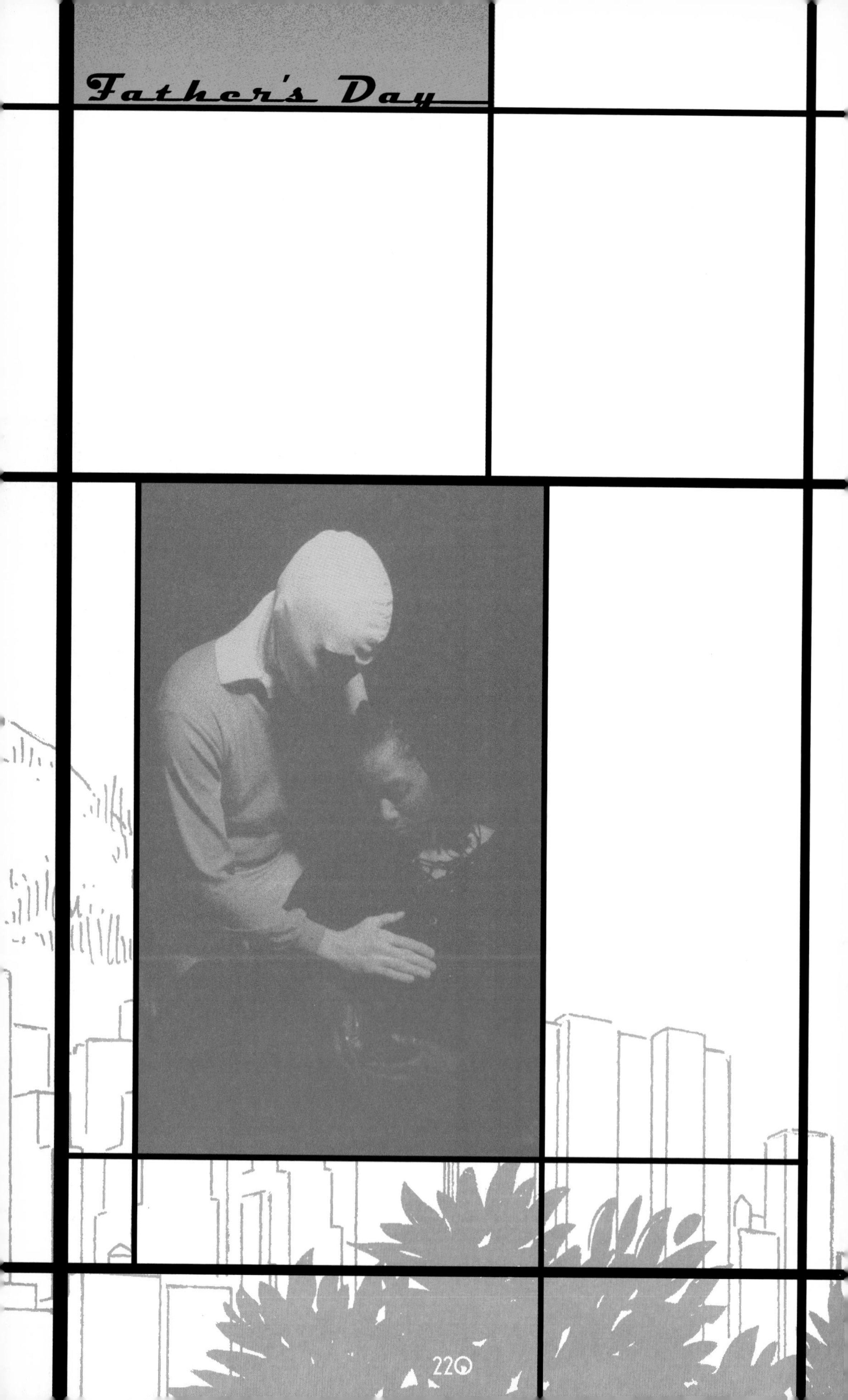

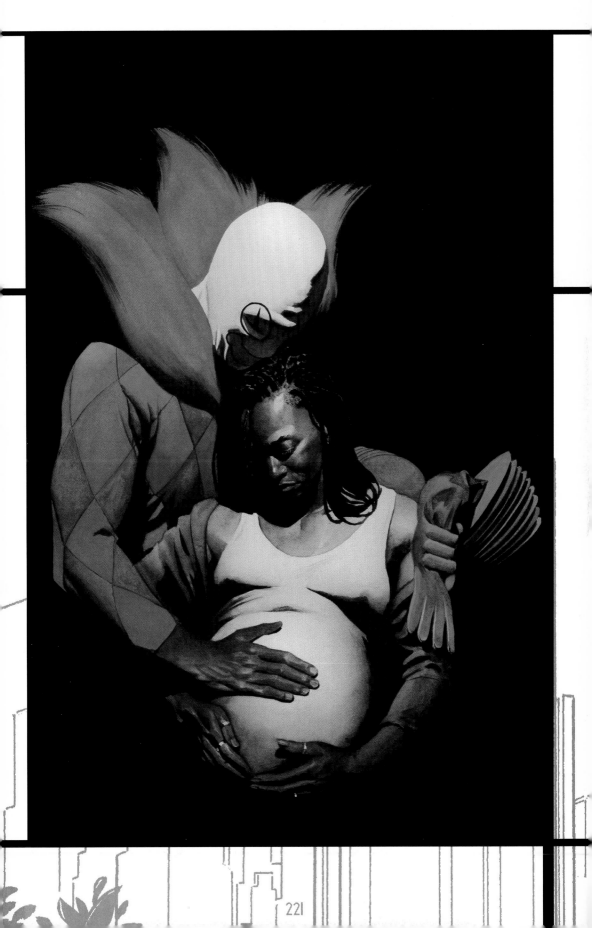

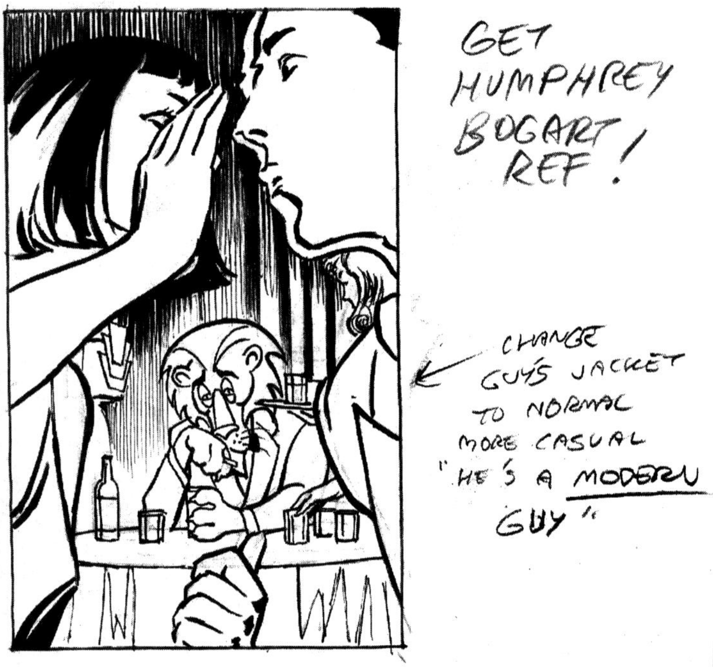
GET HUMPHREY BOGART REF!
CHANGE GUY'S JACKET TO NORMAL MORE CASUAL "HE'S A MODERN GUY"

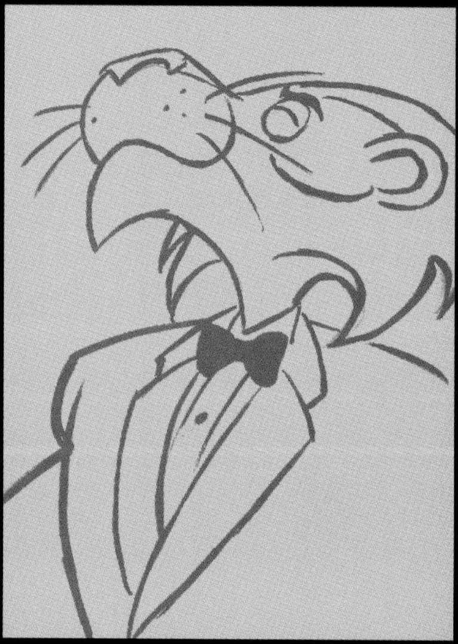

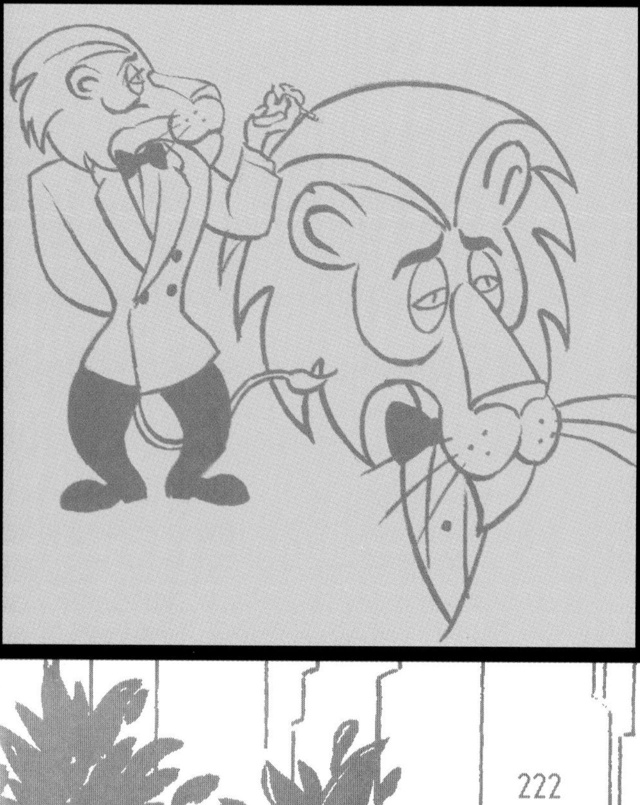

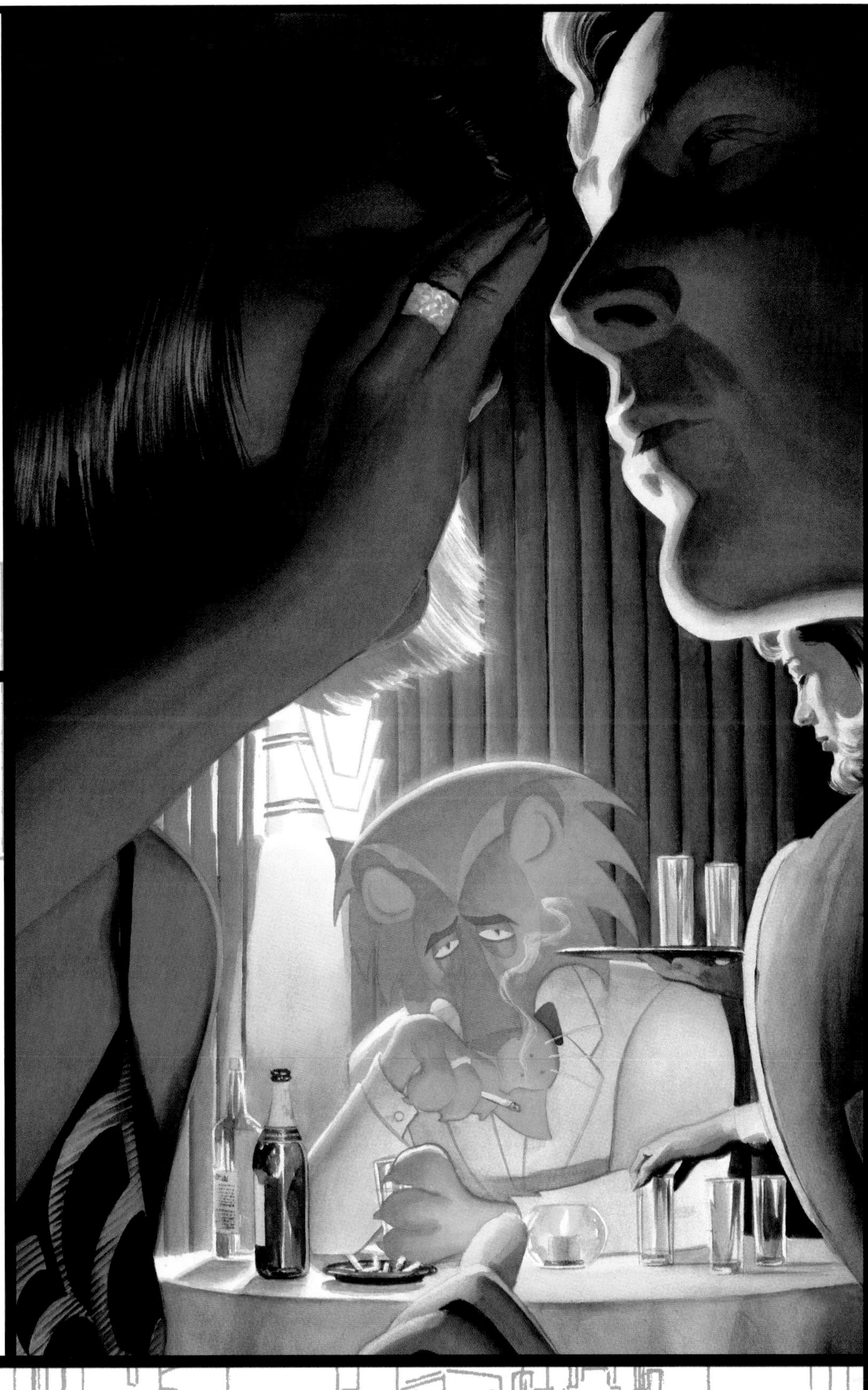

Acknowledgments

My thanks, as always, to the usual subjects for their encouragement and support, from my family bugging me for my next issue to my friends offering up advice, ideas or just an ear when it was needed. And this time around, specific thanks to Lawrence and Julie Evans for chemistry advice, and to Barbara Kesel's father, Jim Randall, for the 414B Hotshot. Also, special thanks to Jonathan Peterson, Astro City's editor for all of the stories included in this volume and the previous one — we may have given you ulcers and made you tear out your hair, Jonathan, but it was a pleasure working with you.

– Kurt Busiek

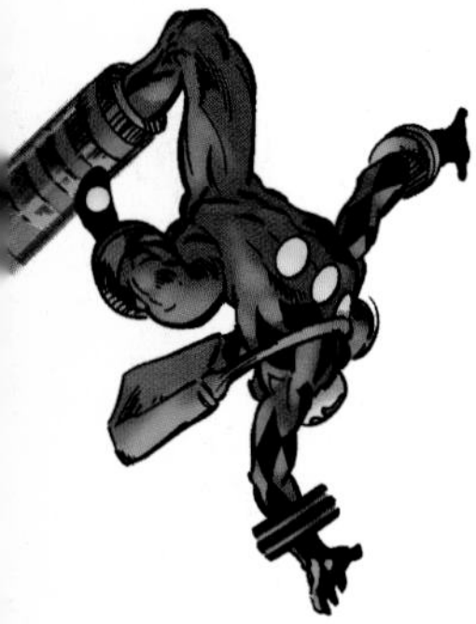

Thanks go to the many concentric rings of family around me; to my wife Shirley and son Bryce, for the hours they grant me to draw this book; to my mom Carol, sister Cinda, nephew Cody, my brother Aaron and his new family Carol, Adam, Ben and Robyn for their support; to my eternal brothers Frank, Ken, Gary, Chuck, Ron, and Stan for being a constant source of joy and irritation; to Walter Sauers, a Spellbinder forever; to Archie Goodwin, an uncle to us all; and a heartfelt thank-you to two guys in Oaktown who had the courage to say this book makes a difference.

– Brent Eric Anderson

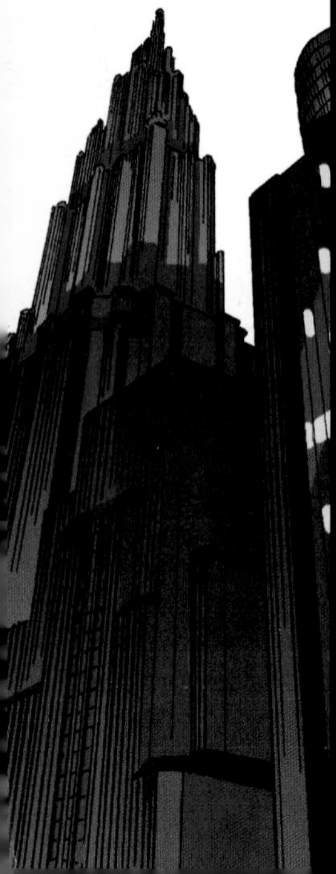

My thanks to my models Ophelia Clark, Greg Gill, Mike Reidy, Ken Kooi, my pop and all my dolls for posing for the covers. I have a brother and two sisters if anybody cares, but they really didn't do anything to contribute to this so they don't bear mentioning by name.

– Alex Ross